# A Natural Introduction to Computer Programming with Java™

**Kari Laitinen**

www.naturalprogramming.com

Note for Librarians: A cataloguing record for this book is available from Library and Archives Canada at www.collectionscanada.ca/amicus/index-e.html
ISBN 1-4120-8152-1



Cover design by Matjas Jumisko

*Printed in Victoria, BC, Canada. Printed on paper with minimum 30% recycled fibre. Trafford's print shop runs on "green energy" from solar, wind and other environmentally-friendly power sources.*

*Offices in Canada, USA, Ireland and UK*

This book was published *on-demand* in cooperation with Trafford Publishing. On-demand publishing is a unique process and service of making a book available for retail sale to the public taking advantage of on-demand manufacturing and Internet marketing. On-demand publishing includes promotions, retail sales, manufacturing, order fulfilment, accounting and collecting royalties on behalf of the author.

**Book sales for North America and international:**
Trafford Publishing, 6E–2333 Government St.,
Victoria, BC V8T 4P4 CANADA
phone 250 383 6864 (toll-free 1 888 232 4444)
fax 250 383 6804; email to orders@trafford.com
**Book sales in Europe:**
Trafford Publishing (UK) Limited, 9 Park End Street, 2nd Floor
Oxford, UK OX1 1HH UNITED KINGDOM
phone 44 (0)1865 722 113 (local rate 0845 230 9601)
facsimile 44 (0)1865 722 868; info.uk@trafford.com
**Order online at:**
trafford.com/05-3149

10 9 8 7 6 5 4 3 2

## Some reasons to choose this book

Computer programs are textual descriptions written according to the rules of a programming language. By writing computer programs we can make computers behave according to our thoughts. This book explains how computer programs are written using the Java programming language. Java is a popular language that is widely used both in educational institutes and in industry. The main purpose of this book is, however, to teach computer programming in general terms. After you have studied with this book, you'll know how computers operate; you'll be familiar with the fundamentals of programming and the essentials of object-oriented programming; and you'll be prepared to study other books related to computing and programming languages.

This book is written for people who are beginners in the field of computer programming, but experienced people may find it beneficial as well. This book does not assume any previous knowledge of computer programming. Logical operating principles of computers are explained before the actual studies of programming begin. In addition, this book promotes a programming style which prevents programming errors. All the examples of computer programs are written so that the reader encounters a lot of natural-language expressions instead of the traditional abbreviations of the computer world. This approach aims to make learning easier.

The pages of this book are designed to maximize readability and understandability. Examples of computer programs are presented in easy-to-read graphical descriptions. Pages are even composed so that the reader does not need to turn them unnecessarily.

If you later, after having studied with this book, need to study the C++ and C# programming languages, there are familiar books available to you. My two earlier books, *A Natural Introduction to Computer Programming with C#* and *A Natural Introduction to Computer Programming with C++*, have the same "look and feel" as this book. With these books it is easy to switch from one programming language to another because they present the same carefully-written computer programs using different programming languages.

To find more general information about this and my other programming books, please visit *www.naturalprogramming.com*. There you can read, among other things, success stories related to these books. The site provides free sample pages of my books. If you want to know why I ended up writing these books, then you should read the Epilogue and Preface of the C++ book.

## Notes for teachers and other experienced programmers

This book differs from other programming books in that all its computer programs are written with so-called natural names. This means that all names (identifiers) of variables, constants, arrays, methods, classes, etc. consist of several natural words. The names are written without abbreviations, and they thus look like the following

```
character_index   integer_index   character_from_keyboard
given_value   number_of_characters_read
string_to_search   replacement_string
```

Learning should be easier because the programs are written with readable names like those above.

I have been teaching subjects related to computer programming for more than 10 years. My course materials have always contained only programs with natural names, and I have encouraged students to use this kind of naming style in their programming work. My experience is that those students who use only natural names in their programs tend to produce better programs. I have also experienced personally that inventing informative natural names is a way to think during the process of program writing, and when you think clearly, you produce better programs and make less programming errors. For these reasons, I want to recommend the naming style that is used in this book. I know that there are experienced programmers who do not want to give up using abbreviations in programs, and people can have very strong opinions related to naming and other programming style issues. I would, however, like to urge people to try programming without abbreviations. Such programming style changes the physical appearance of programs and makes them slightly longer, but once you get accustomed to such programs you may experience something new in the process of program creation.

The names in the example programs of this book are such that underscore characters ( _ ) are used to separate (or to join) the words of a name. This kind of naming style is, in fact, not very common among Java programmers. For example, in many other Java books names are capitalized, which means that the words of a name are written so that an uppercase (capital) letter begins a new word in a name. According to this naming style, names look like

```
nameToBeKnown          integerFromKeyboard
findSmallestNumberInArray    keyboardInputIsNumerical
```

while in this book these names are written in the following way

```
name_to_be_known    integer_from_keyboard
find_smallest_number_in_array    keyboard_input_is_numerical
```

I have decided not to follow the usual Java naming style for the following two reasons

- The underscore character makes space between the words of a name, and as we are accustomed to the fact that there is generally space between the words of a text, the names that are formed with underscores can be considered more natural and readable than capitalized names. (ConsiderWhatThisBookWouldLookLikeIfItsBodyTextWouldBeWrittenThisWay.)
- The use of the underscore character helps to identify different types of names in this book. Because the names of the standard Java classes and methods are capitalized, they can be easily recognized as standard Java names when most other names contain underscore characters. For example, when the reader of this book finds method names like **nextLine**, **lastIndexOf**, and **charAt**, he or she knows that they are standard Java names because they are capitalized. On the other hand, names like **given_file_name**, **line_number**, and **text_line_from_file** are recognized as names invented by this author because they contain underscores.

The underscore character is most useful when the names in a program are long, and in this book the names are longer than in other programming books. With the advent of the Java language, the popularity of the underscore character has been decreasing. I think, however, that underscores should not be abandoned in programming. The underscore character serves an important purpose in this book, and it could be exploited in a similar way in other contexts.

## Acknowledgments

This book is based on my earlier books *A Natural Introduction to Computer Programming with C#* and *A Natural Introduction to Computer Programming with C++*. For this reason, I would like to thank again the people I have mentioned in my longer acknowledgments in the earlier books.

In addition I would like to thank Charles Hayles, Stephen Rank, Jouni Halleen, Jukka Joutsjoki, Pekka Alaluukas, Teemu Korpela, Katja Kurasto, and the roughly 500 students who have attended my Java courses over the last 5 years.

Oulu, Finland, November 2005

Kari Laitinen

## What kind of computer will you need?

It is assumed in this book that the reader is using a personal computer (PC) that runs a version of the Windows operating system. Various instructions (e.g. advice related to the compilation of Java programs) are based on this assumption. However, if you are able to find out by yourself how to write, compile, and execute Java programs on other types of computers (e.g. Linux, UNIX, or Macintosh computers), those computers will do as well. You just need to ensure that you are using version 5.0 or some later version of the Java Development Kit. As Java is a general-purpose programming language, a Java Development Kit is available for different types of computers.

Regardless of the type of your computer, it is an advantage if you are already able to use the computer for purposes like word processing. A connection to the Internet will also be needed on occasion, for example when you have to download electronic material from the Internet. You do not necessarily have to purchase any programming tools for your computer. In this book, we use programming tools that are freely available on the Internet.

## Some advice for studying

Although I have tried my best while writing this book, and I believe this is a very good textbook for a person who is starting to learn computer programming, it is still a fact that computer programming can be a difficult subject to begin with. When you read about something new in this book, you may not understand it immediately. At the start it might be possible that things just won't begin to become clear. That has happened to me, and still I became quite an expert in computer programming. So my first suggestion is

**Do not worry if you do not understand something immediately.**

It often happens that some things which you're studying may seem difficult in the beginning, and are only understood later, perhaps the following day when you have re-read the text which had been so difficult. Therefore, it is of prime importance to learn to accept that there are difficult things which cannot be understood quickly.

As this book is written so that it should be read sequentially from the beginning towards the end, I advise you to do so. If you encounter something that is already familiar to you, it is up to you if you want to skip some pages. But I would like to remind you, that it may deepen your knowledge, and in any case it does not harm you at all, if you also read the pages that seem to contain something familiar.

While you are reading have a pencil or pen at hand, and do not hesitate to

- underline or otherwise mark those sentences which you think are important;
- write your own thoughts in the margins and empty spaces of the pages;
- add your own explanation texts near the example programs; and
- mark, for example with a question mark (?), those parts of the text which you did not understand, and which you need to read again later.

Because you learn also by doing, it is important that you write about the things you are studying. Sometimes it may even be helpful to write down the things you do not understand.You can write down on the pages of this book (provided that it is your own book), and you should also have a separate notebook for writing. In addition to writing, it is important that you discuss matters of computer programming orally with your friends and fellow students. Sometimes it may help you to understand a computer program when you try to explain it to another person.

You just can't learn computer programming without writing programs by yourself. There are plenty of programming exercises in parts II and III of this book. You should do at least part of those exercises with a computer. One possible approach for doing the exercises is that you first read the text of a section and then do the exercises in that section.

You should also try to invent your own computer programs. It's nice to work with programs which nobody else has. In Part I of this book there are less exercises, but you should read that part before starting programming in the subsequent parts.

When you try programming exercises, you must use the keyboard of your computer. And in the future, you will probably use a computer and its keyboard daily in your work. To write effectively with a computer keyboard, and to prevent writing mistakes, I recommend that you learn to type with all 10 fingers. Computer keyboards are designed so that they can be used effectively with 10 fingers. The skill of typing with all 10 fingers can be learned through daily half-hour exercises over a few weeks. The time you spend learning this skill will be paid back hundreds of times in the future. There are special computer programs with which you can learn the 10-finger typing system. If you can't find a suitable program, you can borrow an old typing manual from a public library.

While you study this book and do exercises of computer programming, you will notice that you need a lot of information to write computer programs, and you cannot simply remember all the necessary information. The needed information may be in this book but you do not know on which page the information is located. To find information, you need to learn to use the index that is at the end of this book. The index lists keywords and phrases which are used on certain pages. It is normal that you may not find a certain piece of information by checking the page of your first search word. In such situations you just need to be patient. The index is a useful tool to search for information, but you must use ingenuity to invent several search words which can be looked up in the index. This advice applies to the indexes in other books as well. (The index of a book is a kind of Internet search engine whose "Internet" is the book. An advantage of a book is that it is a more organized information space than the Internet.)

Some pieces of information are regularly needed when computer programs are being written. For example, you may often have to check things in Appendix A. One possible way to make it easier to find frequently-used data is to take copies of the important pages and hang the copies on the wall near the place where you study or use your computer. Another possibility is to make the frequently-used pages easy to find by attaching pieces of tape or paper clips to them. With these kinds of little arrangements it is possible to make learning and computer programming somewhat easier for you.

The purpose of this book is to be your first book about computer programming. In the beginning, this book should be enough. However, as you proceed towards the end of this book, you shall become more and more experienced in computer programming, and you may not consider yourself a beginner any more. You may want to write longer computer programs or try other fields of computer programming. When you become more experienced, I recommend that you also acquire other programming books. I have personally found out that what cannot be found in one book, may be found in another book. After studying this book, you should be able to read books that are written for more experienced programmers. Especially if you start working as a computer programmer, you or your employer should not hesitate to invest in computer programming books. An appropriate book may easily save many working hours, and the price of the book is usually not much more than the price of a single working hour.

It might be a good idea to re-read this introductory section after you have done some computer programming.

## The structure of this book

This book is a textbook, a book for studying purposes. This is very much like other textbooks. The text and other elements of the book are organized in chapters. Then there are some things that do not belong to chapters. The overall structure of this book is the following

- introductory pages (this page belongs to these)
- chapters (there are 16 of them)
- appendices (these are identified with letters A, B, ...)
- index (this is very important to find information contained in the book)
- some useful tables for computer programmers

When you are learning computer programming, it is important that you learn to understand various structures of a text. This book has a certain structure which is described here. Like this book, computer programs are written according to certain structural rules.

Most of the text of this book is found in the chapters. Each chapter has a number. Chapters consist of sections which are numbered 1.1, 1.2, ... 2.1, 2.2, ... 3.1, 3.2, ... etc. Each section in this book consists of

- body text which is present in every section
- zero or more figures which are referred to in the body text by, for example, "Figure 3-2 shows how ..."
- zero or more tables which are referred to in the body text by, for example, "... is summarized in Table 6-3."
- zero or more program descriptions which are referred to with a file name in the body text by, for example, "Program **Weddingdates.java** is an example ..."
- zero or more information boxes which give interesting information related to the subject discussed in the section
- zero or more exercise boxes which present exercises related to the subject of the section.

Figures and tables are numbered so that the chapter number is mentioned. For example, when Figure 10-4 is discussed, you know that it is the fourth figure in Chapter 10 and there are three preceding figures in that chapter. Figures and tables are usually numbered this way in textbooks.

Program descriptions are a unique feature of this book. They form a systematic way to present computer programs, and to show how programs behave when they are executed on a computer. The structure of program descriptions is explained in the following introductory section.

### Example of an information box

In some sections you can find boxes like this one. There are two types of boxes:

- An information box usually presents information that is related to the subject discussed in the section, but the contents of an information box are usually not so important as the matters discussed in the body text of the section.
- An exercise box contains exercises which you should do after reading the text of the section. After the table of contents of this book, you can find a list which helps you to find those pages which contain exercise boxes.

## The structure of program descriptions

Computer programs are presented in a unique and exact manner in this book. These presentations are called program descriptions. The program descriptions resemble figures but they are not figures because their captions are different, and they do not follow the numbering system of figures. The first program descriptions are included in Chapter 2, and they are used throughout parts II and III of the book. The program descriptions may look a little bit strange at first, but after you become familiar with them, you'll find out that they are a very informative way to describe computer programs and their operation. This introductory section explains the notations used in program descriptions. You might read this section after you have studied some source programs.

The following is the simplest form of a program description that describes an executable program:

Program descriptions contain text "balloons" in which the structure and behavior of the program in question is explained. You are now reading a text balloon. The arrow points to that part of the program which is being explained by the balloon. The arrow of this balloon points to the beginning of the actual program text. It is important to note that the balloons are not part of the program, they just explain it.

There can be several balloons with varying sizes in a single source program description, and several arrows can originate from a single balloon. The arrow of this balloon points to the last line in the program text. The balloons make the program descriptions look a little bit like cartoons. That should make this book fun to read.

```
//  Filename.java

using System ;

class  Filename
{
   public static void main( String[] not_in_use )
   {
      // The actual program is always written by using
      // this Courier font. In the Courier font all
      // characters have the same physical width.

      // This program is an example which does nothing.
   }
}
```

**Filename.java - 1. Caption which describes the source program.**

```
What appears on the screen of the computer when the program is
executed is shown in this kind of box.
```

**Filename.java - X. Caption which says something about the execution of the program.**

A simple program description consists of two separate sub-descriptions which both have their own captions, i.e., some text below the descriptions:

- The source description presents the source program text of the program. The caption of the source description begins **Filename.java - 1. ...**
- The execution description shows what happens on the screen of a computer when the program is executed. The caption of the execution description is identified by the letter X and it begins **Filename.java - X. ...**

The key idea here is that both a program, and its program description, are identified with a file name. You can use the same file name that is used in a caption of a program description to search for the program among the electronic material associated with this book. For example, because the captions of the first program description on the first pages of Chapter 2 begin **First.java - ...**, you know that you can find the actual program in a file named **First.java**.

When program descriptions are referred to in the body text of this book, they are identified using the file name. For example, when I write "Program **First.java** is the first example of a Java program", I refer to all descriptions which have captions which begin **First.java - ...**

Many examples of computer programs in this book are so long that their text does not fit into a single source description. In these cases several source descriptions are needed to present the program. For example, a program description in Chapter 15 consists of four sub-descriptions with the captions

**Events.java - 1: The declaration of ...**

**Events.java - 2: Using an ArrayList array ...**

**Events.java - 3. Sorting and combining ...**

**Events.java - X. Three lists printed ...**

When there is a colon (:) written in the caption of a source description, it means that the program text continues in the following source description. In the final source description there is a full stop (.) after the number.

In some cases, it is necessary to explain just part of a program in a separate source description. In these situations, the plus sign (+) is used in the caption of a source description. For example, the first program in Chapter 6, **Largeint.java**, has a caption that begins

**Largeint.java - 1.+ A program to find ...**

The full stop (.) means that this is the final source description of the program, but the plus sign (+) means that some part of the text shown in this description is presented in more detail in another source description. The caption of the detailed description is equipped with a new level number and it begins

**Largeint.java - 1-1. The if constructs that ...**

The captions used in program descriptions form a kind of language where numbers, the colon, the full stop, the plus sign, and the letter X convey certain meanings. When you see a caption like

**Somefile.java - 2:+ ...**

you should be able to deduce that the entire program is presented in at least three separate source descriptions, and one or more parts of this second source description are explained in descriptions that have captions like

**Somefile.java - 2 -1 ...**

**Somefile.java - 2 - 2 ...**

## Table of contents

INTRODUCTORY PAGES
Some reasons to choose this book ..... iii
Notes for teachers and other experienced programmers ..... iii
Acknowledgments ..... iv
What kind of computer will you need? ..... v
Some advice for studying ..... v
The structure of this book ..... vii
The structure of program descriptions ..... viii
Table of contents ..... x
Java programs in this book ..... xiv
Pages where exercises can be found ..... xvii

PART I: THE WORLD OF COMPUTERS ..... 1

1 COMPUTING: SOME CONCEPTS AND TERMINOLOGY ..... 3
1.1 Hardware and software ..... 4
1.2 Operating systems, main memory, and memory devices ..... 4
1.3 Source programs and executable programs ..... 8
1.4 Programs, applications, and systems ..... 9

2 A FIRST LOOK AT JAVA SOURCE PROGRAMS ..... 11
2.1 A program that can print text to the screen ..... 12
2.2 A program that can read from the keyboard and calculate ..... 14
2.3 Getting a Java compiler to your computer ..... 20
2.4 Installing the electronic material of this book ..... 23
2.5 Compiling programs in a command prompt window ..... 25
2.6 Editor tools for writing and modifying source programs ..... 27
2.7 Modifying and compiling programs – introduction to exercises ..... 29

3 HOW INFORMATION IS STORED IN THE MEMORY OF A COMPUTER ..... 31
3.1 Numerical information: numbering systems ..... 32
3.2 Numerical information: the binary world of computers ..... 40
3.3 Textual information: character coding systems ..... 45
3.4 More information: pictures, sound, and moving pictures ..... 48

4 LOGICAL OPERATING PRINCIPLES OF COMPUTERS ..... 49
4.1 How does the main memory operate? ..... 50
4.2 The components of an imaginary computer ..... 54
4.3 Inside the imaginary processor ..... 56
4.4 Machine instructions ..... 59
4.5 The steps and states of program execution ..... 66
4.6 Programs to print text "Hello!" ..... 68
4.7 Programming language IML and compilation ..... 73
4.8 IC8 and ICOM – simulator programs for the imaginary computer ..... 80
4.9 A program that contains a loop ..... 82
4.10 Subroutine calls and stack operations ..... 84
4.11 Programs that use the keyboard, memory area, and stack ..... 87
4.12 Chapter summary – towards high-level programming ..... 94

**PART II: FUNDAMENTALS OF PROGRAMMING ........................... 97**

**5 VARIABLES AND OTHER BASIC ELEMENTS IN JAVA PROGRAMS ................ 99**

5.1 Integer variables (int, short, long, byte, char) ........................ 100
5.2 Keywords, names, spaces, and newlines ........................ 108
5.3 Floating-point variables ........................ 110
5.4 Operators, assignments, and literal constants ........................ 113
5.5 Reading data from the keyboard – a first look at strings ........................ 118
5.6 The double role of operator + ........................ 121
5.7 Formatting the output on the screen ........................ 125
5.8 Chapter summary ........................ 131

**6 DECISIONS AND REPETITIONS: BASIC ACTIVITIES IN PROGRAMS ................ 133**

6.1 Making decisions with keywords if and else ........................ 134
6.2 Making decisions with switch-case constructs ........................ 147
6.3 while loops enable repetition ........................ 152
6.4 for loops repeat a known number of times ........................ 158
6.5 do-while loops execute at least once ........................ 164
6.6 The block structure of Java programs ........................ 167
6.7 try-catch constructs handle exceptions ........................ 171
6.8 Truth values and variables of type boolean ........................ 174
6.9 Chapter summary ........................ 176

**7 ARRAYS: SETS OF SIMILAR DATA ITEMS ........................ 177**

7.1 Creating arrays and referring to array elements ........................ 178
7.2 Array declaration vs. array creation ........................ 189
7.3 Initialized arrays ........................ 191
7.4 Multidimensional arrays ........................ 196
7.5 Chapter summary ........................ 197

**8 STRINGS STORE SEQUENCES OF CHARACTER CODES ........................ 199**

8.1 "Variables" of type String ........................ 200
8.2 String literals ........................ 203
8.3 Accessing individual characters of a string ........................ 204
8.4 String methods ........................ 208
8.5 Class StringBuilder – mutable strings ........................ 226
8.6 Arrays of strings ........................ 231
8.7 Chapter summary ........................ 236

**9 METHODS – LOGICAL PERFORMING UNITS IN PROGRAMS ........................ 239**

9.1 Simple static methods and the concept of calling ........................ 240
9.2 Methods that take parameters ........................ 244
9.3 Methods that return data to the caller ........................ 254
9.4 Calling static methods of another class ........................ 262
9.5 The role of the stack in method calls ........................ 268
9.6 Scope of variables ........................ 275
9.7 Parameters for the method main() ........................ 278
9.8 Overloading method names ........................ 282
9.9 Chapter summary ........................ 286

**PART III: OBJECT-ORIENTED PROGRAMMING . . . . . 287**

**10 CLASSES AND OBJECTS . . . . . 289**

10.1 Classes, fields, and instance methods . . . . . 290
10.2 Constructors are methods that build objects . . . . . 300
10.3 Several constructors in a class . . . . . 306
10.4 Arrays containing references to objects . . . . . 310
10.5 Value types vs. reference types . . . . . 324
10.6 When objects become garbage . . . . . 325
10.7 A stack that grows dynamically . . . . . 326
10.8 Java packages . . . . . 334
10.9 Chapter summary . . . . . 337

**11 MORE ADVANCED CLASSES . . . . . 341**

11.1 Class Date – an example of a larger class . . . . . 342
11.2 The this keyword . . . . . 362
11.3 Graphical UML class diagrams . . . . . 365
11.4 "Objects inside objects" . . . . . 366
11.5 Using object references as method parameters . . . . . 379
11.6 Chapter summary . . . . . 382

**12 INHERITANCE AND CLASS HIERARCHIES . . . . . 383**

12.1 Base classes and derived classes . . . . . 384
12.2 Larger class hierarchies . . . . . 400
12.3 Polymorphism – redefining methods in derived classes . . . . . 414
12.4 Chapter summary . . . . . 428

**13 SOME STANDARD JAVA CLASSES . . . . . 431**

13.1 Wrapper classes Byte, Short, Integer, Long, Float, Double, etc. . . . . . 432
13.2 Object: the class above all classes . . . . . 434
13.3 Exception classes . . . . . 438
13.4 Class Math provides static mathematical methods . . . . . 446
13.5 Chapter summary . . . . . 448

**14 STORING INFORMATION IN FILES . . . . . 449**

14.1 Classes to read and write files . . . . . 450
14.2 Reading and writing text files . . . . . 452
14.3 Handling files as binary files . . . . . 469
14.4 A larger program that uses a binary file . . . . . 478
14.5 Chapter summary . . . . . 496

**15 MORE STANDARD JAVA TYPES . . . . . 501**

15.1 ArrayList class . . . . . 502
15.2 Comparable and other interfaces . . . . . 514
15.3 Class GregorianCalendar and its superclass Calendar . . . . . 521
15.4 Chapter summary . . . . . 528

**16 GOING CLOSER TO THE MACHINE . . . . . 529**

16.1 Bit operators &, |, ^, ~. >>, and << . . . . . 530
16.2 Playing with the time in programs – introduction to threads . . . . . 538
16.3 Chapter summary . . . . . 551

**APPENDIX A: SUMMARY OF IMPORTANT JAVA FEATURES .......... 555**
A - 1: Literals .......... 555
A - 2: Variables, constants, and arrays of basic types .......... 556
A - 3: String objects, other objects, and arrays of objects .......... 557
A - 4: Expressions .......... 558
A - 5: Assignments and left-side expressions .......... 558
A - 6: The most important Java operators in order of precedence .......... 559
A - 7: Control structures to make decisions (selections) .......... 560
A - 8: Control structures to perform repetitions (iterations) .......... 561
A - 9: Some basic Java method structures .......... 562
A - 10: String methods .......... 563
A - 11: Mechanisms for keyboard input and screen output .......... 564
A - 12: Input/output from/to files .......... 564
A - 13: Data conversions .......... 565
A - 14: Java class declaration .......... 566
**APPENDIX B: JAVA KEYWORDS (RESERVED WORDS) .......... 567**
**APPENDIX C: PRACTICAL ADVICE FOR PROGRAMMING EXERCISES .......... 571**
C - 1: Starting an exercise .......... 571
C - 2: Writing your program .......... 571
C - 3: Compiling and executing your program .......... 572
C - 4: Correcting compilation errors .......... 573
C - 5: Searching for errors that compilers do not detect .......... 574
C - 6: Programs that do not terminate .......... 575
C - 7: Incremental program development .......... 576
C - 8: Printing your program on paper .......... 577
C - 9: Program versions and backups .......... 577
**INDEX .......... 579**
**USEFUL TABLES .......... 593**

## *Java programs in this book*

The Java programs that are presented and explained in this book are listed below in alphabetical order according to their file names. If you know the file name of a program, the list below helps you to find the page on which the program is explained. The physical files of the source programs that are discussed in the chapters of this book can be found in the directories (folders) **javafiles1**, **javafiles2**, and **javafiles3** among the electronic material associated with this book. The numbers in the directory names refer to the three parts of this book. For example, the programs that are discussed in Part II of this book are stored in directory **javafiles2**. In addition to the programs that are listed below, the electronic material provides programs in the **javafilesextra** directory. Those programs are not widely discussed in this book. Then there is the directory **javasolutions** which contains solutions to programming exercises.


Additions.java - 1. Demonstrating the use of the + operator. . . . . 124
Animals.java - 1: Class Animal with two constructors and two other methods. . . . . 308
ArrayDemo.java - 1.+ A program that demonstrates the use of an array. . . . . 180
ArrayListDemo.java - 1: Demonstrating the standard class ArrayList. . . . . 506
BankBetter.java - 1: A program with a BankAccount class that has a constructor. . . . . 302
BankPolymorphic.java - 1: A program with several bank account classes. . . . . 416
BankSimple.java - 1: The declaration of class BankAccount. . . . . 296
BetterDate.java - 1: Deriving a new class from an existing class. . . . . 386
Binary.java - 1: A method that prints an integer value in binary form. . . . . 536
Birthdays.java - 1. A program that finds the dates for the most important birthday parties. . . . . 346
BirthdaysGregorianCalendar.java - 1. A rewritten version of program Birthdays.java. . . . . 522
Boxings.java - 1: Boxing and unboxing activities demonstrated.. . . . . 437
Calculate.java - 1: First part of the program. . . . . 280
Calendars.java - 1: A program with which calendars can be printed. . . . . 394
Capitals.java - 1.+ A simple program to find the capitals of some countries.. . . . . 218
Celsius.java - 1. Converting temperature values with an initialized array. . . . . 193
Clock.java - 1: A program which acts as a kind of clock. . . . . 546
Collect.java - 1: The first part of a program to maintain data about a collection. . . . . 482
Columbus.java - 1. Demonstrating the use of Date objects. . . . . 345
Commanding.java - 1. A method main() that prints the given command line parameters. . . . . 279
Convert.java - 1 - 1. Method convert() of class Conversion. . . . . 320
Convert.java - 1+: A program to make conversions between units of measure. . . . . 318
CurrentDate.java - 1. The declaration of class CurrentDate. . . . . 390
Date.java - 1: A general-purpose class to handle date information. . . . . 350
DateDistance.java - 1. A class that represents a chronological distance between two dates. . . . . 361
Decorations.java - 1.+ Method main() calls a method that takes a string as a parameter. . . . . 248
Distance.java - 1.+ A program to convert meters to other units of distance. . . . . 114
DotsAndDollars.java - 1: A program that runs as three threads. . . . . 541
Elvis.java - 1. Modifying some characters of a StringBuilder object. . . . . 227
Evenodd.java - 1. A program to find out whether a given integer is even or odd. . . . . 139
Events.java - 1: The declaration of class Event. . . . . 516
ExceptionalNumbers.java - 1: Throwing and catching some exceptions. . . . . 440
Filecopy.java - 1: A program that makes a copy of a text file. . . . . 460
Fileprint.java - 1.+ A program that reads a text file and prints the text lines to the screen. . . . . 458
FileToNumbers.java - 1: A program to show the contents of a file as hexadecimal bytes. . . . . 474
Findreplace.java - 1: A program to replace a string with another string in a text file. . . . . 464
First.java - 1. A Java program that prints a single line of text to the screen. . . . . 13
For20.java - 1. Program While20.java implemented with a for loop. . . . . 159
Forcodes.java - 1.+ A program that prints a character code table. . . . . 162
Formatting.java - 1. Demonstrating the use of format specifiers.. . . . . 126
Friday13.java - 1. A program that demonstrates how certain kinds of dates can be searched. . . . . 348
Friday13GregorianCalendar.java - 1. A rewritten version of program Friday13.java. . . . . 524

Fullname.java - 1. The input/output of strings. . . . . 201
Game.java - 1.+ A program that implements a simple computer game. . . . . 102
Highmiddlelow.java - 1: Declarations of classes MemberClass, HighClass, and MiddleClass. . . . . 402
Iffing.java - 1. A program that contains a complex if construct. . . . . 144
Interest.java - 1.+ Calculating interest on interest with a multidimensional array. . . . . 194
Largeint.java - 1.+ A program to find the largest of three integers. . . . . 136
LargestWithIntParameter.java - 1: A rewritten version of LargestWithReturn.java. . . . . 380
LargestWithReturn.java - 1. A method that returns data to its caller with a return statement. . . . . 256
Letters.java - 1. Method main() calling a method that calls two other methods. . . . . 243
Likejava.java - 1.+ A program containing an if-else if-else construct. . . . . 142
Likejavas.java - 1. Program Likejava.java rewritten using a switch-case construct. . . . . 148
Marilyn.java - 1. The use of string method compareTo(). . . . . 212
MathDemo.java - 1. Using some mathematical methods of the standard class Math. . . . . 447
Meanvalue.java - 1. A program to calculate the mean value of a set of integers. . . . . 165
MeanvalueArray.java - 1.+ An improved version of program MeanvalueException.java. . . . . 186
MeanvalueException.java - 1. A rewritten version of Meanvalue.java. . . . . 172
MeanvalueMethod.java - 1: The first part of the program. . . . . 260
Messages.java - 1. Method main() calling a simple method named print_message(). . . . . 241
Miles.java - 1. A program that uses floating-point variables. . . . . 111
Months.java - 1.+ Demonstration of an initialized array of strings. . . . . 232
MorseCodes.java - 1. Using class ArrayList to store String objects. . . . . 509
NumbersToFile.java - 1. A program that stores numerical values to a binary file. . . . . 476
Olympics.java - 1: The declaration of class Olympics. . . . . 313
Overload.java - 1. A program containing several versions of the method print_array(). . . . . 284
Person.java - 1. A class that has public data fields. . . . . 298
Planets.java - 1: A program that gives information about planets. . . . . 321
Playtime.java - 1: A program that displays time information after every 5 seconds. . . . . 544
Presidents.java - 1: A program that provides information about U.S. presidents. . . . . 368
Rectangles.java - 1: The declaration of class Rectangle. . . . . 292
Reverse.java - 1.+ A program that inputs integers and prints them in reverse order. . . . . 184
ScopeExploration.java - 1. Using classwide and local data. . . . . 277
Search.java - 1: A method that searches for a string in a text file. . . . . 462
Sentence.java - 1. Using a switch-case construct with no break statements. . . . . 150
Showtime.java - 1. Extracting time/date information from a GregorianCalendar object. . . . . 526
Sleepings.java - 1. Demonstrating the use of the Tread.sleep() method. . . . . 540
Sort.java - 1: A program whose methods are in three classes. . . . . 264
SplittingAtoms.java - 1.+ Splitting a string with method split(). . . . . 234
Stack.java - 1: The fields and constructors of class Stack. . . . . 328
States.java - 1: Using method substring() and the concatenation operator +. . . . . 214
StatesStringBuilder.java - 1: A rewritten version of program States.java. . . . . 228
StringEquality.java - 1: Demonstrating the equality operator and method equals(). . . . . 210
Stringing.java - 1: Demonstrating string construction and character access. . . . . 216
StringMethodsMore.java - 1. contains(), indexOf(), regionMatches(), and substring() in use. . . . . 213
StringReverse.java - 1. Printing the characters of a string in reverse order. . . . . 207
Sum.java - 1.+ A program to calculate the sum of two integers. . . . . 15
SumImproved.java - 1. A slightly improved version of program Sum.java. . . . . 18
Sums.java - 1.+ Method main() calls a method that takes two parameters of type int. . . . . 246
Times.java - 1: Demonstrating the use of an abstract class named CurrentTime. . . . . 424
Titanic.java - 1. A program that uses both a Date object and a CurrentDate object. . . . . 391
Translate.java - 1: The declaration of class BilingualTranslation. . . . . 510
TruthValues.java - 1. A program that prints truth values. . . . . 175
Uplow.java - 1. A program that demonstrates the use of the bitwise-AND operator &. . . . . 535
Weddingdates.java - 1.+ Using a CurrentDate object to find the next best wedding dates. . . . . 392
While20.java - 1. A program containing a simple while loop. . . . . 155

Whilesum.java - 1. A program to calculate the sum of integers in a while loop. . . . . . . . . . 156
Widename.java - 1. Referring to individual characters of a string. . . . . . . . . . 205
Windows.java - 1: A program with a long class hierarchy. . . . . . . . . . 406
Words.java - 1.+ A program that contains many blocks of statements. . . . . . . . . . 168

## Pages where exercises can be found

Programming exercises are presented in special exercise boxes in this book. An exercise box is not always located at the end of a chapter. A chapter may have several exercise boxes among the body text. The list below helps you to find those pages that contain an exercise box.


Exercises with program Sum.java . . . . . 17
Exercises related to numbering systems . . . . . 39
Exercise related to main memory usage . . . . . 52
Exercises related to machine-level programming . . . . . 72
Exercise with the IC8 simulator program . . . . . 81
Exercises with programs abcde.iml and aaaabbbbcccc.iml . . . . . 86
Exercises with programs reverse_in_memory.iml and reverse_in_stack.iml . . . . . 89
Exercises with program Game.java . . . . . 105
Exercises with program Distance.java . . . . . 116
Exercises – write some simple programs . . . . . 123
Exercises related to if constructs . . . . . 146
Exercises related to boolean expressions . . . . . 149
Exercises related to while loops . . . . . 161
Exercises with loops . . . . . 166
Exercises with program ArrayDemo.java . . . . . 179
Exercises related to arrays . . . . . 192
More exercises related to arrays . . . . . 197
Exercises related to strings . . . . . 206
Exercises with Marilyn.java . . . . . 230
Exercises related to strings and arrays . . . . . 237
Exercises related to methods . . . . . 252
More exercises related to methods . . . . . 253
Still more exercises related to methods. . . . . . 263
Exercises related command line parameters . . . . . 285
Exercises with program BankBetter.java . . . . . 304
Exercises with program Animals.java . . . . . 307
Exercises related arrays containing object references . . . . . 312
Exercise with program Stack.java . . . . . 330
Exercises related to classes . . . . . 338
A first exercise with Date objects . . . . . 344
Second exercise with Date objects . . . . . 349
More exercises with class Date . . . . . 364
Exercises to improve class Date . . . . . 364
Exercises with program Presidents.java . . . . . 378
Exercises related to inheritance . . . . . 399
Exercises with program Windows.java . . . . . 412
Exercise with program BankPolymorphic.java . . . . . 421
Exercise with program Times.java . . . . . 428
Exercises with program ExceptionalNumbers.java . . . . . 444
Exercises related to text files . . . . . 468
Exercises related to binary files . . . . . 477
Exercises with program Collect.java . . . . . 481
Exercises with program Translate.java . . . . . 513
Exercises related to ArrayList-based arrays . . . . . 513
Exercise related to program Events.java . . . . . 519
Exercise related to sorting of arrays . . . . . 519
Exercises with class GregorianCalendar . . . . . 528
Exercises related to bit operators . . . . . 549

Exercises related to timing ........ 549
Exercises related to timing (continued) ........ 550
Exercises related to timing (continued) ........ 551

# PART I: THE WORLD OF COMPUTERS

Chapters

1 Computing: some concepts and terminology
2 A first look at Java source programs
3 How information is stored in the memory of a computer
4 Logical operating principles of computers

Use empty pages for your own notes

# CHAPTER 1

## COMPUTING: SOME CONCEPTS AND TERMINOLOGY

Practically all learning involves the learning of new terms and concepts. When we learn new things, we have to learn the language of the new area or field. For example, if you want to learn to play the game of golf, you have to learn what terms like "birdie", "bogey", and "eagle" mean. Similarly, to learn computer programming, you need to learn what is a "source program", what "compilation" means, what is a "floating-point variable" etc.

In this first chapter we shall study some of the basic terms of computing. We will examine the basic structure of a computer and the role of an operating system in a computer. You will be shown a Java source program but we shall not try to understand it yet. Be patient! It is important to learn some basics before starting to study computer programming. You should also realize that this is not the only chapter where new terminology is introduced. The whole book is full of new terms which you should learn gradually as you proceed with your studies.

## 1.1 Hardware and software

Electronic computers were brought into commercial use shortly after World War II. During their history, computers have evolved tremendously. The first computers were large machines occupying entire rooms. Today, computers are small because electronic components and integrated circuits, which they are made of, are small. The early computers were used only by a few scientists and engineers. Nowadays, personal computers have become equally as common as radios and TVs. In addition to electronic devices which we call computers, there are hidden or embedded computers inside much commonplace equipment. For instance, modern mobile telephones contain computers that control the equipment.

Computers consist of hardware and software. Hardware is everything which we can see and touch in a computer. For example, in a personal computer (PC), the screen, the keyboard, the mouse, the hard disk, the integrated circuits, and other electronic components on the greenish boards inside the control unit are hardware. Software, on the other hand, is much more difficult to describe. Software is not visible in the same way as hardware. We cannot touch software.

Software makes computers do things. The user of a computer communicates with software that is being run (or executed) on the computer. The software of a computer consists of applications. Word processing programs, which are also called word processors, are a good example of application software. Microsoft Word is an example of a commercially available word processing program. You can run a word processing program on your computer, and thereby you apply your computer to word processing purposes. Other kinds of applications are, for example, computer games, Internet browsers, and compilers. There are certainly thousands of different computer applications in the world. By studying this book, you will learn to create your own computer applications.

It is very hard to define the word "software" exactly, but after reading this book you will understand what this word means. Software makes computers "live", operate, and be useful. A computer without software is a little bit like a CD player without any music stored on CDs, or a TV without any VCRs, DVD players, or broadcasting or cable-TV companies. Because software is so important for computers, it is useful to learn how to develop software, and that is what this book will teach you.

## 1.2 Operating systems, main memory, and memory devices

In every modern computer, there is an operating system which is software. An operating system is software that makes the hardware of the computer come alive. Computers would be very difficult to use without operating systems. Operating systems are software that control all the basic operations of a computer. With the help of an operating system, it is possible to use other software packages, such as word processing programs, computer games, and Internet browsers.

Probably the most widely-known commercial operating system is Microsoft Windows of which there are several variations. An imitation of the MS-DOS operating system, the first operating system for personal computers, is hidden inside the Windows operating system. UNIX is the operating system for larger workstation computers. Apple Macintosh computers also have their own operating system. Linux is a free UNIX-like operating system for PCs.

An operating system is software that controls the essential hardware components of a computer. An operating system serves as a link between the application software and the hardware (see Figure 1-1). When you operate a personal computer, you always have to interact with the operating system.

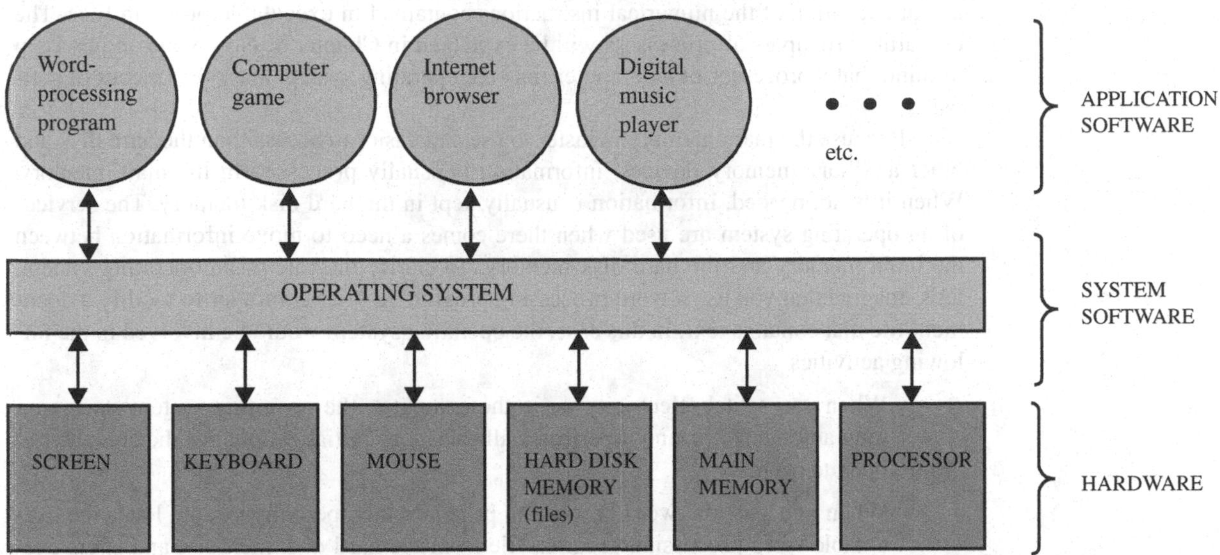


***Figure 1-1. An operating system is a link between hardware and application software.***

Computers need memory devices in order to operate and store information. The most important piece of memory in a computer is its main memory. The main memory is also called "the immediate access memory" or "the main storage". The main memory of a PC is made of RAM components. RAM is an abbreviation of "random access memory" which means that a processor of a computer can access all memory locations with a certain numerical memory address. (Don't panic if this sounds somewhat difficult. The operation of computer memory will be studied more thoroughly later.)

In addition to the main memory, a computer usually has various kinds of memory devices which we can refer to with the term "auxiliary memory". Auxiliary memory devices are usually slower and cheaper than the components of the main memory. In a PC, the most important auxiliary memory device is a hard disk where information is stored magnetically on rotating plates. Other auxiliary memory devices in a typical PC are USB memory devices, CDs, and DVDs.

The auxiliary memory devices of a computer could be called the file memory because all information in the auxiliary memory is stored in files. Every file must have a unique name that identifies it. A file name usually consists of the actual file name and a file name extension. For example, in the name **Sum.java** (pronounced "sum dot java"), **Sum** is the actual file name and **.java** is the file name extension. A file name extension usually shows what is contained in a file or how a file ought to be used. For example, the extension **.java** reveals that the file contains a Java source program, the extension **.exe** is for files that contain executable computer programs, and **.txt** terminates the names of files that contain readable unformatted texts.

Because the memory devices of a computer can contain thousands of files, there must be some kind of system to organize the files into groups so that they can be easily found. For this reason, it is possible to create directories on hard disks and other memory devices. Directories are also called folders. A directory can contain a set of files and other directories that are called subdirectories.

There must also be a means to identify different memory devices. In PCs that run the Windows operating system, different memory devices are identified with letters like A, C, D, E, etc. These letters are called drives. Usually drive A: is a floppy disk drive, drive C: and often also drive D: are on the hard disk, then drive E: might be a CD drive, and so on. All the memory devices, the drives, have a root directory that contains files and other directories that are stored on the memory device.

A processor is the most important component in a computer. Processors perform the actual execution of the numerical instructions contained in executable program files. The operating principles of processors will be explained in Chapter 4. Now you can just keep in mind that a processor of a computer runs the operating system and other pieces of software.

Because the main memory is faster to use and easier to access than the hard disk and other auxiliary memory devices, information is usually processed in the main memory. When it is not needed, information is usually kept in the hard disk memory. The services of an operating system are used when there comes a need to move information between the main memory and the hard disk memory. To clarify the role of an operating system, let's imagine that you use a word processing program in your computer to modify a document file that contains text. In this case, the operating system would be involved in the following activities:

- When you switch electricity on in the computer, the operating system starts running automatically, and it performs all necessary initializations for the computer to operate properly.
- When you start the word processing program, the operating system loads the executable word processing program file from the hard disk memory, and starts executing it in the computer's main memory.
- When the word processing program that is being executed loads the document file from the hard disk memory, it loads the file by using the file reading services which are provided by the operating system.
- When a word processing program displays the text from the document file on the screen and reads characters from the keyboard, it does all these operations through the operating system.
- When you want to save the modified text, the word processing program uses the file storing services provided by the operating system.
- When you terminate (exit) the word processing program, the operating system frees the main memory that was occupied by the word processing program.

When a file is being processed with a text processing program, the operating system, the text processing program, and the text being processed reside in the computer's main memory. This situation is illustrated in Figure 1-2. The processor executes the text processing program until it is terminated. The operating system of the computer takes care of what is executed by the processor, and what resides in the main memory. When an application (e.g. a text processing program) is being executed, the processor executes the application and the operating system at the same time. Modern operating systems can usually handle situations where several applications are simultaneously executed by one processor.

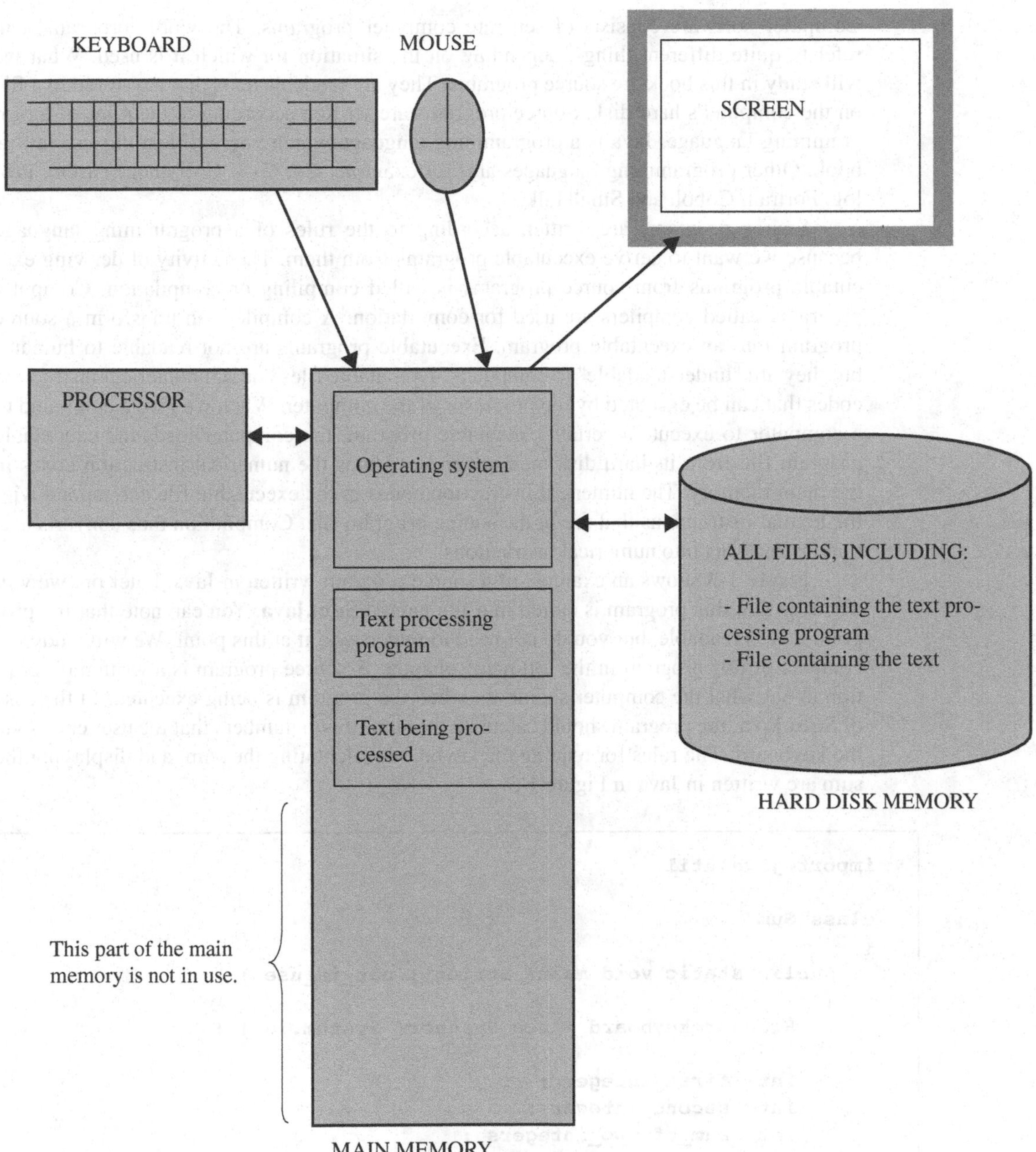


*Figure 1-2. A text processing program being executed on a computer.*

## 1.3 Source programs and executable programs

Computer software consists of separate computer programs. The word "program" can refer to quite different things, depending on the situation for which it is used. What we will study in this book are source programs. They are readable texts that are stored in a file on the computer's hard disk. Source programs are written according to the rules of a programming language. Java is a programming language which you will learn to use in this book. Other programming languages are, for example, C#, C++, C, Python, Pascal, Prolog, Fortran, Cobol, and SmallTalk.

Source programs are written according to the rules of a programming language because we want to derive executable programs from them. The activity of deriving executable programs from source programs is called compiling or compilation. Computer programs called compilers are used for compilation. A compiler can transform a source program into an executable program. Executable programs are not readable to humans, but they are "understandable" to computers. Executable files contain numerical instruction codes that can be executed by the processor of the computer. When we give a command to a computer to execute a certain executable program, the computer loads the executable program file from its hard disk memory and executes the numerical instruction codes in the main memory. The numerical instruction codes in the executable file correspond with the textual instructions that are in the source program file. Compilation thus converts textual instructions into numerical instructions.

Figure 1-3 shows an example of a source program written in Java. Later on, we will discover that this program is stored in a file named **Sum.java**. You can note that the program text is readable, but you do not need to understand it at this point. We will study the contents of this program in the following chapter. A source program is a written description about what the computer should do when the program is being executed. In the case of **Sum.java**, the program should calculate the sum of two numbers that the user enters via the keyboard. The rules for reading the keyboard, calculating the sum, and displaying the sum are written in Java in Figure 1-3.

```
import java.util.* ;

class Sum
{
   public static void main( String[] not_in_use )
   {
      Scanner keyboard = new Scanner( System.in ) ;

      int  first_integer ;
      int  second_integer ;
      int  sum_of_two_integers ;

      System.out.print( "\n Please, type in an integer:       " ) ;
      first_integer   =  keyboard.nextInt() ;

      System.out.print( "\n Please, type in another integer: " ) ;
      second_integer   =  keyboard.nextInt() ;

      sum_of_two_integers   =   first_integer   +   second_integer ;

      System.out.print( "\n The sum of the given integers is "
                           +  sum_of_two_integers ) ;
   }
}
```

*Figure 1-3. An example of a Java source program, Sum.java.*

Source programs are usually written using a program editor, which is a special kind of text processing program, tailored to write source program texts. Source programs must be compiled with a compiler program before they can be executed. Program editors and compilers are executable programs which you can buy or download freely for your computer. These programs are called software development tools or programming tools. Nowadays it is common that the programming tools are combined into one tool. Source programs can be edited, compiled, and executed with a single tool, called an integrated program development environment.

Figure 1-4 shows the phases of program development. When you have written a source program with a program editor, you must compile it before you can execute it. Source programs can be compiled and executed in different ways, depending on what kind of a compiler is in use. We shall learn about the compilation and execution of programs in the following chapter. For now, we can say that a new file is created when a source program is transformed into an executable program. The original source program file remains untouched. In the case of **Sum.java**, the compilation would produce a file named **Sum.class**. The commonly used file name extension for Java source programs is **.java**. Executable files resulting from compilation end with **.class**.

Figure 1-5 describes the execution of programs that are written with the Java language. Java programs need a special runtime environment, the Java virtual machine, that is installed together with the Java compiler. Java programs thus differ from traditional computer programs whose execution is controlled solely by the operating system.

Depending on the situation, the word "program" means a source program or an executable program. Executable programs can be generated from source programs, but they can also be purchased. Compilers, editors, and other computer tools are executable programs that are often bought for a computer. Many computer tools are also freely available on the Internet.

Sometimes the word "code" is used instead of the word "program". People use the term "source code" instead of "source program", or they may say "executable code" or "machine code" instead of "executable program". The word "code" is relevant in the world of computers because everything we input to a computer is coded somehow. Even letters and pictures are coded using numbers. An executable program contains numerical codes to be executed by a processor or by a virtual machine. Therefore, it is relevant to call executable programs with the term "executable code". The term "source code" can be used, because source programs are coded according to the rules of a programming language.

## 1.4 Programs, applications, and systems

The words "application" and "program" are used to speak about computer programs, but is is hard to distinguish their meanings. These words can mean the same thing in some cases. A word processing application can be called a word processing program. An application is usually a larger program, which has originally been built by writing many source programs which have then been integrated into a single larger application.

The word "system" is also used in the context of computers and software. A "system" means something that is even bigger than an application. A system usually includes both the computer and its software. A large computer system may include several computers that interact with each other. The term "system development" is sometimes used to mean the software development of large systems.

Small computer applications can simply be called computer programs. The Java programs that will be presented in this book are called programs, not applications or systems. Programs are readable texts written according to the rules of a programming language. The act of writing computer programs is called programming. The people who write programs are called (computer) programmers. After you have learned what is said in this book, you can say that you can program computers. If computer programming becomes your profession, you might call yourself a computer programmer or software developer.

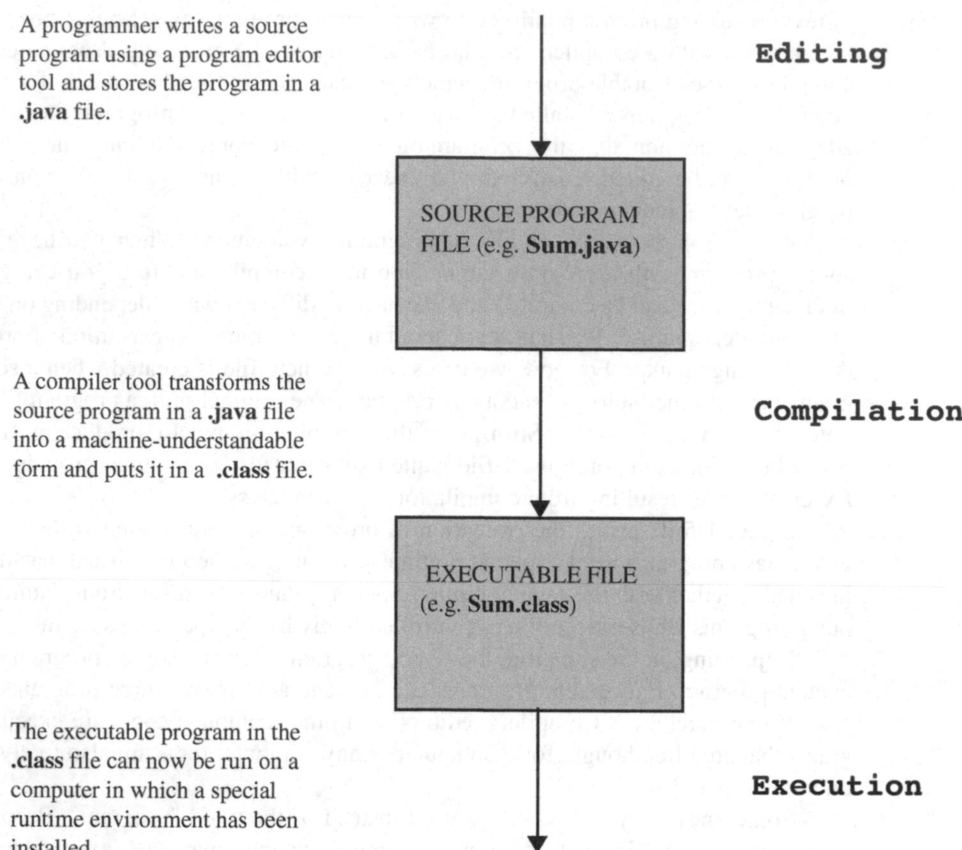

A programmer writes a source program using a program editor tool and stores the program in a .java file.
Editing
SOURCE PROGRAM FILE (e.g. Sum.java)
A compiler tool transforms the source program in a .java file into a machine-understandable form and puts it in a .class file.
Compilation
EXECUTABLE FILE (e.g. Sum.class)
The executable program in the .class file can now be run on a computer in which a special runtime environment has been installed.
Execution

***Figure 1-4. The process of Java computer program development.***

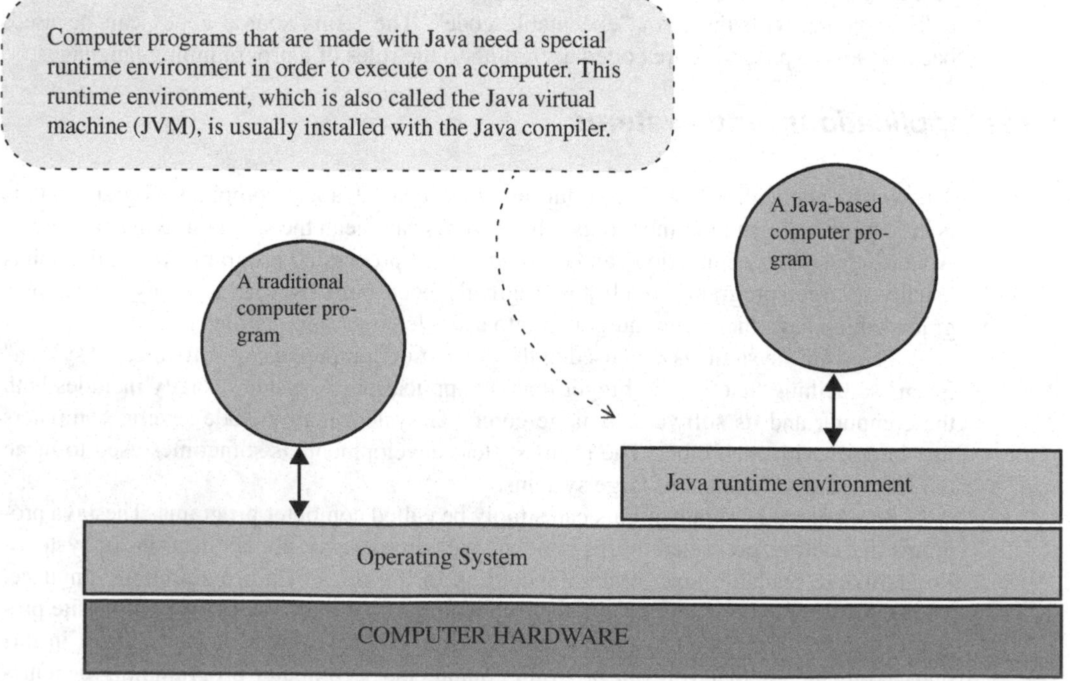

Computer programs that are made with Java need a special runtime environment in order to execute on a computer. This runtime environment, which is also called the Java virtual machine (JVM), is usually installed with the Java compiler.
A traditional computer program
A Java-based computer program
Java runtime environment
Operating System
COMPUTER HARDWARE

***Figure 1-5. The execution of traditional and Java-based computer programs.***

# CHAPTER 2

## A FIRST LOOK AT JAVA SOURCE PROGRAMS

We have already seen one Java source program in the previous chapter in Figure 1-3, but we have not yet tried to understand it. In this chapter, we shall study a couple of computer programs, including the one in Figure 1-3. You will learn some basic things, such as

- how a Java program displays text on the screen,
- how a Java program reads in numbers from the keyboard,
- how simple calculations can be made in Java programs, and
- how Java programs can be compiled and executed.

After this chapter, you will know something about Java programming, but it is likely that you will have many questions in your mind. You may want to know

- how can a variable store information?
- what is actually happening during compilation?
- how does a computer execute programs?

It is perfectly natural to have these questions in your mind. In chapters 3 and 4 we shall study some basics of computing, and these questions will be answered then.

## 2.1 A program that can print text to the screen

The simplest things computer programs can do is to read in some data (e.g. numbers or text) from the keyboard, do something to that data, and then print something to the screen. Perhaps the simplest computer program is one that just prints a single sentence of text to the screen. Such a computer program is **First.java** which is presented in a program description on the opposite page. Later on in this chapter, you will be instructed how to get the file **First.java** to your own computer. When the program is compiled and executed on a computer, the following line will appear on the screen of the computer:

```
I am a simple computer program.
```

By studying program **First.java** you will discover that, in some ways, computer programs resemble texts written in natural languages such as English. For example, the program **First.java** contains such natural words as **`public`** and **`print`**. On the other hand, program texts are in many ways much more complex than natural-language texts. For example, there are special characters like { } ( ) ; in use in program **First.java**. All these characters have a special meaning in the program. The special characters are interpreted by the compiler of the Java programming language when the program is transformed into an executable form.

The act of printing text to the screen of a computer is called output. We say that a program can output text to the screen. In program **First.java** text output is performed by the output statement

```
System.out.print( "I am a simple computer program." ) ;
```

The output mechanism of the Java programming language is such that **`System.out`** represents the screen and **`print`** is a method that is used to print, or move, text to the screen. The text to be printed must be written inside double quotation marks.

All Java programs must be written according to a certain structure, that is, the syntax of the programming language. All Java programs up until Chapter 8 in this book follow the structure

```
class ClassName
{
   public static void main( String[] not_in_use )
   {
      ...
   }
}
```

The meaning of the three dots is "some program lines written with Java". In the place of the three dots there is something different in each program, but there is always **`class ClassName`** followed by an opening brace { followed by **`public static void main( String[] not_in_use )`** followed by another opening brace {. After the program statements there is a closing brace } that marks the end of method **`main()`**, and another closing brace that marks the end of the class. In the above program structure, a method named **`main()`** is inside a class named **`ClassName`**. According to the rules of Java, this kind of class would have to be stored in a file named **ClassName.java**. As we shall see in the next section of this chapter, in some programs we have **`import`** statements before the line that begins with the word **`class`**.

A peculiarity in the program structure described above is the definition **`String[] not_in_use`**. The rules of Java require that we must write these definitions although they specify something that is not used. We will study and use these definitions in Chapter 9. Then we'll have something else in place of the name **`not_in_use`**.

In this book, examples of computer programs are described so that the actual program text is explained within "balloons" such as these. These balloons are not part of the computer program. Instead, they are a means to teach you. The arrow originating from this balloon points to the first line of program **First.java**. This program has only 7 lines. Note that the actual program is always written with the font called **courier**.

This is the line in this source program which specifies what will be printed to the screen when the program is executed. The text to be printed to the screen must be written "inside double quote characters", and there must be a semicolon (;) at the end.

```
class First
{
   public static void main( String[] not_in_use )
   {
      System.out.print( "I am a simple computer program." ) ;
   }
}
```

Pairs of braces { } are used to group program statements in Java. The first closing brace (}) terminates the **main()** method. The second closing brace terminates the class named **First** inside which the **main()** method is located.

This text is not part of the computer program. Instead, it contributes to how computer programs are described in this book. Note that these caption texts always show what the physical file name of the program is. This program can be found by name **First.java**.

**First.java - 1. A Java program that prints a single line of text to the screen.**

```
D:\javafiles1>java First
I am a simple computer program.
D:\javafiles1>
```

**First.java - X. The execution of the compiled program First.exe**

In this book the execution of an example program is shown in a box which has its own caption text. The text inside the box is what appears on the screen when the program is executed in a command prompt window. The letter X in the caption text means that this describes the execution of the program. The original file name of the program is always shown in the caption of a program description.

## 2.2 A program that can read from the keyboard and calculate

In the same way as writing text to the screen is called output, the act of reading text from the keyboard of a computer is called input. We say that a program can input text or numerical data from the keyboard. The screen is an output device, whereas the keyboard is an input device for a computer program. (Also the mouse is an input device, but our programs are not using the mouse.)

**Sum.java** is an example program which can read two integers from the keyboard and calculate the sum of the integers read. Program **Sum.java** is presented as a program description on the opposite page. The execution of the program is described below the source program, and some parts of the program are explained in more detail on the next page.

Integers are one data type in the Java programming language. Integer variables can be declared with the reserved keyword **`int`**. An integer variable can store an integer value. Integers are whole numbers ( ... -2, -1, 0, 1, 2, 3, ...) which do not have any decimal points or decimal fractions. Program **Sum.java** first declares the necessary integer variables, then it asks the user to give values for the integer variables, then it calculates their sum, and finally the sum of the integers is printed to the screen.

An important element of a computer program is a statement. In Java, statements are terminated so that a semicolon (;) is written at the end of every statement. When the compiler of the programming language finds a semicolon in the program text, it knows that that is the end of a statement. In our first Java programs, all action takes place inside a method that is called **`main()`**. The **`main()`** method is written inside a class for which a name is given. Inside every method **`main()`** there are one or more statements. In program **First.java** there is only one statement inside the method **`main()`**, but the **`main()`** method in program **Sum.java** contains ten statements, each having a semicolon at the end. (Like many other writers of programming books, I use a pair of empty parentheses () after method names such as **`main`**.)

When a computer executes a program, the statements are executed one at a time, in a sequential order. As a general rule, the statements which are written earlier in a program are executed before those statements which are written later in the program. For example, in program **Sum.java**, the statement

```
System.out.print( "\n The sum of the given integers is " +
                  sum_of_two_integers ) ;
```

is the last statement to be executed because it is the last statement in the program.

There are basically two kinds of statements in Java programs:

- *Declaration statements* introduce names and define data. They do not cause any action to happen in a program. An example of this kind of a statement is

  ```
  int  first_integer ;
  ```

  which declares a variable named **`first_integer`**. In program **Sum.java**, this variable is used to store the first integer that is read from the keyboard.

- *Action statements* make a program perform some actions. These statements can be thought of as commands to the computer, and they usually come after data declaration statements in a program. In program **Sum.java**, an example of this kind of statement is

  ```
  sum_of_two_integers  =  first_integer  +  second_integer ;
  ```

  This statement can be described in a command form such as: "Calculate the sum of the contents of variables **`first_integer`** and **`second_integer`** and store the sum into variable **`sum_of_two_integers`**." The variables must be declared in data declaration statements before these kinds of action statements can be allowed in a program.

In those programs in which data is read from the keyboard, we have these two program lines. The line that begins **Scanner keyboard = ...** declares and creates a keyboard object, which represents the physical keyboard in the program. The line **import java.util.* ;** is needed because the **Scanner** utility is declared in the **java.util** package.

Here, three variables of type **int** are declared. These variables can store integers (whole numbers). **int** is simply an abbreviation of the word integer. All statements in Java programs are terminated with a semicolon (;).

```
import java.util.* ;

class Sum
{
   public static void main( String[] not_in_use )
   {
      Scanner keyboard = new Scanner( System.in ) ;

      int  first_integer ;
      int  second_integer ;
      int  sum_of_two_integers ;

      System.out.print( "\n Please, type in an integer:        " ) ;
      first_integer  =  keyboard.nextInt() ;

      System.out.print( "\n Please, type in another integer: " ) ;
      second_integer  =  keyboard.nextInt() ;

      sum_of_two_integers  =  first_integer  +  second_integer ;

      System.out.print( "\n The sum of the given integers is "
                          + sum_of_two_integers ) ;
   }
}
```

These two statements read numerical values from the keyboard. The numbers which the user of the program types in from the keyboard become the values of the variables **first_integer** and **second_integer**.

This statement prints the calculated sum to the screen. The value of variable **sum_of_two_integers** is printed after the text inside the double quotes. Operator + joins the value of the variable to the text. In this statement operator + has a different meaning than in the previous statement.

This plus sign means that this program will be further explained on following pages.

**Sum.java - 1.+ A program to calculate the sum of two integers.**

```
D:\javafiles1>java Sum

 Please, type in an integer:      17

 Please, type in another integer: 95

 The sum of the given integers is 112
```

**Sum.java - X. The program is executed here by typing in the integers 17 and 95.**

**int** is a reserved keyword in Java. That means that it cannot be used as a name in a Java program. When the Java compiler reads the word **int** in a program, it knows that an integer variable is being declared.

**first_integer**, **second_-integer**, and **sum_of_two_integers** are names of variables in this program. The names of variables must be chosen by the person who writes a program. In this book we write the names so that they consist of natural words which are joined with underscore characters _ (No space characters are allowed in a name.)

```
import java.util.* ;

class Sum
{
   public static void main( String[] not_in_use )
   {
      Scanner keyboard = new Scanner( System.in ) ;

      int  first_integer ;
      int  second_integer ;
      int  sum_of_two_integers ;

      System.out.print( "\n Please, type in an integer:      " ) ;
      first_integer  =  keyboard.nextInt() ;

      System.out.print( "\n Please, type in another integer: " ) ;
      second_integer  =  keyboard.nextInt() ;
```

This statement reads a numerical value from the keyboard and stores (assigns) the value to variable **first_integer**. The execution of the program stays on this line until the user of the program types in the number. When **keyboard.nextInt() ;** is written to the right side of the assignment operator (=), the next integer is read from the keyboard, and it is stored to the variable on the left side of the assignment operator.

These statements print text lines to the screen. The marking **\n** at the beginning of the text causes the text to be printed on a new line. Therefore **\n** is called the newline character.

**Sum.java - 1 - 1: The first part of the complete program Sum.java.**

This is called an assignment statement. Assignment statements are executed "from right to left". The values of the variables **first_integer** and **second_integer** are summed first, and then the calculated sum is assigned as a value to the variable **sum_of_two_integers**.

Mathematical notations are used here. The plus sign (+) is used as an addition operator. The equal sign (=) is an assignment operator.

```
      sum_of_two_integers  =  first_integer  +  second_integer ;

      System.out.print( "\n The sum of the given integers is "
                        +  sum_of_two_integers ) ;
   }
}
```

**Sum.java - 1 - 2. The last part of the complete program Sum.java.**

Usually, there is no single way of writing a computer program. Because programming languages provide a great variety of means to perform various computing activities, computing problems, like the problem of calculating the sum of two integers, can be solved with different kinds of programs. Program **SumImproved.java**, on the following page, is an improved version of program **Sum.java**, and it shows another possible way to write a simple computer program. Although the two programs are doing the same calculation, program **SumImproved.java** introduces some new features of the Java programming language:

- At the beginning of the program, there are some English sentences which explain briefly what the program does. These sentences are called the comments of the program. Comments are actually not part of the program text because they are discarded by the compiler. Comments are intended to be read by humans who want to study the program. The compiler recognizes comment lines through the double slash //. Whenever the compiler finds a double slash on some program line, it discards the double slash and everything that follows until the end of that line.
- Two variables have been given different names in **SumImproved.java** than they had in **Sum.java**. The following modifications have been made to variable names:

```
first_integer   ->   first_integer_from_keyboard
second_integer  ->   second_integer_from_keyboard
```

  The names of variables can be chosen by the author of a program. Every variable must have a name that is different from any other variable name in the same program. When a variable name is used, it must always be written in exactly the same way. The names of variables should be chosen so that they describe the purpose of the variable. Java allows short and abbreviated variable names like `val` or `i`, or variable names containing numbers like `val2`, but we will not use them in this book. Instead, the programs in this book have meaningful variable names which consist of natural words joined together with underscore characters.
- In program **SumImproved.java**, variables are declared and given values in single statements, such as

```
int  first_integer_from_keyboard  =  keyboard.nextInt() ;
```

  This single statement performs the same activities as the declaration statement

```
int  first_integer ;
```

  and the assignment statement

```
first_integer  =  keyboard.nextInt() ;
```

  which are used in program **Sum.java**.

## Exercises with program Sum.java

Before you can do these exercises, you must read the following sections where you will learn how to edit, compile, and execute Java programs.

Exercise 2-1. Modify program **Sum.java** so that when it is given the numbers 17 and 95 it prints the line

```
17 + 95  =  112
```

The aim is that the program will print the plus sign (+) and the equal sign (=) instead of words.

Exercise 2-2. Modify program **Sum.java** so that it calculates the sum of three integers.

These lines are so-called comment lines which explain in plain English what this particular program does. Two adjacent slash characters // (a double slash) begin a comment line. When a compiler sees a double slash // it ignores those characters and the rest of the program line. It is a good programming practice to mention the program file name and the author of the program on some comment lines.

```
//  SumImproved.java (c) Kari Laitinen

//   This is a simple calculator program that can
//   calculate the sum of the two integers that are
//   typed in from the keyboard.

import java.util.* ;

class SumImproved
{
   public static void main( String[] not_in_use )
   {
      Scanner keyboard = new Scanner( System.in ) ;

      System.out.print( "\n Please, type in an integer:      " ) ;
      int first_integer_from_keyboard  =  keyboard.nextInt() ;

      System.out.print( "\n Please, type in another integer: " ) ;
      int second_integer_from_keyboard =  keyboard.nextInt() ;

      int sum_of_two_integers  =  first_integer_from_keyboard  +
                                  second_integer_from_keyboard  ;

      System.out.print( "\n The sum of " +  first_integer_from_keyboard
                      + " and "  +  second_integer_from_keyboard
                      + " is "   +  sum_of_two_integers   +   ".\n" ) ;
   }
}
```

The plus sign functions here, not as an addition operator, but as as a link joining the values of the variables to the texts that are given inside double quotes.

Sometimes, program statements are so long that they need to be written on several lines of program text. The semicolon (;) is the symbol which marks the end of each statement

**SumImproved.java - 1. A slightly improved version of program Sum.java.**

```
D:\javafiles1>java SumImproved

 Please, type in an integer:      115

 Please, type in another integer: 43

 The sum of 115 and 43 is 158.
```

**SumImproved.java - X. Program execution with integers 115 and 43.**

### The MS-DOS command prompt window (console window) in Windows computers

It might be useful to read this box if you are not familiar with the use of the command prompt window in a computer that runs some version of the Microsoft Windows operating system. The command prompt window can be used to compile and execute Java programs. In addition, you may need the command prompt window to perform the installations described in this chapter. In Windows XP, for example, the command prompt window can be opened by selecting **Start > All Programs > Accessories > Command Prompt**. The opening of the command prompt window can be somewhat different in different Windows versions.

Through the command prompt window it is possible to carry out many operations by using the commands of the old MS-DOS operating system, and thereby control the entire computer. The command prompt window imitates the operation of the old MS-DOS operating system, and, therefore, it is also called the MS-DOS window. In many cases, you can use either an MS-DOS command or the mouse of your computer. For example, you can copy a file with the COPY command, or you can use the mouse in the copying operation.

The MS-DOS commands are lines of text written according to a certain syntax. You need to know at least some of the MS-DOS commands in order to compile and execute Java programs in the command prompt window. Here are some examples of the commands you may need:

| Command | Description |
|---|---|
| `D:` | Select drive D. |
| `CD \` | Change to the root directory in the current drive. |
| `CD myjava` | Change to the directory (folder) named **myjava**. |
| `CD ..` | Change to the parent directory of the current directory. |
| `COPY \javafiles1\Sum.java` | Copy file **Sum.java** from the directory named **javafiles1** to the current directory. |
| `COPY \javafiles1\*.java` | Copy all files which have the name extension **.java** from the directory **javafiles1** to the current directory. |
| `COPY Sum.java MySum.java` | Copy a file named **Sum.java** to file named **MySum.java** in the current directory. |
| `DIR` | Display a list of all files and subdirectories in the current directory. |
| `DIR *.java` | Display a list of files whose names terminate with **.java**. |
| `DIR s*` | Display a list of files whose names begin with letter s. |
| `DIR *sum*` | Display a list of files that have the word **sum** in their name. |
| `HELP \| MORE` | Display a list of all MS-DOS commands. |
| `HELP dir` | Display information of the DIR command. |
| `HELP path` | Display information of the PATH command. |
| `MD myjava` | Create (make) a subdirectory named **myjava** into the current directory. |
| `REN test.txt test.old` | Rename a file named **test.txt** to **test.old** in the current directory. |

Although the example commands above are written with uppercase letters, you can also write them with lowercase letters.

When you use the command prompt window in your work, it may be better for your eyes if you adjust the properties of the window. The properties can be adjusted, at least in Windows XP, by clicking the symbol in the upper left corner of the window. I always set the background color to white, text color to black, and the window size to 10 x 18. I also set the screen buffer size to 80 columns x 25 rows (the same as the window size). When you modify the properties of the command prompt window, remember to press the OK button in order to make the modifications permanent.

## 2.3 Getting a Java compiler to your computer

As you have now seen a couple of computer programs, you may be eager to experiment with them on a computer. In order to compile and run Java programs on your computer, you need to have in your computer a Java compiler to transform Java source programs into an executable form. I'm supposing here that you use a personal computer that runs the Windows operating system, and I'll explain below how to install a Java compiler to a Windows computer. You can, however, use a Linux, UNIX, or Macintosh computer in your studies, but you must study other sources to find out how a Java compiler can be installed into those computers.

The Java programming language is a language provided by a company called Sun Microsystems. Sun provides a Java compiler that can be freely downloaded from their Internet pages. In this section, I will explain how to download the free Java compiler, and how to install it into your computer. The free Java compiler is an excellent compiler, although you do not need to pay any money for it. (You can, of course, use more commercial programming tools while you are studying with this book if you have such tools at your disposal.)

To install the free Java compiler into your computer, you actually have to install a larger software package named Java Development Kit, which is usually abbreviated as JDK. The Java compiler is included in the JDK which contains also other tools and necessary libraries that are needed when Java programs are executed on a computer.

To get the installation file of the Java Development Kit from the Sun web pages, you'll need an Internet connection to your PC. The connection should be a fast one because the installation file that you have to download from Sun can have a size of more than 50 MB (megabytes). If you have trouble downloading the installation file from the Sun web pages, you should consult somebody who knows more about downloading larger files from the Internet.

The installation file that you need to download from Sun Microsystems is an executable file, **.exe** file, which you need to execute on your computer after you have downloaded it. When the installation file is executed, it creates other files and folders on your computer. To store the installation file on your computer, it is good to have a particular folder (directory) for it. Such a folder is also useful later when you download other material from the Internet. I keep the installation files in a folder named **D:\setupfiles**, and I suggest that you might also use this kind of folder. **D:\setupfiles** is a descriptive folder name for installation files because these files are used to set up programs on your computer. The **D:\setupfiles** folder can be created by writing the following commands in a command prompt window

```
D:
CD \
MD setupfiles
```

Alternatively you can create the **D:\setupfiles** folder in Windows XP by selecting **Start > My Computer > Local Disk D: > Make a new folder** (in **File and Folder Tasks**), and writing **setupfiles** as the new folder name. If your computer does not have the **D:** drive (**Local Disk D:**) you should use the **C:** drive (**Local Disk C:**) and create a folder named **setupfiles** there.

I'm providing detailed instructions for downloading and installing the Java Development Kit on the Internet pages of this book. So, when you are ready to do the installation, go to the Internet address

```
http://www.naturalprogramming.com/
```

with your Internet browser (e.g. Internet Explorer). At the above address[1], you should first select the homepage of this book. Then you should select the link named "Support for readers", and finally you should click on "Download and install Java Development Kit".

When you see a page which contains instructions for downloading and installing the Java Development Kit software package, you should follow the instructions given on that page.

The detailed instructions for the JDK installation are provided on an Internet page because it is possible that the installation instructions need to be changed when new versions of the JDK become available. I'll modify the Internet page when it is necessary to change the instructions. (It is quite impossible to modify the pages of this book when you are holding the book in your hands!) While I'm writing these lines, the JDK version 5.0 Update 4 is the latest valid version of the software package. It is important that you download JDK version 5.0 or some later version. JDK versions whose version number is smaller than 5.0 cannot be used with this book because the Java programs presented in this book are written so that they utilize the new Java features that were introduced in version 5.0. The update number that is associated with the JDK is less essential than the version number.

The Java compiler that is included in the Java Development Kit is a so-called command line compiler that can be invoked by giving a command like

```
javac Test.java
```

in a command prompt window. The above command would compile a Java program in a file named **Test.java**. The compiler itself is in a file named **javac.exe** in a folder that was created during the installation of the JDK. The Internet page that gives instructions for installing the JDK also explains how you have to set an environment variable named **Path** on your computer. The value of the **Path** variable is a list of folders (directories) where executable programs (e.g. **javac.exe**) are searched when they are activated from a command line. If you are not able to set the **Path** variable correctly, your Java compiler may not work although the installations were done properly. If you cannot make the Java compiler work on your computer, you might ask somebody who is experienced in installing programs to help you. On the other hand, it is not absolutely necessary that you learn to operate the Java compiler from the command line. As I'll explain later in this chapter, there is a tool called JCreator which can automatically find the Java compiler and compile a program with it.

When the installations have been done correctly, your computer should contain the following things:

- A Java interpreter that is able to interpret and run compiled Java programs. The Java interpreter is also called the Java virtual machine because the interpreter behaves like a computer inside a computer. The Java interpreter and software components that are associated with it form the Java runtime environment (JRE).
- A large class library to be used with Java programs. You'll learn more about classes later.
- A Java compiler and other tools to be used in the development of Java programs.

1. If, for whatever reason, this Internet address does not work, use the Internet search engines to find the electronic material of this book. If you search with the full name of this book or with phrases like "Homepage of Kari Laitinen", you should be able to find the homepage of this book.

### Uppercase and lowercase letters in file names

When you work with files and directories in the Windows operating systems, you should remember that the file and directory (folder) names can be written both in uppercase and lowercase letters. This means, for example, that the directory names **TEMP** and **temp** mean the same, and the file names **SUM.JAVA** and **Sum.java** can refer to the same file in Windows.

We say that the Windows operating system is not case sensitive in regard to file and directory names. The UNIX and Linux operating systems are different in this respect. They are case sensitive, which means, for example, that a UNIX/Linux directory may contain two different files that have names **SUM.JAVA** and **Sum.java**.

The difference between uppercase and lowercase letters is important also in programming languages. You will learn that the Java language is case sensitive, which means, for example, that names like **`SOME_VARIABLE`** and **`some_variable`** are considered different names.

### Electronic Java documentation

As you gradually proceed with your studies about computer programming, and become more experienced with Java, you will need information about the Java class library. The class library is a collection of standard Java classes that are needed when more advanced Java programs are written. The class library is installed to your computer when the Java Development Kit (JDK) is installed.

At the beginning of your studies you do not need to worry about the class library as you do not even have to know what the term "class" means, but in the later chapters of this book, terms like "standard class" and "electronic Java documentation" become more and more frequent. Then you probably need to find information about the standard Java class library, and this information is provided in electronic form by Sun Microsystems. This electronic Java documentation is available in the form of **.html** files, and you can read it with a browser program (e.g. Internet Explorer or Mozilla Firefox).

The electronic Java documentation can be accessed over the Internet via the address *http://java.sun.com.* Because it may be difficult to quickly find the documentation via this address, the "Support for readers" page of this book provides suitable links to the Sun pages. To find the electronic Java documentation, you can first go to *http://www.naturalprogramming.com*, then select the homepage of this book, and then click on "Support for readers". There you'll find the following links:

- Read Java class library documentation (API specification)
  This is an important link that you are likely to need during your studies with this book. After you have selected this link, you'll see a page whose title is *Java 2 Platform Standard Edition 5.0, API Specification*. In this title API is an abbreviation of *Application Programming Interface*. The standard classes of Java constitute an API. The page that you'll see shows on the left a huge list of names of the standard classes. The names are in alphabetical order. When you click on a class name, information about the selected class is displayed on the right part of the page. The standard classes are grouped into packages of classes. If you do not want to view the names of all classes, you can select a certain package before selecting a class.

- Read Java Development Kit documentation
  This link leads to a page that provides more general information about the Java Development Kit. You should spend some time to explore what is said and shown on this page.

If you have a reliable connection to the Internet, you can use the electronic Java documentation over the Internet. Another possibility is to download the documentation as a **.zip** file and install it locally into your own computer. The "Support for readers" page provides instructions for downloading and unzipping the needed **.zip** file.

## 2.4 Installing the electronic material of this book

In order to study with this book, you need to install some electronic material to your computer. That material includes all the Java source programs (**.java** files) presented in this book, some extra Java programs, and programs discussed in Chapter 4.

To obtain the electronic material, go to the web address

```
http://www.naturalprogramming.com/
```

with your Internet browser. (I'm supposing below that you use the Microsoft Internet Explorer as your browser program.) At the above address you must first choose a link for the homepage of this book, then select the link named "Support for readers", and finally click on "Download Java source programs and other electronic material".

After you have made the above selections, you will see the following information

```
ALL_JAVA_FILES_ETC.ZIP
icom
javafiles1
javafiles2
javafiles3
javafilesextra
javasolutions
```

If you are familiar with **.zip** files, or want to learn how to use **.zip** files, you should click with the right mouse button the file **ALL_JAVA_FILES_ETC.ZIP** and store it locally in the directory **D:**. **D:** is the root directory of drive D: on your computer. (If your computer does not have drive D: you should use drive C:.)

The file **ALL_JAVA_FILES_ETC.ZIP** contains all the **.java** files and other files in a special compressed format. You should be able to unzip the file on your computer. Unzipping means that **.java** and other files are extracted from the **.zip** file. The file can be unzipped in Windows XP by selecting **My Computer > Drive D:**, clicking the icon of the **.zip** file and selecting the extraction of all files. When you unzip the file, it automatically creates a set of directories on your computer, and puts the **.java** and other files into those directories. I recommend that you extract the files to the directory **D:**, the root of drive D. When the above file is unzipped, it creates the following directories on your computer

| | |
|---|---|
| **icom** | Contains programs related to the imaginary computer that is discussed in Chapter 4 of this book. |
| **javafiles1** | Contains the **.java** files that are discussed in Part I (Chapter 2) of this book |
| **javafiles2** | Contains the **.java** and other files that are presented in Part II (Fundamentals of programming) of this book. |
| **javafiles3** | Contains the **.java** and other files that are presented in Part III (Object-oriented programming) of this book. |
| **javafilesextra** | Contains extra **.java** files such as special versions of some of the programs that are discussed in the chapters. |
| **javasolutions** | Contains **.java** files that are solutions to programming exercises. |

If you are using the Windows 2000 operating system, you should also be able to unzip the **.zip** file easily by clicking the file's icon. You may try this in other operating systems as well, but in older Windows operating systems you may need special unzipping tools.

If you were not able to use the standard Windows unzipping tools, or if you are using another operating system, there is another possibility to unzip the **.zip** file. Among the tools that were installed to your computer when the Java Development Kit (JDK) was installed, is a tool called **jar**. The **jar** tool is a Java archives management tool, and it can be used to create and unzip **.zip** files. The **jar** tool works on your computer provided that you were able to correctly set the **Path** environment variable when you installed the Java Development Kit. If the file **ALL_JAVA_FILES_ETC.ZIP** was downloaded to the root directory of drive D: on your computer, you can unzip the file by giving the following commands in a command prompt window

```
D:
CD \
jar xvf ALL_JAVA_FILES_ETC.ZIP
```

If you were not able to unzip the **.zip** file, you can create the above directories on your own computer by yourself, and download the **.java** files and other files one file at a time. You can create the directories using the following commands in a command prompt window:

```
D:
CD \
MD javafiles1
MD javafiles2
MD javafiles3
MD javafilesextra
MD javasolutions
MD icom
```

Then you can use your Internet browser to go to the corresponding directories on the Internet. For example, if you click **javafiles1** on this book's pages on the Internet, the following list of files will be displayed

```
First.java
Sum.java
SumImproved.java
```

If you use the Internet Explorer browser and click, for example, the file name **First.java** with the right mouse button, and then select **Save Target As ...**, the browser lets you save the program locally on your own computer. In the **Save As** dialog box, you should have the local directory (folder) **D:\javafiles1** in the **Save in:** field, and you probably have to select **All files** to the **Save as type:** field before you save the file. By using the **Back** button of your browser, and by selecting other files and other directories, you can get all the **.java** and other files to your computer. Obtaining the Java programs this way is more time consuming than unzipping the **.zip** file, but you do not have to download all files at once.

### Downloading files with Microsoft Internet Explorer

Microsoft Internet Explorer is the most popular so-called browser program in personal computers. Usually a browser is used to view Internet pages written with the HTML language, but a browser can also download files from the Internet. The Internet Explorer works so that normally you use the left mouse button to do selections, but if you want to download a file from the Internet, you have to click on the file name with the right mouse button.

When you click on a file name with the right mouse button and then select **Save Target As ...**, the Internet Explorer lets you to store the file locally on your computer. After making this selection, the Internet Explorer displays a **Save As** dialog box in which you must specify into which local directory (folder) you want the file to be stored, and how you want the file to be stored. When downloading simple text files like **.java** files, it is best to select **All Files** to the **Save as type:** field before you save the file. If you do not make this selection, the browser may add the ending **.txt** to the end of the file name.

## 2.5 Compiling programs in a command prompt window

In this section, I'll explain how the Java compiler can be used in a command prompt window. Compiling programs by giving commands in a command prompt window is a somewhat old-fashioned way to use a compiler, but it is important that you know that a compiler can be used this way. Later on in this chapter, I'll explain how a tool called JCreator can be used to compile Java programs. This tool simplifies the compilation process.

I am assuming here that you were able to install the Java Development Kit (JDK), which includes the Java compiler, and at least the example programs **First.java**, **Sum.java**, and **SumImproved.java** to your computer. The **Path** environment variable must be set so that the compiler can be activated from the command line.

Assuming that you have installed the program **First.java** in the directory (folder) **D:\javafiles1**, you can go to see the contents of that directory by first opening a command prompt window, and then typing the commands

```
D:
cd \javafiles1
dir
```

After these commands, you should see a list of files that are in the directory **D:\javafiles1**. If the file **First.java** is there, you can compile it by typing

```
javac First.java
```

When the compilation is successful, the compiler does not print anything to the window. Only the so-called prompt appears after a successful compilation.

If your compiler prints something to the screen, it is likely that the compilation was not successful. In such a case you should ensure that you did not make any typing mistakes, and the compiler installation was successful. If you type, after a successful compilation, the command

```
dir First.*
```

you will see that the compiler produced a file named **First.class**. (The above command means "list all files whose file name body is **First**". The asterisk in the command means "any file name extension".)

The file **First.class** is the file that can be executed on your computer. To execute the file, you should type

```
java First
```

In this command, the word **`java`** activates the Java interpreter, which will interpret the numerical instructions inside the **First.class** file. When you give the above execution command, you must give the second word in capitalized form (i.e. you may not write **`first`**) because **`First`** is written as a capitalized word inside the Java source program. When a correct command is given, the program should produce the following screen output

```
I am a simple computer program.
```

The command with which you invoke the Java compiler is **javac** which is obviously an abbreviation of the words "java compiler". To compile the other **.java** files that have been presented in this chapter, you should type

```
javac Sum.java
javac SumImproved.java
```

These commands make the compiler to produce the executable files **Sum.class** and **SumImproved.class**. The file **Sum.class** can be executed by typing

```
java Sum
```

In general, if there is a Java source program which contains a class named `Somefile`, and which is placed in a file named **Somefile.java**, it can be compiled by the command

```
javac Somefile.java
```

A successful compilation produces a file named **Somefile.class** which can be executed with the command

```
java Somefile
```

The compilation process produces a **.class** file that corresponds to the **.java** file that was given in the compilation command. The **.class** file contains numerical data that corresponds to the textual program contained in the **.java** file. When the **.class** file is executed, the Java interpreter makes the computer behave according to the numerical instructions in the **.class** file.

The name of the **.class** file that is produced by the compiler is based on the class name that is given inside the **.java** file. For example, because program **First.java** looks like

```
class  First
{
   public static void main( String[] not_in_use )
   {
      System.out.print( "I am a simple computer program." ) ;
   }
}
```

and the name written after the keyword `class` is `First`, the compiler produces a file named **First.class**. The general rule in Java is that the file name of a program must correspond to the class name inside the program, i.e., the file name must be **First.java** because the class name inside the program is `First`. Therefore, it seems that the name of a **.class** file depends on the name of the corresponding **.java** file. Later on, when you compile more complicated programs which contain several class definitions, you will find out that the compiler produces a separate **.class** file from each class that is defined inside a program.

Typically, when you work with a program so that you do the compilation in a command prompt window, you have two windows, an editor window and a command prompt window, open on the screen. The editor window belongs to a program editor with which you can modify your program. In the editor window you modify the program and in the command prompt window you compile and execute the program. You can move from one window to another by clicking on the window you want to use. Whenever you start compiling a program in the command prompt window, you must first save the program in the editor window.

When doing a programming exercise or writing some other program, it is usual that you have to modify, compile, and execute your program many times before the program works as you want. In such a program development process, you need to repeat the compilation and execution commands over and over. Fortunately, the command prompt window is designed so that you can recompile and re-execute your programs easily, without having to retype the commands. If you have once typed the compilation and execution commands, like those above, you can find the commands again by using the Arrow Up key on the keyboard of your computer. You can scroll through the old commands with the Arrow Up and Arrow Down keys. After you find an old command which you want to re-execute, you just press the Enter key. This way, once-written compilation and execution commands can be executed repeatedly, and recompilation and re-execution of your program is rather easy. To recompile after the modification of a program, you just need to click the command prompt window and use the Arrow Up and Arrow Down keys to find the previous compilation command.

## 2.6 Editor tools for writing and modifying source programs

To write and modify computer programs, you need a tool called a program editor on your computer. There are many tools that can serve as a program editor. For example, in the Windows operating system there is a standard text editor called Notepad that can be used as a program editor. You can use Notepad as your program editor for a while. The Notepad editor can be activated in Windows XP by selecting **Start > All Programs > Accessories > Notepad**. When you work with source programs, it is important that the program editor is able to show the line number where the cursor is. Therefore, you need to make the selection **View > Status Bar** in the Notepad editor. After this selection, Notepad shows the line and column numbers of the cursor at the bottom of its window. A program writer may need to know the line numbers of a program because the compiler may display a message which says that there is an error on a certain line of a program.

You can start your programming career with the Notepad editor, but, because there are better tools available, you should get a program editor that has more features. The program editor I'm recommending to you is called JCreator. The JCreator tool is actually something more than a conventional program editor. Yet it is a simple tool which is tailored for writing and modifying Java programs. A "lite" version of JCreator can be freely downloaded from the Internet. The following is a list of features that make JCreator particularly suitable for the development of Java programs:

- Provided that a Java compiler has been installed on a computer, the compiler is automatically located by JCreator when the tool is activated for the first time. Similarly, JCreator can automatically find the Java interpreter and other tools that belong to the Java Development Kit.
- JCreator has buttons with which you can compile and execute Java programs.
- JCreator can, to some extent, understand the syntax of the Java programming language. This means in practice that it shows certain parts of the program text with different color and/or font. For example, Java keywords (e.g. `class` and `int`) are shown with a different color than the texts that are written inside double quotation marks.

When you compile a Java program with the JCreator tool, it automatically stores the modified source program into its file, and after this it invokes the Java compiler. The compiler produces **.class** files in the same way as if it were activated in a command prompt window. When you execute a Java program with JCreator, it opens a command prompt window where it shows the output of the program. You must close the opened command prompt window after the execution of the program terminates.

If you do not want to use the JCreator tool or the simple Notepad editor, there are other possible free editors available on the Internet. Any working text editor can be used to write Java programs when the programs are compiled and executed in a command prompt window.

On the Internet pages of this book, I'm providing instructions for downloading and installing the JCreator tool, and alternatively some free program editors. To get a free editing tool, you should go to the address

**`http://www.naturalprogramming.com/`**

with your Internet browser, and first select the homepage of this book. Then you have to select "Support for readers", and finally you have to click on the link "Download and install JCreator" or alternatively the link "Download and install free program editors". By following the instructions given on the Internet page, you should be able to download and install the tool you have selected.

Program editors, including the JCreator tool, should not be difficult to use. They are tools to create and modify text files such as source programs. Once you have a program editor at your disposal, it is important to spend some time in investigating the various features of the editor. A program editor typically provides menus through which you can perform certain activities. Typical menus include the following:

- The **File** menu is used to open, save, and close files that you are editing. When you select the **New** operation in a **File** menu, you can create a new file. With the **Save As** option you can save a file with a new file name, which can actually mean that you make a copy of a file.
- Via the **Edit** menu you can do **Cut**, **Copy**, and **Paste** operations as well as search for certain words or character combinations in the text being edited, or you can replace certain character combinations with other character combinations. Some editors provide a separate **Search** menu for searching operations.
- Usually an editor has a **Settings**, **Configure**, or **Options** menu through which it is possible to configure the editor. Configuring means that you can select how an editor behaves in certain situations.
- A **View** menu allows you to adjust what you see on the screen while you are using an editor. A **View** menu is thus also a kind of configuration menu.

In addition to the menus, a program editor may contain buttons which you can press with the mouse. Usually the buttons are alternative "shortcuts" to some of the operations which can be done through the menus.

## What really happens when a .class file is executed

There are a lot of **.exe** files in a computer that runs the Windows operating system. These **.exe** files are executable files containing numerical machine instructions according to which the processor of the computer performs basic computing activities. Computer programs are in executable form in **.exe** files. (Also in other computers, that are based on an operating system other than Windows, there are executable files but their file name extension may be something else than **.exe**.)

Traditionally, **.exe** files are produced when programs are transformed into executable programs in compilation. The compilers of older programming languages (e.g. C++ compilers) operate so that they produce **.exe** files which are ready for execution. The Java compiler, however, does not produce any **.exe** files. Instead, it produces **.class** files. The execution of the **.class** files differs in some ways from the execution of the **.exe** files.

As is explained in Chapter 1, Java programs require the Java runtime environment (JRE) in order to be executed on a computer. The Java runtime environment includes a Java interpreter which is able to execute the **.class** files that are produced by the Java compiler. The interpreter is also called the Java virtual machine. The **.class** files do not contain machine instructions that can immediately be executed by the processor. Instead, they contain numerical bytecode instructions which are processed by the Java interpreter. When you execute a **.class** file on your computer, you activate the Java interpreter which then executes the bytecode instructions in the **.class** file. The Java interpreter is the "real" executable program that is being executed by the processor of the computer. The interpreter imitates a processor or a computing machine while it executes bytecode instructions. For this reason, it is also called the Java virtual machine.

As the executable form of a Java program is a **.class** file, Java programs can be executed on every computer that provides the Java runtime environment. Java programs are portable from one computer to another. The Sun Microsystems corporation provides Java runtime environments for all common operating systems, which makes it possible to run the same Java **.class** files on different computers and operating systems. Traditional executable files are not portable. For example, you cannot take a Windows **.exe** file and execute it in some other operating system.

There are many Java runtime environments and interpreters available on the market. Although they process Java **.class** files identically, there can be differences in the internal operation of the interpreters. Some Java interpreters compile bytecode instructions to real machine instructions and they let the processor execute those generated machine instructions.

## 2.7 Modifying and compiling programs – introduction to exercises

To learn computer programming, you have to do practical programming exercises. This book contains a lot of programming exercises which can be found by using the list presented on the introductory pages. The purpose of this section is to give some advice related to programming exercises, as well as to help you to use the Java programming tools. More advice related to programming exercises can be found in Appendix C. In the discussion below it is supposed that a program is modified with the JCreator tool in the Windows XP operating system.

When you start doing programming exercises, it is best to create a special directory (folder) for those **.java** files that you write by yourself. Such a directory can have, for example, the name **D:\myjava**. To create this directory, you can type the following commands in a command prompt window

```
D:
CD \
MD myjava
```

To explore the process of program modification, let's suppose that you have to do a programming exercise in which you have to modify program **First.java** that was discussed in Section 2.1. Your task is to modify the program so that it produces, instead of just a single line, the following two lines to the screen:

```
I am a simple computer program.
It is nice to be a computer program.
```

When you start modifying an example program that is presented in this book, it is best to make a copy of the program, give a new file name to the new **.java** file, and store the program into your own working directory. First you could just make a copy of the existing program and check that the copied program works. Provided that you have installed the electronic material as described in Section 2.4, you can copy the program **First.java** with JCreator (and with other typical editors) in the following way:

- First open the file by selecting **File > Open ... > Local Disk D: > javafiles1 > First.java** and finally push the **Open** button. The file is opened successfully when the editor displays the program text. In the file opening operation, the text from the file **First.java** is copied inside the program editor.
- You make a copy of the file when you select **File > Save As ... > Local Disk D: > myjava**, change the file name to **MyFirst.java** in the **File name:** field, and finally push the **Save** button. After these operations, a copy of the file **First.java** is in directory (folder) **D:\myjava**, the new file has name **MyFirst.java**, and the new file is open in the editor window ready to be modified.

There is the general rule in Java that the name of a class defined inside a **.java** file must correspond to the name of the file. Because now the file name of your program file is **MyFirst.java**, you should modify the program so that you write `class MyFirst` in place of `class First`.

After this you can try to compile the program. With JCreator you can do it by selecting **Build > Compile File**. Before the actual compilation, JCreator saves the modified program text to the file. If the compilation is successful, JCreator displays only "Process completed." at the bottom of the window. If error messages are printed, the compilation was not successful.

If the compilation is successful, you can try to execute the program by selecting **Build > Execute File**. If the program can be executed, JCreator opens a command prompt window which shows the output generated by the program. In the command prompt window, there is the additional text "Press any key to continue ..." JCreator produces this extra text to the window, because otherwise the window would close immediately after the program has displayed its texts to the screen. The window would close so quickly that you would not have time to see what your program displayed.

After you are sure that your program can be compiled and executed, you can make the modification that is the actual task in the exercise. You can make the program display the required second line of text when you insert the lines

```
System.out.print(
                 "\nIt is nice to be a computer program." ) ;
```

before the first closing brace } in the program. After you have made this modification, you can recompile and re-execute the program as explained above. If the program can be compiled, and it produces the specified output, you have successfully done this exercise.

JCreator is a very nice tool when you want to create Java programs. If you explore the tool, you will find out that it provides buttons with which you can compile and execute programs. Using the buttons is quicker than making selections from the **Build** menu. JCreator provides the possibility to create projects and open workspaces, but those features are not needed when you work with small programs.

# CHAPTER 3

## HOW INFORMATION IS STORED IN THE MEMORY OF A COMPUTER

Now, after having looked at a couple of computer programs, we know that it is possible to declare variables inside programs, and it is possible to store numerical values into the declared variables. When a program has been compiled and it is being run (executed) on a computer, the variables are in the memory of the computer, or we can say that memory space has been reserved to represent the variables of the program. Thus, the information that is stored in a variable is actually stored in the memory of the computer.

This chapter discusses how it is possible for the electronic circuitry of computers to store information, and how the memory of computers should be thought of by a programmer. A computer's memory can be considered a logical device which is built using electronic components. To understand how the memory in computers works, a programmer does not necessarily need to understand electronics or memory technology. It is enough to understand how the memory works in a logical sense.

In the following sections, we will study how different types of information (e.g. numbers, texts, and pictures) can be stored in the memory of a computer. The memory is such that it can hold information stored in a certain manner. The memory in a computer "remembers" what was written to it. The memory of a computers is, however, fundamentally different from human memory. Information stored in a computer's memory will be lost when some other information is written in the same place in the memory. Moreover, there is always a limit how much information a computer memory can hold.

## 3.1 Numerical information: numbering systems

The most typical way of showing numerical information is to use the ten familiar numerical symbols 0, 1, 2, 3, 4, 5, 6, 7, 8, and 9. With these symbols, it is possible to express any number. There are certain rules how to combine these symbols to form larger numbers. The numerical symbols are called digits when they appear in a larger number. For example, number 6378 has four digits, 6 is called the most significant digit, and 8 is the least significant digit.

Actually, it is quite amazing that with ten basic symbols it is possible to express a countless number of values. We could ask: why exactly ten different numerical symbols? Why not nine, or eleven, or three hundred, or one, or two? Probably the reason why we use ten different symbols for counting is that we have ten fingers and ten toes. Our counting system was invented by people who lived a long time ago, and they probably ended up in a ten-symbol system after counting with their fingers. In any case, it is possible to formulate a working numbering system for nearly any number of numerical symbols. We shall see that computers use only two numerical symbols to represent and store numerical information. To study different numbering systems, we must first take a closer look at our commonly used numbers, the Arabic numbers.

With the ten different symbols, we can basically express only ten different quantities, but our minds are accustomed to combine the ten numerical symbols in a sophisticated manner. When we want to express larger numbers, we start thinking in terms of times of ten. For example, the number 6378 is:

6 times 10 times 10 times 10 plus
3 times 10 times 10 plus
7 times 10 plus
8

By deciding that * means "times" (the multiplication operation), that + means "plus" (the addition operation), and that multiplication operations are carried out before additions in mathematics, we can express the number 6378 in a more mathematical way with the following expression

$$6 * 10 * 10 * 10 + 3 * 10 * 10 + 7 * 10 + 8$$

Furthermore, by deciding that $10^0$ is 1, $10^1$ is 10, $10^2$ is 10 * 10, $10^3$ is 10 * 10 * 10, etc., we can write the above expression even more elegantly, as follows:

$$6 * 10^3 + 3 * 10^2 + 7 * 10^1 + 8 * 10^0$$

In the mathematical expression above, it is important to note that ten to the power of zero is considered to be one. In mathematics, any number to the power of zero is one. It is possible to express any number in our commonly used numbering system in the same way as the number 6378 above. For example, the number 285024 can be expressed as

$$2 * 10^5 + 8 * 10^4 + 5 * 10^3 + 0 * 10^2 + 2 * 10^1 + 4 * 10^0$$

Because the Arabic numbering system has ten different symbols (0, 1, 2, 3, 4, 5, 6, 7, 8, and 9) to express numerical information, the number 10 is an important number in the mathematical expressions above. As we have ten different numerical symbols in use, our numbering system is said to be the base-10 numbering system.

The advantage of having such a numbering system as our base-10 system is that we can concisely write down numerical information. We can understand how much is 299 without thinking that it is actually $2 * 10^2 + 9 * 10^1 + 9 * 10^0$. We are so accustomed to using the base-10 system that in everyday life we do not need any other numbering systems. However, to understand how information is stored in the memory of a computer, and how computers process information, it is necessary to also know and understand other numbering systems.

It is possible to formulate new numbering systems from the base-10 system by removing the most significant numerical symbols from it. For example, we get a base-9 numbering system by leaving the symbol 9 out from the base-10 system. When we leave both the symbols 9 and 8 out from the base-10 system, we get a base-8 numbering system which is also called the octal numbering system. The most minimal numbering system is the base-2 system which contains only two numerical symbols, 0 and 1. That is called the binary numbering system. Another possibility to formulate new numbering systems is to add new numerical symbols to the symbols of the base-10 system. For example, we get a base-16 system by introducing six new numerical symbols A, B, C, D, E, and F to the symbols of the base-10 system. The base-16 system is called the hexadecimal numbering system.

Table 3-1 shows some numbers written down in different numbering systems. The essential difference between different numbering systems is the number of numerical symbols in use. By studying Table 3-1, you can see that whenever we count upwards and run out of symbols (i.e. reach symbol 9 in the base-10 system, reach symbol 7 in the base-8 system, reach symbol 1 in the base-2 system, or reach symbol F in the base-16 system) we start to use a new column of symbols, or we can say that we start to use a new digit which has more significance. In all numbers, in all numbering systems, the column to the left bears symbols of greater value, or more significant digits, and the rightmost digit of a number is the least significant. All the numbering systems are basically similar. The only fundamental difference is how many numerical symbols are in use.

## Roman numbers

Our normal numbers are called Arabic numbers because they were introduced to Western Europe by Arabs who had learned them in India. The Arabic numbering system and the numbering systems that can be derived from it are not the only numbering systems in use these days. For example at the end of movies, the year when the movie was made is often expressed with a so-called Roman number. The letters MCMXCVI at the end of a movie mean that the movie was made in the year 1996. In the Roman numbering system, certain letters are used to denote certain numerical quantities, and there are rules how the numerical letters can be combined to form bigger numbers. The basic meanings of the numerical letters are the following:

| | | | |
|---|---|---|---|
| I | one | V | five |
| X | ten | L | fifty |
| C | one hundred | D | five hundred |
| M | one thousand | | |

The letters I, X, C, and M can be combined so that two or three consecutive letters represent two or three times the value of that symbol (e.g. XX means twenty, XXX means thirty, C means one hundred, and CC means two hundred). When a lower-valued letter precedes a higher-valued letter, the numerical meaning of the higher-valued letter is reduced (e.g. XC means ninety, CM means nine hundred, IX means nine, and CD means four hundred). Full-valued letter combinations and letters with decreased values can be combined to express various quantities. In the Roman system, the numbers from one to twenty are I, II, III, IV, V, VI, VII, VIII, IX, X, XI, XII, XIII, XIV, XV, XVI, XVII, XVIII, XIX, and XX; 1234 is MCCXLVII; 333 is CCCXXXIII; and 444 is CDXLIV. It must be noted, that there is no quantity "zero" in the Roman numbering system. For that reason, it is not mathematically convenient and therefore it has been replaced by the Arabic system. When you learn more while reading this book, try to write a program that can convert from Roman numbers to Arabic ones and vice versa.

## Table 3-1: Numbers expressed in different numbering systems.

| Base-10 (decimal numbers) | Base-8 (octal numbers) | Base-2 (binary numbers) | Base-16 (hexadecimal numbers) |
|---|---|---|---|
| 0 | 0 | 0 | 0 |
| 1 | 1 | 1 | 1 |
| 2 | 2 | 10 | 2 |
| 3 | 3 | 11 | 3 |
| 4 | 4 | 100 | 4 |
| 5 | 5 | 101 | 5 |
| 6 | 6 | 110 | 6 |
| 7 | 7 | 111 | 7 |
| 8 | 10 | 1000 | 8 |
| 9 | 11 | 1001 | 9 |
| 10 | 12 | 1010 | A |
| 11 | 13 | 1011 | B |
| 12 | 14 | 1100 | C |
| 13 | 15 | 1101 | D |
| 14 | 16 | 1110 | E |
| 15 | 17 | 1111 | F |
| 16 | 20 | 10000 | 10 |
| 17 | 21 | 10001 | 11 |
| 18 | 22 | 10010 | 12 |
| 19 | 23 | 10011 | 13 |
| 20 | 24 | 10100 | 14 |
| 21 | 25 | 10101 | 15 |
| 22 | 26 | 10110 | 16 |
| 23 | 27 | 10111 | 17 |
| 24 | 30 | 11000 | 18 |
| 25 | 31 | 11001 | 19 |
| 26 | 32 | 11010 | 1A |
| 27 | 33 | 11011 | 1B |
| 28 | 34 | 11100 | 1C |
| 29 | 35 | 11101 | 1D |
| 30 | 36 | 11110 | 1E |
| 31 | 37 | 11111 | 1F |
| 32 | 40 | 100000 | 20 |
| 33 | 41 | 100001 | 21 |
| 34 | 42 | 100010 | 22 |
| 35 | 43 | 100011 | 23 |
| 36 | 44 | 100100 | 24 |
| 37 | 45 | 100101 | 25 |
| 38 | 46 | 100110 | 26 |
| 39 | 47 | 100111 | 27 |
| 40 | 50 | 101000 | 28 |
| 41 | 51 | 101001 | 29 |
| 42 | 52 | 101010 | 2A |
| 43 | 53 | 101011 | 2B |
| 44 | 54 | 101100 | 2C |
| 45 | 55 | 101101 | 2D |

**Table 3-2: Important numbers in computing.**

| $2^n$ | Decimal | Hex | $16^{(n/4)}$ | "slang" |
|---|---|---|---|---|
| $2^0$ | 1 | 1H | $16^0$ | |
| $2^1$ | 2 | 2H | | |
| $2^2$ | 4 | 4H | | |
| $2^3$ | 8 | 8H | | |
| $2^4$ | 16 | 10H | $16^1$ | |
| $2^5$ | 32 | 20H | | |
| $2^6$ | 64 | 40H | | |
| $2^7$ | 128 | 80H | | |
| $2^8$ | 256 | 100H | $16^2$ | |
| $2^9$ | 512 | 200H | | |
| $2^{10}$ | 1024 | 400H | | 1 k |
| $2^{11}$ | 2048 | 800H | | 2 k |
| $2^{12}$ | 4096 | 1000H | $16^3$ | 4 k |
| $2^{13}$ | 8192 | 2000H | | 8 k |
| $2^{14}$ | 16384 | 4000H | | 16 k |
| $2^{15}$ | 32768 | 8000H | | 32 k |
| $2^{16}$ | 65536 | 10000H | $16^4$ | 64 k |
| $2^{17}$ | 131072 | 20000H | | 128 k |
| $2^{18}$ | 262144 | 40000H | | 256 k |
| $2^{19}$ | 524288 | 80000H | | 512 k |
| $2^{20}$ | 1048576 | 100000H | $16^5$ | 1 M |
| $2^{21}$ | 2097152 | 200000H | | 2 M |
| $2^{22}$ | 4194304 | 400000H | | 4 M |
| $2^{23}$ | 8388608 | 800000H | | 8 M |
| $2^{24}$ | 16777216 | 1000000H | $16^6$ | 16 M |

Numbers in different numbering systems can be expressed using mathematical expressions. For example, the base-8 number 40572 can be expressed as

$$4 * 8^4 + 0 * 8^3 + 5 * 8^2 + 7 * 8^1 + 2 * 8^0$$

The base-2 number 10110101B can be expressed as

$$1 * 2^7 + 0 * 2^6 + 1 * 2^5 + 1 * 2^4 + 0 * 2^3 + 1 * 2^2 + 0 * 2^1 + 1 * 2^0$$

The base-16 number 85ADFH can be expressed as

$$8 * 16^4 + 5 * 16^3 + A * 16^2 + D * 16^1 + F * 16^0$$

The base number of the numbering system makes all the difference in the expressions above. Remember that * means a multiplication operation. Note also the convention of using the letter B at the end of a binary number to show that it is a binary number. Similarly, the letter H at the end of a hexadecimal number is used to denote that the number is of the hexadecimal numbering system. For base-8 octal numbers we do not have any special letters, because we do not use base-8 often in this book. By using letters at the end of numbers other than base-10 decimal numbers, we can write all numbers down without the possibility of misunderstanding. For example, numbers 16H, 10110B, and 22 mean the same.

The binary numbering system and the hexadecimal numbering system are important in the world of computers. It is often necessary to make conversions between these numbering systems and our base-10 decimal system. To make the conversions easily, you should buy a calculator which is capable of operating with binary and hexadecimal numbers. However, a computer specialist must be able to make the conversions by hand, if necessary. At this phase of your becoming a computer specialist, it is good practice to learn to make the conversions that will be explained below.

Conversions to the decimal system can be made by writing expressions like the ones above. For example, 101011B can be converted to a decimal number in the following way

$$\begin{aligned} 101011B &= 1 * 2^5 + 0 * 2^4 + 1 * 2^3 + 0 * 2^2 + 1 * 2^1 + 1 * 2^0 \\ &= 32 + 0 + 8 + 0 + 2 + 1 \\ &= 43. \end{aligned}$$

Table 3-2 shows how much $2^0$, $2^1$, $2^2$, $2^3$, etc. is in the decimal system. That table is therefore useful when making conversions like the one above. Converting a binary number to the decimal system is basically a matter of taking the correct numbers from the second column of Table 3-2 and calculating the sum of these numbers.

Converting a hexadecimal number to the decimal system resembles the conversion of binary numbers. For example, 3AF2H can be converted to a decimal number in the following way

$$\begin{aligned} 3AF2H &= 3 * 16^3 + A * 16^2 + F * 16^1 + 2 * 16^0 \\ &= 3 * 4096 + 10 * 256 + 15 * 16 + 2 * 1 \\ &= 12288 + 2560 + 240 + 2 \\ &= 15090. \end{aligned}$$

In these kinds of conversions you can also exploit the important numbers shown in Table 3-2. And always remember that any number to the power of zero is one.

Conversions from the decimal system to the binary numbering system can be carried out by performing subtraction operations with the "magical numbers" in the second column of Table 3-2. Those numbers are somewhat magical because, provided that new rows are added to the table if necessary, any whole number (integer) can be expressed as the sum of a set of numbers from the second column of the table. For example, let's convert the number 2841 to the binary system. Beforehand, we know that the result of the conversion will be a series of 1s and 0s. We also know that the result begins with a 1 because leading zeroes in numbers are insignificant (e.g. 001101B is the same as 1101B). The decimal-to-binary conversion procedure is the following:

- Search for the largest number from the second column in Table 3-2 which can be subtracted from the number being converted. In the case of 2841, 2048 is the largest number that can be subtracted. Because 2048 is 2 to the power of 11, we can deduce that the binary number we are trying to construct has a 1 in the exponent position 11, and the binary number has 12 digits. The number thus looks like

| $2^{11}$ | $2^{10}$ | $2^9$ | $2^8$ | $2^7$ | $2^6$ | $2^5$ | $2^4$ | $2^3$ | $2^2$ | $2^1$ | $2^0$ |
|---|---|---|---|---|---|---|---|---|---|---|---|
| 1 | x | x | x | x | x | x | x | x | x | x | x |

  Now the rest of our task is to find out whether there is 0 or 1 in place of each x.

- Subtract the number found in the second column from the number being converted. In our example case 2841 - 2048 makes 793.

- Moving upwards from the position found in Table 3-2, find the largest number that can be subtracted from what is left from the original decimal number. In our example case we go upwards from the exponent position 11 in the table, and search for a number in the second column that can be subtracted from 793. We can see that 1024 in the exponent position 10 cannot be subtracted, but 512 in the exponent position 9 can be subtracted from 793. This means that there is a 0 in the exponent position 10 and a 1 in the exponent position 9, and the binary number now looks like

| $2^{11}$ | $2^{10}$ | $2^9$ | $2^8$ | $2^7$ | $2^6$ | $2^5$ | $2^4$ | $2^3$ | $2^2$ | $2^1$ | $2^0$ |
|---|---|---|---|---|---|---|---|---|---|---|---|
| 1 | 0 | 1 | x | x | x | x | x | x | x | x | x |

- Subtract the number found in the second column from what is left from the original number. By calculating 793 - 512 we get 281.

- Continue going upwards in the second column of Table 3-2, searching for the largest numbers that can be subtracted from what is currently left from the original decimal number. Mark a 1 in those exponent positions where subtraction is possible and carry out the subtraction. Mark a 0 to the exponent positions where no subtraction is possible. Stop the procedure when there is nothing left from the original number, and mark a 0 to any remaining unsolved exponent positions. In our example case we are searching for a number that can be subtracted from 281. The procedure goes as follows

| | | | |
|---|---|---|---|
| 256 | can subtract | result is 25 | binary digit is 1 |
| 128 | cannot subtract | | binary digit is 0 |
| 64 | cannot subtract | | binary digit is 0 |
| 32 | cannot subtract | | binary digit is 0 |
| 16 | can subtract | result is 9 | binary digit is 1 |
| 8 | can subtract | result is 1 | binary digit is 1 |
| 4 | cannot subtract | | binary digit is 0 |
| 2 | cannot subtract | | binary digit is 0 |
| 1 | can subtract | result is 0 | binary digit is 1 |

The last binary digit, the least significant bit, in our example was 1 because it was an odd number that was being converted. The final result of our conversion example is

| $2^{11}$ | $2^{10}$ | $2^9$ | $2^8$ | $2^7$ | $2^6$ | $2^5$ | $2^4$ | $2^3$ | $2^2$ | $2^1$ | $2^0$ |
|---|---|---|---|---|---|---|---|---|---|---|---|
| 1 | 0 | 1 | 1 | 0 | 0 | 0 | 1 | 1 | 0 | 0 | 1 |

Making a decimal-to-binary conversion needs a little bit of work if you do it by hand (and brains), but converting between hexadecimal and binary numbers is an easier thing to do. One reason why hexadecimal numbers are loved so much by computing specialists is that it is very easy to convert a binary number to a hexadecimal number and vice versa. The relationship between binary numbers and hexadecimal numbers is such that four bits (binary digits) in a binary number correspond directly to a single digit in the same number in the hexadecimal form. Therefore, a binary number can be converted to a hexadecimal number in groups of four bits. Figure 3-1 shows how binary number 10101101101100B can be converted to a hexadecimal number. By applying the procedure described in Figure 3-1 in the reverse sense, it is possible to make hexadecimal-to-binary conversions. For example hexadecimal number 6F1DH is 0110111100011101B because 6H is 0110B, FH is 1111B, 1H is 0001B, and DH is 1101B.

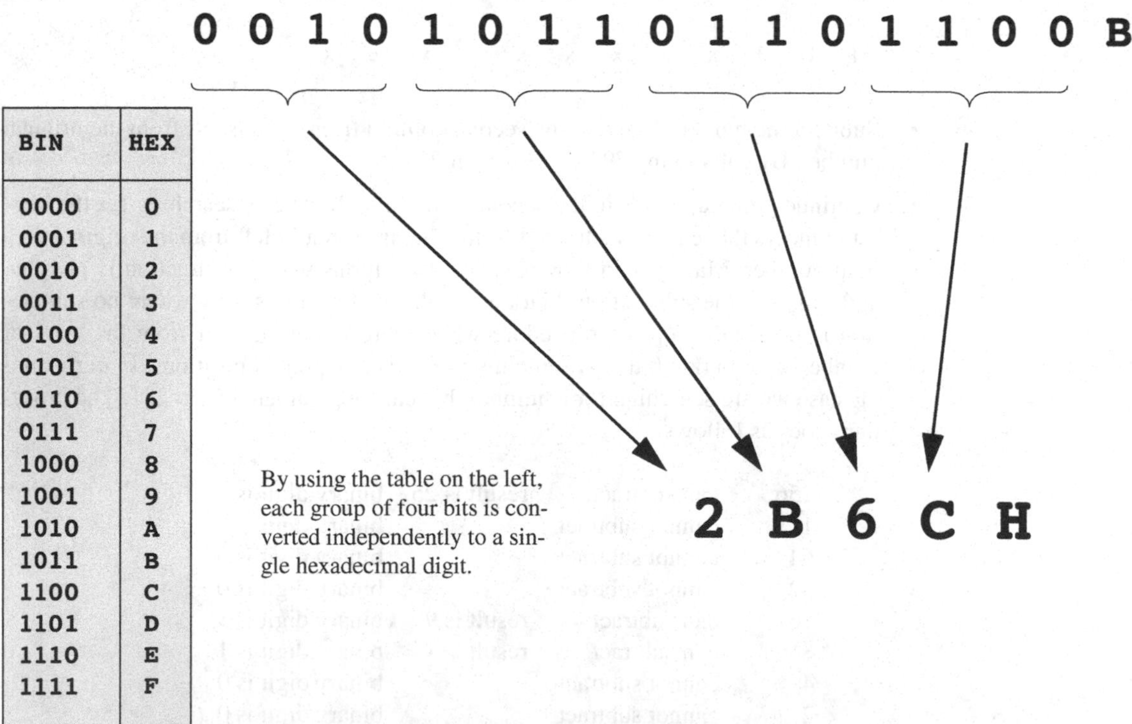


*Figure 3-1. Converting 10101101101100B to a hexadecimal number.*

The "slang" column of Table 3-2 may require some explanation. When speaking about things in the world of computers, we often need to speak about large numbers. It is a nice coincidence of the binary numbering system and the decimal numbering system that numbers 1024 and 1000, as well as numbers 1048576 and 1000000 are so close to each other. On the other hand, the word kilo (k) means 1000 times something and Mega (M) means 1000000 times something. Outside the world of computers it is usual to say 1 kilometer to mean 1000 meters, or 1 Megaton to mean 1000000 tons. Therefore, it has become customary to say, for example,

64 kilobits (kb) to mean 65 536 bits,
1 Megabit (Mb) to mean 1 048 576 bits, and
8 Megabytes (MB) to mean 8 388 608 bytes.

## Conventions for writing hexadecimal numbers

Hexadecimal numbers are expressed by using the normal numerical symbols 0, 1, 2, 3, 4, 5, 6, 7, 8, and 9, and six additional numerical symbols A, B, C, D, E, and F. To indicate that a number is a hexadecimal number, it is common to add the letter H at the end of the number. These are not, however, the only conventions. Another commonly used notation is to use the prefix 0x, a zero and letter x, to indicate that a number is a hexadecimal number. The additional hexadecimal symbols may also be written as lowercase letters a, b, c, d, e, and f. Thus we have the following four different possibilities to write hexadecimal numbers:

| DECIMAL | HEXADECIMAL | HEXADECIMAL | HEXADECIMAL | HEXADECIMAL |
|---|---|---|---|---|
| 22 | 16H | 16H | 0x16 | 0x16 |
| 31 | 1FH | 1fH | 0x1F | 0x1f |
| 254 | FEH | feH | 0xFE | 0xfe |
| 15090 | 3AF2H | 3af2H | 0x3AF2 | 0x3af2 |
| 55236 | D7C4H | d7c4H | 0xD7C4 | 0xd7c4 |

## Exercises related to numbering systems

In the exercises below you should do the conversions manually as described in this section. You can verify your answers with a calculator which is capable of handling binary and hexadecimal numbers.

Exercise 3-1. Convert the binary numbers 10111010B and 101010110110B to decimal numbers and hexadecimal numbers.

Exercise 3-2. Convert the hexadecimal numbers AF21H and B29DH to binary numbers and decimal numbers.

Exercise 3-3. Convert the decimal numbers 1234 and 5678 first to binary numbers. Convert then the binary numbers to hexadecimal numbers.

## 3.2 Numerical information: the binary world of computers

Now you have learned that numerical information can be expressed in different ways. We are accustomed to using decimal numbers in our everyday life, but it is the binary numbering system that is THE numbering system in the world of computers. The binary numbers can be written with only two symbols, 0 and 1, but they are equally as adequate numbers as our common decimal numbers. Everything that can be written down as a decimal number can also be expressed as a binary number.

Binary numbers are convenient for computers because they need only two symbols. Binary numbers can be stored in the memory of computers in the form of electric phenomena. For example, a voltage present in a certain part of an electronic component can mean the binary 1. No voltage present can then mean a binary 0, and thereby we have all binary symbols expressed in electric form.

The most important electronic components inside modern computers are integrated circuits, the black components on greenish boards. Integrated circuits contain many transistors that are connected to each other in a special way. Transistors are the basic electronic elements inside integrated circuits. A single integrated circuit may contain thousands if not millions of transistors. The transistors inside integrated circuits are used to store information in binary form. By setting a voltage to a certain wire it is possible to store binary information into an integrated circuit, and by setting a voltage to another wire, it is possible to read the previously stored binary information.

Although computers are rather complex electronic constructions, a person who wants to write programs to be run on computers does not have to understand all the electronic details of computers. A programmer needs merely a logical view of a computer's electronics. A computer can be considered a device that contains very many logical memory cells which are able to store one bit of information. The memory cells are made of transistors. A bit (binary digit) is the smallest unit of information inside a computer. A memory cell which can hold a bit of information can contain a zero (0) or one (1). The key idea in electronic computing is that, although information is stored in small bits, it is possible to handle large amounts of information when there are very many of these single-bit memory cells.

Figure 3-2 shows a simple memory cell which is capable of storing one bit of information. The memory cell operates with a voltage of +5V and it has lines (wires) for writing and reading information. The information that can be stored is either 0 or 1. We can assume that zero Volts means 0 and +5 Volts means 1. The memory cell is capable of holding the voltage that has been stored in it, and it simply outputs a voltage of 0V or +5V depending on which of these two voltages has been stored in the memory cell. Information can be stored in the memory cell by switching a voltage of +5V to the WRITE MEMORY line and simultaneously setting the INPUT line to the voltage that represents the information which is being stored. Information can be read from the memory cell by switching a voltage of +5V to the READ MEMORY line. As long as the READ MEMORY line has an active voltage of +5V, the OUTPUT line has the voltage (0V or +5V) that has previously been stored in the memory cell. The lines WRITE MEMORY and READ MEMORY are control signals which are used to transfer information to or from the memory cell. The actual data transfer occurs via the INPUT and OUTPUT lines. The GROUND line is the basis for which all voltages are measured. The line that connects the memory cell to the operating voltage is also marked in Figure 3-2, though that line does not affect the logical operation of the cell.

Figure 3-3 shows a timing diagram that describes the operation of the single-bit memory cell. It is assumed that the memory cell is somewhere among the other electronic circuitry and the outside circuitry changes the voltages on the lines that are connected to the memory cell. Note that the line OUTPUT has a defined voltage only when the line READ MEMORY has a voltage with which the memory cell is ordered to deliver its contents to the outside world.

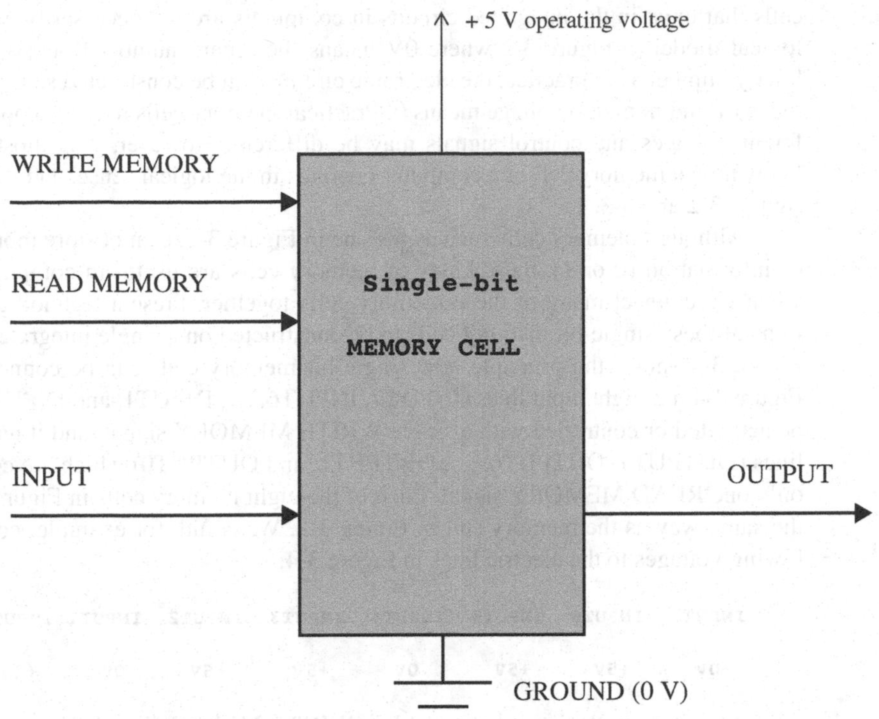
+ 5 V operating voltage
WRITE MEMORY
READ MEMORY
Single-bit
MEMORY CELL
INPUT
OUTPUT
GROUND (0 V)

***Figure 3-2. A logical model of a single-bit memory cell.***

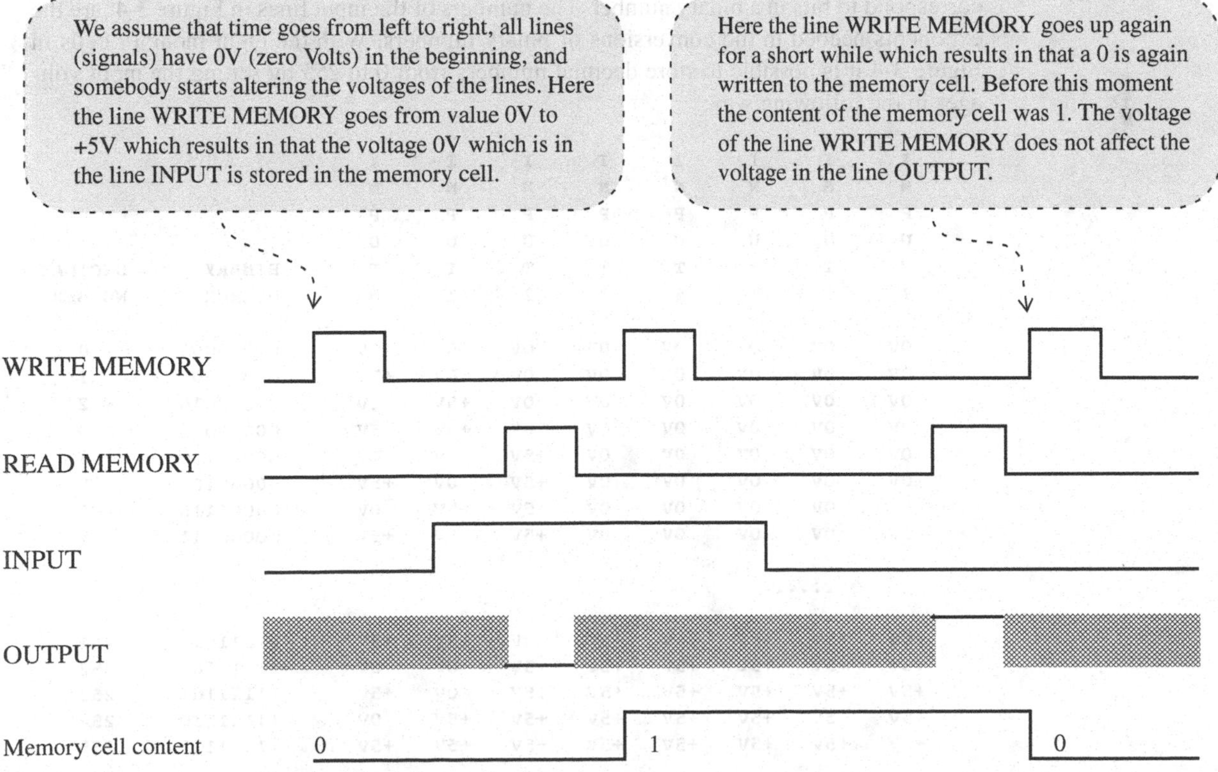
We assume that time goes from left to right, all lines (signals) have 0V (zero Volts) in the beginning, and somebody starts altering the voltages of the lines. Here the line WRITE MEMORY goes from value 0V to +5V which results in that the voltage 0V which is in the line INPUT is stored in the memory cell.
Here the line WRITE MEMORY goes up again for a short while which results in that a 0 is again written to the memory cell. Before this moment the content of the memory cell was 1. The voltage of the line WRITE MEMORY does not affect the voltage in the line OUTPUT.
WRITE MEMORY
READ MEMORY
INPUT
OUTPUT
Memory cell content
0
1
0

***Figure 3-3. Writing and reading a single-bit memory cell.***

Memory cells are called flip-flops in the literature of digital electronics. The memory cells that exist in the integrated circuits in computers are not necessarily exactly like the logical model in Figure 3-2 where 0V means the binary number 0 and +5V means the binary number 1. In practice, the electronic circuits can be constructed so that zero voltage means 1 and non-zero voltage means 0. Practical memory cells may also operate with different voltages and control signals may be different. However, it is most important to know how a memory cell of a computer operates in the logical sense, and that is shown in figures 3-2 and 3-3.

Although memory cells such as the one in Figure 3-2. cannot store more than one bit of information (0 or 1), these kinds of memory cells are useful in computer electronics when we connect many of these memory cells together. Present technology allows millions of these single-bit memory cells to be constructed on a single integrated circuit chip. Figure 3-4 shows the principle how single bit memory cells can be connected together. Figure 3-4 has eight input lines (INPUT7, INPUT6, ... , INPUT1, and INPUT0) which can be activated or controlled with a single WRITE MEMORY signal, and it has eight output lines (OUTPUT7, OUTPUT6, ... , OUTPUT1, and OUTPUT0) which are controlled with only one READ MEMORY signal. Each of the eight memory cells in Figure 3-4 works in the same way as the memory cell in Figure 3-2. We could, for example, connect the following voltages to the electric lines in Figure 3-4:

| INPUT7 | INPUT6 | INPUT5 | INPUT4 | INPUT3 | INPUT2 | INPUT1 | INPUT0 | WRITE MEMORY |
|---|---|---|---|---|---|---|---|---|
| 0V | +5V | +5V | 0V | +5V | +5V | 0V | +5V | +5V |

After setting the input lines and line WRITE MEMORY to these voltages, the voltages in the input lines would be stored in the eight memory cells. Supposing that +5V means 1 and 0V means 0, we can say that by having stored the above voltages, we have actually stored the binary number 01101101B into the memory cells. The key idea here is that numeric information is stored in the form of electronic voltages, and the input lines correspond to bits in a binary number. The numbers of the input lines in Figure 3-4 are the exponents needed in the conversions of binary numbers. With the eight memory cells in Figure 3-4 it is possible to store decimal numbers from 0 to 255 by setting the input voltages in the following way:

| INPUT7 | INPUT6 | INPUT5 | INPUT4 | INPUT3 | INPUT2 | INPUT1 | INPUT0 | BINARY NUMBER | DECIMAL NUMBER |
|---|---|---|---|---|---|---|---|---|---|
| 0V | 0V | 0V | 0V | 0V | 0V | 0V | 0V | 00000000 | 0 |
| 0V | 0V | 0V | 0V | 0V | 0V | 0V | +5V | 00000001 | 1 |
| 0V | 0V | 0V | 0V | 0V | 0V | +5V | 0V | 00000010 | 2 |
| 0V | 0V | 0V | 0V | 0V | 0V | +5V | +5V | 00000011 | 3 |
| 0V | 0V | 0V | 0V | 0V | +5V | 0V | 0V | 00000100 | 4 |
| 0V | 0V | 0V | 0V | 0V | +5V | 0V | +5V | 00000101 | 5 |
| 0V | 0V | 0V | 0V | 0V | +5V | +5V | 0V | 00000110 | 6 |
| 0V | 0V | 0V | 0V | 0V | +5V | +5V | +5V | 00000111 | 7 |
| | ........ | | | | | | | ... | .. |
| +5V | +5V | +5V | +5V | +5V | 0V | +5V | +5V | 11111011 | 251 |
| +5V | +5V | +5V | +5V | +5V | +5V | 0V | 0V | 11111100 | 252 |
| +5V | +5V | +5V | +5V | +5V | +5V | 0V | +5V | 11111101 | 253 |
| +5V | +5V | +5V | +5V | +5V | +5V | +5V | 0V | 11111110 | 254 |
| +5V | +5V | +5V | +5V | +5V | +5V | +5V | +5V | 11111111 | 255 |

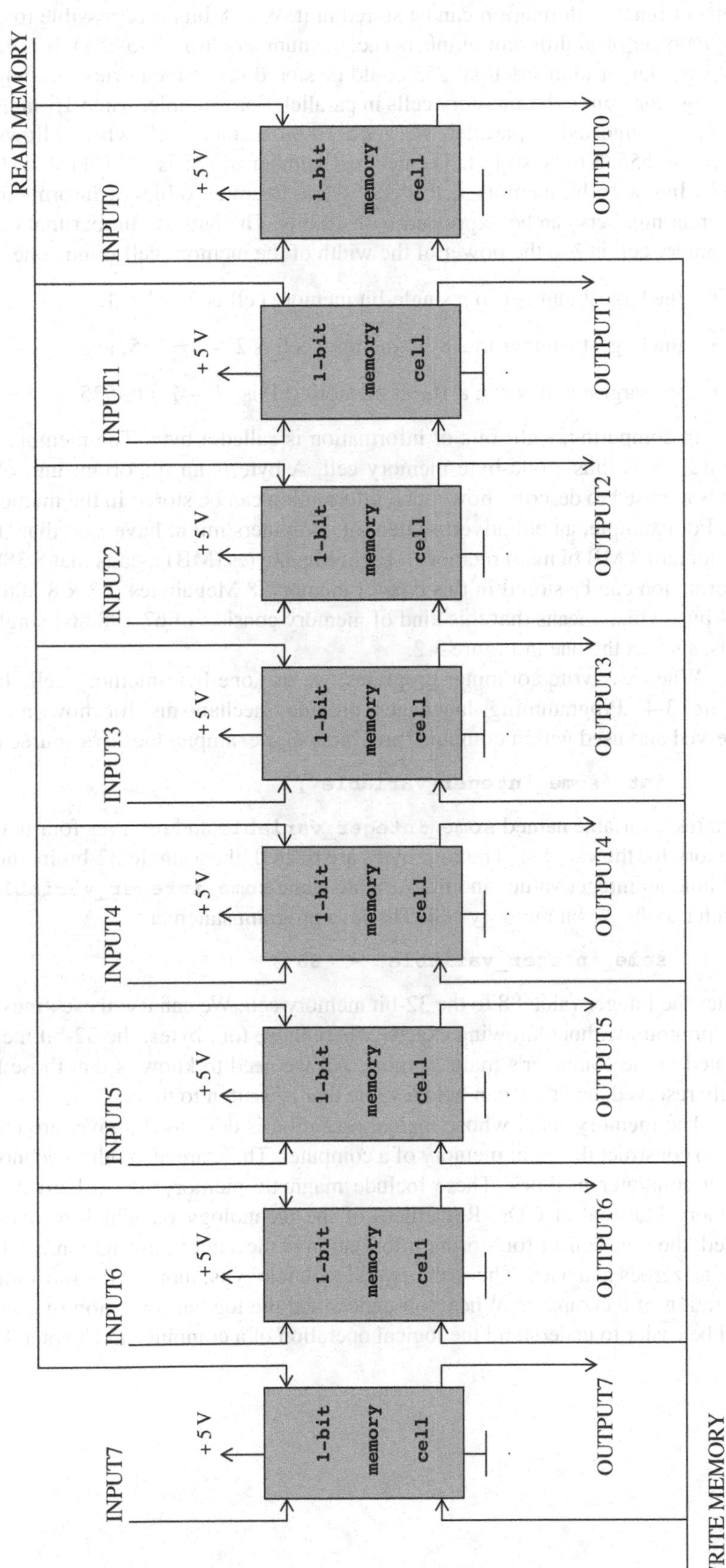


*Figure 3-4. Eight single-bit memory cells connected in parallel.*

The configuration in Figure 3-4 can be called an 8-bit memory cell which means that 8 bits of binary information can be stored in it. With 8 bits it is possible to express 256 (2 to the power of 8) different numbers (i.e. the numbers from 0 to 255). It is easy to imagine that even larger numbers than 255 could be stored in the memories of computers by connecting more single-bit memory cells in parallel. For example, when 16 single-bit memory cells are connected in parallel, we get a 16-bit memory cell which allows the numbers from 0 to 65535 to be stored. The decimal number 65535 is 1111111111111111B (sixteen ones). Into a 16-bit memory cell it is possible to store 16 bits of information, and 65536 different numbers can be expressed with 16 bits. The largest number that can be stored in a memory cell is 2 to the power of the width of the memory cell minus one. Therefore

- the largest number in a single-bit memory cell is $2^1 - 1 = 1$,
- the largest number in a 8-bit memory cell is $2^8 - 1 = 255$, and
- the largest number in a 16-bit memory cell is $2^{16} - 1 = 65535$.

In computing, eight bits of information is called a byte. The memory cell shown in Figure 3-4 is thus a one-byte memory cell. A byte is an important unit of information. Bytes are used to describe how much information can be stored in the memory of computers. For example, an old advertisement of computers might have said that "these computers contain 8 MB of main memory". Eight Megabytes (MB) means that 8 388 608 bytes of information can be stored in this type of memory. 8 Megabytes is 8 x 8 388 608 = 67 108 864 bits, which means that this kind of memory consists of 67 108 864 single-bit memory cells, such as the one in Figure 3-2.

When we write computer programs, we use one-byte memory cells like the one in Figure 3-4. Programming languages provide mechanisms for how memory can be reserved and used within computer programs. For example, the Java source program line

```
int  some_integer_variable ;
```

declares a variable named **some_integer_variable** and reserves four bytes (32 bits) of memory for the variable. The four bytes are treated like a single 32-bit memory cell which can hold an integer value, and the variable name **some_integer_variable** can be used to refer to the 32-bit memory cell. The Java program statement

```
some_integer_variable  =  88 ;
```

writes the integer value 88 to the 32-bit memory cell. We can use these kinds of statements in a program without knowing exactly where those four bytes, the 32-bit memory cell, are located in the computer's main memory. All we need to know is that those four bytes are really reserved, and they can hold a value that is written to them.

The memory cells, whose logical operation is described above, are used, for example, to construct the main memory of a computer. There are also other technologies to construct computer memory. These include magnetic memory like a hard disk and optical memory like that of CDs. Regardless of the technology on which a memory device is based, the mechanism for storing information is the same: information can be stored only as bits, zeroes and ones. The memory cell technology is, though, the most important in the operation of a computer. When you understand the logical operation of a memory cell, it will be easier to understand the logical operation of a computer in Chapter 4.

## 3.3 Textual information: character coding systems

Information is stored in the memory of computers as zeroes and ones. We learned this in the previous section, and, in fact, this is the most important thing to be learned about how computers store information. There is nothing else but zeroes and ones, represented by two voltage levels, in the memory of computers. Zeroes and ones are convenient when we want to store numerical information, but these two digits can also be used to store other types of information, such as various texts.

When we want to store a number, say 123, in a computer's memory, we can store it in binary form. 123 is 1111011B as a binary number. Since 1111011B consists of seven binary digits, a one-byte memory cell such as the one in Figure 3-4 is sufficient for storing this number. When larger numbers need to be stored, several bytes of memory can be used.

It is not difficult to store whole numbers in a computer memory since these numbers can be expressed clearly in binary form. But when we want to store text in a computer's memory, the situation becomes somewhat more complicated. Because computer memories can only store zeroes and ones, there has to be a way to code textual information to zeroes and ones. A traditional coding system for textual information is the ASCII coding system. ASCII is an acronym of "American Standard Code for Information Interchange". The ASCII coding system is an agreement made by organizations working in the computing business. As its name implies, the coding system was developed in the United States where the commercial use of computers began.

There are ASCII character codes for all those textual symbols that can be found on the keyboard of a computer. The ASCII coding system is based on the idea that each letter or symbol must fit in one byte of memory. Because one byte is 8 bits, there can be 256 different character codes. 256 different codes is sufficient to represent all uppercase English letters (A, B, C, etc.), all lowercase English letters (a, b, c, etc.), all decimal numerical symbols (0, 1, 2, 3, 4, 5, 6, 7, 8, and 9), many special printable characters (!, ", #, $, %, &, ', (, ), -, /, etc.), and many non-English letters and special symbols (Ä, Ö, å, etc.).

At the end of this book on page 594 you can find a table which lists the first 128 most commonly used ASCII character codes. You can see, for example, that the code for the letter A is 41H (0100 0001 binary, 65 decimal), and the code for the plus sign + is 2BH (0010 1011 binary, 43 decimal). By carefully studying the table you can find out the following facts about the ASCII coding system:

- The codes from 30H to 39H are reserved for numerical symbols from 0 to 9.
- The codes from 41H to 5AH are reserved for uppercase letters from A to Z.
- The codes from 61H to 7AH are reserved for lowercase letters from a to z.
- You get the code for a lowercase letter by adding 20H to the code of the corresponding uppercase letter. For example, because the character code of uppercase letter R is 52H, the character code of lowercase letter r is 52H + 20H = 72H.
- You get the character code of a numerical symbol by adding 30H to the number in question. For example, the character code of 8 is 30H + 8 = 38H
- The first codes from 0 to 1FH are not printable or visible characters. Instead, they represent special control characters. Some of the special control characters like BACKSPACE, TABULATOR, NEWLINE, and ESCAPE can be produced by computer keyboards. BELL is a special "character" that represent a sound that computers can produce. A special "character" is also NULL which has code 0. The NULL character has its own name so that it can be clearly distinguished from the character code of zero which is 30H.
- You cannot find character codes for non-English letters such as Ä, Ö, Å, Ñ, É, etc. in the table. The codes of these letters are in the range from 80H to FFH, and there exist different code tables for this code range.

Once you have a character code chart like the table on page 594 available, it is easy to convert textual information to character codes. For example, the word HELLO is coded in the following way:

```
48H  45H  4CH  4CH  4FH     ( hexadecimal codes )

72   69   76   76   79      ( decimal codes )

H    E    L    L    O
```

The sentence "Computing is fun." is coded with the following sequence of numbers:

```
43H 6FH 6DH 70H 75H 74H 69H 6EH 67H 20H 69H 73H 20H 66H 75H 6EH 2EH

67  111 109 112 117 116 105 110 103 32  105 115 32  102 117 110 46

'C' 'o' 'm' 'p' 'u' 't' 'i' 'n' 'g' ' ' 'i' 's' ' ' 'f' 'u' 'n' '.'
```

Note that spaces between the words in the sentence above have character codes (20H), and the full stop '.' at the end of the sentence has the code 2EH. Storing the text "Computing is fun." requires 17 bytes of memory: the letters require 14 bytes altogether, two spaces require two bytes, and the full stop needs one byte.

It is possible to express numbers with character codes. For example, number 123 could be coded as follows

```
31H   32H   33H    ( hexadecimal codes )

49    50    51     ( decimal codes )

'1'   '2'   '3'
```

Storing the number 123 coded with character codes would require 3 bytes of memory. If the number was stored as a binary number, it could be stored in a single byte of memory

ASCII coding is widespread in computing and telecommunications. For example, when you send an e-mail message on the Internet, the text is converted to character codes which are sent in electronic form. When you press some key on the keyboard of your computer, the program which is being run by the computer receives the character code of the key that was pressed. Even source programs are sequences of character codes in a file on a hard disk of a computer.

One problem with the ASCII coding system is that only the codes from 0 to 7FH (0 to 127) are the same for most computer operating systems. The codes from 80H to FFH (128 to 255) can have different meanings in different operating systems.

A further limitation of the ASCII coding system is that it defines only 256 different codes. Those codes represent letters and other symbols used in English and Western-European languages. There are many natural languages which use characters and symbols which cannot be expressed with the ASCII coding system. Because this kind of limitation causes problems, a new and more universal coding system for textual information has been developed. The name of the new system is Unicode, and it uses 16 bits to code each textual symbol. With 16 bits it is theoretically possible to code 65536 different symbols.

The Unicode system has codes for the characters of many natural languages. Each character set has been reserved a certain range of character codes. The following are examples of hexadecimal code ranges

| | |
|---|---|
| **0370 ... 03FF** | Greek and Coptic characters |
| **0400 ... 04FF** | Cyrillic characters |
| **0530 ... 058F** | Armenian characters |
| **0590 ... 05FF** | Hebrew characters |
| **0600 ... 06FF** | Arabic characters |

Because the Unicode system attempts to cover the characters of all natural languages, it is impossible to show all the character codes and the actual characters here. To see the character code tables and the actual characters, please visit the Internet address *www.unicode.org*.

The first 256 character codes in the Unicode system are the same as the codes of the standardized ASCII coding system. The following list compares Unicode character codes to ASCII character codes (Note that all codes are expressed as hexadecimal codes):

| CHARACTER | Unicode | ASCII |
|---|---|---|
| NULL | 0000 | 00 |
| BACKSPACE | 0008 | 08 |
| NEWLINE | 000A | 0A |
| ESCAPE | 001B | 1B |
| SPACE | 0020 | 20 |
| ! | 0021 | 21 |
| " | 0022 | 22 |
| # | 0023 | 23 |
| $ | 0024 | 24 |
| * | 002A | 2A |
| + | 002B | 2B |
| 0 | 0030 | 30 |
| 1 | 0031 | 31 |
| 2 | 0032 | 32 |
| 3 | 0033 | 33 |
| A | 0041 | 41 |
| B | 0042 | 42 |
| C | 0043 | 43 |
| D | 0044 | 44 |
| a | 0061 | 61 |
| b | 0062 | 62 |
| c | 0063 | 63 |
| d | 0064 | 64 |

For example, the Unicode character code for the uppercase letter A is

```
0041H          0000 0000 0100 0001 B
```

and the corresponding ASCII code is

```
41H            0100 0001 B
```

The 8 most significant bits of the Unicode character code of A are zeroes. As leading zeroes in a number are not mathematically significant, the two codes above can be considered equal.

We shall see later that the Java programming language encodes textual information according to the Unicode system. Therefore, when a Java program stores a character, it reserves 16 bits (2 bytes) of memory to store the code of the character. Of those 16 bits, however, 8 most significant bits are zeroes when the character is one that belongs to the English alphabet.

Because the first 256 Unicode character codes are the same as the ASCII codes, you can use the table on page 594 to find out the Unicodes of characters. For example, when you want to find out the Unicode character code of the letter R, you can pick up the code 52H from the table, and add two leading zeroes to the hexadecimal code.

The Unicode character coding system is still evolving, and it includes character codes that need more than 16 bits of storage capacity. In this book, however, we use only the traditional 16-bit codes.

## 3.4 More information: pictures, sound, and moving pictures

The memory of a computer, whether it is silicon-based main memory, magnetic disk memory, or optical memory such as CD, contains just bits, zeroes and ones. All these types of memory store information in digital binary form. Numbers and texts are stored in binary form, and so it is in the case of such forms of information as pictures, sound, and even moving pictures.

We learned in the previous section that to store textual information in computer memory, there has to be a commonly accepted standard. The Unicode system is a standard according to which textual information can be stored and transferred in digital form. To store pictures, sound (music), and moving pictures in digital form, there are own special standards for each type of information. These standards can be called storage formats. One storage format can be more widely accepted than another storage format.

A picture can be put into digital form so that the picture area is divided into thousands of tiny points, and the color and brightness of each point is then described with a numerical value which is stored in binary form. The picture area of a digital picture can be, for example, 2048 points wide and 1536 points high. If the color and brightness of each point were stored in an 8-bit byte, storing this kind of a digital picture would require 2048 * 1536 = 3145728 bytes of storage capacity. This is the basic idea for how pictures can be stored in digital form. The existing standard formats for storing picture information are, however, more complex than the description above. Examples of digital picture formats are:

- GIF, Graphics Interchange Format,
- JPEG, the format of Joint Photographic Experts Group, and
- TIFF, Tagged Image File Format.

Sound can be converted to digital form so that extremely many samples are taken from the original sound, and each sample is then described with a numerical value which is stored in binary form. The music on audio CDs, for example, is made by taking every second thousands of samples from the music. The millions of resulting samples are stored on a CD in binary form. When the CD is played with a CD player, the player constructs the original sound from the binary sound samples. The audio CD standard is one way to store sound in digital form. Another example of a digital sound standard is called MP3.

Moving pictures are in digital form on video DVDs and on the tapes used in digital video cameras. Storing moving pictures in digital form requires a lot of storage capacity because moving pictures are made of many still pictures. Standards for storing moving pictures in digital form are set by Moving Pictures Experts Group (MPEG). The standard for storing digital video pictures on CD is called MPEG-1. The standard that is used on DVDs and digital TV is called MPEG-2. It is likely that companies that manufacture digital video cameras have their own standards for storing moving pictures on tape.

The purpose of this section was to give you an overview of the possibilities which exist to store digital information in computer memory. Storing and handling of digital information requires computer programs, and the purpose of this book is to teach you to write computer programs. While learning computer programming we will concentrate only on numerical and textual information in this book. The reason for this is that the handling of numerical and textual information is much easier for a beginner than the handling of pictures, sound, and moving pictures. After you have learned computer programming sufficiently well, you may one day write programs which do something smart with sound or moving pictures.

# CHAPTER 4

## LOGICAL OPERATING PRINCIPLES OF COMPUTERS

The most important parts in a computer are its processor and its main memory that can be read and written by the processor. For a computer to do something useful, there must be an executable program in its main memory. An executable program is a sequence of machine instructions which the processor of the computer can read and interpret.

In this chapter, we shall study machine instructions and some general operating principles of computers. First, we will examine the operation of the main memory. Then we will study a processor and programs which are executed by the processor. You will learn how some basic computing activities, like repetition and subroutine calling, are performed at the machine level. This will help you to understand high-level Java programming in later chapters.

The general operating principles of computers will be explained with the help of an imaginary computer which can be regarded as a logical model of real computers. All computers which are commonly used operate according to the same principles as the imaginary computer, although the imaginary computer is simpler than a real computer. The simplicity of the imaginary computer makes it an ideal instrument for learning the basics of computer operation. The computer is imaginary because it has not been built by using electronic or any other physical components. The Internet site of this book provides, however, simulation programs that imitate the imaginary computer on a real computer.

## 4.1 How does the main memory operate?

Computers are able to process information that is stored in their memory in binary form. There are basically two kinds of memory devices in a computer. The main memory is built of RAM memory devices. (RAM is an abbreviation of Random Access Memory.) All other memory devices can be considered auxiliary memory devices. The main memory of a computer is more important than the auxiliary memory devices because programs that are being executed must be kept in the main memory. A computer must have a main memory in order to operate. Although computers like PCs are equipped with auxiliary memory devices (e.g. hard disk), it is possible to build computers without the auxiliary devices.

The main memory of a computer is a device which can be read from and written to by the processor of the computer. Figure 4-1 illustrates a small main memory that is only 16 bytes (16 x 8 bits) in size. Computers generally have a much larger main memory, but we can study the memory operations with just this small main memory. Figure 4-1 shows that four address lines A0, A1, A2, and A3 are needed to select one of the 16 bytes in the memory. The memory addressing control takes care that the right memory location is selected when a certain bit combination is switched to the address lines.

While studying the memory device in Figure 4-1, we suppose that it can be used by switching either zero Volts (0V) or five Volts (5V) to the lines of the device. By switching various voltages to the address lines, it is possible to select certain memory locations, for example in the following way:

| A3 A2 A1 A0 | MEANING |
|---|---|
| 0V 0V 0V 0V | memory address 0 is selected |
| 0V 0V 0V 5V | memory address 1 is selected |
| 0V 5V 0V 5V | memory address 5 is selected |
| 5V 0V 0V 5V | memory address 9 is selected |
| 5V 5V 5V 5V | memory address 15 is selected |

The main memory of a computer has data lines through which information is either moved into the memory (writing of data), or information is moved out of the memory (reading of data). In Figure 4-1 there are 8 data lines D0, D1, D2, D3, D4, D5, D6, and D7 through which one byte of information can either be written to or read from the memory.

Address lines are used to select the desired location in the memory, and data lines are needed to carry information to/from the memory. In addition to address and data lines, there are usually control lines and power supply lines in memory devices. The control lines ensure that the reading and writing operations are carried out in an accurate manner. The memory device in Figure 4-1 has two control lines which have names READ MEMORY and WRITE MEMORY. With these lines (signals) the processor which is using the memory device can perform either a writing operation or a reading operation. Power supply lines are needed to supply electricity for physical memory components, but for simplicity these lines are left out from Figure 4-1.

The control signals of a memory device are activated by the processor that is using the memory. The control signals of the memory device in Figure 4-1 can have the following values and meanings

| WRITE MEMORY | READ MEMORY | MEANING |
|---|---|---|
| 0 (0V) | 0 (0V) | No memory operations |
| 0 (0V) | 1 (5V) | Read selected memory address |
| 1 (5V) | 0 (0V) | Write selected memory address |
| 1 (5V) | 1 (5V) | Not allowed combination |

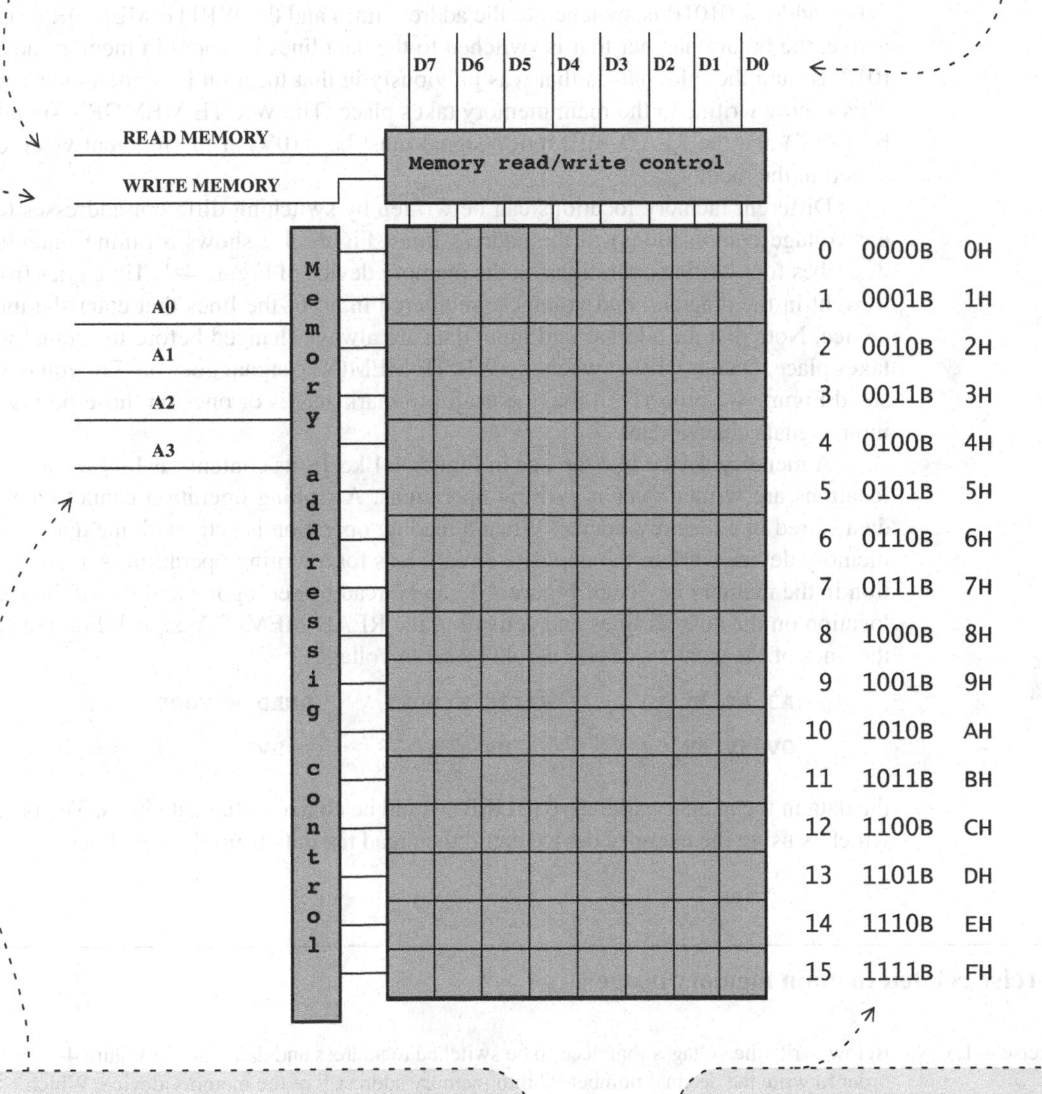


*Figure 4-1. A theoretical 16-byte main memory device.*

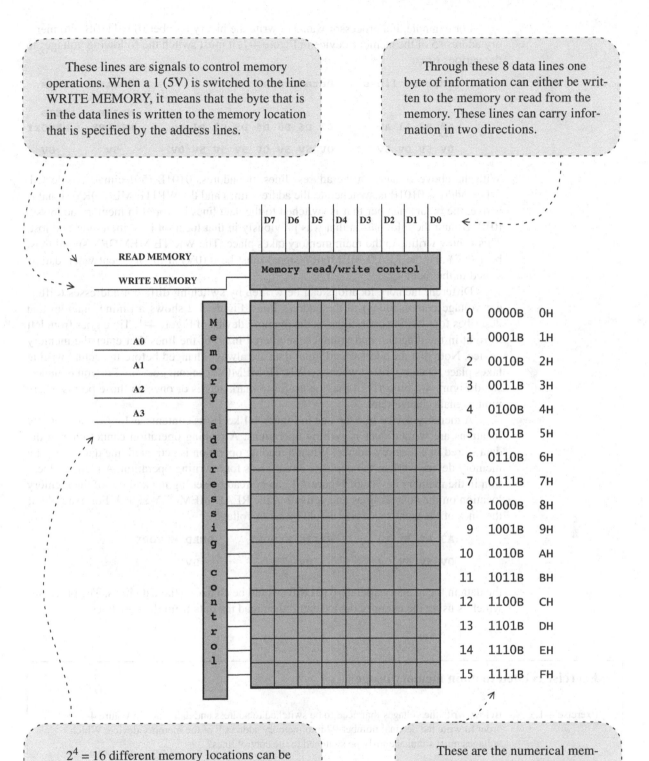

For example, if a processor wants to write the binary number 01101110B into memory address 5 of the memory device in Figure 4-1, it must switch the following voltages to the various lines:

| Address lines | Data lines | Control lines | |
|---|---|---|---|
| | | WRITE MEMORY | READ MEMORY |
| A3 A2 A1 A0 | D7 D6 D5 D4 D3 D2 D1 D0 | | |
| 0V 5V 0V 5V | 0V 5V 5V 0V 5V 5V 5V 0V | 5V | 0V |

With the above voltages in the address lines, the address 0101B (5 decimal) is selected. When address 0101B is switched to the address lines and the WRITE MEMORY signal is active, the binary number that is switched to the data lines is stored in memory address 5 (0101B) and the information that was previously in that location is written over and lost. This is how writing to the main memory takes place. The WRITE MEMORY signal must be 1 (5V) and the READ MEMORY signal must be 0 (0V) at the moment when data is stored in the memory.

Different memory locations can be written by switching different addresses (different voltage combinations) to the address lines. Figure 4-2 shows a timing diagram that describes four writing operations on the memory device of Figure 4-1. Time goes from left to right in the diagram, and voltages are altered in all of the lines that enter the memory device. Note that the address and input data are always changed before the actual writing takes place. Data is written when the WRITE MEMORY signal goes up. For you to understand Figure 4-2 properly, it may be useful to mark zeroes or ones on those points where input signals change state.

A memory device like the one in Figure 4-1 keeps its contents as long as no memory locations are written over in writing operations. A reading operation cannot change the data stored in a memory device. When a reading operation is activated, the data lines of a memory device work in the opposite direction as for a writing operation. A memory location in the memory device of Figure 4-1 can be read by setting the address of the memory location on the address lines and activating the READ MEMORY signal. For example, if the lines of the memory device would be set to voltages

| A3 A2 A1 A0 | WRITE MEMORY | READ MEMORY |
|---|---|---|
| 0V 5V 5V 0V | 0V | 5V |

the data in the memory address 6 (0110B) would be copied to the data lines. The processor which is using the memory device could then read the data from the data lines.

## Exercise related to main memory usage

Exercise 4-1. Below, write the voltages that need to be switched to address and data lines in Figure 4-1 in order to write the decimal number 97 into memory address 9 of the memory device. Which voltages must simultaneously be switched to the control lines?

| Address lines | | | | Data lines | | | | | | | |
|---|---|---|---|---|---|---|---|---|---|---|---|
| A3 | A2 | A1 | A0 | D7 | D6 | D5 | D4 | D3 | D2 | D1 | D0 |
| | | | | | | | | | | | |

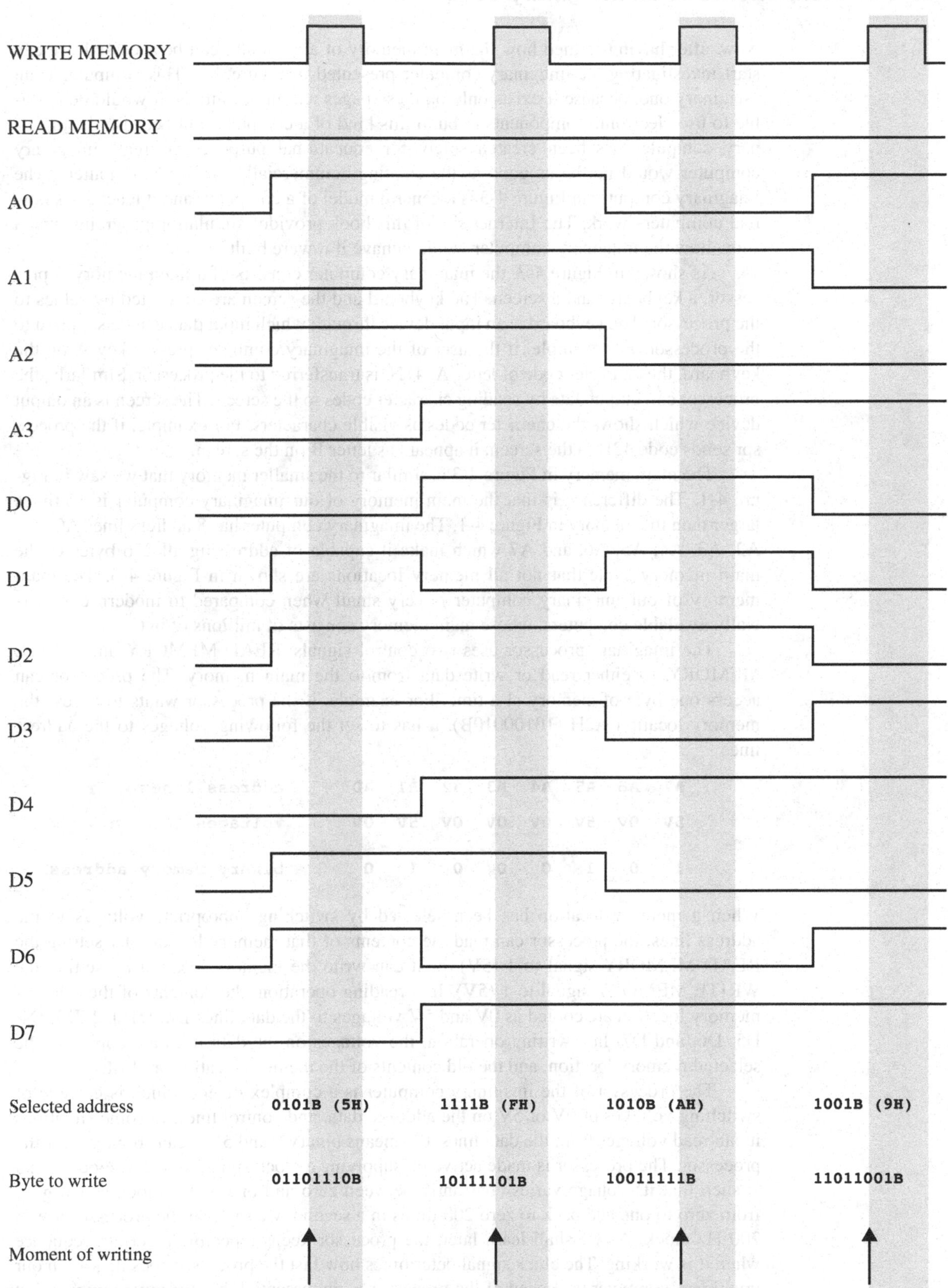


***Figure 4-2. Writing four memory locations in the memory device of Figure 4-1.***

## 4.2 The components of an imaginary computer

Now, after having studied how the main memory of a computer can be accessed, we can start investigating the imaginary computer presented in Figure 4-3. This computer is an imaginary one, because it exists only on these pages and in our minds. It would be possible to use electronic components to build this kind of a computer, but because the imaginary computer has been created solely for educational purposes, a "real" imaginary computer would not be as good as the existing commercially available computers. The imaginary computer in Figure 4-3 is a general model of a computer, and it teaches us how real computers work. The Internet site of this book provides simulation programs which show how the imaginary computer would behave if it were built.

As shown in Figure 4-3, the imaginary computer consists of a main memory, a processor, a keyboard, and a screen. The keyboard and the screen are connected by cables to the processor. The keyboard is an input device through which input data can be supplied to the processor. For example, if the user of the imaginary computer presses key A on the keyboard, the character code of letter A, 41H, is transferred to the processor. Similarly, the processor can output data by sending character codes to the screen. The screen is an output device which shows the character codes as visible characters. For example, if the processor sends code 42H to the screen, it appears as letter B on the screen.

The main memory in Figure 4-3 is similar to the smaller memory that we saw in Figure 4-1. The difference is that the main memory of our imaginary computer is 16 times larger than the memory in Figure 4-1. The imaginary computer has 8 address lines A0, A1, A2, A3, A4, A5, A6, and A7 which make it capable of addressing all 256 bytes of the main memory. Note that not all memory locations are shown in Figure 4-3. The main memory of our imaginary computer is very small when compared to modern commercially available computers, whose main memory consists of millions of bytes.

The imaginary processor uses two control signals, READ MEMORY and WRITE MEMORY, to either read or write data from/to the main memory. The processor can access one byte of memory at a time. For example, if the processor wants to access the memory location A2H (10100010B), it has to set the following voltages to the address lines

```
A7   A6   A5   A4   A3   A2   A1   A0        address lines

5V   0V   5V   0V   0V   0V   5V   0V        voltages

1    0    1    0    0    0    1    0         binary memory address
```

When a memory location has been selected by switching appropriate voltages to the address lines, the processor can read the contents of that memory location by setting the READ MEMORY signal to 1 (5V), or it can write the memory location by setting the WRITE MEMORY signal to 1 (5V). In a reading operation, the contents of the selected memory location are copied as 0V and 5V voltages to the data lines D0, D1, D2, D3, D4, D5, D6, and D7. In a writing operation, the voltages on the data lines are copied to the selected memory location, and the old contents of the memory location are lost.

The processor of the imaginary computer is a complex device which is capable of switching voltages of 0V or 5V on the address, data, and control lines. In some situations it can read voltages from the data lines. 0V means binary 0 and 5V means binary 1 for the processor. The processor is made active by supplying a clock signal to it. The clock signal is such that its voltage varies constantly between zero and one. If the clock signal goes from zero to one and back to zero 200 times in a second, we say that the processor uses a 200 Hz clock. As we shall learn later, the processor keeps repeating a certain sequence when it is working. The clock signal determines how fast the processor does its job. In our imaginary computer the speed of the processor is not essential, but we must imagine that there is a clock signal which makes the processor active.

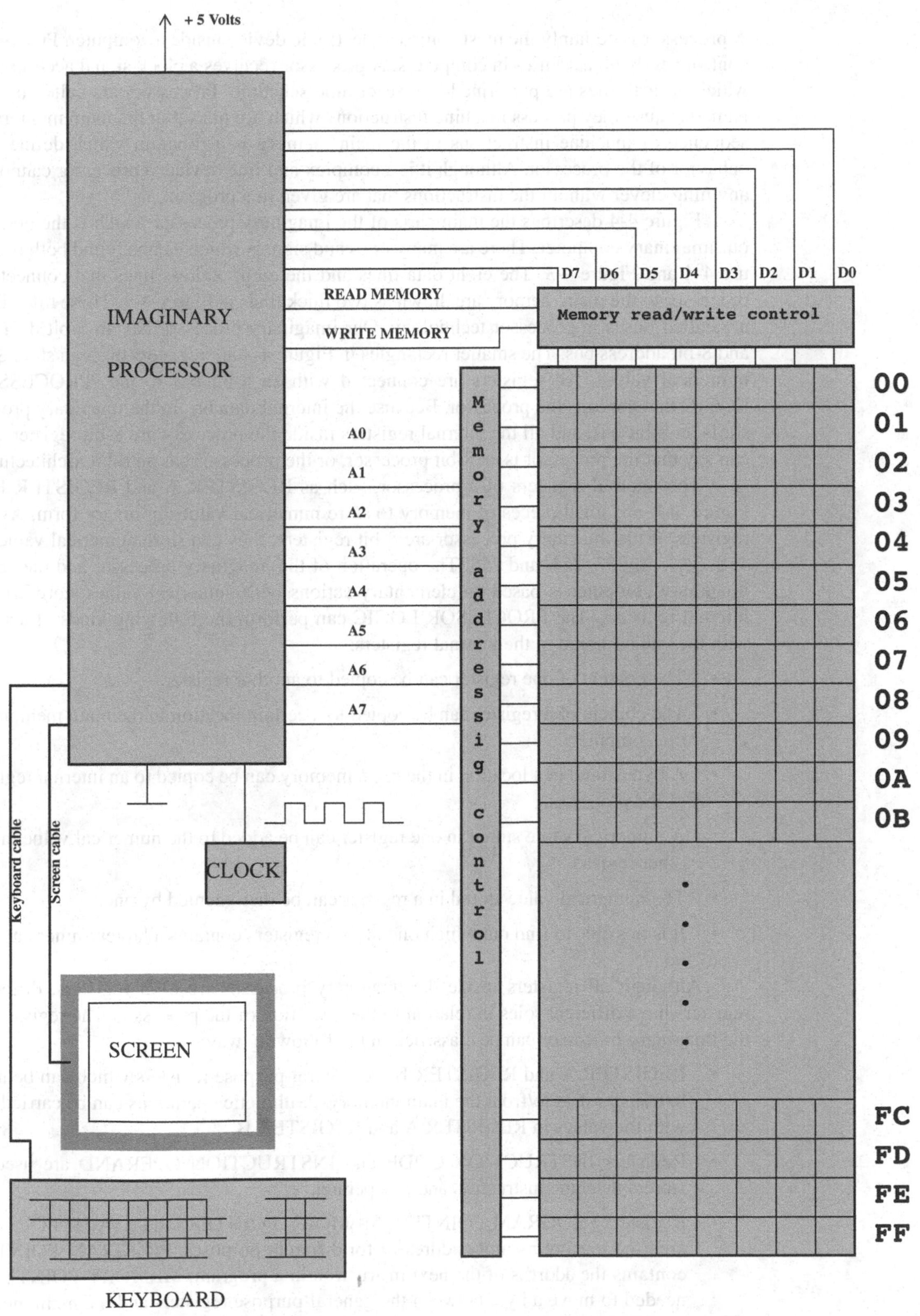


***Figure 4-3. An imaginary computer with a 256-byte main memory.***

## 4.3 Inside the imaginary processor

A processor is certainly the most complex electronic device inside a computer. Processors control nearly all activities in computers. A processor receives a clock signal according to which all activities are performed in a strict time schedule. Processors are called by that name because they process machine instructions which are placed in the main memory. A sequence of machine instructions in the main memory is a program which defines the behavior of the processor. Although it is a complex and fine device, a processor cannot do anything clever without the instructions that are given in a program.

Figure 4-4 describes the main parts of the imaginary processor which is the brain of our imaginary computer. There are many lines and signals which can be found both in Figure 4-4 and Figure 4-3. The eight data lines and the eight address lines that connect the processor to the main memory are drawn as two thick lines in Figure 4-4. These thick lines are called buses in processor technology. Our imaginary processor has an 8-bit data bus and 8-bit address bus. The smaller rectangles in Figure 4-4 are registers that can store 8-bit numerical values. All registers are connected with an 8-bit bus to the PROCESSOR LOGIC that controls the processor. Because the internal data bus in the imaginary processor is an 8-bit bus, and all the internal registers inside the processor are 8-bit registers, we can say that the processor is an 8-bit processor, or the processor has an 8-bit architecture.

The internal registers of a processor, such as REGISTER A and REGISTER B in Figure 4-4, are small pieces of memory to store numerical values in binary form. As the registers of the imaginary processor are 8-bit registers, they can store numerical values 0, 1, 2, 3, 4, ..., 253, 254, and 255. The operation of the imaginary processor and the entire imaginary computer is based on elementary actions with numerical values stored in the internal registers. The PROCESSOR LOGIC can perform the following kinds of actions with the values stored in the internal registers:

- The content of one register can be copied to another register.
- The content of a register can be copied to a certain location in the main memory of the computer.
- A byte stored in a location in the main memory can be copied to an internal register of the processor.
- A numerical value stored in one register can be added to the numerical value in another register.
- The numerical value stored in a register can be incremented by one.
- It is possible to find out which one of two registers contains a larger numerical value.

Although all registers inside the imaginary processor are 8-bit registers, different registers have different roles in relation to the operation of the processor. The registers of the imaginary processor can be classified in the following way:

- REGISTER A and REGISTER B are general-purpose registers which can be used to transfer data to/from the main memory. Arithmetic operations can be carried out with the values in REGISTER A and REGISTER B.
- Registers INSTRUCTION CODE and INSTRUCTION OPERAND are used to store a machine instruction and its operand.
- Registers PROGRAM POINTER, MEMORY POINTER, and STACK POINTER are used to store memory addresses for different purposes. PROGRAM POINTER contains the address of the next instruction in a program. MEMORY POINTER is needed to move a byte between the general-purpose registers and the main memory. STACK POINTER contains the address of the first free position on the stack.

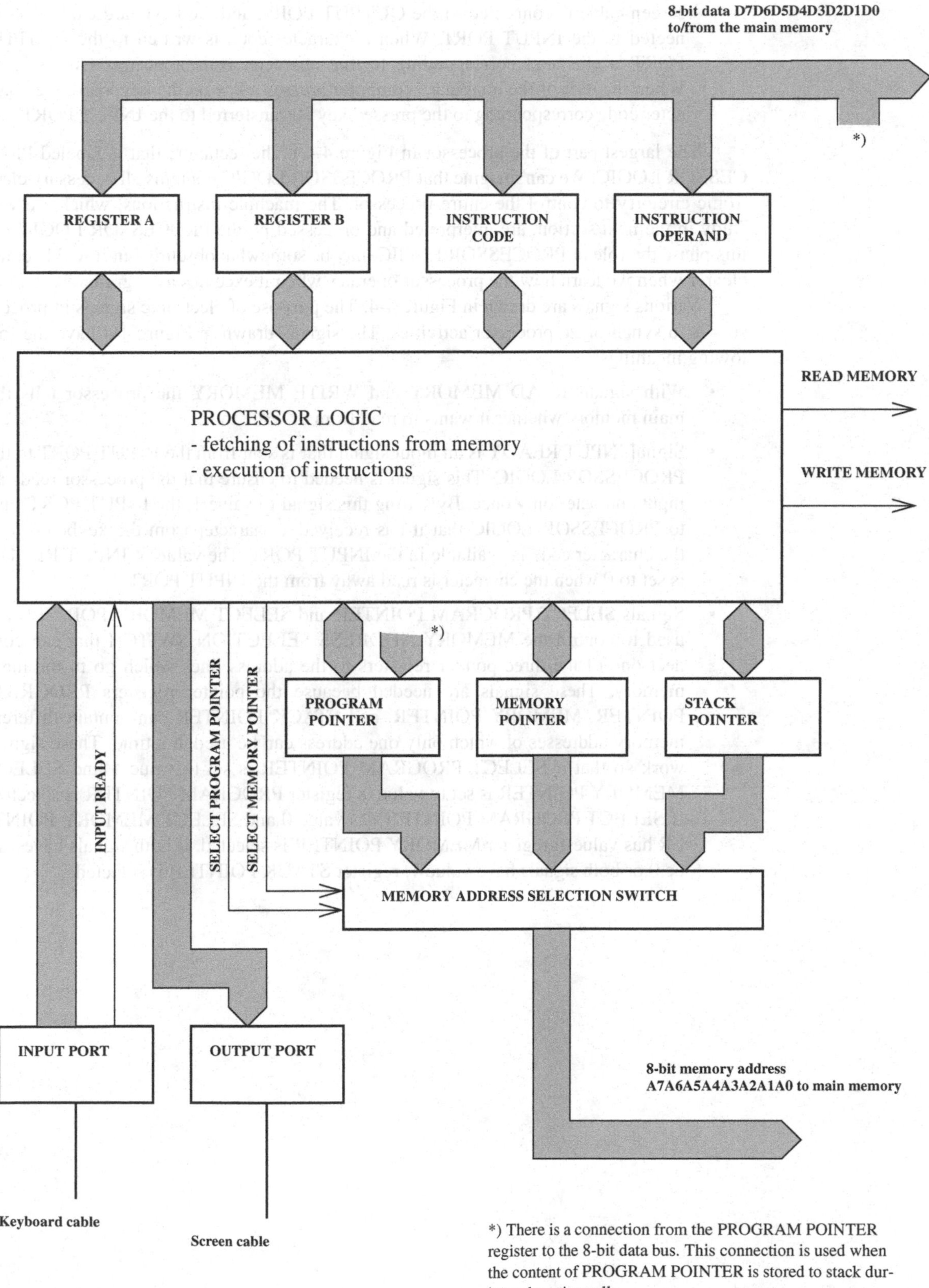
8-bit data D7D6D5D4D3D2D1D0
to/from the main memory
*)
REGISTER A
REGISTER B
INSTRUCTION
CODE
INSTRUCTION
OPERAND
READ MEMORY
PROCESSOR LOGIC
- fetching of instructions from memory
- execution of instructions
WRITE MEMORY
*)
INPUT READY
SELECT PROGRAM POINTER
SELECT MEMORY POINTER
PROGRAM
POINTER
MEMORY
POINTER
STACK
POINTER
MEMORY ADDRESS SELECTION SWITCH
INPUT PORT
OUTPUT PORT
8-bit memory address
A7A6A5A4A3A2A1A0 to main memory
Keyboard cable
Screen cable
*) There is a connection from the PROGRAM POINTER register to the 8-bit data bus. This connection is used when the content of PROGRAM POINTER is stored to stack during subroutine calls.

*Figure 4-4. The internal structure of the imaginary processor.*

- INPUT PORT and OUTPUT PORT are different from the other registers. They are ports through which the processor can communicate with the outside world. The screen cable is connected to the OUTPUT PORT, and the keyboard cable is connected to the INPUT PORT. When a character code is written to the OUTPUT PORT, a character corresponding to that character code appears on the screen. When the user of the imaginary computer presses a key on the keyboard, the character code corresponding to the pressed key is transferred to the INPUT PORT.

The largest part of the processor in Figure 4-4 is the rectangle that is labeled PROCESSOR LOGIC. We can imagine that PROCESSOR LOGIC contains all necessary electronic circuitry to control the entire processor. The machine instructions, which we will study in the next section, are interpreted and processed by the PROCESSOR LOGIC. At this phase the role of PROCESSOR LOGIC may be somewhat obscure, but it will become clearer when we learn how the processor operates when it executes a program.

Various signals are drawn in Figure 4-4. The purpose of electronic signals in processors is to synchronize processor activities. The signals drawn in Figure 4-4 have the following meanings:

- With signals READ MEMORY and WRITE MEMORY the processor tells the main memory whether it wants to read from or write to it.
- Signal INPUT READY is an input signal that is sent from the INPUT PORT to the PROCESSOR LOGIC. This signal is needed to ensure that the processor reads an input character only once. By setting this signal to value 1, the INPUT PORT says to PROCESSOR LOGIC that it has received a character from the keyboard, and the character code is available in the INPUT PORT. The value of INPUT READY is set to 0 when the character is read away from the INPUT PORT.
- Signals SELECT PROGRAM POINTER and SELECT MEMORY POINTER are used to control the MEMORY ADDRESS SELECTION SWITCH that can connect one of the three pointer registers to the address lines which go to the main memory. These signals are needed because the pointer registers PROGRAM POINTER, MEMORY POINTER, and STACK POINTER can contain different memory addresses of which only one address can be used at a time. These signals work so that if SELECT PROGRAM POINTER is set to value 1 and SELECT MEMORY POINTER is set to value 0, register PROGRAM POINTER is selected. If SELECT PROGRAM POINTER has value 0 and SELECT MEMORY POINTER has value 1, register MEMORY POINTER is selected. If both signals have value 0 or both signals have value 1, register STACK POINTER is selected.

## 4.4 Machine instructions

Computers are machines that process information. For this reason, the most elementary instructions that are interpreted by a processor of a computer are called machine instructions. A series of machine instructions form a program that can be executed by a processor. The program is placed in the main memory, from where the processor can automatically read the program, instruction by instruction.

The machine instructions of a processor are unique numerical codes which cause the processor to act in a certain way. Machine instructions determine what the processor does. We can say that a processor can understand machine instructions which are fed to it via the main memory. Machine instructions thus form a machine language which is uniquely meaningful to the processor.

The machine instructions of our imaginary processor consist of either one or two bytes. The first byte is the numerical instruction code, according to which the processor determines what it should do next. Each machine instruction has a different numerical instruction code. The codes must be different, because otherwise the processor could not distinguish its machine instructions from one another. Some machine instructions, like the one in Figure 4-5, are two bytes long. In these instructions, the second byte is an operand for the actual machine instruction, the first byte. The operand byte can be a numerical value to be used in an arithmetic operation, or it can be a memory address.

The machine instructions of the imaginary computer are small pieces of information which the processor reads from the main memory. A complete computer program of the imaginary processor consists of a sequential list of these small pieces of information.When the processor reads the machine instructions from the main memory, it places them in the registers INSTRUCTION CODE and INSTRUCTION OPERAND. When the processor has done what is required by the current instruction contained in these registers, it copies a new instruction to these registers, and starts processing that. This kind of one-instruction-at-a-time processing goes on until the processor finds a "stop processing" instruction in the main memory.

All machine instructions of the imaginary processor are listed in Table 4-1. The table contains all the numerical instruction codes, and explains the meaning of each for the programmer who creates computer programs by using these instructions. The last column of the table describes what actions the processor performs when it processes each instruction. The table is called an "instruction decoding table" because we can imagine that there is such a table, in electronic form, inside the PROCESSOR LOGIC of the imaginary processor. We can think that when the imaginary processor reads a machine instruction from the main memory, it consults this kind of a table and, according to what is said in this "instruc-

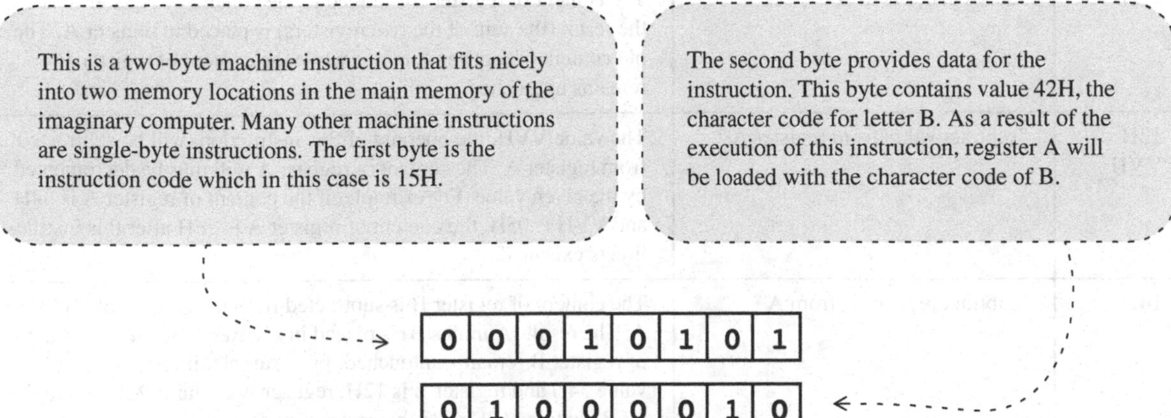

This is a two-byte machine instruction that fits nicely into two memory locations in the main memory of the imaginary computer. Many other machine instructions are single-byte instructions. The first byte is the instruction code which in this case is 15H.
The second byte provides data for the instruction. This byte contains value 42H, the character code for letter B. As a result of the execution of this instruction, register A will be loaded with the character code of B.
0 0 0 1 0 1 0 1
0 1 0 0 0 0 1 0


*Figure 4-5. Instruction "load register A with value" of the imaginary computer.*

tion decoding table", it then determines what it should do. For example, if the processor read the instruction 14H, it would use the fourth line of the instruction decoding table because the instruction with code 14H is explained there. The processor would find out that it must subtract the content of REGISTER B from the content of REGISTER A, and place the result in REGISTER A.

You will need to consult Table 4-1 when we start studying example computer programs in the next section. The nature of the machine instructions will become clearer when you learn how the imaginary computer actually processes a program. At this point, you can find out that there are seven categories of instructions in Table 4-1. The category an instruction belongs to can be identified from the first hexadecimal digit of the instruction code. For example, instructions for arithmetic and moving operations have codes that start with 1, and the codes of memory-related instructions start with 2. When an instruction is a two-byte instruction, its instruction code is odd. Single-byte instructions have even instruction codes. The operand byte of two-byte instructions is marked either VVH or MMH in Table 4-1. The values of operand bytes can be anything from 0 to FFH. The creator of a program determines which values are needed as operands for various machine instructions. VVH means a value to be loaded to some register or to be used in an arithmetic operation. MMH means a memory address which is needed by the instruction.

## Table 4-1: Instruction decoding table of the imaginary processor

| **Instruction code and optional operand.** | **Meaning for the programmer** | **Actions taken by the processor** |
|---|---|---|
| | **INSTRUCTIONS FOR ARITHMETIC AND MOVING OPERATIONS** | |
| 11H VVH | "add value to register A" | The value VVH, the operand of this instruction, will be added to the content of register A. The content of register A will thus be incremented by the given value. For example, if the content of register A is 34H and VVH is 05H, the content of register A is 39H after the execution of this instruction. |
| 12H | "add register B to A" | The content of register B is added to the content of register A and the result (the sum of the two registers) is placed in register A. The old content of register A is lost while the content of register B remains untouched. |
| 13H VVH | "subtract value from register A" | The value VVH, the operand of this instruction, will be subtracted from register A. The content of register A will thus be decremented by the given value. For example, if the content of register A is 34H and VVH is 05H, the content of register A is 2FH after this instruction is executed. |
| 14H | "subtract register B from A" | The content of register B is subtracted from the content of register A. The result (A minus B) is placed in register A, while the content of register B remains untouched. For example, if register A has value 34H and register B is 12H, register A contains 22H and register B contains 12H after this instruction is executed. |

**Table 4-1: Instruction decoding table of the imaginary processor (Continued)**

| | | |
|---|---|---|
| 15H<br>VVH | "load register A with value" | The value VVH, the operand byte, will be copied to register A. The old content of register A will be lost. For example, if the value VVH is 05H, the content of register A will be 05H regardless of its previous value. |
| 16H | "increment register A" | The content of register A will be incremented by 1. For example, if the content of register A is 34H, its content will be 35H after the execution of this instruction. |
| 17H<br>VVH | "load register B with value" | The value VVH will be copied to register B. The old content of register B will be written over and lost. This instruction is similar to 15H but this one affects register B. |
| 18H | "increment register B" | The content of register B will be incremented by 1. For example, if the content of register B is 12H, its content will be 13H when this instruction is executed. |
| 1AH | "decrement register A" | The content of register A will be decremented by 1. For example, if the content of register A is 34H, it will change to 33H as a result of this instruction. |
| 1CH | "decrement register B" | The content of register B will be decremented by 1. For example, if the content of register B is 12H, it will be 11H after the execution of this instruction. |
| 1EH | "move content of register A to B" | The content of register A is copied to register B. The old content of register B is written over. After this instruction has been executed, both registers have the same content. |
| | **MEMORY-RELATED INSTRUCTIONS** | |
| 21H<br>MMH | "set memory pointer" | The memory address MMH that is given as the operand for this machine instruction is copied to register MEMORY POINTER. With this instruction, it is possible to start manipulating new areas of the computer's main memory. The content of MEMORY POINTER determines which memory address is affected by instructions "store register A to memory", "load register A from memory", "store register B to memory", and "load register B from memory". |
| 22H | "increment memory pointer" | The content of MEMORY POINTER is incremented by 1. For example, if the old content of MEMORY POINTER is 9BH, its new content will be 9CH. |
| 24H | "decrement memory pointer" | The content of MEMORY POINTER is decremented by 1. For example, if the content of MEMORY POINTER is B3H, its content will change to B2H. |
| 26H | "store register A to memory" | The content of register A will be written to that memory location which is currently the content of MEMORY POINTER. For example, if the content of register A is 34H and the content of MEMORY POINTER is 9BH, the memory location in address 9BH will contain value 34H after this instruction has been executed. |

**Table 4-1: Instruction decoding table of the imaginary processor (Continued)**

| | | |
|---|---|---|
| 28H | "load register A from memory" | This is the opposite of instruction "store register A to memory". This instruction copies one byte from the main memory to register A. The byte that will be copied will be determined by the content of MEMORY POINTER. For example, if the content of MEMORY POINTER is B3H, this instruction loads register A with the byte that is in memory location B3H. |
| 2AH | "store register B to memory" | This is similar to the instruction with code 26H, but this copies the contents of register B to a location in the main memory. |
| 2CH | "load register B from memory" | This is similar to the instruction with code 28H, but this instruction modifies the content of register B. |
| | **INSTRUCTIONS RELATED TO JUMPING IN PROGRAMS** | These instructions modify the content of PROGRAM POINTER. "jump to address" modifies it always. Other instructions modify the content of PROGRAM POINTER only if certain conditions are valid. All these instructions are two-byte instructions. Instruction operand MMH is a possible new value for PROGRAM POINTER. |
| 41H MMH | "jump to address" | This instruction performs an unconditional jump in the program by modifying the content of register PROGRAM POINTER. The next instruction that will be executed after this instruction is the one that resides in the address given in MMH, the operand of this instruction. For example, if the value of MMH is 08H, the value of PROGRAM POINTER is 08H after this instruction has been executed. |
| 43H MMH | "jump if registers equal" | This instruction is a conditional jump within the program. If the contents of register A and register B are the same, MMH is copied to PROGRAM POINTER, and the next instruction to be executed is the one in the address that is given in the operand of this instruction. |
| 45H MMH | "jump if register A zero" | This is another conditional jump. If the content of register A is zero, PROGRAM POINTER is loaded with the value MMH. If register A is not equal to zero, the program execution continues in the normal way from the instruction that follows this instruction. |
| 47H MMH | "jump if register A smaller than B" | A jump to memory location MMH occurs if the content of register A is smaller than the content of register B. If register A is larger than or equal to register A, no jump takes place, and the program execution continues from the instruction that follows this instruction. |
| 49H MMH | "jump if register A greater than B" | This is a kind of opposite instruction to the previous one. A jump occurs when the content of register A is greater than the content of register B. For example, if register A is 34H, register B is 12H, and the operand byte MMH is 08H, the value of PROGRAM POINTER is changed to 08H because 34H is greater than 12H. |
| 4BH MMH | "jump if input not ready" | This instruction tests whether a byte is ready to be read from the input port. This instruction causes a jump if the input is not ready, i.e., INPUT READY signal has value 0, which means logically FALSE. This instruction is used when a program is waiting for a human to give it a byte of data. Because humans tend to be slower than computers, a computer program usually has to jump and wait until the user of the computer has entered its input. |

**Table 4-1: Instruction decoding table of the imaginary processor (Continued)**

| | | |
|---|---|---|
| | **INSTRUCTIONS TO HANDLE SUBROUTINE CALLS** | |
| 81H MMH | "call subroutine" | The execution of this instruction causes a jump to address MMH but the execution will eventually return to the instruction that follows this instruction. This kind of behavior is accomplished by storing the current value of PROGRAM POINTER to the stack. Three separate actions take places when this instruction is executed. First the content of register PROGRAM POINTER is stored to that memory address which is the content of register STACK POINTER. Then the content of register STACK POINTER is decremented by one. Finally, value MMH is copied to register PROGRAM POINTER.<br>This way the program execution continues from address MMH. PROGRAM POINTER is stored on the stack to be used by the subroutine which starts in address MMH. Instruction "call subroutine" can be explained with the phrase "go and execute the machine instructions starting from address MMH, but come back when you encounter the instruction code 82H". |
| 82H | "return to calling program" | This instruction is a kind of counterpart to the instruction "call subroutine". "return to calling program" must be the last instruction in a subroutine. It marks the end of a called subroutine and causes a return to the calling program. This instruction loads PROGRAM POINTER with the memory address that was put to the stack by instruction "call subroutine". This causes a return to the instruction that immediately follows the "call subroutine" instruction in the calling program. The following two actions take place when this instruction is executed:<br>The value in register STACK POINTER is incremented by one.<br>Register PROGRAM POINTER is loaded from the memory address which is the content of register STACK POINTER. |
| | **INPUT/OUTPUT INSTRUCTIONS** | |
| 92H | "output byte from register A" | This instruction is used when a program wants to output a character to the screen. The instruction copies the content of register A to OUTPUT PORT. A character code must be present in register A before this instruction can be successfully executed. The result of the execution is that the character corresponding to the character code in register A is displayed on the screen. The OUTPUT PORT works so that always when a character code is written to it, the corresponding character appears on the screen. |
| 94H | "output byte from register B" | This is similar to the previous instruction, but this one outputs the content of register B. |
| 96H | "input byte to register A" | This instruction is used when a program wants to input a character code from the keyboard to register A. The instruction copies a byte from the INPUT PORT to register A. Signal INPUT READY indicates whether a character code of a character has been received from the keyboard to INPUT PORT. INPUT READY must have value 1 (i.e. TRUE) before this instruction can be executed. After the input character code has been copied to register A, INPUT READY is set back to zero. |

## Table 4-1: Instruction decoding table of the imaginary processor (Continued)

| | **STACK INSTRUCTIONS** | |
|---|---|---|
| A1H MMH | "set stack pointer" | This instruction is rarely needed because register STACK POINTER is set to value FFH when the imaginary computer is switched on. The last bytes of the main memory are thus used as stack. With this instruction it is possible to select a new memory area to be used as stack memory. Value MMH is copied to register STACK POINTER when this instruction is executed. |
| A2H | "push register A to stack" | This instruction stores (pushes) register A to the top of the stack. Register STACK POINTER always contains a value that "points" to the first free memory location on the stack. This instruction causes two separate actions: first the content of register A is stored to that memory address which is the content of register STACK POINTER, and then the memory address in STACK POINTER is decremented by one. The stack thus grows towards the smaller memory addresses. After this instruction has been executed, the topmost element on the stack and register A contain the same information. |
| A4H | "pop register A from stack" | This instruction performs an opposite operation compared to the actions caused by the previous instruction. First, the memory address in register STACK POINTER is incremented by one, and then register A is loaded from the memory address that is in register STACK POINTER. This instruction takes away that byte that was the last one pushed to the stack. The stack gets smaller when this instruction is executed. |
| | **INSTRUCTION TO HALT THE PROCESSOR AT THE END OF A PROGRAM** | |
| B2H | "stop processing" | This is a special kind of instruction which stops the imaginary processor entirely. This instruction marks the end of the program. No more instructions will be executed after this one until imaginary electricity is switched off and on again. |

## A classification of computers

Both the technology and terminology related to computers are evolving rapidly, and there exist different terms to describe different types of computers. Much of this terminology may be somewhat confusing. The following list may reduce the confusion to some extent.

- Supercomputers are large computers and they are the fastest computers in the world. Supercomputers have been built by using special electronic components and processors. Supercomputers are used to run applications that perform massive calculations. Such applications include various scientific and military applications. Weather forecasting is one application domain where supercomputers have traditionally been used.
- Mainframe computers are those computers that, at least some decades ago, tended to occupy entire air-conditioned rooms. Mainframe computers are used by large organizations like government offices, banks, and insurance companies who need to process massive amounts of data. The most famous provider of mainframe computers is without doubt IBM (International Business Machines).
- Minicomputers are something smaller than mainframe computers. The term "minicomputer" is not widely used any more, probably because minicomputers have become equally small as microcomputers or microcomputers have become equally efficient as the traditional minicomputers.
- The term "microcomputer" was brought into use to describe computers that could be placed on a table, and were built by using the commercially available microprocessors. Obviously the world's most well-known software company was originally named as Microsoft because the company produced software for microcomputers.
- The term "personal computer" (PC) was brought into use when IBM introduced its IBM Personal Computer in 1981. The original IBM PC was running an operating system from Microsoft. After IBM introduced its PC, many computer manufacturers started to build computers that were compatible with the IBM PC. Nowadays, a personal computer (PC) is any computer that runs the Windows operating system. The command prompt window of Windows imitates the MS-DOS operating system that was used in the first personal computers.
- The term "workstation computer", or simply "workstation", has traditionally meant a powerful desktop computer that runs the UNIX operating system. Nowadays the distinction between a workstation and a personal computer is harder to make.
- A server computer serves other computers connected to a local network of computers. Server computers are typically connected to other servers. The Internet is a worldwide network of server computers. The Linux operating system has become popular in servers.
- Laptop computers are portable computers whose size is small, but they have a normal-size keyboard and display.
- Palmtop computers are small enough to be carried in a pocket. The display of a palmtop computer is small. Because they do not have a traditional keyboard, some palmtop computers are operated by using a special pen. Top models of modern mobile phones are like palmtop computers.
- Nanocomputers ... these are something that may exist in the future.
- Theoretical computers do not exist in reality. The imaginary computer that is presented in this chapter is an example of a theoretical computer, but there are many other theoretical computers. For example, in 1937 Alan Turing published an article that presented a theoretical computer that was later named the Turing machine. The architecture of the Turing machine differs significantly from the architecture of the modern computers. Therefore, the Turing machine is not appropriate for educational purposes these days.

## 4.5 The steps and states of program execution

Because the imaginary computer does not exist in reality, we must make some assumptions about how it would operate in reality. Since no computer can operate without a program in its main memory, we must assume that a program can somehow be loaded to the main memory of the imaginary computer. A program is always loaded so that the first instruction is in the memory address 00H, and other instructions of the program are in the subsequent memory addresses.

We assume also that there is an ON/OFF switch in the imaginary computer. When there is a program loaded in the main memory, and the computer is switched on, it starts executing the program according to the following steps:

STEP 1: Load value 00H to register PROGRAM POINTER, and value FFH to register STACK POINTER. So at the beginning PROGRAM POINTER points to the first location in the main memory, and STACK POINTER points to the last memory location. Go to STEP 2.

STEP 2: Fetch the instruction code of a machine instruction from that memory address which is stored in register PROGRAM POINTER. Store the instruction code to register INSTRUCTION CODE. Increment the address in register PROGRAM POINTER by one. Go to STEP 3.

STEP 3: If the content of register INSTRUCTION CODE is odd (i.e. if the instruction is a two-byte instruction), fetch a byte from the memory address which is stored in PROGRAM POINTER, store the byte to register INSTRUCTION OPERAND, and increment the address in register PROGRAM POINTER by one. Otherwise, if the content of INSTRUCTION code is even, do nothing. Go to STEP 4.

STEP 4: If the content of register INSTRUCTION CODE is B2H (the code for instruction "stop processing"), go to STEP 6. Otherwise, go to STEP 5.

STEP 5: Interpret the instruction by using the instruction decoding table (Table 4-1) and execute the actions required by that instruction. After all necessary actions are performed, go to STEP 2.

STEP 6: Stop processing. Do nothing. The end of the program has been encountered.

The six steps above describe what the processor of the imaginary computer is doing when it is running. What really happens is determined by the program that is stored in the main memory. The processor repeats steps from 2 to 5 over and over, depending on how many instructions and which instructions there are in the program.

A computer is a machine that can have different states while it is operating. Figure 4-6 is a diagram which describes the operation of the imaginary computer as a machine which changes states. The rounded rectangles in the figure are states in which certain activities are carried out. After the activities of a state have been performed, it is possible to make a transition to another state. The arrows describe transitions from one state to another. The texts in brackets near some arrows mean conditions under which the transition can occur. For example, the transition from state FETCH INSTRUCTION CODE to state FETCH INSTRUCTION OPERAND occurs only when the instruction code is odd. The first state of the computer is RESET PROCESSOR, and that state is entered only once. The final state of the computer is PROCESSOR STOPPED. That state is reached when the instruction code is B2H.

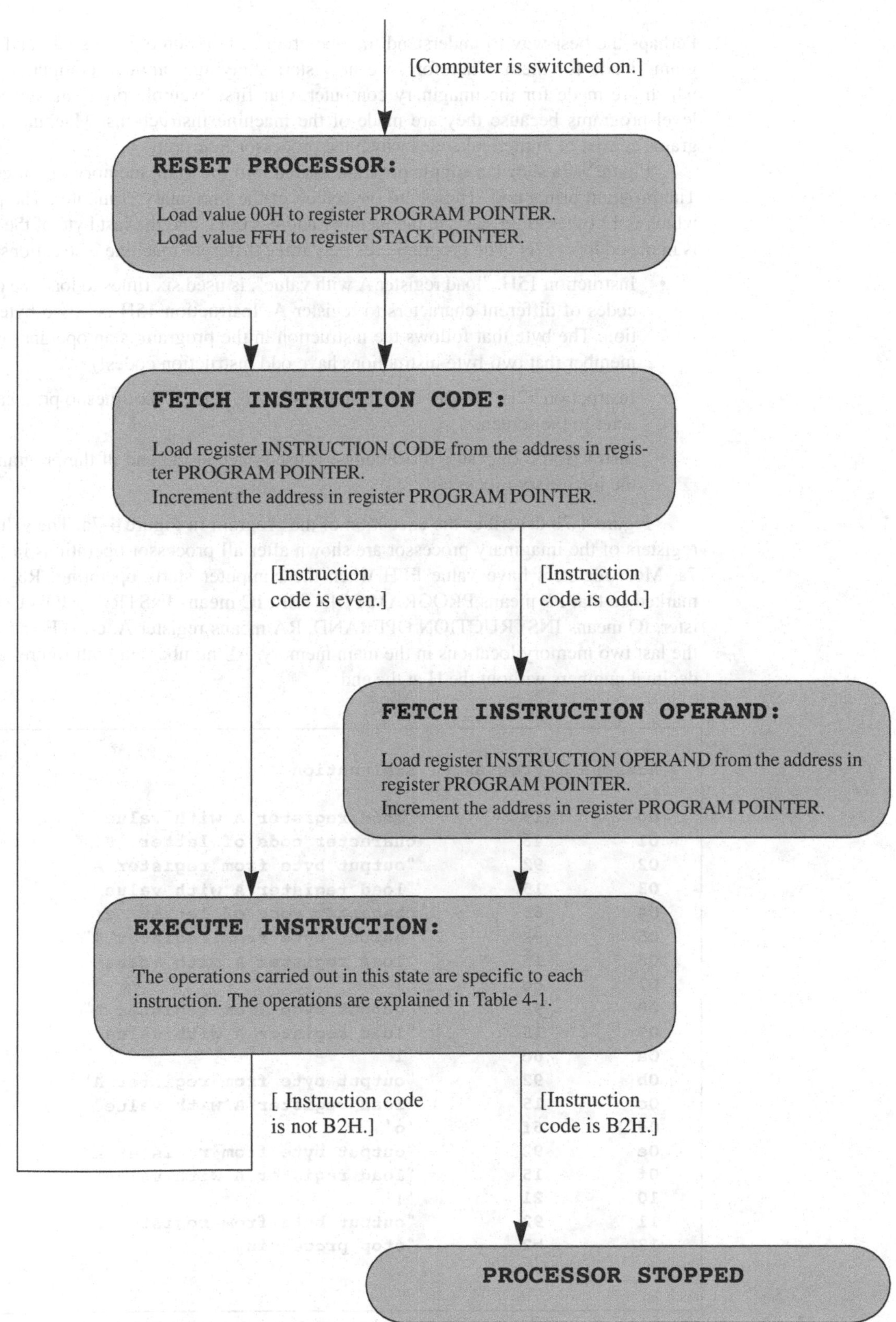
[Computer is switched on.]
RESET PROCESSOR:
Load value 00H to register PROGRAM POINTER.
Load value FFH to register STACK POINTER.
FETCH INSTRUCTION CODE:
Load register INSTRUCTION CODE from the address in register PROGRAM POINTER.
Increment the address in register PROGRAM POINTER.
[Instruction code is even.]
[Instruction code is odd.]
FETCH INSTRUCTION OPERAND:
Load register INSTRUCTION OPERAND from the address in register PROGRAM POINTER.
Increment the address in register PROGRAM POINTER.
EXECUTE INSTRUCTION:
The operations carried out in this state are specific to each instruction. The operations are explained in Table 4-1.
[ Instruction code is not B2H.]
[Instruction code is B2H.]
PROCESSOR STOPPED

*Figure 4-6. A state diagram that describes the operation of the imaginary computer.*

## 4.6 Programs to print text "Hello!"

Perhaps the best way to understand the operation of computers is to study and run programs made for them. Therefore, we now start studying complete computer programs which are made for the imaginary computer. Our first example programs are machine-level programs because they are made of the machine instructions. Machine-level programs consist of numerical codes which the processor interprets.

Figure 4-7a shows a simple program loaded into the main memory of our computer. The program prints text "Hello!" to the screen of the imaginary computer. The program, which is 13 bytes long, starts in the memory address 00H, and the last byte of the program is in the address 12H. The program uses only three different machine instructions:

- Instruction 15H, "load register A with value", is used six times to load the character codes of different characters to register A. Instruction 15H is a two-byte instruction. The byte that follows the instruction in the program is an operand byte. (Remember that two-byte instructions have odd instruction codes!)
- Instruction 92H, "output byte from register A", is used six times to print each character to the screen.
- Instruction B2H, "stop processing", is used once at the end of the program to stop the imaginary processor.

Figure 4-7b describes the execution of the program in Figure 4-7a. The values of all registers of the imaginary processor are shown after all processor operations in Figure 4-7a. Most registers have value FFH when the computer starts operating. Registers are marked so that PP means PROGRAM POINTER, IC means INSTRUCTION CODE register, IO means INSTRUCTION OPERAND, RA means register A, etc. FE and FF mean the last two memory locations in the main memory. All numbers in both figures are hexadecimal numbers without the H at the end.

```
Address   Program   Explanation

00        15        "load register A with value"
01        48        character code of letter 'H'
02        92        "output byte from register A"
03        15        "load register A with value"
04        65        character code of letter 'e'
05        92        "output byte from register A"
06        15        "load register A with value"
07        6c        'l'
08        92        "output byte from register A"
09        15        "load register A with value"
0a        6c        'l'
0b        92        "output byte from register A"
0c        15        "load register A with value"
0d        6f        'o'
0e        92        "output byte from register A"
0f        15        "load register A with value"
10        21        '!'
11        92        "output byte from register A"
12        b2        "stop processing"
```

*Figure 4-7a. A machine-level program that prints text "Hello!"*

The first status of the processor is always RESET. Here the processor performs two fetch operations because the first machine instruction, 15H, "load register A with value", is a two-byte instruction. After the last fetch operation, register INSTRUCTION OPERAND (IO) contains value 48H which is the character code of uppercase letter H.

At the beginning, the screen of the computer is empty. Text "Hello!" emerges gradually on the screen, character by character, as the program execution proceeds.

| Status | PP | IC | IO | RA | RB | MP | SP | FE | FF | Screen contents |
|---|---|---|---|---|---|---|---|---|---|---|
| RESET | 00 | ff | ff | ff | ff | ff | ff | ff | ff | |
| FETCH | 01 | 15 | ff | ff | ff | ff | ff | ff | ff | |
| FETCH | 02 | 15 | 48 | ff | ff | ff | ff | ff | ff | |
| EXECUTE | 02 | 15 | 48 | 48 | ff | ff | ff | ff | ff | |
| FETCH | 03 | 92 | 48 | 48 | ff | ff | ff | ff | ff | |
| EXECUTE | 03 | 92 | 48 | 48 | ff | ff | ff | ff | ff | H |
| FETCH | 04 | 15 | 48 | 48 | ff | ff | ff | ff | ff | H |
| FETCH | 05 | 15 | 65 | 48 | ff | ff | ff | ff | ff | H |
| EXECUTE | 05 | 15 | 65 | 65 | ff | ff | ff | ff | ff | H |
| FETCH | 06 | 92 | 65 | 65 | ff | ff | ff | ff | ff | H |
| EXECUTE | 06 | 92 | 65 | 65 | ff | ff | ff | ff | ff | He |
| FETCH | 07 | 15 | 65 | 65 | ff | ff | ff | ff | ff | He |
| FETCH | 08 | 15 | 6c | 65 | ff | ff | ff | ff | ff | He |
| EXECUTE | 08 | 15 | 6c | 6c | ff | ff | ff | ff | ff | He |
| FETCH | 09 | 92 | 6c | 6c | ff | ff | ff | ff | ff | He |
| EXECUTE | 09 | 92 | 6c | 6c | ff | ff | ff | ff | ff | Hel |
| FETCH | 0a | 15 | 6c | 6c | ff | ff | ff | ff | ff | Hel |
| FETCH | 0b | 15 | 6c | 6c | ff | ff | ff | ff | ff | Hel |
| EXECUTE | 0b | 15 | 6c | 6c | ff | ff | ff | ff | ff | Hel |
| FETCH | 0c | 92 | 6c | 6c | ff | ff | ff | ff | ff | Hel |
| EXECUTE | 0c | 92 | 6c | 6c | ff | ff | ff | ff | ff | Hell |
| FETCH | 0d | 15 | 6c | 6c | ff | ff | ff | ff | ff | Hell |
| FETCH | 0e | 15 | 6f | 6c | ff | ff | ff | ff | ff | Hell |
| EXECUTE | 0e | 15 | 6f | 6f | ff | ff | ff | ff | ff | Hell |
| FETCH | 0f | 92 | 6f | 6f | ff | ff | ff | ff | ff | Hell |
| EXECUTE | 0f | 92 | 6f | 6f | ff | ff | ff | ff | ff | Hello |
| FETCH | 10 | 15 | 6f | 6f | ff | ff | ff | ff | ff | Hello |
| FETCH | 11 | 15 | 21 | 6f | ff | ff | ff | ff | ff | Hello |
| EXECUTE | 11 | 15 | 21 | 21 | ff | ff | ff | ff | ff | Hello |
| FETCH | 12 | 92 | 21 | 21 | ff | ff | ff | ff | ff | Hello |
| EXECUTE | 12 | 92 | 21 | 21 | ff | ff | ff | ff | ff | Hello! |
| FETCH | 13 | b2 | 21 | 21 | ff | ff | ff | ff | ff | Hello! |
| STOP | 13 | b2 | 21 | 21 | ff | ff | ff | ff | ff | Hello! |

This line shows the situation after the instruction 15H has been executed. The execution resulted in the value 21H, the character code of exclamation mark !, being copied from register INSTRUCTION OPERAND (IO) to register A (RA). Register PROGRAM POINTER (PP) already points to the address of the next instruction in the program.

*Figure 4-7b. Step-by-step execution of the program in Figure 4-7a.*

I advise you to study Figure 4-7b very carefully. You should read all the lines which show the values of the registers, and note changes in the values. It may be useful to re-read the processing steps which were discussed in the previous section. You should also read Table 4-1 to find out how the used machine instructions should work. If you can understand what is said in Figure 4-7b, you have learned the basics about the operation of the imaginary computer.

Usually there are several possibilities to construct a computer program that performs a certain activity. The program in Figure 4-7a is one way to print text "Hello!" to the screen. In Figure 4-8a, there is another program that prints the text "Hello!" to the screen of the imaginary computer. The program in Figure 4-7a is rather simple because the two instructions "load register A with value" and "output byte from register A" are repeated six times in it. The program in Figure 4-8a is constructed in such a way that necessary instructions are repeated six times although they exist only once in the program.

In the program in Figure 4-8a, the characters of the text "Hello!" are separated from the actual program. The character codes of the characters are in different memory area than the machine instructions. The last machine instruction is in address 09H, and the first character of the text is in address 0AH. The character codes are in the order in which they should be printed, and 00H, the NULL character, marks the end of the text to be printed.

The program in Figure 4-8a uses the following instructions not used in the program in Figure 4-7a:

- With instruction 21H, "set memory pointer", register MEMORY POINTER is set to point to address 0AH which is the beginning of text "Hello!" in the main memory.
- Instruction 28H, "load register A from memory" is used to read the characters of the text "Hello!" from the main memory. The value of MEMORY POINTER specifies which memory location is read by instruction "load register A from memory". Since MEMORY POINTER points to address 0AH at the beginning, the character code of letter H is the first value that is loaded to register A.
- Instruction 22H, "increment memory pointer", adds 1 to the value of MEMORY POINTER. This ensures that instruction "load register A from memory" loads different character codes from the main memory when the program is executed.

```
Address   Program   Explanation

00        21        "set memory pointer"
01        0a        value to register MEMORY POINTER
02        28        "load register A from memory"
03        45        "jump if register A zero"
04        09        address for possible jump
05        92        "output byte from register A"
06        22        "increment memory pointer "
07        41        "jump to address"
08        02        address for unconditional jump
09        b2        "stop processing"
0a        48        'H'
0b        65        'e'
0c        6c        'l'
0d        6c        'l'
0e        6f        'o'
0f        21        '!'
10        00        NULL  (zero)
```

*Figure 4-8a. Another program that prints text "Hello!"*

Here instruction 41H, "jump to address", is executed. The execution modifies the content of register PROGRAM POINTER so that the next instruction to be executed is in address 02H.

| Status | PP | IC | IO | RA | RB | MP | SP | FE | FF | Screen contents |
|---|---|---|---|---|---|---|---|---|---|---|
| RESET | 00 | ff | ff | ff | ff | ff | ff | ff | ff | |
| FETCH | 01 | 21 | ff | ff | ff | ff | ff | ff | ff | |
| FETCH | 02 | 21 | 0a | ff | ff | ff | ff | ff | ff | |
| EXECUTE | 02 | 21 | 0a | ff | ff | 0a | ff | ff | ff | |
| FETCH | 03 | 28 | 0a | ff | ff | 0a | ff | ff | ff | |
| EXECUTE | 03 | 28 | 0a | 48 | ff | 0a | ff | ff | ff | |
| FETCH | 04 | 45 | 0a | 48 | ff | 0a | ff | ff | ff | |
| FETCH | 05 | 45 | 09 | 48 | ff | 0a | ff | ff | ff | |
| EXECUTE | 05 | 45 | 09 | 48 | ff | 0a | ff | ff | ff | |
| FETCH | 06 | 92 | 09 | 48 | ff | 0a | ff | ff | ff | |
| EXECUTE | 06 | 92 | 09 | 48 | ff | 0a | ff | ff | ff | H |
| FETCH | 07 | 22 | 09 | 48 | ff | 0a | ff | ff | ff | H |
| EXECUTE | 07 | 22 | 09 | 48 | ff | 0b | ff | ff | ff | H |
| FETCH | 08 | 41 | 09 | 48 | ff | 0b | ff | ff | ff | H |
| FETCH | 09 | 41 | 02 | 48 | ff | 0b | ff | ff | ff | H |
| EXECUTE | 02 | 41 | 02 | 48 | ff | 0b | ff | ff | ff | H |
| FETCH | 03 | 28 | 02 | 48 | ff | 0b | ff | ff | ff | H |
| EXECUTE | 03 | 28 | 02 | 65 | ff | 0b | ff | ff | ff | H |
| FETCH | 04 | 45 | 02 | 65 | ff | 0b | ff | ff | ff | H |
| FETCH | 05 | 45 | 09 | 65 | ff | 0b | ff | ff | ff | H |
| EXECUTE | 05 | 45 | 09 | 65 | ff | 0b | ff | ff | ff | H |
| FETCH | 06 | 92 | 09 | 65 | ff | 0b | ff | ff | ff | H |
| EXECUTE | 06 | 92 | 09 | 65 | ff | 0b | ff | ff | ff | He |
| FETCH | 07 | 22 | 09 | 65 | ff | 0b | ff | ff | ff | He |
| EXECUTE | 07 | 22 | 09 | 65 | ff | 0c | ff | ff | ff | He |
| FETCH | 08 | 41 | 09 | 65 | ff | 0c | ff | ff | ff | He |
| FETCH | 09 | 41 | 02 | 65 | ff | 0c | ff | ff | ff | He |
| EXECUTE | 02 | 41 | 02 | 65 | ff | 0c | ff | ff | ff | He |
| FETCH | 03 | 28 | 02 | 65 | ff | 0c | ff | ff | ff | He |
| EXECUTE | 03 | 28 | 02 | 6c | ff | 0c | ff | ff | ff | He |
| FETCH | 04 | 45 | 02 | 6c | ff | 0c | ff | ff | ff | He |
| FETCH | 05 | 45 | 09 | 6c | ff | 0c | ff | ff | ff | He |
| EXECUTE | 05 | 45 | 09 | 6c | ff | 0c | ff | ff | ff | He |
| FETCH | 06 | 92 | 09 | 6c | ff | 0c | ff | ff | ff | He |
| EXECUTE | 06 | 92 | 09 | 6c | ff | 0c | ff | ff | ff | Hel |

Execution of instruction 45H, "jump if register A zero", results in a jump only when register A contains value 00H.

Not all lines are printed here because of space limitations.

| Status | PP | IC | IO | RA | RB | MP | SP | FE | FF | Screen contents |
|---|---|---|---|---|---|---|---|---|---|---|
| FETCH | 06 | 92 | 09 | 21 | ff | 0f | ff | ff | ff | Hello |
| EXECUTE | 06 | 92 | 09 | 21 | ff | 0f | ff | ff | ff | Hello! |
| FETCH | 07 | 22 | 09 | 21 | ff | 0f | ff | ff | ff | Hello! |
| EXECUTE | 07 | 22 | 09 | 21 | ff | 10 | ff | ff | ff | Hello! |
| FETCH | 08 | 41 | 09 | 21 | ff | 10 | ff | ff | ff | Hello! |
| FETCH | 09 | 41 | 02 | 21 | ff | 10 | ff | ff | ff | Hello! |
| EXECUTE | 02 | 41 | 02 | 21 | ff | 10 | ff | ff | ff | Hello! |
| FETCH | 03 | 28 | 02 | 21 | ff | 10 | ff | ff | ff | Hello! |
| EXECUTE | 03 | 28 | 02 | 00 | ff | 10 | ff | ff | ff | Hello! |
| FETCH | 04 | 45 | 02 | 00 | ff | 10 | ff | ff | ff | Hello! |
| FETCH | 05 | 45 | 09 | 00 | ff | 10 | ff | ff | ff | Hello! |
| EXECUTE | 09 | 45 | 09 | 00 | ff | 10 | ff | ff | ff | Hello! |
| FETCH | 0a | b2 | 09 | 00 | ff | 10 | ff | ff | ff | Hello! |
| STOP | 0a | b2 | 09 | 00 | ff | 10 | ff | ff | ff | Hello! |

*Figure 4-8b. Step-by-step execution of the program in Figure 4-8a.*

- Instruction 45H, "jump if register A zero", is a so-called conditional jump. The execution of the program jumps to address 09H if the content of register A is zero. If the content of register A is not zero, the program execution continues from the instruction that follows "jump if register A zero". Instruction "jump if register A zero" causes a jump in the program when all characters of text "Hello!" have been displayed on the screen. Because there is a zero at the end of the text, register A becomes zero and a jump to address 09H takes place. Because address 09H contains the instruction "stop processing", the program terminates.
- Instruction 41H, "jump to address", is an unconditional jump which causes a jump to address 02H in the program. With this instruction, the program prepares to read and display the next character of text "Hello!".

The execution of the program in Figure 4-8a is described in Figure 4-8b. Again, it is very important that you study carefully how the values in the registers of the imaginary computer change while the program is being executed. While you study Figure 4-8b, you should note the following points:

- During the FETCH operations, when the processor is reading instructions and their operands from the main memory, the values of registers A (RA), B (RB), MEMORY POINTER (MP), and STACK POINTER (SP) do not change, but the value of register PROGRAM POINTER (PP) grows after every FETCH operation.
- Values of registers INSTRUCTION CODE (IC) and INSTRUCTION OPERAND (IO) do not change during EXECUTE operations.
- When the processor reads an instruction which has an odd instruction code, it performs another FETCH operation that reads an operand for the instruction. After the second FETCH operation, register INSTRUCTION OPERAND (IO) has a new value. The imaginary computer is designed in such a way that two-byte instructions have odd instruction codes and single-byte instructions have even instruction codes.

## Exercises related to machine-level programming

Exercise 4-2. Study the program in Figure 4-7a. Which instruction can be taken away from the program without affecting the output of the program? The program should still print "Hello!" if the instruction were removed from the program.

Exercise 4-3. Modify one (and only one) byte in the program of Figure 4-8a so that the program prints "Hello" instead of "Hello!".

Exercise 4-4. Modify one (and only one) byte in the program of Figure 4-8a so that the program prints "ello!" instead of "Hello!".

## 4.7 Programming language IML and compilation

Now we have seen that executable computer programs are sequences of numerical machine instructions. By putting the right machine instructions into a program, it is possible to make a computer behave in a certain manner. But it is quite difficult to construct a program if you only have the numerical machine instructions in your mind. It is also hard to read the computer programs which are made of numerical machine instructions. For these reasons, different kinds of textual programming languages have been invented. Textual programming languages allow us to write computer programs in text form. Textual programming languages are defined in such a way that the numerical machine codes can be generated automatically in a process that is called compilation.

Here we will define and study a simple textual programming language for the imaginary computer. The name of the simple language is IML, an abbreviation of "Imaginary Computer's Machine-Level Language". IML is a machine-level language because you still have to think about the registers of the imaginary processor when you are writing programs with it. But when you use IML, you do not have to remember the numerical machine instructions, and the programs become readable. IML is presented here just to show you some principles of programming languages. IML helps you also to understand what happens in the compilation of computer programs. The purpose is not that you will become an expert in IML programming. You may forget most of IML after you have read this chapter and understood how the programs work. Languages like IML should not be used if there are languages like Java available. When you write programs with a high-level programming language like Java, programming is easier, because you do not have to think about the registers of the processor that is being used.

The following is the program of Figure 4-7a written with the IML programming language:

```
// hello.iml  (c) Kari Laitinen

//  A program that prints the text "Hello!" on the screen.

     load_register_a_with_value    'H'
     output_byte_from_register_a
     load_register_a_with_value    'e'
     output_byte_from_register_a
     load_register_a_with_value    'l'
     output_byte_from_register_a
     load_register_a_with_value    'l'
     output_byte_from_register_a
     load_register_a_with_value    'o'
     output_byte_from_register_a
     load_register_a_with_value    '!'
     output_byte_from_register_a
     stop_processing
```

This program is largely made of the explanations which are present in Figure 4-7a. The numerical instruction codes of the imaginary processor are represented by textual instructions in an IML program. As IML is a programming language, it is possible to make a compiler which can translate an IML program from the textual form to numerical form. An IML compiler would process the above program according to the following rules:

- A program is translated line by line, from the beginning to the end.
- All empty lines, lines that contain no text, are omitted.
- All lines starting with character pair // are omitted. Lines starting with // are comment lines which do not belong to the actual program.

- All other lines are translated to machine instructions:

```
load_register_a_with_value    'H'   translates to   15H  48H
load_register_a_with_value    'e'   translates to   15H  65H
load_register_a_with_value    'l'   translates to   15H  6CH
    etc.
output_byte_from_register_a         translates to   92H
stop_processing                     translates to   B2H
```

Textual IML instructions like

```
load_register_a_with_value
add_register_b_to_a
```

correspond to the numerical instruction codes of the imaginary processor. You can think that the textual IML instructions are names invented for the numerical instructions. The textual instructions are formed of the phrases which can be found in the second column of Table 4-1. The words of the phrases must be concatenated with underscores so that an IML compiler can interpret them as whole textual entities. An IML compiler translates each textual instruction to a numerical instruction code, and, if the instruction uses an operand, adds an operand byte after the instruction code. Table 4-2 lists all textual instructions together with the corresponding numerical instruction codes. If an instruction needs a value or a memory address as an operand, there is VVH or MMH on the instruction's line in Table 4-2. The table also shows which registers of the imaginary processor are modified when the instructions are executed. To compile an IML source program, an IML compiler must have an internal instruction translation table that resembles Table 4-2 and describes which textual instruction corresponds to which numerical instruction.

Because many of the instructions of the imaginary processor need an operand byte, there have to be special notations in the IML programming language to present the operand bytes. When numerical constants are needed as operands in IML programs, they can be expressed in the following ways:

| | |
|---|---|
| 'H' | means 48H, the character code of uppercase letter H |
| 'a' | means 61H, the character code of lowercase letter a |
| ' ' | means 20H, the character code of the space character |
| '\n' | means 0AH, the character code of the newline character |
| 'n' | means 6EH, the character code of lowercase letter n |
| 123 | means 7BH, the decimal number 123 |
| 0x22 | means 22H, the decimal number 34 |
| 0x1F | means 1FH, the decimal number 31 |

So if you need a character code of a letter in an IML program, you do not have to remember the character code. You can write the letter inside single quote characters, and let the IML compiler translate it to the correct character code. If you need a number in your program, you can write it as a normal decimal number. In the case that you want to write a number in hexadecimal form you must put the prefix 0x before the hexadecimal digits. Because there are several ways to express operand values in an IML program, there are many possibilities to write IML program lines. For example, as the character code of letter A is 65 as a decimal number and 41H as a hexadecimal number, the following three IML program lines mean the same

```
load_register_a_with_value      'A'
load_register_a_with_value      65
load_register_a_with_value      0x41
```

## Table 4-2: IML instruction translation table.

| TEXTUAL INSTRUCTION | CODE | OPERAND | REGISTERS WRITTEN RA | RB | PP | MP | SP | Memory |
|---|---|---|---|---|---|---|---|---|
| add_value_to_register_a | 11H | VVH | x | | | | | |
| add_register_b_to_a | 12H | | x | | | | | |
| subtract_value_from_register_a | 13H | VVH | x | | | | | |
| subtract_register_b_from_a | 14H | | x | | | | | |
| load_register_a_with_value | 15H | VVH | x | | | | | |
| increment_register_a | 16H | | x | | | | | |
| load_register_b_with_value | 17H | VVH | | x | | | | |
| increment_register_b | 18H | | | x | | | | |
| decrement_register_a | 1AH | | x | | | | | |
| decrement_register_b | 1CH | | | x | | | | |
| move_content_of_register_a_to_b | 1EH | | | x | | | | |
| set_memory_pointer | 21H | MMH | | | | x | | |
| increment_memory_pointer | 22H | | | | | x | | |
| decrement_memory_pointer | 24H | | | | | x | | |
| store_register_a_to_memory | 26H | | | | | | | x |
| load_register_a_from_memory | 28H | | x | | | | | |
| store_register_b_to_memory | 2AH | | | | | | | x |
| load_register_b_from_memory | 2CH | | | x | | | | |
| jump_to_address | 41H | MMH | | | x | | | |
| jump_if_registers_equal | 43H | MMH | | | ?[a] | | | |
| jump_if_register_a_zero | 45H | MMH | | | ? | | | |
| jump_if_register_a_smaller_than_b | 47H | MMH | | | ? | | | |
| jump_if_register_a_greater_than_b | 49H | MMH | | | ? | | | |
| jump_if_input_not_ready | 4BH | MMH | | | ? | | | |
| call_subroutine | 81H | MMH | | | x | | x | x |
| return_to_calling_program | 82H | | | | x | | x | |
| output_byte_from_register_a | 92H | | | | | | | |
| output_byte_from_register_b | 94H | | | | | | | |
| input_byte_to_register_a | 96H | | x | | | | | |
| set_stack_pointer | A1H | MMH | | | | | x | |
| push_register_a_to_stack | A2H | | | | | | x | x |
| pop_register_a_from_stack | A4H | | x | | | | x | |
| stop_processing | B2H | | | | | | | |

a. The question mark ? means that the register is possibly written. The conditional jump instructions write register PROGRAM POINTER only when certain conditions exist.

Most instructions for the imaginary processor are plain instructions which do not need any operands, some instructions take numerical values as operands, and some instructions must be given memory addresses as operands. The memory addresses are numerical values, but they are different kinds of numerical values than, for example, character codes. In the program of Figure 4-8a, memory addresses are needed by instructions which cause jumps in the program, and the memory address of the text "Hello!" needs to be stored to MEMORY POINTER at the beginning of the program.

In the IML programming language, memory addresses are described with address names which have to be invented by the program author. When memory addresses are correctly described with names, an IML compiler can find correct numerical values for the memory addresses. This helps a lot when programs must be created for the imaginary computer.

Figure 4-8c shows what the program of Figure 4-8a looks like when it is written with the IML programming language, and translated to machine instructions with an IML compiler. There are four address names in the program. The compiler has found numerical values for the address names in the following way:

```
ADDRESS NAME                      NUMERICAL ADDRESS

beginning_of_program              00H
display_characters                02H
end_of_program                    09H
address_of_text                   0AH
```

The address names refer to memory locations in the program. For example, the name **address_of_text** refers to the memory address of the first letter of the text "Hello!", the name **display_characters** refers to the address where instruction **load_-register_a_from_memory** is, and the name **end_of_program** refers to the address where the instruction **stop_processing** is located. An address name must be written before the instruction whose address is referred to by the name. The colon character : must be written after an address name in that place where it specifies a memory location.

When an IML compiler processes an IML source program, it first finds all address names which are followed by the colon character (:). Then the compiler counts how many instructions and what kinds of instructions precede each address name in the program. That way the compiler is able to find numerical values for the address names. In the program in Figure 4-8c, address name **display_characters** is given the value 02H because it is preceded by a single two-byte instruction in the program. Address name **end_of_program** is given the value 09H because its position in the program is such that it is preceded by three single-byte instructions and three two-byte instructions which occupy addresses 00H, 01H, ..., and 08H.

After the IML compiler has found numerical values for the address names, it is able to translate those instructions which use an address name as an operand. For example, when the compiler has found out that the name **end_of_program** refers to address 09H in the program of Figure 4-8c, it is able to make the following translation

```
jump_if_register_a_zero    end_of_program      -->    45H  09H
```

The compiler has an internal instruction translation table from which it can find out that the textual instruction **jump_if_register_a_zero** must be translated with the numerical code 45H, and the address value 09H it has calculated by itself.

As IML is a programming language for which it is possible to build a compiler, it is possible to write a program which does not compile because some rules of the IML language are violated in the program. For example, if the above instruction were written like

```
jump_if_register_aaa_zero    end_of_program
```

an IML compiler could not compile the instruction because it could not find the textual instruction **jump_if_register_aaa_zero** in its internal instruction translation table. Similarly, the instruction

```
jump_if_register_a_zero      end_of_programmm
```

would result in a compilation error because the compiler could not find the address name **end_of_programmm** in its internal table of address names. It is important that a name in a computer program is always written in exactly the same way. This is equally important both in IML programs and in Java programs.

The text "Hello!" is defined

```
address_of_text:        STRING        "Hello!"
```

in the program in Figure 4-8c. When an IML compiler recognizes this definition, it puts the character codes of characters H, e, l, l, o, and ! to those memory locations where the declaration is. In addition to the character codes of the characters, the compiler inserts 00H, a zero, after the last character. Thus the above line is translated to codes 48H, 65H, 6CH, 6CH, 6FH, 21H, and 00H in memory addresses from 0AH to 10H in Figure 4-8c.

```
//   hello_loop.iml   (c) Kari Laitinen

//   This program prints the characters of text "Hello!"
//   in a loop. The text is defined with the keyword STRING
//   at the end of the program. As the IML compiler puts a
//   zero at the end of the string, the program knows when
//   to stop printing characters.

beginning_of_program:
      set_memory_pointer                 address_of_text

display_characters:
      load_register_a_from_memory
      jump_if_register_a_zero            end_of_program
      output_byte_from_register_a
      increment_memory_pointer
      jump_to_address                    display_characters

end_of_program:
      stop_processing

address_of_text:        STRING        "Hello!"
```

```
00    21  0A

02    28
03    45  09
05    92
06    22
07    41  02

09    B2

0A    48
0B    65
0C    6C
0D    6C
0E    6F
0F    21
10    00
```

This is the compiled version of the program. All numbers are hexadecimal without the letter H at the end. Memory addresses are shown on the left and generated numerical codes are on the right.

*Figure 4-8c. The program of Figure 4-8a written with IML and translated to machine instructions.*

The word STRING is a reserved keyword in the IML programming language. This means that the word STRING cannot be used as an address name in an IML program. STRING is reserved for situations when textual strings need to be defined (or declared). The characters of the textual string must be given inside double quotation marks "". An IML compiler automatically converts the characters of the textual string to character codes and adds a NULL character, a zero, to the end of the visible characters. When there is a NULL character, 00H, at the end of the visible characters, a program can easily recognize where the text ends, and, for example, stop printing the text. Because a textual string can be defined this way in an IML program, it is very easy to make the program of Figure 4-8c print other texts. For example, if the last line of the textual program were changed to

```
address_of_text:          STRING          "How are you doing?"
```

the program would print

```
How are you doing?
```

if it were compiled with an IML compiler and executed in the imaginary computer.

In addition to word STRING there are two other similar reserved keywords in the IML language. These words are DATA and CONSTANT. If you write in an IML program

```
result_of_calculation:   DATA        2
```

you reserve two bytes from the main memory and the address name **result_of_-calculation** refers to the address of the first reserved byte. By using a larger number in place of 2, it is possible to reserve larger areas from the main memory.

With the reserved keyword CONSTANT it is possible to reserve a single byte from the main memory, and initialize the reserved memory location with a certain numerical value. For example, the definition

```
number_of_states_in_usa:   CONSTANT   50
```

would reserve one byte of memory and store the value 50 in that memory location. By using the address name **number_of_states_in_usa**, it would be possible to refer to the reserved memory location. The definition

```
year_of_french_revolution:  CONSTANT  1789
```

would be incorrect in the case of IML and the imaginary computer because numbers larger than 255 cannot be stored in a single byte. It is true, though, that a historical revolution started in France in 1789.

In the example definitions above, all reserved memory locations are given an address name with which they can be referred to. It is common in computer programming that the program writer must invent and write various names in programs. The program writer must follow the rules of the programming language when he or she invents the names. In IML, the names must consist of letters and underscore characters. There may not be any space characters in a name, and a name may not be STRING, DATA, CONSTANT, or any of the textual instructions in the first column of Table 4-2.

### How do real computers differ from the imaginary computer?

The imaginary computer is an 8-bit computer with only 256 bytes of main memory. Although this kind of a computer operates, and can be programmed, like a real computer, computers like the imaginary computer are not used in the real world. There can be 8-bit processors in use in some special applications, but no modern computer works with a small 256-byte main memory. If we, for example, compare the imaginary computer to a personal computer, we can find the following essential differences:

- The processors which are used in personal computers are usually 32-bit processors in which all internal registers can hold 32-bit values. The registers of the imaginary processor are all 8-bit registers.
- The processors of personal computers have more machine instructions than our imaginary processor. The machine instructions are more complicated, they can perform a wide range of operations, and they can operate with many general-purpose registers. The imaginary processor has only a simple set of machine instructions with which some basic computing activities can be performed.
- The main memory of a personal computer can be a million times larger than the main memory of the imaginary computer. Personal computers use auxiliary memory devices in addition to the main memory. The imaginary computer works only with its small main memory.
- Various peripheral equipment such as modems, printers, scanners, cameras, etc. can be connected to personal computers. The imaginary computer has only two ports to which a screen and a keyboard are connected.
- In a personal computer there is always an operating system, a program which can control the execution of other programs. In the imaginary computer, programs are loaded to the main memory with some imagination, and they are executed by switching the computer on.

### Compiler for IML?

You may be wondering why I do not provide a compiler for the IML language. The truth is that I do have a rudimentary compiler for the language, but I'm afraid that it does not work well enough to be distributed for wider use. Compilers are extremely complicated computer programs, and it is not easy to make a reliable compiler even for such a simple language like IML. The existing compiler inputs an IML source program file and produces another file which contains the machine instructions of the program. For example, when the file **hello_loop.iml** is compiled, a file named **hello_loop.ice** is produced. Files ending with **.ice** can be loaded to the ICOM simulator. (Simulators for the imaginary computer will be discussed in the following section.) The file name extension **.ice** means "imaginary computer executable". There are some **.ice** files available among the electronic material of this book, but the same programs can be found built in the simulators.

Another reason for not providing an IML compiler is that IML is just a language for educational purposes. It is not necessary to write more IML programs than those that are presented in this book and built in the IC8 and ICOM simulators. You should start learning Java and compiling Java programs as soon as you have learned the basics of computer technology in this chapter.

## 4.8 IC8 and ICOM – simulator programs for the imaginary computer

Although the imaginary computer described in this chapter does not exist as a computer built of hardware components, there are two programs which simulate the imaginary computer on a personal computer. The older one of the simulator programs is called ICOM, and you can find information about it if you read the sample pages of Chapter 4 of my C++ book. You can find those pages via the Internet address *www.naturalprogramming.com*. The ICOM simulator runs in a command prompt window, and you can command it only with the keyboard of your computer. It does not recognize mouse commands. If you decide to use the ICOM simulator, please read the help pages that are built in it.

A better simulation program[1] for the imaginary computer is called IC8. This program is a so-called Java applet that can be executed on an Internet page. To use the IC8 simulator, you must go with your Internet browser (e.g. Internet Explorer) to a certain page on the Internet. That page can be reached through the address *www.naturalprogramming.com*. In order to run the simulator, the settings of your Internet browser must be such that Java applets can be executed. (I'll put some information about the browser settings on the Internet pages.)

When you have found the page on which the IC8 simulator is located, and the execution of Java applets is enabled in your browser, the browser should display a view like the one that is shown in Figure 4-9. The IC8 simulator is a program which you can control by using the mouse to press its buttons. The most important rule in the use of the simulator is that you must first load a program into its main memory with the **Load Program** button, and only after that can you actually start using the simulator. Some of the buttons of the simulator are explained in Figure 4-9. The rest of the buttons have the following effects

- The **Reset** button loads value 00H to register PROGRAM POINTER and value FFH to all other important processor registers. The INPUT READY signal is set to 0. The screen is cleared, but the contents of the main memory are not modified.
- By pressing the **Translate** button, you can see a kind of textual form of the program in the main memory. Repressing the button brings back the normal view.
- With the **Modify** button you can put the simulator to a mode in which you can modify the contents of the main memory. After the **Modify** button has been pressed, you can click on memory locations with the mouse and enter new values to the selected locations through the keyboard. You must repress the **Modify** button to get back to the normal simulation mode.
- By selecting one of the buttons **HEX**, **BIN**, or **DEC**, you can choose the numbering system in which numbers are shown.

While you are using the IC8 simulator program, you should remember that it is a program that has not been widely tested, and there may be errors in it. Although I do not know about any serious errors in IC8, I cannot guarantee that it operates correctly. And most importantly, I shall not assume any kind of responsibility for any kind of damages the IC8 simulator (or the ICOM simulator) causes while you are using it. Because IC8 is an applet, not a real application, it should not cause any serious troubles on your computer. If it seems that the program is not operating properly, a wise thing to do is to first close your browser, restart the browser, and then go back to the page of the simulator.

Using the IC8 simulator, or the ICOM simulator, helps you to understand how computers operate. Of course, if you feel that you understand the example IML programs of this chapter by just studying them on paper, it is not necessary to use any simulator programs. The programs are in any case an easy way to verify the answers which you got for the exercises in this chapter.

---

1. The word "simulation" is common in the world of computers. It means that a computer program imitates a real-life phenomenon or something that could exist in reality.

Here, the simulator shows the first 31 locations of the main memory. The machine instructions of program **hello.iml** are loaded into the memory. An important feature of this simulator is that if you click with the mouse on an instruction in a memory location, when the simulator is executing a program, the execution goes with maximum speed until the clicked instruction, and continues then with the normal, selected speed.

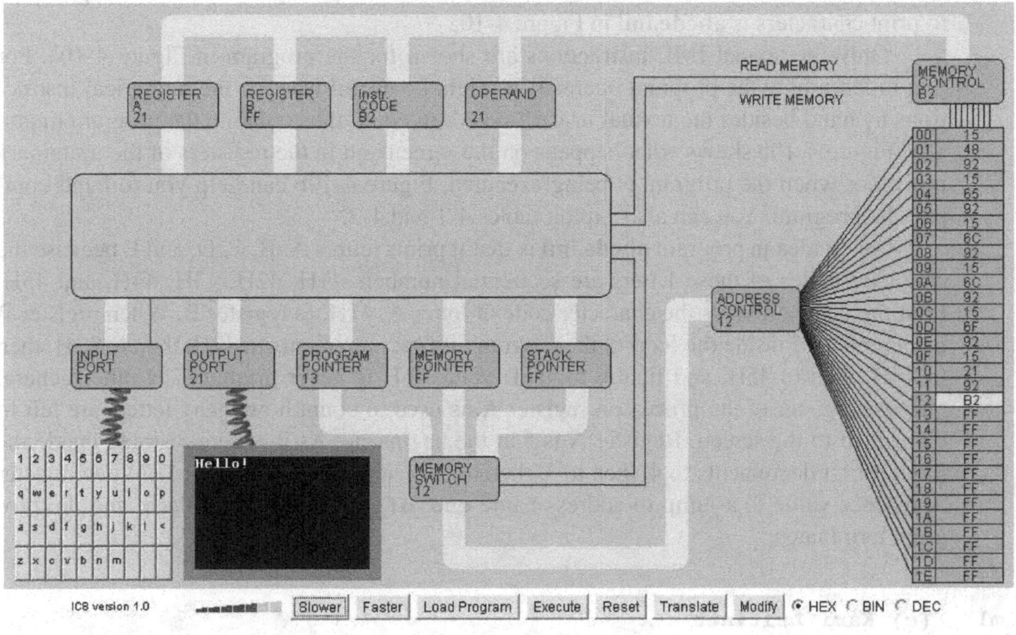


By pressing the **Load Program** button, you can load an executable program into the main memory of the imaginary computer. There are many compiled ready-to-run executable programs built in the simulation program. All the example programs of this chapter are there for you to try. After this button is pressed, you'll see a menu from which you can select a program when you know the file names of the IML programs. For example, if you want to run the program of Figure 4-8c in the simulator, you can easily load the correct program because the file name **hello_loop.iml** is mentioned in Figure 4-8c.

After a program has been loaded with the **Load Program** button, it can be executed by pressing the **Execute** button. The **Execute** button transforms to **Pause** button with which you can stop the execution temporarily. When the program is stopped, this button is the **Continue** button with which you can resume program execution. The execution speed of the simulator can be altered with the **Slower** and **Faster** buttons.

***Figure 4-9. The screen of the IC8 simulator after the program hello.iml has been executed.***

### Exercise with the IC8 simulator program

Exercise 4-5. Verify your answers to exercises 4-3 and 4-4 by using the IC8 simulator program. Use the Load Program button to load program **hello_loop.iml** to the simulator, and then modify the program by pressing the Modify button. Finally you must execute it to see how it works.

## 4.9 A program that contains a loop

In principle, programs are executed so that those instructions which are at the beginning of a program are executed first, and the program execution proceeds instruction by instruction towards the end of the program. By using jump instructions it is possible to violate this principle. A jump instruction can cause a jump from the end of a program to the beginning of the program. We say that jump instructions can create a loop in a program. Loops are sequences of instructions which are repeated many times during the execution of a program. In program **hello_loop.iml** in Figure 4-8c we have already seen a loop which prints the characters of the text "Hello!". Another program in which a loop is used to print characters is **abcde.iml** in Figure 4-10a.

Only the textual IML instructions are shown for the program in Figure 4-10a. For you to learn how the program operates, it might be useful to write the numerical instructions by hand besides the textual instructions. You could thus compile the program manually. Figure 4-10b shows what happens on the screen and in the registers of the imaginary processor when the program is being executed. Figure 4-10b can help you to hand-compile the program. You can also exploit tables 4-1 and 4-2.

A key idea in program **abcde.iml** is that it prints letters A, B, C, D, and E because the character codes of these letters are sequential numbers 41H, 42H, 43H, 44H, and 45H. First the program loads the character code of letter A, 41H, to register B. When register B is incremented inside the loop of the program, it first increments to 42H, then to 43H, then to 44H, then to 45H, and finally to 46H. Value 46H is never printed. The other general purpose register of the processor, register A, is used to count how many letters are left to be printed to the screen. Register A is 5 at the beginning. As it is decremented inside the loop, it first decrements to 4, then to 3, then to 2, then to 1, and finally to 0. When register A reaches value 0, a jump to address name **`end_of_program`** takes place, and the program terminates.

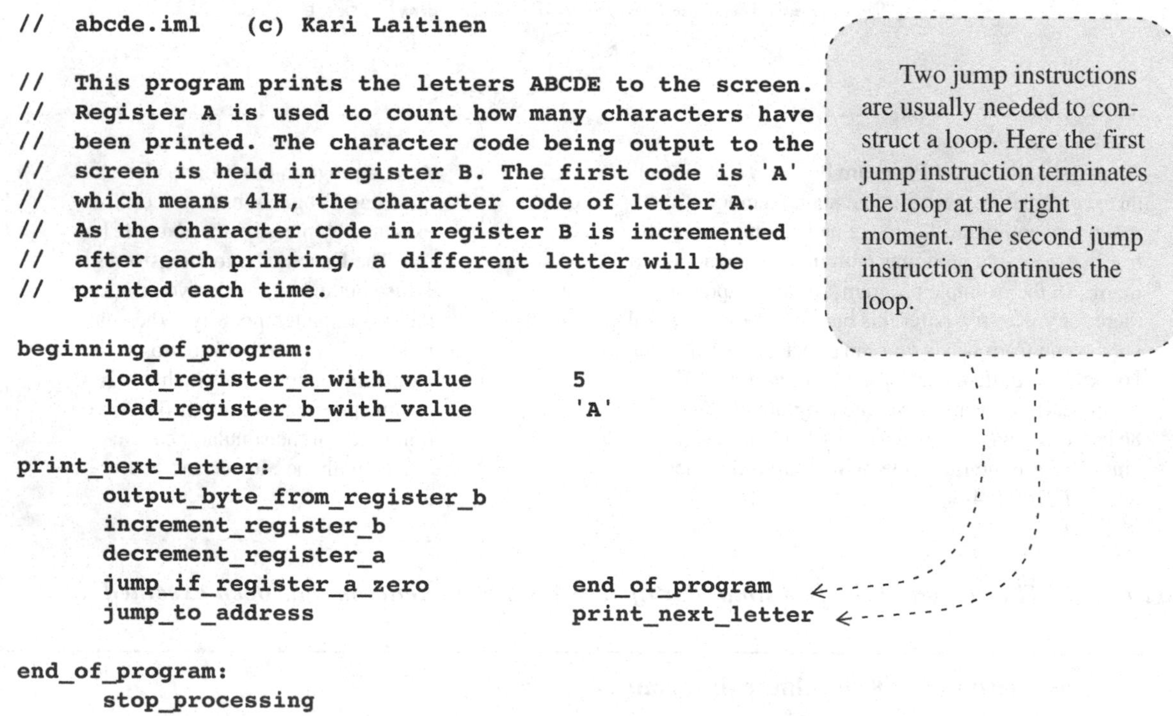

```
//  abcde.iml    (c) Kari Laitinen

//  This program prints the letters ABCDE to the screen.
//  Register A is used to count how many characters have
//  been printed. The character code being output to the
//  screen is held in register B. The first code is 'A'
//  which means 41H, the character code of letter A.
//  As the character code in register B is incremented
//  after each printing, a different letter will be
//  printed each time.

beginning_of_program:
      load_register_a_with_value         5
      load_register_b_with_value         'A'

print_next_letter:
      output_byte_from_register_b
      increment_register_b
      decrement_register_a
      jump_if_register_a_zero            end_of_program
      jump_to_address                    print_next_letter

end_of_program:
      stop_processing
```

Two jump instructions are usually needed to construct a loop. Here the first jump instruction terminates the loop at the right moment. The second jump instruction continues the loop.



*Figure 4-10a. A program that prints letters ABCDE in a loop.*

> Here the first jump in the program takes place. Instruction 41H, "jump to address", is executed. The execution modifies PROGRAM POINTER (PP) so that the address of the next instruction is 04H.

> Register A (RA) reaches value 0 at the end. At that moment register B has already value 46H, the character code of letter F. That letter is, though, never printed because the program terminates when register A has value 0.

| Status | PP | IC | IO | RA | RB | MP | SP | FE | FF | Screen contents |
|---|---|---|---|---|---|---|---|---|---|---|
| **RESET** | 00 | ff | ff | ff | ff | ff | ff | ff | ff | |
| **FETCH** | 01 | 15 | ff | ff | ff | ff | ff | ff | ff | |
| **FETCH** | 02 | 15 | 05 | ff | ff | ff | ff | ff | ff | |
| **EXECUTE** | 02 | 15 | 05 | 05 | ff | ff | ff | ff | ff | |
| **FETCH** | 03 | 17 | 05 | 05 | ff | ff | ff | ff | ff | |
| **FETCH** | 04 | 17 | 41 | 05 | ff | ff | ff | ff | ff | |
| **EXECUTE** | 04 | 17 | 41 | 05 | 41 | ff | ff | ff | ff | |
| **FETCH** | 05 | 94 | 41 | 05 | 41 | ff | ff | ff | ff | |
| **EXECUTE** | 05 | 94 | 41 | 05 | 41 | ff | ff | ff | ff | A |
| **FETCH** | 06 | 18 | 41 | 05 | 41 | ff | ff | ff | ff | A |
| **EXECUTE** | 06 | 18 | 41 | 05 | 42 | ff | ff | ff | ff | A |
| **FETCH** | 07 | 1a | 41 | 05 | 42 | ff | ff | ff | ff | A |
| **EXECUTE** | 07 | 1a | 41 | 04 | 42 | ff | ff | ff | ff | A |
| **FETCH** | 08 | 45 | 41 | 04 | 42 | ff | ff | ff | ff | A |
| **FETCH** | 09 | 45 | 0b | 04 | 42 | ff | ff | ff | ff | A |
| **EXECUTE** | 09 | 45 | 0b | 04 | 42 | ff | ff | ff | ff | A |
| **FETCH** | 0a | 41 | 0b | 04 | 42 | ff | ff | ff | ff | A |
| **FETCH** | 0b | 41 | 04 | 04 | 42 | ff | ff | ff | ff | A |
| **EXECUTE** | 04 | 41 | 04 | 04 | 42 | ff | ff | ff | ff | A |
| **FETCH** | 05 | 94 | 04 | 04 | 42 | ff | ff | ff | ff | A |
| **EXECUTE** | 05 | 94 | 04 | 04 | 42 | ff | ff | ff | ff | AB |
| **FETCH** | 06 | 18 | 04 | 04 | 42 | ff | ff | ff | ff | AB |
| **EXECUTE** | 06 | 18 | 04 | 04 | 43 | ff | ff | ff | ff | AB |
| **FETCH** | 07 | 1a | 04 | 04 | 43 | ff | ff | ff | ff | AB |
| **EXECUTE** | 07 | 1a | 04 | 03 | 43 | ff | ff | ff | ff | AB |
| **FETCH** | 08 | 45 | 04 | 03 | 43 | ff | ff | ff | ff | AB |
| **FETCH** | 09 | 45 | 0b | 03 | 43 | ff | ff | ff | ff | AB |
| **EXECUTE** | 09 | 45 | 0b | 03 | 43 | ff | ff | ff | ff | AB |
| **FETCH** | 0a | 41 | 0b | 03 | 43 | ff | ff | ff | ff | AB |
| **FETCH** | 0b | 41 | 04 | 03 | 43 | ff | ff | ff | ff | AB |
| **EXECUTE** | 04 | 41 | 04 | 03 | 43 | ff | ff | ff | ff | AB |
| **FETCH** | 05 | 94 | 04 | 03 | 43 | ff | ff | ff | ff | AB |
| **EXECUTE** | 05 | 94 | 04 | 03 | 43 | ff | ff | ff | ff | ABC |
| **FETCH** | 06 | 18 | 04 | 03 | 43 | ff | ff | ff | ff | ABC |
| **EXECUTE** | 06 | 18 | 04 | 03 | 44 | ff | ff | ff | ff | ABC |
| **FETCH** | 07 | 1a | 04 | 03 | 44 | ff | ff | ff | ff | ABC |

Because of space limitation, 16 lines have been left out here.

| Status | PP | IC | IO | RA | RB | MP | SP | FE | FF | Screen contents |
|---|---|---|---|---|---|---|---|---|---|---|
| **FETCH** | 0a | 41 | 0b | 01 | 45 | ff | ff | ff | ff | ABCD |
| **FETCH** | 0b | 41 | 04 | 01 | 45 | ff | ff | ff | ff | ABCD |
| **EXECUTE** | 04 | 41 | 04 | 01 | 45 | ff | ff | ff | ff | ABCD |
| **FETCH** | 05 | 94 | 04 | 01 | 45 | ff | ff | ff | ff | ABCD |
| **EXECUTE** | 05 | 94 | 04 | 01 | 45 | ff | ff | ff | ff | ABCDE |
| **FETCH** | 06 | 18 | 04 | 01 | 45 | ff | ff | ff | ff | ABCDE |
| **EXECUTE** | 06 | 18 | 04 | 01 | 46 | ff | ff | ff | ff | ABCDE |
| **FETCH** | 07 | 1a | 04 | 01 | 46 | ff | ff | ff | ff | ABCDE |
| **EXECUTE** | 07 | 1a | 04 | 00 | 46 | ff | ff | ff | ff | ABCDE |
| **FETCH** | 08 | 45 | 04 | 00 | 46 | ff | ff | ff | ff | ABCDE |
| **FETCH** | 09 | 45 | 0b | 00 | 46 | ff | ff | ff | ff | ABCDE |
| **EXECUTE** | 0b | 45 | 0b | 00 | 46 | ff | ff | ff | ff | ABCDE |
| **FETCH** | 0c | b2 | 0b | 00 | 46 | ff | ff | ff | ff | ABCDE |
| **STOP** | 0c | b2 | 0b | 00 | 46 | ff | ff | ff | ff | ABCDE |

***Figure 4-10b. Step-by-step execution of the program in Figure 4-10a.***

## 4.10 Subroutine calls and stack operations

It is common that larger computer programs are organized so that they consist of smaller pieces of programs. The smaller pieces are usually subroutines. A subroutine typically performs a certain well-defined operation in a program. Such an operation can be, for example, printing a line of text, or reading a character from the keyboard. In every computer program there must be a main program. In addition to the main program, there can be subroutines which are called by the main program. The term "calling" is used to describe the relation between a main program and a subroutine. A main program calls a subroutine to perform a certain activity. When the subroutine has performed its activity, there is a return to the main program, the calling program.

The programs which we have studied so far are just main programs which do not call any subroutines. Program **aaaabbbbcccc.iml** in Figure 4-11a is an example where a subroutine is called. Figure 4-11b shows what happens in the execution of the program. The first part of **aaaabbbbcccc.iml** is the main program. The last part of the program is subroutine named **`output_register_a_four_times`**. As its address name suggests, the subroutine outputs the content of register A four times. As the subroutine is called three times with register A contents 'a', 'b', and 'c', the text aaaabbbbcccc emerges on the screen when the program is executed. (It may again be a good idea to hand-compile the program by writing numerical instruction codes and their addresses besides the textual instruction codes.)

STACK POINTER is an important processor register in subroutine calls. It is one of the three registers with which the main memory can be accessed. The value of STACK POINTER is FFH when the imaginary computer starts operating. At the beginning, the STACK POINTER thus points to the last memory location in the main memory.

```
//   aaaabbbbcccc.iml

//   This program prints the text "aaaabbbbcccc" to the
//   screen. It calls a subroutine which prints the contents
//   of register A four times to the screen.

//   First register A is loaded with 'a', the character code
//   of letter a (61H). When register A is incremented, its
//   content becomes first 61H and later 62H. These are the
//   character codes of letters b and c.

beginning_of_program:
      load_register_a_with_value     'a'
      call_subroutine                output_register_a_four_times
      increment_register_a
      call_subroutine                output_register_a_four_times
      increment_register_a
      call_subroutine                output_register_a_four_times
      stop_processing

output_register_a_four_times:
      output_byte_from_register_a
      output_byte_from_register_a
      output_byte_from_register_a
      output_byte_from_register_a
      return_to_calling_program
```

The start address of the subroutine is the operand of instruction **`call_subroutine`**. The address name that is written here is the name of the subroutine.

*Figure 4-11a. A program in which subroutine output_register_a_four_times is called.*

Here the first subroutine call, instruction 81H, is executed. PROGRAM POINTER gets the value 0BH which is the beginning of the subroutine. The return address 04H is stored onto the stack in memory location FFH. STACK POINTER is decremented to value FEH.

When the subroutine is called for the second time, the return address stored on the stack is 07H. The second instruction to increment register A is in that address.

Here instruction 82H is executed, and a return to calling program takes place. 0AH is the return address in the calling program which is copied from the stack to PROGRAM POINTER (PP). The value of STACK POINTER is incremented to FFH.

| Status | PP | IC | IO | RA | RB | MP | SP | FE | FF | Screen contents |
|---|---|---|---|---|---|---|---|---|---|---|
| RESET | 00 | ff | ff | ff | ff | ff | ff | ff | ff | |
| FETCH | 01 | 15 | ff | ff | ff | ff | ff | ff | ff | |
| FETCH | 02 | 15 | 61 | ff | ff | ff | ff | ff | ff | |
| EXECUTE | 02 | 15 | 61 | 61 | ff | ff | ff | ff | ff | |
| FETCH | 03 | 81 | 61 | 61 | ff | ff | ff | ff | ff | |
| FETCH | 04 | 81 | 0b | 61 | ff | ff | ff | ff | ff | |
| EXECUTE | 0b | 81 | 0b | 61 | ff | ff | fe | ff | 04 | |
| FETCH | 0c | 92 | 0b | 61 | ff | ff | fe | ff | 04 | |
| EXECUTE | 0c | 92 | 0b | 61 | ff | ff | fe | ff | 04 | a |
| FETCH | 0d | 92 | 0b | 61 | ff | ff | fe | ff | 04 | a |
| EXECUTE | 0d | 92 | 0b | 61 | ff | ff | fe | ff | 04 | aa |
| FETCH | 0e | 92 | 0b | 61 | ff | ff | fe | ff | 04 | aa |
| EXECUTE | 0e | 92 | 0b | 61 | ff | ff | fe | ff | 04 | aaa |
| FETCH | 0f | 92 | 0b | 61 | ff | ff | fe | ff | 04 | aaa |
| EXECUTE | 0f | 92 | 0b | 61 | ff | ff | fe | ff | 04 | aaaa |
| FETCH | 10 | 82 | 0b | 61 | ff | ff | fe | ff | 04 | aaaa |
| EXECUTE | 04 | 82 | 0b | 61 | ff | ff | ff | ff | 04 | aaaa |
| FETCH | 05 | 16 | 0b | 61 | ff | ff | ff | ff | 04 | aaaa |
| EXECUTE | 05 | 16 | 0b | 62 | ff | ff | ff | ff | 04 | aaaa |
| FETCH | 06 | 81 | 0b | 62 | ff | ff | ff | ff | 04 | aaaa |
| FETCH | 07 | 81 | 0b | 62 | ff | ff | ff | ff | 04 | aaaa |
| EXECUTE | 0b | 81 | 0b | 62 | ff | ff | fe | ff | 07 | aaaa |
| FETCH | 0c | 92 | 0b | 62 | ff | ff | fe | ff | 07 | aaaa |
| EXECUTE | 0c | 92 | 0b | 62 | ff | ff | fe | ff | 07 | aaaab |
| FETCH | 0d | 92 | 0b | 62 | ff | ff | fe | ff | 07 | aaaab |
| EXECUTE | 0d | 92 | 0b | 62 | ff | ff | fe | ff | 07 | aaaabb |
| FETCH | 0e | 92 | 0b | 62 | ff | ff | fe | ff | 07 | aaaabb |
| EXECUTE | 0e | 92 | 0b | 62 | ff | ff | fe | ff | 07 | aaaabbb |
| FETCH | 0f | 92 | 0b | 62 | ff | ff | fe | ff | 07 | aaaabbb |
| EXECUTE | 0f | 92 | 0b | 62 | ff | ff | fe | ff | 07 | aaaabbbb |
| FETCH | 10 | 82 | 0b | 62 | ff | ff | fe | ff | 07 | aaaabbbb |
| EXECUTE | 07 | 82 | 0b | 62 | ff | ff | ff | ff | 07 | aaaabbbb |
| FETCH | 08 | 16 | 0b | 62 | ff | ff | ff | ff | 07 | aaaabbbb |
| EXECUTE | 08 | 16 | 0b | 63 | ff | ff | ff | ff | 07 | aaaabbbb |
| FETCH | 09 | 81 | 0b | 63 | ff | ff | ff | ff | 07 | aaaabbbb |
| FETCH | 0a | 81 | 0b | 63 | ff | ff | ff | ff | 07 | aaaabbbb |
| EXECUTE | 0b | 81 | 0b | 63 | ff | ff | fe | ff | 0a | aaaabbbb |
| FETCH | 0c | 92 | 0b | 63 | ff | ff | fe | ff | 0a | aaaabbbb |
| EXECUTE | 0c | 92 | 0b | 63 | ff | ff | fe | ff | 0a | aaaabbbbc |
| FETCH | 0d | 92 | 0b | 63 | ff | ff | fe | ff | 0a | aaaabbbbc |
| EXECUTE | 0d | 92 | 0b | 63 | ff | ff | fe | ff | 0a | aaaabbbbcc |
| FETCH | 0e | 92 | 0b | 63 | ff | ff | fe | ff | 0a | aaaabbbbcc |
| EXECUTE | 0e | 92 | 0b | 63 | ff | ff | fe | ff | 0a | aaaabbbbccc |
| FETCH | 0f | 92 | 0b | 63 | ff | ff | fe | ff | 0a | aaaabbbbccc |
| EXECUTE | 0f | 92 | 0b | 63 | ff | ff | fe | ff | 0a | aaaabbbbcccc |
| FETCH | 10 | 82 | 0b | 63 | ff | ff | fe | ff | 0a | aaaabbbbcccc |
| EXECUTE | 0a | 82 | 0b | 63 | ff | ff | ff | ff | 0a | aaaabbbbcccc |
| FETCH | 0b | b2 | 0b | 63 | ff | ff | ff | ff | 0a | aaaabbbbcccc |
| STOP | 0b | b2 | 0b | 63 | ff | ff | ff | ff | 0a | aaaabbbbcccc |

*Figure 4-11b. Step-by-step execution of the program in Figure 4-11a.*

In general, a stack is a memory area that is used so that what is last put to the stack, comes out first from the stack. When a value is put to the stack, we say that a push operation is made. The opposite operation is a pop operation that takes a value away from the stack. The imaginary processor uses the last part of the main memory as its stack. The STACK POINTER register always points to the first free memory address of the stack. When values are pushed to the stack, the value of STACK POINTER is decremented. In pop operations the value of STACK POINTER is incremented. We say that a pop operation takes a value away from the stack although in reality the value remains in a memory location in the main memory. When the pop operation increments the STACK POINTER, it frees a memory location for a push operation.

The stack is always used when subroutine calls are made. After a subroutine has been called and executed, the execution of the calling program must continue from the next statement after the subroutine call. This can be accomplished by storing a return address into the stack. Instruction **`call_subroutine`** automatically pushes the return address, the address of the next instruction, to the stack, and its counterpart instruction **`return_to_calling_program`** pops the return address from the stack when it terminates the execution of the subroutine.

Figure 4-11b shows how the contents of the registers change when the program in Figure 4-11a is being executed. Note that all registers except PROGRAM POINTER contain FFH when the computer starts operating. Note also, that in addition to the contents of all registers, the contents of memory locations FEH and FFH are shown in Figure 4-11b. The value in memory location FFH, the first free position of the stack, changes when a subroutine call is made. Figure 4-11b shows that after the **`call_subroutine`** instruction, 81H, is executed, both PROGRAM POINTER (PP) and STACK POINTER (SP) have new values, and stack memory location FFH contains a return address to the calling program. An appropriate return address is on the stack during the time when the subroutine is being executed. At the end of the subroutine, when the instruction with code 82H is executed, the return address is read from the stack and STACK POINTER is incremented by one.

The stack is simply one particular area of the main memory. This special memory area is automatically used in subroutine calls to store return addresses in calling programs. The stack is particularly useful in subroutine calls because it can also handle the difficult situation when a called subroutine calls another subroutine. In such situations, many return addresses are pushed onto the stack, and when they are popped away from the stack, they automatically come out in the correct order.

## Exercises with programs abcde.iml and aaaabbbbcccc.iml

Exercise 4-6. Which small modification should be made to program **abcde.iml** in order to make it print letters ABCDEFGHI (nine letters from the beginning of the alphabet instead of just five letters) ?

Exercise 4-7. With very small modification to the textual form of **abcde.iml** the program would print HIJKL. What should be done to make this happen?

Exercise 4-8. Program **abcde.iml** can be made to print EDCBA by making two modifications to the program. The first modification is that 'A' should be changed to 'E' in Figure 4-10a. The other modification involves replacing an instruction with another similar instruction. Which are these instructions?

Exercise 4-9. How can program **abcde.iml** be made to print AABBCCDDEE ? This can be achieved by inserting one new instruction inside the loop of the program.

Exercise 4-10 With which small modification can **aaaabbbbcccc.iml** be made to print xxxxyyyyzzzz ? Which instruction should be removed to make it print aaaabbbbbbbb ?

Remember that you can verify your answers with the IC8 simulator!

## 4.11 Programs that use the keyboard, memory area, and stack

In this section we will study two IML programs which both read a text from the keyboard, and display the characters of the text in reverse order. This means that if, for example, the text "Hello " is typed in from the keyboard, the screen of the imaginary computer will look like

```
Hello  olleH
```

after program execution. These programs again show us that there are usually several possibilities to write a computer program to perform a certain activity.

Program **reverse_in_memory.iml**, which is shown in Figure 4-12a, is the first program to print the characters of a text in reverse order. The program reads characters from the keyboard until a space character ' ' has been entered. Each character is stored in a reserved memory area. When the program has read the space character from the keyboard, it starts printing the whole text in reverse order. The text is printed in reverse order because the memory area is processed backwards.

You should consult tables 4-1 and 4-2 to find out what the instructions in Figure 4-12a do. In addition, Figure 4-12b shows what happens inside the imaginary processor and on the screen when program **reverse_in_memory.iml** is being executed. The execution of the program takes so long that only the beginning of it can be seen in Figure 4-12b. If you study Figure 4-12b carefully, you will notice that the start address of the memory area is 19H. The name **memory_for_characters** refers to this address. For example, if the text "Hello " is given to the program, it is stored in the memory in the following way:

| ADDRESS | CHARACTER CODE | CHARACTER |
|---|---|---|
| 19H | 00H | |
| 1AH | 48H | 'H' |
| 1BH | 65H | 'e' |
| 1CH | 6CH | 'l' |
| 1DH | 6CH | 'l' |
| 1EH | 6FH | 'o' |
| 1FH | 20H | ' ' |

The program uses a kind of trick as it stores the value 00H to the first location of the reserved memory area. When the program reads the characters from the memory, while it is printing them in reverse order, the value 00H tells it when to stop reading and printing. The program does not need to know how many characters were entered from the keyboard. The value 00H marks the end of the characters in their reverse order. 00H is a convenient value for this kind of purpose because it is not a character code of any visible character.

Program **reverse_in_memory.iml** contains three loops. The shortest loop is

```
waiting_a_character:
        jump_if_input_not_ready          waiting_a_character
```

When the above instruction is executed, it causes a jump to itself, the same instruction, if the input is not ready. The program waits in this loop until the user of the program types in a character from the keyboard. The program keeps waiting forever if the user decides not to touch the keyboard. The loop terminates when signal INPUT READY inside the imaginary processor is set to value 1 (true). That happens when the INPUT PORT receives a character code from the keyboard.

The short loop is inside another loop which has the following structure

```
read_character:

            ...

            jump_if_registers_equal       print_characters
            jump_to_address               read_character

print_characters:
```

This loop can be called the input loop. As usual, the loop is constructed by using first a conditional jump instruction, and then an unconditional jump instruction. The conditional jump instruction makes the loop terminate when the code of the space character ' ' is in both registers A and B.

The last loop, the output loop, is also made with two jump instructions. The instruction

```
jump_if_register_a_zero       all_characters_printed
```

makes the program jump to its end when register A contains value 00H. That value is the trick value which marks the beginning of the reserved memory area.

You may be wondering why there is an output instruction inside the input loop. The output instruction is written right after the input instruction:

```
input_byte_to_register_a
output_byte_from_register_a
```

The reason for having the output instruction in the input loop is that it is convenient for the user of the program to see what he or she is typing into the computer. When a low-level programming language like IML is used, programs must be written so that they take care that input data is displayed on the screen. This activity is called echoing. Program **reverse_in_memory.iml** thus echoes the input to the screen.

Program **reverse_in_stack.iml**, which is shown in Figure 4-13a and "executed" in Figure 4-13b, is another program which prints the characters of its input text in reverse order. The main difference between the two programs is that, instead of a memory area, **reverse_in_stack.iml** uses the stack to store the input text.

The last bytes of the main memory of the imaginary computer are used as stack memory. Register STACK POINTER controls the use of the stack. For example, when instruction

```
push_register_a_to_stack
```

is executed for the first time in program **reverse_in_stack.iml**, value 00H is written to memory location FFH which is the current value of register STACK POINTER. After that the value of STACK POINTER is decremented to value FEH. This way the next push instruction writes memory location FEH.

When program **reverse_in_stack.iml** is executed by giving it text "Hello ", the last part of the main memory looks like the following

| ADDRESS | CHARACTER CODE | CHARACTER |
|---|---|---|
| F9H | 20H | ' ' |
| FAH | 6FH | 'o' |
| FBH | 6CH | 'l' |
| FCH | 6CH | 'l' |
| FDH | 65H | 'e' |
| FEH | 48H | 'H' |
| FFH | 00H | |

after the execution of the program. The stack is a particularly useful means to reverse the characters of a text because the stack always gives away the last byte that was put onto it.

Therefore, the last character of the input text comes out first from the stack. Characters are popped away from the stack with the instruction

```
pop_register_a_from_stack
```

which first increments the value of register STACK POINTER, and then copies the content of the memory location whose address is in STACK POINTER to register A.

Another difference between programs **reverse_in_memory.iml** and **reverse_in_stack.iml** is that the latter calls a subroutine to read characters from the keyboard. You should note, while studying the program execution in Figure 4-13b, that values on the stack change also because the subroutine calling mechanism uses the stack. A subroutine which reads a character from the keyboard is particularly useful. The subroutine `read_and_echo_a_character` could be copied from program **reverse_in_stack.iml** and used in many other programs.

## Exercises with programs reverse_in_memory.iml and reverse_in_stack.iml

Exercise 4-11. Now the programs stop reading characters from the keyboard when they encounter a space character ' ', 20H. It is thus not possible to type in complete sentences which contain spaces between words. Modify program **reverse_in_memory.iml** so that, instead of a space character, it stops reading characters when it encounters character '.', the full stop.

Exercise 4-12. Modify program **reverse_in_stack.iml** so that you take away the call to subroutine `read_and_echo_a_character`, and input the characters inside the first loop of the main program. This can be achieved by moving the instructions which are inside the subroutine to the input loop of the calling program. (I'm asking you to do this just as an exercise. In general, it is a good habit to use subroutines in computer programming.)

Exercise 4-13. Modify program **reverse_in_memory.iml** so that you put there the subroutine `read_and_echo_a_character` which is in **reverse_in_stack.iml**. You should call the subroutine in the input loop in the same way as it is called in **reverse_in_stack.iml**. The behavior of the program may not change.

The last two exercises require quite a lot of modifications to the programs. You must hand-compile the programs and carefully calculate correct memory addresses if you test your answers with the IC8 simulator.

## Other IML programs

The electronic material that is available for the readers of this book contains many IML programs which are not discussed in this chapter. These programs are also built in the simulators. In this chapter only the most essential programs are shown and explained.

If you are interested, you can study the other programs by printing them on paper, and by running them with a simulator. Among the extra programs there is one which shows what happens when a subroutine calls another subroutine. Another interesting program shows how numbers can be multiplied with the imaginary computer. Although the imaginary processor does not have machine instructions to perform multiplication operations, it is possible to multiply by executing many addition operations in a loop.

```
//   reverse_in_memory.iml   (c) Kari Laitinen

//   The following program reads text from the keyboard. After the
//   space key has been pressed, the program displays the characters
//   of the entered text in reverse order. Thus if the user typed in
//
//      Hello
//
//   the computer would respond
//
//       olleH

beginning_of_program:
       load_register_a_with_value         0
       set_memory_pointer                 memory_for_characters
       store_register_a_to_memory

read_character:
       increment_memory_pointer
waiting_a_character:
       jump_if_input_not_ready            waiting_a_character
       input_byte_to_register_a
       output_byte_from_register_a
       store_register_a_to_memory
       load_register_b_with_value         ' '      // code for space
       jump_if_registers_equal            print_characters
       jump_to_address                    read_character

print_characters:
       output_byte_from_register_a
       decrement_memory_pointer
       load_register_a_from_memory
       jump_if_register_a_zero            all_characters_printed
       jump_to_address                    print_characters

all_characters_printed:
       stop_processing

memory_for_characters:      DATA          20
```

This definition reserves a memory area of 20 bytes where the character codes, which are read from the keyboard, are stored. An IML compiler puts this memory area to those memory locations which follow the executable machine instructions. Because the machine instructions need the first 25 (19H) bytes from the main memory, this memory area starts from address 19H. The executable program starts, as always, from address 00H.

The text that follows the character pair //, double slash, on this line is a comment, which is ignored by the compiler. The double slash is part of the comment. The text before the double slash on this line is a valid IML instruction.

***Figure 4-12a. A program that prints the characters of an input text in reverse order.***

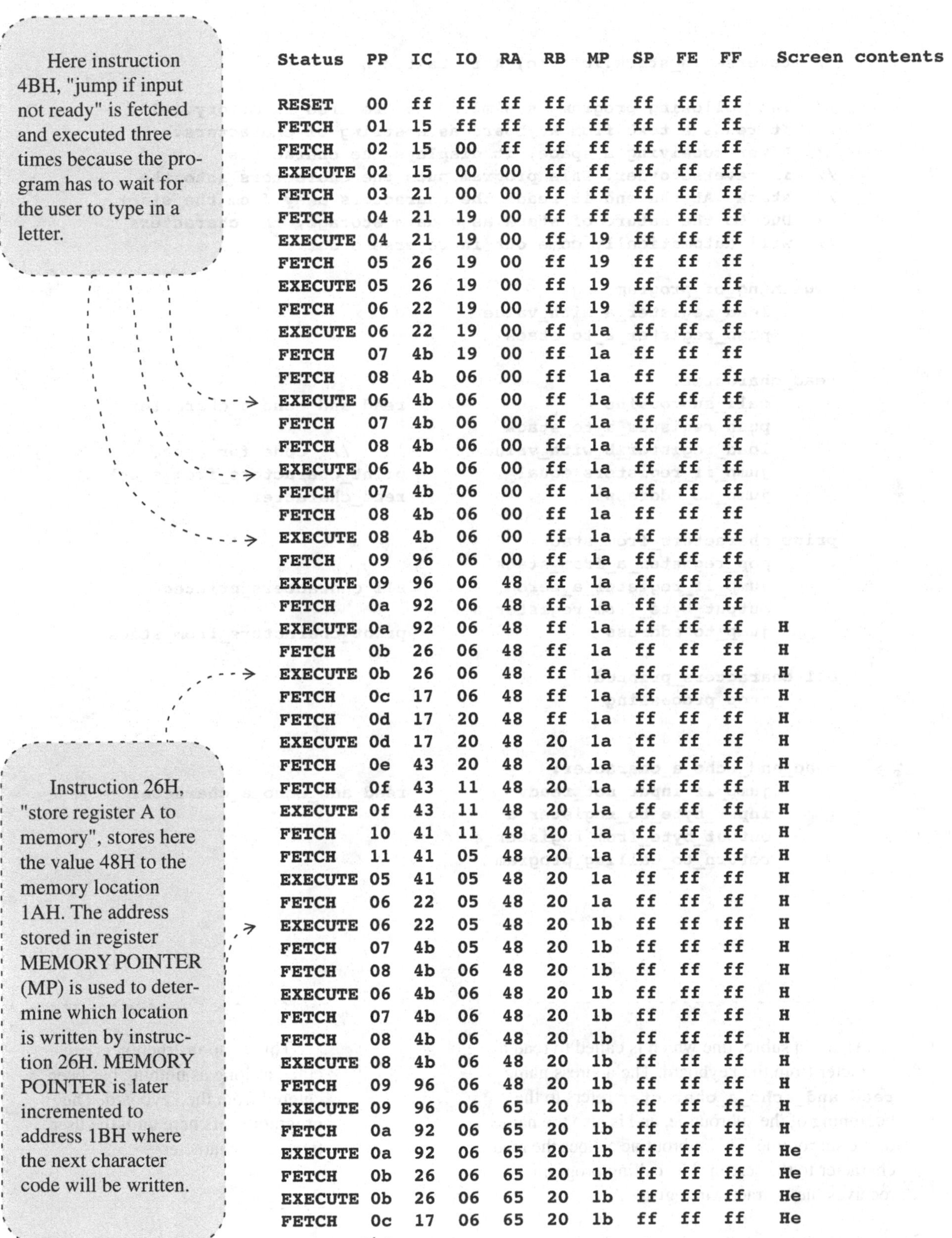

| Status | PP | IC | IO | RA | RB | MP | SP | FE | FF | Screen contents |
|---|---|---|---|---|---|---|---|---|---|---|
| RESET | 00 | ff | ff | ff | ff | ff | ff | ff | ff | |
| FETCH | 01 | 15 | ff | ff | ff | ff | ff | ff | ff | |
| FETCH | 02 | 15 | 00 | ff | ff | ff | ff | ff | ff | |
| EXECUTE | 02 | 15 | 00 | 00 | ff | ff | ff | ff | ff | |
| FETCH | 03 | 21 | 00 | 00 | ff | ff | ff | ff | ff | |
| FETCH | 04 | 21 | 19 | 00 | ff | ff | ff | ff | ff | |
| EXECUTE | 04 | 21 | 19 | 00 | ff | 19 | ff | ff | ff | |
| FETCH | 05 | 26 | 19 | 00 | ff | 19 | ff | ff | ff | |
| EXECUTE | 05 | 26 | 19 | 00 | ff | 19 | ff | ff | ff | |
| FETCH | 06 | 22 | 19 | 00 | ff | 19 | ff | ff | ff | |
| EXECUTE | 06 | 22 | 19 | 00 | ff | 1a | ff | ff | ff | |
| FETCH | 07 | 4b | 19 | 00 | ff | 1a | ff | ff | ff | |
| FETCH | 08 | 4b | 06 | 00 | ff | 1a | ff | ff | ff | |
| EXECUTE | 06 | 4b | 06 | 00 | ff | 1a | ff | ff | ff | |
| FETCH | 07 | 4b | 06 | 00 | ff | 1a | ff | ff | ff | |
| FETCH | 08 | 4b | 06 | 00 | ff | 1a | ff | ff | ff | |
| EXECUTE | 06 | 4b | 06 | 00 | ff | 1a | ff | ff | ff | |
| FETCH | 07 | 4b | 06 | 00 | ff | 1a | ff | ff | ff | |
| FETCH | 08 | 4b | 06 | 00 | ff | 1a | ff | ff | ff | |
| EXECUTE | 08 | 4b | 06 | 00 | ff | 1a | ff | ff | ff | |
| FETCH | 09 | 96 | 06 | 00 | ff | 1a | ff | ff | ff | |
| EXECUTE | 09 | 96 | 06 | 48 | ff | 1a | ff | ff | ff | |
| FETCH | 0a | 92 | 06 | 48 | ff | 1a | ff | ff | ff | |
| EXECUTE | 0a | 92 | 06 | 48 | ff | 1a | ff | ff | ff | H |
| FETCH | 0b | 26 | 06 | 48 | ff | 1a | ff | ff | ff | H |
| EXECUTE | 0b | 26 | 06 | 48 | ff | 1a | ff | ff | ff | H |
| FETCH | 0c | 17 | 06 | 48 | ff | 1a | ff | ff | ff | H |
| FETCH | 0d | 17 | 20 | 48 | ff | 1a | ff | ff | ff | H |
| EXECUTE | 0d | 17 | 20 | 48 | 20 | 1a | ff | ff | ff | H |
| FETCH | 0e | 43 | 20 | 48 | 20 | 1a | ff | ff | ff | H |
| FETCH | 0f | 43 | 11 | 48 | 20 | 1a | ff | ff | ff | H |
| EXECUTE | 0f | 43 | 11 | 48 | 20 | 1a | ff | ff | ff | H |
| FETCH | 10 | 41 | 11 | 48 | 20 | 1a | ff | ff | ff | H |
| FETCH | 11 | 41 | 05 | 48 | 20 | 1a | ff | ff | ff | H |
| EXECUTE | 05 | 41 | 05 | 48 | 20 | 1a | ff | ff | ff | H |
| FETCH | 06 | 22 | 05 | 48 | 20 | 1a | ff | ff | ff | H |
| EXECUTE | 06 | 22 | 05 | 48 | 20 | 1b | ff | ff | ff | H |
| FETCH | 07 | 4b | 05 | 48 | 20 | 1b | ff | ff | ff | H |
| FETCH | 08 | 4b | 06 | 48 | 20 | 1b | ff | ff | ff | H |
| EXECUTE | 06 | 4b | 06 | 48 | 20 | 1b | ff | ff | ff | H |
| FETCH | 07 | 4b | 06 | 48 | 20 | 1b | ff | ff | ff | H |
| FETCH | 08 | 4b | 06 | 48 | 20 | 1b | ff | ff | ff | H |
| EXECUTE | 08 | 4b | 06 | 48 | 20 | 1b | ff | ff | ff | H |
| FETCH | 09 | 96 | 06 | 48 | 20 | 1b | ff | ff | ff | H |
| EXECUTE | 09 | 96 | 06 | 65 | 20 | 1b | ff | ff | ff | H |
| FETCH | 0a | 92 | 06 | 65 | 20 | 1b | ff | ff | ff | H |
| EXECUTE | 0a | 92 | 06 | 65 | 20 | 1b | ff | ff | ff | He |
| FETCH | 0b | 26 | 06 | 65 | 20 | 1b | ff | ff | ff | He |
| EXECUTE | 0b | 26 | 06 | 65 | 20 | 1b | ff | ff | ff | He |
| FETCH | 0c | 17 | 06 | 65 | 20 | 1b | ff | ff | ff | He |

... etc.

Here instruction 4BH, "jump if input not ready" is fetched and executed three times because the program has to wait for the user to type in a letter.
Instruction 26H, "store register A to memory", stores here the value 48H to the memory location 1AH. The address stored in register MEMORY POINTER (MP) is used to determine which location is written by instruction 26H. MEMORY POINTER is later incremented to address 1BH where the next character code will be written.



*Figure 4-12b. Step-by-step execution of the program in Figure 4-12a.*

```
//  reverse_in_stack.iml  (c) Kari Laitinen

//  The following program is similar to "reverse_in_memory.iml".
//  It reads a text from keyboard as a string of characters.
//  After receiving a space, it displays the characters
//  in reverse order. This program puts the characters into the
//  stack. At the end it reads the characters away from the stack.
//  Due to the nature of stack as a data storage, the characters
//  will automatically come out in reverse order.

beginning_of_program:
      load_register_a_with_value        0
      push_register_a_to_stack

read_character:
      call_subroutine                   read_and_echo_a_character
      push_register_a_to_stack
      load_register_b_with_value        ' '  //  code for space
      jump_if_registers_equal           print_characters_from_stack
      jump_to_address                   read_character

print_characters_from_stack:
      pop_register_a_from_stack
      jump_if_register_a_zero           all_characters_printed
      output_byte_from_register_a
      jump_to_address                   print_characters_from_stack

all_characters_printed:
      stop_processing

read_and_echo_a_character:
      jump_if_input_not_ready           read_and_echo_a_character
      input_byte_to_register_a
      output_byte_from_register_a
      return_to_calling_program
```

This is a subroutine which is called to read a character from the keyboard. The address name **read_and_echo_a_character** refers to the beginning of the subroutine, and is also the name of the subroutine. This subroutine echoes the read character to the screen. The calling program receives the character in register A.

This jump instruction is executed as long as nothing has been entered from the keyboard. The program waits here until the user types in a character.

*Figure 4-13a. Another version of a program to reverse the characters of a text.*

Here instruction 81H, "call subroutine", is executed. The subroutine is in address 13H. At this moment the value 00H and the return address 05H are on the stack.

When instruction A2H is executed here, the content of register A (48H, the character code of letter H) is copied to the top of the stack which is in address FEH. After that the value of register STACK POINTER is decremented to value FDH which is the new top location of the stack. Note that the stack locations FDH, FCH, FBH, etc. are not shown here because of space limitations.

| Status | PP | IC | IO | RA | RB | MP | SP | FE | FF | Screen contents |
|---|---|---|---|---|---|---|---|---|---|---|
| RESET | 00 | ff | ff | ff | ff | ff | ff | ff | ff | |
| FETCH | 01 | 15 | ff | ff | ff | ff | ff | ff | ff | |
| FETCH | 02 | 15 | 00 | ff | ff | ff | ff | ff | ff | |
| EXECUTE | 02 | 15 | 00 | 00 | ff | ff | ff | ff | ff | |
| FETCH | 03 | a2 | 00 | 00 | ff | ff | ff | ff | ff | |
| EXECUTE | 03 | a2 | 00 | 00 | ff | ff | fe | ff | 00 | |
| FETCH | 04 | 81 | 00 | 00 | ff | ff | fe | ff | 00 | |
| FETCH | 05 | 81 | 13 | 00 | ff | ff | fe | ff | 00 | |
| EXECUTE | 13 | 81 | 13 | 00 | ff | ff | fd | 05 | 00 | |
| FETCH | 14 | 4b | 13 | 00 | ff | ff | fd | 05 | 00 | |
| FETCH | 15 | 4b | 13 | 00 | ff | ff | fd | 05 | 00 | |
| EXECUTE | 13 | 4b | 13 | 00 | ff | ff | fd | 05 | 00 | |
| FETCH | 14 | 4b | 13 | 00 | ff | ff | fd | 05 | 00 | |
| FETCH | 15 | 4b | 13 | 00 | ff | ff | fd | 05 | 00 | |
| EXECUTE | 15 | 4b | 13 | 00 | ff | ff | fd | 05 | 00 | |
| FETCH | 16 | 96 | 13 | 00 | ff | ff | fd | 05 | 00 | |
| EXECUTE | 16 | 96 | 13 | 48 | ff | ff | fd | 05 | 00 | |
| FETCH | 17 | 92 | 13 | 48 | ff | ff | fd | 05 | 00 | |
| EXECUTE | 17 | 92 | 13 | 48 | ff | ff | fd | 05 | 00 | H |
| FETCH | 18 | 82 | 13 | 48 | ff | ff | fd | 05 | 00 | H |
| EXECUTE | 05 | 82 | 13 | 48 | ff | ff | fe | 05 | 00 | H |
| FETCH | 06 | a2 | 13 | 48 | ff | ff | fe | 05 | 00 | H |
| EXECUTE | 06 | a2 | 13 | 48 | ff | ff | fd | 48 | 00 | H |
| FETCH | 07 | 17 | 13 | 48 | ff | ff | fd | 48 | 00 | H |
| FETCH | 08 | 17 | 20 | 48 | ff | ff | fd | 48 | 00 | H |
| EXECUTE | 08 | 17 | 20 | 48 | 20 | ff | fd | 48 | 00 | H |
| FETCH | 09 | 43 | 20 | 48 | 20 | ff | fd | 48 | 00 | H |
| FETCH | 0a | 43 | 0c | 48 | 20 | ff | fd | 48 | 00 | H |
| EXECUTE | 0a | 43 | 0c | 48 | 20 | ff | fd | 48 | 00 | H |
| FETCH | 0b | 41 | 0c | 48 | 20 | ff | fd | 48 | 00 | H |
| FETCH | 0c | 41 | 03 | 48 | 20 | ff | fd | 48 | 00 | H |
| EXECUTE | 03 | 41 | 03 | 48 | 20 | ff | fd | 48 | 00 | H |
| FETCH | 04 | 81 | 03 | 48 | 20 | ff | fd | 48 | 00 | H |
| FETCH | 05 | 81 | 13 | 48 | 20 | ff | fd | 48 | 00 | H |
| EXECUTE | 13 | 81 | 13 | 48 | 20 | ff | fc | 48 | 00 | H |
| FETCH | 14 | 4b | 13 | 48 | 20 | ff | fc | 48 | 00 | H |
| FETCH | 15 | 4b | 13 | 48 | 20 | ff | fc | 48 | 00 | H |
| EXECUTE | 13 | 4b | 13 | 48 | 20 | ff | fc | 48 | 00 | H |
| FETCH | 14 | 4b | 13 | 48 | 20 | ff | fc | 48 | 00 | H |
| FETCH | 15 | 4b | 13 | 48 | 20 | ff | fc | 48 | 00 | H |
| EXECUTE | 15 | 4b | 13 | 48 | 20 | ff | fc | 48 | 00 | H |
| FETCH | 16 | 96 | 13 | 48 | 20 | ff | fc | 48 | 00 | H |
| EXECUTE | 16 | 96 | 13 | 65 | 20 | ff | fc | 48 | 00 | H |
| FETCH | 17 | 92 | 13 | 65 | 20 | ff | fc | 48 | 00 | H |
| EXECUTE | 17 | 92 | 13 | 65 | 20 | ff | fc | 48 | 00 | He |
| FETCH | 18 | 82 | 13 | 65 | 20 | ff | fc | 48 | 00 | He |
| EXECUTE | 05 | 82 | 13 | 65 | 20 | ff | fd | 48 | 00 | He |
| FETCH | 06 | a2 | 13 | 65 | 20 | ff | fd | 48 | 00 | He |
| EXECUTE | 06 | a2 | 13 | 65 | 20 | ff | fc | 48 | 00 | He |
| FETCH | 07 | 17 | 13 | 65 | 20 | ff | fc | 48 | 00 | He |

... etc.

*Figure 4-13b. Step-by-step execution of the program in Figure 4-13a.*

## 4.12 Chapter summary – towards high-level programming

In this chapter, we have studied an imaginary computer and the simple IML language which we used to write programs for the computer. Our aim was to learn how computers work in general: how they execute sequences of machine instructions which are called programs. Machine instructions are numerical codes which the processor executes in a certain way.

A computer programmer needs to know something about the logical operation of computers. That is the reason why the imaginary computer and its machine-level programming language were introduced here. However, I would like to emphasize that a serious computer programmer should not write programs using languages like IML. It is better to use high-level languages such as Java, which allow one to think in terms of application domain concepts.

During the early days of computing, machine-level programming languages similar to IML were widely used in software development. They have been traditionally called assembly languages. However, because software development was found to be rather difficult with assembly languages, high-level programming languages were invented. Writing programs with assembly languages is difficult because of the following reasons:

- The program writer must know the registers and the behavior of the processor for which he or she is writing a program.
- An assembly language programmer must think in terms of memory locations and register contents.
- Even for simple operations, many lines of source program code must be written with an assembly language.

High-level languages allow programmers to pay more attention to what the programs should do, and they free programmers from knowing the internal structure of the used processor. High-level programming languages are usually machine-independent, which means that a program written with a high-level language can be run by different computers. Many high-level programming languages require that every type of computer must have its own compiler to transform a high-level program into machine instructions of that particular computer. Java is a high-level programming language that requires a special runtime environment in which compiled Java programs can be executed. As Java runtime environments are available for different types of computers, Java-based programs can be executed on most modern computers.

Programs written with a high-level language are usually shorter than programs written with a language like IML. To demonstrate this, let's consider the following piece of IML source program:

```
// Some values should be stored beforehand to memory
// locations first_number and second_number.

      set_memory_pointer                    first_number
      load_register_a_from_memory
      set_memory_pointer                    second_number
      load_register_b_from_memory

      add_register_b_to_a
      set_memory_pointer                    sum_of_numbers
      store_register_a_to_memory

first_number:       DATA        1
second_number:      DATA        1
sum_of_numbers:     DATA        1
```

The instructions above first calculate the sum of the numbers that are in the memory locations which have names **first_number** and **second_number**. Then the sum is stored in the memory location which has name **sum_of_numbers**. If a high-level language like the Java programming language existed for the imaginary computer, the above IML instructions could be written with the high-level language in the following way

```
int  first_number ;
int  second_number ;
int  sum_of_numbers ;

// Some values should be stored to variables
// first_number and second_number.

sum_of_numbers  =  first_number  +  second_number ;
```

By comparing the two pieces of program it is easy to see that the program written with the high-level language is shorter. Later on, after you have learned Java programming, you will most likely say that the high-level program is also easier to understand.

You may wonder why we studied the IML language if high-level programming languages are more convenient. The answer is, that in order to understand high-level languages properly, it is important to know something about processors and machine-level programming. These matters are easy to explain with a simple processor and with a simple language. Without knowing anything about machine-level programming, it is hard to understand why high-level programs need to be compiled, and what is happening in compilation. Just like an IML compiler, the compiler of a high-level programming language translates textual source programs to list of numerical machine instructions. If there existed a compiler to translate the above high-level program for the imaginary computer, the compiler could produce the same machine instructions which would result in the translation of the corresponding piece of an IML source program. (In reality, however, it is very difficult to build such a compiler.)

Making comparisons between the Java programming language and the IML language is difficult because the Java compiler does not compile programs to machine instructions of a particular processor. Instead, the Java compiler produces bytecode instructions which are "translated" to real machine instructions in the Java runtime environment. You can, however, think that the Java compiler produces low-level instructions that are similar to the machine instructions of the imaginary computer. Also the Java runtime environment operates in many ways according to the same principles as the imaginary computer presented in this chapter.

## "Bugs" in computer programs

While reading this chapter you may have realized, or you may have experienced personally with the IC8 simulator, that it is possible to make computer programs which do not behave as intended, or which never terminate. The following is an example of a program that never terminates:

```
beginning_of_program:
          load_register_a_with_value          'X'
          output_byte_from_register_a
          jump_to_address                     beginning_of_program
```

The above program is an infinite (endless) loop which keeps displaying the letter X forever. These kinds of loops can be made accidentally in computer programs. When a computer program does not work as originally planned, we say that there is an error in the program. A never-terminating program is one example of an erroneous program. There can be many kinds of errors in programs, and it is common in the world of computers to call errors by the word "bug". The activity of searching and removing errors in computer programs is called "debugging". Computer programs which can help in the search of errors in other programs are called debugging tools, or simply debuggers.

The English word "bug" can mean any small insect. That word started to mean a problem in a computer because small insects really did cause malfunctions in early computers. A small insect could cause an erroneous electrical connection among the relays of an early computer, and make the computer behave in an unexpected manner. Small insects are no threat to modern computers because their electronic circuits are so small that no bug can walk inside them, but humans can still make all kinds of errors when they write computer programs.

# PART II: FUNDAMENTALS OF PROGRAMMING

Chapters

5 Variables and other basic elements in Java programs
6 Decisions and repetitions: basic activities in programs
7 Arrays: sets of similar data items
8 Strings store sequences of character codes
9 Methods – logical performing units in programs

# CHAPTER 5

## VARIABLES AND OTHER BASIC ELEMENTS IN JAVA PROGRAMS

Now, finally, we really begin studying computer programming with the Java language. Variables are important elements in computer programs, and they are needed in almost every computer program. In this chapter we shall study different types of variables and use the variables in simple arithmetic computations. We shall also explore names and keywords which are very basic elements in source programs.

This chapter, as well as the following chapters, introduces many examples of Java source programs for you to study. A source program is a textual description of what the computer should do when the compiled version of the source program is executed by a computer. The source programs that you will see in this chapter contain variable declarations followed by executable program statements, action statements, which do something with the variables. The general structure of the programs is the following:

```
import java.util.* ;

class ClassName
{
   public static void main( String[] not_in_use )
   {
      Scanner keyboard = new Scanner( System.in ) ;

      Variable declarations.

      Action statements that modify and print
      the contents of the variables that
      were declared above.
   }
}
```

These lines are present only in those programs which read data from the keyboard.

As was already discussed in Chapter 2, the structure of our first programs is such that a static method named **main()** contains the action statements of the program, and the **main()** method is written inside a class declaration. At this phase, we do not attempt to profoundly understand the meaning of the class declaration. We'll just try to figure out how the internal statements of method **main()** operate.

## 5.1 Integer variables (int, short, long, byte, char)

A variable in a source program is a basic program element that can be used to store a numerical value. The value of a variable usually changes when the program is being executed. When we declare a variable in a program, we actually reserve a few bytes of computer's main memory to be used for a special purpose. The following is an example of a *variable declaration*:

```
int   integer_from_keyboard ;
```

This source program line which introduces a variable into a program can also be called a *variable definition*. The above source program line means that four bytes (32 bits) of memory are reserved to store an integer that will be read from the keyboard, and these four bytes can be referred to with the name **`integer_from_keyboard`**. Integers are whole numbers that have no decimal point. Integers can be positive or negative. Variables of type **`int`** are said to be 32-bit variables because they occupy 32 bits (four bytes) in the main memory of the computer

A variable always has a type, such as **`int`** which is an abbreviation of the word "integer". The programmer, the person who writes the variable declarations in a program, must give a unique name to each variable. In the declaration above, the name of the variable is **`integer_from_keyboard`**. Variable declarations, like all Java statements, must be terminated with a semicolon (;).

Program **Game.java**, presented as a program description on the following page opening, is an example program where two variables of type **`int`** are declared and used. The program is an extremely simple computer game. Unfortunately it is not a fair game because the user of the program will always lose. The program always wins by presenting an integer that is one larger than the number given by the user of the program.

A source program like **Game.java** is a text file in a computer's hard disk memory before it is compiled. When a source program is compiled, we get an executable version of the program. The compiler is a computer tool that can convert a source program into executable form. The compiler reads and processes a source program file in the same order in which it is written. While compiling program **Game.java**, the compiler sees first the variable declarations and reserves main memory for the variables. It then transforms the remaining statements, the action statements, to numerical instructions to be processed during program execution.

The action statements in a source program describe the activities a computer performs when the executable version of the program is run by a computer. The action statements of a program are executed in an order that corresponds with the order in which the statements are written in the source program. In the case of the program **Game.java**, the computer performs the following activities:

- First it asks the user to enter an integer from the keyboard.
- It then reads the integer entered from the keyboard and stores it in variable **`integer_from_keyboard`**.
- Then it calculates a value that is one larger than the user-given integer and stores that value in variable **`one_larger_integer`**.
- In the end, it displays the values of both variables and informs the user that the computer won the game.

There are four action statements in **Game.java**. Each statement is terminated with a semicolon (;). The variable declarations at the beginning are also statements, but they are not action statements. Variable declarations just reserve memory to store information.

Although the memory space that is reserved for an **int** variable is rather large, 4 bytes, there are limitations how large values can be stored in an **int** variable. A 4-byte **int** variable can store values in the ranges

-2,147,483,648, ... , -1, 0, 1, ... , 2,147,483,647 (decimal numbering system)

-80000000H, ..., -1, 0, 1, ... , 7FFFFFFFH (hexadecimal numbering system)

A 4-byte **int** can thus store 4,294,967,296 (100000000H) different values. To demonstrate the difficulties that arise when the storage capacity of an **int** variable is exceeded, program **Game.java** is also executed with an exceedingly large input value in the program description. The computer tries to increment the value 2,147,483,647 which is stored in a 4-byte **int** variable. This results in the number -2,147,483,648 and not in 2,147,483,648. To explain this strange behavior of the program, we must remember that the memories of computers can contain only non-negative binary numbers. Negative numbers are represented so that some positive values stored in memory are considered as negative numbers. For example, the value 2,147,483,648 is treated as -2,147,483,648. The values that can be contained in 4-byte **int** variables have the following meanings:

```
VALUE IN MEMORY                          MEANING IN PROGRAM

2,147,483,648 (80000000H)                -2,147,483,648
2,147,483,649 (80000001H)                -2,147,483,647
2,147,483,650 (80000002H)                -2,147,483,646
.                                        .
.                                        .
4,294,967,294 (FFFFFFFEH)                -2
4,294,967,295 (FFFFFFFFH)                -1
0                                        0
1                                        1
.                                        .
.                                        .
2,147,483,646 (7FFFFFFEH)                2,147,483,646
2,147,483,647 (7FFFFFFFH)                2,147,483,647
```

Figure 5-1 shows how the variables of program **Game.java** look like in the main memory of a computer, and how the values of the variables change when the program is executed with input value 1234. A variable declaration like

```
int   integer_from_keyboard ;
```

reserves four bytes from contiguous memory locations somewhere in the main memory. Right after the declaration of the variable, the contents of the four bytes are unspecified. After an assignment statement like

```
integer_from_keyboard  =  keyboard.nextInt() ;
```

is executed, the four bytes are given values that represent the number that was typed in from the keyboard.

The illustration in Figure 5-1 shows the general principle according to which memory is reserved for variables. The compiler may, however, optimize the use of memory if it finds out that it can save memory.

This line is not actually part of the program. This is a comment line that gives documentary information to the reader of the program. A double slash // marks the beginning of a comment line. The compiler ignores the double slash and the text that follows it on the same line.

As was explained in Chapter 2, we need to have these lines in those programs which read data from the keyboard.

Here two integer variables are declared. The names of the variables are **`integer_from_keyboard`** and **`one_larger_integer`**. The variables are referred to with these names later in the program.

```
//  Game.java  (c) Kari Laitinen

import java.util.* ;

class Game
{
   public static void main( String[] not_in_use )
   {
      Scanner keyboard = new Scanner( System.in ) ;

      int  integer_from_keyboard ;
      int  one_larger_integer ;

      System.out.print(
         "\n This program is a computer game. Please, type in "
       + "\n an integer in the range  1 ... 2147483646 : " ) ;

      integer_from_keyboard  =  keyboard.nextInt() ;

      one_larger_integer  =  integer_from_keyboard  +  1 ;

      System.out.print( "\n You typed in " + integer_from_keyboard + "."
                      + "\n My number is " + one_larger_integer    + "."
                      + "\n Sorry, you lost. I won. The game is over.\n") ;
   }
}
```

This line of source code reads an integer from the keyboard and stores the read integer into variable **`integer_from_keyboard`**. The execution of the program stays on this line until the user of the program has entered an integer. The integer is read by the **`nextInt()`** method which is invoked for the defined **`keyboard`**.

Texts inside double quote characters " " are strings of characters that will be displayed on the screen. **`\n`** among the text means that the text will begin from a new line. **`\n`** is said to be the newline character.

**Game.java - 1.+ A program that implements a simple computer game.**

When we write **System.out**, we can refer to the screen of the computer. **print()** is a method that can be invoked by writing **System.out.print( ... )**, and this method invocation (or method call) writes data to the screen. Here, the text that is going to be displayed on the screen consists of two strings of characters. These two character strings are concatenated with operator +.

After this assignment statement has been executed, the value of variable **one_larger_integer** is one greater than the value stored in **integer_from_keyboard**.

```
System.out.print(
   "\n This program is a computer game. Please, type in "
 + "\n an integer in the range  1 ... 2147483646 : " ) ;

integer_from_keyboard  =  keyboard.nextInt() ;

one_larger_integer  =  integer_from_keyboard  +  1 ;

System.out.print( "\n You typed in " + integer_from_keyboard + "."
            +  "\n My number is " + one_larger_integer    + "."
            +  "\n Sorry, you lost. I won. The game is over.\n") ;
```

It is possible to output many types of data in a single call to method **System.out.print()**. Here the values of the integer variables are displayed between strings of characters given inside double quotes. Operator + is placed between different types of data. The + operator converts the numerical values stored in the variables to character strings, and joins these character strings to the other character strings given inside double quotes. A semicolon (;) terminates the entire statement.

**Game.java - 1 - 1. The action statements of the program.**

```
D:\javafiles2>java Game

 This program is a computer game. Please, type in
 an integer in the range  1... 2147483646 : 1234

 You typed in 1234.
 My number is 1235.
 Sorry, you lost. I won. The game is over.

D:\javafiles2>java Game

 This program is a computer game. Please, type in
 an integer in the range  1 ... 2147483646 : 2147483647

 You typed in 2147483647.
 My number is -2147483648.
 Sorry, you lost. I won. The game is over.
```

**Game.java - X. In the second execution too large an input value is given to the program.**

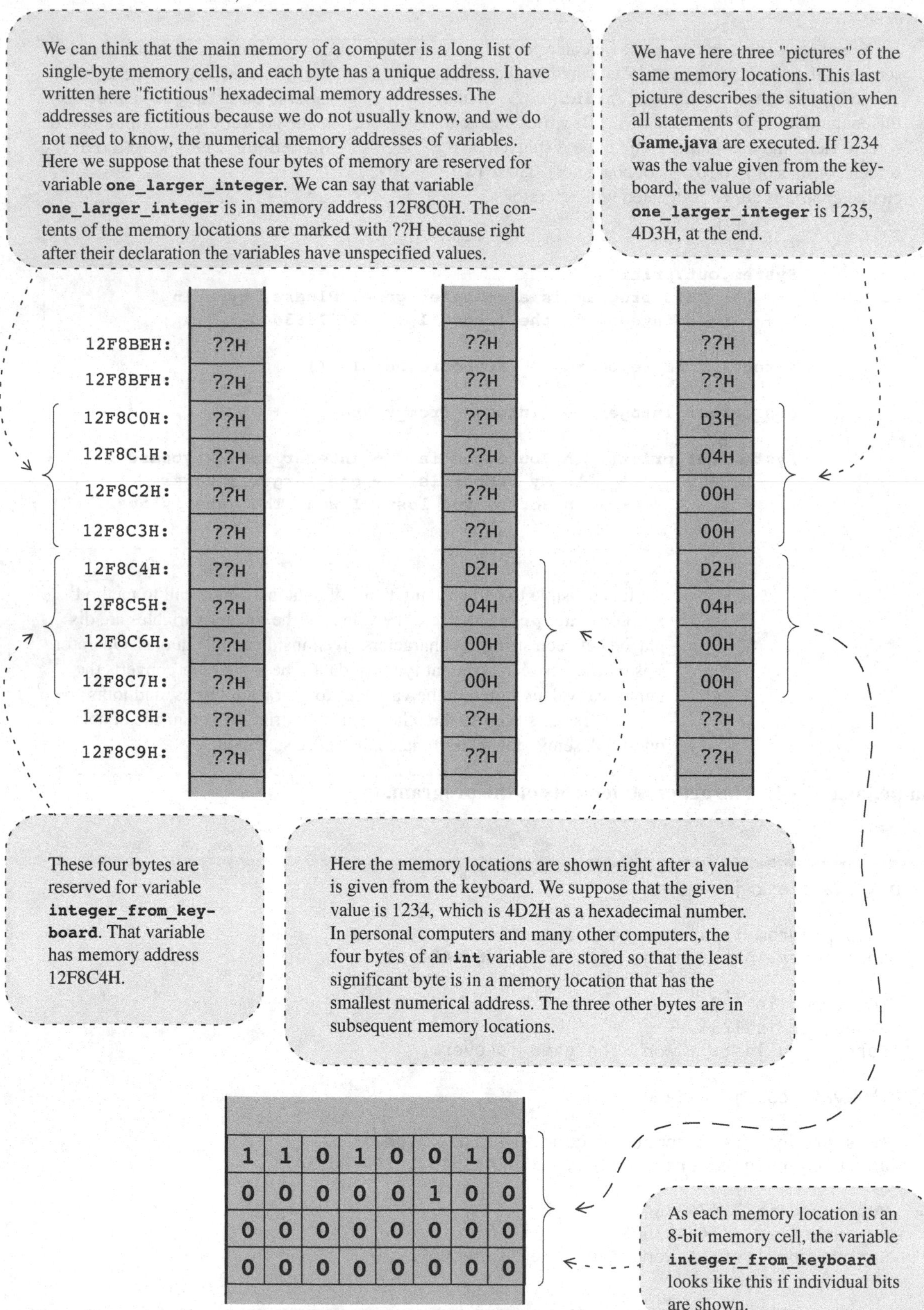
We can think that the main memory of a computer is a long list of single-byte memory cells, and each byte has a unique address. I have written here "fictitious" hexadecimal memory addresses. The addresses are fictitious because we do not usually know, and we do not need to know, the numerical memory addresses of variables. Here we suppose that these four bytes of memory are reserved for variable one_larger_integer. We can say that variable one_larger_integer is in memory address 12F8C0H. The contents of the memory locations are marked with ??H because right after their declaration the variables have unspecified values.
We have here three "pictures" of the same memory locations. This last picture describes the situation when all statements of program Game.java are executed. If 1234 was the value given from the keyboard, the value of variable one_larger_integer is 1235, 4D3H, at the end.
12F8BEH: ??H ??H ??H
12F8BFH: ??H ??H ??H
12F8C0H: ??H ??H D3H
12F8C1H: ??H ??H 04H
12F8C2H: ??H ??H 00H
12F8C3H: ??H ??H 00H
12F8C4H: ??H D2H D2H
12F8C5H: ??H 04H 04H
12F8C6H: ??H 00H 00H
12F8C7H: ??H 00H 00H
12F8C8H: ??H ??H ??H
12F8C9H: ??H ??H ??H
These four bytes are reserved for variable integer_from_keyboard. That variable has memory address 12F8C4H.
Here the memory locations are shown right after a value is given from the keyboard. We suppose that the given value is 1234, which is 4D2H as a hexadecimal number. In personal computers and many other computers, the four bytes of an int variable are stored so that the least significant byte is in a memory location that has the smallest numerical address. The three other bytes are in subsequent memory locations.
1 1 0 1 0 0 1 0
0 0 0 0 0 1 0 0
0 0 0 0 0 0 0 0
0 0 0 0 0 0 0 0
As each memory location is an 8-bit memory cell, the variable integer_from_keyboard looks like this if individual bits are shown.

***Figure 5-1. The variables of program Game.java in a computer's main memory.***

In addition to variables of type **int**, Java has other types of integer variables. These variables are sometimes called integral types. Type **long** is another integer type. Variables of type **long** occupy 8 bytes (64 bits) of memory. They are thus longer integer variables than variables of type **int**. If we declared the variables of program **Game.java** as

```
long  integer_from_keyboard ;
long  one_larger_integer ;
```

the program would work correctly with much larger numbers as it does now.

A third integer variable type is **short** which is a 2-byte, 16-bit, variable. This type may be useful when your program uses only integer values that are smaller than 32,767. If you need to store very many such values, you can save some memory by using type **short** instead of type **int**. In small programs, though, there is no need to use variables of type **short** because memory is rather abundant in modern computers.

**byte** is a variable type to store 8-bit values in the range -128 ... 127. A variable of type **byte** occupies a single byte of memory.

Variables of type **char** are 2-byte (16-bit) variables that are used to store 16-bit Unicode character codes. The first 256 Unicodes are the same as the codes in the ASCII coding system. **char** variables are like integer variables because the used character codes are integer values. However, it is better not to use **char** variables in situations where integer variables are needed.

The integer types **int**, **short**, **long**, etc. will be used when we need to store whole numbers in our computer programs. The most common integer type is **int**. Integer variables are convenient when we want to count something in our programs. Table 5-1 summarizes the integer types and other variable types in Java. Figure 5-2 shows how some variables look like in the main memory of a computer. The other variable types will be discussed later in this chapter. Type **boolean** is a special variable type to declare so-called boolean variables. Boolean variables can be given only two values: **true** and **false**. We shall study these variables in more detail when we encounter them in some example programs.

Some other programming languages (e.g. C++ and C#) have "unsigned" integral variable types. In such variables it is possible to store only non-negative whole numbers. These variable types are not available in the Java programming language.

## Exercises with program Game.java

Exercise 5-1. Modify the program so that it always loses the game by presenting a number which is one smaller than the number given by the user. With operator - it is possible to perform subtractions in Java.

Exercise 5-2. Modify the program so that it prints three numbers that are larger than the number given by the user. For example, if the user types in 144, the program must print 145, 146, and 147.

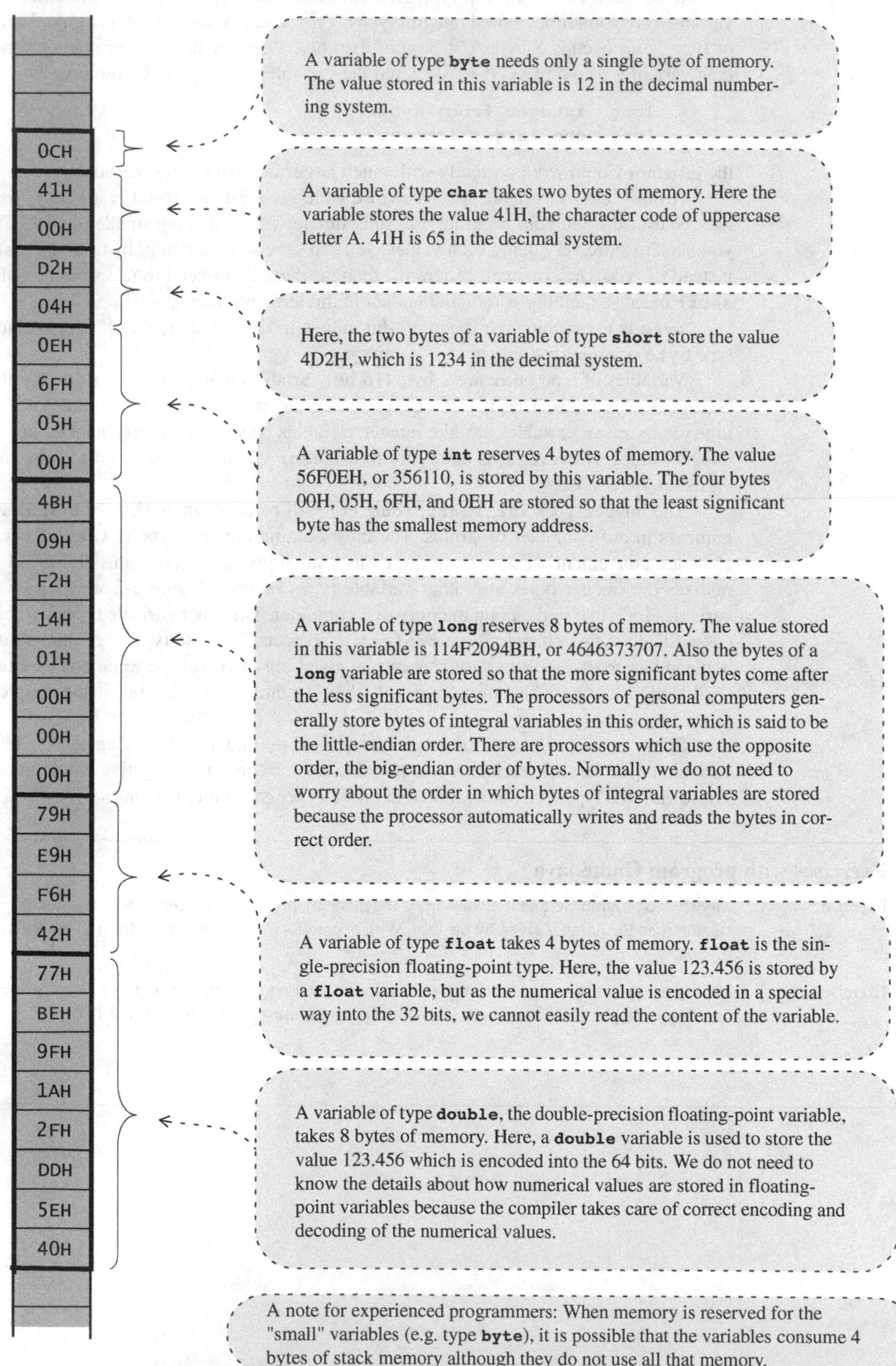


*Figure 5-2. Different types of variables in a computer's main memory.*

**Table 5-1. Variable types of Java.**

| Type | Size | Storage capacity |
|---|---|---|
| `int` | `4 bytes 32 bits` | `-2,147,483,648 ... 2,147,483,647`<br>`-80000000H ... 7FFFFFFFH` |
| `short` | `2 bytes 16 bits` | `-32,768 ... 32,767`<br>`-8000H ... 7FFFH` |
| `long` | `8 bytes 64 bits` | `-9,223,372,036,854,775,808 ... 9,223,372,036,854,775,807`<br>`-8000000000000000H ... 7FFFFFFFFFFFFFFFH` |
| `byte` | `1 byte 8 bits` | `-128 ... 127`<br>`-80H ... 7FH` |
| `boolean` | `1 byte 8 bits` | `false or true` |
| `char` | `2 bytes 16 bits` | `Unicode 0 ... 65535` |
| `float` | `4 bytes 32 bits` | `Precision: 7 decimal digits`<br>`Range: +/- 1.5e-45 ... 3.4e38`[a] |
| `double` | `8 bytes 64 bits` | `Precision: 15 decimal digits`<br>`Range: +/- 5.0e-324 ... 1.7e308` |
| `memory address`[b] | `4 bytes 32 bits` | `Sufficient for addressing up to 4,294,967,296 bytes (4 gigabytes) of main memory.` |

a. The ranges that are given here are approximate.
b. "memory address" is not a variable type in Java. This row describes how much memory is allocated when a so-called object reference is declared.

## 5.2 Keywords, names, spaces, and newlines

Java source programs contain special characters or character pairs such as {, }, (, ), =, ;, ", \n, and +; and natural-language expressions such as **static**, **void**, **main**, **int**, **System**, and **integer_from_keyboard**. Both the special characters and natural-language expressions are meaningful for the Java compiler. When the compiler starts compiling a Java source program, it reads a text file that contains character codes. Depending on what the compiler reads from the source program file, it creates a corresponding executable file, the result of the compilation process. With the special characters and natural-language expressions we tell the compiler what kind of executable file it should create.

Keywords of a programming language are words or abbreviations borrowed from a natural language for special purposes. The compiler of the programming language uses the keywords to detect syntactic structures in source programs. Keywords cannot be used as names in programs. For this reason keywords are called reserved words of the programming language. Java has the following keywords:

```
abstract    boolean  break     byte      case         catch
char        class    const     continue  default      do
double      else     enum      extends   final        finally
float       for      goto      if        implements   import
instanceof  int      interface long      native       new
null        package  private   protected public       return
short       static   super     switch    synchronized this
throw       throws   transient try       void         volatile
while
```

Keywords will be explained in the following chapters, as we encounter them in example programs. All keywords are listed and discussed briefly in Appendix B.

A name in a source program is a natural-language expression invented by the writer of the program. Names are also called symbols or identifiers in programming terminology. Program **Game.java** contains variable names **integer_from_keyboard** and **one_larger_integer**. **main()** is the name of the main method of the program, **print()** is the name of the method with which we can write text to the screen, and **nextInt()** is the name of a method with which we can read an integer value from the keyboard. Although **main**, **print**, and **nextInt** are not official keywords of Java, they should almost be treated as such because the main method of a Java program must be called **main()**, and **print()** and **nextInt()** are method names defined in standard Java classes. (Note that there is a pair of empty parentheses () at the end of the method names. Those parentheses do not belong to the method names. They are just a means to distinguish method names from other names in the body text of this book.)

In this book, we use so-called natural names in the source programs. Natural names are such that they consist of natural English words. The name of a variable should describe the purpose of the variable. Natural names with carefully selected words usually fulfil this requirement. Because computer programs are generally rather complex, they should be made as easy to read as possible. The use of natural naming makes source programs readable and understandable.

The words of a natural name can be joined with the underscore character ( _ ) or capitalization can be used to mark the beginning of a new word in a name. In this book, the names of variables are constructed so that the words are joined with underscore characters. Standard Java names like **nextInt** are constructed by using capitalization, i.e., an uppercase letter starts a new word in a name.

Natural names are important for human readers, but compilers treat source programs in a very technical manner. From the compiler's point of view, a name does not necessarily need to be natural. The following are the technical rules for writing a name in Java:

- A name must be a continuous sequence of characters. You may not include spaces, newline characters, or other special characters in a name. (In the body text and text balloons of this book, a name is sometimes hyphenated, i.e., a name continues on the following line. Hyphenation is not, however, allowed in source programs. A name may not continue on the following line in program text.)
- The first character of a name must be a letter or an underscore ( _ ).
- The characters following the first character must be letters, digits, or underscores. This means that a digit cannot start a name, but digits are allowed after the first character.

According to these rules, all the following variable declarations would be acceptable for the Java compiler:

```
int  i ;
int  __xxx ;
int  some_integer ;
int  SOME_INTEGER ;
int  someInteger ;
int  x2 ;
```

Although these names contain the same words, all these names are considered different names by the compiler.

The Java compiler allows short and abbreviated names, but it is better to use natural names because they increase the readability of programs.

When the compiler detects something illegal in a source program, it displays an error message on the screen. It is also possible to make errors with the names. For example, the declaration

```
int  1_larger_integer ;
```

is illegal because a digit may not start a name. The declarations

```
int  integer from keyboard ;
int  some-other-integer ;
```

are not acceptable because a name may not contain characters ' ' and '-'.

The use of space characters is important in Java programs. There must be at least one space character between a keyword and a name. For example, the variable declaration

```
intinteger_from_keyboard ;
```

would result in a compilation error because the compiler could not distinguish keyword **int** from the variable name. Generally, you do not need spaces between special characters and names, but the use of spaces makes the source code more readable. The two source code lines

```
one_larger_integer=integer_from_keyboard+1;
one_larger_integer  =  integer_from_keyboard  +  1 ;
```

are the same in technical sense but the latter is easier to read because of the use of spaces.

If you want, you may write more than one space in all those places of a Java program where spaces are allowed. In all those places where a space character is allowed, a newline character or a tabulator character is also allowed. There is a newline character at the end of every line of a Java program. When you insert empty lines in a program, you actually insert newline characters into the source program file.

When you use a long statement, it is sometimes necessary to split the statement on several source program lines. The general rule in splitting statements is that you may add a newline character to all those places where a space can be added. This means in practice that names must remain intact when a statement continues on the following line.

## 5.3 Floating-point variables

Integer variables are convenient when we want to count something. But when we want to deal with something related to the real world, integer variables are often not sufficient. To store such values as 3.1416, the value of pi, and 6,378.16, the equatorial radius of the Earth in kilometers, Java has floating-point variables. They can be declared by using keywords **float** or **double**.

Program **Miles.java** is an example that uses floating-point variables of type **float**. The program asks the user to give a distance in miles, and then converts the given distance to kilometers. Because one mile is 1.6093 kilometers, the program must use floating-point variables to make these conversions accurately. An integer variable cannot contain a value which has a decimal point.

Floating-point variables are based on the idea that every number with a decimal point can be expressed in exponential notation, a notation frequently used by scientists who make calculations with very large or very small numbers. The following are examples of numbers presented in exponential notations (* means multiplication and . is the decimal point)

| "NORMAL" NOTATION | EXPONENTIAL NOTATIONS | |
|---|---|---|
| 2,000,000,000,000 | $2.0 * 10^{12}$ | 2.0e12 |
| 299,800,000 | $2.998 * 10^{8}$ | 2.998e8 |
| 0.000,000,123 | $1.23 * 10^{-7}$ | 1.23e-7 |
| 0.000,000,000,002 | $2.0 * 10^{-12}$ | 2.0e-12 |

In exponential notation, a number is presented with two parts: a mantissa and an exponent. In the case of the first number above, the mantissa is 2.0 and the exponent is 12. The mantissa indicates "how much" the number is and the exponent tells how many times the mantissa must be multiplied by ten, or divided by ten in the case of negative exponents, to get the "normal" form of the number. The exponential notation is thus based on the fact that every number can be expressed as its "mantissa" times 10 to the power of its "exponent". Here you must again remember that 10 to the power of zero is one.

Floating-point variables store numbers in exponential notation. The mantissa and exponent are stored separately as binary numbers. A floating-point variable of type **float** occupies 4 bytes of memory, and a variable of type **double** occupies 8 bytes of memory.

The internal structure of floating-point variables is rather complex. The Java compiler uses the 32 bits of a **float** variable so that 8 bits are used to store the exponent, 23 bits are used to store the mantissa, and the remaining 1 bit is used to store the sign (plus or minus). The more precise floating-point type **double** uses more bits for the mantissa and exponent.

Usually a programmer does not need to worry about the internal structure of floating-point variables. The compiler and the computer ensure that calculations with floating-point variables are carried out in a correct manner. If we declare a floating-point variable like

```
float  a_float_variable ;
```

the compiler reserves four bytes of main memory for the variable. When we assign a value for the variable with statement

```
a_float_variable  =  12.34F ;
```

the compiler takes care that the floating-point literal constant 12.34F is converted to the exponential notation used in **float** variables, and stores the literal to the reserved four bytes for that notation. Note that the letter F must be written at the end of a literal constant of type **float**.

Here, keyword **float** is used to declare two single-precision floating-point variables. These variables can store numbers that have a decimal point.

* is the multiplication operator of Java. As one mile is 1.6093 kilometers, miles can be converted to kilometers by multiplying the distance in miles by 1.6093. After this statement has been executed, the contents of variable **distance_in_kilometers** is 1.6093 times the contents of variable **distance_in_miles**. Note that the letter F is written after the numerical digits in the literal 1.6093F. That letter indicates that the literal is of type **float**.

```
// Miles.java

import java.util.* ;

class Miles
{
   public static void main( String[] not_in_use )
   {
      Scanner keyboard = new Scanner( System.in ) ;

      float distance_in_miles ;
      float distance_in_kilometers ;

      System.out.print( "\n This program converts miles to kilometers."
                      + "\n Please, give a distance in miles:   " ) ;

      distance_in_miles    =  keyboard.nextFloat() ;

      distance_in_kilometers  =  1.6093F * distance_in_miles ;

      System.out.print( "\n "  +  distance_in_miles  +  " miles is "
                      +  distance_in_kilometers  +  " kilometers." ) ;

      System.out.printf( "\n %.3f miles is %.3f kilometers.",
                         distance_in_miles,  distance_in_kilometers ) ;
   }
}
```

Here the distance in miles is read from the keyboard with method **nextFloat()**. The program waits here until the user has typed in the distance. After this statement has been executed the given distance is stored in variable **distance_in_miles**.

These two statements print the same information to the screen. There are thus two different mechanisms for printing numerical information among textual information. In the latter statement, a printing method named **printf()** is in use, and **%.3f** marks the places where the values of the variables should be printed.

**Miles.java - 1. A program that uses floating-point variables.**

```
D:\javafiles2>java Miles

 This program converts miles to kilometers.
 Please, give a distance in miles:  250

 250.0 miles is 402.325 kilometers.
 250.000 miles is 402.325 kilometers.
```

**Miles.java - X. The execution of the program with input value 250.**

A programmer must know when to use floating-point variables instead of integer variables. Floating-point variables are often used when we are dealing with things that can be measured: distances, weights, currencies, temperatures, etc. Integer variables are used in counting. When a floating-point variable is used, the programmer needs to select the correct floating-point type. The capacities of floating-point variables are shown in Table 5-1. Generally, the type **double** is used when a high level of precision is required in calculations, but the type **float** is sufficient for many situations. The floating-point variable types **float** and **double** can also be found in other programming languages like C++ and C#.

## Precedence and associativity of operators

Operators have two fundamentally important characteristics: precedence and associativity. The precedence of an operator can be either higher, the same, or lower when compared to the precedence of another operator. Precedence means that operators having a higher precedence take effect first in a complex expression. For example, the value of the arithmetic expression 3 + 4 * 5 is 23 because the multiplication operator * takes effect first, as it has a higher precedence than operator +. If you cannot remember which operator has the higher precedence, you can always use parentheses to ensure the correct evaluation of an expression. The subexpressions in parentheses are evaluated first in a complex expression. The value of ((3 + 4) * 5) is thus 35.

The associativity of operators is a more subtle matter. The assignment operators and unary operators of Java are generally right-to-left associative and other operators are left-to-right associative. Associativity needs to be considered when two operators of the same precedence level are used in the same expression. For example, the expression 3 * 4 / 5 means (3 * 4) / 5, not 3 * (4 / 5) because the used operators have the same precedence and they are left-to-right associative. The compiler evaluates this expression from left to right. Right-to-left associativity means, for example, that in assignment operations the expression that is to the right of the assignment operator = is evaluated before carrying out the assignment.

## 5.4 Operators, assignments, and literal constants

Program **Game.java**, which we studied earlier, has the following assignment statement

```
one_larger_integer  =  integer_from_keyboard  +  1 ;
```

In this statement

- the two variable names refer to previously declared variables,
- 1 is a literal constant, or integer literal,
- + is the addition operator,
- = is the assignment operator, and
- ; terminates the entire statement.

All these separate elements of the statement are recognized and processed by the compiler. An assignment statement is executed so that what is on the right side of the assignment operator = is processed first, and then the result is assigned as a value to the left side. When a computer executes the statement above, it first calculates the value of the arithmetic expression

```
integer_from_keyboard  +  1
```

and then it assigns the result as a value to variable **`one_larger_integer`**. In an assignment operation only the left side gets a new value. The value of variable **`integer_from_keyboard`** does not change in the above statement. The variable **`one_larger_integer`** loses its previous value and gets a new value.

We have thus far encountered two arithmetic operators, the addition operator (+) and the multiplication operator (*). A new arithmetic operator, the division operator /, is used in program **Distance.java**. The program converts meters to other units of distance. For example, the conversion from meters to light years is made with the assignment statement

```
distance_in_light_years  =  distance_in_meters  /
                           ( 2.99793e8 * 365 * 24 * 3600 ) ;
```

When the computer executes this statement, it performs activities in the following order:

- It first evaluates the value of the expression 2.99793e8 * 365 * 24 * 3600 because this expression is written inside parentheses. The calculated value is 9.45427e15 which is nearly the correct value of the length of one light year in meters.
- It divides the contents of the variable **`distance_in_meters`** by the calculated value 9.45424e15. The value of **`distance_in_meters`** does not change in this operation.
- The result of the division is stored in the variable **`distance_in_light_years`** whose previous contents are overwritten. The previous contents are not important because they are what happened to be in those memory locations which were reserved for the variable.

In addition to arithmetic operators +, *, and /, Java also has the arithmetic operator - which performs subtraction operations. All these operators will be used throughout the book. All Java operators are summarized in Appendix A.

As usual, method **main()** is written inside a class. Here the name of the class is **Distance**. At this point of our studies, we write static methods inside class declarations, but we do not pay much attention to the class itself.

All values are stored in double-precision floating-point variables in this program. It is possible to declare several variables of the same type in a long declaration statement. In this declaration, variable names are separated with commas, and there is only one semicolon (;) at the end. When you declare variables in this way, you avoid repeating the type keyword, which is **double** in this case.

```
//  Distance.java  (c) Kari Laitinen

import  java.util.* ;

class Distance
{
   public static void main( String[] not_in_use )
   {
      Scanner keyboard = new Scanner( System.in ) ;

      double  distance_in_meters,  distance_in_kilometers,
              distance_in_miles,   distance_in_yards,
              distance_in_feet,    distance_in_inches ;
      double  distance_in_light_years ;

      System.out.print(
           "\n This program converts meters to other units of"
         + "\n distance. Please, enter a distance in meters:  " ) ;

      distance_in_meters   =   keyboard.nextDouble() ;

      distance_in_kilometers   =  distance_in_meters / 1000.0 ;
      distance_in_miles        =  6.21371e-4 *  distance_in_meters ;
      distance_in_yards        =  1.093613   *  distance_in_meters ;
      distance_in_feet         =  3.280840   *  distance_in_meters ;
      distance_in_inches       =  12         *  distance_in_feet ;
      distance_in_light_years  =   distance_in_meters /
                                ( 2.99793e8 * 365 * 24 * 3600 ) ;

      System.out.print( "\n " + distance_in_meters + " meters is: \n\n" ) ;

      System.out.printf( "%15.3f  kilometers\n",distance_in_kilometers) ;
      System.out.printf( "%15.3f  miles \n",  distance_in_miles ) ;
      System.out.printf( "%15.3f  yards \n",    distance_in_yards ) ;

      System.out.printf( "%15.3f  feet   \n%15.3f  inches \n",
                    distance_in_feet, distance_in_inches ) ;

      System.out.printf( "%15.5e  light years \n",
                                  distance_in_light_years) ;
   }
}
```

**Distance.java - 1.+ A program to convert meters to other units of distance.**

Assignment statements are executed so that, what is on the right side of the assignment operator = is calculated (evaluated) first, and after that the result of the calculation is copied to the variable that is on the left side of the = operator.

As one meter is 1.093613 yards, you can get the distance in yards simply by multiplying the metric distance by this literal constant. After this statement is executed, the result of the multiplication is stored in **distance_in_yards**.

```
distance_in_kilometers  =  distance_in_meters / 1000.0 ;
distance_in_miles       =  6.21371e-4  *  distance_in_meters ;
distance_in_yards       =  1.093613    *  distance_in_meters ;
distance_in_feet        =  3.280840    *  distance_in_meters ;
distance_in_inches      =  12          *  distance_in_feet ;
distance_in_light_years  =  distance_in_meters /
                         ( 2.99793e8 * 365 * 24 * 3600 ) ;
```

This literal constant, which shows the speed of light in meters per second, is a floating-point literal written in exponential notation. The same value could be written without the exponent as 299793000. No space characters are allowed in a literal constant. 2.99793  e8 would be an illegal constant.

The calculations inside parentheses are carried out before any other calculations. In this case, the length of one light year is calculated first, before it is used as a divider. In these calculations, 365 means the number of days in a year, 24 is the number of hours in each day, and 3600 is the number of seconds in every hour.

**Distance.java - 1 - 1: The assignment statements of the program.**

```
D:\javafiles2>java Distance

 This program converts meters to other units of
 distance. Please, enter a distance in meters:   40075160

 4.007516E7 meters is:

      40075.160   kilometers
      24901.542   miles
   43826715.953   yards
  131480187.934   feet
 1577762255.213   inches
    4.23884e-09   light years
```

This is the length of the equator of the Earth in meters.

**Distance.java - X. The program executed with input value 40075160.**

As you can see from the output of the program, the contents of the distance variables are printed so that, although the numbers are of various lengths, all numbers end up in the same right-hand column. This is accomplished by using the printing method **printf()** instead of the **print()** method. **printf()** is a method for formatted printing. The **printf()** method is able to use so-called format specifiers to format the output on the screen. For example, the format specifier **%15.3f** stipulates that a floating-point variable is printed to the right side of a printing field that is 15 character positions wide, and the variable is printed with such a precision that 3 digits follow the decimal point. The unused positions in the 15 character printing field are filled with spaces. The format specifiers themselves are not printed to the screen. Instead, the value of a variable is printed in that position of the text where a format specifier is written.

```
System.out.print( "\n " + distance_in_meters + " meters is: \n\n" ) ;

System.out.printf( "%15.3f  kilometers\n",distance_in_kilometers) ;
System.out.printf( "%15.3f  miles \n",    distance_in_miles ) ;
System.out.printf( "%15.3f  yards \n",    distance_in_yards ) ;

System.out.printf( "%15.3f  feet   \n%15.3f  inches \n",
                   distance_in_feet, distance_in_inches ) ;

System.out.printf( "%15.5e  light years \n",
                            distance_in_light_years) ;
```

The format specifier **%15.5e** means that the value of variable **distance_in_light_years** is shown in the exponential notation with the precision of 5 digits after the decimal point. Letter e thus indicates that exponential notation must be used. The value of the variable is output in a printing field that is 15 character positions wide.

In this statement, method **printf()** prints the contents (values) of two variables, **distance_in_feet** and **distance_in_inches**. The value of variable **distance_in_feet** is printed in the space of the first **%15.3f**, and the value of **distance_in_inches** is printed to the position of the second **%15.3f**.

**Distance.java - 1 - 2. The output statements of the program.**

## Exercises with program Distance.java

Exercise 5-3. A light year is the distance which light travels in one year. It is a huge distance. Program **Distance.java** makes a small mistake when it calculates the length of a light year because it supposes that there are exactly 365 days in a year. A more correct duration for a year is 365 days and 6 hours. Modify program **Distance.java** so that it calculates a better value for the length of a light year. Remember that those calculations which are inside parentheses are executed first.

Exercise 5-4. A furlong is a unit of distance which has been in use in some countries. 1 furlong is exactly 660 feet. Improve program **Distance.java** so that it prints the distance also in furlongs.

Programming languages have operators in order to perform various operations in a program. The term *operand* is used to describe the participants of an operation. For example, in the arithmetic operation

```
1.6093F * distance_in_miles
```

both 1.6093F and **distance_in_miles** are operands to the multiplication operator *. The value 1.6093F, which is a literal constant of type **float**, is the left operand. The variable **distance_in_miles** is the right operand. Operands can be complex expressions such as (2.99793e8 * 365 * 24 * 3600). Complex expressions themselves contain operators and operands. When a complex expression is an operand, the value of the expression is evaluated before it is used as an operand.

The numerical values that are used in programs are called literal constants or just literals in the programming terminology. Program **Distance.java** contains, for example, the literal constants

```
1000.0       6.21371e-4       1.093613
```

which are all floating-point literals because they include a decimal point. A floating-point literal represents a value that can be stored in a floating-point variable. Floating-point literals should not be assigned as values to integer variables. Integer literals such as 12, 365, and 3600 do not contain a decimal point. Usually it is possible to assign an integer literal as a value to a floating-point variable. Sometimes you may need an integer literal that is of type **long**. Such a literal can be specified by writing letter L to the end of the literal (e.g. 12345678L). As you saw in program **Miles.java**, a floating-point literal must have suffix F or f at the end before it can be assigned to a variable of type **float**.

The world of computers is a binary one. Because hexadecimal numbers are convenient to express binary quantities, numbers stored in integer variables are sometimes expressed as hexadecimal numbers. To assign hexadecimal values to variables, Java provides hexadecimal literals which are written by using the prefix 0x, a zero followed by the letter x. For example, the decimal numbers 10, 255, 258, and 65535 can be written as hexadecimal literals in the following way

```
0xA     0xFF     0x102     0xFFFF
```

The following two statements are the same from the Java compiler's point of view

```
some_variable   =  31 ;
some_variable   =  0x1F ;
```

The compiler recognizes numerical literals in program text because they start with a numerical character. To make literals different from names, Java has a rule that names may not begin with a numerical character. The letter x in a hexadecimal literal makes the compiler treat the numerical characters as hexadecimal digits. When the compiler reads a literal, it detects the end of the literal when it sees a character which is not a numerical digit. Spaces may not be used inside literals. For example, it would be an error to write

```
mean_distance_to_moon_in_kilometers   =   384 400 ;
```

because the compiler would not understand the literal as 384400 but as two separate literals 384 and 400.

Although both literals and variables represent information that is processed by the action statements of a program, a literal in a source program is a kind of opposite to a variable. The value of a literal is fixed, while the value of a variable usually changes when a program is being executed. Literals may appear only on the right side of assignment statements. The left side of an assignment statement is a variable in the programs of this chapter.

## 5.5 Reading data from the keyboard – a first look at strings

The mechanism with which the Java programs of this book read data from the keyboard is such that first a **keyboard** is declared and created with the statement

```
Scanner keyboard = new Scanner( System.in ) ;
```

When this statement is executed in a program, the name **keyboard** starts referring to an object which represents the physical keyboard of the computer. At this phase of your studies it is not necessary to understand the above statement thoroughly. The operation of the above statement becomes clear when we study objects and classes in Part III of this book.

The above statement uses a standard Java class named **Scanner**. The object referred to by the name **keyboard** is such that it can be used to scan data from the physical keyboard. **System.in** in the above statement refers to the standard input device, which is the physical keyboard. Because the **Scanner** class is declared in a package of classes named **java.util**, it is necessary to have the **import** statement

```
import  java.util.* ;
```

at the beginning of every program which uses the **Scanner** class. This statement imports to "this" program everything that belongs to the **java.util** package.

Whenever you need to read data into your own Java program from the keyboard, you can write the above two statements into the program, and the keyboard is at the disposal of your program. When the above two statements are present in your program, you can use a statement like

```
integer_from_keyboard   =  keyboard.nextInt() ;
```

to read an **int** value from the keyboard. This statement invokes a method named **nextInt()** for the defined **keyboard**. The **nextInt()** method waits until the user of the program has typed in data from the keyboard and pressed the Enter key. After the **nextInt()** method gets data from the user, it converts it to an integer value, and the integer value is stored to variable **integer_from_keyboard**.

When a numerical value is read from the keyboard, a data conversion must take place because the data from the keyboard arrives in the form of character codes. Although a method like **nextInt()** makes this conversion automatically, it is important to know that such a conversion occurs. Figure 5-3 explains how character codes are converted when the above statement is executed.

In addition to the **nextInt()** method, there exist other methods to read other types of numerical values from the keyboard. For example, to read a value of type **short**, you can first declare a variable like

```
short  a_short_variable ;
```

and then you can write the statement

```
a_short_variable  =  keyboard.nextShort() ;
```

which uses (calls) method **nextShort()** to read a value for the variable. For other numerical types, there exist methods **nextLong()**, **nextByte()**, **nextFloat()**, and **nextDouble()** which can be invoked with statements like

```
a_long_variable     =  keyboard.nextLong() ;

a_byte_variable     =  keyboard.nextByte() ;

a_float_variable    =  keyboard.nextFloat() ;

a_double_variable   =  keyboard.nextDouble() ;
```

The illustration below describes what happens when this statement is executed when the user of the program types in 556601. The program execution stays in method **nextInt()** until the user has typed in the number from the keyboard. After the **nextInt()** method has received data from the keyboard and converted it to an **int** value, the **int** value is stored to variable **integer_from_keyboard**.

```
integer_from_keyboard   =   keyboard.nextInt() ;
```

The "raw" data that is received from the keyboard is a sequence of 16-bit character codes. As we suppose that the user types in number 556601, the input from the keyboard looks like this sequence of bytes in the main memory. Here each 16-bit character code is stored in two bytes so that the more significant byte comes after the less significant byte. (In this book it is supposed that the computer in use stores bytes in this order, but not all computers use this byte order.) In every character code, the more significant byte is zero because the values of the character codes are small numbers, less than FFH. The character codes of numerical characters and other characters are presented in the table on page 594.

When the input from the keyboard is converted, and stored in **integer_from_keyboard**, it looks like this in the main memory. 556601 is 00087E39H in hexadecimal form. The least significant byte is stored first in the memory.

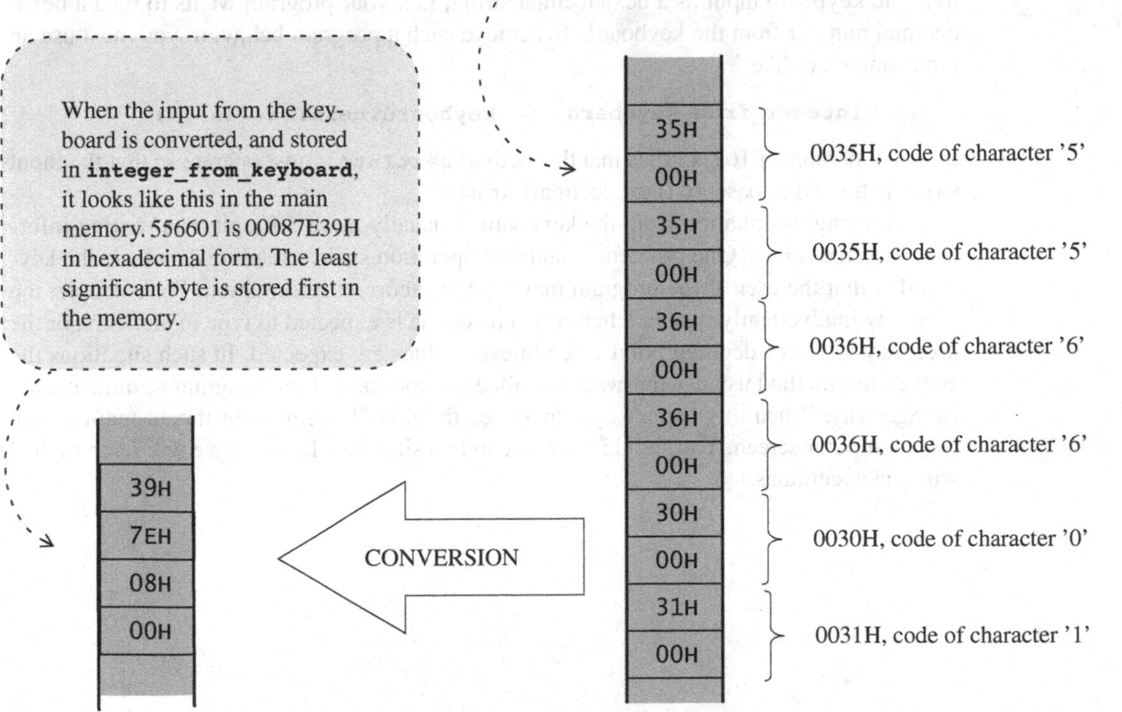


*Figure 5-3. Reading value 556601, 87E39H, from the keyboard.*

All the methods that read values for variables from the keyboard perform necessary data conversions according to the variable type in question. The methods **nextInt()**, **nextShort()**, etc., can be called **Scanner** methods because they are defined in the standard class named **Scanner**. We can use these methods although we do not yet know much about the structure of classes.

There is also a **Scanner** method named **nextLine()** with which we can read a line of text from the keyboard. To do this, we first have to declare a **String** variable with a statement like

```
String   line_of_text ;
```

After this declaration is made, we can read a line of text from the keyboard with the statement

```
line_of_text   =   keyboard.nextLine() ;
```

The **String** variables will be discussed more thoroughly in Chapter 8. **String** variables, which can store sequences of character codes, differ from the variables we have encountered so far.

The **nextLine()** method can also be used when we want to read a single character from the keyboard, i.e., when we want to get a value for a variable of type **char**. For example, if we first declare a variable like

```
char   character_from_keyboard ;
```

we can assign a value for it with the statement

```
character_from_keyboard = keyboard.nextLine().charAt( 0 ) ;
```

When this statement is executed, the **nextLine()** method first reads a line of text from the keyboard, then the **charAt()** method copies the first character from the text, and finally the code of the character is stored to variable **character_from_keyboard**. The number 0 in the above statement refers to the first character of the text line. (It is usual in the programming world to count 0, 1, 2, 3, ... instead of 1, 2, 3, 4, ...)

In some cases, when numerical values are read from the keyboard, it is necessary to treat the keyboard input as a hexadecimal string, i.e., your program wants to read a hexadecimal number from the keyboard. To achieve such a program behavior, you must use an input statement like

```
integer_from_keyboard   =   keyboard.nextInt( 16 ) ;
```

in which parameter 16 specifies that the method **nextInt()** must operate so that the input string is treated as base-16 (hexadecimal) string.

Reading information from the keyboard is usually more difficult than writing information to the screen. One problem in an input operation such as reading data from the keyboard is that the user of the program may type in incorrect information. For example, the user may inadvertently type in letters when he or she is expected to type in numbers, or the user may type in a decimal point when integer values are expected. In such situations the conversion method usually throws a so-called exception, and the program terminates in a strange way. When this happens you may see the text "Exception in thread main ..." on your computer screen. You should not panic in this situation. Later on we will learn to deal with the exceptions.

## 5.6 The double role of operator +

You have certainly learned to use the plus sign (+) when you have attended mathematics lessons at school. The statements of Java resemble mathematical notations in that the plus sign serves as the addition operator that can be used to write statements like

```
one_larger_integer  =  integer_from_keyboard  +  1 ;

sum_of_integers  =  first_integer  +  second_integer ;
```

In the case of these statements, the Java compiler detects that the plus sign is used between an integer variable and an integer literal constant, or between two integer variables, and the compiler treats the plus sign as the addition operator. Similarly, the plus sign serves as the addition operator when it is used between floating-point variables or between some other program constructs that represent numerical values.

The plus sign has also another role in Java. It can be used as a concatenation operator to link together strings of characters. Concatenation means joining two character strings to produce a single longer character string. Concatenation is needed, for example, when you want to produce several lines of text to the screen with a single call to method **System.out.print()**. In the following statement, method **System.out.print()** is called so that the string that is printed to the screen is made by concatenating three separate string literals that are written inside double quotes:

```
System.out.print(  "\n This is first line."
                +  "\n This is second line."
                +  "\n This is third line." ) ;
```

When the Java compiler processes the above statement, it detects that the plus sign is used between string literals, and therefore interprets the plus sign as the concatenation operator and not as the addition operator. In Java, a string literal such as

```
"some text"
```

is of type **String**. The double quote characters are the symbols that make the compiler to distinguish string literals from other program constructs. The double quotes do not belong to the characters of the string literals above.

When the concatenation operator (+) is used between a string literal and a variable, a conversion operation is carried out before the actual concatenation. For example, in the statement

```
System.out.print( "Number is " + some_integer ) ;
```

the concatenation operator is written between the string literal "**Number is** " and variable **some_integer**. When this statement is executed, the value of variable **some_integer** is first converted to a string of characters , and then the resulting string is joined to the string literal "**Number is** ". Figure 5-4 describes what happens in the conversion and concatenation operations.

The + operator can be used several times in a single statement. How the operator is interpreted by the compiler, depends on what is written to the left side and right side of the operator. Because the + operator is left-to-right associative, longer expressions are evaluated so that the leftmost plus sign is applied first. For example, when the expression

```
some_integer + some_integer + "xxxx" + "yyyy"
```

is processed, the leftmost plus sign is first used as an addition operator, and the sum

```
some_integer + some_integer
```

is calculated. The other two plus signs are interpreted as concatenation operators, which means that the calculated sum is converted to a string of characters, and the string literals "**xxxx**" and "**yyyy**" are joined to the calculated sum.

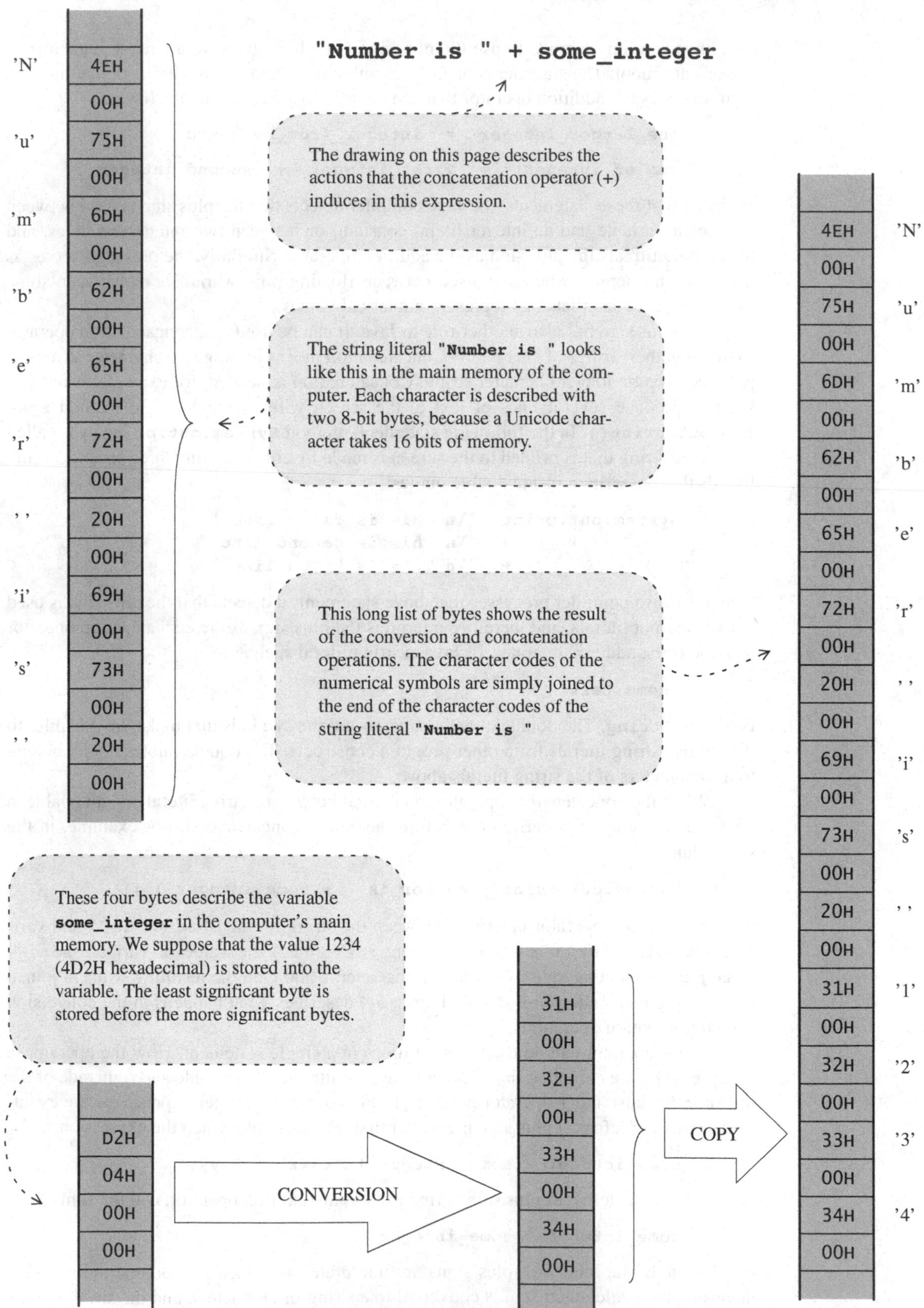


*Figure 5-4. Using the + operator between a character string and an integer variable.*

In complex expression, parentheses can be used to override the left-to-right rule. This means that what is written inside parentheses in a complex expression is evaluated before the rest of the expression. Therefore, the two expressions

```
"xxxx" + ( some_integer + some_integer ) + "yyyy"
"xxxx" + some_integer + some_integer + "yyyy"
```

are different expressions. The use of parentheses in complex expressions is often useful, even if the parentheses do not have any technical effect. For example, in the expression

```
(( some_integer + some_integer ) + "xxxx" ) + "yyyy"
```

the parentheses do not affect the evaluation of the expression, but they may clarify the expression. When there are several pairs of parentheses in an expression, the innermost pair takes effect first.

Program **Additions.java** provides example statements where the plus sign (+) is interpreted both as the concatenation operator and the addition operator. In this section we have added only integer values with the addition operator. The operator works, though, similarly with other numerical types like **`float`**, **`double`**, **`long`**, etc. Operators and expression will be further discussed in later chapters when we study some other operators of Java.

## Exercises – write some simple programs

Exercise 5-5. Write a program with which you can convert a human height given in feet and inches to centimeters. The program should ask the user to type in his or her height in two parts: first the height in feet and then the inches part for the height. There can be thus two separate input statements in the program. After the program has received the feet and the inches, it should calculate the corresponding value in centimeters and print it to the screen. The following data should be useful: 1 foot is 30.48 centimeters, 1 inch is 2.54 centimeters, and 1 foot is 12 inches.

Exercise 5-6. Write a program that inputs the height of a person in centimeters and converts it to light years. One light year is the distance that light travels in one year. The speed of light is 2.99793e8 meters per second.

Exercise 5-7. There are two common systems for measuring temperature. Degrees of Fahrenheit (ºF) are used in the U.S. and some other countries, while degrees of Celsius (ºC) are in use in most European countries and in many countries throughout the world. The freezing point of water is 0 degrees Celsius and 32 degrees Fahrenheit, 10ºC is 50ºF, 20ºC is 68ºF, 30ºC is 86ºF, and so on. You can see that 10 degrees on the Celsius scale corresponds to 18 degrees on the Fahrenheit scale. Write a program that can convert degrees Fahrenheit to degrees Celsius, or vice versa.

When you are doing the programming exercises, it is very likely that you encounter various kinds of problems. In these situations, Appendix C can be helpful.

The + operator works as an addition operator only when there is a numerical value, numerical expression, or a variable on both sides of the operator. In this statement, the + operator in the middle is between two integer variables, but because the leftmost + operator is applied first, the left side of the + operator in the middle becomes a string of characters, and therefore all plus signs are treated as concatenation operators.

```
//  Additions.java

class Additions
{
   public static void main( String[] not_in_use )
   {
      int  some_integer  =  1234 ;

      System.out.print( "\n " ) ;
      System.out.print( "xxxx" + some_integer + "zzzz" ) ;
      System.out.print( "\n " ) ;
      System.out.print( "xxxx" + some_integer + some_integer + "zzzz" ) ;
      System.out.print( "\n " ) ;
      System.out.print( "xxxx" + ( some_integer + some_integer ) + "zzzz" ) ;
      System.out.print( "\n " ) ;
      System.out.print( some_integer + some_integer + "xxxx" + "zzzz" ) ;
      System.out.print( "\n " ) ;
      System.out.print( some_integer + ( some_integer + "xxxx" ) + "zzzz" ) ;
      System.out.print( "\n " ) ;
      System.out.print( "xxxx" + "zzzz" + some_integer + ( some_integer + 1));
      System.out.print( "\n " ) ;
      System.out.print( "xxxx" + "zzzz" + some_integer + some_integer + 1 ) ;
   }
}
```

The general rule in Java is that, what is written inside parentheses, is executed before other stuff in a statement. As the arithmetic expression

`( some_integer + some_integer )`

is inside parentheses in this statement, it is evaluated before other parts of the statement. Because the plus sign is between two integer variables in the above expression, the + operator is interpreted as an addition operator.

**Additions.java - 1. Demonstrating the use of the + operator.**

```
D:\javafiles2>java Additions

 xxxx1234zzzz
 xxxx12341234zzzz
 xxxx2468zzzz
 2468xxxxzzzz
 12341234xxxxzzzz
 xxxxzzzz12341235
 xxxxzzzz123412341
```

**Additions.java - X. The output of the program is always the same.**

## 5.7 Formatting the output on the screen

Programs output numbers and text to the screen. It is often necessary to format the output so that what is presented on the screen is legible to the user of the program. When you want to format the output, you should use the method **System.out.printf()** instead of the simpler **System.out.print()** method. In this section we'll examine some of the formatting mechanisms provided by the **System.out.printf()** method. At this point it is not absolutely necessary that you learn to use all the formatting mechanisms. You can, however, return to this section later if you want to know more about formatting.

The **System.out.printf()** method works so that usually several parameters are supplied to it inside parentheses. The first parameter is a string literal, a sequence of characters given inside double quotation marks. The rest of the parameters are usually names of variables. Parameters are separated with commas.

When the **System.out.printf()** method is used to print the value of a single integer variable, it can be invoked (called) in the following way

```
System.out.printf( "The value is %d.", some_integer ) ;
```

This statement would print

```
The value is 112.
```

if the value of **some_integer** were 112. The **printf()** method thus inserts the value of the variable to that position in the text where **%d** is written. **%d** is a format specifier that itself is not printed. Instead, a format specifier dictates the position where a value of a variable should be printed. In addition, a format specifier can tell the **printf()** method how the value of the variable should appear on the screen.

It is possible to use several format specifiers, and thereby print the values of several variables, in a single call to method **System.out.printf()**. For example, the statement

```
System.out.printf( "The values are %d and %d.",
                   some_integer, some_other_integer ) ;
```

would print

```
The values are 112 and 622.
```

if variables **some_integer** and **some_other_integer** had values 112 and 622, respectively. The above statement works as follows: the value of the first variable following the text given inside the double quotation marks is inserted into the text position of the first **%d**, while the value of the second variable goes to the position of the second **%d**.

Program **Formatting.java** shows different ways for printing an integer variable with format specifiers. In program **Distance.java** we saw how floating-point variables can be printed in certain format. There exist the following general rules for writing format specifiers:

- The percent sign **%** in the character string that is supplied to the **printf()** method marks the beginning of a format specifier.
- A letter at the end of a format specifier marks the type of data that is being printed (e.g., **d** means integers in the decimal numbering system and **f** means floating-point values.)
- Numbers and other characters between the percent sign and the last letter define printing fields and provide other formatting information. A format specifier (e.g. **%d**) can be written without any other characters between the percent sign and the last letter.
- By adding markings like **1$**, **2$**, **3$**, etc., after the percent sign it is possible to specify which parameter is referred to by a format specifier, and a single parameter can be printed several times. For example, the statement

The value of **some_integer** is printed here according to the format specifier **%9d** which means that the value of the variable is printed right-justified to a printing field that is 9 character positions wide. A minus sign (-) specifies left justified printing, a missing minus sign specifies right-justified printing.

```
//  Formatting.java

import  java.util.* ;

class Formatting
{
   public static void main( String[] not_in_use )
   {
      int  some_integer  =  123456 ;

      System.out.print(  "\n 12345678901234567890 \n" ) ;

      System.out.printf( "\n %9d   right justified",  some_integer ) ;
      System.out.printf( "\n %-9d   left justified",   some_integer ) ;
      System.out.printf( "\n %9X   right hexadecimal", some_integer ) ;
      System.out.printf( "\n %-9X   left hexadecimal", some_integer ) ;
      System.out.printf( "\n %d  no printing field",  some_integer ) ;
      System.out.printf( "\n %X  hexadecimal uppercase", some_integer ) ;
      System.out.printf( "\n %x  hexadecimal lowercase", some_integer ) ;
      System.out.printf( "\n %012d  leading zeroes", some_integer ) ;
      System.out.printf( "\n %012X  hexadecimal",  some_integer ) ;
      System.out.printf( "\n %,d  digit grouping", some_integer ) ;
      System.out.print( "\n" ) ;

      Formatter text_to_print  =  new  Formatter() ;

      text_to_print.format( "\n %9d   right justified", some_integer ) ;
      System.out.print( text_to_print ) ;

      String another_text_to_print  =
             String.format( "\n %09d  leading zeroes", some_integer ) ;
      System.out.print( another_text_to_print ) ;

      another_text_to_print  =  "SOME TEXT" ;
      System.out.printf( "\n %s is a string.", another_text_to_print ) ;
      System.out.printf( "\n %c is a character.", 'k' ) ;
   }
}
```

These program lines demonstrate that the format specifiers can also be used with methods other than the **printf()** method. The **String.format()** method will be useful when you learn to use strings in your programs. (You do not need to understand these lines when you are still studying the first chapters of this book.)

**%s** is the format specifier used to print texts stored in **String** objects. With the format specifier **%c** it is possible to print single characters.

**Formatting.java - 1. Demonstrating the use of format specifiers.**

```
D:\javafiles2>java Formatting

 12345678901234567890

     123456  right justified
 123456      left justified
      1E240  right hexadecimal
 1E240       left hexadecimal
 123456  no printing field
 1E240  hexadecimal uppercase
 1e240  hexadecimal lowercase
 000000123456  leading zeroes
 00000001E240  hexadecimal
 123,456  digit grouping

     123456    right justified
 000123456   leading zeroes
 SOME TEXT is a string.
 k is a character.
```

When the value of a variable is printed to a printing field, it can be justified either right or left. This means usually that either the left side or the right side of the printing field is unused and filled with space characters.

Hexadecimal numbers can be printed in two different ways, either so that uppercase letters (A,B,C,D,E,F) or lowercase letters (a,b,c,d,e,f) are used as hexadecimal digits. Lowercase hexadecimal digits can be selected by putting lowercase x instead of uppercase X to the format specifier.

A number can be printed so that its digits are grouped into groups of three digits. Here the digit groups are separated with commas because the computer on which this program was executed was set to use U.S. number formats. If your computer's location information is set to an European country, it is likely that digits are separated by periods, and comma is used as decimal point.

**Formatting.java - X. Using printing fields, leading zeroes, etc.**

```
System.out.printf( "%1$d is %1$d, but %1$d is not %2$d",
                   some_integer, some_other_integer ) ;
```

would print

```
112 is 112, but 112 is not 622
```

if variables **some_integer** and **some_other_integer** had values 112 and 622, respectively. **1$** in the format specifiers refers to the first variable after the text, and **2$** refers to the second variable after the text. Hence, the value of **some_integer** is printed three times, whereas the value of **some_other_integer** is printed only once.

The **System.out.printf()** method is indeed a very powerful method. Here I have explained only the most common ways to use it. The most common letters and other characters used in format specifiers are summarized in Table 5-2. If you want to get more information about formatting with the format specifiers, you should read the electronic Java documentation about the standard Java class **Formatter**.

It may be difficult to learn to use the format specifiers by just reading these pages. One way to better understand the operation of the format specifiers and other things in programming is to write small test programs. You could, for example, make small modifications to program **Formatting.java** in order to discover how the formatting mechanisms work.

**Table 5-2. Letters and other codes used in format specifiers.**

| Letter or character | Effect on output |
|---|---|
| **d** | Letter d means that an integer value will be shown in the decimal numbering system. When a number precedes letter d, the number specifies a printing field of certain width. For example, **%9d** specifies right-justified printing, **%-9d** specifies left-justified printing, and **%09d** specifies printing with leading zeroes. |
| **X** | Letter X indicates that integers must be printed in the hexadecimal numbering system. For example, the specifier **%04X** means that an integer must be shown in hexadecimal form in a printing field of 4 character positions wide, and the unused positions of the printing field are filled with zeroes. If the integer value does not fit to the specified printing field, the printing field is automatically enlarged. The value 1234 would be printed 04D2 with the format specifier **%04X**. |
| **x** | Letter x functions just as X, except that with letter x it is possible to print hexadecimal numbers so that the lowercase letters a, b, c, d, e, and f are used as hexadecimal symbols instead of the uppercase letters A,B,C,D,E, and F. Thus, the hexadecimal number 4FFE would be printed 004ffe if **%06x** were in use. |
| **f** | Letter f specifies that a floating-point value must be shown in fixed point form. It is possible to specify a printing field for a floating-point value as well as how many digits should follow the decimal point. The desired number of digits is written after a period. For example, with specifier **%.4f** the value 123.456 is shown as 123.4560 (four digits after the decimal point) and with specifier **%012.4f** it would be shown as 0000123.4560 (in a printing field of 12 positions; unused positions filled with zeroes). |

**Table 5-2. Letters and other codes used in format specifiers.**

| Letter or character | Effect on output |
|---|---|
| `e` | Letter e specifies that a number must be printed in exponential form. Sometimes the exponential form is called the scientific form. If you specify **`%.5e`**, a number like 123.456 appears 1.23456e+02.The desired number of digits after the decimal point is written after a period. |
| `E` | Letter E functions in the same way as letter e. The difference is that numbers specified with the letter E are formatted so that an uppercase E is shown in the exponential number (e.g. 1.23456E+02). |
| `g` | Letter g can be used to print floating-point numbers so that a suitable notation (the fixed-point notation or the exponential notation) is selected automatically according to the numerical value being printed. |
| `c` | Letter c can be used to print a single character, a value of type **`char`**. |
| `s` | Traditionally, letter s is used to print strings of characters, i.e., those character sequences that are stored in **`String`** objects or given inside double quotation marks. Letter s can, however, be used to print all objects for which either **`formatTo()`** or **`toString()`** method is provided. As we shall learn later on, a **`toString()`** method is available for all objects, and, therefore, all objects can be printed with letter s. |
| `t` | Letter t, or an uppercase T, is used to print time-related information. Actually, to get working format specifiers for time-related information, t has to be used with other letters. For example, **`%tT`** prints time in 24-hour format and **`%tF`** prints a date in YYYY-MM-DD format. (See program **Showtime.java** for more information.) |
| `0 (zero)` | By adding 0 (a zero) before the number that specifies a printing field, you can dictate that the unused positions of the printing field are filled with zeroes. If you use a format specifier like **`%06d`** instead of **`%6d`**, the unused positions of the printing field of 6 positions are filled with zeroes instead of space characters. |
| `-` | Printing-fields are used by default so that what is printed is put to the rightmost positions of the printing field, and the positions on the left are filled with space characters or zeroes. This means right-justified printing. When the hyphen sign (-) is added to a format specifier, it is possible to specify left-justified printing. |
| `,` | By using a comma in a format specifier, the digits of a number can be printed so that they are arranged into groups of three digits. For example, the value 1234567.89 might look like 1,234,567.890 when the format specifier **`%,.3f`** is used. Numbers can be grouped in different ways, depending on the settings of the computer being used. In the United States, the decimal point is the full stop and a comma is used to separate digits, but in many European countries these characters are used in the opposite way, i.e., the comma is the European decimal point. |
| `%` | The percent sign marks the beginning of a format specifier. Because % is a special character in format specifiers, and format specifiers themselves are not printed, there must be a special way to print the percent sign. The rule is that you have to write **`%%`** when you want to print %. |

## How a compiler "sees" a source program

Although the discussion below is somewhat inaccurate, it may help you to better understand the nature of source programs and the process of compilation. For us source programs are readable texts, but compilers treat them in a very technical manner. To examine the process of compilation, let's consider the following short Java program:

```
//  SomeProgram.java

class SomeProgram
{
   public static void main( String[] not_in_use )
   {
      int some_variable  = 9 ;

      System.out.print( "The value is " + some_variable ) ;
   }
}
```

Let's suppose that this program is placed in a file named **SomeProgram.java**, and the Java compiler is activated to compile the program in the file. When the compiler starts processing this file, it starts reading the characters of the program text from the beginning of the file. The compiler reads the characters of the program text line by line, continuing the reading process towards the end of the file. During this process, the compiler makes various decisions, and finally it produces an executable form of the program.

Although the compiler is just an executable computer program that does not see or taste anything, we can imagine that the compiler would "see" the above program in the following form:

```
0D 0A
2F 2F 20 20 53 6F 6D 65 50 72 6F 67 72 61 6D 2E 6A 61 76 61 0D 0A
0D 0A
63 6C 61 73 73 20 53 6F 6D 65 50 72 6F 67 72 61 6D 0D 0A
7B 0D 0A
20 20 20 70 75 62 6C 69 63 20 73 74 61 74 69 63 20 76 6F 69 64 20 6D ... 0D 0A
20 20 20 7B 0D 0A
20 20 20 20 20 20 69 6E 74 20 73 6F 6D 65 5F 76 61 72 69 61 62 6C 65 ... 0D 0A
0D 0A
20 20 20 20 20 20 53 79 73 74 65 6D 2E 6F 75 74 2E 70 72 69 6E 74 28 ... 0D 0A
20 20 20 7D 0D 0A
7D 0D 0A
```

The characters of the program are written above as hexadecimal character codes. (I do not use here the letter H to indicate that the numbers are hexadecimal.) You can find the codes of the characters in the table on page 594. The three dots `...` mean that all codes of the line in question are not shown. As is usual in the example programs in this book, there is an empty, textless, line at the beginning of the source program file. The compiler would thus first see the character codes 0D and 0A, and it would take no action because these are the line termination characters in (Windows) text files, and in this case they indicate an empty line. Empty lines are insignificant in Java programs.

Then the compiler would find the character codes 2F and 2F which are the character codes of the slash character /. The compiler would determine that this is the beginning of a comment line, and it would read and ignore characters until it finds the following line termination characters 0D and 0A. After processing the comment, the compiler would again find the character codes 0D and 0A and ignore the empty line.

Then the compiler would find the character code 63, the code of the lowercase letter c. Now the compiler would think that either the beginning of a name or the beginning of a reserved keyword has been found. The compiler would start reading the subsequent character codes until it finds a character that terminates a name. It would read the character codes 6C, 61, 73, and 73, the codes of letters l, a, s, and s. Then it would read the character code 20, the code of the space character, and it would think that the end of the name has been found since the space character is among the characters that cannot belong to a name. The compiler would think that the character codes 63, 6C, 61, 73, and 73 form a name or a keyword. It would not yet know whether this is a name or a keyword. Therefore, the compiler would compare the found name to the character codes in its internal list of keywords, and it would discover that the found character codes match with the keyword **`class`**. (The compiler might think that this is so far a valid Java program as the **`class`** keyword can start a Java program.)

*(This box continues on the following page)*

## 5.8 Chapter summary

At this point you should have learned the basic structure of Java source programs. You have studied programs that perform simple calculations, output text and contents of variables to the screen, and input numerical values from the keyboard. You have seen how different kinds of variables can be declared, and how assignment statements work. In general, we can say that Java source programs consist of

- reserved keywords such as **`int`**, **`long`**, and **`double`**
- names invented by the programmer (e.g. **`integer_from_keyboard`**)
- names of standard classes (e.g. **`System`** and **`Scanner`** )
- names of standard methods (e.g. **`print`**, **`printf`**, and **`nextInt`** )
- operators such as =, +, -, *, and /
- strings of characters for output (e.g. "**`\n Type in a number:  `**")
- numerical literals like 3600 and 2.99793e8
- pairs of braces { } and parentheses ( )
- commas (,) and semicolons (;)

### How a compiler "sees" a source program *(Continued)*

The compilation would continue this way so that the file being compiled would be examined character by character. Compilation is actually a process that consists of several phases. During the first phase, which is called the lexical analysis, the compiler identifies program elements such as names, keywords, literals, operators, parentheses, braces, brackets, commas, and semicolons.

In the later phases of compilation, the compiler actually examines how various program elements are used, and produces an executable program that corresponds to the source program. The compiler stops the compilation process and displays error messages if it finds out that the program being compiled is not written according to the rules of the programming language.

# CHAPTER 6

## DECISIONS AND REPETITIONS: BASIC ACTIVITIES IN PROGRAMS

So far, our programs have been made of statements that declare variables, assignment statements, input statements, and output statements. Assignment statements, which we studied in the previous chapter, are fundamentally important action statements in computer programs. With an assignment statement, we can copy the contents of one variable into another variable, or we can produce a new value for a variable by inserting an arithmetic expression to the right side of an assignment operation. Assignment statements always write to a location in the main memory of a computer.

In this chapter, we will study more fundamental statements used in computer programming. You will learn to write statements that make decisions (selections) and perform repetitions. Decisions made in a program result in some statements being executed and others not being executed. Performing repetitions means that one or more statements can be executed many times. Java provides **`if`** and **`switch`** statements for making decisions, and **`while`**, **`for`**, and **`do-while`** statements for performing repetitions. In this book, **`if`** statements are usually called **`if`** constructs, and **`while`**, **`for`**, and **`do-while`** statements are called loops.

## 6.1 Making decisions with keywords if and else

The word "if" in our natural language expresses a condition. We can say: "If the weather is warm and sunny tomorrow, let's go to the beach." The word "if" is used in a similar way in Java. **`if`** is a keyword that identifies the basic decision-making mechanism of Java.

**`if`** statements, which we often call **`if`** constructs, are used to make decisions in Java. The structure of the simplest **`if`** construct is described in Figure 6-1. An **`if`** construct always contains a *boolean expression* that can be either true or false. Boolean expressions are named after George Boole (1815 - 1864) whose ideas have deeply influenced computing and programming.

Boolean expressions define conditions. In **`if`** constructs, the boolean expression is given in parentheses ( ) after the keyword **`if`**. Every boolean expression has a truth value which is always either true or false, but not both. Provided that the boolean expression is true, the statements inside the braces { } after the boolean expression will be executed. If the boolean expression is false (i.e. not true), the statements inside the braces will not be executed, and the execution of the program continues from the statement that follows the closing brace of the **`if`** construct.

```
if  ( boolean expression  )
{
      One or more statements that will be executed if the boolean
      expression, given in parentheses above, is true. These statements
      will not be executed at all if the boolean expression  is false (i.e.
      not true).
}
```

*Figure 6-1. The structure of a simple if construct*

```
if  ( boolean expression  )
{
      One or more statements that will be executed if the boolean
      expression, given in parentheses above, is true.
}
else
{
      One or more statements that will be executed if the boolean
      expression, given in parentheses above, is false (i.e. not true).
}
```

*Figure 6-2. The structure of an if-else construct*

A more advanced form of **`if`** statement is an **`if-else`** construct which contains two Java keywords, **`if`** and **`else`**. The structure of **`if-else`** construct is explained in Figure 6-2. The **`if-else`** construct has two blocks of statements, and only one block of statements will be executed. When one or more statements are inside braces { }, we can call the group of statements an embraced block of statements, or simply a block. In **`if-else`** constructs, depending on the truth value of the boolean expression, either the first block of statements or the second block, but never both, will be executed. The **`if-else`** construct thus makes a decision as to which program block will be executed.

Program **Largeint.java** is an example where two decisions are made with keywords **`if`** and **`else`**. The first decision is made with an **`if-else`** construct. The second decision is made with a simple **`if`** construct. The program is able to find the largest of three integers that the user types in from the keyboard. First the program decides which is larger of the first two integers. Then it decides whether the third integer is larger than the largest of the first two integers.

Boolean expressions have a truth value, either true or false. To write a boolean expression we need operators that can describe situations that are either true or false. Relational operators, which are listed in Table 6-1, are common in boolean expressions. In program **Largeint.java**, the relational operator < is used in the boolean expression

```
( first_integer  <  second_integer )
```

to test whether it is true that the value of the variable **`first_integer`** is less than the value of the variable **`second_integer`**. A common use for relational operators is to compare values of variables, but relational operators can also take numerical values as operands. For example, the boolean expression

```
( some_variable   ==   0 )
```

tests whether the contents of **`some_variable`** is zero. If the contents of **`some_variable`** is zero, then the expression above is true, otherwise it is false. Because relational operators compare variables and other values, they are also called comparison operators.

Operator ==, like most of the relational operator symbols, consists of two characters. There should be no spaces between the two characters. Writing, for example, = = will result in a compilation error. The compiler would interpret the two equal signs separated with a space as two adjacent assignment operators.

## Table 6-1: The relational operators of Java

| Operator symbol | Operator name |
|---|---|
| < | less than |
| <= | less than or equal |
| > | greater than |
| >= | greater than or equal |
| == | equal |
| != | not equal |

This program shows that variable declarations do not need to be the first statements of a program. This statement, which is written after a couple of action statements, both declares a variable of type **int** and assigns a value to the declared variable by reading a value from the keyboard. By using these kinds of statements it is possible to make programs somewhat shorter. This single statement means the same as the two statements

```
int first_integer ;
first_integer = keyboard.nextInt();
```

```
// Largeint.java

import java.util.* ;

class Largeint
{
   public static void main( String[] not_in_use )
   {
      Scanner keyboard = new Scanner( System.in ) ;

      System.out.print( "\n This program can find the largest of three"
                      + "\n integers you enter from the keyboard. "
                      + "\n Please, enter three integers separated "
                      + "\n with spaces : " ) ;

      int first_integer    =  keyboard.nextInt() ;
      int second_integer   =  keyboard.nextInt() ;
      int third_integer    =  keyboard.nextInt() ;

      int found_largest_integer ;

      if ( first_integer  >  second_integer )
      {
         found_largest_integer  =  first_integer ;
      }
      else
      {
         found_largest_integer  =  second_integer ;
      }

      if ( third_integer  >  found_largest_integer )
      {
         found_largest_integer  =  third_integer ;
      }

      System.out.print( "\n The largest integer is "
                      +  found_largest_integer  +  ".\n" ) ;
   }
}
```

This is the simplest form of an **if** construct, containing only the keyword **if**. If the contents of **third_integer** is greater than the contents of **found_largest_integer**, the contents of variable **third_integer** will be copied to variable **found_largest_integer**.

This is an **if-else** construct. If the contents of **first_integer** is greater than the contents of **second_integer**, the contents of **first_integer** will be copied to **found_largest_integer**. Otherwise, the contents of **second_integer** will be copied to **found_largest_integer**.

**Largeint.java - 1.+ A program to find the largest of three integers.**

The relational operator >, greater than, is used to define a boolean expression which determines which variable shall be copied to **found_largest_integer**.

Note that there are no semicolons (;) following the boolean expressions of **if** constructs.

```
if ( first_integer  >  second_integer )
{
   found_largest_integer  =  first_integer ;
}
else
{
   found_largest_integer  =  second_integer ;
}

if ( third_integer  >  found_largest_integer )
{
   found_largest_integer  =  third_integer ;
}
```

**Largeint.java - 1-1. The if constructs that find the largest integer.**

```
D:\javafiles2>java Largeint

 This program can find the largest of three
 integers you enter from the keyboard.
 Please, enter three integers separated
 with spaces :   111 222 211

 The largest integer is 222.
```

**Largeint.java - X. The program finds 222 to be the largest of 111, 222, and 211.**

Program **Evenodd.java** is another example of the use of an **`if-else`** construct. This program asks the user to type in an integer, and it decides whether the given integer is an even or odd number. Because even numbers are equally divisible by two, the **`if-else`** construct in the program **Evenodd.java** simply tests whether it is true that if the given number divided by two would result in a zero remainder. The boolean expression in **Evenodd.java** is

```
( ( integer_from_keyboard  %  2 )   ==   0 )
```

and it contains the arithmetic expression (**`integer_from_keyboard`** % 2). The % operator is an arithmetic operator belonging to the same category as +, -, *, and /. Operator % returns the remainder that would result if its left operand were divided by its right operand. In the expression above, % returns the remainder that would result if the value of variable **`integer_from_keyboard`** were divided by two. The value of the variable is not modified. In the above expression the remainder is calculated first and then the remainder is compared to zero. The relational comparison operator returns true when the remainder is zero. Otherwise it returns false.

When integers are divided by two, the remainder is always zero or one, depending on whether the integer is even or odd. As there are only two possible values for the remainder in divisions by two, the boolean expression

```
( ( integer_from_keyboard  %  2 )   !=   1 )
```

could replace the boolean expression used in the program **Evenodd.java** and the program would work equally well. Operator != returns true when its operands are not equal. Boolean expressions can often be written either with operator == (equal) or with operator != (not equal). When possible, it is better to use operator ==, because it is usually easier to understand.

## The remainder operator %

The remainder operator %, which is sometimes called the modulus operator, is used with integers only. Division operations with integers are sometimes inaccurate because computers do not round numbers upwards. For example, the division operation 11/4, eleven divided by four, would be evaluated to 2 although 3 would be closer to the correct value. Computers do not obey human division rules. In division operations involving integers, computers always round downwards. For this reason, the remainder operator % is sometimes useful. To understand operators / and % properly, below are some correct calculations for you to study.

```
1 / 2  is  0              1 % 2  is  1
2 / 2  is  1              2 % 2  is  0
7 / 4  is  1              7 % 4  is  3
9 / 4  is  2              9 % 4  is  1
14 / 5  is  2             14 % 5  is  4
101 / 10 is 10            101 % 10 is 1
```

This program is based on the fact that even numbers are equally divisible by two. ( **integer_from_keyboard** % 2) is an arithmetic expression that is part of the boolean expression of this **if** construct. % is the remainder operator of Java. In this case, % returns the remainder that would result if **integer_from_keyboard** were divided by two. With even numbers the remainder is zero, making the boolean expression true.

```
//  Evenodd.java   (c) Kari Laitinen

import java.util.* ;

class Evenodd
{
   public static void main( String[] not_in_use )
   {
      Scanner keyboard = new Scanner( System.in ) ;

      int  integer_from_keyboard ;

      System.out.print( "\n This program can find out whether an integer"
                     +  "\n is even or odd. Please, enter an integer: " ) ;

      integer_from_keyboard  =  keyboard.nextInt() ;

      if ( ( integer_from_keyboard  %  2 )  ==  0 )
      {
         System.out.print( "\n " + integer_from_keyboard + " is even.\n") ;
      }
      else
      {
         System.out.print( "\n " + integer_from_keyboard + " is odd. \n") ;
      }
   }
}
```

This statement will be executed when the boolean expression, given in parentheses after the keyword **if**, is false.

**Evenodd.java - 1. A program to find out whether a given integer is even or odd.**

```
D:\javafiles2>java Evenodd

 This program can find out whether an integer
 is even or odd. Please, enter an integer: 12345

 12345 is odd.
```

**Evenodd.java - X. The program executed with input value 12345.**

In most cases, there is no single way to write a computer program to accomplish the desired program behavior and functionality. This is generally true also for boolean expressions. For example, all the following boolean expressions mean the same

```
( first_integer  <  second_integer )
( second_integer  >  first_integer )
( ( second_integer - first_integer )  >  0 )
( ( first_integer  -  second_integer )  <  0 )
( ( first_integer + 1 )  <=  second_integer )
```

It is, however, good programming practice to try to write simple, non-complex, and elegant programs. For this reason, the last three boolean expressions would not be appropriate choices because they are made unnecessarily complex by using arithmetic operators.

Figure 6-3 shows the structure of a large **if** construct, the **if-else if-else** construct. Such a construct consists of three parts: an **if** part, an **else if** part, and an **else** part. Each part contains an embraced program block. The execution of the program blocks is controlled by two boolean expressions. To be accurate, the program construct described in Figure 6-3 actually consists of two **if-else** constructs. The **else-if** part starts the second **if-else** construct. The second **else-if** construct does not have any braces around itself. You will understand this more clearly when the use of braces in Java program constructs is discussed in more detail in Section 6.6.

The **if** structure explained in Figure 6-3 is used in program **Likejava.java**. The **if-else if-else** construct selects one of three program blocks to be executed. It is possible to write even more complex **if** constructs by adding more **else if** parts between the **if** part and **else** part. Program **Iffing.java** is an example where three **else if** parts are used in a single **if** construct. In summary, we can state the following facts about **if** constructs:

- Every **if** construct contains an **if** part.
- **if** constructs can contain zero, one, or more **else if** parts.
- **if** constructs contain zero or one **else** parts.

```
if ( boolean expression 1 )
{
     One or more statements that will be executed if and only if
     boolean expression 1 is true.
}
else if ( boolean expression 2 )
{
     One or more statements that will be executed if and only if
     boolean expression 2 is true and boolean expression 1 is false.
}
else
{
     One or more statements that will be executed if and only if
     neither boolean expression 1 nor boolean expression 2 is true.
}
```

***Figure 6-3. The structure of an if-else if-else construct.***

Both programs **Likejava.java** and **Iffing.java** investigate what is the character code of the character that the user typed in from the keyboard. Character coding systems were discussed in Chapter 3. Java uses a character coding system called Unicode in which each character is coded with a 16-bit value. In practice, however, the character codes of the English characters as well as many other European characters can be expressed with 8 bits, and the 8 most significant bits of these character codes are zeroes. In Java, single quotes are used to refer to the character codes of characters. For example,

`'Y'` means the character code of Y (89, 59H)

`'n'` means the character code of n (110, 6EH)

`'9'` means the character code of 9 (57, 39H)

`' '` means the character code of space (32, 20H)

By using single quotes it is possible to refer to a character code without remembering the numerical value of the character code. When 'Y' appears in a program, it means the same as the numerical literal constant 89, the character code of uppercase letter Y. For a Java compiler, the relational expression

```
( character_from_keyboard  ==  'Y' )
```

and the relational expression

```
( character_from_keyboard  ==  89 )
```

are technically the same, but for a human reader they are different and the first form is easier to understand. It is difficult to remember the character codes of all characters. Therefore, the meaning of 'Y' is easier to grasp than the meaning of 89. In the terminology of programming languages, characters inside single quotes, such as 'Y', 'n', '9', and ' ', are called character literals. In addition to character literals, we also need string literals like "Hello!" in our programs. In Java, character literals are written with single quotes and string literals are written with double quotes.

Programs **Likejava.java** and **Iffing.java** introduce new operators called logical operators. These operators can combine several relational expressions into a single boolean expression. For example, in the boolean expression

```
( ( character_from_keyboard  ==  'Y' )  ||
  ( character_from_keyboard  ==  'y' )  )
```

the logical-OR operator || combines two relational expressions. The logical-OR operator || returns true if either or both of its operands, the relational expressions, are true. The logical-OR returns false only when both of its operands are false. The truth value of the boolean expression above is evaluated so that the truth values of the relational expressions are evaluated first, and these truth values are then joined with the logical-OR operator ||. If the contents of variable **`character_from_keyboard`** were 121, which is 'y', the relational expressions would have the following truth values

```
( character_from_keyboard  ==  'Y' )     would be false
( character_from_keyboard  ==  'y' )     would be true
```

The truth value of the entire boolean expression would be true because the logical-OR operation result for false and true is true. (To be accurate, the logical-OR operator || works so that it does not check the truth value of its second operand if its first operand makes the entire boolean expression true.)

This statement reads a value for the **char** variable **character_from_keyboard**. This is achieved by first reading a line of text from the keyboard, and then using the **charAt()** method to take the first character of the text line.

'Y' is a character literal which means 59H, the character code of uppercase letter Y. Single quotes are used to write character literals in Java. Character literals are sometimes called character constants or literal character constants.

```
// Likejava.java (c) Kari Laitinen

import java.util.* ;

class Likejava
{
   public static void main( String[] not_in_use )
   {
      Scanner keyboard = new Scanner( System.in ) ;

      char character_from_keyboard ;

      System.out.print( "\n Do you like the Java programming language?"
                      + "\n Please, answer Y or N :  " ) ;

      character_from_keyboard = keyboard.nextLine().charAt( 0 ) ;

      if ( ( character_from_keyboard == 'Y' ) ||
           ( character_from_keyboard == 'y' ) )
      {
         System.out.print( "\n That's nice to hear. \n" ) ;
      }
      else if ( ( character_from_keyboard == 'N' ) ||
                ( character_from_keyboard == 'n' ) )
      {
         System.out.print( "\n That is not so nice to hear. "
                         + "\n I hope you change your mind soon.\n" ) ;
      }
      else
      {
         System.out.print( "\n I do not understand \""
                         + character_from_keyboard + "\".\n" ) ;
      }
   }
}
```

This statement will be executed if **character_from_keyboard** contains something other than 'Y', 'y', 'N', or 'n'. Note that if you want to include a double quote character (") among the text to be printed, you must write a backslash \ before it.

This boolean expression is true if **character_from_keyboard** contains either the character code for uppercase N or lowercase n. || is the logical-OR operator which can combine relational expressions.

**Likejava.java - 1.+ A program containing an if-else if-else construct.**

This is a relational expression which is true when variable **character_from_keyboard** contains the character code of uppercase Y (59H). The relational expression is inside parentheses and it is made with relational operator ==.

This logical-OR operator || combines the two relational expressions into one boolean expression, which is true when at least one of the relational expressions is true. The entire boolean expression is false only when both relational expressions are false.

```
if ( ( character_from_keyboard  ==  'Y' ) ||
     ( character_from_keyboard  ==  'y' ) )
```

This is another relational expression, and it is true when **character_from_keyboard** contains 79H, the character code of lowercase y.

**Likejava.java - 1-1. The first boolean expression in the program.**

```
D:\javafiles2>java Likejava

 Do you like the Java programming language?
 Please, answer Y or N :  y

 That's nice to hear.

D:\javafiles2>java Likejava

 Do you like the Java programming language?
 Please, answer Y or N :  z

 I do not understand "z".
```

**Likejava.java - X. The program is executed here twice, with inputs y and z.**

Character codes are tested in these boolean expressions. Codes that are less than 20H are non-printable characters. Numbers are in the range from 30H to 39H, uppercase letters in the range from 41H to 5AH, and lowercase letters in the range from 61H to 7AH. ' ' means the character code of space (20H), '9' means the character code of digit 9 (39H). && is the logical-AND operator which returns true only if the relational expressions on both sides of && are true.

```
//  Iffing.java

import java.util.* ;

class Iffing
{
   public static void main( String[] not_in_use )
   {
      Scanner keyboard = new Scanner( System.in ) ;

      char  given_character ;

      System.out.print( "\n Please, type in a character:  " ) ;

      given_character  =   keyboard.nextLine().charAt( 0 ) ;

      if ( given_character  <  ' ' )
      {
         System.out.print( "\n That is an unprintable character \n" ) ;
      }
      else if ( given_character >= '0'  &&  given_character <= '9' )
      {
         System.out.print( "\n You hit the number key "
                         +  given_character   + ". \n" ) ;
      }
      else if ( given_character >= 'A'  &&  given_character <= 'Z' )
      {
         System.out.print( "\n "   +  given_character
                         +  " is an uppercase letter. \n" ) ;
      }
      else if ( given_character >= 'a'  &&  given_character <= 'z' )
      {
         System.out.print( "\n "   +  given_character
                         +  " is a lowercase letter. \n" ) ;
      }
      else
      {
         System.out.print( "\n "   +  given_character
                         +  " is a special character. \n" ) ;
      }
   }
}
```

**Iffing.java - 1. A program that contains a complex if construct.**

```
D:\javafiles2>java Iffing

 Please, type in a character:  z

 z is a lowercase letter.
```

**Iffing.java - X. The program executed with input z.**

Program **Iffing.java** examines the character code of the character that it receives from the keyboard. It can find out whether the character is an unprintable character, a number, an uppercase letter, or a lowercase letter. If the character is none of these, the program assumes that the character is a punctuation character or some other special character. **Iffing.java** has the boolean expression

```
( given_character   >=   '0'   &&  given_character   <=   '9' )
```

to check whether variable **given_character** contains the character code of a number. In this boolean expression the logical-AND operator (&&) is used to combine the two relational expressions. The logical-AND operator returns true only when both of its operands are true. In the above boolean expression, the relational expressions are the operands of the logical-AND operator. If either or both of the relational expressions is false, the entire boolean expression is false. When variable **given_character** contains a value that is greater or equal to the character code of zero (30H) and less than or equal to the character code of nine (39H), the boolean expression above is true.

The boolean expression above could be written, without changing its meaning, with extra parentheses, in the following way

```
((given_character   >=   '0') && (given_character   <=   '9'))
```

but the extra parentheses are not necessary because the operator && has a lower precedence than the relational operators >= and <=. Precedence of operators means the order in which the operators take effect. Operators with higher precedence are applied before operators with lower precedence. In the boolean expression above, operators >= and <= take precedence over operator &&. You can think that the program first evaluates the truth values of the relational expressions

```
given_character   >=   '0'
given_character   <=   '9'
```

and then the calculated truth values are used in a logical-AND operation. In reality, however, the truth value of the second operand is not checked in a logical-AND operation if the first operand of && is false.

Java operators are listed in the order of their precedence in Appendix A. The official precedence of operators can always be overridden with parentheses. For example, the multiplication operator * has a higher precedence than the addition operator +, but with parentheses this precedence can be changed. The following example shows the effect of the use of parentheses:

```
2  *  5  +  4       would be evaluated to 14, but
2  *  ( 5 + 4 )     would be evaluated to 18.
```

The logical operators are listed in Table 6-2 and their behavior is summarized in Table 6-3. The NOT operator ! is said to be an unary operator because it takes only one operand. The NOT operator complements the truth value of its operand expression. Complementing is sometimes called inverting or reversing. Complementing means that either true becomes false or false becomes true. The NOT operator can be used to write complex expressions. For example, the expressions

```
( given_character   <=   '9' )
( ! ( given_character   >   '9' ) )
```

mean the same but the latter expression is more difficult to read and understand. It is better to favor simple expressions. The NOT operator (!) is often useful, but it should not be used unnecessarily.

## Table 6-2: The logical operators of Java.[a]

| Operator symbol | Operator name | Explanation |
|---|---|---|
| `\|\|` | Logical OR | Logical OR returns true if either or both of its operand expressions is true. |
| `&&` | Logical AND | Logical AND returns true only if both of its operand expressions are true. |
| `!` | NOT | NOT operator complements the truth value of the expression to the right of the operator symbol !. |

a. Java has operators & and | which work in many cases like operators && and ||, respectively. It is, however, better to use operators && and || when you write boolean expressions for **`if`** constructs and loops. Operators & and | will be discussed in Chapter 16.

## Table 6-3: The truth values of logical operations. (a and b can be variables or expressions.)

| `a` | `b` | `a \|\| b` | `a && b` | `! a` | `! b` |
|---|---|---|---|---|---|
| false | false | false | false | true | true |
| false | true | true | false | true | false |
| true | false | true | false | false | true |
| true | true | true | true | false | false |

### Exercises related to if constructs

Exercise 6-1. Make a copy of program **Largeint.java**. You might name the new file **Largest4.java**. Modify the new file so that it asks for four integers from the keyboard and finds the largest of the four integers. Having done that, make the program find both the smallest and the largest of the four integers.

Exercise 6-2. Write a program that can convert amounts of currency given in U.S. dollars to Japanese yen and vice versa. Check out the latest currency exchange rates in a newspaper. Your program must first ask whether the user wants to change dollars to yen or yen to dollars. The program must have an **`if`** construct which selects the right conversion statements. Naturally, if you prefer, you can also use other currency units in your program.

Remember that Appendix C contains advice for programming exercises.

## 6.2 Making decisions with switch-case constructs

Various kinds of **if** constructs are the principal means for making decisions in Java programs. In addition to **if** constructs, Java provides **switch-case** constructs to make decisions. **switch** and **case** are keywords in Java. You can make all decisions with **if** constructs, but with **switch-case** constructs you can sometimes make the decisions with less writing.

In this section we shall study programs that contain **switch-case** constructs. You need to learn these constructs in order to master Java, and to understand programs you find in the literature. However, because **switch-case** constructs are not used much in this book, you can temporarily skip this section if you are eager to learn more interesting things about Java. You can come back to this section when you see the keywords **switch** and **case** somewhere.

A **switch-case** construct is sometimes convenient when you need to test the value of some variable many times. For example, in program **Likejava.java** the value of variable **character_from_keyboard** is tested altogether four times in two boolean expressions. To demonstrate the use of a **switch-case** construct, the **if-else if-else** construct of **Likejava.java** is replaced with a **switch-case** construct in **Likejavas.java**. Program **Likejavas.java** is thus a rewritten version of **Likejava.java**. This again proves that there can be two programs that behave precisely in the same way although they are written in different ways.

Figure 6-4 shows how **switch-case** constructs usually look like. The structure of a **switch-case** construct is often such that you test the value of an arithmetic expression, and jump to different cases in the construct depending on the value of the tested arithmetic expression. When the program execution goes to some **case** inside the braces of the construct, the execution continues from that point until a **break** statement is encountered. **break**, which is a reserved word and a statement of its own, has the effect that the execution of the program breaks out from the area surrounded by braces. Program **Sentence.java** is an example which further clarifies the role of **break** statements in **switch-case** constructs.

```
switch ( arithmetic expression )
{
case v1:
     Statements which will be executed if the arithmetic expression
     has value v1
        break ;
case v2:
     Statements which will be executed if the arithmetic expression
     has value v2
        break ;
case vn:
     Statements to be executed when the arithmetic expression has
     value vn
        break ;
default:
     Statements which will be executed if none of the cases matched
     the value of the arithmetic expression
        break ;
}
```

***Figure 6-4. The structure of a typical switch-case construct.***

Often, **switch-case** constructs test the value of a single variable of type **char** or **int**. The variable that is tested is written in parentheses after the keyword **switch**. A single variable is, in fact, a simple arithmetic expression. It is also possible to write a more complex arithmetic expression inside the parentheses. In that case, switching is carried out according to the evaluated value of the arithmetic expression.

```
//  Likejavas.java

import java.util.* ;

class Likejavas
{
   public static void main( String[] not_in_use )
   {
      Scanner keyboard = new Scanner( System.in ) ;

      char  character_from_keyboard ;

     System.out.print( "\n Do you like the Java programming language?"
                     + "\n Please, answer Y or N :  " ) ;

      character_from_keyboard  =  keyboard.nextLine().charAt( 0 ) ;

      switch ( character_from_keyboard )
      {
      case  'Y':
      case  'y':
         System.out.print( "\n That's nice to hear. \n" ) ;
         break ;
      case  'N':
      case  'n':
         System.out.print( "\n That is not so nice to hear. "
                         + "\n I hope you change your mind soon.\n" ) ;
         break ;
      default:
         System.out.print( "\n I do not understand \""
                         + character_from_keyboard   +  "\".\n" ) ;
         break ;
      }
   }
}
```

A **switch-case** construct is indeed like a switch that you can turn to many positions. The cases inside braces are the possible positions where the program execution can go in the switching operation. The execution of the program jumps from the keyword **switch** into this position when **character_from_keyboard** contains either 'N' or 'n'. The **break** statements cause the program execution to jump outside the **switch-case** construct.

The case marked with keyword **default** is the place where the program execution jumps to if none of the other cases match the contents of **character_from_keyboard**.

**Likejavas.java - 1. Program Likejava.java rewritten using a switch-case construct.**

```
D:\javafiles2>java Likejavas

 Do you like the Java programming language?
 Please, answer Y or N :  5

 I do not understand "5".
```

**Likejavas.java - X. The program is executed here with input 5.**

## Exercises related to boolean expressions

Exercise 6-3. Let's suppose that **first_variable** has value 5, **second_variable** has value 8, and **third_variable** contains value 14. Write T or F after the following boolean expressions depending on whether they are true or false!

```
( first_variable  <  second_variable )
( third_variable  <  first_variable )
( ! ( first_variable  <  second_variable ) )
( third_variable  >  first_variable )
( ( first_variable + second_variable )  <  third_variable )
( ( first_variable + second_variable ) <= third_variable )
( ( third_variable - second_variable )  >  first_variable )
( first_variable  ==  0 )
( ! ( first_variable == 0 ) )
( first_variable  >  0  ||  second_variable  <  0 )
( first_variable  ==  8  ||  second_variable  == 5 )
( first_variable  <  second_variable  &&  third_variable >=  14 )
( first_variable  ==  5  &&  second_variable  >  8 )
```

Exercise 6-4. Write the following complex boolean expressions in a simpler form

```
( ! ( some_variable  == 8 ) )
( ( some_variable - 10 )  >  0 )
( some_variable  <  88  ||  some_variable  ==  88 )
( ( some_variable - other_variable )  <  0 )
( ! ( ! ( some_variable  <  99 ) ) )
```

This program, which is a somewhat illogical program, clarifies the role of the **break** statements in **switch-case** constructs. As a general rule, programs should not be written like this. There should always be a **break** statement after the statements of each **case** in a **switch-case** construct.

This statement reads a value for the **char** variable **character_from_keyboard**. The input from the keyboard is processed so that first the method **nextLine()** reads a line of text, then the method **toUpperCase()** converts all characters of the given text line to uppercase letters, and finally method **charAt()** takes the first character of the text line. As the text characters are converted to uppercase letters, the user of the program does not need to worry about the case of the letters.

```
//  Sentence.java

import java.util.* ;

class Sentence
{
   public static void main( String[] not_in_use )
   {
      Scanner keyboard = new Scanner( System.in ) ;

      char  character_from_keyboard ;

      System.out.print(
                "\n Type in L, M, or S, depending on whether you want"
           +    "\n a long, medium, or short sentence displayed:  "  ) ;

      character_from_keyboard  =
                   keyboard.nextLine().toUpperCase().charAt( 0 ) ;

      System.out.print( "\n This is a" ) ;

      switch  ( character_from_keyboard )
      {
      case   'L':
         System.out.print( " switch statement in a \n" ) ;
      case   'M':
         System.out.print( " program in a" ) ;
      case   'S':
         System.out.print( " book that teaches Java programming." ) ;
      default:
         System.out.print( "\n I hope that this is an interesting book.\n");
      }
   }
}
```

Because there are no **break** statements in this **switch-case** construct, all statements following a certain **case** will be executed. For example, when the user of the program types in the letter L, all statements inside the **switch-case** construct will be executed because **case 'L':** happens to be the first case.

**Sentence.java - 1. Using a switch-case construct with no break statements.**

```
D:\javafiles2>java Sentence

  Type in L, M, or S, depending on whether you want
  a long, medium, or short sentence displayed:  s

  This is a book that teaches Java programming.
  I hope that this is an interesting book.

D:\javafiles2>java Sentence

  Type in L, M, or S, depending on whether you want
  a long, medium, or short sentence displayed:  L

  This is a switch statement in a
  program in a book that teaches Java programming.
  I hope that this is an interesting book.
```

**Sentence.java - X. The program is executed here twice, with inputs s and L.**

## 6.3 while loops enable repetition

At this point you should have realized that computers are actually quite stupid machines. To make them do something, you have to very carefully and precisely describe that thing in a source program. But what computers lack in intelligence they gain in speed. Once you have written a program that works correctly, computers can execute the program extremely fast–that is, millions of machine instructions per second. And you can run the same program equally fast, as many times as you like, in many different computers if you choose. Since computers can do things so fast, they can be made to be very effective by making them repeat things.

Loops are program constructs with which we can make computers repeat things over and over. As computers are so fast, we can accomplish many things simply by making a computer repeat a few simple statements. There are several different loop structures in Java, but the **`while`** loop can be considered the basic loop. The structure of **`while`** loops is described in Figure 6-5.

Programs that we have studied so far have been such that they are executed from the beginning to end, statement by statement. When there are **`if`** constructs in a program, they have the effect that some statements may be left unexecuted, but programs with **`if`** constructs are also executed from the beginning to end. When there are loops in a program, the execution of statements is not always from the beginning to end. With a **`while`** loop, for example, there is a possibility to jump backwards in a program, and execute the internal statements of the loop over and over. The statements of a program are always executed in the order they are written in the source program, but a loop allows the program execution to go through the same statements many times. When a **`while`** loop is encountered in a program during its execution, we can imagine that the computer follows these three steps:

Step 1. Check the truth value of the boolean expression given in parentheses.

Step 2. If the boolean expression is true, execute the internal statements once and go back to Step 1.

Step 3. If the boolean expression is false (not true), continue by executing the statements that follow the **`while`** loop in the program.

Statements preceding the **`while`** loop.

**`while`** **`(`** *boolean expression* **`)`**
**`{`**

One or more internal statements that will be repeatedly executed as long as the boolean expression, given in parentheses above, is true.

**`}`**

Statements following the **`while`** loop.

***Figure 6-5. The structure of while loops.***

## Describing while loops with flowcharts

A flowchart is a traditional way to describe the operation of a program. A flowchart shows graphically how the program control flows within a program. Flowcharts are particularly useful to explain how loops operate. Below on the left you find a flowchart that describes the general operation principle of a `while` loop. The flowchart on the right shows how the `while` loop in program **While20.java** operates. The arrows in the flowcharts represent movements from one activity to another in the program. The rectangles describe activities, and the diamond shapes describe conditions.

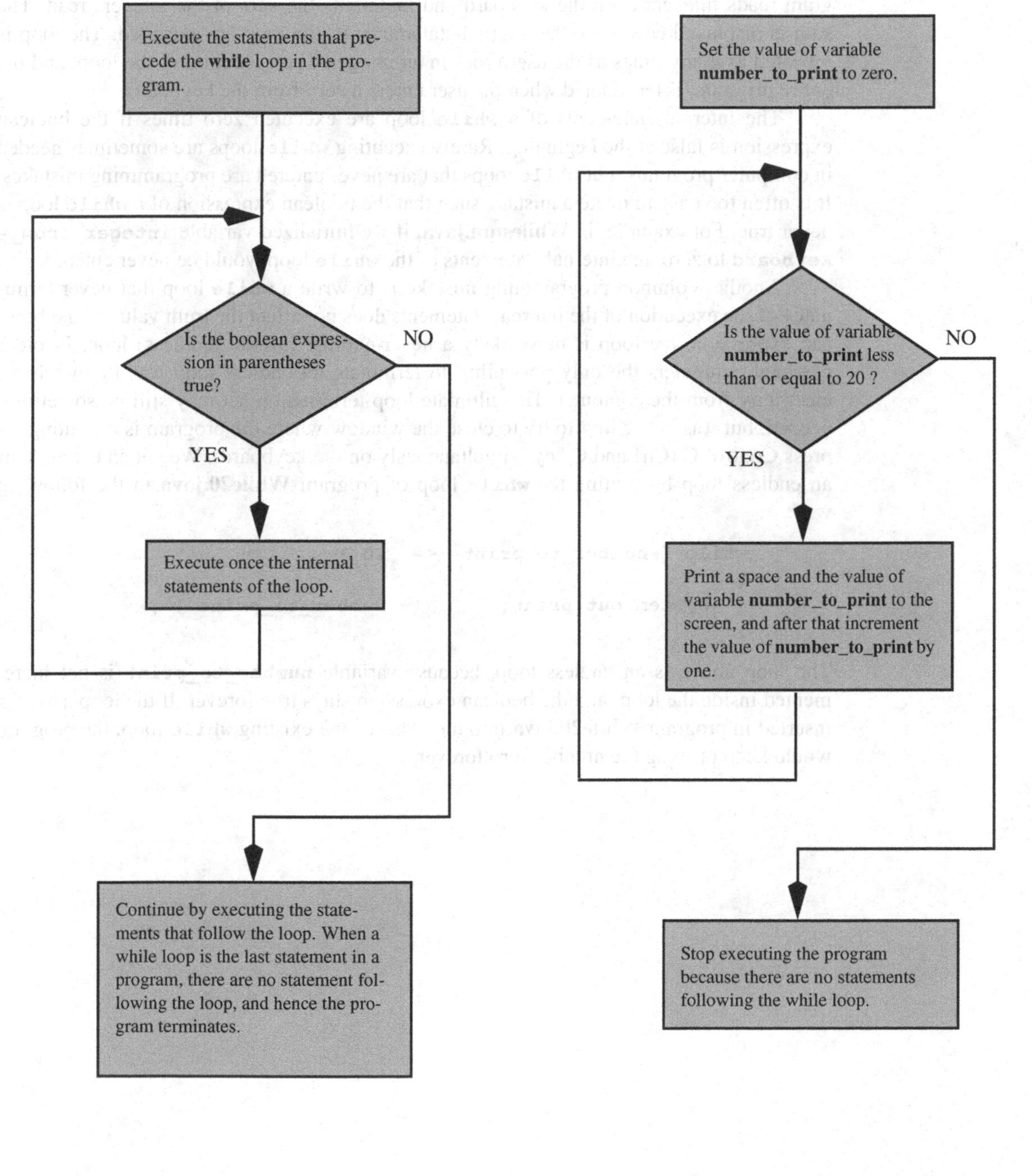

Program **While20.java** is an example where a **while** loop is used to print the numbers from zero to 20 to the screen. The two statements inside the **while** loop will be repeated 21 times when the program is run. The essential idea in the **while** loop is that the internal statements of the loop modify a variable that affects the truth value of the boolean expression. In **While20.java**, the value of variable **number_to_print** grows inside the loop. The same variable is tested in the boolean expression, and ultimately the value of **number_to_print** is so big that the boolean expression becomes false, and the loop terminates. When the boolean expression of a **while** loop is not true any more, the program execution continues from the statement that follows the **while** loop in the program. In **While20.java**, the whole program terminates when the **while** loop terminates because there are no statements following the **while** loop.

Program **Whilesum.java** is another example of the use of a **while** loop. The program reads integers from the keyboard and maintains the sum of the integers read. The sum is displayed each time the internal statements of the loop are executed. The loop is repeated as many times as the user types in an integer. The execution of the loop, and the entire program, is terminated when the user enters a zero from the keyboard.

The internal statements of a **while** loop are executed zero times if the boolean expression is false at the beginning. Rarely executing **while** loops are sometimes needed in computer programs, but **while** loops that are never entered are programming mistakes. It is often too easy to make a mistake such that the boolean expression of a **while** loop is never true. For example, in **Whilesum.java**, if we initialized variable **integer_from_keyboard** to zero, the internal statements of the **while** loop would be never entered.

Another common programming mistake is to write a **while** loop that never terminates. If the execution of the internal statements does not affect the truth value of the boolean expression, the loop is most likely a never-ending, infinite (endless) loop. In older personal computers the only possibility to terminate an endless loop was to switch off electricity from the computer. This ultimate loop-termination act may still be sometimes needed, but it is better first to try to close the window where the program is executing, or press Control-C (Ctrl and C keys simultaneously on the keyboard). We get an example of an endless loop by writing the **while** loop of program **While20.java** in the following way:

```
while ( number_to_print  <=  20 )
{
   System.out.print( " "  +  number_to_print ) ;
}
```

The loop above is an endless loop, because variable **number_to_print** is not incremented inside the loop, and the boolean expression stays true forever. If the loop above is inserted in program **While20.java** into the place of the existing **while** loop, the program would keep printing the number zero forever.

It is possible to declare a variable and assign a value to it in a single statement. This line means the same as

```
int number_to_print ;
number_to_print  =  0 ;
```

When a variable is assigned a value at the same time when it is declared, we say that the variable is an initialized variable.

```
//  While20.java

class While20
{
   public static void main( String[] not_in_use )
   {
      int  number_to_print  =  0 ;

     System.out.print( "\n Numbers from 0 to 20 are the following:\n\n " ) ;

      while ( number_to_print  <= 20 )
      {
         System.out.print( " "  +  number_to_print ) ;
         number_to_print  ++  ;
      }
   }
}
```

++ is called the increment operator. In this case the operator increments the value of **number_to_print** by one. This line means the same as

```
number_to_print = number_to_print + 1 ;
```

The two statements inside braces after the boolean expression will be repeatedly executed as long as the boolean expression is true. As the value of **number_to_print** is initially zero, and it is incremented by one every time the loop is executed, the loop will terminate after 21 repetitions.

The above program could be constructed without a loop by writing the two statements 21 times in the program:

```
System.out.print( " "  +  number_to_print ) ;
number_to_print  ++  ;
System.out.print( " "  +  number_to_print ) ;
number_to_print  ++  ;
System.out.print( " "  +  number_to_print ) ;
number_to_print  ++  ;
  ... etc. etc.
```

It is easier, though, to write the program by using a loop.

**While20.java - 1. A program containing a simple while loop.**

```
D:\javafiles2>java While20

 Numbers from 0 to 20 are the following:

  0 1 2 3 4 5 6 7 8 9 10 11 12 13 14 15 16 17 18 19 20
```

**While20.java - X. The output from the program is always the same.**

These variables are assigned initial values at the same time they are declared. **integer_from_keyboard** must be initialized with a non-zero value because otherwise the boolean expression of the **while** loop would not be true at the beginning. **sum_of_integers** must be zero at the beginning because no integers have been read from the keyboard so far.

This boolean expression is true as long as **integer_from_keyboard** contains something other than a zero. != is the "not equal" operator of Java

```
//  Whilesum.java  (c) Kari Laitinen

import java.util.* ;

class Whilesum
{
   public static void main( String[] not_in_use )
   {
      Scanner keyboard = new Scanner( System.in ) ;

      int  integer_from_keyboard   =  -1 ;
      int  sum_of_integers         =   0 ;

      System.out.print( "\n This program calculates the sum of the integers"
                      + "\n you type in from the keyboard. By entering a"
                      + "\n zero you can terminate the program. \n\n" ) ;

      while ( integer_from_keyboard  !=  0 )
      {
         System.out.printf( "  Current sum: %8d    Enter an integer: ",
                          + sum_of_integers   ) ;

         integer_from_keyboard  =  keyboard.nextInt() ;

         sum_of_integers   =  sum_of_integers + integer_from_keyboard ;
      }
   }
}
```

Variable **integer_from_keyboard** gets a new value each time the internal statements of the loop are executed. Immediately after the integer is read from the keyboard, it is added to the sum of the integers.

The value of variable **sum_of_integers** is printed right-justified into a printing field that is 8 character positions wide. This is achieved by using the format specifier **%8d** with the **printf()** method. When the internal statements of the loop are executed for the first time, **sum_of_integers** is zero.

**Whilesum.java - 1. A program to calculate the sum of integers in a while loop.**

```
D:\javafiles2>java Whilesum

  This program calculates the sum of the integers
  you type in from the keyboard. By entering a
  zero you can terminate the program.

   Current sum:         0   Enter an integer: 5
   Current sum:         5   Enter an integer: 16
   Current sum:        21   Enter an integer: 107
   Current sum:       128   Enter an integer: 1008
   Current sum:      1136   Enter an integer: 9999
   Current sum:     11135   Enter an integer: 0
```

**Whilesum.java - X. The program calculates the sum of six integers here.**

**while** loops, and also other loops, are such that we often use a particular integer variable to control the correct termination of the loop. The technique works by having a variable as part of the boolean expression of the loop, and this same variable is incremented or decremented inside the loop. To increment and decrement the values of variables, Java provides two operators ++ and --. Operator ++ is the increment operator which increments the value of a variable by one. Operator -- is the decrement operator which subtracts one from the value of the variable. Incrementing the value of a variable by one is the same as assigning the variable a value which is one larger than its current value. Thus the meaning of the following two statements is the same:

```
some_variable  ++ ;
some_variable  =  some_variable  +  1 ;
```

Also the meaning of the following two statements is the same:

```
some_variable  -- ;
some_variable  =  some_variable  -  1 ;
```

Increment and decrement operators are useful because incrementing and decrementing operations are so common inside loops, and these operators allow us to write things down in a concise way. When you use an increment or decrement operator in a program, you may not write any spaces between the two plus or minus signs. If you write, for example, + +, the compiler interprets these separate plus signs as two adjacent addition operators, and most likely displays an error message.

Assignment statements and increment/decrement statements, such as the ones above, are usually short, occupying only one line in a program. They look very different from loops or **if** constructs. However, it is important to realize also that **while** loops, and the other loops that will be introduced in the following sections, are statements. Various kinds of **if** constructs are also statements. Because loops and **if** constructs are usually long and consist of many lines of source program, they do not look very similar to the shorter statements. For this reason, they are just called loops and constructs in this book, but you must remember that loops and **if** constructs are statements. A loop can have another loop or an **if** construct as an internal statement.

## 6.4 for loops repeat a known number of times

Program **While20.java** uses a `while` loop to print numbers from 0 to 20. The internal statements of the loop are repeated 21 times. The termination of the loop depends on the value of variable `number_to_print`. Program **For20.java** is a rewritten version of program **While20.java**. A `for` loop is used in **For20.java** instead of a `while` loop. Although they are written by using different looping mechanisms, programs **For20.java** and **While20.java** perform in exactly the same way.

`for` loops are convenient when we want to repeat something a certain number of times in a program. Typically, `for` loops are controlled by a single integer variable (`number_to_print` in **For20.java**) which is either incremented or decremented each time the internal statements of the loop have been executed. The general structure of a typical `for` loop is described in Figure 6-6. `for` loops are not that much different from `while` loops. The termination of both loops is controlled by a single boolean expression. When the boolean expression is or becomes false, the execution of the program continues from the statement that follows the loop. The essential difference between a `while` loop and a `for` loop is that a `for` loop has three "things" inside parentheses ( ) after keyword `for`, whereas a `while` loop has only one "thing", the boolean expression, inside parentheses after keyword `while`. The assignment statement that is the first thing in parentheses in Figure 6-6 will be executed before anything else takes place, and that statement is executed only once. The third thing in parentheses, the increment or decrement statement, is executed always after the internal statements of the loop have been executed.

Everything that can be done with a `for` loop in a program can also be done with a `while` loop. Figure 6-7 shows how a `for` loop can be converted into a `while` loop. The assignment statement, that is the first item inside parentheses of the `for` loop, can be written as a statement that precedes the `while` loop. The increment or decrement statement, that is the last item inside parentheses of the `for` loop, can be added as the last statement to the body of the `while` loop. As the increment or decrement statement is executed equally as many times as the internal statements of a `for` loop, it is logical to include it in the internal statements of the corresponding `while` loop.

```
Statements preceding the for loop.

for ( assignment statement ;
      boolean expression ;
      increment or decrement statement )
{
   One or more internal statements that will be repeatedly executed
   as long as the boolean expression given above is true. When the
   boolean expression becomes false, the statements that follow this
   for loop will be executed.
}

Statements following the for loop.
```

*Figure 6-6. Typical structure of a for loop.*

Inside the parentheses after the keyword **for**, **for** loops have three "things" separated with two semicolons. In this loop

- the assignment statement **number_to_print = 0** will be executed before the program actually starts looping,
- the boolean expression **number_to_print <= 20** decides when the loop terminates, and
- the increment statement **number_to_print ++** will be executed each time after the internal statement of the loop has been executed.

```
//  For20.java  (c) Kari Laitinen

class For20
{
   public static void main( String[] not_in_use )
   {
      int  number_to_print ;

      System.out.print( "\n Numbers from 0 to 20 are the following:\n\n " ) ;

      for ( number_to_print  =  0  ;
            number_to_print  <= 20 ;
            number_to_print  ++  )
      {
         System.out.print( " "  +  number_to_print ) ;
      }
   }
}
```

In the same way as in the case of **while** loops, the internal statements of **for** loops are written inside braces. The internal statements of a loop can also be called with the term "body of the loop".

This statement is the only statement inside the loop. The statement will be executed 21 times. When the value of **number_to_print** is 20, it will be incremented to 21, resulting in that the boolean expression **number_to_print <= 20** is not true any more, and the loop terminates.

**For20.java - 1. Program While20.java implemented with a for loop.**

```
D:\javafiles2>java For20

 Numbers from 0 to 20 are the following:

  0 1 2 3 4 5 6 7 8 9 10 11 12 13 14 15 16 17 18 19 20
```

**For20.java - X. The program produces the same output as program While20.java**

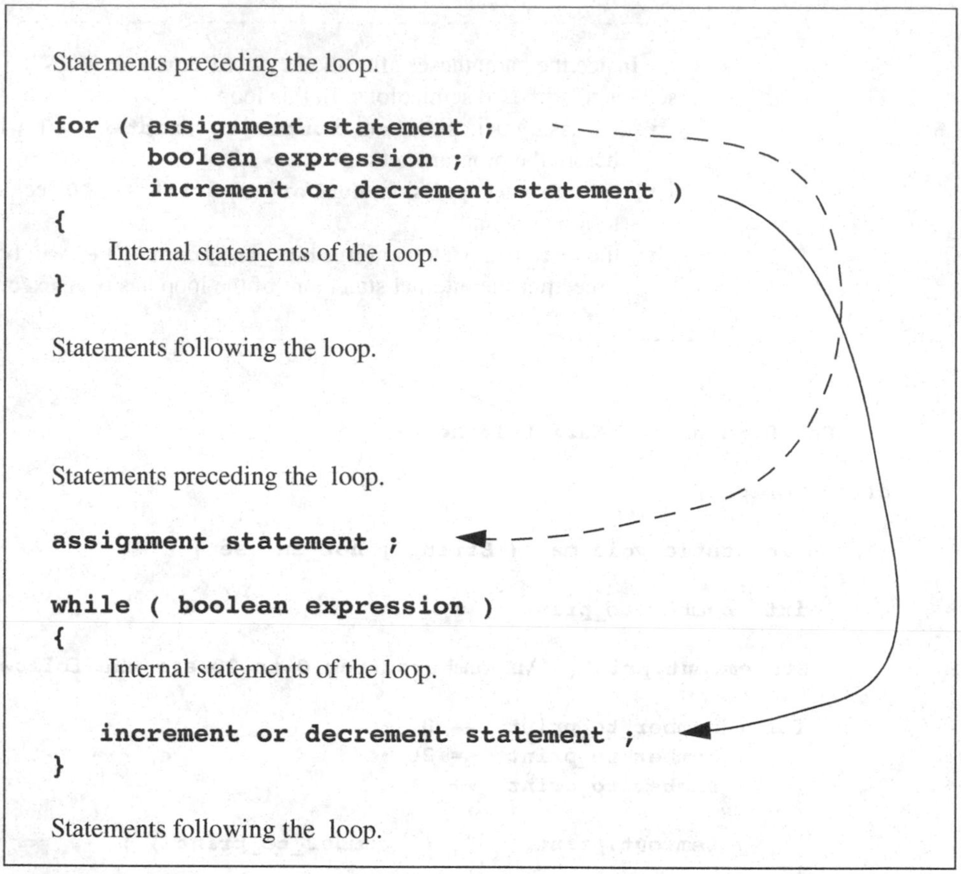

Statements preceding the loop.

```
for ( assignment statement ;
      boolean expression ;
      increment or decrement statement )
{
    Internal statements of the loop.
}
```

Statements following the loop.

Statements preceding the loop.

```
assignment statement ;

while ( boolean expression )
{
    Internal statements of the loop.

    increment or decrement statement ;
}
```

Statements following the loop.

*Figure 6-7. Converting a for loop into a while loop*

Loops and **`if`** constructs can be mixed in a program. A loop can contain an **`if`** construct, and a loop can be written inside an **`if`** construct. Program **Forcodes.java** shows how an **`if`** construct can be one of the internal statements of a **`for`** loop. When the internal statements of the **`for`** loop of **Forcodes.java** are repeated, the internal statements of the **`if`** construct are executed when the boolean expression of the **`if`** construct is true.

**Forcodes.java** prints characters and their character codes in the range from 20H to 7FH (from 32 to 127 in decimal). The program must repeat the internal statements of the loop 96 times to perform the entire printing operation. Because we know beforehand how many times the loop must be repeated, a **`for`** loop is convenient in this program. To print the characters and character codes from 20H to 7FH, the loop control variable named **`numerical_code`** is set to value 0x20 at the beginning and the loop terminates when **`numerical_code`** reaches value 0x80. A **`for`** loop is typically such that its loop control variable is given a certain initial value, and its value is incremented or decremented until it reaches a certain terminal value. In program **Forcodes.java**, the loop control variable **`numerical_code`** passes through all values from 20H to 7FH while the loop is being executed.

Hexadecimal literals 0x20 and 0x80 are used in **Forcodes.java**. The prefix 0x is needed when a programmer wants to write a numerical literal in hexadecimal form in Java. When the compiler recognizes the prefix 0x, it knows that it is a hexadecimal number. Without a prefix, the compiler assumes numerical literals to be in the normal decimal form. It is often convenient to think of character codes in hexadecimal form. However, if you found hexadecimal literals difficult in **Forcodes.java**, you could replace 0x20 with 32 and 0x80 with 128 without making any functional changes in the program.

As program **Forcodes.java** must print 96 different characters and their character codes and also insert spaces to separate the characters and codes, it is impossible to print everything on a single line on the computer's screen. For this reason, the program brings a new line into use after it has printed 8 characters and codes on the current line. The program uses the variable **number_of_codes_on_this_line** to count how many character codes it has processed. The **if** construct in the body of the **for** loop monitors the value of this variable. When **number_of_codes_on_this_line** reaches the value 8, a newline character is printed and the value of the variable is made zero again.

In the case of each numerical code **Forcodes.java** first prints the character and then the numerical code in hexadecimal form. For example, when the value of variable **numerical_code** is 54H, the program prints "T 54 ". The program does not use letter H to indicate hexadecimal numbers. To convert a numerical code into a character, the program copies the numerical code into a variable of type **char** in the statement

```
char character_to_print  = (char) numerical_code ;
```

which both declares the variable and copies a value to it. The marking **(char)** in the above statement is an explicit type conversion that converts the value of **numerical_code** to type **char** before the assignment takes place. Without the explicit type conversion, the above assignment is not possible. After the above statement has been executed, both variables, **character_to_print** and **numerical_code**, contain the same numerical value. But the contents of variable **character_to_print** will be printed as a character because it is of type **char**. Here you must remember that all variables in a computer's main memory contain nothing but binary numbers, zeroes and ones. But in a program which uses the variables in a computer's memory, the binary information stored in the variables can be interpreted in different ways, depending on the type of the variable. In **Forcodes.java**, the numerical information stored in variable **numerical_code** is considered to be numerical information, but when the same information is stored in the variable **character_to_print**, it is treated as a character symbol.

## Exercises related to while loops

Exercise 6-5. Which numbers would be printed to the screen if the lines

```
int  growing_number    =  1 ;
int  shrinking_number  =  20 ;

while ( growing_number  <  shrinking_number )
{
   System.out.print(  " "  +  growing_number
                   +  " "  +  shrinking_number ) ;

   growing_number   =  growing_number  +  2 ;
   shrinking_number  =  shrinking_number  -  3 ;
}
```

were executed on a computer? How would the output of the above **while** loop change if the internal statements of the loop were put in an opposite order, i.e., if the output statement came after the assignment statements?

Exercise 6-6. Make a copy of program **While20.java**, and name the new file **Whileodd.java**. Modify the new program so that it prints only the odd numbers in the range from 0 to 20.

Here a variable of type **char** is declared inside the **for** loop, and the value of **numerical_code** is copied into the variable. Variable **character_to_print** is printed as a character because it is of type **char**. Variable **numerical_code** is printed as numerical digits because it is of type **int**.

By using the **printf()** method and the format specifier **%x**, it is possible to print the value of an **int** variable in hexadecimal form. The current value of **numerical_code** replaces the format specifier **%x** in the string **"%x "**. In practice this means that a space character is printed after each hexadecimal code.

```
//  Forcodes.java  (c) Kari Laitinen

class Forcodes
{
   public static void main( String[] not_in_use )
   {
      int   number_of_codes_on_this_line   =   0 ;

      System.out.print( "\n The visible characters with codes from 20"
                    +  "\n to 7F (hexadecimal) are the following:\n\n ");

      for ( int numerical_code     =  0x20 ;
                numerical_code     <  0x80 ;
                numerical_code     ++ )
      {
         char  character_to_print  =  (char) numerical_code  ;

         System.out.print( character_to_print  +  " " ) ;
         System.out.printf( "%x ", numerical_code ) ;

         number_of_codes_on_this_line   ++   ;

         if (  number_of_codes_on_this_line  ==  8  )
         {
            System.out.print( "\n " ) ;
            number_of_codes_on_this_line   =   0 ;
         }
      }
   }
}
```

We say that a program prints a newline, when a new empty line is started on the screen. A newline can be printed simply by outputting character \n which means actually a character which has character code 0AH (10 decimal).

This **if** construct ensures that the program prints a newline after eight characters and their character codes have been printed. The boolean expression of the **if** construct becomes true in every 8th repetition of the loop. The program prints altogether 96 characters and character codes on 12 lines.

**Forcodes.java - 1.+ A program that prints a character code table.**

It is possible to declare and initialize a variable inside the parentheses of a **for** loop. Because the initial value of the variable **numerical_code** is 20H (32 decimal), a space is the first character to be printed. 20H is the character code of the space character. By adding the prefix 0x before the actual number, you can define a hexadecimal literal constant in Java. 0x20 means the same as 32.

The internal statements of the loop will be repeatedly executed as long as the value of **numerical_code** is less than 80H (128 decimal).

Variable **numerical_code** is incremented by one every time after the internal statements of the loop have been executed once.

```
for ( int numerical_code  =  0x20 ;
          numerical_code  <  0x80 ;
          numerical_code  ++ )
{
   char  character_to_print  =  (char) numerical_code  ;

   System.out.print( character_to_print  +  " " )  ;
   System.out.printf( "%x " , numerical_code ) ;

   number_of_codes_on_this_line  ++  ;

   if (  number_of_codes_on_this_line  ==  8  )
   {
      System.out.print( "\n " ) ;
      number_of_codes_on_this_line   =  0 ;
   }
}
```

**Forcodes.java - 1 - 1. The for loop which prints the characters and character codes.**

```
D:\javafiles2>java Forcodes

 The visible characters with codes from 20
 to 7F (hexadecimal) are the following:

   20 ! 21 " 22 # 23 $ 24 % 25 & 26 ' 27
 ( 28 ) 29 * 2a + 2b , 2c - 2d . 2e / 2f
 0 30 1 31 2 32 3 33 4 34 5 35 6 36 7 37
 8 38 9 39 : 3a ; 3b < 3c = 3d > 3e ? 3f
 @ 40 A 41 B 42 C 43 D 44 E 45 F 46 G 47
 H 48 I 49 J 4a K 4b L 4c M 4d N 4e O 4f
 P 50 Q 51 R 52 S 53 T 54 U 55 V 56 W 57
 X 58 Y 59 Z 5a [ 5b \ 5c ] 5d ^ 5e _ 5f
 ` 60 a 61 b 62 c 63 d 64 e 65 f 66 g 67
 h 68 i 69 j 6a k 6b l 6c m 6d n 6e o 6f
 p 70 q 71 r 72 s 73 t 74 u 75 v 76 w 77
 x 78 y 79 z 7a { 7b | 7c } 7d ~ 7e ¦ 7f
```

**Forcodes.java - X. The 96 characters and character codes printed by the program.**

## 6.5 do-while loops execute at least once

Both **while** loops and **for** loops have a boolean expression which decides whether the internal statements of the loop are executed or not. The boolean expression is checked first, and the internal statements are executed afterwards if the boolean expression was true. The statements inside **while** and **for** loops are not executed at all if the boolean expression is false at the beginning. Sometimes it is necessary that a loop is executed zero times, but in some other cases we need loops to execute their body, the internal statements, at least once. For such situations, Java provides a third possibility to construct a loop. These loops are called **do-while** loops.

Figure 6-8 shows the basic structure of a **do-while** loop. The essential difference between **while** loops and **do-while** loops, is that in **while** loops the value of the boolean expression is evaluated at the beginning, whereas in **do-while** loops the boolean expression is evaluated after the internal statements have been executed. For this reason, the internal statements of a **do-while** loop are executed at least once.

Program **Meanvalue.java** calculates the mean value of the integers read from the keyboard. It uses a **do-while** loop to read the integers and simultaneously calculate the sum of the integers read. The boolean expression of the **do-while** loop causes it to terminate when the user types in a zero from the keyboard. After the **do-while** loop the program calculates the mean value as it knows the sum of the integers and how many integers were entered from the keyboard. Note that an **if** construct is used in the program **Meanvalue.java** to ensure that there were non-zero number of integers entered from the keyboard. No mean value can be calculated if no integers other than the zero were entered.

In program **Meanvalue.java** the following statement calculates the mean value:

```
mean_value  =  (float) sum_of_integers /
               (float) number_of_integers_given ;
```

The term (**float**) in the assignment statement above means that the **int** variables **sum_of_integers** and **number_of_integers_given** are converted to type **float** before division. This kind of conversion is called explicit type conversion. In the above case, type conversion is necessary to get accurate division results. You can make these kinds of type conversions for any variable type by writing the destination type in parentheses before the variable name. Explicit type conversion has a local effect to the type of a variable. The converted value is used only in that place of a program where (*some type*) is written. For example in the statement above, the value of **int** variable **sum_of_integers** is treated as a **float** value, but the variable still remains as an **int** variable, and it would be treated as such if it were used later in the program.

```
do
{
     One or more statements that will be first executed once, and then
     repeatedly executed as long as the boolean expression, given
     below in parentheses, is true.
}
 while ( boolean expression ) ;
```

*Figure 6-8. The structure of do-while loops.*

This **do-while** loop reads the integers and calculates their sum. **do** is a reserved keyword of Java. The internal statements of a **do-while** loop, which are always executed at least once, are given inside braces immediately after the keyword **do**.

-1 is the initial value of the variable that counts how many integers have been entered from the keyboard. This way the last integer, a zero, is not calculated in the sum of the integers.

```
//  Meanvalue.java  (c) Kari Laitinen

import java.util.* ;

class Meanvalue
{
   public static void main( String[] not_in_use )
   {
      Scanner keyboard = new Scanner( System.in ) ;

      int   integer_from_keyboard      =  0 ;
      int   number_of_integers_given   =  -1 ;
      float mean_value                 =  0 ;
      int   sum_of_integers            =  0 ;

      System.out.print( "\n This program calculates the mean value of"
                      + "\n the integers you enter from the keyboard."
                      + "\n Please, start entering numbers. The program"
                      + "\n stops when you enter a zero. \n\n" ) ;

      do
      {
         System.out.print( "   Enter an integer: " ) ;
         integer_from_keyboard  =  keyboard.nextInt();

         number_of_integers_given  ++  ;
         sum_of_integers  =  sum_of_integers + integer_from_keyboard ;
      }
       while  ( integer_from_keyboard  !=  0 ) ;

      if ( number_of_integers_given  >  0 )
      {
         mean_value  =  (float) sum_of_integers /
                        (float) number_of_integers_given ;
      }

      System.out.print( "\n The mean value is: " + mean_value + " \n" ) ;
   }
}
```

This program calculates the mean value only if some numbers were actually entered from the keyboard. Without this **if** construct, the program could carry out a division by zero which might result in serious problems when the program is executed.

There must be a semicolon to terminate a **do-while** loop. The boolean expression is always evaluated after the internal statements of the loop have been executed once. Here, the boolean expression is constructed by using operator !=, "not equal".

**Meanvalue.java - 1. A program to calculate the mean value of a set of integers.**

```
D:\javafiles2>java Meanvalue

 This program calculates the mean value of
 the integers you enter from the keyboard.
 Please, start entering numbers. The program
 stops when you enter a zero.

   Enter an integer: 222
   Enter an integer: 333
   Enter an integer: 444
   Enter an integer: 555
   Enter an integer: 0

 The mean value is: 388.5
```

**Meanvalue.java - X. The program calculates here the mean value of four integers.**

## Exercises with loops

Exercise 6-7. Make a copy of program **Whilesum.java**, and modify the new file so that the program calculates how many integers the user has entered from the keyboard. The program must stop reading in new integers when the user has entered 10 integers.

Exercise 6-8. Make a copy of program **Meanvalue.java**, and modify the new file so that the program prints the current mean value each time a new integer has been entered from the keyboard.

Exercise 6-9. Write a program that prints a conversion table from miles to kilometers or from kilometers to miles. The program must first ask what kind of conversion table the user wants. After having asked this, you need an **`if`** construct in the program. The program must use either a **`for`** or a **`while`** loop to print the conversion table. The program must print at least 15 conversion lines, for example, in the following way:

```
miles     kilometers

10        16.09
20        32.19
30        48.28
.         .
.         .
.         .
140       225.30
150       241.40
```

Exercise 6-10. In Chapter 5 there is an exercise which explains how to convert degrees Celsius to degrees Fahrenheit. Write a program that prints a Celsius to Fahrenheit conversion table. Use a **`for`** loop in your program.

Exercise 6-11. Write a program that can display the character code of any character that is entered from the keyboard. The program should read characters in a loop and print their character codes. The character code must be printed both in hexadecimal and decimal form. You can use program **Forcodes.java** as an example, but it is better to use a **`while`** loop in this kind of a program. The program should stop asking new characters when the user enters a special character like % or &.

## 6.6 The block structure of Java programs

The braces { and } are important in Java programming. Without braces it is not possible to write a valid Java program. At least, you must use braces to declare a class inside which you put the **`main()`** method, and it is necessary to have an opening brace and a closing brace to tell the compiler where the statements of the method **`main()`** begin and where they end. Groups of statements that are surrounded by braces are called blocks of statements, program blocks, or simply blocks. Program blocks are used in **`if`** constructs and in all kinds of loops. We can say, for example, that the internal statements of a **`while`** loop make up a **`while`** block.

Program **Words.java** clarifies the block structure of Java programs. We can identify the following program blocks in **Words.java**:

- Class **`Words`** inside which method **`main()`** is written is the outmost block of the program.
- The statements of method **`main()`** form one block.
- One statement in method **`main()`** is a **`while`** loop which contains a **`while`** block.
- The **`if-else`** construct which belongs to the **`while`** block contains two program blocks, an **`if`** block and an **`else`** block.

In **Words.java**, the **`if`** block and the **`else`** block are inside the **`while`** block which in turn is inside the block of method **`main()`**, and method **`main()`** is inside class **`Words`**. A program block that belongs to some other program block, the outer block, is said to be a nested block. For example, the **`if`** and **`else`** blocks in **Words.java** belong to the **`while`** block, and they are thus nested blocks in relation to the **`while`** block.

It is a nice programming style to write the statements of nested blocks three or four character positions to the right of the statements of the outer block. Those statements that are written deeper to the right than other statements are said to be indented statements. Indentation clarifies the logical structure of programs.

When you write your own programs, it is useful to learn to indent the nested program blocks properly. As indentation highlights the logical structure of your programs, you may make less programming errors, or you are able to discover errors more easily when you indent statements inside program blocks. Indentation, although it has no technical effect on how your programs work, helps you to think more logically. It also helps other people to read your programs.

The braces that are used in **`if`** constructs and loops in the program examples of this book are written according to certain rules. As you can see in program **Words.java** and in other programs, the braces are written so that the opening brace and the closing brace are always in the same column (character position) as the first letter of the reserved word which defines the program block. In **`while`** loops, for example, { is written right below letter w, and } is in the same column somewhere later in the program. The same kind of writing style is used in **`for`** loops and in **`if`** constructs. You should follow this programming style in your own programs.

To be accurate, many program examples in this book contain more pairs of braces than is officially required by the Java compiler. In **`if`** constructs and loops, Java does not necessarily require any braces around program blocks that are made of a single statement. The **`if-else`** construct in program **Words.java** could be written without braces in the following way

```
if ( character_in_sentence.charAt( 0 )  ==  ' ' )

   System.out.print( "\n  " ) ;
else

   System.out.print( " "  +  character_in_sentence ) ;
```

In Java programs, methods are written inside class declarations. The statements of every method in a source program file form a program block. The statements of a method must be written inside braces after the method's name. Inside this class named **Words**, there is only the **main()** method, but, as we shall see later, a class can contain many methods which form logically independent program blocks.

```
//  Words.java  (c) Kari Laitinen

import java.util.* ;

class Words
{
   public static void main( String[] not_in_use )
   {
      Scanner keyboard = new Scanner( System.in ) ;

      System.out.print( "\n This program separates the words of a"
                      + "\n sentence and prints them in wide form."
                      + "\n Type in a sentence, and write a PERIOD '.'"
                      + "\n at the end of the sentence.\n\n   " ) ;

      String character_in_sentence  =  keyboard.findInLine( "." ) ;

      System.out.print( "\n   " ) ;

      while ( character_in_sentence.charAt( 0 )  !=  '.' )
      {
         if ( character_in_sentence.charAt( 0 )  ==  ' ' )
         {
            System.out.print( "\n   " ) ;
         }
         else
         {
            System.out.print( " "  +  character_in_sentence ) ;
         }

         character_in_sentence  =  keyboard.findInLine( "." ) ;
      }
   }
}
```

The internal statements of **while**, **for**, and **do-while** loops form program blocks that need to be surrounded with braces. In this book we write the braces so that the opening brace and the closing brace of a program block are in the same column.

Note that the internal statements of any program block are indented, i.e., written so that the source program lines begin three character positions to the right of the statements outside of the block. Indentation is not required by the compiler, but it is an important way to clarify the logical structure of a program.

Every **if-else** construct has two program blocks, an **if** block and an **else** block. In this particular case, the **if**-construct is inside a larger program block, a **while** block.

**Words.java - 1.+ A program that contains many blocks of statements.**

Text is read in here character by character. The **findInLine()** method is used to read the characters one at a time. The parameter "." makes the **findInLine()** method accept any character except the newline character.

Characters are read in until a period (full stop) is encountered.

```
String character_in_sentence  =  keyboard.findInLine( "." ) ;

System.out.print( "\n   " ) ;

while ( character_in_sentence.charAt( 0 )  !=  '.' )
{
   if ( character_in_sentence.charAt( 0 ) == ' ' )
   {
      System.out.print( "\n   " ) ;
   }
   else
   {
      System.out.print( " " + character_in_sentence ) ;
   }

   character_in_sentence  =  keyboard.findInLine( "." ) ;
}
```

This program is probably too difficult for this early chapter. So, don't panic if you cannot understand everything about it.

When the character is a space, a newline is printed. This way the words of the sentence will be printed on separate lines on the screen.

**Words.java - 1 -1. The operation of the program explained.**

```
D:\javafiles2>java Words

 This program separates the words of a
 sentence and prints them in wide form.
 Type in a sentence, and write a PERIOD '.'
 at the end of the sentence.

   Apple Macintosh was introduced in 1984.

   A p p l e
   M a c i n t o s h
   w a s
   i n t r o d u c e d
   i n
   1 9 8 4
```

Apple Macintosh was the first commercially available computer with a mouse and a graphical user interface (GUI). The graphical Windows operating system is a later invention. The example programs of this book do not react to the mouse or use any real graphical features of the operating system.

**Words.java - X. The program finds five spaces in the input sentence.**

and the compiler would accept it. However, in this book braces are used around each program block for the following reasons:

- All **if** constructs and loops have the same logical structure and visual appearance when braces are always used. This should make the programs more readable and easy to understand.
- Often you need to modify a program by adding more statements in a single-statement program block. When the block already has braces, it is less likely that you will make a programming error by forgetting to add the braces. Using braces in every program block is thus a technique to prevent errors. These kinds of techniques are especially important in companies where programs are written to build commercial software systems. In companies, existing programs need to be modified very often, and programming mistakes can cost a lot of money.
- When we always use braces we have only one kind of basic **if** structure and one kind of basic loop structure. This way the language we use becomes simpler. It is possible that the entire grammar of Java would be simpler if the language required the use of braces in every **if** construct and in every loop.
- In single-statement methods, such as

```
public static void main( String[] not_in_use )
{
   System.out.print( "I am a program." ) ;
}
```

  we must use braces. Therefore, it is logically relevant to use braces in the case of other single-statement program blocks.

The **if-else if-else if-...** constructs are a special case regarding the use of braces. These program constructs are made by combining two or more **if-else** constructs. These constructs are the only case in this book where braces are not used in the way discussed above.

## 6.7 try-catch constructs handle exceptions

A computer program that is being run on a computer communicates with the world outside the computer. Computers operate in a very logical manner, but the outside world is, unfortunately, less logical. Especially we, the human users of computer programs, can cause many error situations from which computer programs must recover. Because it is very human that people make mistakes, it is very important that computer programs are written so that they can handle mistakes. A typical error situation that a human user can cause is that he or she enters the wrong type of data into a program. For example, a user may type in letters when a program asks for a number.

Because it is mandatory that computer programs can recover from error situations, programming languages provide standard mechanisms for handling errors. In Java, the standard mechanism to handle errors is to use so-called exception objects. The exception objects can simply be called exceptions. In this section we shall take a quick look at exceptions. Later on, when we have learned more about classes and objects, we'll explore the exception handling mechanism more thoroughly. Because exceptions are an essential feature in a language like Java, we must study them a little bit this early. Also, some discussion about exceptions is relevant under the title of this chapter because exception handling means decision making in abnormal situations and exceptions affect the block structure of Java programs.

If you execute the program **Meanvalue.java**, which we studied earlier in this chapter, so that you type in a letter when the program asks you to type in an integer, the execution of the program terminates in a strange way, and you get the following lines to the screen

```
Exception in thread "main" java.util.InputMismatchException
        at java.util.Scanner.throwFor(Unknown Source)
        at java.util.Scanner.next(Unknown Source)
        at java.util.Scanner.nextInt(Unknown Source)
        at java.util.Scanner.nextInt(Unknown Source)
        at Meanvalue.main(Meanvalue.java:30)
```

This message means that an exception of type **`InputMismatchException`** was thrown when a letter character was found in the input string that should have contained only numerical characters. Because this exception was not handled in the program, the program was terminated abruptly.

We say that an exception (object) is thrown in an error situation. In program **Meanvalue.java**, it is the method **`nextInt()`** that can cause exception throwing. When the **`nextInt()`** method reads an integer from the keyboard, it needs to convert a string of characters to a numerical value. When it is found that the input string is not in a correct format, an exception is thrown. (To be accurate, the above lines say that there are two other methods, **`next()`** and **`throwFor()`**, involved in the process of exception throwing. We can, however, think that the **`nextInt()`** method is the one that causes exception throwing. The above message tells also that the methods in question are methods of class **`Scanner`** which belongs to a software package named **`java.util`**. Number 30 is mentioned because the call to the **`nextInt()`** method is on line 30 in the source program file **Meanvalue.java**.)

Just as exceptions can be thrown, they can also be caught. The mechanism for catching exceptions is demonstrated in program **MeanvalueException.java**, which is a rewritten version of program **Meanvalue.java**. Program **MeanvalueException.java** does not terminate in a strange way if the user types in a letter. Instead, a letter in the input causes the program to terminate correctly and to calculate the mean value.

Exceptions are caught in Java by using so-called **`try-catch`** constructs. **`try`** and **`catch`** are reserved keywords in Java. Figure 6-9 explains the structure of a simple **`try-catch`** construct that can catch only one kind of exception. Later on, we'll study somewhat more complicated **`try-catch`** constructs that can catch several types of exceptions.

A variable of type **boolean** can be given values **true** and **false**. This variable is set initially to value **true**, and it is used to control the correct termination of the **while** loop.

Integers are read from the keyboard inside a **try-catch** construct. Here, this program construct operates so that program execution jumps from this input statement to the statement inside the **catch** block when a letter is found in the input string. The jump is caused by an exception object that is thrown by method **nextInt()** whenever it attempts to convert letters to an **int** value.

```
// MeanvalueException.java
import java.util.* ;

class MeanvalueException
{
   public static void main( String[] not_in_use )
   {
      Scanner keyboard = new Scanner( System.in ) ;

      System.out.print( "\n This program calculates the mean value of"
                      + "\n the integers you enter from the keyboard."
                      + "\n The program stops when you enter a letter."
                      + "\n\n   Enter an integer: " ) ;

      int    number_of_integers_given    =  0 ;
      int    sum_of_integers             =  0 ;

      boolean  keyboard_input_is_numerical  =  true ;

      while ( keyboard_input_is_numerical ==  true )
      {
         try
         {
            int integer_from_keyboard  =  keyboard.nextInt() ;
            number_of_integers_given  ++  ;
            sum_of_integers  =  sum_of_integers + integer_from_keyboard ;
            System.out.print(  "   Enter an integer: " ) ;
         }
         catch ( Exception  not_numerical_input_exception )
         {
            keyboard_input_is_numerical  =  false ;
         }
      }

      float mean_value  =  0 ;

      if ( number_of_integers_given  >  0 )
      {
         mean_value  =  (float) sum_of_integers /
                        (float) number_of_integers_given ;
      }

      System.out.print( "\n The mean value is: " + mean_value + " \n" ) ;
   }
}
```

The **catch** part of a **try-catch** construct specifies what kinds of exceptions will be caught, and contains the block of statements that will be executed when an exception is caught. This construct can catch many types of exceptions. **not_numerical_input_exception** is the name referring to the exception object.

**MeanvalueException.java - 1. A rewritten version of Meanvalue.java.**

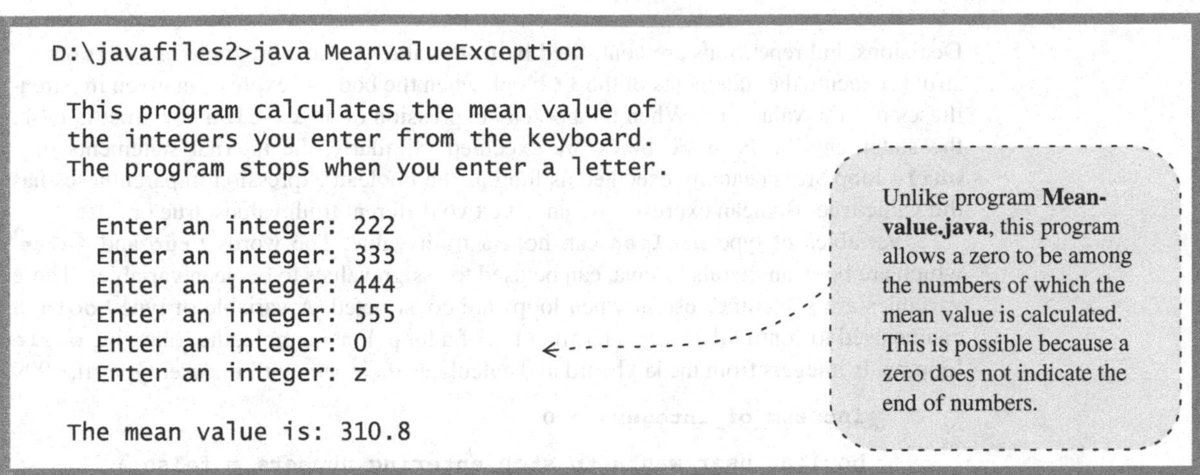


Unlike program Meanvalue.java, this program allows a zero to be among the numbers of which the mean value is calculated. This is possible because a zero does not indicate the end of numbers.

**MeanvalueException.java - X. The program calculates here the mean value of five integers.**

Statements preceding the **try-catch** construct.

```
try
{
```

One or more statements that are executed after the statements preceding this **try-catch** construct. If some of these statements throws an exception of type **ExceptionType**, the rest of these statements are left unexecuted, and the program execution continues in the **catch** block. Otherwise, if no exceptions are thrown, all of these statements are executed, and the program execution continues with the statements following this **try-catch** construct.

```
}
catch ( ExceptionType exception_name )
{
```

One or more statements that will be executed only if an exception of type **ExceptionType** was thrown by some of the statements in the try block.

```
}
```

Statements following the **try-catch** construct.

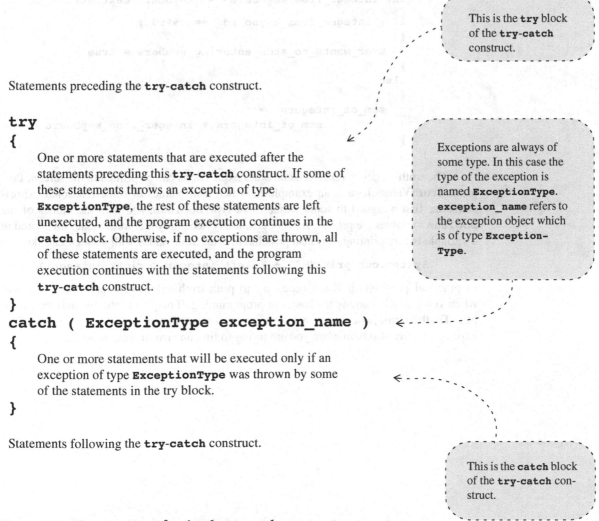

This is the **try** block of the **try-catch** construct.

Exceptions are always of some type. In this case the type of the exception is named **ExceptionType**. **exception_name** refers to the exception object which is of type **ExceptionType**.

This is the **catch** block of the **try-catch** construct.

*Figure 6-9. The structure of a simple try-catch construct.*

## 6.8 Truth values and variables of type boolean

Decisions and repetitions are controlled by truth values in Java programs. **if-else** constructs execute the statements of the **if** block when the boolean expression given in parentheses has the value true. When the boolean expression of an **if-else** construct is false, the statements in the **else** block are executed. Similarly, the internal statements of a **while** loop are repeatedly executed as long as the boolean expression in parentheses has the value true. Boolean expressions can have two different truth values: true or false.

Variables of type **boolean** can hold a truth value. The words **true** and **false**, which are boolean literals in Java, can be used to assign values to boolean variables. These variables are sometimes useful when loops are constructed. A variable of type **boolean** can be used to control the correct termination of a loop. For example, the following **while** loop reads integers from the keyboard and calculates their sum until the user types in 9999

```
int sum_of_integers = 0 ;

boolean user_wants_to_stop_entering_numbers = false ;

while ( user_wants_to_stop_entering_numbers == false )
{
   System.out.print( "\n Give a number: " ) ;

   int integer_from_keyboard  =  keyboard.nextInt() ;

   if ( integer_from_keyboard  ==  9999 )
   {
      user_wants_to_stop_entering_numbers = true ;
   }
   else
   {
      sum_of_integers  =
               sum_of_integers + integer_from_keyboard ;
   }
}
```

The truth values of relational and other expressions can be printed to the screen. Program **TruthValues.java** is an example in which truth values of some relational expressions are first assigned to some variables of type **boolean**, and then the values of the **boolean** variables are printed. It is not absolutely necessary that truth values are stored in a variable before printing. It is also possible to print truth values with a statement like

```
System.out.print( "" + ( left_integer < right_integer ) ) ;
```

In practical programs it is not necessary to print truth values of expressions, but now, when you are still learning the basics of programming, it may be useful to study programs like **TruthValues.java**. Using a temporary statement that prints the truth value of an expression may also help when you are trying to find an error in your program.

```
//  TruthValues.java

class TruthValues
{
   public static void main( String[] not_in_use )
   {
      int left_integer  =  4 ;

      System.out.print( "\n left  right   <     >=    !=  \n" ) ;

      for ( int right_integer  =  0 ;
                right_integer  <  7 ;
                right_integer  ++ )
      {
         System.out.print( "\n    "  +  left_integer
                         + "     "  +  right_integer ) ;

        boolean  first_truth_value   =  ( left_integer  <  right_integer ) ;
        boolean  second_truth_value  =  ( left_integer  >= right_integer ) ;
        boolean  third_truth_value   =  ( left_integer  != right_integer ) ;

         System.out.print( "   "  +  first_truth_value
                          +  "  "  +  second_truth_value
                          +  "  "  +  third_truth_value  ) ;
      }
   }
}
```

**boolean** is a variable type that can store a truth value. In this statement, the value of the relational expression **( left_integer < right_integer )** is stored into the variable **first_truth_value**. The truth value changes when the loop is executed.

When the plus sign, i.e., the string concatenation operator, is placed between a string value and a **boolean** variable, the value stored in the **boolean** variable is converted either to the string "true" or "false".

**TruthValues.java - 1. A program that prints truth values.**

```
D:\javafiles2>java TruthValues

 left  right   <     >=    !=

   4     0   false  true  true
   4     1   false  true  true
   4     2   false  true  true
   4     3   false  true  true
   4     4   false  true  false
   4     5   true  false  true
   4     6   true  false  true
```

**TruthValues.java - X. Truth values of expressions changing in a loop.**

## 6.9 Chapter summary

- Decisions and repetitions are two very important and fundamentally essential programming concepts. Decision making through **if** constructs and repetition through loop constructs are the two basic mechanisms that make programs work.
- **if** constructs and loops are statements containing other statements, which we call internal statements. An **if** construct can have other **if** constructs or loops as internal statements. Similarly, a loop may have **if** constructs or other loops as internal statements.
- Every **if** construct and loop must have a boolean expression that determines which decisions are made, or for however long looping goes on. Boolean expressions are either true or false.
- Boolean expressions are mainly written using relational operators (**<**, **<=**, **>**, **>=**, **==**, and **!=**) together with logical operators (**&&**, **||**, and **!**). Typically, logical operators are used to combine several relational operations.

### "foreach" loops

In addition to the basic **while**, **for**, and **do-while** loops, Java has a fourth kind of loop structure that I call here the "foreach" loop. A "foreach" loop is a new kind of **for** loop that has been introduced in the Java version 5.0. The "foreach" loop of Java is similar to the loops that are written with the **foreach** keyword in some other programming languages (e.g. C#). (Obviously, because it is difficult to add new keywords to an existing programming language, the developers of Java could not add the **foreach** keyword to the language when the "foreach" loop was introduced in version 5.0.)

"foreach" loops can be exploited when arrays are used in a program. (At this point you do not necessarily have to understand what I say here because arrays are the subjects of later chapters.) With a "foreach" loop it is possible to process an array without having to write too many source program lines. For example, the traditional **for** loop

```
for ( int integer_index  =  0 ;
          integer_index  <  array_of_integers.length ;
          integer_index  ++ )
{
   System.out.print( "  "  +  array_of_integers[ integer_index ] )
}
```

can be replaced with the following "foreach" loop that has less lines

```
for ( int integer_in_array : array_of_integers )
{
   System.out.print( "  "  +  integer_in_array ) ;
}
```

A "foreach" loop is written with the keyword **for**, and it processes the elements of an array from the beginning to the end. "foreach" loops do not contain a boolean expression. Instead, they always process all elements of an array. "foreach" loops are not as flexible as the conventional **for** loops. Everything that can be done with a "foreach" loop in a program can also be done with a traditional **for** loop. However, not all traditional **for** loops can be replaced with a "foreach" loop.

Among the extra programs of this book, in the **javafilesextra** folder, you can find a file named **ForeachDemo.java** that demonstrates the use of the "foreach" loop.

# CHAPTER 7

## ARRAYS: SETS OF SIMILAR DATA ITEMS

Computers process information and usually they need to process masses of information. In previous chapters we have studied programs that contain a few variables where information is stored. These kinds of programs are not sufficient to handle practical information processing tasks. Therefore, programming languages provide data structures that can store larger quantities of information.

Arrays are data structures in which it is possible to store many similar data items. Arrays can thus hold large amounts of information. In this chapter we shall learn how traditional arrays are declared, created, and used in Java. A traditional array is such that it can store data items of certain type (e.g. **`int`**, **`long`**, **`byte`**, or **`double`**). A traditional array has a certain length which specifies how many data items it can store.

## 7.1 Creating arrays and referring to array elements

Arrays are collections of similar data items, such as integers. We usually need an array when we want to handle many similar data items in a single program. Everything that can be stored in a variable can also be stored in an array. The difference between a variable and an array is that, while a variable stores exactly one data item, an array can hold hundreds of similar data items.

The declaration of an array is rather complex when we compare it to the declaration of a variable. A variable of type **int** can be declared by writing

```
int  some_name ;
```

but to declare and create an array that can hold 5 values of type **int**, we must write

```
int[]  some_name  =  new  int[ 5 ] ;
```

Both declarations above begin with the keyword **int** to indicate that we are declaring something that can hold integer values. In the array declaration a pair of empty brackets [] after the keyword **int** tells the Java compiler that now we are declaring an array, and not a variable. The expression to the right of the assignment operator = actually creates the array and reserves necessary memory space for it. When we write

```
new  int[ 5 ]
```

we specify that new memory space must be reserved to store 5 data items of type **int**. An array like the one above is said to have 5 array elements or positions, and the length of the array is 5. The storage capacity of this array is the same as the capacity of five separate variables of type **int**.

Arrays are used in the same way as variables. First we declare an array and then we store information in it. Storing information in a variable is simple because a variable holds only one piece of information at a time. An assignment statement can store a value in a variable, for example, in the following way

```
some_integer_variable  =  7  ;
```

Storing a value in an array is more complex because we have to somehow specify exactly where in the array we want the value to be stored. To store a number in an array, we need to use an index value which dictates in which element in the array the number will be stored. Let us suppose that we have the following array of integers created

```
int[] array_of_integers  =  new  int[ 50 ] ;
```

This array can be used to store up to 50 integer values. At the beginning, when the array is created, it does not contain meaningful data. We can refer to some array element by writing an index value in brackets after the array name. This way numbers can be stored in an array. For example, the following assignment statements write numbers 7 and 77 to the first and second element in the above array

```
array_of_integers[ 0 ]  =   7 ;
array_of_integers[ 1 ]  =  77 ;
```

Index values start counting from zero, not from one. When we want to refer to the first element of an array, we use index 0. The index of the second element is 1, the index of the third element is 2, and so on. The maximum index that the above array of integers can have is 49, one less than the defined array length. You should note that the number inside brackets has a different meaning in array creation and in a reference to an array element. In an array creation the number means the array length. In a reference to an array element, the number specifies which array element is going to be affected.

The above array of integers has a storage capacity that is equal to 50 variables of type **int**. Because a variable of type **int** requires 4 bytes (32 bits) of memory space, the above array requires 200 bytes (50 times 4 bytes) of memory. We can think that the array is a 200-byte memory area that is divided into 50 slots, and each 4-byte slot can hold an **int** value. By writing **array_of_integers[ 0 ]** we can refer to the first slot or position in the array. **array_of_integers[ 49 ]** refers to the last position in the array. When an array is allocated memory space from a computer's main memory, we do not need to know the exact memory address of the array. We can, however, think that the first array position has the smallest numerical memory address, and the last position has the largest numerical memory address.

Program **ArrayDemo.java** shows different ways to assign values to the elements of an array whose type is **int[]**. The array in program **ArrayDemo.java** has 50 array elements which are filled with various integer values. You can see that a loop is the most efficient way to fill an array. Usually, **for** loops are used when entire arrays are processed. Figure 7-1 shows what the array of program **ArrayDemo.java** looks like in a computer's main memory after the program has been executed.

An index variable, such as **integer_index** in **ArrayDemo.java**, is the most efficient and common way to access the elements of an array. With an index variable we specify which position of an array we are currently accessing. An index variable is usually initialized before the processing of an array begins. During the processing of an array in a loop, the index variable is either incremented or decremented inside the loop. To understand how index variables work, let us suppose that we have made the following declarations:

```
int[] array_of_integers  =  new  int[ 50 ] ;
int   integer_index  =  4 ;
```

The index variable **integer_index** having been initialized with the value 4,

- **array_of_integers[ integer_index ]** refers to the 5th array element in the array of integers,
- **array_of_integers[ integer_index - 1 ]** refers to the 4th element,
- **array_of_integers[ integer_index + 2 ]** refers to the 7th element, and
- **array_of_integers[ integer_index * 2 ]** refers to the 9th element.

The above examples demonstrate that it is possible to write an arithmetic expression inside the brackets in an array reference.When we use an index variable, it is easy to move to the following or previous element in an array by incrementing or decrementing the index variable by one. An array reference that contains an arithmetic expression does not alter the value of the index variable. In the array reference **array_of_integers[ integer_index + 1 ]** the value of **integer_index** is not modified. The program calculates the value of **integer_index + 1** (i.e. the program evaluates expression **integer_index + 1**), but that value is discarded once the array reference is processed.

## Exercises with program ArrayDemo.java

Exercise 7-1. Written twice in the program is "+ 2". How would the behavior of the program change if the plus sign and number 2 were taken away from the program?

Exercise 7-2. Modify the first **for** loop so that values 8, 11, 14, 17, 20, 23, 26, 29, etc. will be written to those array positions which currently hold values 7, 9, 11, 13, 15, 17, 19, 21, etc. This is not a large modification.

Exercise 7.3. What would happen if the beginning of the second **for** loop was written like

```
for ( integer_index  =  1 ;
      integer_index  <  29 ;
      integer_index  =  integer_index + 2 )
```

Exercise 7-4. Modify the second **for** loop, or replace it with a **while** loop, so that the loop prints out the integers from the array in reverse order. Studying program **Reverse.java** may help in this task.

The first three elements in the array are assigned values 333, 33, and 3.

The fourth element in the array gets a value that is the value of the third element plus 2. As the index value of an array element is always one less than the "serial number" of the element, the fourth element is accessed with index 3, and the third element with index 2.

```
//  ArrayDemo.java

class ArrayDemo
{
   public static void main( String[] not_in_use )
   {
      int[]  array_of_integers  =  new  int[ 50 ] ;

      int   integer_index ;

      array_of_integers[ 0 ]  =  333 ;
      array_of_integers[ 1 ]  =   33 ;
      array_of_integers[ 2 ]  =    3 ;
      array_of_integers[ 3 ]  =  array_of_integers[ 2 ]  +  2 ;

      for ( integer_index  =  4 ;
            integer_index  <  50 ;
            integer_index  ++ )
      {
         array_of_integers[ integer_index ]  =
                array_of_integers[ integer_index - 1 ]  +  2 ;
      }

      System.out.print( "\n The contents of \"array_of_integers\" is:\n" ) ;

      for ( integer_index  =  0 ;
            integer_index  <  50 ;
            integer_index  ++ )
      {
         if ( ( integer_index  %  10 )  ==  0 )
         {
            System.out.print( "\n" ) ;
         }

         System.out.printf( "%5d", array_of_integers[ integer_index ] ) ;
      }
   }
}
```

**ArrayDemo.java - 1.+ A program that demonstrates the use of an array.**

```
D:\javafiles2>java ArrayDemo

 The contents of "array_of_integers" is:

  333   33    3    5    7    9   11   13   15   17
   19   21   23   25   27   29   31   33   35   37
   39   41   43   45   47   49   51   53   55   57
   59   61   63   65   67   69   71   73   75   77
   79   81   83   85   87   89   91   93   95   97
```

**ArrayDemo.java - X. 10 array elements are printed on each row.**

This **for** loop writes numbers to array positions with index values from 4 to 49. As variable **integer_index** is assigned value 4 at the beginning, the 5th element in the array will be written first.

The value of variable **integer_index** is incremented by one always after the internal statements of the **for** loop have been executed. The variable will reach a value of 50 but that value is not used because the loop terminates.

```
for ( integer_index  =  4 ;
      integer_index  <  50 ;
      integer_index  ++ )
{
   array_of_integers[ integer_index ]  =
          array_of_integers[ integer_index - 1 ]  +  2 ;
}
```

Here the index is an arithmetic expression. This means that the value of this expression is used as an index to access the array. The computer calculates how much is "**integer_index** minus one" before accessing the array. The value of **integer_index** is not modified in this operation.

This statement means that the array element currently referred to with **integer_index** gets a value that is the value of the preceding array element plus 2. By writing **integer_index - 1** it is possible to refer to the preceding element in the array. Because the value of **array_of_integers[ 3 ]** is 5, the values of subsequent elements will be 7, 9, 11, 13, 15, etc.

**ArrayDemo.java - 1 - 1: The for loop that writes array elements with indexes from 4 to 49.**

Usually, when we want to go through an entire array in a **for** loop, the first index is zero, and the upper limit is the array length, which is 50 in this case. The value 50 is never used in array access because the operator <, "less than", terminates the loop with that value.

This **if** construct ensures that a newline character is printed after ten values from the array have been printed. Here the remainder operator % returns the remainder for the case where the **integer_index** is divided by 10. A newline will be printed if the remainder is zero. This results in a newline being printed with **integer_index** values 0, 10, 20, 30, and 40. The use of operator % does not affect the value of **integer_index**.

```
for ( integer_index  =  0 ;
      integer_index  <  50 ;
      integer_index  ++ )
{
   if ( ( integer_index  %  10 )  ==  0 )
   {
      System.out.print( "\n" ) ;
   }

   System.out.printf( "%5d", array_of_integers[ integer_index ] ) ;
}
```

Method **printf()** prints the values of the array elements. This format specifier stipulates that the values are printed right-justified to a printing field that is 5 character positions wide. This ensures that all numbers end in the same column on the screen, regardless of how many digits the numbers may have.

**ArrayDemo.java - 1 - 2. The for loop that prints the entire array to the screen.**

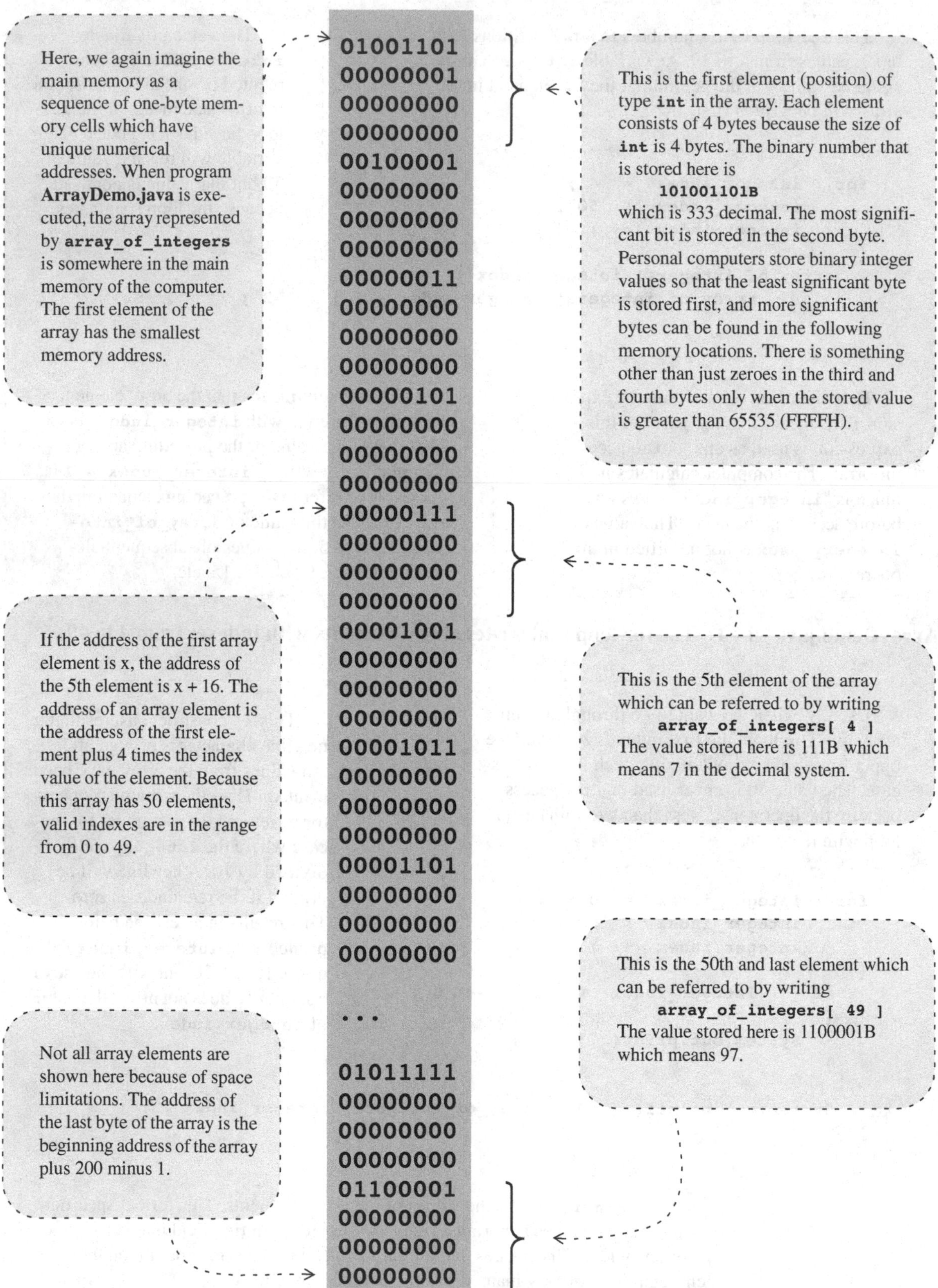

Here, we again imagine the main memory as a sequence of one-byte memory cells which have unique numerical addresses. When program ArrayDemo.java is executed, the array represented by array_of_integers is somewhere in the main memory of the computer. The first element of the array has the smallest memory address.
01001101
00000001
00000000
00000000
00100001
00000000
00000000
00000000
00000011
00000000
00000000
00000000
00000101
00000000
00000000
00000000
00000111
00000000
00000000
00000000
00001001
00000000
00000000
00000000
00001011
00000000
00000000
00000000
00001101
00000000
00000000
00000000
...
01011111
00000000
00000000
00000000
01100001
00000000
00000000
00000000
This is the first element (position) of type int in the array. Each element consists of 4 bytes because the size of int is 4 bytes. The binary number that is stored here is
101001101B
which is 333 decimal. The most significant bit is stored in the second byte. Personal computers store binary integer values so that the least significant byte is stored first, and more significant bytes can be found in the following memory locations. There is something other than just zeroes in the third and fourth bytes only when the stored value is greater than 65535 (FFFFH).
If the address of the first array element is x, the address of the 5th element is x + 16. The address of an array element is the address of the first element plus 4 times the index value of the element. Because this array has 50 elements, valid indexes are in the range from 0 to 49.
This is the 5th element of the array which can be referred to by writing
array_of_integers[ 4 ]
The value stored here is 111B which means 7 in the decimal system.
Not all array elements are shown here because of space limitations. The address of the last byte of the array is the beginning address of the array plus 200 minus 1.
This is the 50th and last element which can be referred to by writing
array_of_integers[ 49 ]
The value stored here is 1100001B which means 97.

*Figure 7-1. The array of integers in the main memory after the execution of ArrayDemo.java.*

Program **Reverse.java** is another example of using an array of integers. This program reads integers from the keyboard and stores the read numbers in an array. The reading loop terminates when the user types in a zero. The reading loop is followed by another loop that outputs the integers from the array so that the integers are printed in reverse order. This is achieved by decrementing the index variable towards zero. Arrays are used in programs when many similar data items need to be stored and manipulated. Program **Reverse.java** has to store all the input integers because it needs to remember them all in order to print them in reverse order.

When we create an array, we must specify a length for the array. For example, when we write

```
int[] array_of_integers  =  new  int[ 50 ] ;
```

we create an array whose length is 50, i.e., this array has 50 different positions for storing `int` values. The length of an array cannot be modified after the array is created.

The length of an array dictates which are the legal index values when we refer to the individual array elements. For an array whose length is 50, the legal index values are in the range from 0 to 49. The Java compiler can compile a program in which an illegal index value is used, but the program cannot be executed. For example, a program containing the statements

```
int[] array_of_integers  =  new  int[ 50 ] ;
array_of_integers[ 52 ]  =   88 ;
array_of_integers[ 99 ]  =  888 ;
```

can be compiled, but it cannot be successfully executed because the index values 52 and 99 are larger than the largest legal index value 49.

Program **Reverse.java** does not have any protection against the use of too large index values. If you had the patience to type in more than 100 integers into **Reverse.java**, the program would terminate with the text

```
Exception in thread "main"
java.lang.ArrayIndexOutOfBoundsException: 100
```

appearing on the screen. **Reverse.java** was written without any protection against the use of too large index values because it is easier at first to study simple programs. However, when you write programs that have purposes other than educational, you must take care that array indexes are not growing too large.

Program **MeanvalueArray.java** is an example of a safer program that ensures that the index variable `number_index` does not exceed the length of the used array. The `while` loop that writes data to the array is equipped with the boolean expression

```
number_index  <  array_of_numbers.length
```

which terminates the loop if `number_index` becomes too large. By writing `.length` in the above boolean expression we can find out what length was specified for the array when it was created.

`length` is a data field that is associated with every array. This data field stores the length of an array and it can be read by using the dot operator . in the following way

```
array_name.length
```

The `length` field provides an integer value that tells what is the length of the array in question. This integer value can be used in many ways. For example, the program lines

```
int[] some_array  =  new  int[ 33 ] ;
System.out.print( "Array length is " + some_array.length ) ;
```

would produce the following line to the screen

```
Array length is 33
```

Here we declare and create an array that has space to store 100 **int** values. This array reserves 400 bytes of memory. **integer_index** is a variable that is used to index the array. With initial value 0, **integer_index** refers to the first position in the array.

The value of variable **integer_-from_keyboard** is copied to an array position specified by the value of variable **integer_index**. As the value of **integer_index** is incremented by one after this statement, the next integer will be written to the next position in the array.

```
//  Reverse.java  (c) Kari Laitinen

import java.util.* ;

class Reverse
{
   public static void main( String[] not_in_use )
   {
      Scanner keyboard = new Scanner( System.in ) ;

      int[] array_of_integers      =  new  int[ 100 ] ;
      int   integer_index          =  0 ;
      int   integer_from_keyboard  =  0 ;

      System.out.print("\n This program reads integers from the keyboard."
                     + "\n After receiving a zero, it prints the numbers"
                     + "\n in reverse order. Please, start entering numbers."
                     + "\n The program will stop when you enter a zero.\n\n") ;
      do
      {
         System.out.print( " "  +  integer_index  +  "  Enter an integer: ") ;
         integer_from_keyboard  =  keyboard.nextInt() ;

         array_of_integers[ integer_index ]  =  integer_from_keyboard ;
         integer_index  ++ ;
      }
       while ( integer_from_keyboard  !=  0 ) ;

      System.out.print( "\n Reverse order:  " ) ;

      while  ( integer_index  >  0 )
      {
         integer_index  -- ;
         System.out.print( array_of_integers[ integer_index ]  +  "   " ) ;
      }
   }
}
```

This **while** loop prints the contents of the array to the screen. Because **integer_index** is decremented inside the loop, the numbers are printed in reverse order.

This **do-while** loop terminates when the user of the program types in a zero. Also the zero is written to the array. When this loop terminates, **integer_index** has a value that is exactly the same as the number of integers written to the array. The zero is included in that count.

Remember that **do-while** loops execute at least once. This program works also when the user enters nothing but the zero.

**Reverse.java - 1.+ A program that inputs integers and prints them in reverse order.**

When this loop is entered, **integer_index** contains a value that equals the number of integers that were originally typed in and stored to the array. **integer_index** thus refers to the first array element that has not been written in the program. Therefore, **integer_index** must be decremented before anything is printed. Operator -- decrements the value of a variable by one.

This loop can be approximately translated into natural language: "As long as it is possible to decrement variable **integer_index** without it becoming negative, decrement it, and use the value to print an integer from the array of integers."

```
while  ( integer_index  >  0 )
{
   integer_index  -- ;
   System.out.print( array_of_integers[ integer_index ] +  "   " ) ;
}
```

Three spaces are used to separate the printed integers.

**Reverse.java - 1 - 1. The while loop that prints the array in reverse order.**

```
D:\javafiles2>java Reverse

 This program reads integers from the keyboard.
 After receiving a zero, it prints the numbers
 in reverse order. Please, start entering numbers.
 The program will stop when you enter a zero.

 0  Enter an integer: 22
 1  Enter an integer: 33
 2  Enter an integer: 444
 3  Enter an integer: 555
 4  Enter an integer: 6666
 5  Enter an integer: 7777
 6  Enter an integer: 88
 7  Enter an integer: 99
 8  Enter an integer: 0

 Reverse order:  0   99   88   7777   6666   555   444   33   22
```

**Reverse.java - X. Here the program is executed with 9 integers.**

An array is created here so that its length is 100. The array is thus capable of holding 100 different values of type **double**. Later, the **length** field is used to refer to the previously specified length of the array.

```
//  MeanvalueArray.java

import java.util.* ;

class MeanvalueArray
{
   public static void main( String[] not_in_use )
   {
      Scanner keyboard = new Scanner( System.in ) ;
      System.out.print( "\n This program calculates the mean value of"
                      + "\n the numbers you enter from the keyboard."
                      + "\n The program stops when you enter a letter."
                      + "\n\n   Enter a number: " ) ;

      double[]  array_of_numbers  =  new double[ 100 ] ;
      int       number_index   =  0  ;
      boolean  keyboard_input_is_numerical  =  true ;

      while ( keyboard_input_is_numerical ==  true  &&
              number_index  <  array_of_numbers.length  )
      {
         try
         {
            double  number_from_keyboard  =  keyboard.nextDouble() ;

            array_of_numbers[ number_index ]  =  number_from_keyboard ;
            number_index  ++ ;
            System.out.print(  "   Enter a number: " ) ;
         }
         catch ( Exception  not_numerical_input_exception )
         {
            keyboard_input_is_numerical  =  false ;
         }
      }

      int  number_of_numbers_in_array  =  number_index ;
      double  sum_of_numbers  =  0 ;

      for (  number_index  =  0 ;
             number_index  <  number_of_numbers_in_array ;
             number_index  ++ )
      {
         sum_of_numbers  =  sum_of_numbers  +
                            array_of_numbers[ number_index ] ;
      }

      double  mean_value  =  0 ;

      if ( number_of_numbers_in_array  >  0 )
      {
         mean_value  =  sum_of_numbers /
                        (double) number_of_numbers_in_array ;
      }

      System.out.print( "\n The mean value is: " + mean_value + " \n" ) ;
   }
}
```

**MeanvalueArray.java - 1.+ An improved version of program MeanvalueException.java.**

As in program **MeanvalueException.java**, numerical values are read from the keyboard inside a **try-catch** construct. When method **nextDouble()** detects that non-numerical data were read from the keyboard, the **catch** block is executed.

The boolean expression of this **while** loop consists of two subexpressions. The latter part of the boolean expression takes care that too large index values are not used. The length of the array was defined to be 100 at the beginning of the program. If **number_index** reaches this value, the loop terminates. The logical-AND operator && combines the two parts of the boolean expression.

```
      while ( keyboard_input_is_numerical ==  true  &&
              number_index  <  array_of_numbers.length  )
      {
         try
         {
            double  number_from_keyboard  =  keyboard.nextDouble() ;

            array_of_numbers[ number_index ]  =  number_from_keyboard ;
            number_index  ++ ;
            System.out.print(  "   Enter a number:  " ) ;
         }
         catch ( Exception  not_numerical_input_exception )
         {
            keyboard_input_is_numerical  =  false ;
         }
      }
```

This statement is executed when the user of the program types in something else than valid numbers. When the boolean variable is given the value **false**, the loop terminates.

This statement copies the number typed in from the keyboard into the array position determined by the value of **number_index**.

**MeanvalueArray.java - 1 -1. The while loop that inputs numbers from the keyboard.**

```
D:\javafiles2>java MeanvalueArray

 This program calculates the mean value of
 the numbers you enter from the keyboard.
 The program stops when you enter a letter.

   Enter a number: 1040.609
   Enter a number: 2030.456
   Enter a number: 2345
   Enter a number: 2346.789
   Enter a number: 3344.99
   Enter a number: z

 The mean value is: 2221.5688
```

**MeanvalueArray.java - X. Calculating the mean value of five input numbers.**

Program **MeanvalueArray.java** is an improved version of programs **Meanvalue.java** and **MeanvalueException.java** which we studied in Chapter 6. These programs are able to calculate mean values of integers, but **MeanvalueArray.java** is also able to handle floating-point numbers and even the zero. The array in **MeanvalueArray.java** is of type **double**, the double-precision floating-point type. Although the array is a floating-point array, it is indexed with an **int** variable.

Every variable type in Java can also be the type of an array (see Figure 7-2). All types of arrays are indexed in the same way, using indexes of type **int**. The arrays

```
int[]    array_of_integers   =  new  int[ 50 ] ;
float[]  array_of_floats     =  new  float[ 50 ] ;
double[] array_of_numbers    =  new  double[ 50 ] ;
char[]   array_of_characters =  new  char[ 50 ] ;
```

are all acceptable to the Java compiler. The length of all these arrays is 50, but they would need different amounts of memory. The array of type **float[]** would need 200 bytes of memory because a variable of type **float** needs 4 bytes. The array of type **char[]** would need only 100 bytes because a variable of type **char** is a two-byte variable.

When we use arrays in our programs, we usually need index variables to access the array. In this book the index variables are mostly named so that the name of the index variable indicates what is stored in the array being indexed. For example, if an array stores integers, the name of the index variable is **integer_index**; arrays that store other kinds of numbers are indexed with a variable named **number_index**; an array of type **char[]** is indexed with **character_index**; and so on.

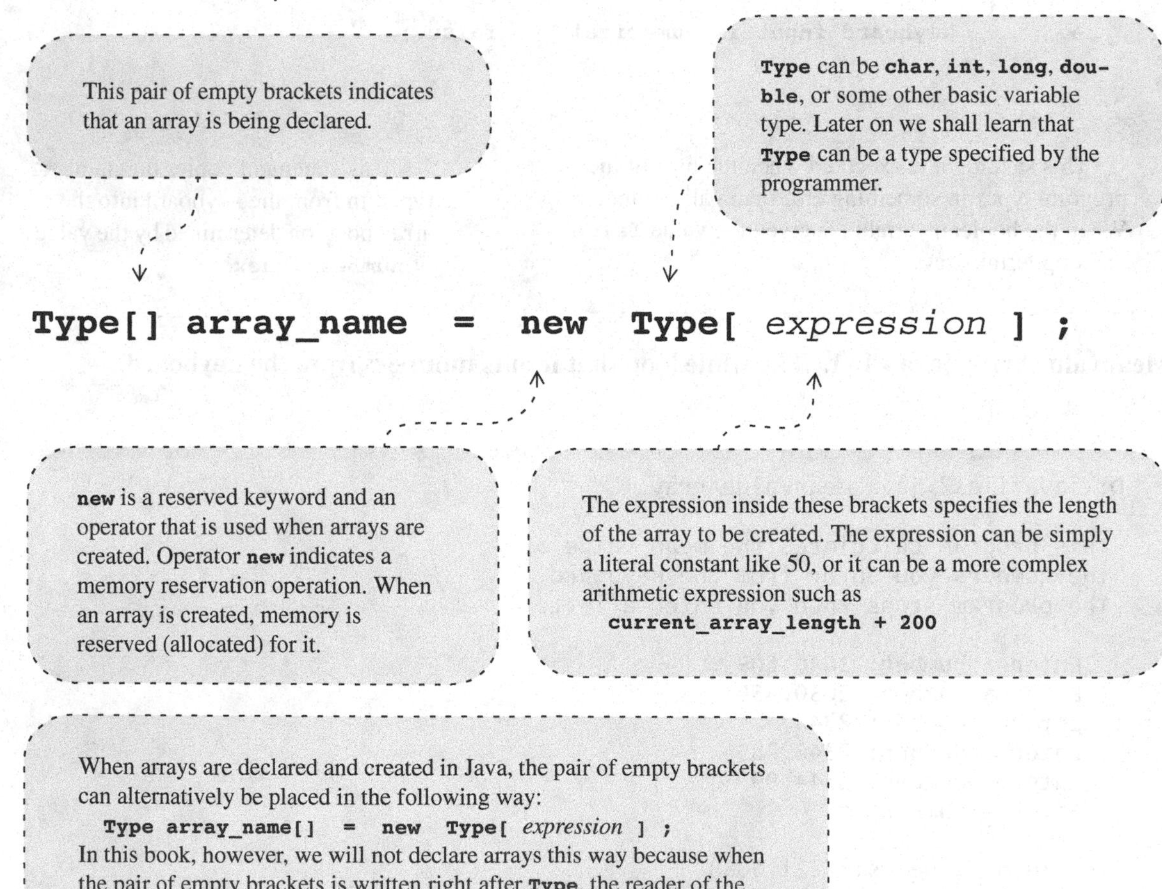

This pair of empty brackets indicates that an array is being declared.
Type can be char, int, long, double, or some other basic variable type. Later on we shall learn that Type can be a type specified by the programmer.
Type[] array_name = new Type[ expression ] ;
new is a reserved keyword and an operator that is used when arrays are created. Operator new indicates a memory reservation operation. When an array is created, memory is reserved (allocated) for it.
The expression inside these brackets specifies the length of the array to be created. The expression can be simply a literal constant like 50, or it can be a more complex arithmetic expression such as
current_array_length + 200
When arrays are declared and created in Java, the pair of empty brackets can alternatively be placed in the following way:
Type array_name[] = new Type[ expression ] ;
In this book, however, we will not declare arrays this way because when the pair of empty brackets is written right after Type, the reader of the program can discover it more easily that an array is being introduced.


*Figure 7-2. The syntax of a simple array creation statement.*

## 7.2 Array declaration vs. array creation

In the example programs of the preceding section, arrays were created with statements such as

```
int[] array_of_integers  =  new  int[ 50 ] ;
```

This statement actually includes two separate operations: the declaration of an array and the creation of an array. The above statement can be replaced with the two statements

```
int[] array_of_integers ;

array_of_integers  =  new  int[ 50 ] ;
```

of which the first statement declares an array and the latter statement creates an array. The array declaration statement

```
int[] array_of_integers ;
```

specifies an array reference that can refer to or point to an array that will be created later. The pair of empty brackets informs the compiler that here we are declaring an array, and not a variable. Keyword **int** in the declaration stipulates that the array can contain only values of type **int**.

The array creation statement

```
array_of_integers  =  new  int[ 50 ] ;
```

actually creates the array by reserving necessary memory area for it. An array of type **int[]** whose length is 50 needs a memory area whose size is equal to the memory needed by 50 separate variables of type **int**.

When a Java program is being run on a computer, the program uses separate memory areas from the main memory in the following way:

- The program needs "program memory" for itself. The Java interpreter (the Java virtual machine) stores the executable Java program from a **.class** file to a memory area which we can call "program memory". (An executable Java program consists of bytecode instructions which are processed by the Java interpreter. The Java interpreter is itself a "real" computer program consisting of executable machine instructions.)
- The stack memory is a memory area from which memory space is allocated for small data items such as variables.
- The heap memory is a memory area from which the program can reserve memory space for large pieces of data. The large pieces of data include arrays and other large objects that we'll study later in this book.

When an array is declared and created in a Java program, both the stack memory and the heap memory are needed. These separate memory areas, that reside "somewhere" in the main memory, are used so that an array creation statement reserves memory space from the heap memory, and an array declaration statement reserves four bytes from the stack memory. The four bytes that are reserved from the stack memory are able to store a 32-bit memory address, the address of the memory space in the heap memory. Figure 7-3 describes the usage of these two memory areas.

When we speak about the separate memory areas in the main memory of a computer, we can only say that they reside "somewhere" in the main memory. We do not need to know exactly where these memory areas are. The operating system of the computer manages these memory areas, and takes care that program executing on the computer can access them. We, programmers, need to understand how these memory areas are used when we specify different kinds of data constructs in our programs.

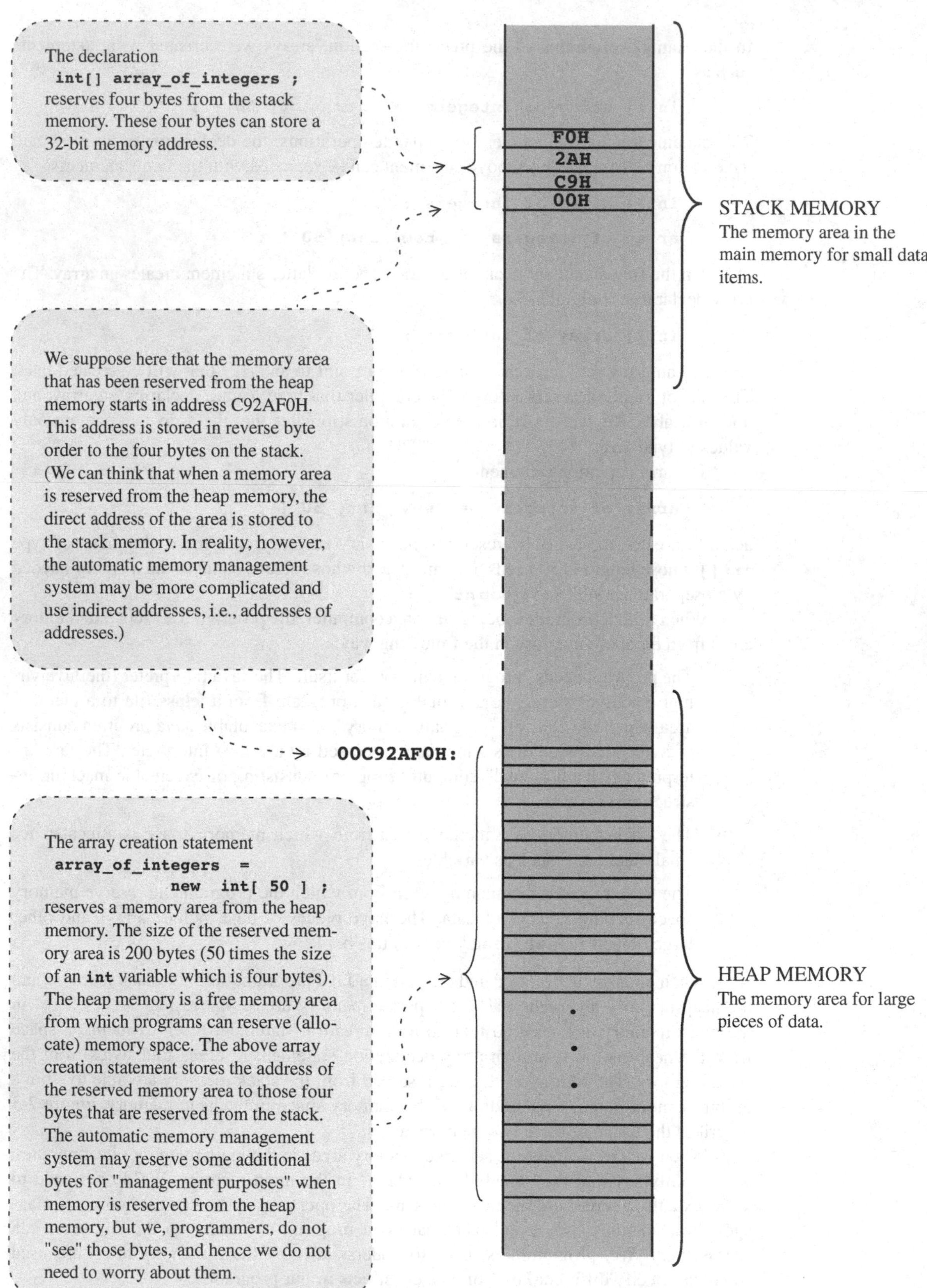

The declaration
int[] array_of_integers ;
reserves four bytes from the stack memory. These four bytes can store a 32-bit memory address.
F0H
2AH
C9H
00H
STACK MEMORY
The memory area in the main memory for small data items.
We suppose here that the memory area that has been reserved from the heap memory starts in address C92AF0H. This address is stored in reverse byte order to the four bytes on the stack. (We can think that when a memory area is reserved from the heap memory, the direct address of the area is stored to the stack memory. In reality, however, the automatic memory management system may be more complicated and use indirect addresses, i.e., addresses of addresses.)
00C92AF0H:
The array creation statement
array_of_integers =
new int[ 50 ] ;
reserves a memory area from the heap memory. The size of the reserved memory area is 200 bytes (50 times the size of an int variable which is four bytes). The heap memory is a free memory area from which programs can reserve (allocate) memory space. The above array creation statement stores the address of the reserved memory area to those four bytes that are reserved from the stack. The automatic memory management system may reserve some additional bytes for "management purposes" when memory is reserved from the heap memory, but we, programmers, do not "see" those bytes, and hence we do not need to worry about them.
HEAP MEMORY
The memory area for large pieces of data.


***Figure 7-3. Memory used by an array.***

## 7.3 Initialized arrays

Sometimes we need arrays to contain certain data before they are referred to in a program. In other words, arrays may need to be initialized. Initialization means giving a data item a value at the same time as it is declared. We have already learned how to initialize single variables. Very often, an index variable is initialized to the value zero in the following way

```
int   some_index   =   0 ;
```

Just as we can initialize single variables, it is possible to initialize arrays. However, because arrays need to be both declared and created before they can be used, their initialization is somewhat complicated. One possibility to declare, create, and initialize an array in Java is to use the following kind of statement

```
int[]  days_in_months   =   new  int[]
   { 0, 31, 28, 31, 30, 31, 30, 31, 31, 30, 31, 30, 31 } ;
```

In the above statement, the initialization values are given inside braces { } with individual values separated by commas. The length of the created array is 13 because there are 13 initialization values given inside the braces. Initialized in this way, the elements of the array contain the following values

```
days_in_months[ 0 ]      contains 0
days_in_months[ 1 ]      contains 31
days_in_months[ 2 ]      contains 28
days_in_months[ 3 ]      contains 31
....
days_in_months[ 11 ]     contains 30
days_in_months[ 12 ]     contains 31
```

The array referenced by **days_in_months** could be used in a program that needs to know how many days there are in a given month. (This array would not be convenient to handle leap years which have 29 days in February.) By indexing the above array with the number of the month in question, the program would get the number of days in that month. Note that there is also a month with number zero which has zero days. This extra "month" allows the array to be indexed with the real month number.

The above statement in which an array is declared, created, and initialized is somewhat complicated. Luckily, Java provides another possibility to create an initialized array. The above statement can be replaced with the statement

```
int[]  days_in_months   =
   { 0, 31, 28, 31, 30, 31, 30, 31, 31, 30, 31, 30, 31 } ;
```

from which **new int[]** has been left out. Also in this simpler statement, the array is created and the length of the array is determined by the number of initialization values inside the braces. Similarly, initialized arrays of other types can be declared in different ways. The following two array declarations are identical

```
double[]  us_gallons_to_liters  =  new  double[]
     { 0.0, 3.785, 7.570, 11.355, 15.140, 18.925 } ;

double[]  us_gallons_to_liters  =
     { 0.0, 3.785, 7.570, 11.355, 15.140, 18.925 } ;
```

These arrays could be used to convert U.S. gallons to liters (e.g. 2 gallons is 7.570 liters). The latter array creation statement is simpler. Generally, it is easier to create initialized arrays without writing **new int[]**, **new double[]**, etc. to the array creation statements.

The following are examples of initialized arrays of types **float** and **char**

```
float[] liters_to_us_gallons =
            { 0.0F, 0.264F, 0.528F, 0.793F, 1.057F, 1.321F } ;

char[] arithmetic_operators = { '+', '-', '*', '/', '%' };
```

You must remember to add the letter F to the end of the initialization values, the floating-point literals, when you are initializing an array of type **float**. Without the suffix F, a floating-point literal is considered to be of type **double**.

If an array is not explicitly initialized by giving the initialization values in braces, all the elements of the array are initialized implicitly with default values for the type that is stored in the array. The default initialization value is zero. Therefore, the following two array creations are identical

```
int[] array_of_zeroes = new int[ 6 ] ;

int[] array_of_zeroes = { 0, 0, 0, 0, 0, 0 } ;
```

As you can see by studying program **Celsius.java**, the use of an initialized array is not different from the use of a non-initialized array. Initialization is just a means to easily put some meaningful data to an array. Once the data exists in the array, the elements of the array can be referred to in the normal way.

## Exercises related to arrays

Exercise 7-5. Modify program **ArrayDemo.java** so that it calculates and prints the sum of the numbers which are stored in the array of integers. This can be achieved, for example, by adding a third loop to the program. Studying program **MeanvalueArray.java** may be useful.

Exercise 7-6. Below, you will find a method **main()**, without the last closing brace, that reads integers from the keyboard and stores them in an array. Your task is to continue the program by adding a new loop which goes through the array of integers and prints all integers that are greater than 99. You can also add new variables at the beginning of method **main()**. Inside the new loop, you must test, using an **if** construct, which integers are greater than 99. For example, if the program received numbers

```
2 301 44 100 1999 13 99 222 177 98 0
```

it should print numbers

```
301 100 1999 222 177
```

You should continue the following program

```
import java.util.* ;

class IntegersLargerThan99
{
   public static void main( String[] not_in_use )
   {
      Scanner keyboard = new Scanner( System.in ) ;

      int[] array_of_integers     = new int[ 100 ] ;
      int   integer_index         =   0 ;
      int   integer_from_keyboard = 999 ;

      while ( integer_from_keyboard  != 0 )
      {
         System.out.print( "\nEnter an integer: " ) ;
         integer_from_keyboard = keyboard.nextInt( ) ;
         array_of_integers[ integer_index ] =
                                  integer_from_keyboard ;
         integer_index ++ ;
      }
```

An array can be initialized by giving the initialization values inside braces and separated by commas. Here, the initialization operation both creates the array and initializes it. The entire array is initialized so that we get the temperature in degrees Fahrenheit when we use the degrees Celsius as an index.

```
//  Celsius.java

import java.util.* ;

class Celsius
{
   public static void main( String[] not_in_use )
   {
      Scanner keyboard = new Scanner( System.in ) ;

      int[]  array_of_degrees_fahrenheit  =

      { 32, 34, 36, 37, 39, 41, 43, 45, 46, 48,
        50, 52, 54, 55, 57, 59, 61, 63, 64, 66,
        68, 70, 72, 73, 75, 77, 79, 81, 82, 84,
        86, 88, 90, 91, 93, 95, 97, 99, 100, 102 } ;

      System.out.print(
         "\n This program converts temperatures given in"
       + "\n degrees Celsius to degrees Fahrenheit."
       + "\n Please, give a temperature in degrees Celsius:  " ) ;

      int degrees_celsius  =  keyboard.nextInt() ;

      System.out.print(
         "\n " +  degrees_celsius  +  " degrees Celsius is "
       +  array_of_degrees_fahrenheit[ degrees_celsius ]
       + " degrees Fahrenheit. \n" ) ;
   }
}
```

The conversion from degrees Celsius to degrees Fahrenheit is simply an array reference. This approach to solve the conversion problem is simple, but it has serious limitations. The program can convert only positive temperatures only up to 39 degrees Celsius because 39 is the maximum index for the conversion array.

**Celsius.java - 1. Converting temperature values with an initialized array.**

```
D:\javafiles2>java Celsius

 This program converts temperatures given in
 degrees Celsius to degrees Fahrenheit.
 Please, give a temperature in degrees Celsius:  16

 16 degrees Celsius is 61 degrees Fahrenheit.
```

**Celsius.java - X. Executing the program with input value 16**

Compound interest is a financial term meaning the payment of interest on interest. This line in the table describes how much interest you have to pay for a sum of 100.0 if the annual interest percentage is 5%. The last number on this line gives the compound interest after eight years.

```
//  Interest.java  (c) 2004 Kari Laitinen

import java.util.* ;

class Interest
{
   public static void main( String[] not_in_use )
   {
      Scanner keyboard = new Scanner( System.in ) ;

      double[][]  compound_interest_table  =
      {
        { 5.00, 10.25, 15.76, 21.55, 27.63, 34.01, 40.71, 47.75 },
        { 6.00, 12.36, 19.10, 26.25, 33.82, 41.85, 50.36, 59.38 },
        { 7.00, 14.49, 22.50, 31.08, 40.26, 50.07, 60.58, 71.82 }
      } ;

      double given_sum_of_money ;
      int    interest_percentage,  loan_period_in_years ;

      System.out.print( "\n This program calculates the compound interest"
                      + "\n for a given sum of money (principal). \n"
                      + "\n  Give the loan amount: " ) ;
      given_sum_of_money   =  keyboard.nextDouble() ;

      System.out.print( "\n  Give the interest percentage (5, 6, or 7): ");
      interest_percentage    =  keyboard.nextInt() ;

      System.out.print( "\n  Give the loan period in years (max. 8): ") ;
      loan_period_in_years   =  keyboard.nextInt() ;

      System.out.print( "\n  For a loan of "  +  given_sum_of_money
                      +  " you must pay \n  "
                      +  ( given_sum_of_money / 100.0 ) *
                         compound_interest_table[ interest_percentage - 5 ]
                                                [ loan_period_in_years - 1 ]
                      +  " as compound interest after "
                      +  loan_period_in_years  +  " years." ) ;
   }
}
```

Because there are two dimensions in the array referenced by **compound_interest_table**, we need two indexes to refer to an element. The first index selects a line in the table, and the second index selects a column. The two indexes are adjusted so that they start increasing from zero. In the case of the first index, 5 must be subtracted because the 5% line has index value 0.

**Interest.java - 1.+ Calculating interest on interest with a multidimensional array.**

A two-dimensional array is declared by writing two pairs of empty brackets after the array type. When the array elements are accessed in a statement, you need as many indexes as there are dimensions in the array declaration.

This table has three lines which each contain 8 elements of type **double**.There are braces inside braces when the initialization values for a multidimensional array are listed. The values for each line have their own braces. The three brace-enclosed initializers for every line are separated by commas and enclosed in master braces.

```
double[][]  compound_interest_table  =
{
   { 5.00, 10.25, 15.76, 21.55, 27.63, 34.01, 40.71, 47.75 },
   { 6.00, 12.36, 19.10, 26.25, 33.82, 41.85, 50.36, 59.38 },
   { 7.00, 14.49, 22.50, 31.08, 40.26, 50.07, 60.58, 71.82 }
} ;
```

**Interest.java - 1 - 1. The two-dimensional array of the program.**

```
D:\javafiles2>java Interest

 This program calculates the compound interest
 for a given sum of money (principal).

 Give the loan amount: 7500.00

 Give the interest percentage (5, 6, or 7): 5

 Give the loan period in years (max. 8): 5

 For a loan of 7500.0 you must pay
 2072.25 as compound interest after 5 years.
```

**Interest.java - X. Calculating compound interest for a sum of 7500.**

## 7.4 Multidimensional arrays

Arrays can be made multidimensional by using several dimension specifiers. So far, we have discussed only one-dimensional arrays. The term "array length" has been used to speak about the single dimension of a one-dimensional array. But in the case of multidimensional arrays we can speak about array dimensions. The array

```
int[][]  matrix  =  new int[ 4 ] [ 5 ] ;
```

has two dimensions as there are two dimension specifiers given inside the brackets. The elements of a multidimensional array can be referred to by giving an index value for each dimension. We can think that the matrix declared above has 4 rows and 5 columns. The following statements would write a 1 to each corner of the matrix.

```
matrix[ 0 ][ 0 ]  =  1 ;
matrix[ 0 ][ 4 ]  =  1 ;
matrix[ 3 ][ 0 ]  =  1 ;
matrix[ 3 ][ 4 ]  =  1 ;
```

It is possible to declare three-dimensional arrays by writing three dimension specifiers in the array declaration. Multidimensional arrays will not be used much in this book. Multidimensional arrays tend to be difficult to understand, especially when there are more than two dimensions. Instead of multidimensional arrays it is often easier to use arrays of objects which we will study later in this book.

Program **Interest.java** is an example in which an initialized multidimensional array is used. **Interest.java** calculates compound interests for the given sums of money. A two-dimensional initialized array of pre-calculated sums of interest is used to simplify the calculation process. Both **Celsius.java** and **Interest.java** could be written without any initialized arrays to gain the same functionality, but the use of initialized arrays makes the functional source programs simpler. When there is something pre-calculated available in the form of initialized arrays, there is less to be calculated in arithmetic operations.

Multidimensional arrays in Java are actually arrays of arrays. This means that a multidimensional array contains subarrays. A subarray inside a multidimensional array can be created separately from the array that represents the first array dimension. For example, the two-dimensional array that is used in program **Interest.java** could alternatively be created by first creating the array that represents the first dimension. This could be achieved with the statement

```
double[][] compound_interest_table  =  new double [ 3 ] [] ;
```

After the array that can contain subarrays is created, the subarrays could be created with the statements

```
compound_interest_table[ 0 ]  =  new  double[]
  { 5.00, 10.25, 15.76, 21.55, 27.63, 34.01, 40.71, 47.75 } ;

compound_interest_table[ 1 ]  =  new  double[]
  { 6.00, 12.36, 19.10, 26.25, 33.82, 41.85, 50.36, 59.38 };

compound_interest_table[ 2 ]  =  new  double[]
  { 7.00, 14.49, 22.50, 31.08, 40.26, 50.07, 60.58, 71.82 };
```

If the array in **Interest.java** were created with the above statements, the program would work in the same way as it does now.

The subarrays inside a two-dimensional array do not necessarily have to be of the same length. When the subarrays have different lengths, the two-dimensional array is called a ragged array or a jagged array. When the lengths of the subarrays are equal, the two-dimensional array is a rectangular array because we can imagine that such an array has the form of a rectangle. (For more information, see programs **InterestAnotherVersion.java** and **InterestJaggedArray.java** in the **javafilesextra** folder.)

## 7.5 Chapter summary

- A statement like

```
int[]  some_array ;
```

declares a name that can later on refer to (point to) a created array.

- Operator **new** is used to reserve (allocate) memory space from the heap memory for an array. The following statement creates an array by using a previously declared array name

```
some_array  =  new  int[ 300 ] ;
```

- Arrays are declared and created with statements like the following

```
int[]    array_of_integers  =  new  int[ 100 ] ;
float[] temperatures_of_last_month  =  new float[ 31 ] ;
char[]  character_buffer  =  new char[ current_buffer_size ];
```

- Arrays may be initialized when they are declared. The following statements both create and initialize arrays

```
int[]    smallest_prime_numbers  =
               { 1, 2, 3, 5, 7, 11, 13, 17, 19, 23 } ;
double[] square_roots  =  { 0.0,      1.0,   1.414214,
                          1.732051, 2.0,   2.236068 } ;
```

- Individual array elements can be referred to by writing an index in brackets after the array name. An index value can be a numerical literal constant or it can be evaluated from an arithmetic expression. The index of the first array element is zero. If the length of an array is n, relevant index values are 0, 1, 2, ..., n-2, and n-1.
- The length of an array can be found out by using the **length** field that is associated with every array.

### More exercises related to arrays

Exercise 7-7. Even numbers are equally divisible by two. If a number is not an even number, it is an odd number. Write a program that reads integers into an array and searches all even numbers from the array. The beginning of the program can be the same as in the previous exercise. You need a new loop to search the even numbers. You can use the remainder operator % to test whether an array element is even. For example, the boolean expression

```
( ( some_integer % 2 )  ==  0 )
```

is true if variable **some_integer** contains an even value.

Exercise 7-8. Improve program **Celsius.java** so that it works also when the user gives a Celsius temperature that is negative. You can do this by declaring a separate array which contains those Fahrenheit temperatures which correspond to negative Celsius temperatures. With an **if** construct you can test the input temperature to find out which temperature array should be used.

## 7.5 Chapter summary

# CHAPTER 8

## STRINGS STORE SEQUENCES OF CHARACTER CODES

Computers perform many kinds of text processing tasks. Therefore, programming languages must have mechanisms to handle textual information. In Java, the basic mechanism for storing and handling text is an object of type **`String`**. Texts consist of sequences of characters, and a **`String`** object can contain a sequence of character codes.

**`String`** objects are like variables, but they are different from the variables that we have studied so far. **`String`** objects are actually instances of a class named **`String`**, and they can be manipulated with special string methods. In this chapter, we shall study the nature of **`String`** objects and string methods. Because methods and classes will be the subjects of the following chapters, it is possible that the last part of this chapter (string methods etc.) will be too difficult for you. So my suggestion is that, please, study the first three sections of this chapter, and, if the rest of the sections turn out to be too difficult, return to those sections after chapters 9 and 10. These "difficult" sections were included in this chapter because I wanted to have all string-related stuff presented in a single chapter.

## 8.1 "Variables" of type String

So far, we have studied programs that handle mostly numerical information. In addition to numerical information, programs often handle textual information. Textual information consists of sequences of letters, punctuation characters, and other special characters. Computers process textual information in the form of character codes (see the table on page 594). Every character that can be input from the keyboard has a unique character code. Uppercase and lowercase letters have different codes. Although character codes are nothing but binary numbers when they are stored in a computer's memory, programming languages have special features that enable them to handle character information in a different way from that of pure numerical information.

In Java, textual information is stored in strings which resemble both variables and arrays. A string can store a sequence of character codes that represent a text. Strings can be declared in the following way

```
String  name_from_keyboard ;
String  file_name ;
```

These declarations clearly resemble variable declarations. **String** is the name of a standard Java class. It is not a reserved keyword like the keywords **int**, **long**, **double**, etc. By studying program **Fullname.java**, you can find out that, like variables, strings can be assigned values and strings can be printed to the screen.

Although strings in some ways resemble variables, they are, however, in some ways different from the traditional variables. A string declaration like

```
String  first_name ;
```

specifies a reference, a name that can reference or refer to a **String** object. A **String** object can be created, for example, by invoking (calling) the method **nextLine()** for the keyboard object. For example, the statement

```
first_name  =  keyboard.nextLine() ;
```

creates a **String** object of those characters that are read by method **nextLine()**, and makes the name **first_name** reference the created object. A string name like **first_name** references a **String** object so that the address of the object is stored in the memory that is reserved in the declaration of the string. Figure 8-1 clarifies how string declarations and string object creations consume memory.

When a variable stores a numerical value, it stores the value as it is. A variable does not refer to a value stored elsewhere in the main memory. A string is different. A string references a **String** value (object) that is located in a different part of the main memory, the heap memory. For this reason, string can be said to be a reference type. Basic variable types such as **int**, **long**, **double**, etc., can be called value types to distinguish them from **String** and other reference types.

Here, two "variables" of type **String** are declared. These "variables" are not like the traditional variables although these declarations resemble the declarations of the variables of the basic types **int**, **long**, **short**, **double**, etc.

```
//  Fullname.java (c) Kari Laitinen

import  java.util.* ;

class Fullname
{
   public static void main( String[] not_in_use )
   {
      Scanner keyboard = new Scanner( System.in ) ;

      String  first_name ;
      String  last_name ;

      System.out.print( "\n Please, type in your first name: " ) ;
      first_name  =  keyboard.nextLine() ;
      System.out.print( "\n Please, type in your last name:  " ) ;
      last_name   =  keyboard.nextLine() ;

      System.out.print( "\n Your full name is "
                   +  first_name  +  " "  +  last_name  +  ".\n" ) ;
   }
}
```

Here we read values for the string "variables" from the keyboard by calling method **nextLine()** for the keyboard object. **nextLine()** reads a line of characters and constructs a **String** object of those characters. The **String** objects that are returned by the **nextLine()** method are assigned as values for the string "variables".

Strings can be joined with the string concatenation operator +. The **String** values (objects) which the names **first_name** and **last_name** reference are printed among the string literals that are given between double quotes.

**Fullname.java - 1. The input/output of strings.**

```
D:\javafiles2>java Fullname

 Please, type in your first name: Kari

 Please, type in your last name:  Laitinen

 Your full name is Kari Laitinen.
```

**Fullname.java - X. A space is inserted between the first name and the last name in the output.**

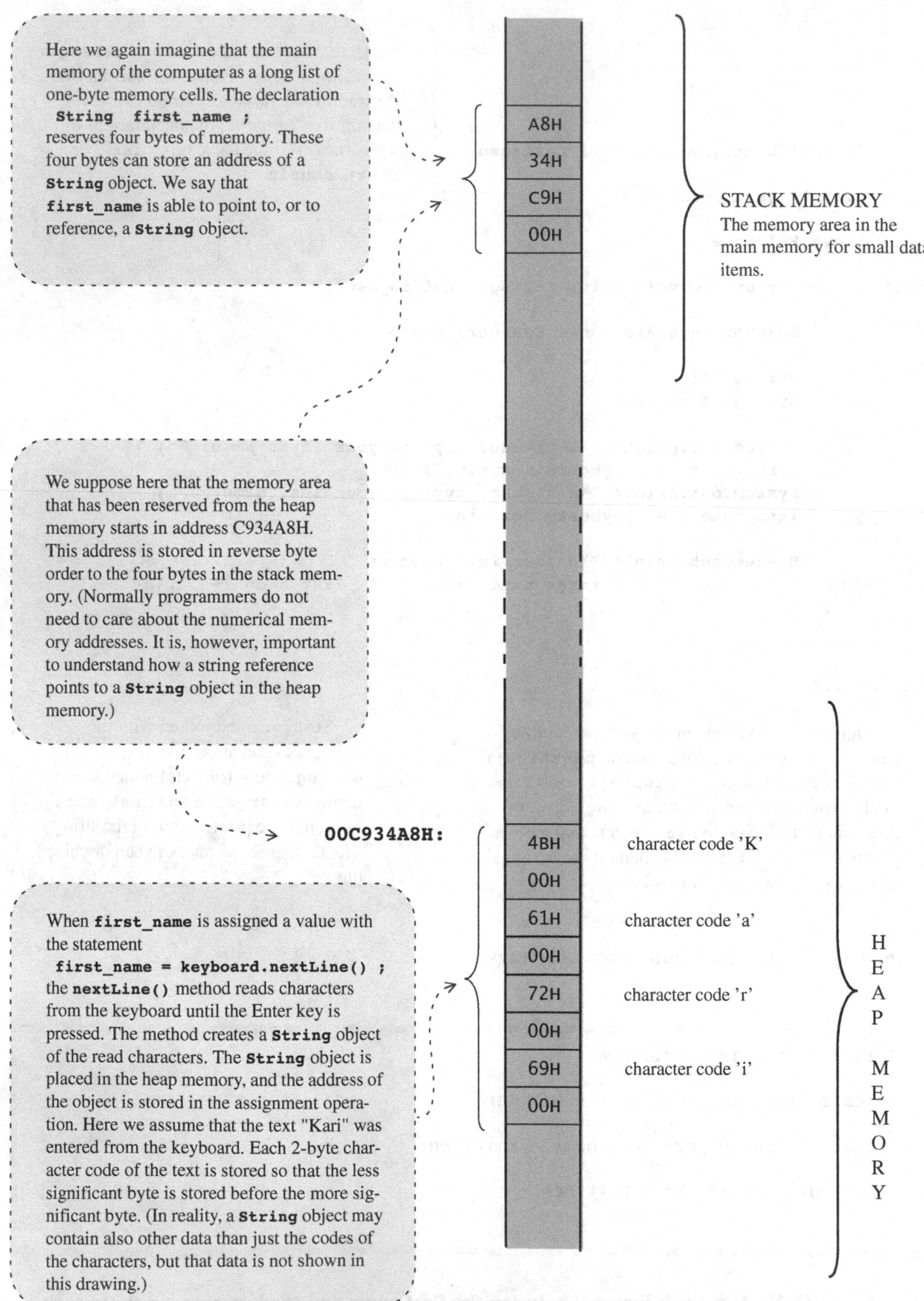

Here we again imagine that the main memory of the computer as a long list of one-byte memory cells. The declaration
String first_name ;
reserves four bytes of memory. These four bytes can store an address of a String object. We say that first_name is able to point to, or to reference, a String object.
A8H
34H
C9H
00H
STACK MEMORY
The memory area in the main memory for small data items.
We suppose here that the memory area that has been reserved from the heap memory starts in address C934A8H. This address is stored in reverse byte order to the four bytes in the stack memory. (Normally programmers do not need to care about the numerical memory addresses. It is, however, important to understand how a string reference points to a String object in the heap memory.)
00C934A8H:
4BH
character code 'K'
00H
61H
character code 'a'
00H
72H
character code 'r'
00H
69H
character code 'i'
00H
HEAP MEMORY
When first_name is assigned a value with the statement
first_name = keyboard.nextLine() ;
the nextLine() method reads characters from the keyboard until the Enter key is pressed. The method creates a String object of the read characters. The String object is placed in the heap memory, and the address of the object is stored in the assignment operation. Here we assume that the text "Kari" was entered from the keyboard. Each 2-byte character code of the text is stored so that the less significant byte is stored before the more significant byte. (In reality, a String object may contain also other data than just the codes of the characters, but that data is not shown in this drawing.)


*Figure 8-1. The text "Kari" stored in a String object.*

## 8.2 String literals

Although it has not been explicitly mentioned, we have actually been using string information throughout this book. In most output statements there are constant texts inside double quotes. These constant texts are called string literals. They may also be called string constants. For example, the following statement outputs a string literal to the screen.

```
System.out.print( "I am a string literal." ) ;
```

String literals can be used to create **String** objects by assigning a string literal as a value to a declared string. For example, when a string like

```
String  some_string  ;
```

is declared, it can be assigned a value with a statement like

```
some_string  =  "I am a text inside a String object." ;
```

The above statement creates a **String** object of the characters that are given between the double quotes, and makes **some_string** reference (point to) the created **String** object. If necessary, the two statements above can be combined into the following single statement that both declares the string and assigns a value to it

```
String  some_string  = "I am a text inside a String object.";
```

A string literal is a data item of type **String**, and stored somewhere in the computer's main memory. String literals cannot be modified. They belong to the same category as integer, floating-point, or character literals. Integer literals are plain numbers (e.g. 4 or 1909). Floating-point literals are numbers with a decimal point (e.g. 25.106). Character literals are characters inside single quotes (e.g. 'A', 'n', or '+'). It is important to understand the difference between single-quoted character literals and double-quoted string literals. For example,

'A' is a literal of type **char** and it means the character code of letter A (i.e. the numerical value 65 or 41H), but

"A" means a string inside which the character code of letter A is stored.

The rule for writing string literals is that you include the characters of the string literal inside double quotes. A problem arises when you want to include the double quote character itself in a string literal. In Java, this problem has been solved so that, if you want to include a double quote character in a string literal, you simply have to add one backslash character \ before the double quote. A backslash preceding a double quote means that the double quote character is not the terminator of that string literal. A backslash in a string literal generally means that the character following the backslash will be interpreted in a special way. For example, the output statement

```
System.out.print( "\"C:\\TEMP\" is a directory. " ) ;
```

would produce the text

```
"C:\TEMP" is a directory.
```

on the screen. You can note that \" means a double quote and \\ means a backslash in the above string literal. Previously we have learned that \n means a newline in texts to be printed. Other characters that need to be printed with the help of a backslash are backspace \b, carriage return \r, the tabulator character \t, and single quote \'. In addition to string literals, the backslash sequences are applied in character literals. For example, '\n' means the character code for a newline and '\'' is the character code for a single quote. The characters that are written with a backslash are called escape sequence characters. The backslash character \ is an escape character with which we can escape from the general rules for writing string literals and character literals.

## 8.3 Accessing individual characters of a string

An object of type **String** contains zero or more character codes that represent a text. The character codes can be codes of letters (A, B, C, D, ..., a, b, c, d,...), codes of numerical digits (0, 1, 2, 3, ...), codes of special and punctuation characters (*, [, }, -, +, ., \, /, ...), or codes of "invisible" characters such as newlines (\n) or tabulators (\t). The character codes stored in a **String** object are arranged in such an order that the position of each character (e.g. the first character and the last character) can be identified. Actually, there is an array of character codes inside every **String** object. The individual characters stored in the array can be accessed with a special method named **charAt()**.

Programs **Widename.java** and **StringReverse.java** are examples that demonstrate how individual characters of **String** objects can be read and printed to the screen. By studying these programs you can see that a string can be processed in a loop in the same way as an array. A single character of a string can be read by using (calling) the **charAt()** method. An index expression is written between the parentheses when **charAt()** is called. Valid index values start counting from zero, and the last valid index value is one less than the length of the string.

For **String** objects there exists a method named **length()** that tells what is the length of the string in question, i.e., how many characters are stored in the string. The **length()** method can be called (invoked) for a **String** object by using the dot operator . in the following way

```
string_name.length()
```

Also the "invisible" characters like newlines and tabulators are counted as characters when the length of a string is determined. For example, the statements

```
String  short_text_lines  =  "\n aaa \n bbb \n ccc " ;

System.out.print( short_text_lines.length() ) ;
```

would print 18 to the screen because the string **short_text_lines** is made of 3 newlines, 6 space characters, and 9 letter characters. The newline character \n is a single character although we have to write it with two separate character symbols in our programs.

An empty string is a string that has been created, but that does not contain any characters. The length of an empty string is zero. You cannot access any characters of an empty string because all index values are illegal. The following is an example of the creation of an empty string

```
String  some_empty_string  =  "" ;
```

In general, the following facts apply to every string provided that the string is not empty:

- **string_name.charAt( 0 )** refers to the first character of the string.
- **string_name.charAt( string_name.length() - 1 )** refers to the last character of the string.
- **string_name.charAt(** *any valid index expression* **)** refers to a data item of type **char**.

A **String** object is an immutable entity once it has been created. This means that it is possible to read the characters of a **String** object, but it is not possible to modify them. Later on in this chapter we shall study **StringBuilder** objects which are mutable strings.

Method **nextLine()** reads a string from the keyboard. The program waits here until the user types in something and presses the Enter key. The newline character \n that represents the Enter key is not included in the read character string. After this statement has been executed, the input from the keyboard is stored in the **String** object referenced by **name_from_keyboard**.

In this **while** loop, the string **name_from_keyboard** is processed from the beginning to the end. The **while** loop stops when **character_index** reaches a value that is the length of the string. Method **length()** is used here to find out how many characters the **String** object contains.

```
// Widename.java  (c) Kari Laitinen

import java.util.* ;

class Widename
{
   public static void main( String[] not_in_use )
   {
      Scanner keyboard = new Scanner( System.in ) ;

      String  name_from_keyboard ;
      int     character_index  =  0 ;

      System.out.print( "\n Please, type in your name: " ) ;
      name_from_keyboard  =  keyboard.nextLine() ;

      System.out.print( "\n Here is your name in a wider form: \n\n  " ) ;

      while ( character_index  <  name_from_keyboard.length() )
      {
         System.out.print(
              " "  +   name_from_keyboard.charAt( character_index ) ) ;
         character_index  ++  ;
      }
   }
}
```

To achieve widely spaced printing, this output statement prints one space character before each character from **name_from_keyboard**. Method **charAt()** returns a single character from the string. The value of **character_index** determines which character is currently being printed.

**Widename.java - 1. Referring to individual characters of a string.**

```
D:\javafiles2>java Widename

 Please, type in your name: Charles Babbage

 Here is your name in a wider form:

   C h a r l e s   B a b b a g e
```

Charles Babbage was a man who built mechanical computing machines more than 150 years a ago.

**Widename.java - X. Here "wide" printing means spaces between characters.**

## Exercises related to strings

Exercise 8-1. Program **Widename.java** shows how a string can be printed in wide form, with a space between the characters of the string. Program **StringReverse.java** shows how the characters of a string can be printed in reverse order. Your task is to now write a program that does both these activities. The program should ask for a string from the keyboard, and print the characters of the string both in wide form and in reverse order. If string "Hello!" were entered from the keyboard, your program should print

```
! o l l e H
```

Exercise 8-2. Write a program that asks for a string from the keyboard, and explores each character in the given string and counts how many uppercase letters, lowercase letters, numbers, and other characters there are in the given string. By writing **keyboard.nextLine()** you can read the string from the keyboard. You can use normal integer variables to count different types of characters. When you use the **charAt()** method, you need an index variable (e.g. **character_index** ). Studying program **Iffing.java** in Chapter 6 may help you in this exercise.

Exercise 8-3. Write a program that reads a string from the keyboard, and prints the character codes of the string in hexadecimal form. If string "Hello!" were entered from the keyboard, the program should print

```
48 65 6C 6C 6F 21
```

where 48 is the hexadecimal code for the uppercase letter H, 65 the hexadecimal code for the lowercase letter e, etc. When the **charAt()** method is called, it returns a value of type **char**. One possibility to print a value of type **char** in hexadecimal form is to first convert the **char** value to an **int** value, and then print the **int** value in hexadecimal form with the **printf()** method. For example, if **some_character** is a variable of type **char**, it can be printed in hexadecimal form with the statement

```
System.out.printf(  " %X",   (int) some_character ) ;
```

Exercise 8-4. Write a program that inputs a string from the keyboard, and prints the string in uppercase form. For example, if the string "Steven Jobs" were typed in from the keyboard, your program should print

```
STEVEN JOBS
```

Your program must find all lowercase letters in the given string and convert them to uppercase. A lowercase letter can be converted to uppercase by subtracting 20H from the lowercase character code. The following expression is true when **character_in_string** contains a lowercase letter

```
( character_in_string  >=  'a'  &&
  character_in_string  <=  'z' )
```

Another possibility to create this program is to use the string method **toUpperCase()**.

Exercise 8-5. Write a program that reads a string from the keyboard and checks whether the given string is a palindrome, a string that is the same were it read from left to right or from right to left. The following strings are examples of palindromes

```
aabbbccbbbaa
*xx12zzz21xx*
saippuakauppias
```

One possibility to make this program is to read the characters of the string with two indexes, one index incrementing from zero and the other index decrementing from the last character. The program should check whether corresponding letters at each end of the string are the same. Another possibility is to make a reversed copy from the original string, and use either the string method **compareTo()** or the string method **equals()** to check whether the strings are equal. Class **StringBuilder**, which will be studied later in this chapter, provides a **reverse()** method to reverse strings.

```
//  StringReverse.java

import java.util.* ;

class StringReverse
{
   public static void main( String[] not_in_use )
   {
      Scanner keyboard = new Scanner( System.in ) ;

      System.out.print("\n This program is able to reverse a string."
                     + "\n Please, type in a string.\n\n   " ) ;

      String  string_from_keyboard  =  keyboard.nextLine() ;

      System.out.print("\n String length is " + string_from_keyboard.length()
                     + ".\n\n String in reverse character order: \n\n   " ) ;

      int character_index  =  string_from_keyboard.length() ;

      while (  character_index  >  0 )
      {
         character_index  --  ;
         System.out.print( string_from_keyboard.charAt( character_index ) ) ;
      }
   }
}
```

This statement both declares and creates a string. After this statement has been executed, **string_from_keyboard** points to a **String** object containing the characters that were typed in from the keyboard.

The method **length()** reveals the length of a string, i.e., it returns the number of characters in the string.

Inside the **while** loop, **character_index** is first decremented, and then the character referred to by that index value is printed. This way characters are printed from the end to the beginning of the string. Before this loop is entered, **character_index** has a value that is the first illegal index value. Note that method **System.out.print()** prints here a value of type **char** because we refer to an individual character in a string.

**StringReverse.java - 1. Printing the characters of a string in reverse order.**

```
D:\javafiles2>java StringReverse

 This program is able to reverse a string.
 Please, type in a string.

   Alan Turing is a famous man in the history of computing.

 String length is 56.

 String in reverse character order:

   .gnitupmoc fo yrotsih eht ni nam suomaf a si gniruT nalA
```

In 1937, before any electronic computers were built, Alan Turing published a mathematical model for a computer.

**StringReverse.java - X. Reversing a long input string.**

## 8.4 String methods

String methods are services with which we can perform various activities related to **String** objects. For example, there is a method named **indexOf()** that can search a certain substring in a string, and a method named **compareTo()** checks how two **String** objects relate alphabetically to each other.

A method is a piece of code that performs a well-defined task. Methods are used in relation to objects. Because we have not yet profoundly studied methods, and our knowledge about objects is still quite limited, it is possible that this section is too difficult for you. <u>If it turns out that you cannot understand these pages, it might me a good idea to study the rest of the sections in this chapter after you have read chapters 9 and 10.</u>

String methods are declared in a standard Java class named **String**, and **String** objects are objects of class **String**. String methods can be used to do something to **String** objects, or we can say that with the string methods we can manipulate strings. The most important string methods are explained in the large information box that starts on page 220. In addition, you can find information about these methods if you use the electronic Java documentation.

Some of the string methods are static methods (class methods), but most of the methods are non-static methods (instance methods). A non-static method is called

```
string_name.methodName( ...
```

where **string_name** is a reference that is pointing to (referencing) a **String** object. The static methods can be called by writing

```
String.methodName( ...
```

where **String** is the name of the **String** class.

On the following pages you can find the following example programs in which string methods are used.

- Program **StringEquality.java** demonstrates the use of the string method **equals()**, and compares it to the use of the equality operator. Figure 8-2 shows how string objects occupy memory at the end of program **StringEquality.java**.
- Program **Marilyn.java** shows how to use method **compareTo()**.
- Program **StringMehodsMore.java** exploits methods **substring()**, **regionMatches()**, **contains()**, and **indexOf()**.
- Program **States.java** demonstrates the use of string methods **substring()**, **lastIndexOf()**, and **replace()**.
- Program **Stringing.java** shows, among other things, how a string can be converted to an array of type **char[]** with the **toCharArray()** method.
- Program **Capitals.java** demonstrates string methods **substring()**, **toLowerCase()**, **toUpperCase()**, and **trim()**.

Don't worry if there is something you do not understand about methods. You are not yet supposed to fully understand methods because they are the topic of Chapter 9. It is common even for experienced programmers that they have to reread books and documents to find information about topics such as string methods. You do not need to try to remember, for instance, in what order you have to write parameters in parentheses when you use the string methods. These things you can always look up in books and, for example, in the electronic Java documentation. As you grow more experienced in programming, you will automatically remember the most essential things. The less essential things you can always find in some kind of documents.

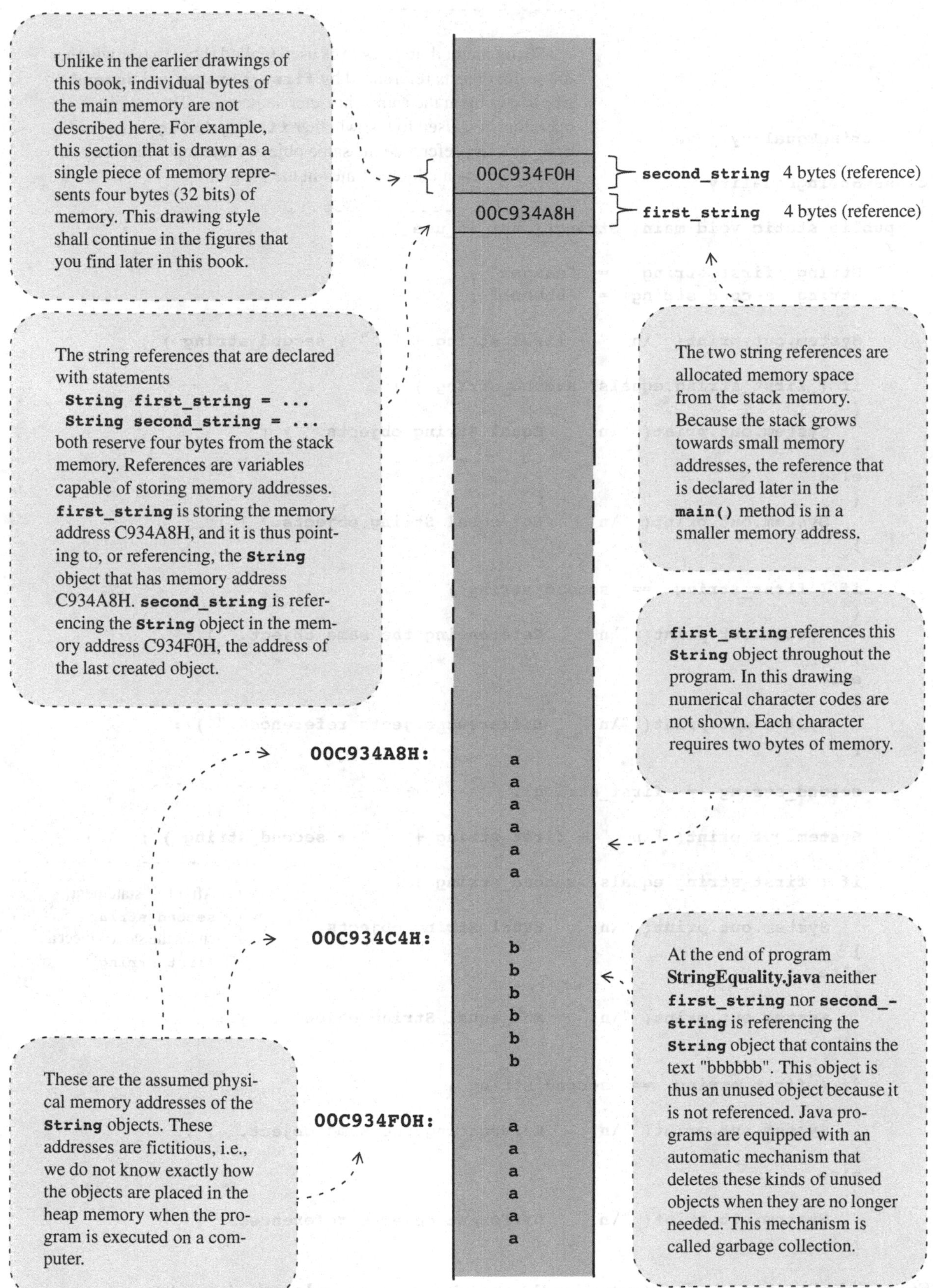

Unlike in the earlier drawings of this book, individual bytes of the main memory are not described here. For example, this section that is drawn as a single piece of memory represents four bytes (32 bits) of memory. This drawing style shall continue in the figures that you find later in this book.
00C934F0H
00C934A8H
second_string 4 bytes (reference)
first_string 4 bytes (reference)
The string references that are declared with statements
String first_string = ...
String second_string = ...
both reserve four bytes from the stack memory. References are variables capable of storing memory addresses. first_string is storing the memory address C934A8H, and it is thus pointing to, or referencing, the String object that has memory address C934A8H. second_string is referencing the String object in the memory address C934F0H, the address of the last created object.
The two string references are allocated memory space from the stack memory. Because the stack grows towards small memory addresses, the reference that is declared later in the main() method is in a smaller memory address.
first_string references this String object throughout the program. In this drawing numerical character codes are not shown. Each character requires two bytes of memory.
00C934A8H:
a a a a a a
00C934C4H:
b b b b b b
00C934F0H:
a a a a a a
These are the assumed physical memory addresses of the String objects. These addresses are fictitious, i.e., we do not know exactly how the objects are placed in the heap memory when the program is executed on a computer.
At the end of program StringEquality.java neither first_string nor second_string is referencing the String object that contains the text "bbbbbb". This object is thus an unused object because it is not referenced. Java programs are equipped with an automatic mechanism that deletes these kinds of unused objects when they are no longer needed. This mechanism is called garbage collection.

***Figure 8-2. The String objects in memory when program StringEquality.java reaches its end.***

String method **equals()** is used (called) here to test whether the string objects referenced by **first_string** and **second_string** contain the same character sequences. The equality operator == is used to test whether **first_string** and **second_string** reference the same object. Note that these **if** constructs are repeated three times in the program.

```
//  StringEquality.java

class StringEquality
{
   public static void main( String[] not_in_use )
   {
      String  first_string   =  "aaaaaa" ;
      String  second_string  =  "bbbbbb" ;

      System.out.print( "\n   " + first_string + "   " + second_string ) ;

      if ( first_string.equals( second_string ) )
      {
         System.out.print( "\n     Equal String objects." ) ;
      }
      else
      {
         System.out.print( "\n     Not equal String objects." ) ;
      }

      if ( first_string  ==  second_string )
      {
         System.out.print( "\n     Referencing the same object." ) ;
      }
      else
      {
         System.out.print( "\n     Different objects referenced." ) ;
      }

      second_string  =  first_string ;

      System.out.print( "\n   " + first_string + "   " + second_string ) ;

      if ( first_string.equals( second_string ) )
      {
         System.out.print( "\n     Equal String objects." ) ;
      }
      else
      {
         System.out.print( "\n     Not equal String objects." ) ;
      }

      if ( first_string  ==  second_string )
      {
         System.out.print( "\n     Referencing the same object." ) ;
      }
      else
      {
         System.out.print( "\n     Different objects referenced." ) ;
      }
```

After this statement, **second_string** references the same object as **first_string**.

**StringEquality.java - 1: Demonstrating the equality operator and method equals().**

This statement creates a new **String** object which becomes a copy of the **String** object referenced by **first_string**. After this statement has been executed, **second_string** references the created new object.

Because **second_string** references an object that is an identical copy of the object referenced by **first_string**, the method **equals()** finds out here that the two objects are identical.

```
      second_string  =  new  String( first_string ) ;

      System.out.print( "\n   " + first_string + "   " + second_string ) ;

      if ( first_string.equals( second_string ) )
      {
         System.out.print( "\n      Equal String objects." ) ;
      }
      else
      {
         System.out.print( "\n      Not equal String objects." ) ;
      }

      if ( first_string ==  second_string )
      {
         System.out.print( "\n      Referencing the same object." ) ;
      }
      else
      {
         System.out.print( "\n      Different objects referenced." ) ;
      }
   }
}
```

**StringEquality.java - 2. Making a copy of a String object.**

```
D:\javafiles2>java StringEquality

   aaaaaa  bbbbbb
      Not equal String objects.
      Different objects referenced.
   aaaaaa  aaaaaa
      Equal String objects.
      Referencing the same object.
   aaaaaa  aaaaaa
      Equal String objects.
      Different objects referenced.
```

Whenever two string references are referencing the same object, method **equals()** finds out that the objects are equal.

**StringEquality.java - X. Testing the equality of string objects and string references.**

```
//  Marilyn.java (c) Kari Laitinen

import java.util.* ;

class Marilyn
{
   public static void main( String[] not_in_use )
   {
      Scanner  keyboard  =  new  Scanner( System.in ) ;

      String  name_to_be_known  =  "Marilyn Monroe" ;

      System.out.print("\n Who played the main role in the movies:"
                  +  "\n\n   \"How To Marry a Millionaire\" (1953)"
                  +    "\n   \"The Seven Year Itch\" (1955)"
                  +    "\n   \"The Misfits\" (1961) \n\n   ? " ) ;

      String  name_from_keyboard  =  keyboard.nextLine() ;

      if ( name_from_keyboard.compareTo( name_to_be_known ) == 0 )
      {
         System.out.print( "\n   Yes, that is correct.\n" ) ;
      }
      else
      {
         System.out.print( "\n   No, it\'s Marilyn Monroe.\n" ) ;
      }
   }
}
```

If you want to include double quote characters in string literals, they have to be preceded by a backslash character \.

String method **compareTo()** is used here to compare whether the string typed in from the keyboard is the same as the string referenced by **name_to_be_known**. Method **compareTo()** produces (returns) a zero when the strings are equal. Otherwise, it returns a non-zero value. Instead of the **compareTo()** method, it would be possible to use the **equals()** method:

```
 if ( name_from_keyboard.equals( name_to_be_known ) )
 { ...
```

**Marilyn.java - 1. The use of string method compareTo().**

```
D:\javafiles2>java Marilyn

 Who played the main role in the movies:

   "How To Marry a Millionaire" (1953)
   "The Seven Year Itch" (1955)
   "The Misfits" (1961)

   ? Marilyn Monroe

   Yes, that is correct.
```

**Marilyn.java - X. Executing the program with the "correct" input.**

Method **regionMatches()** is used here to compare the first 5 character positions in the two **String** objects. The zeroes mean that comparison starts from index position 0 in both strings.

Method **substring()** can be used to take a substring from an existing string. Here, the method is used to make a substring of the first five characters of **second_string**, and another substring in which the first five characters are excluded from **first_string**.

Method **contains()** returns **true** if a string contains another string. Method **indexOf()** returns the index position where another string is found, or it returns -1 if the string being searched for was not found. Here the methods are used to search for "CCCD" in the string referenced by **first_string**.

```
//  StringMethodsMore.java

class StringMethodsMore
{
   public static void main( String[] not_in_use )
   {
      String  first_string    =  "AAABBBCCCDDD" ;
      String  second_string   =  "xxxyyyzzz" ;

      System.out.print( "\n CHARACTER POSITIONS      : 01234567890123456" ) ;
      System.out.print( "\n Original first_string    : " + first_string ) ;
      System.out.print( "\n Original second_string : " + second_string ) ;

      first_string    =   second_string.substring( 0, 5 ) +
                                   first_string.substring( 5 ) ;
      System.out.print( "\n Modified first_string    : " + first_string ) ;

      if ( first_string.regionMatches( 0, second_string, 0, 5 ) )
      {
         System.out.print(
          "\n The first five characters in both strings are the same" ) ;
      }

      if ( first_string.contains( "CCCD" ) )
      {
         System.out.print( "\n String \"" +  first_string
              + "\"includes string \"CCCD\" in index position "
              + first_string.indexOf( "CCCD" )  + ".\n" ) ;
      }
   }
}
```

**StringMethodsMore.java - 1. contains(), indexOf(), regionMatches(), and substring() in use.**

```
D:\javafiles2>java StringMethodsMore

 CHARACTER POSITIONS     : 01234567890123456
 Original first_string   : AAABBBCCCDDD
 Original second_string : xxxyyyzzz
 Modified first_string   : xxxyyBCCCDDD
 The first five characters in both strings are the same
 String "xxxyyBCCCDDD"includes string "CCCD" in index position 6.
```

**StringMethodsMore.java - X. The first 5 characters in both strings are made to be the same.**

Objects of class **String** can be created by assigning a string literal as a value to a string reference.

**String** objects can be concatenated (joined) with the + operator, and a string reference can be copied with the = operator. This statement contains two concatenation operations and one copy operation. The concatenations are carried out before the copy operation because the + operator has a higher precedence than the = operator.

```
// States.java (c) Kari Laitinen

class States
{
   public static void main( String[] not_in_use )
   {
      String  states_in_usa ;

      String  westmost_state   =  "Hawaii" ;
      String  prairie_state    =  "Illinois" ;

      states_in_usa  =  westmost_state  +  " "  +  prairie_state ;

      System.out.print( "\n   "  +  states_in_usa ) ;

      String  golden_state    =  "California" ;

      states_in_usa  =  states_in_usa.substring( 0, 6 )  +  "  "
                     +  golden_state
                     +  states_in_usa.substring( 6 ) ;

      System.out.print( "\n   "  +  states_in_usa ) ;
```

**String** objects are immutable, i.e., they cannot be modified once they have been created. For this reason, the string methods return new **String** objects that are modified versions of old **String** objects. In this statement, for example, the **substring()** method produces new **String** objects which are concatenated with the old **String** object referenced by **golden_state**. After this statement has been executed, **states_in_usa** references a new **String** object which is the result of the concatenation operations.

The first call to method **substring()** takes a substring that contains the first six characters of an existing string. The second call takes a substring which excludes the first six characters. This statement inserts the string "California" into the middle of the string referenced by **states_in_usa**.

A colon here indicates that this program continues in the following program description.

**States.java - 1: Using method substring() and the concatenation operator +.**

The purpose of method **lastIndexOf()** is to find something starting from the end of a **String** object. Here, method **lastIndexOf()** is called to find the last position that contains two adjacent spaces in the string referenced by **states_in_usa**. The index that is returned by method **lastIndexOf()** is used later to make method **substring()** produce a substring that ends in the specified index position.

```
      String   eastmost_state   =   "Maine" ;

      states_in_usa  =  states_in_usa  +   "  Virginia  " ;
      states_in_usa  =  states_in_usa  +   eastmost_state  ;

      System.out.print( "\n   "  +  states_in_usa ) ;

      int index_of_last_state  =  states_in_usa.lastIndexOf( "  " ) ;

      states_in_usa  =  states_in_usa.substring( 0, index_of_last_state ) ;

      states_in_usa  =  states_in_usa  +  "  Massachusetts"  ;

      System.out.print( "\n   "  +  states_in_usa ) ;

      states_in_usa  =  states_in_usa.replace( "Illinois", "Michigan" ) ;

      System.out.print( "\n   "  +  states_in_usa  +  "\n" ) ;
   }
}
```

Here, method **replace()** searches for the string "Illinois" in string **states_in_usa**. When "Illinois" is found, it is replaced with string "Michigan". Method **replace()** creates a new **String** object in which the replacement is made, and **states_in_usa** is set to reference the new **String** object.

A full stop (period, dot) means that this is the last description of this program.

**States.java - 2. Calling string methods lastIndexOf(), substring(), and replace().**

```
D:\javafiles2>java States

   Hawaii  Illinois
   Hawaii  California  Illinois
   Hawaii  California  Illinois  Virginia  Maine
   Hawaii  California  Illinois  Virginia  Massachusetts
   Hawaii  California  Michigan  Virginia  Massachusetts
```

**States.java - X. String states_in_usa is printed five times during program execution.**

Here, a **String** object is created of an array of type **char[]**. The **String** constructor simply creates the string of the characters stored in the array. The same object could be made with the statement
**String xxxxxxxx_string = "xxxxxxxx" ;**

Here a **String** object is initialized with four characters from index positions 3, 4, 5, and 6 in the string referenced by **abcdefgh_string**. Method **substring()** extracts a substring from an existing string. The first parameter of **substring()** specifies the index position from which the substring starts. The second parameter specifies the first index position whose character is not included in the substring.

```
//  Stringing.java (c) Kari Laitinen

class Stringing
{
   public static void main( String[] not_in_use )
   {
      String  abcdefgh_string  =  "abcdefgh" ;

      char[]  xxxxxxxx_array  =  { 'x', 'x', 'x', 'x', 'x', 'x', 'x', 'x' } ;

      String  xxxxxxxx_string  =  new  String( xxxxxxxx_array ) ;

      String  defgzzzz_string  =  abcdefgh_string.substring( 3, 7 ) ;

      defgzzzz_string  =  defgzzzz_string  +  "zzzz" ;

      String  text_to_print  =  "  "  +  abcdefgh_string  +
                                "  "  +  xxxxxxxx_string  +
                                "  "  +  defgzzzz_string  +  "  " ;
      System.out.print( "\n" ) ;

      int  character_index  =  0 ;

      while ( character_index  <  text_to_print.length() )
      {
         System.out.print( text_to_print.charAt( character_index ) ) ;
         character_index  ++ ;
      }

      System.out.print( "\n\n" ) ;
```

Method **length()** returns the length of a **String** object. The length of a string means the number of characters that are in it. An empty string has length zero.

This boolean expression says that the loop terminates when **character_index** reaches a value that equals to the length of the string referenced by **text_to_print**.

**Stringing.java - 1: Demonstrating string construction and character access.**

A **String** object can be converted to an array of type **char[]** with the **toCharArray()** method. The array that is created contains the same characters in the same order that are stored in the **String** object.

All the elements of an array can be processed with the "foreach" loop, which is a special type of **for** loop to handle each element of an array. This "foreach" loop prints all characters from the previously created array of type **char[]**.

Although **String** objects contain an internal array of character codes, **String** objects cannot be processed with a "foreach" loop.

```
      char[] characters_to_print  =  text_to_print.toCharArray() ;

      for ( char character_in_text : characters_to_print )
      {
         System.out.print( " " +  character_in_text ) ;
      }

      System.out.print( "\n" ) ;

      character_index  =  text_to_print.length() ;

      while ( character_index  >  0 )
      {
         character_index  -- ;
         System.out.print( " " +  text_to_print.charAt( character_index ) ) ;
      }
   }
}
```

This loop prints the characters of the string in reverse order. The characters are accessed with the string method **charAt()**.

**Stringing.java - 2. Converting a string to an array of characters.**

```
D:\javafiles2>java Stringing

 abcdefgh  xxxxxxxx  defgzzzz

   a b c d e f g h   x x x x x x x x   d e f g z z z z
   z z z z g f e d   x x x x x x x x   h g f e d c b a
```

**Stringing.java - X. The characters of text_to_print are printed here three times.**

When a country name is read from the keyboard, it is immediately converted to a lowercase string with the string method **toLowerCase()**. This means that those letters of the string which are uppercase letters are converted to lowercase letters. The next statement then converts the first letter of the country name to an uppercase letter. These statements thus ensure that the country name that the user types in is written in the same way as the country names in the string referenced by **countries_and_capitals**.

```
//  Capitals.java
import java.util.* ;

class Capitals
{
   public static void main( String[] not_in_use )
   {
      Scanner keyboard = new Scanner( System.in ) ;

      String  countries_and_capitals  =

        "Finland Helsinki   Usa Washington   Denmark Copenhagen "
      + "Afghanistan Kabul  Russia Moscow    England London "
      + "Italy Rome         France Paris     Spain Madrid "
      + "Portugal Lisbon    Chile Santiago   Japan Tokyo "
      + "Sweden Stockholm   Norway Oslo      Pakistan Islamabad "
      + "Iceland Reykjavik  Hungary Budapest Holland Amsterdam "
      + "Belgium Brussels   Austria Vienna   Israel Jerusalem "  ;

      System.out.print("\n This program may know the capital of a country."
                     + "\n Type in the name of some country: " ) ;

      String  country_name  =  keyboard.nextLine().toLowerCase() ;

      country_name  =  country_name.substring( 0, 1 ).toUpperCase()
                    +  country_name.substring( 1 ) ;

      int index_of_country_name  =  countries_and_capitals.
                                            indexOf( country_name ) ;

      if ( index_of_country_name  !=  -1 )
      {
         // The country name was found in countries_and_capitals

         String  text_after_country_name  =  countries_and_capitals.
             substring( index_of_country_name + country_name.length() ) ;

         // A space at the end of the string ensures that also
         // the last country-capital pair in the string works.

         text_after_country_name  =  text_after_country_name.trim() + " " ;

         String  capital_name  =  text_after_country_name.substring(
                               0, text_after_country_name.indexOf( " " ) ) ;

         System.out.print( "\n The capital of " + country_name
                         + " is " + capital_name  + ".\n" ) ;
      }
   }
}
```

**Capitals.java - 1.+ A simple program to find the capitals of some countries.**

The string referenced by **text_after_country_name** contains the capital's name and all the names of the countries and capitals that follow it in the long string referenced by **countries_and_capitals**.

```
if ( index_of_country_name  !=  -1 )
{
   // The country name was found in countries_and_capitals

   String  text_after_country_name  =  countries_and_capitals.
      substring( index_of_country_name + country_name.length() ) ;

   // A space at the end of the string ensures that also
   // the last country-capital pair in the string works.

   text_after_country_name  =  text_after_country_name.trim() + " " ;

   String  capital_name  =  text_after_country_name.substring(
                        0, text_after_country_name.indexOf( " " ) ) ;

   System.out.print( "\n The capital of " + country_name
                    + " is " + capital_name  + ".\n" ) ;
}
```

Method **trim()** removes space, tabulator, and newline characters both from the beginning and the end of a string. In this case it is used to remove the spaces that precede the capital name.

Before this statement is executed, the capital name is at the beginning of the string referenced by **text_after_country_name**. As a space character follows the capital name, it is possible to determine the end of the capital name by finding out the position of the next single space character.

**Capitals.java - 1 - 1. The if construct that uses several string methods.**

```
D:\javafiles2>java Capitals

 This program may know the capital of a country.
 Type in the name of some country: spain

 The capital of Spain is Madrid.

D:\javafiles2>java Capitals

 This program may know the capital of a country.
 Type in the name of some country: Madrid

 The capital of Madrid is Portugal.
```

The program converts an input string like "spain" to the capitalized word "Spain".

The second program execution results in a silly answer. The program works correctly only when a valid country name is supplied to it.

**Capitals.java - X. The program is executed here twice.**

## Class String methods – read this first

Class **String** provides a large number of methods which allow various operations to be carried out with **String** objects. The most important methods are described below. Sometimes it may be hard to understand how a particular method works in practice. In this kind of situation, it is often a useful idea to write a short test program to see how the method works.

The methods and their parameters are explained on this and the following pages as method calls. Many of the methods are overloaded, i.e., there are several methods that have the same name. Below, **string_object**, **another_string**, and **new_string_object** mean a reference to a **String** object, variables having the words "position", "index", "length", or "number_of_" in their names are integer variables, and variables having the word "character" in their name are of type **char**.

This information box does not explain all the methods of the **String** class. Only the most important methods are presented. To get more information about the string methods, please use the index of this book, and consult the electronic Java documentation.

## Class String methods – charAt(), compareTo(), compareToIgnoreCase()

With the **charAt()** method it is possible to get a single character from a string. The index value that is supplied as a parameter for the method starts counting from zero, i.e., the index of the first character of a string is 0. The largest possible index value is one less than the length of the string.

```
character_in_string  =  string_object.charAt( some_index ) ;

last_character_in_string  =  string_object.charAt( some_string.length() - 1 ) ;
```

To compare **String** objects, there is a method named **compareTo()**, which returns a zero if the **String** objects contain the same characters in the same order. If the return value is less than zero, it means in the example below that **string_object** is alphabetically smaller than **another_string**. If the return value is greater than zero, it means that **string_object** is alphabetically (lexically) greater than **another_string**. For example, string "ABC" is considered alphabetically smaller than "BC" because A comes before B in the alphabet. String "aaab" is greater than "aaaa" because b comes later than a in the alphabet. Method **compareTo()** can be used to arrange a set of strings in alphabetical order. If alphabetical order is not important, the equality of strings can be tested with the **equals()** method.

```
comparison_result  =  string_object.compareTo( another_string ) ;
```

Method **compareToIgnoreCase()** returns the same kind of return values as the **compareTo()** method, but it does not make a distinction between uppercase and lowercase letters. For example, the string "ABC" is considered to be the same as "abc" when **compareToIgnoreCase()** is used.

```
comparison_result  =  string_object.compareToIgnoreCase( another_string ) ;
```

## Class String methods – concat(), contains(), contentEquals(), copyValueOf(), endsWith()

A method named **concat()** concatenates **String** objects to form longer **String** objects. In most cases, it is easier to use the string concatenation operator + instead of the **concat()** method.

```
resulting_string  =  string_object.concat( another_string ) ;
   //  Same as: resulting_string  =  string_object + another_string ;
```

The boolean method **contains()** returns **true** if and only if the string supplied as a parameter is contained in "this" string, i.e., the string given as a parameter is a substring of "this". The parameter for the **contains()** method can be a reference to a **StringBuilder** object. The **contains()** method can be used in an **if** construct in the following way:

```
if ( string_object.contains(  another_string  ) )
{
   ...
```

The above **if** construct means the same as the construct

```
if ( string_object.indexOf(  another_string  )  !=  -1 )
{
   ...
```

Method **contentEquals()** operates in the same way as the **equals()** method, but its parameter can alternatively be a reference to a **String**, **StringBuilder**, or **StringBuffer** object. The following kinds of calls are possible

```
if ( string_object.contentEquals( another_string ) )
{
   ...

if ( string_object.contentEquals( some_string_builder_object ) )
{
   ...

if ( string_object.contentEquals( some_string_buffer_object ) )
{
   ...
```

With method **copyValueOf()** the characters of an array of type **char[]** can be converted to a **String** object. After the statements

```
char[]  some_character_array  =  { 'H', 'e', 'l', 'l', 'o', '!' } ;
String  string_object   =  String.copyValueOf( some_character_array ) ;
```

the object referenced by **string_object** would contain the text "Hello!". The string that is returned by the **copyValueOf()** method can also be created with a constructor of class **String** in the following way:

```
String  string_object  =  new String( some_character_array ) ;
```

Method **endsWith()** returns **true** of **false** depending on whether or not a string ends with a given string. For example, the following **if** construct tests whether **String** object referenced by **file_name** ends with **".java"**.

```
if ( file_name.endsWith( ".java" ) )
{
   //  The ending was ".java"
```

## Class String methods – equals(), equalsIgnoreCase(), format(), getBytes(), getChars()

**equals()** is a method that can be used to test whether two **String** objects contain the same set of characters in the same order. Method **equals()** compares the contents of two **String** objects, and returns **true** if the string objects contain the same strings of characters. If the string objects do not contain the same values, the boolean value **false** is returned. The following is one possible way to call the **equals()** method

```
if ( string_object.equals( another_string ) )
{
   ...
```

Method **equalsIgnoreCase()** compares strings in the same way as the **equals()** method, but it does not make a distinction between uppercase letters and corresponding lowercase letters. Otherwise, the method is used like the **equals()** method:

```
if ( string_object.equalsIgnoreCase( another_string ) )
{
   ...
```

A static method named **format()** is able to, among other things, insert numbers into a string in a certain format. The formatting information must be given in format specifiers like **%06d** for the **format()** method. The **format()** method uses exactly the same format specifiers as the **System.out.printf()** method. See Chapter 5 for more information about format specifiers. The source program lines

```
int given_integer  =  keyboard.nextInt() ;

String  text_to_print  =  String.format(
          "%06d is %06X hexadecimal", given_integer, given_integer ) ;

System.out.print( text_to_print ) ;
```

are an example of the use of the **format()** method. These lines would produce

```
001025 is 000401 hexadecimal
```

to the screen if the user typed 1025 from the keyboard. **format()** is an unusual method in that you can give it almost any number of parameters after the string which contains the format specifiers.

Method **getBytes()** can convert a string to an array of bytes:

```
byte[] array_of_bytes  =  string_object.getBytes() ;
```

When characters of a string are converted to bytes, 16-bit values must be fitted to 8-bit memory positions. This means that characters must be encoded in a certain way.

Method **getChars()** copies characters from "this" string to an array of type **char[]**.

```
string_object.getChars( position_of_first_character_to_be_copied,
                        position_following_last_character_to_be_copied,
                        receiving_array_of_characters,
                        index_of_first_character_in_receiving_array ) ;
```

When all characters of a string need to be put into an array of type **char[]**, it is best to use the **toCharArray()** method.

## Class String methods – indexOf(), lastIndexOf(), length(), matches()

There are various versions of method **indexOf()** that can be used to find substrings or characters inside **String** objects. **indexOf()** returns the first index position where the substring or character is found. If no position is found the methods return the value -1. Note that if no position is given as a second parameter to the method, the search operation is started from position 0, from the beginning of the string. The search always continues to the end of the string.

```
found_index = string_object.indexOf( another_string ) ;

found_index = string_object.indexOf( character_to_search ) ;

found_index = string_object.indexOf( another_string,
                                     position_where_to_start_search ) ;

found_index = string_object.indexOf( character_to_search,
                                     position_where_to_start_search ) ;
```

Method **lastIndexOf()** behaves like method **indexOf()**, but **lastIndexOf()** returns the largest index position where a substring or character is found. **lastIndexOf()** thus searches from the end towards the beginning of a string. If no position is found, the method returns value -1. Also the method versions that start searching from the given index position proceed towards the beginning of the string. If the substring or character is not found, the search stops when the first character of the string is encountered.

```
found_index = string_object.lastIndexOf( another_string ) ;

found_index = string_object.lastIndexOf( character_to_search ) ;

found_index = string_object.lastIndexOf( another_string,
                                         position_where_to_start_search ) ;

found_index = string_object.lastIndexOf( character_to_search,
                                         position_where_to_start_search ) ;
```

Method **length()** returns the length of the **String** object as an integer value. The length means the number of characters in the string.

```
string_length = string_object.length() ;
```

A method named **matches()** can be used to check whether or not a string matches a given *regular expression*. Regular expressions are a special subject in the field of computing, but, unfortunately, it is not possible to cover that subject thoroughly in this book. A regular expression can be used to search certain text patterns in a string of characters. A regular expression can specify a certain set of strings, and it can be used to check whether some string belongs to the specified set of strings. For example, the regular expression [A-G]+ specifies all strings that have at least one character and that consist solely of the uppercase letters A, B, C, D, E, F, and G. In the above regular expression [A-G] specifies a set of characters and + means one or more occurrences of the specified characters. A regular expression is supplied as a string to the **matches()** method, and it returns a **boolean** value. For example, the lines

```
String some_string  =  "BAGDAD" ;
System.out.print( "\n "  +  some_string.matches( "[A-G]+" ) ) ;
```

would produce the text **true** to the screen because the string "BAGDAD" matches the used regular expression.

## Class String methods – regionMatches(), replace(), split(), startsWith(), substring()

The boolean method **regionMatches()** compares a region in "this" string to a region in another string. If the regions are found to contain the same characters in the same order, value **true** is returned. Otherwise, value **false** is returned. The following are possible calls to the method. The second version of the method considers uppercase and lowercase letters the same if its first parameter has value **true**.

```
if ( string_object.regionMatches( beginning_index_of_region_in_this_string,
                                  another_string,
                                  beginning_index_of_region_in_another_string,
                                  length_of_the_regions ) )
{
   ...

if ( string_object.regionMatches( ignore_case_of_characters,  //  true or false
                                  beginning_index_of_region_in_this_string,
                                  another_string,
                                  beginning_index_of_region_in_another_string,
                                  length_of_the_regions ) )
{
   ...
```

Method **replace()** replaces all occurrences of **string_to_replace** with **replacement_string**, or all occurrences of **character_to_replace** with **replacement_character**. If no occurrences of **string_to_replace** or **character_to_replace** are found in **string_object**, the returned string is identical to the original string.

```
new_string_object  =  string_object.replace( string_to_replace,
                                             replacement_string ) ;

new_string_object  =  string_object.replace( character_to_replace,
                                             replacement_character ) ;
```

Method **split()** splits a string to a set of substrings. A regular expression determines the splitting positions. The method is called in the following way

```
String[] array_of_substrings  =  string_object.split( regular_expression_as_string ) ;
```

To find more information about the **split()** method, see program **SplittingAtoms.java** on page 234.

Method **startsWith()** returns **true** of **false** depending on whether or not a string starts with a given string. For example, the following **if** construct tests whether **String** object **name_from_keyboard** starts with **"Joe"**.

```
if ( name_from_keyboard.startsWith( "Joe" ) )
{
   //  The name begins with "Joe".
```

Method **substring()** returns a copy of a substring that is taken from an existing string. It is possible to take the substring from the specified index position until the end of a string, or specify an index value which marks the end of the substring.

```
substring = string_object.substring( position_from_which_to_take_substring )

substring = string_object.substring( position_from_which_to_take_substring,
                                     position_following_last_character_of_substring )
```

**Class String methods – toCharArray(), toLowerCase(), toString(), toUpperCase(), trim(), valueOf()**

Method **`toCharArray()`** converts a **`String`** object to an array of type **`char[]`**. Each character of the string becomes an array element.

```
char[] array_of_characters  =  string_object.toCharArray() ;
```

Method **`toLowerCase()`** returns a modified copy of a **`String`** object. All uppercase letters are converted to the corresponding lowercase letters in the returned copy.

```
new_string_object   =   string_object.toLowerCase() ;
```

Method **`toString()`** returns a reference to this **`String`** object. The **`String`** object is not copied.

```
another_string   =   string_object.toString() ;
```

Method **`toUpperCase()`** returns a modified copy of a **`String`** object. All lowercase letters are converted to the corresponding uppercase letters in the returned copy.

```
new_string_object   =   string_object.toUpperCase() ;
```

With method **`trim()`** it is possible to trim the beginning and end of a string so that so-called whitespace characters are removed both from the beginning and the end of a string. The whitespace characters generally include characters such as newlines '\n', carriage return characters '\r', spaces ' ', and tabulator characters '\t'. The method call

```
String  trimmed_string   =   string_object.trim() ;
```

removes whitespace characters from both ends of the object referenced by **`string_object`**.

The **`String`** class provides many static methods with the name **`valueOf()`**. With these **`valueOf()`** methods it is possible to convert various types of data items to strings. The same conversions can, however, be done with the string concatenation operator (+), and actually it may be easier to use the + operator instead of a **`valueOf()`** method. For example, the following two statements produce the same output to the screen.

```
System.out.print( "\n The value is "  +  String.valueOf( some_integer ) );
System.out.print( "\n The value is "  +  some_integer ) ;
```

## 8.5 Class StringBuilder – mutable strings

**String** objects are immutable data items. That means that they cannot be modified after they have been created. For this reason, string methods operate so that they always create a new **String** object when they modify an existing **String** object. In some larger computer programs (applications), creating many **String** objects may consume too much computing power and slow down the application. As it is not always efficient to manipulate strings as **String** objects, Java provides another class that can be used when working with text strings. The name of this other string manipulation class is **StringBuilder**, and, as its name implies, the **StringBuilder** class can be used to build strings. **StringBuilder** objects (**StringBuilder** strings) are different from regular **String** objects (**String** strings) in that they can be modified without creating new objects.

A **StringBuilder** object can be created with a statement like

```
StringBuilder  text_to_build  =  new  StringBuilder() ;
```

This statement makes **text_to_build** reference a **StringBuilder** object. The object is initially empty, i.e., it does not contain any characters. A **StringBuilder** object can also be created by converting a **String** object to a **StringBuilder** object in the following way

```
String  museum_in_madrid  =  "Prado" ;

StringBuilder  famous_museum  =
                          new  StringBuilder( museum_in_madrid ) ;
```

After the above declarations, **StringBuilder** object (referenced by) **famous_museum** would contain the text "Prado".

Class **StringBuilder** has less methods than class **String**. Among the most important **StringBuilder** methods are **append()**, **delete()**, **insert()**, **replace()**, and **toString()**. These methods are demonstrated in program **StatesStringBuilder.java**, which is a rewritten version of program **States.java**. By comparing these two programs you can find out the differences between **String** and **StringBuilder** objects. **Elvis.java** is an example program that shows how the characters of a **StringBuilder** string can be modified with the **setCharAt()** method.

**StringBuilder** strings can be called dynamic (mutable) strings because these strings can grow dynamically during the execution of a program. The **StringBuilder** class has the method **capacity()** that tells how much memory is reserved for characters in a **StringBuilder** object. If the reserved memory is found to be inadequate, for example, in an **insert()** or **append()** operation, new memory is reserved automatically, and the capacity of the **StringBuilder** object thus increases. For example, by executing the statements

```
StringBuilder  some_text  =  new  StringBuilder() ;
System.out.print( "\n Capacity: " + some_text.capacity() ) ;
some_text.append( "12345678901234567890" ) ;
System.out.print( "\n Capacity: " + some_text.capacity() ) ;
```

the program would print first 16 and then 34. The default capacity of a **StringBuilder** object is 16, i.e., it can store a string that has 16 characters. In the above case the capacity is automatically increased to 34 when a string of 20 characters is appended to **some_text**.

The automatic increase of capacity of a **StringBuilder** object can slow down a program. Especially in programs that process long texts it may be useful to specify **StringBuilder** objects that have a large initial capacity. One possibility to control the capacity a **StringBuilder** object is to use a statement like

```
StringBuilder  long_text  =  new StringBuilder( 2000 ) ;
```

that creates a **StringBuilder** object with an initial capacity of 2000 character positions.

The purpose of this initialized string is to show the positions of various characters in **elvis_sentence**. Note that the count starts from 0.

**elvis_sentence** references a **StringBuilder** object that is almost like a **String** object. Unlike **String** objects, **StringBuilder** objects can be modified after they have been created. Class **StringBuilder** provides a method named **setCharAt()** to change the character in a certain position of a **StringBuilder** string. These statements overwrite some individual characters in **elvis_sentence**. Letters 'r', 'c', and 'k' are overwritten with letters 'm', 'v', and 'i', respectively. The space after the word "rock" is replaced with 'e'. The letter 'r' in word "rock" is the 13th character in the original sentence. That letter can be accessed with index value 12 because we start counting index values from zero.

```
//  Elvis.java

class Elvis
{
   public static void main( String[] not_in_use )
   {
      String  character_positions   =    "0123456789012345678901" ;

      StringBuilder elvis_sentence   =
                       new StringBuilder(  "Elvis was a rock star." ) ;

      System.out.print(   "\n    "  +  character_positions   ) ;

      System.out.print( "\n\n    "  +  elvis_sentence ) ;

      elvis_sentence.setCharAt( 12, 'm' ) ;
      elvis_sentence.setCharAt( 14, 'v' ) ;
      elvis_sentence.setCharAt( 15, 'i' ) ;
      elvis_sentence.setCharAt( 16, 'e' ) ;

      System.out.print( "\n\n    "  +  elvis_sentence   +   "\n" ) ;
   }
}
```

**Elvis.java - 1. Modifying some characters of a StringBuilder object.**

```
D:\javafiles2>java Elvis

   0123456789012345678901

   Elvis was a rock star.

   Elvis was a moviestar.
```

Here **elvis_sentence** is printed for the second time. Because the text was modified after the previous output, the text on the screen is different.

**Elvis.java - X. elvis_sentence before and after modifications.**

Objects of class **StringBuilder** are dynamic strings that are mutable, i.e., they can be modified without creating new objects. This statement declares a **StringBuilder** reference named **states_in_usa**, creates a **StringBuilder** object, and makes **states_in_usa** reference the created object. The **StringBuilder** object is created by passing a **String** object to the **StringBuilder** constructor. The **String** object is first created by concatenating strings with operator +.

```
//  StatesStringBuilder.java (c) Kari Laitinen

class StatesStringBuilder
{
   public static void main( String[] not_in_use )
   {
      String  westmost_state   =  "Hawaii" ;
      String  prairie_state    =  "Illinois" ;

      StringBuilder states_in_usa   =
             new StringBuilder( westmost_state + "  " + prairie_state ) ;

      System.out.print( "\n   " +  states_in_usa ) ;

      String  golden_state     =  "California" ;

      states_in_usa.insert( 6, golden_state ) ;
      states_in_usa.insert( 6, "  " ) ;

      System.out.print( "\n   " +  states_in_usa ) ;
```

These statements call the method **insert()** for the **StringBuilder** object referenced by **states_in_usa**. The first method call inserts the contents of string **golden_state** into the seventh character position of the **StringBuilder** object. The second method call inserts two space characters into the same character position. These insertion operations result in that the **StringBuilder** object is modified so that characters are inserted in the middle of the character string and characters following the insertion point are moved to larger index positions. The length of the **StringBuilder** object thus grows in these operations. These two statements could be replaced by the single statement

```
   states_in_usa.insert( 6, "  " + golden_state ) ;
```

**StatesStringBuilder.java - 1: A rewritten version of program States.java.**

**append()** is a method that exists in the **StringBuilder** class but is missing from the **String** class. With this method it is possible to append a string to the end of a **StringBuilder** string. The **append()** method is not needed in the **String** class because appending operations can be carried out with the string concatenation operator +.

Method **lastIndexOf()** does not exist in class **StringBuilder**. Therefore, the **StringBuilder** string is first converted to a **String** string with method **toString()**, and then method **lastIndexOf()** of class **String** is applied to the **String** string.

```
      String  eastmost_state  =  "Maine" ;

      states_in_usa.append( "  Virginia  " ) ;
      states_in_usa.append( eastmost_state ) ;

      System.out.print( "\n   " + states_in_usa ) ;

      int index_of_last_state  =
               states_in_usa.toString().lastIndexOf( " " ) ;

      states_in_usa.delete( index_of_last_state, states_in_usa.length());
      states_in_usa.append( "  Massachusetts" ) ;

      System.out.print( "\n   " + states_in_usa ) ;

      states_in_usa.replace( states_in_usa.toString().indexOf("Illinois"),
                             states_in_usa.toString().indexOf("Virginia"),
                             "Michigan   " ) ;

      System.out.print( "\n   " + states_in_usa + "\n" ) ;

   }
}
```

Method **replace()** of class **StringBuilder** takes three parameters. The first two parameters specify two index positions between which the text is replaced with the string supplied by the third parameter. **replace()** of class **StringBuilder** operates in a slightly different way when compared to the **replace()** method of class **String**.

**StringBuilder** method **delete()** deletes characters between two index positions. Here, the latter index position is returned by method **length()**, which means that characters are deleted from the end of the **StringBuilder** string.

**StatesStringBuilder.java - 2. The last part of the program that uses a StringBuilder object.**

```
D:\javafiles2>java StatesStringBuilder

   Hawaii  Illinois
   Hawaii  California  Illinois
   Hawaii  California  Illinois  Virginia  Maine
   Hawaii  California  Illinois  Virginia  Massachusetts
   Hawaii  California  Michigan  Virginia  Massachusetts
```

**StatesStringBuilder.java - X. This program produces the same output as program States.java**

## Exercises with Marilyn.java

Exercise 8-6. Now it is necessary to write the full name "Marilyn Monroe" to make program **Marilyn.java** accept your answer. Modify the program so that it finds the answer correct if the user types in just "Marilyn" or "Monroe". You can make this happen by using either method **`contains()`** or method **`indexOf()`** instead of **`compareTo()`**. Method **`contains()`** returns **`true`** and method **`indexOf()`** returns something else than -1 if the string that is written in parentheses is included in the string for which the method was called. See **StringMethodsMore.java** to find out more information about methods **`contains()`** and **`indexOf()`**.

Exercise 8-7. Improve **Marilyn.java** even further so that it accepts the answer also when the input string is written like "marilyn", "MARILYN" or "MArilyn". One possibility to do this is to convert all uppercase letters to lowercase letters in (the **`String`** object referenced by) **`name_from_keyboard`**. You can use the string method **`toLowerCase()`** to convert the letters of a string to lowercase letters.

## Class StringBuffer

Java has also a standard class named **`StringBuffer`** which works like the **`StringBuilder`** class. Both of these classes provide the same methods to manipulate textual information. The **`StringBuffer`** class can be useful in programs in which several threads (pieces of program running simultaneously) are using the same object to store textual information. In this book we use only the **`StringBuilder`** class.

## 8.6 Arrays of strings

**String** objects resemble arrays in some ways. Inside a **String** object there is an array that contains the character codes of the characters of the string. Like an array, a string stores a set of similar data items. Strings can be indexed with the **charAt()** method. The **length()** method tells how many characters are contained in a string.

An essential difference between arrays and strings is that strings can store only character codes, whereas there can be different types of arrays to store different types of data items. We get a particularly interesting array if we declare an array whose type is **String[]**. For example, the statement

```
String[]  array_of_strings  =  new  String[ 20 ] ;
```

declares and creates an array that can reference 20 **String** objects. The above statement does not create any **String** objects. It only creates an array of 20 **String** references that do not yet reference (point to) any **String** objects. We say that the references in this kind of array are **null** references. The term **null** is a reserved keyword in Java and it means that no object is referenced.

If we create an array of strings with the statement

```
String[] array_of_emperors  =  new  String[ 10 ] ;
```

we can store **String** objects into the created array with statements like

```
array_of_emperors[ 0 ]  = "Napoleon Bonaparte" ;

String  first_emperor_of_rome    =  "Augustus (Octavianus)" ;
String  last_emperor_of_russia   =  "Nicholas II" ;

array_of_emperors[ 1 ]  =  first_emperor_of_rome ;
array_of_emperors[ 2 ]  =  last_emperor_of_russia ;
```

An array of strings like the one above can be printed with the loop

```
for ( int emperor_index  =  0 ;
          emperor_index  <  array_of_emperors.length ;
          emperor_index  ++ )
{
   System.out.print( "\n "  +  emperor_index  + ": "
                   +  array_of_emperors[ emperor_index ] ) ;
}
```

In the example above, array of strings (**String** references) was created first, and then the array elements were made to reference **String** objects. Another possibility to create an array of strings is to specify an initialized array. For example, the statement

```
String[]  names_of_famous_queens  =

   { "Isabella I", "Elizabeth I", "Catherine II the Great",
     "Victoria", "Elizabeth II" } ;
```

creates an initialized array of strings, and each array element references a **String** object. The length of the array is 5 because there are 5 initialization strings given inside the braces. Program **Months.java** demonstrates another initialized array of strings, and shows how the array elements can be accessed.

Program **SplittingAtoms.java** is an example in which the string method **split()** is used. Method **split()** can divide a **String** object into many shorter strings (substrings) and put the shorter strings to an array whose type is **String[]**.

An array of strings is like any array of objects. These types of arrays will be studied further in Part III of this book.

This loop prints the first four month names from the array **names_of_months**. The index variable **month_index** is used to decide which month name is selected from the array. **letter_index** selects a letter in a month name.

An initialized array of strings can be declared and created by giving string literals inside braces { }. Each element in this kind of array is a reference to a **String** object. The array length depends on how many string literals are given inside braces. The length of this array is automatically set to 12 because twelve month names are given as string literals.

The seventh element in **names_of_months** is a reference to the **String** object containing the text "July".

```
// Months.java  (c) Kari Laitinen

class Months
{
   public static void main( String[] not_in_use )
   {
      String[]  names_of_months =

         { "January", "February", "March", "April", "May", "June",
           "July", "August", "September", "October", "November",
           "December"  }  ;

      System.out.print( "\n The first month of year is "
                      + names_of_months[ 0 ] +  "." ) ;

      System.out.print(  "\n\n The seventh month, " + names_of_months[ 6 ]
                      +  ", is named after Julius Caesar.\n" ) ;

      System.out.print( "\n Our calendar has "+  names_of_months.length
                      +  " months. \n" ) ;

      for ( int month_index  =  0 ;
                month_index  <  4 ;
                month_index  ++  )
      {
         int number_of_letters_in_month_name  =
                         names_of_months[ month_index ].length() ;

         System.out.print( "\n " +  names_of_months[ month_index ]
                         +  " is made of "
                         +  number_of_letters_in_month_name
                         +  " letters: " ) ;

         for ( int letter_index   =  0 ;
                   letter_index   <  number_of_letters_in_month_name ;
                   letter_index  ++ )
         {
            System.out.print(  " "  +
                  names_of_months[ month_index ].charAt( letter_index ) ) ;
         }
      }
   }
}
```

**Months.java - 1.+ Demonstration of an initialized array of strings.**

```
int number_of_letters_in_month_name  =
                    names_of_months[ month_index ].length() ;

System.out.print( "\n " + names_of_months[ month_index ]
               +  " is made of "
               +  number_of_letters_in_month_name
               +  " letters: " ) ;

for ( int letter_index  = 0 ;
          letter_index  <  number_of_letters_in_month_name ;
          letter_index  ++ )
{
   System.out.print(  " "  +
       names_of_months[ month_index ].charAt( letter_index ) ) ;
}
```

Each element in an array of strings can reference a **String** object, and each **String** object is a kind of array that can be indexed with the **charAt()** method. When we want to refer to a single character in a string that is an element of an array of strings, we must use one index to index the array and another index as a parameter for the **charAt()** method.

This way we can refer to the length of a single string in an array of strings.

**Months.java - 1 - 1. The internal statements of the outer for loop of the program.**

```
D:\javafiles2>java Months

 The first month of year is January.

 The seventh month, July, is named after Julius Caesar.

 Our calendar has 12 months.

 January is made of 7 letters:  J a n u a r y
 February is made of 8 letters:  F e b r u a r y
 March is made of 5 letters:  M a r c h
 April is made of 5 letters:  A p r i l
```

A string containing a single space character is printed between each letter in a month name.

**Months.java - X. All month names are made of letters.**

If you also read my C++ book *A Natural Introduction to Computer Programming with C++*, please note that the **Months.java** program in this book is somewhat different from the **months.cpp** program in the C++ book. Program **Months.java** is thus an exception to the rule that programs bearing the same name (e.g. **game.cpp**, **Game.cs**, and **Game.java**) that are presented in different books work in the same way.

This statement calls the method **split()**. This operation produces an array of type **String[]**. The return type of method **split()** is thus marked as **String[]**. The returned array contains substrings that are taken from **atomic_text** so that the original string is split in those positions which contain either character **\n** (the newline character) or a comma. These characters are given inside brackets [ ] in the string literal **"[\n,]"** that is supplied as a parameter to the **split()** method. The parameter for the **split()** method is a so-called regular expression.

This loop rejoins the substrings that are in the array of strings.

```
//  SplittingAtoms.java (c) Kari Laitinen

class SplittingAtoms
{
   public static void main( String[] not_in_use )
   {
      String  atomic_text  =
                  "\n Atoms consist of protons, neutrons, and electrons." ;

      System.out.print( atomic_text  +  "\n" ) ;

      String[]  substrings_from_text  =   atomic_text.split( "[\n,]" ) ;

      for ( int  substring_index  =  0 ;
                 substring_index  <  substrings_from_text.length ;
                 substring_index  ++ )
      {
         System.out.print( "\n" + substring_index  +  ":"
                        +  substrings_from_text[ substring_index ] ) ;
      }

      atomic_text  =  "" ;

      for ( int  substring_index  =  0 ;
                 substring_index  <  substrings_from_text.length ;
                 substring_index  ++ )
      {
         atomic_text  =  atomic_text  +
                            substrings_from_text[ substring_index ] ;
      }

      System.out.print( "\n\n"  +  atomic_text  +  "\n" ) ;

      substrings_from_text  =  atomic_text.split( "[ ]" ) ;

      for ( int  substring_index  =  0 ;
                 substring_index  <  substrings_from_text.length ;
                 substring_index  ++ )
      {
         System.out.print( "\n" + substring_index  +  ":"
                        +  substrings_from_text[ substring_index ] ) ;
      }
   }
}
```

**SplittingAtoms.java - 1.+ Splitting a string with method split().**

Method **split()** is invoked here to resplit the string that was constructed in a loop. Now the parameter for the **split()** method is "[ ]". This means that the string should be split in those positions where a space character is to be found. "[ ]" is a regular expression which lists inside brackets those characters which should cause a splitting operation. In "[ ]" there is only the space character listed. Regular expressions are a special subject in the field of computing, and they are not thoroughly covered in this book.

```
substrings_from_text  =  atomic_text.split( "[ ]" ) ;

for ( int  substring_index  = 0 ;
           substring_index  <  substrings_from_text.length ;
           substring_index  ++ )
{
   System.out.print( "\n" + substring_index  +  ":"
                 +  substrings_from_text[ substring_index ] ) ;
}
```

An array that contains references to **String** objects is like any other array. The **length** field reveals the number of array elements, and an element can be referred to with an index expression in brackets.

**SplittingAtoms.java - 1 - 1. Resplitting the rejoined string.**

```
D:\javafiles2>java SplittingAtoms

 Atoms consist of protons, neutrons, and electrons.

0:
1: Atoms consist of protons
2: neutrons
3: and electrons.

 Atoms consist of protons neutrons and electrons.

0:
1:Atoms
2:consist
3:of
4:protons
5:neutrons
6:and
7:electrons.
```

The index values of the substrings are printed before the substrings. The first substring is an empty string because the first splitting position was the first position in the string **atomic_text**.

The reconstructed string does not contain any commas because they were the characters that specified the splitting positions in the first splitting operation. The characters in the splitting positions are discarded by the **split()** method.

**SplittingAtoms.java - X. The program produces always the same output.**

## 8.7 Chapter summary

- Textual strings of characters can be handled in Java by declaring and creating objects of class **String**. A statement like

```
String  some_string ;
```

declares a string reference that can be made to reference a **String** object.

- **String** objects can be created by assigning a string literal as a value to a string reference, by calling some of the special constructors of class **String**, or by calling methods that return **String** objects. For example, the following statements create **String** objects

```
some_string  =  "Some text." ;

String  duplicated_string  =  new  String( some_string ) ;

String  string_from_keyboard  =  keyboard.nextLine() ;

char[]  array_of_vowels  =  { 'A', 'E', 'I', 'O', 'U' } ;

String  string_containing_the_vowels  =
                                  new  String( array_of_vowels ) ;

String  some_substring  =
                    some_existing_string.substring( 3 ) ;
```

- Individual characters of a string can be read with the **charAt()** method. When we write

```
some_string.charAt( 3 )
```

we get the fourth character of the string **some_string**, or, to be more accurate, the above expression returns the fourth character of the **String** object referenced by **some_string**.

- **String** objects are immutable, which means that they cannot be modified after they have been created. If you want to use strings that can be modified after their creation, you can use **StringBuilder** strings that are mutable strings.
- **length()** is an important method for **String** and **StringBuilder** objects. With this method you can find out how many characters are stored in a **String** or **StringBuilder** object.
- Arrays of strings, or more accurately, arrays of string references can be declared and created with statements like

```
String[] some_array_of_strings   =  new  String[ 30 ] ;

String[] some_initialized_array_of_strings   =

     { "text in first object", "text in second object",

       "text in third object" } ;
```

## Exercises related to strings and arrays

Exercise 8-8. Write a program that asks for a string from the keyboard, and then prints the string in "shrinking pieces". For example, if the user types in the string "Hello", the program should print

```
Hello
ello
llo
lo
o
```

The program must have a loop which prints smaller and smaller pieces of the string. One possibility to solve this problem is to use the string method **`substring()`** so that shorter and shorter substrings are taken from the given string inside a loop.

Exercise 8-9. Write a program that asks for a sentence from the keyboard, and then prints the sentence so that each word in the sentence is written on its own line in reverse character order. For example, if the user types in "I like computer programming.", the program should respond

```
I
ekil
retupmoc
.gnimmargorp
```

This problem can be solved by letting the string method **`split()`** break the given sentence on all those positions that contain a space character. Then the substrings (words) that are put into an array of strings can be printed separately in reverse character order.

Exercise 8-10. Write a program (e.g. **MonthsHistory.java**) that asks for a month number from a range of 1 to 12, and prints a sentence according to the given number. For example, if number 8 is given to the program, it must print "August is the month of Emperor Augustus". The program must print a sentence that describes the history of a month. Most of the words for the sentence must be taken from arrays of strings. You can copy the array **`names_of_months`** from **Months.java**. In addition, you can use the following array

```
String[]  history_of_months =
{  "month of Roman god Janus",          // January
   "last month in Roman calendar",      // February
   "month of Roman war god Mars",       // March
   "month of Roman goddess Venus",      // April
   "month of goddess Maia",             // May
   "month of Roman goddess Juno",       // June
   "month of Julius Caesar",            // July
   "month of Emperor Augustus",         // August
   "7th Roman month",                   // September
   "8th Roman month",                   // October
   "9th Roman month",                   // November
   "10th Roman month"  } ;              // December
```

To reduce your typing work, the above array is written in comments at the end of program **Months.java**.

## Some explanation about how I write about strings, arrays, and other objects

In the beginning, it can be difficult to understand strings and arrays because they are objects, and objects are such that in addition to the actual objects there has to be object references with which the objects are handled in programs. Because programs can contain both objects and object references, and only the object references have names, texts that describe such programs can be somewhat complicated. For this reason, I want to clarify how I write about objects and object references.

Let's consider the following statement which both declares a string reference and assigns a value to the reference:

```
String  given_name  =  keyboard.nextLine() ;
```

After this statement is executed, **given_name** references a **String** object that is formed of the characters that are given from the keyboard. When I write about the **String** object, I might use sentences like

"If the string object referenced by **given_name** is such that ... "

"If the string **given_name** is such that ... "

"If **given_name** is such that ... "

All the above sentences speak about the **String** object, not about the string reference. To avoid too complicated sentences, I will not always use the words "referenced by" when I speak about some object that is referenced by some object reference. In those cases when I write about an object reference, I try to clearly indicate it. If I wanted to say something about the above string reference, I would write

"If the string reference **given_name** is such that ... "

Arrays are also objects, and in that respect similar to strings. When there is, in this book, an array declared and created with a statement like

```
int[]  array_of_integers  =  new  int[ 50 ] ;
```

I might write later a sentence that begins

"If **array_of_integers** is such that ... "

This sentence actually means

"If the array referenced by **array_of_integers** is such that ... "

and if I wanted to speak about the array reference, I would explicitly say it, for example in the following way

"If the array reference **array_of_integers** is such that ... "

Later on in this book we shall study other objects which are similar to strings and arrays. An object can be created with a statement like

```
SomeClass  some_object  =  new  SomeClass() ;
```

When I would write about this object, I could use a sentence like

"If **some_object** is such that ..."

to say something about the object. If I wanted to tell something about the object reference, I would use a sentence like

"If the object reference **some_object** is such that ..."

It is important to note that the actual objects do not have names in programs. They are referenced by named object references. Then, because usually we need to discuss the objects, not the object references, it is common to name the object references so that the name of an object reference refers to the object instead of the object reference. This means that we do not use the word "reference" in the names of object references. According to this principle, the above name **given_name** refers to the **String** object that is given from the keyboard, the name **array_of_integers** refers to the array object, and the name **some_object** refers to an object.

# CHAPTER 9

## METHODS – LOGICAL PERFORMING UNITS IN PROGRAMS

The word "method" has already been mentioned many times in this book. A method is a piece of program code that performs a well-defined task. In every program we have had a method named **main()**. Method **main()** is always executed first when the execution of a program begins. We have also encountered methods **print()**, **printf()**, and **nextLine()** which are standard methods to write data to the screen and read data from the keyboard. In Chapter 8 we studied many string methods (**indexOf()**, **substring()**, **compareTo()**, etc.) which are standard methods to manipulate strings. Now we are going to take a closer look at methods and their use. You will learn how to write your own methods. The term "calling" will be an important concept associated with methods.

With Java we can write static methods and non-static instance methods. The methods that we are going to study in this chapter are static methods. The instance methods, which are in some ways different from the static methods, will be studied in the following chapter.

## 9.1 Simple static methods and the concept of calling

All programs that we have studied so far are of the form

```
// SomeName.java

class SomeName
{
   public static void main( String[] not_in_use )
   {
      Statements that declare data (variables, objects, and arrays).

      Functional action statements.
   }
}
```

The source program statements that we have seen so far have been statements of the method named **main()**. Method **main()** has always the reserved words **public**, **static**, and **void** preceding its name, and **String[] not_in_use** is written inside parentheses after the method name **main**. The Java statements that dictate what method **main()** does are inside a pair of braces { }.

From now on, we will start studying programs that may contain several methods. The simplest form of a method is such that the type of the method is **void**, and the parentheses after the method name are empty.

Program **Messages.java** is an example where a simple method is called inside the method **main()**. Although the structure of **Messages.java** is such that the source code of the method **print_message()** is written first and method **main()** is at the end of program, the program execution starts from method **main()**. Method **main()** is the "main program" in the file. When a Java program is executed on a computer, the operating system first activates the Java interpreter, the Java virtual machine, and then the virtual machine starts the program by executing the method that is named **main()**.

Method **print_message()** in program **Messages.java** can be considered a subroutine because its execution is completely controlled by method **main()**. The source code of the subroutine starts

```
static void print_message()
{
   ...
```

Note that there is no semicolon (;) here.

and it is called inside method **main()** simply by writing the method name in the following way

```
print_message() ;
```

What happens in a method call is that the calling method stops running, and the statements of the method that was called are executed. When all statements of the method that was called are executed, the program execution continues in the calling method from the statement that follows the method call.

In **Messages.java**, method **print_message()** is called twice. By studying the output you can find out that **print_message()** always prints the same text lines, while method **main()** prints something else in between the message from **print_message()**. Program **Messages.java** could, of course, be written without method **print_message()**. If the statements inside method **print_message()** were copied to those two places where **print_message()** is called in method **main()**, the program would behave in the same way as it is doing now, but it would not need any method calls.

The statements that form the body of method **print_message()** are inside these braces. The structure of this method is similar to the structure of method **main()**. Generally, the name of a method can be invented by the programmer, but method **main()** must have that name.

All methods must be written inside some class declaration. In this program, class **Messages** contains two separate methods.

```
//  Messages.java (c) Kari Laitinen

class Messages
{
   static void print_message()
   {
      System.out.print( "\n   This is method named \"print_message()\"." ) ;
      System.out.print( "\n   Methods usually contain many statements. " ) ;
      System.out.print( "\n   Let us now return to the calling method." ) ;
   }

   public static void main( String[] not_in_use )
   {
      System.out.print( "\n THE FIRST STATEMENT IN METHOD \"main()\"." ) ;

      print_message() ;

      System.out.print( "\n THIS IS BETWEEN TWO METHOD CALLS." ) ;

      print_message() ;

      System.out.print( "\n END OF METHOD \"main()\".\n" ) ;
   }
}
```

Method **print_message()** is called twice inside method **main()**. A simple static method belonging to the same class as the calling method can be called by writing its name, a pair of empty parentheses, and a semicolon. Method calls are statements in Java. What happens in a method call is that the statements inside the called method are executed, and program execution continues from the statement that follows the method call in the calling method.

**Messages.java - 1. Method main() calling a simple method named print_message().**

```
D:\javafiles2>java Messages

 THE FIRST STATEMENT IN METHOD "main()".
   This is method named "print_message()".
   Methods usually contain many statements.
   Let us now return to the calling method.
 THIS IS BETWEEN TWO METHOD CALLS.
   This is method named "print_message()".
   Methods usually contain many statements.
   Let us now return to the calling method.
 END OF METHOD "main()".
```

Those lines containing mostly lowercase letters are printed by method **print_message()**.

**Messages.java - X. Method print_message() prints always the same message.**

In programming terminology, the method that calls another method is the caller, and the method that is called is the callee. In **Messages.java**, method **`main()`** is the caller and method **`print_message()`** is the callee. A caller calls a callee like an employer employs an employee. A callee is always subordinate to its caller. The caller decides when a callee is executed. The caller continues by executing the statements that follow the method call when the statements of a callee have been executed.

Methods are executed, statement by statement, from the first statement to the last statement. Although computers can execute statements extremely fast, only one statement is being executed at a time. To better understand what is happening when a program is being executed, we can think that there exists such a thing as "program control". The program control is at that statement which is currently being executed. When the current statement has been completely executed, the program control is passed to the following statement. The program control is at the first executable statement of method **`main()`** when the execution of a program begins. When the last statement of method **`main()`** is executed, the program control is passed back to the operating system of the computer.

A method call is a statement that passes the program control to the called method, the callee. Just after the execution of a method call, the program control is at the first executable statement in callee. The program control goes through every statement in callee. After the last statement in the callee has been executed, the program control is passed to the statement that follows the method call in caller.

In large computer programs there are methods that call other methods that call other methods that call other methods ... In well-designed programs there is, of course, always a last method that is called but which does not call any other methods. In large programs, methods are useful because they allow programs to be divided into manageable pieces of source code. Program **Letters.java** is an example where a called method calls two other methods. Method **`print_letters()`** is a callee in relation to method **`main()`**, but it is a caller in relation to the two other methods.

Although **Letters.java** does not do anything that could be considered as creative computing (i.e. the program is a simple textbook program), the program is an example of how a programming task can be divided into smaller programming tasks with the help of methods. What program **Letters.java** does is that it prints all letters of the English alphabet. First it prints all uppercase letters and then it prints all lowercase letters. We can imagine that **Letters.java** is the result of a software development project. A boss in a software company could have started a software project to produce a program that first prints all uppercase letters and then all lowercase letters. The software developers working on the project could have divided the programming work into the subtasks

- print uppercase letters
- print lowercase letters

which would have been implemented (i.e. programmed) as two separate methods by different people.

A method is a piece of source program that performs a certain activity. When a caller calls a method, the call is like a command to perform the activity that is programmed inside the method. Because method calls are like commands, it is usual that method names are in a commanding, imperative form. For example, the method names

```
print_uppercase_letters
print_message
```

are in the form of a command, since an imperative verb is the first word in the name. Technically, programmers are free to name methods according to the general naming rules of Java, but it is useful to name methods so that they are commands. This way method names can be easily distinguished from variable names. Inventing accurate and descriptive names for the methods you write helps you to understand your programming task better.

```
//  Letters.java (c) 2005 Kari Laitinen

class Letters
{
   static void print_uppercase_letters()
   {
      System.out.print( "\n Uppercase English letters are: \n\n" ) ;

      for ( char letter_to_print  =  'A' ;
                 letter_to_print  <= 'Z' ;
                 letter_to_print  ++  )
      {
         System.out.print(  " "  +  letter_to_print ) ;
      }
   }

   static void print_lowercase_letters()
   {
      System.out.print( "\n\n Lowercase English letters are: \n\n" ) ;

      for ( char letter_to_print  =  'a' ;
                 letter_to_print  <= 'z' ;
                 letter_to_print  ++ )
      {
         System.out.print(  " "  +  letter_to_print ) ;
      }
   }

   static void print_letters()
   {
      print_uppercase_letters() ;
      print_lowercase_letters() ;
   }

   public static void main( String[] not_in_use )
   {
      print_letters() ;
   }
}
```

These two methods are called by the method **`print_letters()`**.

The method called by **`main()`** contains two other method calls.

Method **`main()`** has only one statement which is a method call. These methods are in such an order that a callee is always written before the caller. In this book programs are generally written so that the method that will be called later in the program is placed before the calling method in the source program file.

**Letters.java - 1. Method main() calling a method that calls two other methods.**

```
D:\javafiles2>java Letters

 Uppercase English letters are:

 A B C D E F G H I J K L M N O P Q R S T U V W X Y Z

 Lowercase English letters are:

 a b c d e f g h i j k l m n o p q r s t u v w x y z
```

**Letters.java - X. All text is printed here by the two topmost methods.**

## 9.2 Methods that take parameters

The methods that we have studied so far are called in the following way

```
method_name() ;
```

You may have wondered why there always has to be a pair of empty parentheses () at the end of a method's name. In your mind you may have asked: "Can a pair of empty parentheses bear any meaning?" The answer is that they can. A pair of empty parentheses means that the method in question does not take any parameters. This, then, raises yet another question: what are parameters?

Parameters, which are sometimes called arguments, are data that are transferred between a method and its caller. A method usually performs a specific activity, and it may need some data while performing the activity that is programmed inside it. With the help of parameters, a calling method can provide the necessary data for a called method.

Program **Sums.java** contains a method named **print_sum()**, and that method takes parameters. We say that it takes two parameters of type **int** because two variables of type **int** are declared inside the parentheses that have so far been empty. Method **print_sum()** is called in **Sums.java** in the following ways

```
print_sum( 555, 222 ) ;
print_sum( first_integer, second_integer ) ;
```

In the first method call, **print_sum()** calculates and prints the sum of the two integer literals 555 and 222. In the second method call, **print_sum()** calculates and prints the sum of the integers stored in the variables **first_integer** and **second_integer**.

When method **print_sum()** is called, data is transferred from the caller to the callee. When the call statement is executed, the data that is supplied as parameters is copied to the parameter variables declared inside method **print_sum()**, and after that the internal statements of the called method are executed.

To explore the calling mechanism of methods, let's compare the calling of methods that take parameters and the calling of methods that take no parameters. When a method without parameters is called, for example, in the following way

```
print_message() ;
```

the method call means "Go and execute the internal statements of method **print_message()**". When a method that takes parameters is called, for example, as follows

```
print_sum( 1122, 3344 ) ;
```

the call means "First copy value 1122 to the first parameter variable of **print_sum()**, then copy 3344 to the second parameter variable, and then go and execute the internal statements of **print_sum()**". There is much meaning embedded in the latter method call. When the method call is compiled, the compiler generates the necessary bytecode instructions to copy the parameter data to the parameter variables.

The source code of method **print_sum()** begins with the lines

```
static void print_sum( int first_integer_from_caller,
                       int second_integer_from_caller )
{
   ...
```

The first two lines before the opening brace { are said to be the declarator of the method. The declarator specifies the most necessary information for the caller:

- the return type of the method (The return type is **void** in the above declarator, but later we will see methods which have more interesting return types.),
- the method name, and
- the names of the parameters and their types.

For the caller of a method, the information given in the method declarator is sufficient to use the method. The caller must know how a method works, but a method can be called without knowing the internal implementation of the method precisely. The implementation of a method means its internal program structure: what kinds of loops are used, which variables are declared, etc. We have already used methods without knowing how they are written internally. In Chapter 8 we used the string methods **compareTo()**, **substring()**, etc. We called these methods without seeing their actual source code.

A method may be called only with those parameter types that are specified in the declarator of the method. The declarator of **print_sum()** says that it accepts two and only two parameters of type **int**. Therefore, the method calls

```
print_sum( "Hello", "world" ) ;
print_sum( 33, 44, 55 ) ;
print_sum( 6666 ) ;
```

are illegal and result in compilation error. The first call above is not accepted by the Java compiler because the two parameters are not of type **int**. The last two method calls are not acceptable because, although the parameters are integer literals, the number of parameters is not equal to two.

Program **Decorations.java** is another example where methods take parameters. In that program, method **main()** calls a method that takes a string reference as a parameter. The first method call is

```
print_text_in_decorated_box( first_text ) ;
```

which means roughly the following: "Here is the string reference **first_text**. Make the local string reference **text_from_caller** reference the **String** object that is referenced by **first_text**. Then execute the internal statements of method **print_text_in_decorated_box()**". Figure 9-1 describes the situation when the above method call has been executed. As you can see by studying the output of **Decorations.java**, the text that is referenced by **first_text** is printed inside a kind of decorated box. Method **print_text_in_decorated_box()** can read the characters of the **String** object referenced by **first_text**, but no copy of the **String** object is made. When variables are method parameters, they are copied to the parameter variables of the called method, the callee. Also when **String** objects are used as parameters, references to the objects are passed to the callee, but no copies of the objects are made. Also arrays and other types of objects, which we'll study later, are passed to the callee in the same way as **String** objects.

When a called method receives a copy of a parameter, we say that the parameter is passed by value. In Java, parameters are always passed by value. When method parameters are objects, the passed values are references to the objects. In some other programming languages (e.g. C++ and C#) parameters can be passed by reference, which means that the parameters of a method can be declared so that when the method is called it can refer to data items declared in the calling method. The developers of Java wanted to create a simple programming language, and, hence, there is only one way to pass parameters to a called method.

In the method declaration, the parameters that the method takes are declared inside parentheses after the method name. Parameter declarations are separated by commas. Parameters are declared in the same way as variables, except that there are no semicolons (;) to terminate the declarations of parameter data.

```
//  Sums.java

import java.util.* ;

class Sums
{
   static void print_sum( int first_integer_from_caller,
                          int second_integer_from_caller )
   {
      int calculated_sum ;

      calculated_sum  =  first_integer_from_caller  +
                         second_integer_from_caller ;

      System.out.print( "\n The sum of " +  first_integer_from_caller
                      + " and "   +  second_integer_from_caller
                      + " is "    +  calculated_sum  + ".\n" ) ;
   }

   public static void main( String[] not_in_use )
   {
      Scanner keyboard = new Scanner( System.in ) ;

      print_sum( 555, 222 ) ;

      System.out.print( "\n As you can see, this program can print"
                    +   "\n the sum of two integers. Please, type in"
                   +   "\n two integers separated with a space:\n\n  " ) ;

      int first_integer    =  keyboard.nextInt() ;

      int second_integer   =  keyboard.nextInt() ;

      print_sum( first_integer, second_integer ) ;
   }
}
```

When method **print_sum()** is called here, value 555 is copied to variable **first_integer_from_caller**, and value 222 is copied to **second_-integer_from_caller** before the statements inside **print_sum()** are executed. This method call thus prints the sum of 555 and 222.

In this method call, before the internal statements of method **print_sum()** are executed, the contents of variable **first_integer** are copied to variable **first_integer_from_caller**, and the contents of variable **second_integer** are copied to **second_-integer_from_caller**. The data stored in variables inside the method **main()** is thus copied to parameter variables declared inside method **print_-sum()**.

**Sums.java - 1.+ Method main() calls a method that takes two parameters of type int.**

**calculated_sum** is an internal variable inside method **print_sum()**. This local variable is visible only to the statements of this method. This variable cannot be modified by the statements inside method **main()**.

These parameter variables are also local variables of method **print_sum()**. Method **main()** does not "see" these variables, but in method calls the caller must provide values for these variables.

```
static void print_sum( int first_integer_from_caller,
                       int second_integer_from_caller )
{
   int calculated_sum ;

   calculated_sum  =  first_integer_from_caller +
                      second_integer_from_caller ;

   System.out.print( "\n The sum of " +  first_integer_from_caller
                   + " and "  +  second_integer_from_caller
                   + " is "   +  calculated_sum  + ".\n" ) ;
}
```

Method **print_sum()** does not do anything else, but, after calculating the sum of the two given integers, it prints the values of all variables to the screen. Except by providing the necessary parameter values, method **main()** cannot affect the internal behavior of method **print_sum()**.

Parameter variables can be used just like any other variables declared inside a method. Method **print_sum()** "sees" only these three variables. The variables declared inside method **main()** cannot be modified by method **print_sum()**.

**Sums.java - 1 - 1. The method print_sum().**

```
D:\javafiles2>java Sums

 The sum of 555 and 222 is 777.

 As you can see, this program can print
 the sum of two integers. Please, type in
 two integers separated with a space:

  3344 11122

 The sum of 3344 and 11122 is 14466.
```

**Sums.java - X. Two sums of integers calculated and printed with method print_sum().**

This method prints the character given as the first parameter as many times as the second parameter specifies.

```
//  Decorations.java  (c) Kari Laitinen

class Decorations
{
   static void multiprint_character( char character_from_caller,
                                     int  number_of_times_to_repeat )
   {
      int  repetition_counter  =  0 ;

      while ( repetition_counter  <  number_of_times_to_repeat )
      {
         System.out.print( character_from_caller ) ;
         repetition_counter ++ ;
      }
   }

   static void print_text_in_decorated_box( String text_from_caller )
   {
      int text_length   =  text_from_caller.length() ;

      System.out.print( "\n " ) ;
      multiprint_character( '=',  text_length  +  8  ) ;
      System.out.print( "\n " ) ;
      multiprint_character( '*',  text_length  +  8  ) ;
      System.out.print( "\n **" ) ;
      multiprint_character( ' ',  text_length  +  4  ) ;

      System.out.print( "**\n **   " + text_from_caller + "   **\n **" ) ;

      multiprint_character( ' ',  text_length  +  4  ) ;
      System.out.print( "**\n " ) ;
      multiprint_character( '*',  text_length  +  8  ) ;
      System.out.print( "\n " ) ;
      multiprint_character( '=',  text_length  +  8  ) ;
      System.out.print( "\n " ) ;
   }

   public static void main( String[] not_in_use )
   {
      String  first_text  =  "Hello, world." ;

      print_text_in_decorated_box( first_text ) ;

      print_text_in_decorated_box(

                  "I am a computer program written in Java." ) ;
   }
}
```

The parameter for method **print_text_in_-decorated_box()** can be either a reference to a **String** object containing the text to be printed or a string literal.

**Decorations.java - 1.+ Method main() calls a method that takes a string as a parameter.**

This method "decorates" the text with a box that consist of characters = and *. Because texts can be of varied length, the width of the decoration box must be adjusted to correspond to the text length. For this reason, the string method **length()** is used here to find out how many characters there are in the **String** object referenced by **text_from_caller**. After this statement has been executed, **text_length** contains the character count of the text.

Here, reference to a **String** object is passed as a parameter. In this kind of a method call, the object is not copied for the called method, but only a reference to the object is passed to the callee. In practice this means that the physical memory address of the object is passed to the callee. Methods that have objects as parameters use the objects that have been created by the calling method.

```
   static void print_text_in_decorated_box( String text_from_caller )
   {
      int text_length  =  text_from_caller.length() ;

      System.out.print( "\n " ) ;
      multiprint_character( '=',  text_length  +  8  ) ;
      System.out.print( "\n" ) ;
      multiprint_character( '*',  text_length  +  8  ) ;
      System.out.print( "\n **" ) ;
      multiprint_character( ' ',  text_length  +  4  ) ;
```

The caller of a method can give an arithmetic expression as a parameter. In this call to **multiprint_character()**, the space character is printed as many times as is the value of **text_length** plus 4. The value of the arithmetic expression is calculated first, and that value is then passed as a parameter.

**Decorations.java - 1 - 1. Part of the method that prints text inside a decorative border.**

```
D:\javafiles2>java Decorations

 =====================
 *********************
 **                 **
 **  Hello, world.  **
 **                 **
 *********************
 =====================

 ================================================
 ************************************************
 **                                            **
 **  I am a computer program written in Java.  **
 **                                            **
 ************************************************
 ================================================
```

**Decorations.java - X. Texts printed inside decorative frames.**

A method which takes no parameters behaves always in the same way, regardless of when and where it is called. But the behavior of a method that does take parameters depends on what kinds of parameters are given. A method declared with parameters must be given a correct number of parameters of the correct type. A method that takes parameters is a kind of incomplete program until it is given the necessary parameter data.

The terminology of programming languages makes a distinction between those method parameters that are declared in a method declarator and those parameters that are given in a method call. The term *formal parameters* means the parameters in a method declarator. The term *actual parameters* refers to the parameters given in a method call. For example, the method declarator

```
static void
multiprint_character( char character_from_caller,
                      int  number_of_times_to_repeat )
```

specifies formal parameters **character_from_caller** and **number_of_times_to_repeat**. These parameters are formal because, although they are declared, they have no values until method **multiprint_character()** is called in some other method. The formal parameters of a method specify how the method can be called. You can imagine that the above method declarator says: "Hi! I am method **multiprint_character()**. You can call me by giving first an actual parameter of type **char**, and then an actual parameter of type **int**. Before my internal statements will be executed, the first actual parameter is stored in variable **character_from_caller**, and the second actual parameter is stored in variable **number_of_times_to_repeat**."

The actual parameters are given in method calls. For example, in the method call

```
multiprint_character( '=',  text_length  +  8  ) ;
```

'=' and **text_length** + 8 are actual parameters which are evaluated, and the values are copied to the formal parameters. Actual parameters may be variables, arithmetic or other expressions, literal constants, or even calls to other methods. In the above method call, '=' is a character literal meaning the character code of the equal sign, and **text_length** + 8 is an arithmetic expression. Any expression used as an actual parameter is evaluated to find a value to be copied to the corresponding formal parameter. Evaluation means that the current value of the expression is calculated. In the above method call, the value of **text_length** + 8 is calculated, and that value is copied to the formal parameter **number_of_times_to_repeat**.

Those things which are called parameters in this book are called arguments in some other books, especially in the context of other programming languages. The word "argument" is also used in the context of Java, for example, in the electronic Java documentation. To my knowledge, however, "parameter" is the more official word in the Java world. Therefore, I try to avoid saying argument when meaning parameter. However, if somebody speaks/writes about arguments, formal arguments, or actual arguments, it is very likely that what is meant are parameters, formal parameters, and actual parameters, respectively. To make things even more complex, I must warn you that some people use the word "argument" to refer to actual parameters and the word "parameter" to refer to formal parameters.

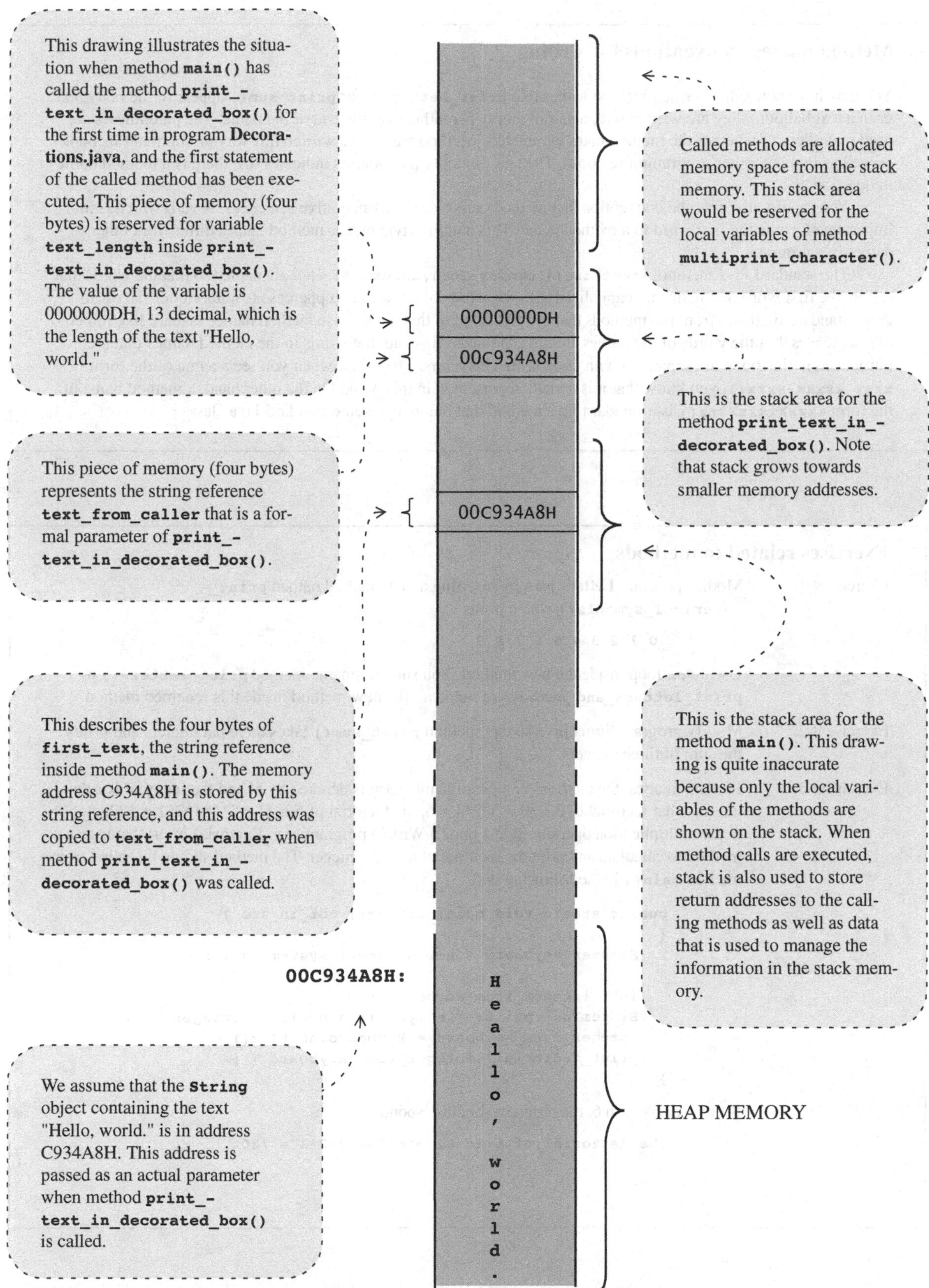

This drawing illustrates the situation when method main() has called the method print_text_in_decorated_box() for the first time in program Decorations.java, and the first statement of the called method has been executed. This piece of memory (four bytes) is reserved for variable text_length inside print_text_in_decorated_box(). The value of the variable is 0000000DH, 13 decimal, which is the length of the text "Hello, world."
This piece of memory (four bytes) represents the string reference text_from_caller that is a formal parameter of print_text_in_decorated_box().
This describes the four bytes of first_text, the string reference inside method main(). The memory address C934A8H is stored by this string reference, and this address was copied to text_from_caller when method print_text_in_decorated_box() was called.
We assume that the String object containing the text "Hello, world." is in address C934A8H. This address is passed as an actual parameter when method print_text_in_decorated_box() is called.
0000000DH
00C934A8H
00C934A8H
00C934A8H:
Hello, world.
Called methods are allocated memory space from the stack memory. This stack area would be reserved for the local variables of method multiprint_character().
This is the stack area for the method print_text_in_decorated_box(). Note that stack grows towards smaller memory addresses.
This is the stack area for the method main(). This drawing is quite inaccurate because only the local variables of the methods are shown on the stack. When method calls are executed, stack is also used to store return addresses to the calling methods as well as data that is used to manage the information in the stack memory.
HEAP MEMORY


*Figure 9-1. The main memory when program Decorations.java is executing.*

## Method names: conventions for writing

You may have noticed that when method names like **print_letters()** or **print_sum()** appear in the body text or in a text balloon, they are written with a pair of empty parentheses at the end of the name. The parentheses are used regardless of whether the method takes parameters. Method names are written this way throughout this book as well as in many other programming books. The pair of empty parentheses indicates that there is a method name in question.

You should also note the convention that method names are like imperative sentences. A verb which is in imperative form is the first word in a method name. This naming style makes method names differ from other names in a program.

The standard Java methods (**nextLine()**, **compareTo()**, **indexOf()**, etc.) are named so that the words that follow the first word of a name are capitalized, i.e., the words begin with an uppercase (capital) letter. To distinguish standard methods from the methods that are presented in this book, I use method names that are like imperative sentences, but the words of the names are not capitalized. Instead, the words in the method names that are introduced in this book are separated with underscore characters. Therefore, when you see a name of the form **xxxx_xxxxx_xxxx()**, you know that it is a method presented in this book. On the other hand, a method name of the form **xxxxXxxxxXxxx()** is a standard Java method that belongs to some standard Java class.

## Exercises related to methods

Exercise 9-1. Modify program **Letters.java** by inserting a new method named **print_numerical_symbols()** which prints

```
0 1 2 3 4 5 6 7 8 9
```

Use a **for** loop inside the new method. You should rename method **print_letters()** to **print_letters_and_numbers()**, and call the new method inside this renamed method.

Exercise 9-2. Modify program **Sums.java** so that method **print_sum()** takes three parameters and prints the sum of three integers.

Exercise 9-3. In mathematics, the factorial of a positive integer n is denoted by n! and the factorial is calculated so that factorial of 3 is 3! = 3*2*1 = 6, the factorial of 5 is 5! = 5*4*3*2*1 = 120, etc. (* is the multiplication operator in this book.) Write a program (e.g. **Factorial.java**) that uses a method to calculate and print the factorial of a given integer. The method should be called from method **main()** in the following way

```
public static void main( String[] not_in_use )
{
   Scanner keyboard = new Scanner( System.in ) ;

   int  integer_from_keyboard ;
   System.out.print( "\n Type in a positive integer: " ) ;
   integer_from_keyboard = keyboard.nextInt();
   print_factorial( integer_from_keyboard ) ;
}
```

If the user types in 6, the program should respond:

```
The factorial of 6 is 6! = 6*5*4*3*2*1 = 720
```

## More exercises related to methods

Exercise 9-4. Write a program (e.g. **Box.java**) which asks for two integers from the keyboard, and, after reading the integers, the program prints a "box" to the screen. The box can be made by printing letters X, and the integers given by the user must be used to specify the width and the height of the box. For example, if the user types in integers 8 and 3, the program must print the following box

```
XXXXXXXX
XXXXXXXX
XXXXXXXX
```

which is 8 character positions wide and 3 rows high. You must copy the method **multiprint_character()** from program **Decorations.java** and use that method in your program. It is important that you learn to reuse existing methods. You need to call **multiprint_character()** inside a loop.

Exercise 9-5. Complete the program

```
// Widecall.java

class Widecall
{
   static void print_wide_string( String given_string )
   {
      // You must add program lines here!


   }

   public static void main( String[] not_in_use )
   {
      String  example_string  =  "Hello, world." ;

      print_wide_string( example_string ) ;
   }
}
```

so that it prints

```
H e l l o ,   w o r l d .
```

Method **print_wide_string()** should be written so that it puts an extra space before or after every character of the given string. Studying program **Widename.java** of Chapter 8 may help in this exercise.

## 9.3 Methods that return data to the caller

So far, we have studied methods which either take no parameters or take parameters which transfer information from the calling method to the called method. For example, method **print_sum()** of **Sums.java** prints the sum of the two integers given by the caller, but it does not give any information to the caller. Method **multiprint_character()** of **Decorations.java** prints the character given by the caller as many times as the caller wants it to be printed, but **multiprint_character()** does not give any data to the caller. In the case of methods **print_sum()** and **multiprint_character()**, the information flow is from caller to callee. These methods input information from the caller. They output information onto the screen, but they don't give anything to their callers.

In this section, we shall study methods that both input and output information from/to their callers. These methods use parameters in the same way as the methods we have already studied. In addition, these methods output data to their callers with a special **return** statement.

Program **LargestWithReturn.java** is an example that shows how the **return** statement can be used. The program contains the following method declarator

```
static int
search_largest_integer( int[] array_of_integers,
                        int   number_of_integers_in_array )
```

where the type of the method is not **void** but **int**. A method of type **int** returns an **int** value to its caller. When the method call

```
found_largest_integer  =
             search_largest_integer( first_array, 5 ) ;
```

is executed in program **LargestWithReturn.java**, the following things happen

- **first_array** is passed to the callee so that **array_of_integers** inside method **search_largest_integer()** refers to **first_array**,
- the integer literal 5 is copied to **number_of_integers_in_array**, and
- after the internal statements of **search_largest_integer()** have been executed, the **int** value returned by the method is assigned to variable **found_largest_integer**.

Statements which return data to the caller are written using the reserved keyword **return**. When a method outputs something with a **return** statement, the method is no longer of type **void** but it is of the same type as the output value. If a method contains a **return** statement like

```
return  some_integer ;
```

and the type of **some_integer** is **int**, the method must also be of type **int** and its declarator must contain the keyword **int** in the following way

```
static int method_name( ...
```

Methods of type **void** are typeless methods because they do not represent any particular type in a call statement. A **void** method can only be called in the following way

**method_name(** *actual parameters* **) ;**

Methods that are not of type **void** are typed methods. A method that is not of type **void** can be called when the returned value is needed. For example, if the returned value is to be stored in a variable, a typed method can be called

**some_variable = method_name(** *actual parameters* **) ;**

If the value returned by a typed method is to be printed but not stored anywhere, the method can be called

```
System.out.print( "" + method_name( actual parameters ) ) ;
```

The returned value from a typed method can be used in a boolean expression like

```
if ( method_name( actual parameters ) > 99 )
```

It is not forbidden to call a typed method the same way typeless methods are called. Method **search_largest_integer()** of program **LargestWithReturn.java** can be called

```
search_largest_integer( first_array, 5 ) ;
```

but that does not make much sense because the calling program does not receive the value for which it is calling the method. However, it is sometimes useful that a method can be called in two ways. A method may return a value that is not always needed in the calling program. Therefore, it is convenient for the caller if it can decide not to use the returned value.

Typed methods must contain a **return** statement. The **return** statement is the final statement in the program **LargestWithReturn.java**, and it is a good programming practice to have the **return** statement always at the end of a method, but the **return** statement does not need to be the last one. When a **return** statement is not the final one, it means that the execution of the method stops there, and the program control returns to the calling program. A **return** statement like

```
return ;
```

can be used in the middle of a typeless **void** method to stop the program execution there, but usually it is not necessary to use these kinds of **return** statements.

The most common use of a **return** statement is at the end of a typed non-**void** method. We have already seen that a **return** statement can return the value of a variable. It is also common to see **return** statements like

```
return  true ;
return  1 ;
```

which return boolean and numerical literal constants. When a **return** statement contains an arithmetic expression, the value of the expression is calculated and returned to the caller. For example, the statement

```
return  ( sum_of_integers / number_of_integers ) ;
```

would first divide the value of **sum_of_integers** with value of **number_of_integers**, and then return the division result to the caller. The values of the variables would not be modified in the processing of the above statement.

The type of this static method is **int**. This means that the method returns a value of type **int**. At the end of this method there is thus a **return** statement that returns the value of variable **largest_integer** to the calling method.

At the beginning the method assumes that the first integer in the array is the largest. While the integers of the array are processed, variable **largest_integer** is rewritten with the new largest integer if necessary.

```
//  LargestWithReturn.java

class LargestWithReturn
{
   static int search_largest_integer( int[] array_of_integers,
                                      int   number_of_integers_in_array )
   {
      int  largest_integer     =  array_of_integers[ 0 ] ;
      int  integer_index  =  1 ;

      while (  integer_index  <  number_of_integers_in_array  )
      {
         if ( array_of_integers[ integer_index ] > largest_integer )
         {
            largest_integer   =  array_of_integers[ integer_index ] ;
         }

         integer_index    ++   ;
      }

      return  largest_integer ;
   }

   public static void main( String[] not_in_use )
   {
      int[]  first_array   =  { 44, 2, 66, 33, 9 } ;
      int[]  second_array  =  { 888, 777, 66, 999, 998, 997 } ;

      int  found_largest_integer   ;

      found_largest_integer =  search_largest_integer( first_array, 5 ) ;

      System.out.print( "\n The largest integer in first_array is "
                      +  found_largest_integer   +   ".\n" ) ;

      System.out.print( "\n The largest integer in second_array is "
           +  search_largest_integer( second_array, 6 )  +   ".\n" ) ;
   }
}
```

Method **search_largest_integer()** is called here before the call to method **System.out.print()** is executed. The value returned by **search_largest_integer()** is printed between the text strings.

Here, **search_largest_integer()** is called on the right side of an assignment statement. When this statement is executed, method **search_largest_integer()** is called first by using the actual parameters in parentheses, and then the value returned by the method is copied to variable **found_largest_integer**.

**LargestWithReturn.java - 1. A method that returns data to its caller with a return statement.**

```
D:\javafiles2>java LargestWithReturn

 The largest integer in first_array is 66.

 The largest integer in second_array is 999.
```

**LargestWithReturn.java - X. Two arrays are processed with method search_largest_integer.**

## Using arrays and other objects as method parameters

Unlike programming languages such as C++ and C#, Java does not have method parameters which would allow a method to pass data to its caller via the parameters. These kinds of parameters, which could be called output parameters, do not exist in Java. The principal means for a Java method to output data to its caller is the **return** statement. However, when an array or some other suitable object is used as a method parameter it is possible to make the parameter behave as an output parameter.

In program **LargestWithReturn.java**, a **return** statement is used to pass an **int** value from the called method to the caller. Another possibility to get information from the called method could be to use an array. To do this, the **LargestWithReturn.java** program could be rewritten in the following way:

```
class LargestWithArrayOutput
{
   static void search_largest_integer( int[] array_of_integers,
                                       int   number_of_integers_in_array,

                                       int[] largest_integer_to_caller )
   {
      //  The internal statements could be as in LargestWithReturn.java except that
      //  the return statement would be replaced with the statement

      largest_integer_to_caller[ 0 ]  =  largest_integer ;
   }

   public static void main( String[] not_in_use )
   {
      int[]  first_array    =  { 44, 2, 66, 33, 9 } ;

      int[]  found_largest_integer  =  new  int[ 1 ] ;

      search_largest_integer( first_array, 5, found_largest_integer ) ;

      System.out.print( "\n The largest integer in first_array is "
                      +  found_largest_integer[ 0 ]  +  ".\n" ) ;
      ...
```

Probably the above program is an example of a misuse of an array, but it nevertheless demonstrates important features of Java arrays. It shows that an array can be used as an "output parameter". The reason for this is that as only an array reference is passed in a method call, and the array itself is not copied, the called method can access the array that was originally created by the caller.

Like arrays, also other kinds of objects can be used to transfer data from a called method to a caller. Later on, when we learn more about objects, we'll see how program **LargestWithReturn.java** can be rewritten so that an object reference is used as a method parameter.

Now, once the typed methods have also been discussed, we can draw a picture of Java methods. Figure 9-2 presents the general structure of Java methods with some essential terms that we have used in this chapter. Some of the information included in Figure 9-2 will be discussed in later chapters.

By using methods, software developers can divide larger programs into smaller, more manageable, sections of programs. Some methods, and especially classes containing certain methods, can also be used in several larger programs. To conclude this section, we will study how a program can be divided into logical functional pieces. In Chapter 7 we had program **MeanvalueArray.java**, an improved version of program **Meanvalue.java**. **MeanvalueArray.java** reads numbers into an array and calculates the mean value of those numbers. On analyzing the activities performed in **MeanvalueArray.java**, the following activity list can be noted

- reading of the numbers from the keyboard
- calculation of the mean value of the numbers
- printing of the mean value onto the screen

In program **MeanvalueMethod.java**, the structure of the program is arranged according to the above list of activities. The first two activities are implemented as separate methods. The last activity is not a separate method because it can be implemented with a single statement. Inside method **`main()`** in **MeanvalueMethod.java**, the above activity list has been converted to the following program activities:

- call method **`ask_numbers_to_array()`**
- call method **`calculate_mean_value()`**
- output variable **`mean_value`**

Both programs **MeanvalueArray.java** and **MeanvalueMethod.java** do the same things. Program **MeanvalueMethod.java** is implemented by using methods, which makes it longer than its predecessor **MeanvalueArray.java**. You may ask: does it really make sense to use methods if they make programs longer? The answer is: oh yes it does. Practical computer programs tend to be much longer than these example programs, and it is usually hard to understand them if they are not divided into smaller methods. Another benefit of using methods is that the same methods can be reused in several applications. For example, if you are asked to write a program that reads numbers from the keyboard and does something to those numbers, you may reuse the method **`ask_numbers_to_array()`** from program **MeanvalueMethod.java** to implement the keyboard-reading part of your programs. Likewise, you can reuse method **`calculate_mean_value()`** when you need to calculate mean values in your programs.

When you want to write a program for yourself, or you have been asked to write a program, it is often difficult in the beginning. Your program should do something but you do not know how to begin to write it. One way to begin program construction is to write down in natural language what the program should do. For example, you can write lists of activities like we did above. The activity lists help you when you then write the actual program. An activity can often be performed with a single Java method. The names of activities can often be converted to method names.

Keyword **public** specifies that a method is visible to methods in all other classes. Instead of the keyword **public**, we can use keywords **protected** and **private** to specify the visibility of a method. If none of the mentioned keywords is used in a method declaration, the method is visible to the methods in classes belonging to the same package of classes.

With keyword **static** we can specify that a method is a static method. If this keyword is missing, the method is a so-called instance method. **Type** can be **void**, **char**, **short**, **int**, **long**, **boolean**, **float**, **double**, or some other type.

This part of a method is the method declarator or method header. The term "method signature" is sometimes used to mean the method declarator without the return type of the method.

```
class ClassName
{
   ...

   public static Type method_name( list of formal
                                        parameters )
   {

      The internal statements of the method:
        -- declarations of local variables and other data items
        -- the action statements of the method

   }

   ...
}
```

Method body

Later on you'll learn that, in addition to keywords like **public** and **static**, there are other keywords that can be written in the method declarator. For example, keyword **abstract** declares abstract methods, and keyword **final** specifies that an instance method may not be overridden in a derived class.

***Figure 9-2. The structure of Java methods.***

The parameter for **ask_numbers_to_array()** is a reference to an array of type **double[]**. When this method is called, a reference to an array is copied, and **array_of_numbers** actually references the array created by the calling method. The array actually functions as an "output parameter" since the calling method gets the numbers that are stored in the array.

```
//  MeanvalueMethod.java

import java.util.* ;

class MeanvalueMethod
{
   static int ask_numbers_to_array( double[] array_of_numbers )
   {
      Scanner keyboard = new Scanner( System.in ) ;

      int  number_of_given_numbers  =  0  ;

      System.out.print( "   Enter a number: " ) ;

      boolean  keyboard_input_is_numerical  =  true ;

      while ( keyboard_input_is_numerical ==  true  &&
              number_of_given_numbers  <  array_of_numbers.length  )
      {
         try
         {
            double  number_from_keyboard  =  keyboard.nextDouble() ;
            array_of_numbers[ number_of_given_numbers ]
                                          =  number_from_keyboard ;
            number_of_given_numbers ++ ;
            System.out.print(  "   Enter a number: " ) ;
         }
         catch ( Exception  not_numerical_input_exception )
         {
            keyboard_input_is_numerical  =  false ;
         }
      }

      return  number_of_given_numbers ;
   }
```

As the type of this method is **int**, it must return an **int** value to its caller.

**MeanvalueMethod.java - 1: The first part of the program.**

```
D:\javafiles2>java MeanvalueMethod

 This program calculates the mean value of
 the numbers you enter from the keyboard.
 The program stops when you enter a letter.

   Enter a number: 999.999
   Enter a number: 998.998
   Enter a number: 997.997
   Enter a number: z

 The mean value is: 998.998
```

**MeanvalueMethod.java - X. The mean of three numbers is calculated here.**

Without this test, there would be a risk of dividing by zero, and that must always be avoided in programs.

This method takes its input data in its parameters, and it outputs a **double** value with a **return** statement. The type of the method is thus **double**. Here, the array works as an "input parameter" because its contents are not modified by this method.

```
   static double calculate_mean_value( double[] array_of_numbers,
                                       int      number_of_numbers_in_array )
   {
      double  calculated_mean_value  =  0 ;
      double  sum_of_numbers         =  0 ;

      for ( int number_index  =  0 ;
                number_index  <  number_of_numbers_in_array ;
                number_index  ++ )
      {
         sum_of_numbers  =  sum_of_numbers  +
                              array_of_numbers[ number_index ] ;
      }

      if ( number_of_numbers_in_array  >  0 )
      {
         calculated_mean_value  = (double) sum_of_numbers /
                                  (double) number_of_numbers_in_array ;
      }

      return  calculated_mean_value  ;
   }

   public static void main( String[] not_in_use )
   {
      double[]  array_of_numbers  =  new  double[ 100 ] ;

      System.out.print( "\n This program calculates the mean value of"
                      + "\n the numbers you enter from the keyboard."
                      + "\n The program stops when you enter a letter.\n\n");

      int  number_of_numbers_read  =
                         ask_numbers_to_array( array_of_numbers ) ;

      double  mean_value  =  calculate_mean_value( array_of_numbers,
                                                   number_of_numbers_read ) ;

      System.out.print( "\n The mean value is: "  +  mean_value  + "\n" ) ;
   }
}
```

After this method call, the array referenced by **array_of_numbers** contains those numbers the user typed in, and **number_of_numbers_read** tells how many numbers were typed in.

**MeanvalueMethod.java - 2. The second and last part of the program.**

## 9.4 Calling static methods of another class

So far the methods we have studied have been such that the calling method, the caller, and the method being called, the callee, have been inside a single class. In this section, we shall study how a method can call another method over a class boundary.

A class is a program structure that can group things. Methods that are written inside a certain class form a group of methods that are "close neighbors" who can call each other by using a method name in the following way

```
method_name( some actual parameters ) ;
```

Then, if a method wants to call a "foreign" static method that is inside another class, the class name of the callee must be written before the method name in the following way

```
ClassName.method_name( some actual parameters ) ;
```

The dot operator (.) is used to link the method name to the class name in these kind of method calls. It is also important to remember that only static methods can be called this way.

A method that will be called by some other method in another class is usually declared with the keyword **public**. This means that such a method is written in the following way

```
class ClassName
{
   ...

   public static void method_name( formal parameters )
   {
      ...
   }
   ...
}
```

When a method is declared with the keyword **public**, permission is given for other methods in all other classes to call the method. (For a more precise discussion about the meaning of the **public** keyword, see page 398.)

**Sort.java** is an example program in which methods have been grouped inside three classes. The program can sort numbers so that the numbers in an array are put to ascending order. The classes of **Sort.java** are the following

- Class **TestingSorting** contains the method **main()** that calls the methods in the other classes.
- Class **InputOutput** contains two methods **ask_numbers_to_array()** and **print_array_of_numbers()** that input data from the keyboard and output data to the screen.
- Class **Sort** contains the sorting method **sort_to_ascending_order()** and the method **get_index_of_smallest_number_in_array()** that is needed by the sorting method. (The sorting algorithm implemented in this class is one possible sorting algorithm. Because sorting is a classical problem in information processing, you may find other, and possibly more efficient, sorting algorithms in the literature of computing.)

The classes and methods in program **Sort.java** are in such an order that the method **main()** is the first method in the source program file. Generally, the Java compiler does not put any restrictions on the order of classes and methods in a source program file. However, the programs of this book are organized so that the method **main()** is the last method in a source program file, and methods are introduced before they are called. **Sort.java** is an exception to this rule.

## Still more exercises related to methods.

Exercise 9-6. Write a program which has methods to reverse and print an array. If the **`main()`** method of your program is the following

```
public static void main( String[] not_in_use )
{
   int[] test_array  =  { 2, 33, 44, 55, 666 } ;

   reverse_array( test_array, 5 ) ;
   print_array(   test_array, 5 ) ;
   reverse_array( test_array, 3 ) ;
   print_array(   test_array, 5 ) ;
}
```

the program should print

```
666  55  44  33  2
44  55  666  33  2
```

A method in program **Overload.java** may be used as the basis for your **`print_array()`** method. Inside method **`reverse_array()`** you need to index the given array from both ends. You need also a variable where you store one array element when you swap the elements at the two ends of the array.

Exercise 9-7. Modify program **Sort.java** so that it sorts the given array into a descending order. Rename the sorting method to **`sort_to_descending_order()`**, and modify it so that it starts moving the largest numbers to the beginning of the array. You also need a method that finds the index of the largest number in an array. Organize the new program so that all methods are inside a single class.

Exercise 9-8. Write a program that has a method to calculate the sum of the elements of an array of type **`int[]`**. The method must use a **`return`** statement to return the sum to the calling program. If the **`main()`** method of your program is

```
public static void main( String[] not_in_use )
{
   int[] example_array = { 22, 33, 44, 55 } ;

   int sum_of_elements  =
               get_sum_of_elements( example_array, 3 ) ;

   System.out.print( "\n Sum of three elements: "
                  +  sum_of_elements ) ;
   System.out.print( "\n Sum of four elements:  "
                  +  get_sum_of_elements( example_array, 4 ) ) ;
}
```

the program should print

```
Sum of three elements: 99
Sum of four elements:  154
```

```
D:\javafiles2>java TestingSorting

 This program sorts the numbers that you enter
 from the keyboard. The program stops asking for new
 numbers when you enter a letter.

   Enter a number: 12.34
   Enter a number: 12.339
   Enter a number: 11.999
   Enter a number: 10
   Enter a number: 9.999
   Enter a number: 11.999
   Enter a number: 9.998
   Enter a number: -9.999
   Enter a number: Z

   -9.999     9.998     9.999    10.000    11.999
   11.999    12.339    12.340
```

When you compile the **Sort.java** program, you'll find out that the compiler produces several **.class** files. The numerical bytecodes of each class in the program will be put in an individual **.class** file whose name is of the form **ClassName.class**.

**Sort.java - X. 8 numbers are put to ascending order here.**

This method call sorts the numbers in the array referenced by **array_of_numbers**. Here, sorting means that the order of numbers changes so that the smallest number becomes the first array element, the second smallest number becomes the second array element, and so on. After this method has done its job, the largest number is in the array position that has index value **number_of_numbers_read** - 1.

```
//  Sort.java

import java.util.* ;

class TestingSorting
{
   public static void main( String[] not_in_use )
   {
      double[]  array_of_numbers  =  new double[ 100 ] ;

      System.out.print(
           "\n This program sorts the numbers that you enter"
         + "\n from the keyboard. The program stops asking for new"
         + "\n numbers when you enter a letter. \n\n" ) ;

      int  number_of_numbers_read  =
                InputOutput.ask_numbers_to_array( array_of_numbers ) ;

      Sort.sort_to_ascending_order( array_of_numbers,
                                    number_of_numbers_read ) ;

      InputOutput.print_array_of_numbers( array_of_numbers,
                                          number_of_numbers_read ) ;
   }
}
```

**Sort.java - 1: A program whose methods are in three classes.**

```
class InputOutput
{
   public static int
   ask_numbers_to_array( double[] array_of_numbers )
   {
      Scanner keyboard = new Scanner( System.in ) ;

      int  number_of_given_numbers  =  0  ;

      System.out.print( "    Enter a number: " ) ;

      boolean  keyboard_input_is_numerical  =  true ;

      while ( keyboard_input_is_numerical ==  true  &&
              number_of_given_numbers  <  array_of_numbers.length  )
      {
         try
         {
            double  number_from_keyboard  =  keyboard.nextDouble() ;
            array_of_numbers[ number_of_given_numbers ]  =
                                        number_from_keyboard ;
            number_of_given_numbers  ++ ;
            System.out.print(  "    Enter a number:  " ) ;
         }
         catch ( Exception  not_numerical_input_exception )
         {
            keyboard_input_is_numerical  =  false ;
         }
      }

      return  number_of_given_numbers  ;
   }

   public static void
   print_array_of_numbers( double[]  array_of_numbers,
                           int       number_of_numbers_in_array )
   {
      for ( int number_index  =  0  ;
                number_index  <  number_of_numbers_in_array ;
                number_index  ++ )
      {
         if ( ( number_index  %  5 )  ==  0  )
         {
            System.out.print( "\n" ) ;
         }

         System.out.printf( "%10.3f", array_of_numbers[ number_index ] ) ;
      }
   }
}
```

This method is almost the same as in the program **MeanvalueMethod.java**. The difference is that this method is declared with keyword **`public`**.

The format specifier **`"%10.3f"`** stipulates that numbers must be printed with three decimals to the right-hand side of a printing field which is 10 character positions wide. Unused character positions are filled with spaces. This way the numbers appear in specific columns on the screen.

This **`if`** construct ensures that a newline is printed after the printing of every 5th element of the array. % is the remainder operator with which it is easy to check whether **`number_index`** is equally divisible by 5.

**Sort.java - 2: The methods of class InputOutput.**

Method **get_index_of_smallest_number_in_array()** processes a subarray within the array that is supplied as the first parameter. **number_index** specifies the beginning of the subarray. **number_of_unsorted_numbers** specifies the length of the subarray. When **number_index** is zero at the beginning, the subarray is the same as the array referenced by **array_of_numbers**. As **number_index** grows, a smaller and smaller part of the array is processed, until only two elements from the end of the array are taken to the subarray. This method is called **number_of_numbers_in_array - 1** times.

```
class Sort
{
   public static void
   sort_to_ascending_order( double[]  array_of_numbers,
                            int       number_of_numbers_in_array )
   {
      for ( int number_index  =  0 ;
                number_index  <  number_of_numbers_in_array - 1 ;
                number_index  ++ )
      {
         int  number_of_unsorted_numbers  =
                       number_of_numbers_in_array - number_index ;

         int index_of_smallest_number  =
                    get_index_of_smallest_number_in_array(
                                          array_of_numbers,
                                          number_index,
                                          number_of_unsorted_numbers ) ;

         double  smallest_number  =  array_of_numbers[
                                           index_of_smallest_number ] ;

         //  Now we simply put the number in current array
         //  position to where the smallest number is, and
         //  then put the smallest number in current position.

         array_of_numbers[ index_of_smallest_number ]  =
                                  array_of_numbers[ number_index ] ;

         array_of_numbers[ number_index ]  =  smallest_number ;
      }
   }
```

These two statements swap the contents of two positions in (the array referenced by) **array_of_numbers**. This way, small numbers are moved towards the beginning of the array.

**Sort.java - 3: The sorting method in the class named Sort.**

In the beginning, it is assumed that the first number that must be processed is the smallest number. Later on, inside the loop, following numbers of the array are checked, and whenever a smaller number is found, it is set as the new smallest number.

```
static int
get_index_of_smallest_number_in_array( double[] array_of_numbers,
                                       int  index_of_first_number_to_process,
                                       int  number_of_numbers_to_process )
{
   double  smallest_number   =
                array_of_numbers[ index_of_first_number_to_process ] ;

   int  index_of_smallest_number  =  index_of_first_number_to_process ;

   for ( int number_index   =   index_of_first_number_to_process   +   1  ;
             number_index   <   index_of_first_number_to_process   +
                                          number_of_numbers_to_process ;
             number_index  ++ )
   {
      if ( array_of_numbers[ number_index ]  <  smallest_number )
      {
         smallest_number   =   array_of_numbers[ number_index ] ;
         index_of_smallest_number  =  number_index ;
      }
   }

   return  index_of_smallest_number ;
}
}
```

**Sort.java - 4. The other method of class Sort. The end of the program.**

## Strong typing vs. weak typing

Java is said to be a strongly-typed programming language. This means that the Java compiler checks that parameters of the correct type are passed in method calls. The language does not allow you to call methods in either the wrong way, with a wrong number of parameters or with parameters that do not match the types specified in a method declarator.

Strong typing also means that the compiler issues error messages in the case of assignment statements where the types on both sides of operator = are not the same. Java is not an extremely strongly-typed language. For example, some assignments between the built-in types **char**, **short**, **int**, and **long** are possible. To some extent, it is possible to circumvent strong typing through the use of explicit type conversion. Explicit type conversion means, for example, that a variable of type **int** can be temporarily converted to type **char** by writing **(char)** before the variable name in the following way

```
char some_character  =  (char) some_int_variable ;
```

Strong typing is a term invented to describe programming languages such as Java which have strong type rules. The opposite of strong typing is weak typing. Compilers of programming languages that are weakly typed do not perform type checking in assignment statements or method calls. An example of a weakly-typed programming language is the original C programming language.

## 9.5 The role of the stack in method calls

When a method is called, the following activities take place during program execution:

- If the called method, the callee, is a method that takes parameters, the actual parameters are copied to the formal parameters.
- The internal statements of the callee are executed.
- Program execution continues in the calling method. Possible return values are processed, and the statements following the method call are executed.

The above activities have been discussed in previous sections of this chapter. If you feel that you understand the mechanism of method calls, you might skip this section, but if you want to gain a more profound understanding about method calls, you should read this section. To understand the discussion below, you probably need to know how subroutine calls are executed by a computer processor. Subroutine calls are explained, for example, in the last three sections of Chapter 4.

A memory area called the stack plays a special role in method calls. The stack memory is a memory area in every computer's main memory. The stack area is used for special purposes such as handling the method calls and the returns to the calling program. In information processing, a stack is a data structure where you can store data items of a certain type. When you put a data item onto a stack, it always goes onto the top of the stack. When a data item is removed from the stack, it is the topmost data item that is removed. We can make stack constructs of objects from the real world. For example, if you build a pile of books on the floor so that you always put a new book on the previous one, the books are in stack formation. You can easily take away only that book which is the topmost book in the book stack. A pack of playing cards also forms a stack: it is easy to take away the topmost card, and put new cards to the top of the card stack.

Computer processors use part of the main memory as stack memory. A processor usually has a special hardware register called the stack pointer that is used to point to the stack area of memory. The stack pointer usually contains the address of the first free memory location on the stack. Processors usually have many other hardware registers. An essential register in program execution is the program pointer (or program counter) which contains the address of the next machine instruction to be executed. The machine instructions are numerical codes. The processor of a computer "understands" the numerical machine instructions, and performs actions according to them. Figure 9-3 illustrates the different memory areas and shows how the registers of the processor point to these areas. Also the memory area called the heap memory is marked in Figure 9-3, but this area is not controlled by the hardware registers.

The execution of Java programs is somewhat complicated when compared to the execution of traditional computer programs. The compiler of a traditional programming language (e.g. the C++ programming language) produces an executable program which consists of the executable numerical instructions which are "understandable" to the processor of a computer. The Java compiler does not produce such executable programs. Instead, the Java compiler produces a program which consists of numerical bytecodes. These bytecodes are then interpreted by the Java virtual machine, which is the runtime environment for Java programs. As the Java virtual machine interprets the bytecode instructions, it is also called the Java interpreter. The Java virtual machine is a "real" executable program which consists of machine instructions, and it acts according to the bytecode program that it is supposed to execute.

Although the Java virtual machine is not a processor made of electronic components, it behaves in many ways like real processors do. It uses the stack memory in the same way as real processors, and it processes method calls largely in the same way as they are processed by real processors.

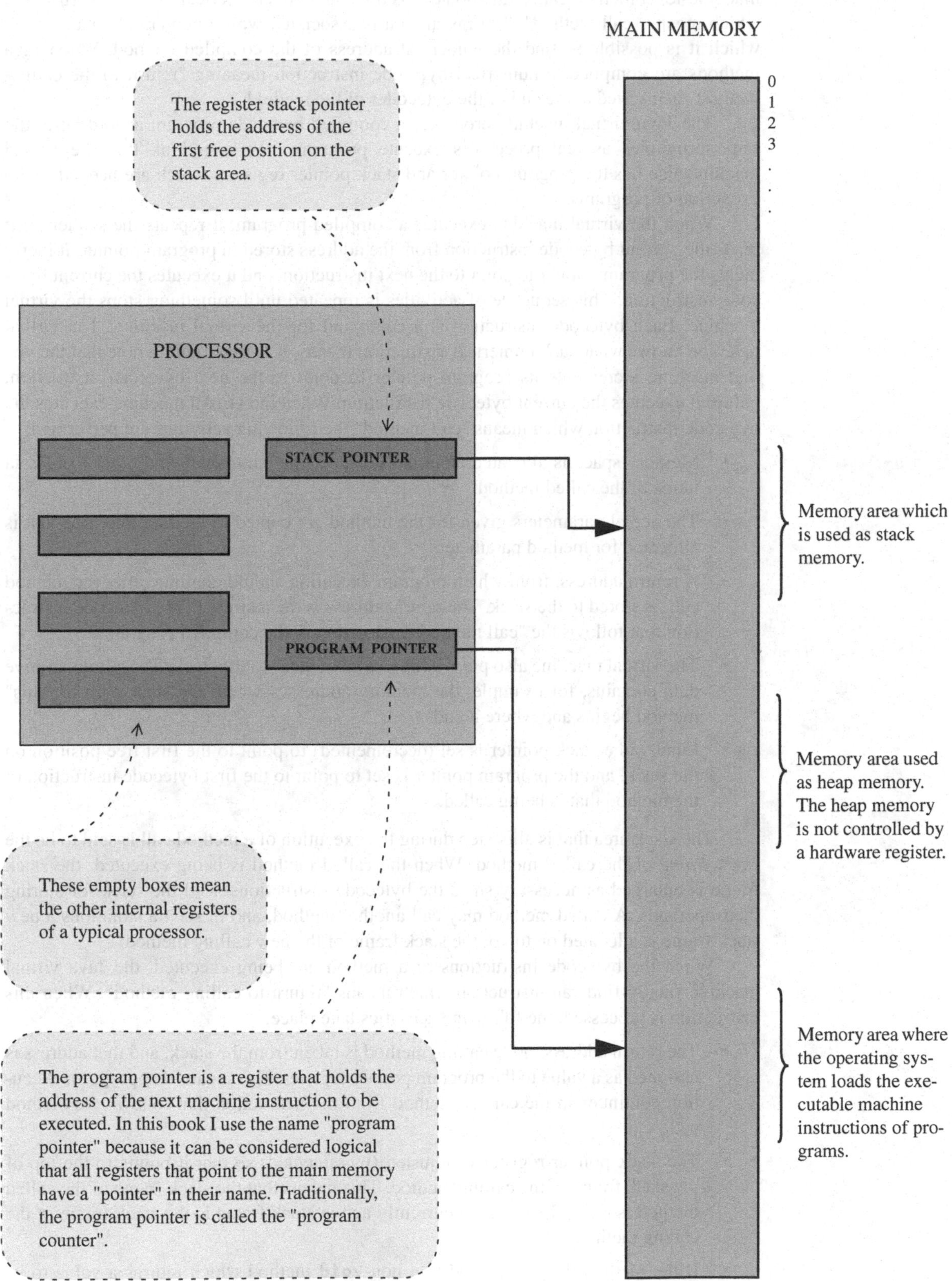
MAIN MEMORY
0
1
2
3
The register stack pointer holds the address of the first free position on the stack area.
PROCESSOR
STACK POINTER
PROGRAM POINTER
Memory area which is used as stack memory.
Memory area used as heap memory. The heap memory is not controlled by a hardware register.
These empty boxes mean the other internal registers of a typical processor.
Memory area where the operating system loads the executable machine instructions of programs.
The program pointer is a register that holds the address of the next machine instruction to be executed. In this book I use the name "program pointer" because it can be considered logical that all registers that point to the main memory have a "pointer" in their name. Traditionally, the program pointer is called the "program counter".

***Figure 9-3. Memory areas in the main memory.***

When there is a method call in a Java program, the Java compiler translates it to a machine-level method call. A method call is translated to a numerical bytecode instruction which means "call method". The instruction is associated with a numerical data through which it is possible to find the numerical address of the compiled method. When Java methods are compiled, a numerical bytecode instruction meaning "return to the calling method" is inserted at the end of the bytecodes of the method.

The Java virtual machine processes a compiled bytecode program according to the same principles as real processors execute programs. We can think that the virtual machine also has the program pointer and stack pointer registers which are needed in the execution of programs.

When the virtual machine executes a compiled program, it repeats the sequence: it reads the current bytecode instruction from the address stored in program pointer, it increments the program pointer to point to the next instruction, and it executes the current bytecode instruction. This sequence of activities is repeated until something stops the virtual machine. Each bytecode instruction is a command for the virtual machine. The virtual machine knows what each numerical instruction means. It is important to note that the virtual machine increments its program pointer to point to the next bytecode instruction, before it executes the current bytecode instruction. When the virtual machine executes the bytecode instruction which means "call method" the following activities are performed:

- Memory space is allocated from the stack for the parameters and other local data items of the called method.
- The actual parameters given for the method are copied to the memory area that is allocated for method parameters.
- A return address, from which program execution should continue after the method call, is stored to the stack. The return address is the address of the bytecode instruction that follows the "call method" instruction in the compiled program.
- The virtual machine also puts "administrative data" to the stack. The administrative data contains, for example, the memory addresses where the stack area of "this" method begins and where it ends.
- Finally, the stack pointer is set (decremented) to point to the first free position on the stack, and the program pointer is set to point to the first bytecode instruction of the method that is being called.

The stack area that is allocated during the execution of a method call is said to be the *stack frame* of the called method. When the called method is being executed, the stack frame is enlarged as necessary since the bytecode instructions need the stack for storing their operands. A called method may call another method, and in such a situations a new stack frame is allocated on top of the stack frame of the new calling method.

When the bytecode instructions of a method are being executed, the Java virtual machine finally finds an instruction which means "return to calling method". When this instruction is processed, the following activities take place:

- The return address in the calling method is taken from the stack, and that address is assigned as a value to the program pointer register. This means that program execution continues in the calling method from the instruction that follows the method call.
- The stack pointer register is adjusted (incremented) so that it points to the top of the stack frame of the calling method. This means that the stack frame of the called method is discarded, and the currently active stack frame is the stack frame of the calling method.
- If the method that was called in a non-**void** method which returns a value to its caller, the value is placed on top of caller's stack frame so that it can be picked by the bytecode instructions that follow the method call in the calling method.

Method calls can be made in chain. A method that is called can call another method, which in turn can call another method, which in turn can call some other method, and so on. A stack is a particularly useful data structure in the processing of method calls. Each called method is allocated a stack frame on top of the stack frame of its caller. When a return to the calling method occurs, the return address can be found from the current stack frame. When the return address is known, the current stack frame can be discarded, and the stack frame of the calling method is made the new current stack frame. This kind of switching from one stack frame to another stack frame allows methods to be called in chain.

At this point, I would like to warn you that this discussion about the use of stack is somewhat inaccurate and simplified. Here I have only explained the general principles according to which the stack is used by the Java virtual machine. Because there can be, and there are, several kinds of Java virtual machines provided by different companies, there can be differences in how they operate. All Java virtual machines, however, must be able to execute the Java bytecode instructions according to specifications, but they do not need to execute exactly in the same way. We have already learned that there are usually several possibilities to write a computer program that performs a certain task. Each Java virtual machine is a computer program that implements *The Java Virtual Machine Specification* (available at *http://java.sun.com*) but there can be differences in the virtual machines. It is possible, for example, that a virtual machine uses two stacks in the processing of the bytecode instructions. In this discussion we have assumed that everything that is put to the stack is put on a single stack.

To further examine the use of stack in method calls, let's go back to program **Decorations.java** that was presented earlier in this chapter. In **Decorations.java**, several methods are called in chain, and Figure 9-1 shows how a reference to a **`String`** object is passed in a method call. Figure 9-4 is an improved version of Figure 9-1, and it describes how memory space is allocated from the stack when **Decorations.java** is executed. By studying Figure 9-4, you will note that each called method has its own stack frame which contains

- the method parameters,
- other local data items,
- the return address to calling method, and
- administrative data.

These data fields are shown in reverse order in Figure 9-4 because the stack grows towards small memory addresses. If a stack is used as shown in Figure 9-4, the method parameters are for each method the first data items that are put to the stack.

In Figure 9-4 I have invented fictitious return addresses that have been stored to the stack. According to these addresses, the bytecode instructions of program **Decorations.java** are somewhere in memory locations after the address 2E70000H. For example, when method **`multiprint_character()`** is called for the first time from method **`print_text_in_decorated_box()`**, the return address inside the calling method is 2E70086H. This means that, if we suppose that the bytecode instruction that indicates a method call is three bytes long, the method call is in address 2E70083H. Thus the address of the bytecode instruction that follows the method call is in address 2E70086H. We can think that, in this case, the bytecode instructions are put to memory in the following way:

| ADDRESS | BYTE | COMMENT |
|---|---|---|
| 02E70083H | XX | operation code for "call method" |
| 02E70084H | ?? | first operand byte to locate the method |
| 02E70085H | ?? | second operand byte to locate the method |
| 02E70086H | YY | the next bytecode instruction |
| 02E70087H | ?? | operand or another instruction |

Still I would like to point out that the discussion here is somewhat theoretical, and the Java virtual machine may work in a slightly different way in practice. The purpose of the fictitious hexadecimal memory addresses shown in Figure 9-4 is to demonstrate the general principles of the mechanisms of method calls. Once you have understood how the method call mechanism works, it is no longer necessary to think about hexadecimal memory addresses. Another essential thing to learn here is that method parameters and other local data items declared inside a method exist only during that time when the method is being executed. The stack is used to allocate memory space for the local variables upon a method call. When the execution of a method terminates and the program control returns to the calling method, the stack frame reserved for the called method is released (deallocated).

The method **`main()`**, which we have in every program and which starts executing automatically, is not much different from other Java methods. Also, the method **`main()`** can have local data which is allocated memory space from the stack. The difference between the method **`main()`** and other methods is that we do not see anything calling method **`main()`**. But from the studies of this section, we can make the deduction that it must be that the Java virtual machine calls method **`main()`**, or at least, that it performs a very call-like operation to start method **`main()`**. The operating system, in turn, activates (or calls) the virtual machine after the user of the computer has given the necessary command.

The operating system of a computer is just another computer program, but it is a very special kind of program. When no application programs are being executed on a computer, we can think that the operating system executes a loop, waiting for someone to command it to execute a program. When someone commands the operating system to execute a Java program, the operating system activates the virtual machine which calls the method **`main()`** of the Java program, and gives the control to that method. Method **`main()`**, in turn, may call other methods, but ultimately the last statement of **`main()`** is executed and method **`main()`** terminates. The program control returns to the virtual machine and ultimately to the waiting loop of the operating system, once the called method **`main()`** has reached its end.

In this section we have explored the nature of Java method calls, but unfortunately we have not yet studied all the different kinds of Java methods in this book. In the following chapter you'll see how so-called instance methods can be written and used. In this chapter we have only studied static methods. You'll see, however, that instance methods are not much different from static methods. Only their invocation is different. Moreover, although the invocation of an instance method is compiled to a special bytecode instruction, instance methods are executed on the bytecode level almost in the same way as static methods. Only the procedure according to which the Java virtual machine finds the called method is different in the case of instance methods. Instance methods use the stack in the same way as static methods.

## Examining the Java stack with a native method

If you want to see how the stack of a Java program looks like in reality, you can study and use program **DecorationsPrintStack.java** that can be found in the **javafilesextra** folder. That program demonstrates how a Java method can call a so-called native method which is written with the C programming language. The program uses a file named **DecorationsPrintStack.dll** which contains a compiled C method. The C method can be called with the name **`print_stack()`** from a Java program, and it prints the contents of the stack to the screen. In this case a native method had to be used because normal Java methods cannot perform the desired task.

A native method is one that is written with a programming language other than Java, and compiled to executable machine instructions with the compiler of the used language. In a Java program, such a method can be used when it is declared, without a method body, with the keyword **`native`**. These kinds of methods are called native methods because they can be run only in the operating system where they are compiled. Normal Java methods can be executed in all operating systems which have the Java virtual machine installed.

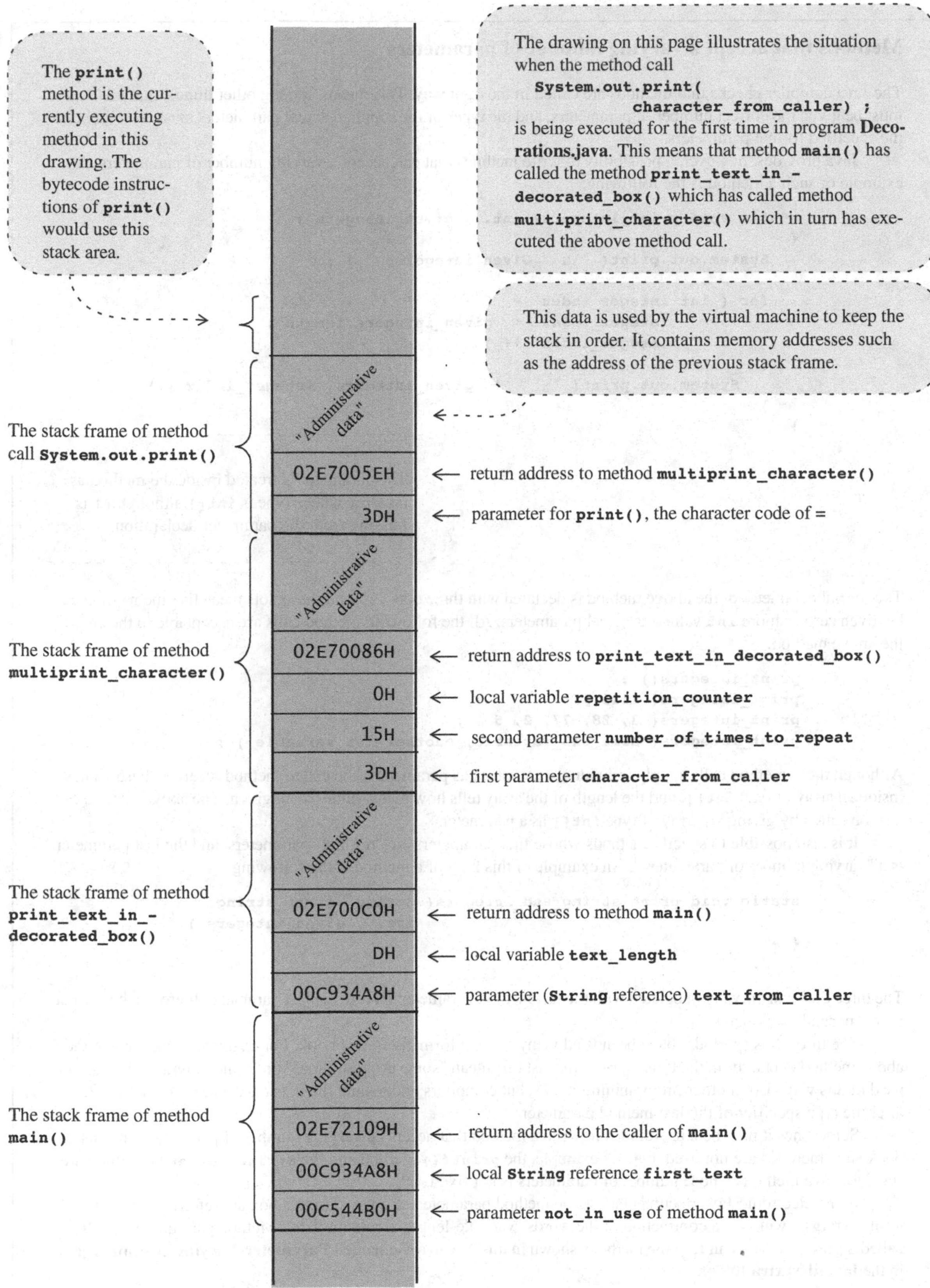

The print() method is the currently executing method in this drawing. The bytecode instructions of print() would use this stack area.
The drawing on this page illustrates the situation when the method call
System.out.print(
character_from_caller) ;
is being executed for the first time in program Decorations.java. This means that method main() has called the method print_text_in_decorated_box() which has called method multiprint_character() which in turn has executed the above method call.
This data is used by the virtual machine to keep the stack in order. It contains memory addresses such as the address of the previous stack frame.
"Administrative data"
The stack frame of method call System.out.print()
02E7005EH
return address to method multiprint_character()
3DH
parameter for print(), the character code of =
"Administrative data"
The stack frame of method multiprint_character()
02E70086H
return address to print_text_in_decorated_box()
0H
local variable repetition_counter
15H
second parameter number_of_times_to_repeat
3DH
first parameter character_from_caller
"Administrative data"
The stack frame of method print_text_in_decorated_box()
02E700C0H
return address to method main()
DH
local variable text_length
00C934A8H
parameter (String reference) text_from_caller
"Administrative data"
The stack frame of method main()
02E72109H
return address to the caller of main()
00C934A8H
local String reference first_text
00C544B0H
parameter not_in_use of method main()

*Figure 9-4. Stack usage during the execution of Decorations.java.*

## Methods that accept a varying number of parameters

The Java compiler checks that methods are called in the right way. This means, among other things, that methods must be given the correct number of parameters, and the types of the supplied actual parameters must correspond to the specified formal parameters.

Java provides, however, a possibility to write methods that can accept a varying number of parameters. An example of such a method is the following:

```
static void print_integers( int... given_integers )
{
   System.out.print( "\n   Given integers: " ) ;

   for ( int integer_index  =  0 ;
             integer_index  <  given_integers.length ;
             integer_index  ++ )
   {
      System.out.print( "  "  +  given_integers[ integer_index ] ) ;
   }
}
```

The parameter is treated inside the method as an array whose type is **int[]** although **[]** is missing from the parameter declaration.

The formal parameter of the above method is declared with three dots **...** and these dots mean that the method can be given zero or more **int** values as actual parameters. All the following method calls are acceptable in the case of the above method:

```
print_integers() ;
print_integers( 1111 ) ;
print_integers( 3, 88, 77, 2, 5 ) ;
print_integers( some_int_variable, another_int_variable ) ;
```

Although these method calls supply individual **int** values as parameters, the called method receives these values inside an array of type **int[]**, and the length of the array tells how many values were given. The above method can also be called by giving an array of type **int[]** as a parameter.

It is also possible to specify methods whose first parameters are "normal" parameters, and the last parameter is a "varying number of parameters". An example of this kind of a method is the following

```
static void print_string_and_integers( String  given_string,
                                       int... given_integers )
{
   ...
```

The three dots can only be associated with the last method parameter. Before the last parameter, there can be zero or more "normal" parameters.

The three dots (periods) have been used many times informally in this book. For example in the case of the above method declaration, the three dots on the last line mean "some program lines" or "some statements". Dots are used in this way also in other programming books, but compilers understand the dots only when they are written after the type specifier of the last method parameter.

Sometimes it may be a useful idea to write a method that accepts a varying number of parameters. In this book such methods are not used, but, for example, the **printf()** method and the **String.format()** method are standard Java methods whose number of parameters is not fixed.

In the electronic Java documentation, the method parameters discussed in this box are referred to with the term "varargs", which is a contraction of the words "variable-length argument lists". Method parameters are also called arguments. You can find the methods shown in this box in a file named **ParametersVaryingInNumber.java** in the **javafilesextra** folder.

## 9.6 Scope of variables

In the previous section, and even earlier, the terms "local variable" and "local data item" have been used in connection with methods. Local variables and other data items (e.g. array and string references), or more generally "local data", are those variables and data items that are declared by the internal statements of a method. A method cannot refer to local variables and data items declared inside another method. We can say that local data is seen only by the internal statements of a method. Local data is not visible to other methods. In the terminology of Java we say that the scope of local data is within the method where they are declared.

As was discussed in the previous section, local variables and other data items are allocated memory space from the stack when the methods containing the local data are called. The stack memory space reserved for local data is deallocated when a method terminates, i.e., when the program control returns to the calling program. In Java terminology, the local variables and other data items go out of scope when a method terminates. Going out of scope means that the local data become nonexistent.

You may already have guessed that there must be non-local variables since there are local variables. Indeed, there can be variables and other data items that are not local to any method. This kind of data can be called classwide data because the data is visible to all methods declared in a class. Variables, arrays, and other data items can be made visible to all methods of a class by declaring them outside the methods in a class. For example, in the declaration

```
class SomeClass
{
   static int first_variable ;
   static void some_method()
   {
      int second_variable ;
      ...
```

**first_variable** is a non-local classwide variable because it is declared outside of any method. **second_variable** is local because it is inside a method. Classwide variables and other data items are declared using the same declaration statement syntax as in the declaration of local data items. The scope of the classwide data items is the class in which they are declared. The methods of the class can refer to the classwide data items simply by using the names of the data items. The classwide data items are also called the data members or data fields of a class. In the example declaration above, the data member **first_variable** is marked with the keyword **static**. As a general rule, static methods can use only static data members. In the following chapter, as we'll learn more about classes, methods, data members, and objects, you will see data members that are not static.

Program **ScopeExploration.java** is an example where static classwide data is used. The methods of the program refer to classwide data, a variable and an array, declared at the beginning of the class. You can see, for example, that **some_array** is referred to in three methods.

Program **ScopeExploration.java** demonstrates also that it is possible to have the same name for a classwide and a local variable. This kind of naming policy cannot, however, be recommended. It is normal that two separate methods have local variables bearing the same name (e.g. **integer_index**), but it is better if a classwide and a local variable have different names. **some_variable** in program **ScopeExploration.java** is used both as a classwide name and a local name just to show how the scope rules of Java work. You can see, for example, that **another_method()** refers to the classwide **some_variable** because there is no local **some_variable** inside **another_method()**. But the statement inside **some_method()** refers to the local variable named **some_variable** because that is closer than the classwide **some_variable**.

The block structure of Java programs was discussed in Chapter 6. Pairs of braces { } are used to form program blocks in Java. The internal statements of each method form a block, and, for example, the internal statements of a loop form a program block. It is possible to declare local variables inside every program block, and the local variables will go out of scope when the statements inside the program block are no longer executed. The local variables declared inside a program block are visible only within the block where they are declared.

Although Java allows the use of identical variable names in nested program blocks (i.e. program blocks inside other program blocks), those kinds of program constructs can be confusing and should therefore be avoided. For example, the variable declarations on the lines

```
static void some_method()
{
   int some_variable ;

   while ( some boolean expression )
   {
      int some_variable ;
      ...
```

would be accepted by the compiler but it is better not to use the same variable name again in a nested program block.

There is one scope-related issue that should be known when **for** loops are used. It is common to declare an index variable inside the parentheses of a **for** loop in the following way

```
for ( int some_index  =  0 ;
          some_index  <  some limit for the index
          some_index  ++ )
{
   internal statements of the for loop
}
```

The scope of the index variable that is declared this way is within the **for** loop. In the above case, **some_index** is visible only to the internal statements of the loop.

```
D:\javafiles2>java ScopeExploration

  some_variable contains 3333
  some_array    contains 1111 and 2222
  some_variable (local) contains 4444
  some_variable contains 3333
  some_array    contains 8888 and 2222
  some_variable contains 7777
  some_array    contains 8888 and 9999
```

**ScopeExploration.java - X. Classwide data is printed three times.**

These are classwide data items. They are declared inside the class **ScopeExploration**, but outside of the methods of the class. These data items are said to be in class scope, meaning that all methods in this class can "see" and use these data items.

In general, it is not good programming practice to use the same names for classwide and local variables. Here, this practice is used only to demonstrate the scope rules of Java. This second **some_variable** is a local variable within the scope of **some_method()**. All statements inside **some_method()** can use this variable. Because **some_method()** has a local variable with the name **some_variable**, it cannot access the classwide variable with the same name.

```
//  ScopeExploration.java

class ScopeExploration
{
   static int[]  some_array     =  { 1111, 2222 } ;
   static int    some_variable  =  3333 ;

   static void some_method()
   {
      int  some_variable  =  4444 ;

      System.out.print( "\n some_variable (local) contains "
                      +  some_variable ) ;

      some_array[ 0 ]   =  8888 ;
   }

   static void another_method()
   {
      some_variable      =  7777 ;

      some_array[ 1 ]   =  9999 ;
   }

   static void print_classwide_data()
   {
      System.out.print( "\n some_variable contains " +  some_variable ) ;

      System.out.print( "\n some_array    contains "
                      + some_array[ 0 ]  + " and "   + some_array[ 1 ] ) ;
   }

   public static void main( String[] not_in_use )
   {
      print_classwide_data() ;
      some_method() ;
      print_classwide_data() ;
      another_method() ;
      print_classwide_data() ;
   }
}
```

Array elements are referred to by all the methods that are called by method **main()**.

**ScopeExploration.java - 1. Using classwide and local data.**

## 9.7 Parameters for the method main()

The method **main()** is a normal Java method which must be written according to the rules of Java. The special feature of method **main()** is that it is called or somehow invoked by the Java interpreter (the Java virtual machine) after a command to execute a Java program is given. The developers of the Java programming language have decided that the method that bears the name **main** is the method that is activated when a program starts executing.

So far, in our programs the parameter of method **main()** has been named **not_in_use** simply because we have not used the parameter. The parameter of method **main()** can, however, bring useful data to a program, and now we are going to study this data transfer mechanism.

A Java program can be executed in a command prompt window with a command like

```
java ClassName
```

where **ClassName** is the name of the class which contains the **main()** method. The above command invokes the Java interpreter (Java virtual machine), and **ClassName** is a parameter for the Java interpreter. In the above command **java** represents a program that is invoked from the command line, and its parameter **ClassName** specifies that the Java bytecode program should be read from a file named **ClassName.class**.

Just like **java**, the command that activates the Java interpreter, receives from the command line a parameter which specifies the Java program that must be executed, the Java program can also be given parameters on the command line. In a command like

```
java ClassName xxxx yyyy
```

**xxxx** and **yyyy** are command line parameters for the **main()** method inside the class named **ClassName**. When the above command is processed, the text strings **xxxx** and **yyyy** are put to an array of strings, and the array of strings is supplied as a parameter for the **main()** method inside class **ClassName**. The data from the command line is first received by the operating system, which passes it to the Java interpreter, which in turn supplies the data as an array of strings to the method **main()**.

In earlier programs, command line parameters have not been used, but from now on, you may see programs in which the declarator of the **main()** method is written in the following way:

```
public static void main( String[] command_line_parameters )
```

The programs in this book are written so that, when you see the name **command_line_-parameters** instead of **not_in_use**, you know that in that particular program the command line parameters are used. The parameter for method **main()** is a normal Java array whose type is **String[]**, i.e., the array contains references to **String** objects.

Program **Commanding.java** is an example that clarifies how the given command line parameters can be found in the parameter array of method **main()**. It is important to note that, although command line parameters and the parameter of method **main()** contain the same data, they are different concepts. They contain the same data in different formats. Regardless of how many parameters are given on the command line, method **main()** takes only a single parameter. Theoretically, there can be an unlimited number of command line parameters.

Command line parameters are a mechanism to transfer data to an application program. It is possible to write an application program so that it checks whether command line data was given or not. If the command line data is not given, the program can be intelligent enough to ask for data from the user. Program **Calculate.java** is an example of this kind of intelligent program. It can accept data from the user in two ways: either through command line parameters or through separate input statements.

In the programs of this book the parameter of method **main()** is named **command_line_parameters** instead of **not_in_use** when the command line parameters are used in the program in question. The parameter is an array of strings, containing the strings that were typed in from the keyboard. As the parameter is an array, the **length** field can be used to find out the length of the array. The length equals to the number of strings that were typed in from the command line.

```
//  Commanding.java

class  Commanding
{
   public static void main( String[]  command_line_parameters )
   {
      System.out.print( "\n Method main() was given the following "
                      +  command_line_parameters.length + " strings"
                      + "\n as command line parameters: \n" ) ;

      int  parameter_index  =  0 ;

      while ( parameter_index  <  command_line_parameters.length )
      {
         System.out.print(
             "\n      " + command_line_parameters[ parameter_index ] ) ;

         parameter_index   ++ ;
      }
   }
}
```

This **while** loop prints out every parameter from the array of command line parameters. This expression refers to a single string in the array of strings. This **while** loop is executed once for each command line parameter.

**Commanding.java - 1. A method main() that prints the given command line parameters.**

```
D:\javafiles2>java Commanding Hello program, how are you?

 Method main() was given the following 5 strings
 as command line parameters:

     Hello
     program,
     how
     are
     you?
```

In this command, **java** invokes the Java interpreter, **Commanding** is a parameter for the Java interpreter, and the rest of the parameters are the actual command line parameters for the **Commanding.java** program.

**Commanding.java - X. Spaces separate the given command line parameters.**

This method is called by method **main()**. It prints the results of the basic arithmetic operations with two integers. This method does not know, and does not need to know, how the two integers were input into this program. This method takes care of data output. It is the job of method **main()** to take care of data input.

Parentheses are needed here to make the addition and subtraction operations happen before string concatenation operations.

```
//  Calculate.java  (c) 2005 Kari Laitinen

import java.util.* ;

class Calculate
{
   static void print_calculations ( int first_integer,
                                    int second_integer )
   {
      System.out.print( "\n    " + first_integer  + " + "
                      + second_integer + " = "
                      + ( first_integer  + second_integer )
                      + "\n    " + first_integer  + " - "
                      + second_integer + " = "
                      + ( first_integer - second_integer )
                      + "\n    " + first_integer + " * "
                      + second_integer + " = "
                      + first_integer * second_integer ) ;

      if ( second_integer  !=  0 )
      {
         System.out.print( "\n    " + first_integer  +  " / "
                         + second_integer  +  " = "
                         + first_integer / second_integer
                         + "\n    " + first_integer  +  " % "
                         + second_integer  + " = "
                         + first_integer % second_integer  +  "\n" ) ;
      }
      else
      {
         System.out.print( "\n    Cannot divide with zero. \n" ) ;
      }
   }
```

Dividing by zero may result in unpredictable behavior in a computer. For this reason, programs should always ensure that division by zero does not occur.

% is the remainder operator in Java. The operator returns the remainder that would result from a division operation with two integers.

**Calculate.java - 1: First part of the program.**

If the number of given command line parameters is two, the program assumes that the user typed in two integers. In this case, it does not ask for any data from the user.

Because numbers given as command line parameters are strings, they must be converted to integer form to suit the method **print_calculations()**. The method **parseInt()** of the standard Java class **Integer** can perform this kind of conversion.

```
   public static void main( String[] command_line_parameters )
   {
      Scanner keyboard = new Scanner( System.in ) ;

      int  first_operand, second_operand ;

      if ( command_line_parameters.length  ==  2 )
      {
         first_operand   =  Integer.parseInt( command_line_parameters[ 0 ] ) ;
         second_operand  =  Integer.parseInt( command_line_parameters[ 1 ] ) ;

         print_calculations( first_operand, second_operand ) ;
      }
      else
      {
         System.out.print( "\n This program calculates with integers."
                         + "\n Give two integers separated by a space:   " ) ;
         first_operand   =  keyboard.nextInt() ;
         second_operand  =  keyboard.nextInt() ;

         print_calculations( first_operand, second_operand ) ;
      }
   }
}
```

**Calculate.java - 2. Method main() that calls the method print_calculations().**

```
D:\javafiles2>java Calculate

 This program calculates with integers.
 Give two integers separated by a space:  99 44

    99 + 44 = 143
    99 - 44 = 55
    99 * 44 = 4356
    99 / 44 = 2
    99 % 44 = 11

D:\javafiles2>java Calculate 44 99

    44 + 99 = 143
    44 - 99 = -55
    44 * 99 = 4356
    44 / 99 = 0
    44 % 99 = 44
```

The program receives these numbers as strings. In string form, 99 is represented by values 39H and 39H, two character codes of digit 9. When converted to an **int**, 99 is 00000063H which is represented by bytes 63H, 00H, 00H, and 00H in the computer's memory.

**Calculate.java - X. The program is executed here in two ways.**

## 9.8 Overloading method names

Since Java is a strongly typed programming language, the Java compiler checks that correct types of actual parameters are used in method calls. This means that calling a method with the wrong types of parameters results in a compilation error. To study this, let's suppose that there is a method with the following declarator

```
static double
find_largest_number( double[] array_of_numbers,
                     int  number_of_numbers_in_array )
```

Supposing that **array_of_integers** is an array of type **int[]** and **largest_integer** is a variable of type **int**, the method call

```
largest_integer  =  find_largest_number(
                              array_of_integers, 5 ) ;
```

would result in a compilation error. The Java compiler would not accept the above method call because, although the second parameter is correct, the first parameter for **find_largest_number()** should be an array of type **double[]**. The above method call would also be illegal because the type of the variable does not correspond with the return type of the method. The compiler requires that the types of actual parameters correspond with the types of declared formal parameters of the method. The compiler also requires that a correct number of parameters is used, and that returned values are treated in a proper manner. Therefore, the method call

```
largest_integer = find_largest_number( array_of_integers );
```

would not be acceptable both because **find_largest_number()** requires two parameters and because it cannot accept an array of type **int[]** as a parameter.

The method calls above are not acceptable if method **find_largest_number()** is declared as it is above. The **find_largest_number()** method above can only accept an array of type **double[]**. But what if we wanted to have a method named **find_largest_number()** that could be called with the above method calls; should the original **find_largest_number()** be modified? The answer is that we would not have to modify anything. We could simply write new versions of the method **find_largest_number()**.

Methods with declarators

```
static int
find_largest_number( int[]  array_of_integers,
                     int    number_of_numbers_in_array )

static int
find_largest_number( int[]  array_of_integers )
```

could be added to the same program file with the original version of **find_largest_number()**. Java allows several methods to have the same name provided that each of the methods takes a different set of parameters. The Java compiler can choose the correct version of a method when it checks the types of the parameters.

When a program contains several versions of a method, we say that the name of the method, or just the method, is overloaded. A method name that is the name of several separate methods has several meanings, or is overloaded with meanings. When the Java compiler is translating a method call, trying to find out which one of the overloaded methods is to be used, it finds the correct method by comparing the given actual parameters to the different sets of formal parameters.

Program **Overload.java** is an example of overloading. It contains three versions of a method bearing the name **print_array()**. The declarators of the three methods are

```
static void print_array( int[]  array_of_integers,
                         int  number_of_integers_to_print )

static void print_array( char[]  character_array,
                        int  number_of_characters_to_print )

static void print_array( char[]  character_array )
```

The first two versions of **print_array()** can be distinguished from each other because the type of the array is **int** in the first version and **char** in the second version. The third **print_array()** differs from the first two in that it has only one parameter. The compiler always selects the correct version of **print_array()** by comparing the actual parameters to the formal parameters. For example, in the method call

```
print_array( second_array ) ;
```

the compiler can direct the call to the third version of **print_array()** because that only takes a single parameter which is an array of type **char[]**, and the type of **second_-array** is **char[]**.

The compiler can also handle the situation when no method matches a method call. For example, if you tried to add the method call

```
print_array( first_array ) ;
```

into the method **main()** of **Overload.java**, the compiler would issue an error message. **first_array** is an array whose type is **int[]**. **Overload.java** does not have a version of **print_array()** that would take just an array of type **int[]** as its only parameter.

The basic rule in Java, as well as in many other programming languages, is that every method must have a unique name, distinguishable from other names in a program. Overloading can be considered a slight loosening of this rule. Two or more methods which perform a similar set of activities (e.g. printing of an array) can have the same name provided that they take a different set of parameters.

Overloading a method name is just one possibility in the naming of methods. An alternative to overloading is to give each method a uniquely distinguishable name. For example, the methods in program **Overload.java** could be named with unique names in the following way

```
static void print_integers_from_array(
                    int[] array_of_integers,
                    int   number_of_integers_to_print )

static void print_characters_from_array(
                    char[] character_array,
                    int    number_of_characters_to_print )

static void print_all_characters_from_array(
                              char[] character_array )
```

Method overloading is an important subject because the overloading of methods is used commonly in the standard Java classes. For example, there are many versions of method **indexOf()** in the standard Java class **String**. My recommendation at this point is, however, that you should not use too much overloading in your own programs. If you use overloading, use it sparingly. The names of methods are important to people who read and try to understand your programs. Those people may include also you, if you need to modify a program you wrote a longer time ago. If a program has only a few method names that are used to mean many methods, the program may be difficult to read and understand.

```
//  Overload.java  (c) 2005 Kari Laitinen

class Overload
{
   static void print_array( int[] array_of_integers,
                            int   number_of_integers_to_print )
   {
      System.out.print( "\n\n Integers in array:" ) ;

      for ( int integer_index  =  0 ;
                integer_index  <  number_of_integers_to_print ;
                integer_index  ++ )
      {
         System.out.print( "   " + array_of_integers[ integer_index ] ) ;
      }
   }

   static void print_array( char[] character_array,
                            int    number_of_characters_to_print )
   {
      System.out.print( "\n\n Characters in array:" ) ;

      for ( int character_index  =  0 ;
                character_index  <  number_of_characters_to_print ;
                character_index  ++ )
      {
         System.out.print( "   " + character_array[ character_index ] ) ;
      }
   }

   static void print_array( char[] character_array )
   {
      System.out.print( "\n\n Characters in array:" ) ;

      for ( int character_index  =  0 ;
                character_index  <  character_array.length ;
                character_index  ++ )
      {
         System.out.print( "   " + character_array[ character_index ] ) ;
      }
   }

   public static void main( String[] not_in_use )
   {
      int[]  first_array  =  { 55, 77, 888, 4444, 33, 22, 11 } ;

      char[] second_array =  { 'A', 'B', 'C', 'D', 'E', 'F', 'G', 'H' } ;

      print_array( first_array, 6 ) ;
      print_array( second_array ) ;
      print_array( second_array, 5 ) ;
   }
}
```

This statement calls the second version of **print_array()** because the first parameter is an array of type **char[]** and the second parameter is an **int**.

**Overload.java - 1. A program containing several versions of the method print_array().**

```
D:\javafiles2>java Overload

   Integers in array:  55   77   888   4444   33   22

   Characters in array:   A   B   C   D   E   F   G   H

   Characters in array:  A   B   C   D   E
```

**Overload.java - X. Three different print_array() methods being called.**

## Exercises related command line parameters

Exercise 9-9. Improve the **main()** method in the program you wrote in Exercise 9-3 so that it checks whether any command line parameters were given. If the program finds out that the integer for which the factorial should be printed was given on the command line, it should call **print_-factorial()** without asking for anything from the user. Otherwise, the program should ask for an integer from the user. Program **Calculate.java** may be a helpful example in this exercise.

Exercise 9-10. Write a program (e.g. **Showcode.java**) that you can use from the command line to find out the character code of a character. The program should work so that when you type

```
java Showcode A
```

the program responds

```
The character code of A is 41H (65)
```

The program must use the parameter of method **main()** to receive the letter that the user typed in while starting the program.

## 9.9 Chapter summary

- The action statements of Java programs are written inside named methods which reside inside named classes. When a Java program is executed, the Java interpreter (the Java virtual machine) is first activated, and then the interpreter calls or activates the method **main()** of the Java program. Method **main()** may call other methods, which in turn may call other methods, and so on.
- A method that calls another method is the caller, and the called method is the callee.
- Method parameters, which are also called arguments, convey information from a caller to a callee. When a method is called, the caller supplies actual parameters which are copied to the formal parameters of the callee.
- In Java, parameters are always passed by value, which means that a value is copied from the calling method to the called method, and a called method cannot access a variable or an object reference declared in the calling method. A called method and a calling method can reference the same object when an object reference is copied in a method call.
- Variables and other data items declared inside a method are its local data. The parameters of a method are also local data. The stack memory area is used to reserve memory space for the local data when methods are called.
- Methods that have **void** as their return type are typeless methods. Typed methods, i.e., methods that are not of type **void**, must have a **return** statement that returns a value to the caller.
- Only static methods have been studied in this chapter. Static methods differ slightly from instance methods which will be studied in the following chapter.

# PART III: OBJECT-ORIENTED PROGRAMMING

Chapters

10 Classes and objects
11 More advanced classes
12 Inheritance and class hierarchies
13 Some standard Java classes
14 Storing information in files
15 More standard Java types
16 Going closer to the machine

# CHAPTER 10

## CLASSES AND OBJECTS

Although the keyword **class** has been used in every example program of this book, only now, after having studied the fundamentals of programming, we can really start exploring the nature of Java classes. Class is a very fundamental concept in modern computer programming. In the programs that we have studied in the previous chapters, classes have played a minor role. Because it is mandatory that all methods of a Java program are written inside some class, we always have had a class declaration in our programs. From now on, however, we'll start using more advanced classes in our programs. You will learn that classes can be your own (data) types with which you can create the kind of objects you want.

As classes are used to create objects, programming based on classes is called object-oriented programming. Therefore, this chapter is the beginning of Part III "Object-Oriented Programming" in this book. In this first object-oriented chapter, we'll examine simple classes that can be used to declare and create objects. In further chapters, the concept of a class will be elaborated. It is not possible to explain the concept of a class with a few words. Therefore, as the concept becomes clearer in further chapters, you might consider the rest of this book as a long answer to the question: "What is a class?"

## 10.1 Classes, fields, and instance methods

The classes that we have studied in the previous chapters have been just program structures that contain a set of static methods, often only the single static **main()** method. Now we are, finally, going to study classes that are the "real" classes that can be used to create objects, that represent (data) types specified by a programmer. Designing these kinds of classes can be called object-oriented programming, and, therefore, this chapter starts the object-oriented Part III of this book.

We need classes in order to create objects. We have already, in Chapter 8, studied objects of type **String**. **String** is a standard class of Java, and, as that class is automatically available for Java programs, we can specify a string reference with a statement like

```
String  some_string ;
```

Then a **String** object can be created, for example, with a statement like

```
some_string  =  "xxxxxx" ;
```

The above statement creates a **String** object whose content is "xxxxxx", a character string in which letter x is repeated 6 times. The statement also makes **some_string** reference the created object. When the string reference **some_string** references a **String** object, it stores the address of the object in the heap memory.

In the case of **String** objects, the class to create objects already exists, and that makes programming quite easy. When you want to create some special kinds of objects, you first have to declare a class that specifies the nature of your objects. Programs **Rectangles.java** and **BankSimple.java** are examples that demonstrate simple classes and the creation of objects that are based on the simple classes. The structure of both programs is the following

```
class SomeClass
{
   Declarations of data items (fields).
   Declarations of instance methods.
}

class SomeTesterClass
{
   public static void main( String[] not_in_use )
   {
      SomeClass  some_object  =  new  SomeClass() ;

      ...
   }
}
```

The program files **Rectangles.java** and **BankSimple.java** both contain two classes. First there is a "real" class that can be used to create objects, and then there is another class that contains the **main()** method which creates the objects.

The classes that are used to create objects usually have data declarations which are called fields in programming terminology. The class **Rectangle** of program **Rectangles.java** begins with the following lines

```
class Rectangle
{
   int  rectangle_width ;
   int  rectangle_height ;
   char  filling_character ;
```

on which **rectangle_width**, **rectangle_height**, and **filling_character** are (data) fields that belong to every object of type **Rectangle**. These fields specify how a simple rectangle looks when it is printed onto the screen of a computer.

The methods of a class that is used to create objects are usually non-static methods that are said to be instance methods. They are instance methods because objects of a class are also called instances of a class, and these methods can only be called in relation to an instance. For example, the method **print_rectangle()** in **Rectangles.java** is called with the statement

```
first_rectangle.print_rectangle() ;
```

where **first_rectangle** is a reference to an object of type **Rectangle** (an instance of class **Rectangle**) and method **print_rectangle()** is called in relation to the object referenced by **first_rectangle**. When **print_rectangle()** is called this way, it prints the **Rectangle** object for which it was called, and it uses those data fields (**rectangle_width**, **rectangle_height**, and **filling_character**) that exist inside the object referenced by **first_rectangle**. (The verb "invoke" is also used when the calling of an instance method is discussed. To describe the activity of calling an instance method for an object, it is commons to say that "a method is invoked for an object".)

It is important to understand that every object of a class contains copies of all data fields of the class. Every object contains instances of the fields of its class. For example, when we create an object of class **Rectangle** in the following way

```
Rectangle  first_rectangle  =  new  Rectangle() ;
```

we actually create a data structure that contains all the data fields declared in class **Rectangle**. The object referenced by **first_rectangle** contains its own **rectangle_width**, **rectangle_height**, and **filling_character**. These internal data fields are accessed through the methods of class **Rectangle**. For example, when the statement

```
first_rectangle.initialize_rectangle( 7, 4, 'Z' ) ;
```

is executed, method **initialize_rectangle()** sets the values of the fields inside the object referenced by **first_rectangle** so that **rectangle_width** is given the value 7, **rectangle_height** is set to 4, and **filling_character** is set to contain the character code of uppercase letter Z. Method **initialize_rectangle()** does not know the name of the object reference when it is executed, but the dot operator . binds it to the correct object in the call. The above call to method **initialize_rectangle()** could be explained in a longer way as "Go and execute the statements inside method **initialize_rectangle()** using the data fields inside the object referenced by **first_rectangle**."

As you already have studied arrays and strings, which also are objects, it should not be very difficult to understand how objects are created to the heap memory, and how they are referenced with a reference in the stack memory. A statement like

```
Rectangle  first_rectangle ;
```

declares an object reference that can be used to reference (or to point to) an object, but this statement does not yet create any objects. An object can be created by using the **new** operator in a statement like

```
first_rectangle  =  new  Rectangle() ;
```

This statement creates a **Rectangle** object to the heap memory, and makes **first_rectangle** reference the created object. An object reference references an object so that it stores the physical memory address of the object. Figure 10-1 shows how the **Rectangle** objects of program **Rectangles.java** are referenced by the references **first_rectangle** and **second_rectangle**. Figure 10-1 describes the situation right before the method **main()** of program **Rectangles.java** terminates.

Class **Rectangle** differs from classes we have seen before so that data items are declared before the methods of the class. **rectangle_width**, **rectangle_height**, and **filling_character** are data items that belong to every object of type **Rectangle**. These data items are called fields in programming terminology. Fields are data members of a class.

```
//  Rectangles.java

class Rectangle
{
   int  rectangle_width ;
   int  rectangle_height ;
   char  filling_character ;

   public void initialize_rectangle( int  given_rectangle_width,
                                     int  given_rectangle_height,
                                     char given_filling_character )
   {
      rectangle_width    =  given_rectangle_width ;
      rectangle_height   =  given_rectangle_height ;
      filling_character  =  given_filling_character ;
   }

   public void print_rectangle()
   {
      for ( int number_of_rows_printed  =  0 ;
                number_of_rows_printed  <  rectangle_height ;
                number_of_rows_printed  ++ )
      {
         System.out.print( "\n      " ) ;

         for ( int number_of_characters_printed  =  0 ;
                   number_of_characters_printed  <  rectangle_width ;
                   number_of_characters_printed  ++ )
         {
            System.out.print( filling_character ) ;
         }
      }

      System.out.print( "\n" ) ;
   }
}
```

The methods of a class can freely read and write the data fields, the classwide data, that are declared at the beginning of the class.

Class **Rectangle** has two methods, **initialize_rectangle()** and **print_rectangle()**, which are written inside the class declaration in the same way as the methods that we have seen before. Because the keyword **static** is not used in the declaration of these methods, they are non-static instance methods than can only be called in relation to a **Rectangle** object according to the following statement syntax

```
object_reference_name.method_name( ... ) ;
```

**Rectangles.java - 1: The declaration of class Rectangle.**

Class **Rectangles** follows class **Rectangle** in file Rectangles.java. Class **Rectangles** exists only because it is logical to have a different class where the **main()** method may be placed. The **main()** method could alternatively be placed inside class **Rectangle**.

This statement declares a reference **first_rectangle** that can reference a **Rectangle** object, creates a **Rectangle** object, and makes **first_rectangle** reference the created object. This statement could be replaced with the statements

```
Rectangle  first_rectangle ;
first_rectangle  =  new  Rectangle() ;
```

```
class Rectangles
{
   public static void main( String[] not_in_use )
   {
      Rectangle  first_rectangle  =  new Rectangle() ;

      first_rectangle.initialize_rectangle( 7, 4, 'Z' ) ;
      first_rectangle.print_rectangle() ;

      Rectangle  second_rectangle  =  new Rectangle() ;

      second_rectangle.initialize_rectangle( 12, 3, 'X' ) ;
      second_rectangle.print_rectangle() ;
   }
}
```

After its creation, an object of type **Rectangle** contains the data fields **rectangle_width**, **rectangle_height**, and **filling_character**, but these fields contain only zeroes. Method **initialize_rectangle()** can be used to give meaningful values to these fields.

**Rectangles.java - 2. The main() method of class Rectangles that creates two Rectangle objects.**

As this chapter belongs to Part III of this book, the example programs are in a directory (folder) that has number 3 in its name.

```
D:\javafiles3>java Rectangles

     ZZZZZZZ
     ZZZZZZZ
     ZZZZZZZ
     ZZZZZZZ

     XXXXXXXXXXXX
     XXXXXXXXXXXX
     XXXXXXXXXXXX
```

This is the **Rectangle** object referenced by **second_rectangle**. The printed rectangle is 12 character positions wide, 3 rows high, and filled with character X.

**Rectangles.java - X. The rectangles are made by printing a single character repeatedly.**

The other simple program **BankSimple.java** shows how a simple bank account class can be declared and used. A banking program may be a useful example, because a large portion of the world's computing power is consumed making calculations related to money. Computers calculate, for example, wages, share prices, and maintain information about money stored in accounts in banks. While studying program **BankSimple.java**, you should bear in mind that real banking programs are much more complicated. The program could not be used in a real bank, but it does demonstrate some operations with objects.

The `BankAccount` objects created in program **BankSimple.java** are somewhat more complicated than the objects created in program **Rectangles.java**. The reason for this complication is that `BankAccount` objects have a string as a data field, and strings are objects themselves. The field `account_owner` of class `BankAccount` references a `String` object. When a `BankAccount` object is initialized with method `initialize_-account()`, `account_owner` starts to reference a separate `String` object where the owner's name is stored. Figure 10-2 shows what the objects look like in the main memory of a computer when all the objects of program **BankSimple.java** have been created.

In order to design useful classes, we should learn to think in object-oriented way. In object-oriented thinking we should think first about data. After having thought what set of data fields could form an entity, an object, we should think what kinds of methods are needed to process that data. In the case of class `BankAccount` in program **BankSimple.java**, object-oriented thinking goes as follows:

- `BankAccount` objects are such that every object contains the name of the account owner (a string), the number of the account, and the balance of the account (i.e. how much money is currently stored in the account).
- As class `BankAccount` has three methods, there are three different possibilities to do something with `BankAccount` objects.
- By calling method `initialize_account()` for a `BankAccount` object, it is possible to initialize data fields `account_owner`, `account_number`, and `account_balance`.
- It is possible to increase the value of data field `account_balance` for a `BankAccount` object by calling method `deposit_money()`.
- By calling `show_account_data()` it is possible to see all data inside a `BankAccount` object.

A central idea in the design of classes is that data is encapsulated inside objects, and the data is accessed only through calls to methods. This principle is used both in program **Rectangles.java** and in **BankSimple.java**. Although the data fields of a class should be accessed only by the methods of the same class, it is possible to write programs in which data fields are accessed by the methods of a foreign class. For example, the data field `account_balance` of a `BankAccount` object can be accessed from method `main()`. The statement

```
first_account.account_balance  =
          first_account.account_balance  +  2222.11 ;
```

would be acceptable in the method `main()` of **BankSimple.java** in place of the method call

```
first_account.deposit_money(  2222.11 ) ;
```

If you want to prevent other classes from accessing the fields of a class, the fields should be declared with keyword `private`. On the other hand, fields declared with keyword `public` are automatically visible to all methods in all classes. Program **Person.java** provides an example of a class with `public` fields. Classes like the class `Person` in program **Person.java** are not, however, very object-oriented classes, and they should not be used too often. The accessibility of class members will be discussed more thoroughly on page 398.

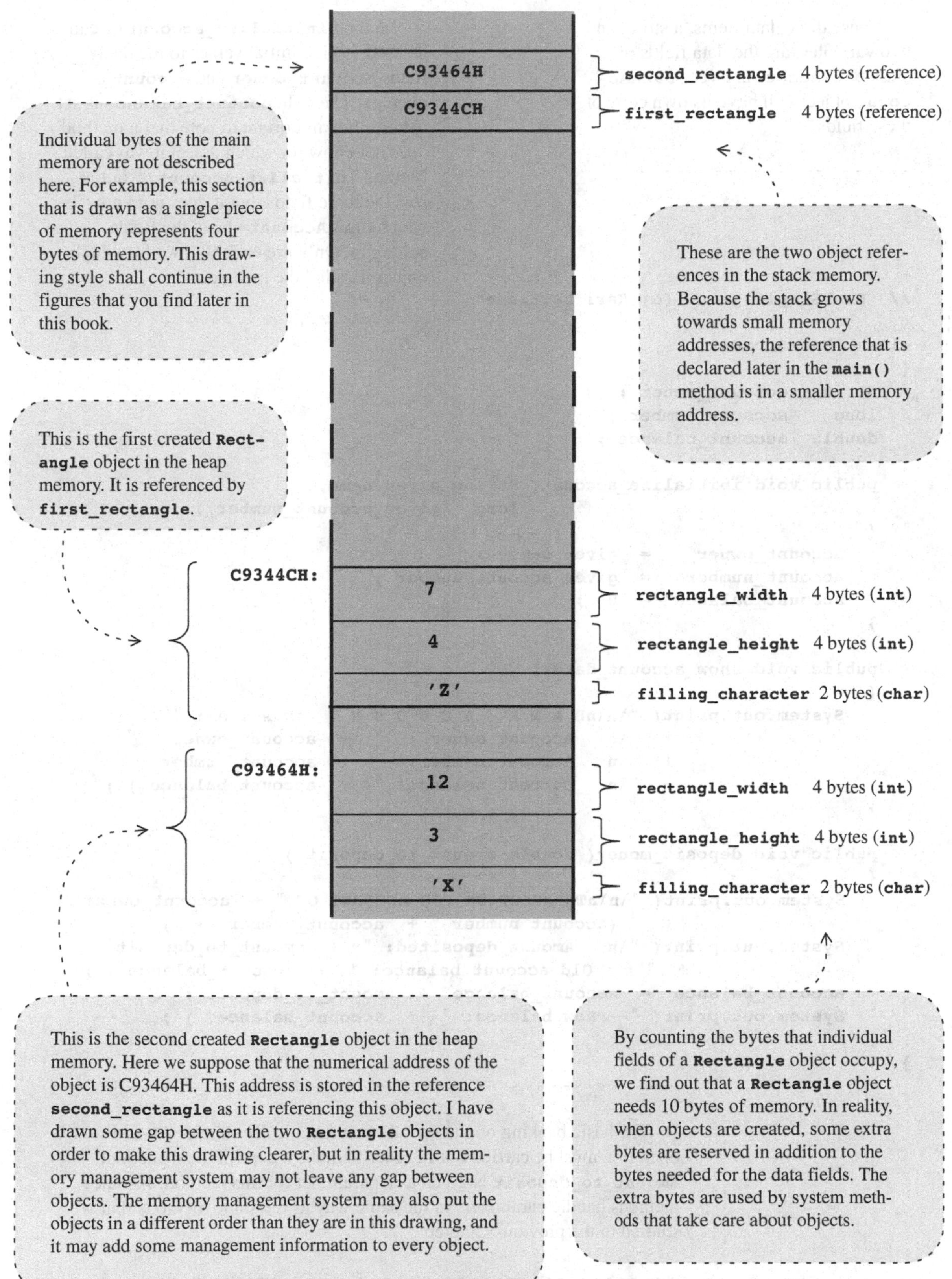

C93464H
C9344CH
second_rectangle 4 bytes (reference)
first_rectangle 4 bytes (reference)
Individual bytes of the main memory are not described here. For example, this section that is drawn as a single piece of memory represents four bytes of memory. This drawing style shall continue in the figures that you find later in this book.
These are the two object references in the stack memory. Because the stack grows towards small memory addresses, the reference that is declared later in the main() method is in a smaller memory address.
This is the first created Rectangle object in the heap memory. It is referenced by first_rectangle.
C9344CH:
7
rectangle_width 4 bytes (int)
4
rectangle_height 4 bytes (int)
'Z'
filling_character 2 bytes (char)
C93464H:
12
rectangle_width 4 bytes (int)
3
rectangle_height 4 bytes (int)
'X'
filling_character 2 bytes (char)
This is the second created Rectangle object in the heap memory. Here we suppose that the numerical address of the object is C93464H. This address is stored in the reference second_rectangle as it is referencing this object. I have drawn some gap between the two Rectangle objects in order to make this drawing clearer, but in reality the memory management system may not leave any gap between objects. The memory management system may also put the objects in a different order than they are in this drawing, and it may add some management information to every object.
By counting the bytes that individual fields of a Rectangle object occupy, we find out that a Rectangle object needs 10 bytes of memory. In reality, when objects are created, some extra bytes are reserved in addition to the bytes needed for the data fields. The extra bytes are used by system methods that take care about objects.


*Figure 10-1. The objects of program Rectangles.java in the main memory.*

These three data items, a string and two variables, are the data fields of class **BankAccount**. Every **BankAccount** object will have its own copy of these fields.

Method **initialize_account()** can be used to give initial values to the data fields **account_owner** and **account_number**. The field **account_balance** is set to zero. It is important to note that a method does not know for which object it was called. Method **initialize_account()** initializes the three fields, but it does not know which **BankAccount** object the fields belong to. Only the caller knows for which object it called the method.

```
//  BankSimple.java  (c) Kari Laitinen

class  BankAccount
{
   String  account_owner ;
   long    account_number ;
   double  account_balance ;

   public void initialize_account( String given_name,
                                   long   given_account_number )
   {
      account_owner    =  given_name  ;
      account_number   =  given_account_number ;
      account_balance  =  0  ;
   }

   public void show_account_data()
   {
      System.out.print( "\n\nB A N K   A C C O U N T   D A T A : "
                     +  "\n   Account owner :  "  +  account_owner
                     +  "\n   Account number:  "  +  account_number
                     +  "\n   Current balance:  "  +  account_balance ) ;
   }

   public void deposit_money( double amount_to_deposit )
   {
      System.out.print( "\n\nTRANSACTION FOR ACCOUNT OF " +  account_owner
                     +  " (Account number " + account_number  + ")" ) ;
      System.out.print( "\n   Amount deposited: "  +  amount_to_deposit
                    +  "\n   Old account balance: "  +  account_balance ) ;
      account_balance  =  account_balance  +  amount_to_deposit ;
      System.out.print( "   New balance: "  +  account_balance  ) ;
   }
}
```

The basic banking operations are mathematically simple. An addition operation must be carried out in order to make a deposit to an account. **amount_to_deposit** is given as a parameter for this method. Instance methods handle parameters in the same way as the static methods that we studied in the previous chapter.

**BankSimple.java - 1: The declaration of class BankAccount.**

```
class BankSimple
{
   public static void main( String[] not_in_use )
   {
      BankAccount  first_account   =  new  BankAccount() ;
      BankAccount  second_account  =  new  BankAccount() ;

      first_account.initialize_account(  "James Bond", 77007007 ) ;
      second_account.initialize_account( "Philip Marlowe", 22003004 ) ;

      first_account.deposit_money(  5566.77 ) ;
      second_account.deposit_money( 9988.77 ) ;
      first_account.deposit_money(  2222.11 ) ;

      first_account.show_account_data() ;
      second_account.show_account_data() ;
   }
}
```

**first_account** and **second_account** are object references that are made to reference the two **BankAccount** objects that are created to the heap memory. Both objects contain the three data fields **account_owner**, **account_number**, and **account_balance**. The fields inside the objects are modified by calling methods for the objects.

**BankSimple.java - 2. Class BankSimple that contains the method main().**

```
D:\javafiles3>java BankSimple


TRANSACTION FOR ACCOUNT OF James Bond (Account number 77007007)
   Amount deposited: 5566.77
   Old account balance: 0.0   New balance: 5566.77

TRANSACTION FOR ACCOUNT OF Philip Marlowe (Account number 22003004)
   Amount deposited: 9988.77
   Old account balance: 0.0   New balance: 9988.77

TRANSACTION FOR ACCOUNT OF James Bond (Account number 77007007)
   Amount deposited: 2222.11
   Old account balance: 5566.77   New balance: 7788.880000000001

B A N K   A C C O U N T   D A T A :
   Account owner :  James Bond
   Account number:  77007007
   Current balance: 7788.880000000001

B A N K   A C C O U N T   D A T A :
   Account owner :  Philip Marlowe
   Account number: 22003004
   Current balance: 9988.77
```

**BankSimple.java - X. The program always produces the same output.**

The fields of class **Person** are declared with keyword **public**, which makes these fields accessible for methods in all other classes. The keyword **public** is an access modifier. Other access modifiers include keywords **private** and **protected**. Also a missing access modifier affects the visibility of a field. See page 398 for more information related to the visibility of class members.

```
//  Person.java  (c) Kari Laitinen

class  Person
{
   public  String  person_name ;
   public  int     year_of_birth ;
   public  String  country_of_origin ;

   public void print_person_data()
   {
      System.out.print( "\n    " + person_name  + " was born in "
                     +  country_of_origin  + " in " + year_of_birth ) ;
   }
}

class  PersonTest
{
   public static void main( String[] not_in_use )
   {
      Person  computing_pioneer  =  new  Person() ;

      computing_pioneer.person_name        =  "Alan Turing" ;
      computing_pioneer.year_of_birth      =  1912 ;
      computing_pioneer.country_of_origin  =  "England" ;

      Person  another_computing_pioneer  =  new  Person() ;

      another_computing_pioneer.person_name        =  "Konrad Zuse" ;
      another_computing_pioneer.year_of_birth      =  1910 ;
      another_computing_pioneer.country_of_origin  =  "Germany" ;

      computing_pioneer.print_person_data() ;
      another_computing_pioneer.print_person_data() ;
   }
}
```

The fields inside a **Person** object can be referred to by using the dot operator (.) which is also used when methods are called for objects.

**Person.java - 1. A class that has public data fields.**

```
D:\javafiles3>java PersonTest

   Alan Turing was born in England in 1912
   Konrad Zuse was born in Germany in 1910
```

The class name **PersonTest** is written on the command line because that class contains the **main()** method.

**Person.java - X. These lines are printed by calling method print_person_data() twice.**

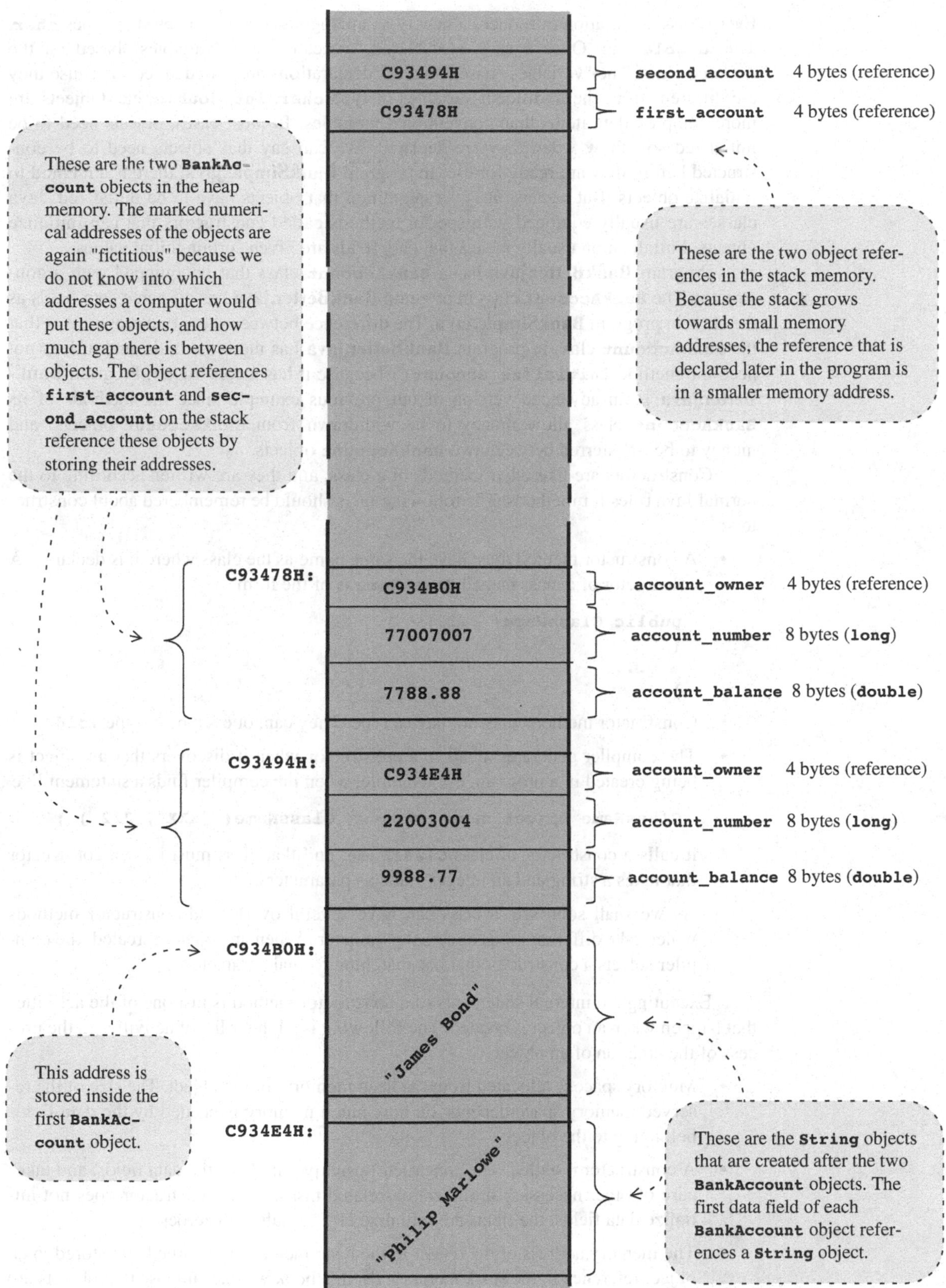


***Figure 10-2. The objects of program BankSimple.java in the main memory.***

## 10.2 Constructors are methods that build objects

Every class declaration introduces a new type, analogous to the basic built-in types **char**, **int**, **double**, etc. Once a class is declared, we can create "variables" based on the declared class. The "variables" based on class declarations are called objects because they are different from the traditional variables of type **char**, **int**, **double**, etc. Objects are more complex data items than conventional variables. In most cases, objects need to be initialized somehow when they are declared. We can say that objects need to be constructed before they are ready for use. In program **BankSimple.java**, there is a method to initialize objects. But because it is very common that objects have to be initialized, Java classes are usually equipped with special methods called constructors that can initialize objects. Initialization usually means that data fields are given certain initial values.

Program **BankBetter.java** has a **BankAccount** class that is equipped with a constructor. The **BankAccount** class in program **BankBetter.java** has the same data fields as the class in program **BankSimple.java**. The difference between these two programs is that the **BankAccount** class in program **BankBetter.java** has more methods, and it does not need the method **initialize_account()** because it has a constructor. Program **BankBetter.java** is an advanced version of our previous example since the methods of its **BankAccount** class allow money to be withdrawn from **BankAccount** objects, and money to be transferred between two **BankAccount** objects.

Constructors are like other methods of a class, and they are written according to the normal Java rules for methods. The following facts should be remembered about constructors:

- A constructor method must have the same name as the class where it is declared. A constructor of a class named **ClassName** is of the form

```
public ClassName( ... )
{
   ...
}
```

- Constructor methods may not have a type. They cannot even be of type **void**.
- The compiler generates a call to a constructor when it discovers that an object is being created in a program. For example, when the compiler finds a statement like

```
ClassName object_name  =  new  ClassName( "XXX", 222 ) ;
```

  it calls a constructor of class **ClassName**, and that class must have a constructor that takes a string and an integer value as parameters.
- As we shall soon see, a class can have several overloaded constructor methods which take different kinds of actual parameters.When an object is created, the compiler selects a constructor that has matching formal parameters.

Executing the internal statements of a constructor method is just one of the activities that happen when an object is created. The following is a longer list of activities in the process of the creation of an object

- Memory space is allocated from the heap memory for the object. The size of the reserved memory space depends on how much memory is needed by the data fields belonging to the object.
- A constructor is called. The constructor usually initializes the data fields, and takes care of other necessary initialization-related tasks. If the constructor does not initialize data fields, the fields are initialized by default with zeroes.
- The memory address of the object in the heap memory is returned and stored in an object reference in the stack memory. (In this book we can suppose that objects are referenced so that their addresses are stored in object references. This kind of logi-

cal thinking is correct from a programmer's point of view although the actual management of objects were more complicated. In reality, depending on how the used Java virtual machine and the automatic memory management system work, an object reference may store an indirect address to an object.)

You may already have wondered that how it is possible that the program **BankSimple.java** contains statements like

```
BankAccount  first_account   =  new  BankAccount() ;
```

where there is clearly a constructor call, but the class `BankAccount` of program **BankSimple.java** does not have a constructor. The explanation of this inconsistency is that if there is no constructors declared in a class, the compiler automatically generates a so-called default constructor that can be called without supplying any parameters. The compiler generates these constructors in programs **BankSimple.java** and **Rectangles.java** where the classes do not have any constructor methods. The compiler-generated default constructors do not actually do anything. They just fulfill the requirement that here has to be a constructor in every class. It is also important to note that the default constructors are not generated if there is a constructor in a class. Therefore, if you try to insert the above statement into the `main()` method of program **BankBetter.java**, it will not work. It works only in **BankSimple.java** where no constructors are present.

Constructors are needed to build objects, but usually no special methods are needed to destroy objects. When an object is created inside a method in the following way

```
public void some_method( ... )
{
   SomeClass  some_object  =  new  SomeClass( ... ) ;
   ...
}
```

the object resides in the heap memory and `some_object` references (or points to) the object. When `some_method()` terminates, all its local data including the object reference `some_object` ceases to exist. The memory space reserved for local data is released from the stack memory when a method terminates. Thus, when `some_method()` above reaches its end, `some_object` simply stops referencing the object in the heap memory, and the object becomes an unnecessary object that is not referenced any more. In such a situation, the object does not need to exist in the heap memory. Therefore, a separate memory management mechanism called the garbage collector sees to it that the object is removed from the heap memory and its memory space is freed for other purposes. The garbage collector is a background program that runs automatically together with Java programs and takes care of automatic memory management activities.

A method that has the same name as the class itself is a constructor method of the class. The compiler generates a call to a constructor when an object is created. Constructors are typeless methods. Not even the type **void** may be specified for them. This constructor simply copies the values of its parameters to the fields of the class.

```
//  BankBetter.java   (c) 2005 Kari Laitinen

class  BankAccount
{
   String  account_owner ;
   long    account_number ;
   double  account_balance ;

   public BankAccount( String  given_account_owner,
                       long    given_account_number,
                       double  initial_balance )
   {
      account_owner    =  given_account_owner ;
      account_number   =  given_account_number ;
      account_balance  =  initial_balance  ;
   }

   public void show_account_data()
   {
      System.out.print( "\n\nB A N K   A C C O U N T   D A T A : "
                      + "\n   Account owner :  "  +  account_owner
                      + "\n   Account number:  "  +  account_number
                      + "\n   Current balance: "  +  account_balance ) ;
   }

   public void deposit_money( double amount_to_deposit )
   {
      System.out.print( "\n\nTRANSACTION FOR ACCOUNT OF " +  account_owner
                      +  " (Account number " +  account_number  + ")" ) ;
      System.out.print( "\n   Amount deposited: "  +  amount_to_deposit
                     +  "\n  Old account balance: "  +  account_balance ) ;
      account_balance  =  account_balance  +  amount_to_deposit ;
      System.out.print( "   New balance: "  +  account_balance  ) ;
   }
```

These two methods are the same as in program **BankSimple.java**.

**BankBetter.java - 1: A program with a BankAccount class that has a constructor.**

There must be enough money for the withdrawal.

```
public void withdraw_money( double amount_to_withdraw )
{
   System.out.print( "\n\nTRANSACTION FOR ACCOUNT OF " + account_owner
         + "  (Account number " +  account_number  + ")" ) ;

   if ( account_balance  <  amount_to_withdraw )
   {
      System.out.print("\n    -- Transaction not completed: "
            + "Not enough money to withdraw " + amount_to_withdraw ) ;
   }
   else
   {
      System.out.print("\n    Amount withdrawn:     "  +  amount_to_withdraw
            + "\n    Old account balance: "  +  account_balance ) ;
      account_balance  =  account_balance  -  amount_to_withdraw ;
      System.out.print("    New balance: "  +  account_balance ) ;
   }
}

public void transfer_money_to( BankAccount  receiving_account,
                               double       amount_to_transfer )
{
   System.out.print( "\n\nTRANSACTION FOR ACCOUNT OF " +  account_owner
         + "  (Account number "+  account_number  +")" ) ;

   if ( account_balance  >=  amount_to_transfer )
   {
      receiving_account.account_balance  =
         receiving_account.account_balance  +  amount_to_transfer ;

      System.out.print(
           "\n   " + amount_to_transfer + " was transferred to "
         +  receiving_account.account_owner  +  " (Account no. "
         +  receiving_account.account_number +  ")."
         +  "\n    Balance before transfer: " +  account_balance ) ;
      account_balance  =  account_balance  -  amount_to_transfer ;
      System.out.print( "    New balance:  " +  account_balance ) ;
   }
   else
   {
      System.out.print( "\n    -- Not enough money for transfer." ) ;
   }
}
}
```

This statement transfers money from "this" account to a receiving account. **receiving_account** is a reference to a **BankAccount** object that is given as a parameter for this method. Because this is a method of class **BankAccount**, it is allowed to access the data fields of another **BankAccount** object by using the syntax
**object_reference_name.data_field_name**

**BankBetter.java - 2: The other part of class BankAccount.**

Here two **BankAccount** objects are created. When the Java compiler sees these **new** operations, it generates calls to the constructor method of class **BankAccount**, and passes the data given in parentheses as parameters to the constructor method.

An object reference is given as a parameter for method **transfer_-money_to()**. Inside the method, **jazz_player_account** is referenced with reference **receiving_account**, and **moon_walker_account** is the "this" account, the account for which the method was called.

```
class BankBetter
{
   public static void main( String[] not_in_use )
   {
      BankAccount  jazz_player_account =
                 new  BankAccount( "Louis Armstrong", 121212, 0 ) ;
      BankAccount  moon_walker_account  =
                 new  BankAccount( "Neil Armstrong",  191919,
                                                      7777.77 ) ;
      jazz_player_account.deposit_money( 3333.33 ) ;

      jazz_player_account.withdraw_money( 4444.44 ) ;

      moon_walker_account.transfer_money_to( jazz_player_account,
                                             2222.22 ) ;

      moon_walker_account.show_account_data() ;
      jazz_player_account.show_account_data() ;
   }
}
```

**BankBetter.java - 3. Method main() that creates and uses two BankAccount objects.**

## Exercises with program BankBetter.java

Exercise 10-1. Write a new method **withdraw_all_money()** to class **BankAccount** in program **BankBetter.java**. The new method should take out all the money from a **BankAccount** object. It should also inform the user how much money was withdrawn. The following method calls could be written in method **main()** to test the new method

```
jazz_player_account.withdraw_all_money() ;
moon_walker_account.withdraw_all_money() ;
```

Exercise 10-2. Write a new method **transfer_money_from()** to class **BankAccount** in program **BankBetter.java**. The new method should transfer money from the other account to "this" account. It should move money in the opposite direction to the direction that the existing method **transfer_money_to()** moves. The new method could be called from method **main()** in the following way

```
jazz_player_account.transfer_money_from(

                        moon_walker_account, 333.33 ) ;
```

```
D:\javafiles3>java BankBetter

TRANSACTION FOR ACCOUNT OF Louis Armstrong (Account number 121212)
   Amount deposited: 3333.33
   Old account balance: 0.0   New balance: 3333.33

TRANSACTION FOR ACCOUNT OF Louis Armstrong (Account number 121212)
   -- Transaction not completed: Not enough money to withdraw 4444.44

TRANSACTION FOR ACCOUNT OF Neil Armstrong (Account number 191919)
   2222.22 was transferred to Louis Armstrong (Account no. 121212).
   Balance before transfer: 7777.77   New balance:  5555.550000000001

B A N K   A C C O U N T   D A T A :
   Account owner :  Neil Armstrong
   Account number:  191919
   Current balance: 5555.550000000001

B A N K   A C C O U N T   D A T A :
   Account owner :  Louis Armstrong
   Account number:  121212
   Current balance: 5555.549999999999
```

**BankBetter.java - X. The output of the program is always the same.**

## Destructors do not exist in Java

Some other programming languages (e.g. C++) have classes that contain destructors in addition to constructors. Destructors are methods that are called when objects are destroyed. So, if you are familiar with C++, you might expect me to explain something about destructors. Unfortunately, or luckily, there is nothing to be explained because destructors do not belong to Java classes. As the automatic memory management system with the Garbage Collector automatically destroys objects which are no longer referenced, there is no need to have destructors in Java classes.

Because, in large and complicated programs, it is possible that something has to be done to objects before they are destroyed from the heap memory, Java provides a possibility to write a method that will be called automatically before an object is destroyed. The name of such a method must be **finalize()** and it is written like this

```
public void finalize()
{
   // Actions needed before the destruction of an object.

}
```

If you put this kind of method to a class, the method will be called automatically before the Garbage Collector destroys the object and deallocates the memory space of the object.

In the programs of this book, we are not going to use **finalize()** methods. If you need more information on this topic, please take a look at program **ObjectClassTests.java** in the **javafilesextra** folder.

## 10.3 Several constructors in a class

The overloading of method names was a subject discussed in Chapter 9. Overloading means that two or more methods may have the same name if their parameters differ sufficiently. The Java compiler can make a distinction between two methods with the same name if parameters have different types, or there is a different number of parameters. Let us, for example, suppose that we have two methods with the declarators

```
void print_numbers( int first_number, int second_number )
void print_numbers( int some_number )
```

If there was the method call

```
print_numbers( 77 ) ;
```

in some other method in the same class, the compiler would call the latter method above, because that takes a single parameter of type **int**.

Overloading is very common in the case of constructor methods. Classes often need to have several constructors because objects need to be constructed in different ways. As the constructor method must always have the same name as the class itself, constructor methods must be overloaded when several constructors are needed.

Program **Animals.java** contains a class declaration that has two constructors. The name of the class is **Animal**. **Animal** objects are quite fictitious, bearing little similarity to real animals. **Animal** objects are such that they can be fed and made to speak. When an **Animal** object is fed, it takes food into its stomach in the form of a string. When an **Animal** object is made to speak, it tells its species' name and what it has eaten. The data fields of class **Animal** are two strings that contain the name of the animal species and maintain information about stomach contents.

The declarators of the two constructors of class **Animal** are

```
public Animal( String  given_species_name )
public Animal( Animal  another_animal )
```

The compiler can distinguish these two methods having the same name since their parameters are of a different type. The first method takes a string reference as a parameter. The latter method takes a reference to type **Animal**. The first constructor initializes the **Animal** object with the given species name. The latter method makes a new copy of the other **Animal** object. It is possible to duplicate, or clone, **Animal** objects with the latter constructor. (Cloning real animals is much more difficult and dubious.)

Constructors that make copies of objects are called copy constructors. The latter constructor above is a copy constructor. It is very common, and sometimes even necessary, that classes are equipped with copy constructors. The copy constructor of a class takes a single parameter that is a reference to an object of the class itself. Thus, the copy constructor inside class **SomeClass** would look like

```
class SomeClass
{
   // declarations of data fields

   public SomeClass( SomeClass object_to_be_copied )
   {
      ...
   }
   // other constructors and methods
}
```

Another common constructor is the default constructor. Default constructors do not require any parameters. If the hypothetical class **SomeClass** above were equipped with the constructor

```
public SomeClass()
{
   ...
}
```

the class would have a default constructor. As was discussed earlier, the compiler automatically generates a default constructor if no constructors are declared in a class.

## Exercises with program Animals.java

Exercise 10-3. Add the new data field

```
String  animal_name ;
```

to class **Animal** in program **Animals.java**. You have to modify the first constructor of the class so that an **Animal** object can be created by writing

```
Animal  named_cat  =  new  Animal( "cat", "Ludwig" ) ;
```

You also need to modify the copy constructor so that it copies the new data field. Method **make_speak()** must be modified so that it prints something like

```
Hello, I am a cat called Ludwig.
I have eaten: ...
```

Exercise 10-4. Modify method **make_speak()** in program **Animals.java** so that it prints something like

```
Hello, I am ...
My stomach is empty.
```

in the case when **stomach_contents** references just an empty string. The stomach is empty as long as method **feed()** has not been called for an **Animal** object. You can use the standard string method **length()** to check if the stomach is empty. Method **length()** can be used, for example, in the following way

```
if ( stomach_contents.length() == 0 )
{
   // stomach_contents references an empty string.
   ...
```

Exercise 10-5. Write a default constructor for class **Animal** in program **Animals.java**. A default constructor is such that it can be called without giving any parameters. The default constructor should initialize the data fields so that the program lines

```
Animal  some_animal  =  new  Animal();
some_animal.make_speak() ;
```

would produce the following output on the screen

```
Hello, I am a default animal called no name.
...
```

Exercise 10-6. Write a new method named **make_stomach_empty()** to class **Animal** in **Animals.java**. The new method could be called

```
animal_object.make_stomach_empty() ;
```

and it should make **stomach_contents** reference an empty string "".

The encapsulated data inside objects of class **Animal** consist of the name of the animal species, and of a stomach where food is put when an **Animal** object is fed.

```
//  Animals.java  (c) Kari Laitinen

class  Animal
{
   String  species_name ;
   String  stomach_contents ;

   public Animal( String  given_species_name )
   {
      species_name      =  given_species_name ;
      stomach_contents  =  "" ;
   }

   public Animal( Animal  another_animal )
   {
      species_name      =  another_animal.species_name ;
      stomach_contents  =  another_animal.stomach_contents ;
   }

   public void feed( String  food_for_this_animal )
   {
      stomach_contents  =
          stomach_contents  +  food_for_this_animal  +  ", "  ;
   }

   public void make_speak()
   {
      System.out.print( "\n Hello, I am a " + species_name     + "."
                      + "\n I have eaten: " + stomach_contents + "\n" ) ;
   }
}
```

**Animal** objects are fed by concatenating (appending) the food string to previous stomach contents. Operator + joins a new string to the end of an existing string. **stomach_contents** references a new **String** object after this operation.

The second constructor simply copies the fields of the object referenced by **another_animal**. As **another_animal** references an **Animal** object, it is possible to access the object's data fields with the dot operator. Note that the name of "this" object, the object for which the constructor was called, is not visible inside methods. The names **species_name** and **stomach_contents** automatically refer to the data fields of "this" object.

To be accurate, this copy constructor does not make a deep copy of the object referenced by **another_animal**. After this constructor has done its job, both "this" object and the object referenced by **another_animal** reference the same **String** objects that represent the stomach contents and species name. However, when "this" object is fed later with method **feed()**, the **feed()** method makes **stomach_contents** reference a new **String** object.

**Animals.java - 1: Class Animal with two constructors and two other methods.**

The first constructor of class **Animal** is called when these statements create objects. The compiler finds out that a string literal is given as a parameter, and that type of parameter is accepted by the first constructor. That constructor initializes the stomachs of the **Animal** objects with an empty string.

```
class  Animals
{
   public static void main( String[] not_in_use )
   {
      Animal  cat_object  =  new Animal( "cat" ) ;
      Animal  dog_object  =  new Animal( "vegetarian dog" ) ;

      cat_object.feed( "fish" ) ;
      cat_object.feed( "chicken" ) ;

      dog_object.feed( "salad" ) ;
      dog_object.feed( "potatoes" ) ;

      Animal  another_cat  =  new Animal( cat_object ) ;

      another_cat.feed( "milk" ) ;

      cat_object.make_speak() ;
      dog_object.make_speak() ;
      another_cat.make_speak() ;
   }
}
```

When **another_cat** is made to speak here, it is no longer an identical copy of **cat_object** because it was fed with milk after the cloning operation.

This object creation invokes the second constructor of class **Animal**. The object referenced by **another_cat** becomes a shallow copy of the object referenced by **cat_object**. The copy operation is shallow because the **String** objects that are referenced by the fields **species_name** and **stomach_contents** are not duplicated.

**Animals.java - 2. Class Animals whose method main() creates and uses Animal objects.**

```
D:\javafiles3>java Animals

 Hello, I am a cat.
 I have eaten: fish, chicken,

 Hello, I am a vegetarian dog.
 I have eaten: salad, potatoes,

 Hello, I am a cat.
 I have eaten: fish, chicken, milk,
```

**Animals.java - X. All these lines are generated through calls to method make_speak().**

## 10.4 Arrays containing references to objects

An array is a data structure where many data items of the same type can be stored. We have already studied arrays of the basic types **char**, **int**, **double**, etc. For example, we get an array whose type is **int[]** when we first declare an array reference like

```
int[]  array_of_integers ;
```

and then create an array with the **new** operator in the following way

```
array_of_integers  =  new  int[ 50 ] ;
```

It is common to combine the array declaration and creation operations into a single statement like

```
int[]  array_of_integers  =  new  int[ 50 ] ;
```

By putting a pair of empty brackets [] after the type name, we tell the compiler that we want to declare an array.

We can also create arrays that are based on the classes that we have declared. It is possible to declare and create arrays of type **Rectangle**, arrays of type **BankAccount**, arrays of type **Animal**, and so on. These arrays can store objects. An array that is based on a class type can be declared and created in the same way as the array above. An array reference named **array_of_objects** can be specified with a statement like

```
SomeClass[]  array_of_objects ;
```

and the actual array is created with a statement like

```
array_of_objects  =  new  SomeClass[ 50 ] ;
```

Also these two statements can be replaced with the single statement

```
SomeClass[]  array_of_objects  =  new  SomeClass[ 50 ] ;
```

The statement above creates an array whose type is **SomeClass[]**, and 50 objects of type **SomeClass** can be referenced by the array elements. What is important to understand is that the above array creation operation does not create any objects of type **SomeClass**. Right after its creation, the array above is a data structure that does not contain any references to objects. In the Java terminology, we say that such an array contain **null** references. **null** in a reserved keyword that means "no object referenced". At the machine level, when a program is executing, the array elements that contain a **null** are set to zero, but at the source program level, we speak about **null**.

To make the above hypothetical array reference objects, one possibility is to create an object for each array element in the following way

```
array_of_objects[ 0 ]  =  new  SomeClass() ;
array_of_objects[ 1 ]  =  new  SomeClass() ;
array_of_objects[ 2 ]  =  new  SomeClass() ;
array_of_objects[ 3 ]  =  new  SomeClass() ;
...
```

As you can see, arrays that contain references to objects can be indexed in the same way as arrays of the basic types. The index value for the first array element is zero, and the largest possible index value is the length of the array minus one.

Program **Olympics.java** is an example that uses an array that contains references to **Olympics** objects. The name of the array reference is **olympics_table**. This name was chosen because these kinds of arrays resemble tables that we can find in books and magazines. If **olympics_table** were a table in a book, it could begin in the following way

| Olympic year | Olympic city | Olympic country |
|---|---|---|
| **1896** | **Athens** | **Greece** |
| **1900** | **Paris** | **France** |
| **1904** | **St. Louis** | **United States** |
| **...** | **...** | **...** |

The names of the columns in the above book-style table are the same as the field names in class **Olympics**, and each row corresponds to an **Olympics** object in the array referenced by **olympics_table**. When you work with arrays like the one in **Olympics.java**, it may be helpful to imagine a book-style table in your mind.

Figure 10-3 shows how the array referenced by **olympics_table** looks like in the main memory of a computer. Because two fields of class **Olympics**, **olympic_city** and **olympic_country**, are string references, each **Olympics** object references two **String** objects. Each **Olympics** object, in turn, is referenced by an array element in the array that is referenced by **olympics_table**.

A method of a class can be called (invoked) for an object referenced by an array element with the call syntax

**array_of_objects[** *index expression* **].method_name( ... ) ;**

The dot operator . can thus be used also in the case of array references. The value of the index expression determines which array element is selected. An array that contains references to objects can be indexed in the same way as the arrays we have studied before. To clarify the indexing mechanism, let's study some examples supposing that we have the **olympics_table** of program **Olympics.java** available:

- The method call

  ```
  olympics_table[ 5 ].print_olympics_data() ;
  ```

  would print the data of year 1912 Olympics in Stockholm, Sweden.

- The method call

  ```
  olympics_table[ 2 ].get_year()
  ```

  would return value 1904.

- The **if** construct

  ```
  if ( olympics_table[ olympics_index + 1 ].get_year() == 9999)
  {
     ...
  ```

  would test if the **olympic_year** of the object referenced by the next array position is 9999.

- If the value of **olympics_index** is 9, the method call

  ```
  olympics_table[ olympics_index - 1 ].print_olympics_data() ;
  ```

  would print the data of year 1928 Olympics in Amsterdam, The Netherlands.

- The method call

  ```
  olympics_table[ 31 ].get_year()
  ```

  would generate a **NullPointerException** because there is a **null** in the 32th position in **olympics_table**. The **null** means that no object is referenced from that array position.

When an array is used in a program, the array is usually filled starting from the beginning of the array. Then, while processing the data in an array, it is usually necessary to test if the end of meaningful data of an array has been encountered. In program **Olympics.java**, the end of meaningful data is marked with a special **`Olympics`** object whose **`olympic_year`** is 9999. The array referenced by **`olympics_table`** has thus the following structure

- The array positions with indexes from 0 to 27 contain references to "real" **`Olympics`** objects.
- The array position with index value 28 references a "surreal" **`Olympics`** object whose purpose is to mark the end of the data.
- The array positions with indexes from 29 to 39 contain **`null`** values (zeroes) which were automatically written to these positions when the array was created. Because no objects were created for these positions, the **`null`** values remained. Also the other array positions were originally set to **`null`**, but these **`null`** values were overwritten when the **`Olympics`** objects were created.

Marking the end of meaningful data with special values is one possible way to make an array store data. Programs **Convert.java** and **Planets.java**, which you can find after **Olympics.java**, are examples that demonstrate two other ways for marking the end of meaningful data. In program **Convert.java**, the array referenced by **`conversion_table`** is such that it does not contain any **`null`** references. The array in **Convert.java** is thus full of meaningful data, and the meaningful data ends when the array ends. The end of the array in **Convert.java** is detected by using the data field **`length`** that belongs to every array in Java. The array in **Planets.java** is like the array of **Olympics.java** in that both arrays contain **`null`** references in those positions that come after the meaningful data. In **Planets.java**, the end of meaningful data is detected when the first **`null`** value is encountered in the array.

Arrays in Java are such that their length, the value stored by the **`length`** field, cannot be altered. The length of an array is the number of array elements. The array length is fixed when an array is created. For example, the statement

```
SomeClass[] array_name  =  new  SomeClass[ some_integer ] ;
```

creates an array whose length is the same as the value of variable **`some_integer`** at the moment when the array is created. If the value of **`some_integer`** is increased later, the length of the array referenced by **`array_name`** does not change. If the length of an array must be increased in a program, one possible way to solve the problem is to create a new longer array, copy all elements from the old array to the new array, and finally make the original array name reference the new array.

## Exercises related arrays containing object references

Exercise 10-7. Modify program **Olympics.java** so that you remove the "surreal" **`Olympics`** object whose **`olympic_year`** is 9999 from the array referenced by **`olympics_table`**. The end of olympics data in the modified program should be detected in the same way as in program **Planets.java**, i.e., the first **`null`** reference in the array marks the end of meaningful data.

Exercise 10-8. By using program **Olympics.java** as an example, write a program that gives information about your favorite sports. For example, if you are interested in football, soccer, basketball, or ice-hockey, you can write a program that can inform which team was the champion in a given year. If your interest is car racing, you can write a program that knows which driver and which team were the champions in a given year.

We have learned that the double slash // is a mechanism for writing comments in Java programs. The pairs of characters /* and */ provide another possibility to write comments. The character pair /* marks the beginning of a comment. When the Java compiler sees the character pair /*, it discards all subsequent characters until it encounters the character pair */ which marks the end of the comment. The character pairs /* and */ are useful when we want to write long comments which occupy several lines of text.

```
/*  Olympics.java  Copyright (c) Kari Laitinen

    This program demonstrates the use of an array of
    objects, or, more precisely, an array that contains
    references to objects. The program first introduces
    a class named Olympics. An Olympics object can contain
    the data of olympic games. By using the class Olympics,
    an array named olympics_table is defined inside
    the main() method of class named OlympicsDataFinder.
    olympics_table is used to search data of olympic games.
*/

import java.util.* ;

class Olympics
{
   int     olympic_year  ;
   String  olympic_city ;
   String  olympic_country ;

   public Olympics( int     given_olympic_year,
                    String given_olympic_city,
                    String given_olympic_country )
   {
      olympic_year    =  given_olympic_year ;
      olympic_city    =  given_olympic_city ;
      olympic_country =  given_olympic_country ;
   }

   public int get_year()
   {
      return  olympic_year ;
   }

   public void print_olympics_data()
   {
      System.out.print( "\n    In " + olympic_year  +
              ", Olympic Games were held in " + olympic_city  +
              ", " + olympic_country  +  ".\n" ) ;
   }
}
```

The constructor of class **Olympics** copies its parameters to the corresponding fields of the class.

**get_year()** is a so-called accessor method with which it is possible to read one field of an object.

**Olympics.java - 1: The declaration of class Olympics.**

This statement both declares and creates an array that contains 40 references to **Olympics** objects. Immediately after the execution of this statement, the 40 references contain a **null** which means that they do not yet reference an object. This statement means the same as the two separate statements

```
Olympics[]  olympics_table ;
olympics_table  =  new  Olympics[ 40 ] ;
```

This and the rest of the statements on this page create 29 **Olympics** objects, and the references to the created objects are stored into the **olympics_table** positions with indexes from 0 to 28.

```
class  OlympicsDataFinder
{
   public static void main( String[] not_in_use )
   {
      Olympics[]  olympics_table  =  new Olympics[ 40 ] ;

      olympics_table[ 0 ] = new Olympics( 1896, "Athens",    "Greece" ) ;
      olympics_table[ 1 ] = new Olympics( 1900, "Paris",     "France" ) ;
      olympics_table[ 2 ] = new Olympics( 1904, "St. Louis", "U.S.A." );
      olympics_table[ 3 ] = new Olympics( 1906, "Athens",    "Greece"  ) ;
      olympics_table[ 4 ] = new Olympics( 1908, "London",    "Great Britain");
      olympics_table[ 5 ] = new Olympics( 1912, "Stockholm","Sweden" ) ;
      olympics_table[ 6 ] = new Olympics( 1920, "Antwerp",   "Belgium"   ) ;
      olympics_table[ 7 ] = new Olympics( 1924, "Paris",     "France"    ) ;
      olympics_table[ 8 ] = new Olympics( 1928, "Amsterdam","Netherlands");
      olympics_table[ 9 ] = new Olympics( 1932, "Los Angeles", "U.S.A.");
      olympics_table[ 10 ] = new Olympics( 1936, "Berlin",   "Germany"   ) ;
      olympics_table[ 11 ] = new Olympics( 1948, "London", "Great Britain");
      olympics_table[ 12 ] = new Olympics( 1952, "Helsinki","Finland"   ) ;
      olympics_table[ 13 ] = new Olympics( 1956, "Melbourne","Australia" ) ;
      olympics_table[ 14 ] = new Olympics( 1960, "Rome",      "Italy"    ) ;
      olympics_table[ 15 ] = new Olympics( 1964, "Tokyo",     "Japan"    ) ;
      olympics_table[ 16 ] = new Olympics( 1968, "Mexico City","Mexico" ) ;
      olympics_table[ 17 ] = new Olympics( 1972, "Munich",    "West Germany");
      olympics_table[ 18 ] = new Olympics( 1976, "Montreal", "Canada"   ) ;
      olympics_table[ 19 ] = new Olympics( 1980, "Moscow",    "Soviet Union");
      olympics_table[ 20 ] = new Olympics( 1984, "Los Angeles","U.S.A.");
      olympics_table[ 21 ] = new Olympics( 1988, "Seoul",     "South Korea");
      olympics_table[ 22 ] = new Olympics( 1992, "Barcelona","Spain"     ) ;
      olympics_table[ 23 ] = new Olympics( 1996, "Atlanta",   "U.S.A." );
      olympics_table[ 24 ] = new Olympics( 2000, "Sydney",    "Australia" ) ;
      olympics_table[ 25 ] = new Olympics( 2004, "Athens",    "Greece"   ) ;
      olympics_table[ 26 ] = new Olympics( 2008, "Beijing",   "China"    ) ;
      olympics_table[ 27 ] = new Olympics( 2012, "London",    "Great Britain");
      olympics_table[ 28 ] = new Olympics( 9999, "end of",    "data"   ) ;
```

This **Olympics** object is used to mark the end of real olympics data.

**Olympics.java - 2: olympics_table at the beginning of method main().**

This variable of type **boolean** is used to control the correct termination of the **while** loop.

Method **get_year()** is used to read the field **olympic_year** from the **Olympics** object whose reference is in the "current position" in the array referenced by **olympics_table**. The "current position" is determined by the value of **olympics_index**. The value returned by the **get_year()** method is compared to the value stored in the variable **given_year**.

```
      System.out.print("\n This program can tell where the Olympic "
                     + "\n Games were held in a given year. Give "
                     + "\n a year by using four digits: "    ) ;

      Scanner  keyboard   =  new Scanner( System.in ) ;
      int  given_year   =  keyboard.nextInt() ;

      int  olympics_index   =   0 ;

      boolean table_search_ready   =   false ;

      while ( table_search_ready    ==   false )
      {
         if ( olympics_table[ olympics_index ].get_year()    ==    given_year )
         {
            olympics_table[ olympics_index ].print_olympics_data() ;

            table_search_ready    =   true ;
         }
         else if ( olympics_table[ olympics_index ].get_year()    ==    9999 )
         {
            System.out.print(  "\n     Sorry, no Olympic Games were held in "
                             +  given_year   +  ".\n"  ) ;

            table_search_ready    =   true ;
         }
         else
         {
            olympics_index   ++   ;
         }
      }
   }
}
```

**Olympics.java - 3. The last part of method main() that performs a search in olympics_table.**

```
D:\javafiles3>java OlympicsDataFinder

 This program can tell where the Olympic
 Games were held in a given year. Give
 a year by using four digits: 1976

     In 1976, Olympic Games were held in Montreal, Canada.
```

**Olympics.java - X. Here the search for olympics data was successful.**

## Initializing data fields with initializers

Constructors are the usual means to build objects and initialize their data fields. Another possibility to initialize fields is to assign initial values when the fields are introduced in a class declaration. It is thus possible to declare a class in the following way

```
class  SomeClass
{
   int      some_integer_field  =  9 ;
   double   some_number         =  33.44 ;
   String   some_string_field   =  "initial text" ;
   int[]    some_integer_array  =  { 66, 77, 88 } ;
   ...
```

The initial values that are given to the fields of a class this way are called initializers. The values that the fields receive through initializers take effect before the constructors are executed. The fields are initialized in the order in which they are written in the class declaration.

Initializers are useful when a class has several constructors, and certain fields must be given certain initial values in every constructor. In such a situation the constructors are simplified if initial values are given by using initializers.

## The order of class members in a class declaration

Class members include data fields, constants, constructors, and methods. Constants are immutable data fields declared with the **final** keyword. The classes in the example programs of this book are written so that different kinds of class members are introduced in a certain order. The order is such that data fields are introduced before constructors and methods. The classes of this book thus have the structure

```
class  ClassName
{
   declarations of data fields and constants

   constructors

   accessor methods

   other methods
}
```

The Java compiler does not, however, require that class members are introduced in the above order. It is possible, for example, to declare a class so that data fields are introduced at the end of the class declaration. The class **Animal** of program **Animals.java** could thus alternatively be written in the following way

```
class  Animal
{
   public void feed( String  food_for_this_animal )
   { ...

   public void make_speak()
   { ...

   public Animal( String  given_species_name )
   { ...

   public Animal( Animal  another_animal )
   { ...

   String  species_name ;
   String  stomach_contents ;
}
```

Although the Java compiler does not set any strict rules for the order of class members in a class declaration, it is a good programming practice to always use a certain order of class members. The order of class members that is used in this book can be considered a logical order because the same order is used in UML class diagrams. (UML diagrams will be discussed in the following chapter.)

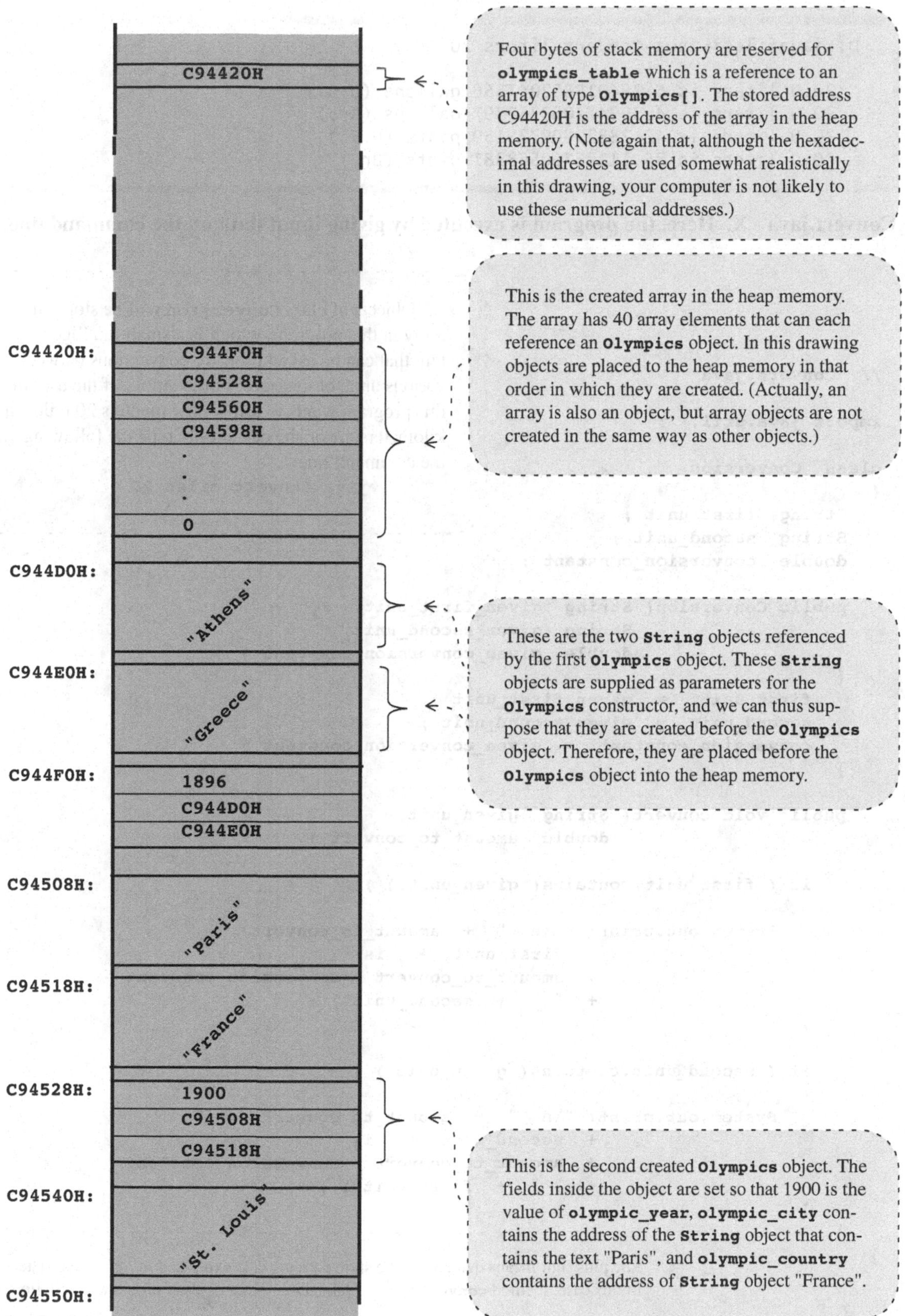


*Figure 10-3. The objects of program Olympics.java in the main memory.*

```
D:\javafiles3>java Convert liters 20

  20.0 liters is 5.284015852047556 gallons (U.S.)
  20.0 liters is 4.399472063352397 gallons (Br.)
  20.0 liters is 42.28329809725159 pints (U.S.)
  20.0 liters is 35.21126760563381 pints (Br.)
```

**Convert.java - X. Here, the program is executed by giving input data on the command line.**

Objects of class **Conversion** will be stored in an array in this program, which is a small intelligent system that can be asked to make conversions between various units of measure. For example, if the user of this program wants to know how much is 20 miles in kilometers, he or she can simply type the following on the command line

**java Convert miles 20**

```
//  Convert.java

import java.util.* ;

class  Conversion
{
   String  first_unit ;
   String  second_unit ;
   double  conversion_constant ;

   public Conversion( String  given_first_unit,
                      String  given_second_unit,
                      double  given_conversion_constant )
   {
      first_unit   =  given_first_unit ;
      second_unit  =  given_second_unit ;
      conversion_constant  =  given_conversion_constant ;
   }

   public void convert( String  given_unit,
                        double  amount_to_convert )
   {
      if ( first_unit.contains( given_unit ) )
      {
         System.out.print(  "\n  "  +  amount_to_convert  +  " "
                         +  first_unit  + " is "
                         +  amount_to_convert * conversion_constant
                         +  " "  +  second_unit ) ;
      }

      if ( second_unit.contains( given_unit ) )
      {
         System.out.print( "\n  "  +  amount_to_convert  +  " "
                         +  second_unit  + " is "
                         +  amount_to_convert / conversion_constant
                         +  " "  +  first_unit ) ;
      }
   }
}
```

The plus sign means that part of the shown program is explained in more detail later. In this case, method **convert()** is explained in a more explicit program description.

**Convert.java - 1+: A program to make conversions between units of measure.**

**conversion_table** references an array that contains references to **Conversion** objects. Each **Conversion** object contains the names of two units of measure, and a constant that tells how these two units relate to each other. The data with which the objects are initialized can be found in Physics books and almanacs. This line, for example, says that one mile is 1.609344 kilometers.

```
class  Convert
{
   public static void main( String[]  command_line_parameters )
   {
      Scanner  keyboard  =  new Scanner( System.in ) ;

      Conversion[]  conversion_table  =  new  Conversion[ 13 ] ;

      conversion_table[ 0 ] = new Conversion("meters", "yards", 1.093613 );
      conversion_table[ 1 ] = new Conversion("meters", "feet",   3.280840 );
      conversion_table[ 2 ] = new Conversion("miles",  "kilometers",1.609344);
      conversion_table[ 3 ] = new Conversion("inches", "centimeters", 2.54 );
      conversion_table[ 4 ] = new Conversion("acres",  "hectares", 0.4046873);
      conversion_table[ 5 ] = new Conversion("pounds", "kilograms",0.4535924);
      conversion_table[ 6 ] = new Conversion("ounces", "grams",       28.35 );
      conversion_table[ 7 ] = new Conversion("gallons (U.S.)","liters", 3.785);
      conversion_table[ 8 ] = new Conversion("gallons (Br.)", "liters", 4.546);
      conversion_table[ 9 ] = new Conversion("pints (U.S.)",  "liters", 0.473);
      conversion_table[ 10 ]= new Conversion("pints (Br.)",   "liters", 0.568);
      conversion_table[ 11 ]= new Conversion("joules",       "calories",4.187);
      conversion_table[ 12 ]= new Conversion("lightyears",   "kilometers",
                                                              9.461e12 ) ;
      String  unit_from_user ;
      int     amount_to_convert ;

      if ( command_line_parameters.length  ==  2 )
      {
         unit_from_user     =  command_line_parameters[ 0 ] ;
         amount_to_convert  =  Integer.parseInt(
                                   command_line_parameters[ 1 ] ) ;
      }
      else
      {
         System.out.print( "\n Give the unit to convert from: " ) ;
         unit_from_user  =  keyboard.nextLine() ;
         System.out.print( " Give the amount to convert:   " ) ;
         amount_to_convert  =  Integer.parseInt( keyboard.nextLine() ) ;
      }

      for ( int conversion_index  =  0 ;
                conversion_index  <  conversion_table.length ;
                conversion_index  ++ )
      {
         conversion_table[ conversion_index ].convert( unit_from_user,
                                                    amount_to_convert ) ;
      }
   }
}
```

**Convert.java - 2. The second part of the program.**

Method **convert()** is called from method **main()** for every created **Conversion** object in the array referenced by **conversion_table**. The method is called without caring whether or not the given unit is represented by the **Conversion** object in question. If the **convert()** method cannot convert the given unit, it does not print anything to the screen.

```
   public void convert( String  given_unit,
                        double  amount_to_convert )
   {
      if ( first_unit.contains( given_unit ) )
      {
         System.out.print(  "\n  " +  amount_to_convert  +  " "
                         +  first_unit  + " is "
                         +  amount_to_convert * conversion_constant
                         +  " "  +  second_unit ) ;
      }

      if ( second_unit.contains( given_unit ) )
      {
         System.out.print( "\n  " +  amount_to_convert  +  " "
                         +  second_unit  + " is "
                         +  amount_to_convert / conversion_constant
                         +  " "   +  first_unit ) ;
      }
   }
}
```

Method **contains()** returns the value **true** when the unit name stored by this object includes the unit string given as a parameter. This method attempts conversions from **first_unit** to **second_unit** and vice versa. Depending on which conversion is possible, either multiplication or division operation is used in conversion.

By using the method **contains()** instead of a more accurate string comparison method like **compareTo()**, it was possible to make this program more flexible. Although all the unit names inside the **Conversion** objects are in plural form (e.g. "pints"), the program also works when the user types in the units in singular form (e.g. "pint").

Instead of the **contains()** method it would be possible to use the **indexOf()** method. An alternative way to write the latter **if** construct would be:

```
if ( second_unit.indexOf( given_unit )  !=  -1 )
{
   ...
```

**indexOf()** is a string method that returns the index of the string that is given as a parameter. For example, if **second_unit** references the string "kilometers" and **given_unit** references the string "meter", the above call to method **indexOf()** returns 4 because the string "meter" starts in position with index 4 in the string "kilometers". **indexOf()** returns -1 when it cannot find the given substring.

**Convert.java - 1 - 1. Method convert() of class Conversion.**

This is the third example program in which an array of objects is used. The class **Planet** is declared here in the same way as the classes in previous example programs. Type **Planet** has 7 data fields.

```
//  Planets.java (c) 2005 Kari Laitinen

import java.util.* ;

class Planet
{
   String  planet_name ;
   double  mean_distance_from_sun ;
   double  circulation_time_around_sun ;
   double  rotation_time_around_own_axis ;
   long    equatorial_radius_in_kilometers ;
   double  mass_compared_to_earth ;
   int     number_of_moons ;

   public Planet( String  given_planet_name,
                  double  given_mean_distance_from_sun,
                  double  given_circulation_time_around_sun,
                  double  given_rotation_time_around_own_axis,
                  long    given_equatorial_radius_in_kilometers,
                  double  given_mass_compared_to_earth,
                  int     given_number_of_moons )
   {
      planet_name  =  given_planet_name ;
      mean_distance_from_sun  =  given_mean_distance_from_sun ;
      circulation_time_around_sun  =  given_circulation_time_around_sun ;
      rotation_time_around_own_axis  =  given_rotation_time_around_own_axis ;
      equatorial_radius_in_kilometers = given_equatorial_radius_in_kilometers ;
      mass_compared_to_earth  =  given_mass_compared_to_earth ;
      number_of_moons  =  given_number_of_moons ;
   }

   public String get_planet_name()
   {
      return  planet_name ;
   }

   public void print_planet_data()
   {
      System.out.print( "\n " + planet_name
                  +  " orbits the sun in average distance of "
                  +  ( mean_distance_from_sun * 149500000 ) + " kilometers."
                  +  "\n It takes "  +  circulation_time_around_sun
                  +  " years for " +  planet_name
                  +  " to go around the sun once. \n The radius of "
                  +  planet_name + " is "
                  +  equatorial_radius_in_kilometers  + " kilometers.\n" ) ;
   }
}
```

The planet name stored inside a **Planet** object needs to be read when planet information is processed. Therefore, the **Planet** class is equipped with an accessor method that returns a reference to **planet_name**.

**Planets.java - 1: A program that gives information about planets.**

**planet_table** references an array that has space for 30 references to **Planet** objects. However, only the first 9 elements of the array are set to reference a **Planet** object. The rest 21 elements of the array are automatically initialized with the value **null**, which means "no object is being referenced".

```
class  Planets
{
   public static void main( String[] not_in_use )
   {
      Scanner  keyboard  =  new Scanner( System.in ) ;

      //  Much of the information given in the following table is
      //  relative to the information concerning the Earth. E.g.,
      //  Pluto is 39.507 times further from the sun than the Earth.
      //  The data concerning the number of moons may be old.

      Planet[]  planet_table  =  new  Planet[ 30 ] ;

      planet_table[ 0 ] = new Planet(
          "Mercury",  0.387,   0.241,  58.815,  2433,   0.05,  0  ) ;
      planet_table[ 1 ] = new Planet(
          "Venus",    0.723,   0.615, 224.588,  6053,   0.82,  0  ) ;
      planet_table[ 2 ] = new Planet(
          "Earth",    1.000,   1.000,   1.000,  6379,   1.00,  1  ) ;
      planet_table[ 3 ] = new Planet(
          "Mars",     1.523,   1.881,   1.029,  3386,   0.11,  2  ) ;
      planet_table[ 4 ] = new Planet(
          "Jupiter",  5.203,  11.861,   0.411, 71370, 317.93, 12  ) ;
      planet_table[ 5 ] = new Planet(
          "Saturn",   9.541,  29.457,   0.428, 60369,  95.07, 10  ) ;
      planet_table[ 6 ] = new Planet(
          "Uranus",  19.190,  84.001,   0.450, 24045,  14.52,  5  ) ;
      planet_table[ 7 ] = new Planet(
          "Neptune", 30.086, 164.784,   0.657, 22716,  17.18,  2  ) ;
      planet_table[ 8 ] = new Planet(
          "Pluto",   39.507, 248.35,    6.410,  5700,   0.18,  0  ) ;
```

**Planets.java - 2: The second part of the program.**

```
D:\javafiles3>java Planets

 This program can give you information about the
 planets in our solar system. Give a planet name: mars

 Mars orbits the sun in average distance of 2.276885E8 kilometers.
 It takes 1.881 years for Mars to go around the sun once.
 The radius of Mars is 3386 kilometers.
```

**Planets.java - X. Some information about our neighbor planet.**

This **while** loop searches for the planet name in the table. The string method **contains()** is used to find out whether **planet_name_from_user** is a substring in the planet name string that is inside a **Planet** object. Both strings are converted temporarily to lowercase strings with the string method **toLowerCase()**. As the two strings are compared this way, the search is successful also when the user of the program types in a lowercase string (e.g. "mars") or a partially correct string (e.g. "mar"). Because the dot operator (.) is left-to-right associative, the method calls are executed in the order from left to right.

```
      System.out.print( "\n This program can give you information about the"
                + "\n planets in our solar system. Give a planet name: ");

      String  planet_name_from_user  =  keyboard.nextLine() ;

      int  planet_index  =  0 ;

      boolean table_search_ready  =  false ;

      while ( table_search_ready  ==  false )
      {
         if ( planet_table[ planet_index ].get_planet_name().toLowerCase()
                   .contains( planet_name_from_user.toLowerCase() ) )
         {
            planet_table[ planet_index ].print_planet_data() ;

            table_search_ready  =  true ;
         }
         else
         {
            planet_index  ++  ;

            if ( planet_table[ planet_index ]  ==  null )
            {
               System.out.print( "\n Sorry, could not find information on \""
                         +  planet_name_from_user  +  "\".\n" ) ;

               table_search_ready  =  true ;
            }
         }
      }
   }
}
```

While processing an array of objects, it is always necessary to check when the last object of the array is encountered. Those array elements that do not reference a **Planet** object contain a **null**, and that information is used here to check when it is time to stop processing the array. **null** is a reserved keyword of Java. Object references in an array contain a **null** when they are not made to point to an object. At the machine level, when a program is executing, the **null** value is a zero, but in programming we use the term **null**.

**Planets.java - 3. The third part of the program.**

## 10.5 Value types vs. reference types

We started studying computer programming in this book by examining simple programs that contain a few variables that can hold numerical values. Now we have ended up studying objects that usually contain several encapsulated data items. A clear difference between variables and objects is that they are allocated memory space from different parts of the main memory of a computer. Variables get their memory space from the stack memory, while objects are created with the **new** operator to the heap memory.

When we declare a variable inside a method in the following way

```
void some_method()
{
   int  some_variable ;

   ...
}
```

the variable is automatically allocated memory space from the stack when the method starts executing. When the program execution reaches the closing brace } of the method, i.e., when the method terminates, the memory space that is allocated for the variable from the stack is released, and the variable ceases to exist. Local data items, like the variable above, keep their memory space only as long as the method inside which they are declared is being executed.

When we write the following declaration inside some method

```
SomeClass  some_object ;
```

the compiler knows that **SomeClass** is a class type, and it allocates stack memory space for an object reference. Later on, when an object of **SomeClass** is created with a statement like

```
some_object  =  new  SomeClass( possible parameters ) ;
```

the object is created to the heap memory. The memory space that is reserved from the heap memory for the object is kept reserved as long as somebody is referencing the object.

Because a declaration like

```
int  some_variable ;
```

reserves stack memory to store a numerical value, types like **int** and other basic variable types can be called value types. Then, types like the classes that programmers can declare are said to be reference types because a declaration like

```
SomeClass  some_object ;
```

reserves stack memory to store a reference to an object in the heap memory. The Java compiler knows which types are value types and which types are reference types, and it can automatically arrange necessary space reservations from the stack.

It is important to note that all arrays are reference types, though arrays of value types and arrays of reference types are somewhat different. For example, the statement

```
int[] array_of_integers  =  new  int[ 50 ] ;
```

creates an array reference to the stack memory and the actual array to the heap memory. The array can store 50 values of type **int**. Then, the statement

```
SomeClass[] array_of_objects  =  new  SomeClass[ 50 ] ;
```

also creates an array reference to the stack memory and the actual array to the heap memory, but this array does not store values. It can store 50 references to objects of type **SomeClass**.

## 10.6 When objects become garbage

Let's suppose that there is the following kind of method

```
void some_method()
{
   SomeClass  some_object     =  new  SomeClass() ;
   SomeClass  another_object  =  new  SomeClass() ;
   ...
   another_object  =  some_object ;
   ...
}
```

which creates two objects at the beginning, and in the middle of the method the object reference **another_object** starts referencing the same object as the reference **some_object**. Then the question is: "What happens to the object that was originally referenced by **another_object**?" The answer is that, because the object is not being referenced any more, it becomes "garbage", and its memory space is freed by the so-called garbage collector, that is part of the automatic memory management mechanism. Thus, in the case of the above example, after the statement

```
another_object  =  some_object ;
```

has been executed, a background program called the garbage collector frees the memory space reserved for the object that **another_object** was referencing before the above statement.

The garbage collector is a system program that runs simultaneously with all Java programs. Its task is to take care of the heap memory. The garbage collector knows which parts of the heap memory are occupied by objects, and which parts are free. The garbage collector also maintains records about who is referencing the objects in the heap memory. When it detects that an object is not referenced any more, it considers that object as garbage, and frees the memory space of the object. The garbage collector may also move objects in the heap memory in order to defragment the memory and make space for larger objects and arrays. When the garbage collector moves objects to different memory locations, it automatically adjusts the references to the objects being moved.

Objects become garbage when they are not referenced any more. The theoretical method above is one example of how an object can become a non-referenced object. Another case is that a new object is created for an existing object reference. For example, the statements

```
SomeClass  some_object  =  new  SomeClass() ;

some_object  =  new  SomeClass() ;
```

create two objects, but the object created by the first statement becomes garbage immediately after its creation because the object reference **some_object** starts referencing the object created by the second statement.

In many cases, objects become non-referenced objects when the methods inside which they are created terminate. Object references declared inside a method are deallocated from the stack memory when the method terminates, and thereby the created objects are not referenced any more. It is, of course, possible that a method creates an object and makes some other object reference the created object. In such a situation, an object can survive after its creator method terminates. For example, method **feed()** in program **Animals.java** creates a new **String** object, and that object continues its existence after the termination of the **feed()** method because a field of the **Animal** object references the created **String** object.

## 10.7 A stack that grows dynamically

So far, we have studied objects that represent, for example, people's possessions (`BankAccount` objects), living creatures (`Animal` objects), and historical events (`Olympics` objects). One category of objects and classes that are widely used in object-oriented programming is objects and classes that represent various data structures such as arrays, queues, lists, and stacks. A stack is a data structure that is widely used as an example in textbooks of programming. It is, therefore, a kind of mandatory exercise to understand what a stack is, and in this section we will study a class named `Stack` that implements a software stack. Class `Stack` is also useful in that it shows how an object can increase its memory space dynamically.

The hardware stack used by processors inside computers has already been discussed in chapters 4 and 9. Processors have a hardware register, usually called Stack Pointer, that contains an address to a stack memory area in the main memory. The stack memory area is used mainly to allocate memory for local data items, and to store return addresses in method calls. The stack that we will study in this chapter is a software stack, but it works according to the same principles as hardware stacks.

A stack is a data structure that can contain many data items of the same type. In this sense, stacks are similar to arrays. The difference between a stack and an array is in how data items are put into and taken out from the two data structures. The following points characterize stacks:

- A stack can be empty. In some cases it can also be full.
- An operation called push inserts a new data item onto a stack. The new item is put on top of the stack. The push operation increases the number of items on the stack by one. A stack cannot be empty after a successful push operation.
- An operation called pop takes one data item away from a stack. The pop operation decreases the number of items on the stack by one. A stack can be empty after a pop operation. The pop operation fails if stack is empty.
- The pop operation always takes away the particular data item that is the last one pushed onto the stack. If a set of items is first pushed onto a stack and then popped away, they will come out in reverse order.

Program **Stack.java** shows how a stack can be implemented with software. The `Stack` class in program **Stack.java** implements a dynamic stack. The memory to store the data items is allocated from the heap. The size of the memory is increased dynamically if the `push()` operation finds out that the memory is too small. The dynamic memory, the heap, is used in the same way as in previous example programs. The physical stack, that is in the heap memory, is implemented as a normal Java array.

Method `push()` in program **Stack.java** always allocates an entirely new area of memory from the heap when the old memory space is full of data items. After a new memory space has been allocated, all data items from the old memory space are copied to the new space. The stack gradually grows this way, moving into a different place in the heap memory. How often the stack grows depends on a constant declared in the program. Now the stack grows in increments of four items, but if the `Stack` class were used in some real application, it might be better to increase the stack size in larger increments.

Figure 10-4 shows what the heap memory looks like when program **Stack.java** is executed by giving it those ten integers described in the program description. The initial stack memory space can store 4 items, the first enlarged memory space can store 8 items, and the final memory space is for 12 items. You should note, while studying Figure 10-4, that the memory area that is allocated for the stack object moves into different places in the heap memory. The old stack memory spaces become free memory areas which could again be taken into use in some other memory allocation operations.

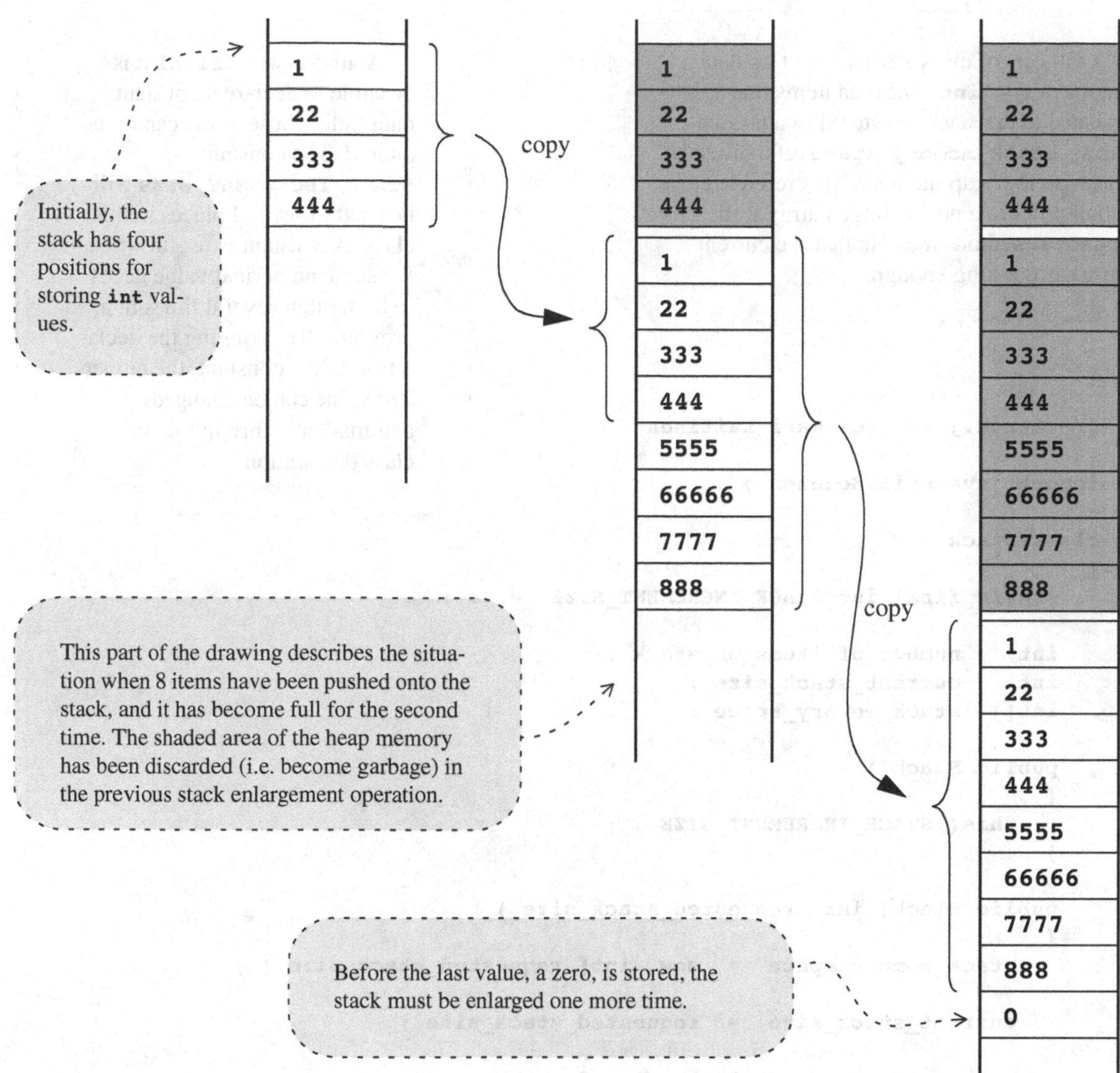


***Figure 10-4. The heap memory during the execution of program Stack.java.***

Objects of class **Stack** can store data items of type **int**. The data items that are pushed to the stack are stored in a normal array. **stack_memory_space** references the array in the heap memory. This reference shall point to a new enlarged array if the **push()** method finds out that the current array is not long enough.

With keyword **final** it is possible to declare a constant data field whose value cannot be altered. The constant **STACK_INCREMENT_SIZE** will be used in several places in this class. A constant is useful when the same numerical value needs to be written several times in a program. By changing the declaration of the constant, the numerical value can be changed automatically throughout the class declaration.

```
//  Stack.java  (c) Kari Laitinen

import java.util.Scanner ;

class Stack
{
   static final int STACK_INCREMENT_SIZE  =  4 ;

   int    number_of_items_on_stack ;
   int    current_stack_size ;
   int[]  stack_memory_space ;

   public Stack()
   {
      this( STACK_INCREMENT_SIZE ) ;
   }

   public Stack( int  requested_stack_size )
   {
      stack_memory_space  =  new  int[ requested_stack_size ] ;

      current_stack_size  =  requested_stack_size ;

      number_of_items_on_stack    =  0 ;
   }
```

This is the default constructor that can be called without supplying any parameters. By using a special syntax and the **this** keyword, the default constructor calls the other constructor of the class. The other constructor is called so that **STACK_INCREMENT_SIZE**, i.e. the numerical value 4, is supplied as a parameter. The initial stack size of a default **Stack** object is thus 4. The **this** keyword shall be discussed more thoroughly later.

This constructor reserves space for the requested number of items of type **int**. Initially, just after the creation of a stack object, the stack is empty, i.e., it contains zero data items.

**Stack.java - 1: The fields and constructors of class Stack.**

A local array reference is needed because, for a short while, this method must have both the old and the new memory space available.

**current_stack_size** is a field that contains information about the size (length) of the currently reserved memory space.

```
   public void push( int item_to_the_stack )
   {
      if ( number_of_items_on_stack  >=  current_stack_size  )
      {
         //  We must increase the memory space of this stack object.

         int[]  new_stack_memory_space ;

         new_stack_memory_space  =  new  int[ current_stack_size +
                                             STACK_INCREMENT_SIZE ] ;

         current_stack_size  =  current_stack_size
                                  + STACK_INCREMENT_SIZE ;

         //  We must copy the old stack contents to the new stack
         //  memory space.

         for ( int item_index  =  0  ;
                   item_index  <  number_of_items_on_stack ;
                   item_index  ++ )
         {
            new_stack_memory_space[ item_index ]  =
                                  stack_memory_space[ item_index ] ;
         }

         //  Let's make stack_memory_space reference the reserved
         //  new memory space. The old memory space shall be freed
         //  by the garbage collector as nobody is referencing that
         //  memory area any more.

         stack_memory_space  =  new_stack_memory_space ;

         System.out.print( " STACK HAS GROWN.\n" ) ;
      }

      //  Here we push the new value to the stack.

      stack_memory_space[ number_of_items_on_stack ]  =
                                        item_to_the_stack ;
      number_of_items_on_stack  ++  ;
   }
```

This data field knows how many items are currently stored in this **Stack** object. It also serves as an index to the first free location on the stack. The physical stack in the heap memory is like a normal array of type **int[]**.

**Stack.java - 2: Method push() of class Stack.**

The return type of method **pop()** is **int** because it has to deliver a value of type **int** to its caller.

The **pop()** operation copies the topmost item from the stack for the calling program. After the **pop()** operation, the item does not, in any logical sense, exist any more on the stack, though it remains in the physical stack memory space.

```
   public int pop()
   {
      int  item_from_the_stack ;

      if  ( number_of_items_on_stack  ==  0 )
      {
         System.out.print( "\n ERROR: Attempt to pop on empty stack !\n" ) ;
         item_from_the_stack  =  -1 ;
      }
      else
      {
         number_of_items_on_stack  -- ;
         item_from_the_stack  =
                 stack_memory_space[ number_of_items_on_stack ] ;
      }

      return  item_from_the_stack ;
   }

   public boolean stack_is_not_empty()
   {
      return  ( number_of_items_on_stack  >  0  ) ;
   }
}
```

This method returns true if there is still something to be popped from the stack.

**Stack.java - 3: Methods pop() and stack_is_not_empty() of class Stack.**

## Exercise with program Stack.java

Exercise 10-9. A stack is a data structure that is frequently used as an example in textbooks of computer programming. Although it is quite difficult to find simple and practical applications where stacks could be used, a stack may be useful in some special applications like computer games. And a stack controlled by hardware is a fundamentally important data structure for the operation of a computer.

To investigate the operation of a stack, modify method **main()** of program **Stacks.java** so that it stores the numbers typed in by the user in one of two different stacks depending on whether the numbers are even or odd. You should create two **Stack** objects (e.g. **even_stack** and **odd_stack**) in the program. The program should print the two stacks in separate loops at the end. For example, if the user typed in numbers

```
1  2  33  44  66  77  99  100  111  222  333  444  0
```

the program should respond

```
0  444  222  100  66  44  2   333  111  99  77  33  1
```

When a `Stack` object is created like this, the constructor uses the default stack size 4 when it allocates the initial memory space. If the object were created

```
Stack  test_stack  =  new  Stack( 20 ) ;
```

there would be initially space for 20 data items of type `int`.

```
class StackTester
{
   public static void main( String[] not_in_use )
   {
      Scanner keyboard = new Scanner( System.in ) ;

      int  value_to_the_stack ;
      int  value_popped_from_the_stack ;

      Stack  test_stack  =  new  Stack() ;

      System.out.print( "\n Let's test a stack. Please, type in integers."
            +  "\n I will push those numbers onto a stack, and later"
            +  "\n take them away from the stack. I will stop reading"
            +  "\n numbers when you type in a zero."
            +  "\n Please, press <Enter> after each number. \n\n" ) ;

      do
      {
         System.out.print( " Give a number:   " ) ;
         value_to_the_stack   =  keyboard.nextInt() ;

         test_stack.push( value_to_the_stack ) ;
      }
       while   ( value_to_the_stack  !=  0  ) ;

      System.out.print( "\n The numbers popped from the stack are:\n\n " ) ;

      while ( test_stack.stack_is_not_empty() )
      {
         value_popped_from_the_stack  =  test_stack.pop() ;

         System.out.print( value_popped_from_the_stack  +  "   "  ) ;
      }

      System.out.print( "\n" ) ;
   }
}
```

The object reference `test_stack` goes out of scope here. That means that the `Stack` object in the heap memory is not referenced any more, and the garbage collector can free the memory area that has been allocated for the `Stack` object.

Values are popped from the `Stack` object referenced by `test_stack` as long as there is something to take away from the stack.

**Stack.java - 4. Method main() that calls methods push() and pop() for a Stack object.**

```
D:\javafiles3>java StackTester

 Let's test a stack. Please, type in integers.
 I will push those numbers onto a stack, and later
 take them away from the stack. I will stop reading
 numbers when you type in a zero.
 Please, press <Enter> after each number.

 Give a number:  1
 Give a number:  22
 Give a number:  333
 Give a number:  444
 Give a number:  5555
 STACK HAS GROWN.
 Give a number:  66666
 Give a number:  7777
 Give a number:  888
 Give a number:  0
 STACK HAS GROWN.

 The numbers popped from the stack are:

 0   888   7777   66666   5555   444   333   22   1
```

Method **push()** always prints the text "STACK HAS GROWN." when it increases the memory space of the stack. That output statement should be removed from the **push()** method if class **Stack** is used in some more serious application.

**Stack.java - X. The program is executed here by typing in 9 integers from the keyboard.**

## Pseudo-code

Sometimes it is useful to describe methods, loops, or other program constructs with so-called pseudo-code. Writing a piece of program with pseudo-code means that you write the program with a language that is something between a programming language and a natural language. Describing a program with pseudo-code may clarify your thoughts, and help you to understand and create programs. Especially in the beginning of the process of program creation, it may be helpful to write down your thoughts in pseudo-code. While writing pseudo-code, you can use the Java reserved words like **if**, **else**, **while**, and **for** to specify the **if** constructs and loops that are needed in the program, but at the same time you can use English or other natural-language sentences to describe what should happen in the program.The last **while** loop in method **main()** of program **Stack.java** can be described with pseudo-code in the following way

```
while ( There is still at least one data item available
        on the stack )
{
   Pop an item from the stack.

   Print the data item to the screen.
}
```

## What does System.out.print() actually mean?

Now, that we have studied the basics of Java classes, you can understand more profoundly the method calls

```
System.out.print( actual parameters ) ;
System.out.printf( actual parameters ) ;
```

If you study the electronic Java documentation dealing with the **System** class, which belongs to the **java.lang** package of classes, you will discover that the class has a public and static field named **out**. The type of the **out** field is **PrintStream**. Thus, when you write **System.out**, you refer to an object of type **PrintStream**. The **PrintStream** object that can be referenced this way is created automatically when the Java interpreter (the Java virtual machine) starts operating, and the object represents the standard output stream, which means in practice the screen of your computer.

The methods **print()** and **printf()**, which we have called many times for the object referenced by **System.out**, are methods of the standard Java class **PrintStream**. If you take a look at the electronic documentation of class **PrintStream**, you'll find out that there are several versions of both the **print()** and **printf()** methods. In addition, the **PrintStream** class provides many versions of the **println()** method which functions like **print()** except that it always adds line termination characters to the end of printed data.

The static **out** field of class **System** is marked with the keyword **final**, which means that its value cannot be changed with an assignment statement. The **System** class provides, however, a method named **setOut()** with which it is possible to change the standard output stream, for example, so that everything that would normally be printed to the screen would be output to a file.

## The mysterious Scanner object referenced by the name keyboard

In this book, we have at the beginning of those **main()** methods which read data from the keyboard the line

```
Scanner keyboard = new Scanner( System.in ) ;
```

Now, that we know the basic structure of Java classes, we can analyze this statement. The statement

- declares an object reference of type **Scanner**,
- creates a **Scanner** object with the **new** operator so that **System.in** is given as a parameter to the constructor of class **Scanner**, and
- makes **keyboard** reference the created **Scanner** object.

The parameter **System.in** that is supplied to the **Scanner** constructor references an existing object. **in** is a static field in the standard class **System**, and the type of the **in** field is **InputStream**. **System.in** refers to an **InputStream** object that is created automatically when the Java interpreter (Java virtual machine) starts operating. The object referenced by **System.in** represents the standard input stream, which in practice means the keyboard of your computer. Therefore, the above statement creates a **Scanner** object that scans the keyboard.

We have already learned to use methods like **nextInt()** and **nextLine()** to read data from the keyboard. These methods are provided by the standard class **Scanner**. If you read the electronic documentation of the **Scanner** class, which belongs to the **java.util** package, you'll see all the methods provided by the class. You will also discover that the **Scanner** class can also be used to scan data sources other than the keyboard.

## 10.8 Java packages

Now, that we have studied classes and their methods, we can take a look at the **import** statements which we sometimes have to use at the beginning of our programs. With the **import** statements we can import standard Java classes so that they can be exploited in our programs. An often used **import** statement is

```
import java.util.* ;
```

This statement specifies that a program that contains the statement is accessing a standard Java package named **java.util**. A Java package contains a number of classes. A program containing the above statement can easily use the classes that belong to the **java.util** package.

Because there exist hundreds of standard classes which belong to the Java programming language, and which are provided with the Java compiler, there must be a means to group those classes in a systematic manner. The possibility of putting certain classes in certain packages is a means to classify classes so that classes having some kind of relationship are put to the same package. Those packages that contain standard Java classes can be called standard Java packages. The following are examples of the standard packages:

- The **java.util** package contains utility classes such as **Scanner**, **Calendar**, **GregorianCalendar**, and **ArrayList**.
- The **java.io** package provides classes which can be used to perform input/output operations. These classes include classes for file handling such as **BufferedReader**, **FileInputStream**, **FileOutputStream**, and **PrintWriter**.

Standard Java packages, as well as other packages, can be brought into a program with an **import** statement. For example, because the **Scanner** class belongs to the **java.util** package, we usually have the statement

```
import java.util.* ;
```

at the beginning of a program when we want to create a **Scanner** object in the program. The above statement imports all classes from the **java.util** package. If we only want to use the **Scanner** class from the **java.util** package, we can alternatively use a statement like

```
import java.util.Scanner ;
```

which imports only the **Scanner** class.

It is actually not always necessary to use an **import** statement when a class from a package is needed. For example, a Java program like

```
import java.util.* ;

class SomeClass
{
   public static void main( String[] not_in_use )
   {
      Scanner  keyboard  =  new  Scanner( System.in ) ;
      ...
   }
}
```

can be written alternatively without an **import** statement as

```
class SomeClass
{
   public static void main( String[] not_in_use )
   {
      java.util.Scanner  keyboard =
                      new  java.util.Scanner( System.in ) ;
      ...
   }
}
```

When the name of a package is specified before a class name (e.g. **java.util.Scanner**), it is possible to use the class in question without having an **import** statement at the beginning of the program. The **import** statements are, however, preferred in this book because they clearly show which packages are in use, and they make many other program statements somewhat shorter.

A special standard package in the Java language is a package named **java.lang**. The **java.lang** package contains classes that are fundamentally important for the language. Because of its central role in the language, the **java.lang** package is automatically imported to every Java program. This means, for example, that the **String** class, which belongs to the **java.lang** package, is available in every Java program although no **import** statements were written to import the class.

A class can be declared as belonging to a certain package by inserting a **package** statement at the beginning of the program file. A **package** statement must precede possible **import** statements at the beginning of the file. As the Java standard classes belong to standard packages, they all contain **package** statements. For example, the declaration of the standard class **Scanner** looks like the following

```
package java.util ;

... // import statements

public class Scanner
{

   ...

   public String nextLine()
   {
      ...
   }

   ...

   public int nextInt()
   {
      ...
   }

   ...

}
```

The above class declaration is preceded by a **package** statement, which means that class **Scanner** belongs to the package whose name is **java.util**.

When a Java class has been declared as belonging to a certain package, the **.class** file of the class has to be placed in a folder (directory) that corresponds with the name of the package. For example, the file **Scanner.class**, the compiled version of the **Scanner** class, is placed in a folder named **java\util** because the **Scanner** class belongs to the **java.util** package. (All the **.class** files of the standard Java classes are in an archive file named **rt.jar** in a subfolder named **jre\lib** in the folder into which the Java Development Kit is installed on the hard disk. Inside the **rt.jar** file there is a folder hierarchy and **Scanner.class** can be found there in folder **java\util**. The Java virtual machine which interprets

Java programs knows where the **rt.jar** file is and it can find the necessary standard **.class** files inside the **.jar** file.)

It would be possible to put all the classes in the example programs of this book into some named packages, but that might complicate matters. Small programs like the example programs in this book are likely to be more understandable when the concept of package has been left out from the programs. Packages should, though, be used when large programs are developed.

When no package is specified in a program, the classes of the program are, nevertheless, in a package that is called the default package. The default package is a nameless package. As the programs in this book do not contain `package` statements, the classes defined in the programs belong to the default package.

When a set of classes belong to the same package, the classes have certain privileges in respect towards each other. For example, if class members are declared without access modifiers such as `private`, `protected`, or `public`, the class members in question can be accessed by methods of other classes in the same package.

## 10.9 Chapter summary

- The most important term in object-oriented programming is class. Classes must exist before objects. When we declare a new class, we introduce a new type.
- The usual members of a class are (data) fields and methods. Fields are usually accessed only by the methods of the class. Methods are usually meant to be called by other methods in other classes.
- Objects are created with the **new** operator. Each object contains the (data) fields that are specified in its class. Upon the creation of an object, memory space is reserved for the object's fields from the heap memory. The memory space reserved for an object is automatically freed by the garbage collector when the object is no longer referenced.
- Objects can be created by first declaring an object reference like

  ```
  ClassName  some_object ;
  ```

  and then creating an object with a statement like

  ```
  some_object  =  new  ClassName( ... ) ;
  ```

  or it is possible to perform these two operations with the single statement

  ```
  ClassName some_object  =  new  ClassName( ... ) ;
  ```

- An object reference references an object by storing the object's memory address. When a reference has value `null`, it does not reference an object. (From a programmer's point of view, it is correct to suppose that an object reference stores the memory address of an object. In reality, depending on how the memory management system works, an object reference may store an indirect address of an object. In indirect addressing, an object reference points to an address of an object.)
- An array of object references can be created with a statement like

  ```
  ClassName[] array_of_objects  =
                      new ClassName[ length expression ] ;
  ```

  The above statement creates an array whose elements can reference objects of type `ClassName`, but it does not create any objects of type `ClassName`. An array element can be set to reference an object with the following kind of statement

  ```
  array_of_objects[ index expression ]  =  new  ClassName( ... ) ;
  ```

- Constructor is a special method that is invoked (i.e. called) when an object is created. Classes usually have several constructors that take a different set of parameters. The name of a constructor must be the same as the name of the class.

## Exercises related to classes

Exercise 10-10. Improve the program **Olympics.java** so that it can also search for olympic cities and olympic countries from the array referenced by `olympics_table`. The program can first ask the user to type in a year, or a city or country name. Then the program checks the input string, and if the string starts with a number, the program searches for a year in the table. Otherwise, the program would search a city or country name in the table. The program can always print the same line of text when it finds something in `olympics_table`. To make the program more elegant, you can write new static methods to class `OlympicsDataFinder` and call them from method `main()`, for example, in the following way

```
if ( string_from_user.charAt( 0 ) >= '0' &&
     string_from_user.charAt( 0 ) <= '9' )
{
   // The user typed in a number.
   int given_year  =  Integer.parseInt( string_from_user ) ;
   search_year_in_olympics_table( given_year ) ;
}
else
{
   search_string_in_olympics_table( string_from_user ) ;
}
```

The method to search for a year is not very much different from the current version of method `main()`. The method to search for a string could use the string method `contains()` in the same way it is used in program **Planets.java**.

In order to access `olympics_table` from different `static` methods you have to declare it as a `static` data member inside class `OlympicsDataFinder`. You can do this by writing

```
class  OlympicsDataFinder
{
   static  Olympics[]  olympics_table  =  new Olympics[ 40 ] ;
   ...
```

Although `olympics_table` is declared outside the methods of `OlympicsDataFinder`, you can still create the `Olympics` objects inside the `main()` method.

Exercise 10-11. By using your imagination, and program **Animals.java** as an example, declare a class named `Car` that can be used in the following ways

```
Car  my_car  =  new  Car( "Honda", "Accord" ) ;
my_car.make_speak() ;
Car your_car  =  new  Car( "Cadillac" ) ;
your_car.start_engine() ;
your_car.increase_speed() ;
your_car.decrease_speed() ;
your_car.stop_engine() ;
```

A `Car` object should not move if its engine is not started, and it should print texts like "Now I'm moving with speed 50." after certain methods are called.

## Accessor methods

Classes and their instances, objects, are usually such that they contain some data items which are manipulated by calling the methods of the class. The data items inside objects are called fields, and usually they are not publicly accessible, which means that they cannot be read or written by methods of all other classes. According to the principle of encapsulation the fields of a class should not be accessible from the outside world. However, sometimes it is necessary to read or write an individual field of a class. In such situations one possibility is to use a so-called accessor method.

We have already used accessor methods that read a single field of a class. For example, class **Olympics** in program **Olympics.java** has the method

```
public int get_year()
{
   return olympic_year ;
}
```

whose only purpose is to read the field **olympic_year** of an **Olympics** object.

We have not yet used an accessor method that would write a single field of a class, but sometimes such methods are needed. For example, in class **Olympics** such method might be

```
public void set_year( int given_olympic_year )
{
   olympic_year  =  given_olympic_year ;
}
```

This accessor method would write the field **olympic_year** of an **Olympics** object. This method is not, however, needed in program **Olympics.java** because **Olympics** objects are not modified after their creation, but in some other kind of Olympics-related program the above method might be useful. An accessor method is usually written so that it does not allow wrong values to be given for a field. Therefore, a better version of the above method would be something like

```
public void set_year( int given_olympic_year )
{
   if ( ( given_olympic_year % 2 )  ==  0  &&
          given_olympic_year     >=  1896 )
   {
      olympic_year  =  given_olympic_year ;
   }
}
```

This accessor method would write the field **olympic_year** only if **given_olympic_year** is even and greater than or equal to 1896. The method would thus prevent using years during which no Olympic games have been arranged.

Accessor methods are sometimes said to be getter and setter methods. The above **get_year()** would be the getter method and **set_year()** would be the setter method for the **olympic_year** field of class **Olympics**. In some sources the word "accessor" means only the read accessor (getter), while the write accessor (setter) is referred to with the word "mutator".

# CHAPTER 11

## MORE ADVANCED CLASSES

In this chapter, we shall explore the nature of Java classes more thoroughly. A key idea in object-oriented programming is that you can use the same classes in several applications. One such general-purpose class is a class named **Date** that will be introduced in this chapter, together with several programs that exploit the **Date** class. When people develop software systems that involve the use of classes, it is helpful if the class designs are described with graphical-textual drawings. This chapter introduces some basics of a systematic graphical-textual drawing method called the Unified Modeling Language (UML).

## 11.1 Class Date – an example of a larger class

One advantage of object-oriented programming is that the same classes can be used over and over again in many application programs. The Java programming environment provides ready-to-use classes which you can exploit in your own programs. It is also important that you learn yourself to design general-purpose classes, and to use them in your programs. For this reason, we will study a general-purpose class named `Date` in this section, and you will be shown several programs that exploit the `Date` class. It is most important that you learn how class `Date` works. You do not necessarily have to understand every program line of the class, but it is important that you understand how an application program can create `Date` objects, and how the methods of the class work.

You have probably already guessed that class `Date` has something to do with presenting information about dates. To calculate time information in days, months, and years is not always such a simple thing to do. Some months have 31 days while others have only 30 days. Then there is the month of February which has only 28 days, except that once in every four years there is a leap year when February has 29 days. Then there is an exception that, although normally years equally divisible by four (e.g. 1992 and 1996) are leap years, years that are full centuries (e.g. 1800 and 1900) are not leap years. Then there is an exception to this exception that full centuries that are equally divisible by four (e.g. 1600, 2000, and 2400) are leap years. These are only some examples of the complexities of time calculation. Most of the complexities related to calculations of time as dates are incorporated in the methods of class `Date`. So this class should be useful when we need to handle date information in our programs.

The reasons why calculating with dates is complex are partly physical, partly historical. The historical reasons include the structure of our calendar and things such as how date information can be written down. In different countries people write dates in different ways. For example, in the United States, dates are written so that 10/18/2001 means the 18th day of October in year 2001. In Europe, it is common to write this date as 18.10.2001. Probably both of these styles to write dates are equally good, but the problem is that there is no single standard way. Class `Date` supports both of these date formats, and it can be made to support other formats if necessary.

The physical reasons why calculating with dates is difficult result from some astronomical facts. For example, a year is defined as the time during which the Earth goes around the Sun once. That is close to 365 and 1/4 days. A month approximates the time that the Moon uses to rotate the Earth once. Our programs for time calculation must be written so that they respect these and other astronomical facts.

Class `Date` solves many of the everyday problems related to calculations with date information. Three short programs demonstrate how class `Date` can be used in application programs. Program **Columbus.java** shows how chronological distances between two `Date` objects can be calculated. Program **Birthdays.java** shows how to easily find out what day of the week is a once-yearly date, such as a birthday. With program **Friday13.java** you can help your superstitious friends. Program **Friday13.java** prints a list of dates that are Fridays and the 13th day of a month. The class `Date` itself, which is exploited in all these example programs, is shown and explained as program **Date.java**.

Class `Date` has three fields that are simple `int` variables to hold the day, month, and year of a `Date` object. The fourth field is `date_print_format` which gets either value 'A' or 'E', depending on whether a `Date` object ought to be printed in the American way MM/DD/YYYY or in the European way DD.MM.YYYY. Class `Date` has four constructor methods. `Date` objects can be created in different ways. For example, `Date` objects for the date 16th of August in year 2004 can be created in the following ways:

```
Date  first_american_date  =  new  Date( 16, 8, 2004, 'A' ) ;
Date  first_european_date  =  new  Date( 16, 8, 2004, 'E' ) ;
Date  second_american_date  =  new  Date( "08/16/2004" ) ;
Date  second_european_date  =  new  Date( "16.08.2004" ) ;
```

The last two ways to create **Date** objects are the easiest to use in practice. Both of these **Date** object creations invoke the same constructor method. The constructor examines the initialization date given as a string, and checks whether '/' or '.' is used to separate the numbers in the string. When '/' is used to separate numbers, the **Date** object becomes an American date, and it will later be printed in the American format. Objects initialized in the European way will later be printed in the European date format.

Class **Date** has almost twenty public methods. Four of these methods are short accessor methods which simply read the fields. For example, the method

```
public int day()   { return this_day ; }
```

reads the field **this_day** and returns it to the caller. Methods like **day()** are commonly used in object-oriented programming, since, according to the principles of object-orientedness, data stored in objects should be protected from the outside world, and accessed only through methods. Methods that either read or write data fields can be labeled with the term "accessor method". Method **day()** is then a read accessor method as it allows a data field to be read.

The longer methods of class **Date** make various calculations related to time in days. The following list describes these methods:

- The boolean method **is_last_day_of_month()** returns **true** or **false**. This method is necessary because the months of a year have different lengths, and during leap years February has an extra day.
- The boolean method **this_is_a_leap_year()** contains the rules that specify whether a year is a leap year or not.
- Method **is_within_dates()** takes two **Date** objects as parameters. It returns **true** if the date for which the method was invoked is equal to or between the dates given as parameters.
- Method **index_for_day_of_week()** returns an integer in the range from 0 to 6. 0 means that the **Date** object is Monday, 6 meaning Sunday.
- Method **get_day_of_week()** calls method **index_for_day_of_week()** and returns a **String** object containing either "Monday", "Tuesday", ..., or "Sunday".
- The methods **increment()** and **decrement()** are used to rotate the dates stored in **Date** objects. These methods take care of leap years and varying lengths of months, so that **Date** objects are incremented and decremented correctly. These methods are called by several other methods of class **Date**.
- Method **get_distance_to()** calculates a chronological distance between two **Date** objects. **get_distance_to()** returns a reference to a **DateDistance** object which contains the distance in whole years, months, and days. The short **DateDistance** class is presented after the **Date.java** file in this chapter.
- Method **get_week_number()** returns an integer that denotes the week of the year. Every **Date** object belongs to some week in the range from 1 to 53. Every year has at least 52 weeks. About every sixth year there is a year that has 53 weeks. The reason for this is that 52 weeks make only 364 days but years are either 365 or 366 days long. Week 53 is a kind of leap week that is used to consume the extra days that do not fit with the normal 52 weeks. Week numbers are commonly used in the calendars of many countries.
- Methods **is_equal_to()**, **is_not_equal_to()**, **is_earlier_than()**, and **is_later_than()** are methods of type **boolean** that return **true** or **false** depending on what is the chronological relation between two **Date** objects.
- Method **toString()** converts a **Date** object to a **String** object and returns it to the caller. When a class has a method with name **toString()**, that method is invoked automatically in situations when objects of the class in question are joined to

**String** objects with the string concatenation operator +. Note that the name of this method is not **to_string()** but **toString()**. The name must be **toString()** in order to make the method automatically invoked in certain situations.

Class **Date** is written into its own source program file named **Date.java**. When you use **Date** objects in a program that is stored in its own source program file, you should ensure that both the file **Date.java** and the **.java** file of your program are located in the same folder (directory) in the hard disk memory of your computer. Because **Date.java** uses the short class declared in **DateDistance.java**, that file must also be present in the compilation folder. The Java compiler automatically compiles necessary files when they are located in the same folder. For example, if you copy the files **Columbus.java**, **Date.java**, and **DateDistance.java** into the same folder, and compile with the command

```
javac Columbus.java
```

the compiler detects that program **Columbus.java** uses classes **Date** and **DateDistance**, and hence it compiles also the **Date.java** and **DateDistance.java** files. The compiler can also detect if some needed file has been modified after the previous compilation, and recompile the file as necessary. The general rule in the development of small Java programs is that all **.java** files should be put in the same folder. (The programs in this book are still "small" programs, though **Date** is an example of a somewhat large class. If you later develop really large Java applications, you should then learn to use several folders as is necessary.)

Class **Date** is a rather simple class that can be used when date information needs to be stored and handled in a program. Because the **Date** class is rather simple, it is a useful tool to study the nature of classes. However, the **Date** class is not a standard Java class, and therefore it cannot be recommended for wider use. Java has the standard classes **Calendar** and **GregorianCalendar** that can be used to handle both date and time information. When you stop doing just programming exercises and start writing more serious programs, it is probably better that you learn to use the **GregorianCalendar** class. That class will be introduced later in this book.

## A first exercise with Date objects

Exercise 11-1. Write a program that calculates the chronological distance in years, months, and days from your birthday to any date that is given from the keyboard. You should, of course, use objects of class **Date** in this program. By studying program **Columbus.java** you can find out how the chronological distance between two **Date** objects can be calculated. Program **Birthdays.java** shows you how a date string can be converted into a **Date** object. You need the following kinds of statements in your program:

```
Date  my_birthday  =  new  Date( ...  // Your birthday here !

String  given_date_as_string  =  ...

Date  given_date  =  new  Date( ...
```

```
D:\javafiles3>java Columbus

   Christopher Columbus discovered America on 10/12/1492
   That was a Wednesday

   Apollo 11 landed on the moon on 20.07.1969
   That was a Sunday

   America was discovered 476 years, 9 months, and 8 days
   before the first moon landing.
```

Those dates that are initialized in format MM/DD/YYYY are also printed this way.

**Columbus.java - X. Outputting information related to dates.**

This program uses class **Date** which is introduced in a separate Java source program file that is explained as a separate program description later in this chapter. You can use class **Date** in your program, when you have the files **Date.java** and **DateDistance.java** in the same folder (directory) where your own program is located.

The first date object that is created here is initialized with an American style date MM/DD/YYYY. The other **Date** object is initialized in the European way DD.MM.YYYY.

**Date** objects can be joined to strings with operator + because there is the method **toString()** in class **Date**. The **toString()** method is called automatically when operator + works as the string concatenation operator. Method **get_day_of_week()** returns either "Monday", "Tuesday", ..., or "Sunday", depending on what is the day of week of the **Date** object.

```
//  Columbus.java

class Columbus
{
   public static void main( String[] not_in_use )
   {
      Date date_of_discovery_of_america = new Date( "10/12/1492" ) ;

      Date date_of_first_moon_landing  =  new Date( "20.07.1969" ) ;

      System.out.print(
         "\n   Christopher Columbus discovered America on "
       +  date_of_discovery_of_america  +  "\n   That was a "
       +  date_of_discovery_of_america.get_day_of_week() ) ;

      System.out.print(
         "\n\n   Apollo 11 landed on the moon on "
       +  date_of_first_moon_landing  +  "\n   That was a "
       +  date_of_first_moon_landing.get_day_of_week() ) ;

      DateDistance  distance_between  =

        date_of_discovery_of_america.get_distance_to(
                                    date_of_first_moon_landing ) ;

      System.out.print( "\n\n   America was discovered "
                   +  distance_between.years    +  " years, "
                   +  distance_between.months   +  " months, and "
                   +  distance_between.days     +  " days"
                   +  "\n   before the first moon landing.\n" ) ;
   }
}
```

Here, method **get_distance_to()** calculates the chronological distance between the **Date** objects referenced by **date_of_discovery_of_america** and **date_of_first_moon_landing**. It returns the calculation result inside a **DateDistance** object. Class **DateDistance** is presented after class **Date** in this chapter.

**Columbus.java - 1. Demonstrating the use of Date objects.**

This object creation results in a call to the fourth constructor that takes a string reference as a parameter. A date that is stored in a string is converted into a **Date** object.

```
//  Birthdays.java  (c) Kari Laitinen

import java.util.Scanner ;

class Birthdays
{
   public static void main( String[] not_in_use )
   {
      Scanner keyboard = new Scanner( System.in ) ;

      System.out.print( "\n Type in your date of birth as DD.MM.YYYY"
                 +  "\n or MM/DD/YYYY. Use four digits for the year"
                 +  "\n and two digits for the month and day:  " ) ;

      String  date_of_birth_as_string   =  keyboard.nextLine() ;

      Date date_of_birth   =   new  Date( date_of_birth_as_string ) ;

      System.out.print(
          "\n    You were born on a "  +  date_of_birth.get_day_of_week()
       + "\n    Here are your days to celebrate. You are\n" ) ;

      int  years_to_celebrate  =  10 ;

      while ( years_to_celebrate  <  80 )
      {
         Date  date_to_celebrate  =  new  Date(

                          date_of_birth.day(),
                          date_of_birth.month(),
                          date_of_birth.year()  +  years_to_celebrate,
                          date_of_birth.get_date_print_format() ) ;

         System.out.print( "\n     "  +  years_to_celebrate
            +  " years old on "  +  date_to_celebrate
            +   " ("  +  date_to_celebrate.get_day_of_week()  +  ")" ) ;

         years_to_celebrate  =  years_to_celebrate  +  10 ;
      }
   }
}
```

As variable **years_to_celebrate** is incremented by 10 at the end of the loop, the program prints the dates for when the person is 10 years old, 20 years old, 30 years old, etc.

Here a new **Date** object is created each time the internal statements of the loop are executed. This statement invokes the **Date** constructor that takes four parameters. **years_to_celebrate** is always added to the birth year. **day()**, **month()**, **year()**, and **get_date_print_format()** are short methods that return the values of the corresponding fields. The values of the fields of an existing **Date** object are used to create a new **Date** object.

**Birthdays.java - 1. A program that finds the dates for the most important birthday parties.**

```
D:\javafiles3>java Birthdays

 Type in your date of birth as DD.MM.YYYY
 or MM/DD/YYYY. Use four digits for the year
 and two digits for the month and day:  14.07.1977

   You were born on a Thursday
   Here are your days to celebrate. You are

   10 years old on 14.07.1987 (Tuesday)
   20 years old on 14.07.1997 (Monday)
   30 years old on 14.07.2007 (Saturday)
   40 years old on 14.07.2017 (Friday)
   50 years old on 14.07.2027 (Wednesday)
   60 years old on 14.07.2037 (Tuesday)
   70 years old on 14.07.2047 (Sunday)
```

When you run this program on your own computer, it is important that you use leading zeroes when you give information of days and months. The program would not work if you wrote here 14.7.1977 or 7/14/1977. This advice also concerns program **Friday13.java**.

**Birthdays.java - X. The program is executed here with the input date July 14, 1977.**

## Some facts about our Gregorian Calendar

The calendar that is commonly used in most countries of the world is called the Gregorian Calendar because its development was initiated by Pope Gregory XIII. The Gregorian Calendar was taken into use in Roman Catholic countries in 1582, and within a couple of centuries the new calendar was in use in most European countries and the United States.

The calendar that was used before the Gregorian Calendar is called the Julian Calendar because it was developed and taken into use by following the orders of Julius Caesar. The problem with the Julian Calendar was that it had too many leap years because every fourth year was a leap year. This resulted in that, after a longer period of use, the Julian Calendar was behind the actual time. The problems of the Julian Calendar were corrected by the Gregorian Calendar that has more complex rules for calculating leap years (see method **`this_is_a_leap_year()`** in class **`Date`**). When the Gregorian Calendar was taken into use in 1582, 10 days were dropped from October. Thursday October 4 was followed by Friday October 15.

Because a new calendar has been taken into use since the days of Christopher Columbus, the information provided in program **Columbus.java** is not entirely true. Columbus was using the Julian Calendar when he found America on October 12, 1492. That day is October 21, 1492, according to the Gregorian Calendar.

Although the Gregorian Calendar is the de facto official calendar of the present world, there are also other calendars in use. The Gregorian Calendar is not perfect either. One of its problems is that the week system of the calendar is not synchronized with the month system. Therefore the calendar is different every year. It is possible to specify calendars that are more stable than the Gregorian Calendar. Such calendars would make it easier to plan various activities in society. You can find information of proposed new calendars if you search the Internet with keywords like "calendar reform" and "world calendar".

```
//  Friday13.java  (c) Kari Laitinen

import java.util.Scanner ;

class Friday13
{
   public static void main( String[] not_in_use )
   {
      Scanner keyboard = new Scanner( System.in ) ;

      System.out.print(
          "\n This program can print you a list of 10 dates"
        + "\n that are Fridays and 13th days of a month."
        + "\n Please, type in a date from which you want"
        + "\n the calculation to begin. Type in the date either"
        + "\n in form DD.MM.YYYY or in form MM/DD/YYYY and use"
        + "\n two digits for days and months and four digits"
        + "\n for the year:  "  ) ;

      String  given_date_as_string  =  keyboard.nextLine() ;

      Date date_to_increment  =  new Date( given_date_as_string ) ;

      int  number_of_friday13_dates_to_print  =  10 ;

      System.out.print( "\n It is a common belief that you may have"
                      +  "\n bad luck on the following dates:\n"  ) ;

      while ( number_of_friday13_dates_to_print  >  0 )
      {
         while ( date_to_increment.index_for_day_of_week()  !=  4  ||
                 date_to_increment.day()  !=  13  )
         {
            date_to_increment.increment() ;
         }

         System.out.print( "\n   " + date_to_increment + ", "
                      + date_to_increment.get_day_of_week() ) ;

         date_to_increment.increment() ;
         number_of_friday13_dates_to_print  --  ;
      }
   }
}
```

Here the date given by the user is converted into an object of type **`Date`**.

Method **`increment()`** increments a **`Date`** object by one day. This method takes care of varying month lengths and leap years. For example, the date 02/28/2003 is incremented to date 03/01/2003, but the date 02/28/2004 is incremented to 02/29/2004 because 2004 was a leap year. Note that when a date has been printed, the **`Date`** object must be incremented to prevent the program from finding the same date again.

This boolean expression specifies the following operation: "Increment **`date_to_increment`** until it contains a date that is Friday and day 13 of some month of some year." The indexes for days of week are such that 0 means Monday, 1 means Tuesday, ... , 4 means Friday, 5 means Saturday, and 6 means Sunday.

**Friday13.java - 1. A program that demonstrates how certain kinds of dates can be searched.**

```
D:\javafiles3>java Friday13

 This program can print you a list of 10 dates
 that are Fridays and 13th days of a month.
 Please, type in a date from which you want
 the calculation to begin. Type in the date either
 in form DD.MM.YYYY or in form MM/DD/YYYY and use
 two digits for days and months and four digits
 for the year:  02/22/2006

 It is a common belief that you may have
 bad luck on the following dates:

   10/13/2006, Friday
   04/13/2007, Friday
   07/13/2007, Friday
   06/13/2008, Friday
   02/13/2009, Friday
   03/13/2009, Friday
   11/13/2009, Friday
   08/13/2010, Friday
   05/13/2011, Friday
   01/13/2012, Friday
```

**Friday13.java - X. Here the program is executed with input date February 22, 2006.**

## Second exercise with Date objects

Exercise 11-2. Normally we calculate our age in years, months, and days, but by using **Date** objects it is easy to calculate one's age in just days. For example, the program lines

```
Date  date_of_birth  =  new  Date( "14.07.1977" ) ;
Date  later_date     =  new  Date( "22.02.2002" ) ;
int   day_counter = 0 ;
while  (  date_of_birth.is_earlier_than( later_date )  )
{
   date_of_birth.increment() ;
   day_counter  ++ ;
}
System.out.print( "\n On " +  later_date + " you are "
                +  day_counter + " days old.\n" ) ;
```

calculate how many days there are between dates July 14, 1977, and February 22, 2002. In the above loop, **date_of_birth** is simply incremented until it reaches **later_date**. Because method **increment()** takes care of correct incrementing of dates also during the leap years, the calculated number of days is correct. Because of the varying lengths of months and the leap years that have 366 days, making calculations like these by hand are not so easy.

By using **Date** objects and method **increment()**, write a program that calculates and prints the dates when you are 10000 days and 20000 days old. A person reaches the age of 10000 days when he or she is something like 27 years and 4 1/2 months old. Remember that by using this program you can find yourself and your friends new days to celebrate!

The fields of this class are declared with keyword **protected**. Actually, the existence of the **protected** keyword here does not affect the behavior of the programs of this book. In this book, the fields of those classes from which we derive new classes are marked as **protected**. For the time being you do not have to worry about the **protected** keyword. Its meaning will be explained in the next chapter.

**WARNING:** Java has also an old standard class named **Date**. The standard **Date** class belongs to package **java.util**. Although the standard **Date** class is not used in this book, it is possible that the two **Date** classes get mixed up. For example, if you intend to use the **Date** class presented in this book but forget to copy the **Date.java** and **DateDistance.java** files to the folder where your program is, the compiler tries to use the standard **Date** class if the entire **java.util** package is imported to your program.

All fields of this class are initialized with initializers. Initializations like these take effect before a constructor is executed.

```
//  Date.java (c) Kari Laitinen

class  Date
{
   protected int this_day     =  1 ;
   protected int this_month   =  1 ;
   protected int this_year    =  1970 ;

   protected char  date_print_format  =  'E' ;

   public Date() {}

   public Date( int  given_day,
                int  given_month,
                int  given_year,
                char given_print_format )
   {
      this_day            =  given_day ;
      this_month          =  given_month ;
      this_year           =  given_year ;
      date_print_format   =  given_print_format ;
   }

   public Date( int  given_day,
                int  given_month,
                int  given_year )
   {
      this_day     =  given_day ;
      this_month   =  given_month ;
      this_year    =  given_year ;
   }
```

General purpose classes are usually equipped with a default constructor, a constructor that does not require any parameters. This constructor is an "empty method" that does not have any internal statements. This constructor is, however, needed because in the next chapter we'll derive new classes from this class.

**Date.java - 1: A general-purpose class to handle date information.**

This constructor method assumes that if character '/' does not separate the numerical parts of the string, it is a European-style date where the day is given before the month. This method cannot interpret the date string correctly if days and months are not given with two numerical digits.

```
   public Date( String  date_as_string )
   {
      //  This constructor accepts date strings in two formats:
      //
      //    MM/DD/YYYY  is the American format.
      //    DD.MM.YYYY  is the format used in Europe.
      //
      //  Member variable date_print_format will be set either
      //  to value 'A' or 'E'. This value will be used to select
      //  correct print format when this date object is converted
      //  to a string with the toString() method.

      if ( date_as_string.charAt( 2 )  ==  '/' )
      {
         date_print_format  =  'A' ;  // American format
         this_day   = Integer.parseInt( date_as_string.substring( 3, 5 ) ) ;
         this_month = Integer.parseInt( date_as_string.substring( 0, 2 ) ) ;
      }
      else
      {
         date_print_format  =  'E' ;  //  European format
         this_day   = Integer.parseInt( date_as_string.substring( 0, 2 ) ) ;
         this_month = Integer.parseInt( date_as_string.substring( 3, 5 ) ) ;
      }

      this_year  = Integer.parseInt( date_as_string.substring( 6, 10 ) ) ;
   }

   public int   day()    {  return  this_day   ; }
   public int   month()  {  return  this_month ; }
   public int   year()   {  return  this_year  ; }
   public char  get_date_print_format()  { return date_print_format ; }
```

These four methods are so-called accessor methods whose purpose is to read the fields of the class.

The numerical substrings of the **String** object referenced by **date_as_string** need to be converted to values of type **int**. This statement first takes a substring (the year) from the index positions from 6 to 9, and then converts the substring into a value of type **int**. The static method **parseInt()** of standard class **Integer** can convert a string to an **int** value.

**Date.java - 2: The fourth constructor and accessor methods of class Date.**

Methods that are of type **boolean** return either **true** or **false**. The names of these boolean methods are often questions or phrases containing the word "is".

If the day of this object is 30 and the month is either February, April, June, September, or November, this **Date** object contains a last day of a month. February is mentioned here, although it should never occur.

```
public boolean is_last_day_of_month()
{
   boolean  it_is_last_day_of_month  =  false ;

   if  (  this_day  >  27  )
   {
      if  (  this_day  ==  31 )
      {
         it_is_last_day_of_month  =  true ;
      }
      else if  ( ( this_day  ==  30 ) &&
                 ( this_month  ==  2  ||  this_month  ==  4  ||
                   this_month  ==  6  ||  this_month  ==  9  ||
                   this_month  ==  11 ) )
      {
         it_is_last_day_of_month  =  true ;
      }
      else if  ( this_day  ==  29  &&  this_month  ==  2 )
      {
         it_is_last_day_of_month  =  true ;
      }
      else if  ( this_day    ==  28  &&
                 this_month  ==   2  &&
                 ! this_is_a_leap_year() )
      {
         it_is_last_day_of_month  =  true ;
      }
   }

   return  it_is_last_day_of_month ;
}
```

Method **this_is_a_leap_year()**, which is called inside this boolean expression, is another boolean method of this class. If method **this_is_a_leap_year()** returns **false** here, the day number 28 of February is the last day of the month.

A method of a class can call another method of the same class without using the dot operator. The method call

**this_is_a_leap_year()**

means the same as

**this.this_is_a_leap_year()**

The **this** keyword is a reference to "this" object, to the object for which this method was called.

**Date.java - 3: A method that returns true if "this" Date is the last day of a month.**

This method returns **true** if the date contained in this **Date** object is a leap year. The **if** constructs inside the method implement the leap year calculation rules of our calendar, the Gregorian Calendar.

Here the remainder operator % returns a zero in those cases when **this_year** is equally divisible by four.

```
public boolean this_is_a_leap_year()
{
   boolean  return_code  =  false ;

   if  ( this_year  %  4   ==  0 )
   {
      //  Years which are equally divisible by 4 and which
      //  are not full centuries are leap years. Centuries
      //  equally divisible by 4 are, however, leap years.

      if  ( this_year  %  100  ==  0 )
      {
         int  century  =  this_year  /  100  ;

         if  ( century  %  4   ==   0 )
         {
            return_code  =  true ;
         }
      }
      else
      {
         return_code  =  true ;
      }
   }

   return  return_code ;
}

public boolean is_within_dates( Date earlier_date,
                                Date later_date   )
{
   return (( equals( earlier_date )  )  ||
           ( equals(  later_date )   )  ||
           ( is_later_than( earlier_date ) &&
             is_earlier_than( later_date ) ) ) ;
}
```

This test is true, for example, for years 1600, 2000, and 2400 because the numbers 16, 20, and 24 are equally divisible by 4. Those years are leap years although they are full centuries.

This method returns **true** if "this" date is later or equal to (the object referenced by) **earlier_date** and earlier or equal to the object referenced by **later_date**. The boolean methods **is_equal_to()**, **is_later_than()**, and **is_earlier_than()** are introduced later in this class.

**Date.java - 4: Methods this_is_a_leap_year() and is_within_dates().**

This method returns the smallest index 0 for Monday and the largest index 6 for Sunday. The week thus begins with Monday, as recommended by the international standard ISO 8601.

To find out the day of the week of "this" **`Date`** object, it is necessary to know the day of the week for some date. October 6th, 1997 has been chosen to be this known date. The program would work equally well if **`known_date`** were October 7, 1997 and **`day_index`** was 1 at the beginning.

```
public int index_for_day_of_week()
{
   //  day_index will get a value in the range from 0 to 6,
   //  0 meaning Monday and 6 meaning Sunday.

   int  day_index  =  0 ;
   Date  known_date  =  new  Date( 6, 10, 1997 ) ;
   // Oct. 6, 1997 is Monday.

   if  ( known_date.is_later_than( this ) )
   {
      while ( known_date.is_not_equal_to( this ) )
      {
         if ( day_index  >  0 )
         {
            day_index  --  ;
         }
         else
         {
            day_index  =  6 ;
         }

         known_date.decrement() ;
      }
   }
   else
   {
      while ( known_date.is_not_equal_to( this ) )
      {
         if ( day_index  <  6  )
         {
            day_index  ++  ;
         }
         else
         {
            day_index  =  0 ;
         }

         known_date.increment() ;
      }
   }

   return  day_index ;
}
```

With the **`this`** keyword a method can reference the object for which it was called.

**`increment()`** and **`decrement()`** are methods of this class. Here, these methods are used to increment or decrement the **`known_date`** until **`known_date`** is the same as "this" date. **`day_index`** is adjusted simultaneously with the increment or decrement operations. In most cases, **`known_date`** must be incremented or decremented thousands of times. This method could be made to execute faster if several known dates were used.

**Date.java - 5: A method that finds out what day of the week it is.**

This method can be called, for example, in the following way

```
System.out.print( "The day of week is "
    +  some_date.get_day_of_week() ) ;
```

Method **index_for_day_of_week()** returns a value in the range from 0 to 6. That value is used to index the array that contains the names of the days of the week.

```
public String get_day_of_week()
{
   String[]  days_of_week  =  { "Monday", "Tuesday", "Wednesday",
                     "Thursday", "Friday", "Saturday", "Sunday" } ;

   return  days_of_week[ index_for_day_of_week() ] ;
}

public void increment()
{
   if  (  is_last_day_of_month() )
   {
      this_day    =  1 ;

      if  (  this_month  <  12  )
      {
         this_month  ++  ;
      }
      else
      {
         this_month  =  1  ;
         this_year  ++ ;
      }
   }
   else
   {
      this_day  ++  ;
   }
}
```

Method **increment()** simply advances the date that is contained in "this" **Date** object on to the next date. Incrementing a date is a somewhat complex operation when the last day of a month has been reached. Method **is_last_day_of_month()** takes care of leap years and other complex matters while finding out whether the date is already the last day of a month.

When we increment days or months, it is sometimes necessary to go back to day one or month one. But when we increment the year, it is always just incremented. Our calendar is such that there is an endless number of years in the future.

**Date.java - 6: Methods get_day_of_week() and increment().**

Method **decrement()** does the opposite operation to that of method **increment()**. It modifies the date information to represent the previous day in the calendar. Fields **this_month** and **this_year** do not need to be modified if the day is not the first day of the month.

May, July, October, and December (months 5, 7, 10, and 12) are months that are preceded by months that have 30 days.

```
public void decrement()
{
   if ( this_day  >  1  )
   {
      this_day  --  ;
   }
   else
   {
      if ( this_month  ==   5  ||  this_month  ==   7 ||
           this_month  ==  10  ||  this_month  ==  12  )
      {
         this_day     =  30 ;
         this_month  -- ;
      }
      else if ( this_month  ==   2  ||  this_month  ==   4  ||
                this_month  ==   6  ||  this_month  ==   8  ||
                this_month  ==   9  ||  this_month  ==  11 )
      {
         this_day     =  31 ;
         this_month  -- ;
      }
      else if (  this_month  ==  1  )
      {
         this_day     =  31  ;
         this_month   =  12  ;
         this_year   -- ;
      }
      else if (  this_month  ==  3  )
      {
         this_month   =  2  ;

         if ( this_is_a_leap_year() )
         {
            this_day  =  29  ;
         }
         else
         {
            this_day  =  28  ;
         }
      }
   }
}
```

When we decrement a date from the first day of March to the last day in February, it is necessary to check whether "this" date object belongs to a leap year. February has 29 days in a leap year.

**Date.java - 7: A method to decrement the date contained in a Date object.**

```
public DateDistance  get_distance_to( Date  another_date )
{
   DateDistance  distance_to_return  =  new DateDistance() ;
   Date  start_date, end_date ;
   int   start_day, end_day ;

   if ( this.is_earlier_than( another_date ) )
   {
      start_date  =  this ;
      end_date    =  another_date ;
   }
   else
   {
      start_date  =  another_date ;
      end_date    =  this ;
   }

   if ( start_date.is_last_day_of_month() ||
        ( start_date.day()     ==  28  &&
          start_date.month()   ==  2  )     )
   {
      start_day    =  30   ;
   }
   else
   {
      start_day    =  start_date.day() ;
   }

   if ( end_date.is_last_day_of_month() ||
        ( end_date.day()     ==  28  &&
          end_date.month()   ==  2  )     )
   {
      end_day    =  30   ;
   }
   else
   {
      end_day    =  end_date.day() ;
   }

   distance_to_return.years   =  end_date.year()   - start_date.year() ;
   distance_to_return.months  =  end_date.month()  - start_date.month() ;
   distance_to_return.days    =  end_day   -  start_day ;

   if ( distance_to_return.days  <  0 )
   {
      distance_to_return.months  --   ;
      distance_to_return.days  =  distance_to_return.days  +  30 ;
   }

   if ( distance_to_return.months  <  0 )
   {
      distance_to_return.years   --   ;
      distance_to_return.months  =  distance_to_return.months +  12 ;
   }

   return  distance_to_return ;
}
```

This method calculates the chronological distance between "this" **Date** object and the object referenced by **another_date**. The calculated chronological distance is returned to the caller as a **DateDistance** object. The short **DateDistance** class is presented after this class in this chapter.

Generally, this method has been found to work accurately, but there is no guarantee that it works correctly in every situation. Because it is taken that day 30 is the last day of each month, this method might sometimes make an error of a day or two.

**Date.java - 8: Calculation of the chronological distance between two Date objects.**

Week numbers are used especially in European printed calendars. Every date belongs to some week that has a week number. Usually there are 52 weeks in a year, but about every 5th year will have 53 weeks. This method returns the number of that week where "this" **Date** object belongs to.

This method uses a known date in the calculation of the week number. This method does not work with dates preceding this date.

```
public int get_week_number()
{
   // January 1, 1883 was a Monday with week number 1.

   Date  date_to_increment  =  new  Date( 1, 1, 1883 ) ;
   int    week_number  =  1 ;
   int    local_index_for_day_of_week  =  0 ; // 0 means Monday

   while ( date_to_increment.is_earlier_than( this ) )
   {
      date_to_increment.increment() ;

      if ( local_index_for_day_of_week  ==  6  ) // 6 means Sunday
      {
         local_index_for_day_of_week  =  0 ; // back to Monday

         if  ( week_number  <   52 )
         {
            week_number  ++  ;
         }
         else  if   ( week_number  ==  52 )
         {
            if ( date_to_increment.day()    <=  28  &&
                 date_to_increment.month()  ==  12  )
            {
               week_number  =  53 ;
            }
            else
            {
               week_number  =  1  ;
            }
         }
         else  // must be week_number  53
         {
            week_number  =  1 ;
         }
      }
      else
      {
         local_index_for_day_of_week  ++  ;
      }
   }

   return  week_number  ;
}
```

This **if** construct decides when week 53 must be used in the calendar. The international standard ISO 8601 specifies that the first Thursday of a year must occur during week 1. In accordance with the ISO standard, weeks start with a Monday in class **Date**.

By using this variable instead of method **index_for_day_of_week()**, this method could be made to execute faster.

**Date.java - 9: A method to return a week number in the range from 1 to 53.**

This **boolean** method returns **true** when the date stored in "this" **Date** object is the same as the date in the object referenced by **another_date**. The field **date_print_format** is not included in the comparison of dates.

```
public boolean is_equal_to( Date another_date )
{
   return ( this_day    ==  another_date.day()    &&
            this_month  ==  another_date.month()  &&
            this_year   ==  another_date.year()   ) ;
}
public boolean is_not_equal_to( Date another_date )
{
   return ( this_day    !=  another_date.day()    ||
            this_month  !=  another_date.month()  ||
            this_year   !=  another_date.year()   ) ;
}

public boolean is_earlier_than( Date another_date )
{
   return ( (  this_year  <   another_date.year()     )  ||
            ( ( this_year  ==  another_date.year() )  &&
              ( this_month <   another_date.month() )  )  ||
            ( ( this_year  ==  another_date.year() )  &&
              ( this_month ==  another_date.month() ) &&
              ( this_day   <   another_date.day() )  )     ) ;
}

public boolean is_later_than( Date another_date )
{
   return ( (   this_year  >   another_date.year()     )  ||
            ( ( this_year  ==  another_date.year() )  &&
              ( this_month >   another_date.month() )  )  ||
            ( ( this_year  ==  another_date.year() )  &&
              ( this_month ==  another_date.month() ) &&
              ( this_day   >   another_date.day() )  )     ) ;
}
```

A **return** statement can include a complex boolean expression. Here, the truth value of the boolean expression is evaluated first, and then the value is returned to the calling method.

**Date.java - 10: Boolean methods for comparing Date objects.**

A method that has the name **toString()** is a special method in a class. Such a method is called automatically in certain situations to convert an object to a string. For example, when the string concatenation operator + is used in the following way

```
System.out.print( "The date is " +
                  some_date_object ) ;
```

the method **toString()** is called for the **Date** object referenced by **some_date_object**. We will study the **toString()** method in the following chapters.

These statements ensure that days and months are always shown with two digits. Leading zeroes are added so that dates have the format 05.08.2004 and not 5.8.2004. These two statements convert the day and month into a string that has two numerical digits. In the format specifier **"%02d"**, **d** refers to the decimal numbering system, **2** means the desired length of the string, and **0** indicates that unused positions of the string should be filled with zeroes.

```
   public String toString()
   {
      String day_as_string    =  String.format( "%02d", this_day ) ;

      String month_as_string  =  String.format( "%02d", this_month ) ;

      String year_as_string   =  "" + this_year ;

      String string_to_caller ;

      if ( date_print_format  ==  'A' )
      {
         string_to_caller  =  month_as_string + "/" + day_as_string
                              + "/"  +  year_as_string  ;
      }
      else
      {
         string_to_caller  =  day_as_string + "." + month_as_string
                              + "."  +  year_as_string  ;
      }

      return  string_to_caller ;
   }
}
```

Day and month are shown in different order, depending on the value of **date_print_format**. 'A' means American date format MM/DD/YYYY. 'E' means the European date format DD.MM.YYYY. This method uses the European format if the American format is not specified. The date print format is set when a **Date** object is created.

**Date.java - 11. The toString() method of class Date.**

The return type of class **Date** method **get_distance_to()** is **DateDistance**. An object of this simple class is used to convey information to the caller of method **get_distance_to()**. As this class has no methods, its data members are accessed directly with the dot operator.

It is important to note that the chronological distance between two dates is a different concept than the concept of a date. Some component (i.e., years, months, or days) of the distance between two dates can be zero, but no component of a date is zero.

```
//   DateDistance.java  (c) Kari Laitinen

class DateDistance
{
   public int years ;
   public int months ;
   public int days ;
}
```

Although this class is very short, it is best to have it in its own source program file. The general rule in Java is that general-purpose classes, which are exploited by several programs, should be put in their own **.java** files.

When the file **Date.java**, or any **.java** file that uses class **Date** is being compiled, this **DateDistance.java** file must be in the same folder (directory). **Date.java** cannot be compiled without this file because the type **DateDistance** is used in method **get_distance_to()**.

**DateDistance.java - 1. A class that represents a chronological distance between two dates.**

## 11.2 The this keyword

A method is a piece of program code that performs a certain task. A method usually reads and/or writes the fields of its class, and it uses local variables that exist only during the execution of the method. When a method is called for an object, the call syntax looks like

```
some_object.method_name( ... ) ;
```

and the called method can be something like

```
public void method_name( ... )
{
   ...
```

Inside the called method, the name of the object reference is not visible. A called method can, in most cases, do its job without knowing the name of the object for which it was called. A called method can access the fields of its class without knowing which object the fields belong to. The calling mechanism ensures that a method is bound to the right object when it is executing. There are, however, some special cases when the called method needs to reference the object for which it was called. In those cases the **this** keyword of Java is useful.

The **this** keyword can be used as a special object reference that always references the object for which a method was called. **this** can only be used inside non-static methods. An example of a method in which the **this** keyword can be useful is a method that takes a parameter whose type is the method's own class. For example, we might want to improve the **Animal** class of program **Animals.java** (see previous chapter) by writing a new **feed()** method to the class. The new **feed()** method would be such that it would make it possible to feed an **Animal** object to some other **Animal** object. A nice feature in such a method might be that an **Animal** object could not eat itself, and in that situation the **this** keyword could be exploited in the following way

```
class Animal
{
   ...
   public void feed( Animal another_animal )
   {
      if ( this  ==  another_animal )
      {
         // The caller tries to feed an Animal object to
         // itself. That is not allowed.
```

The **this** keyword is used inside some of the methods of class **Date**. For example, method **get_week_number()** contains a **while** loop that begins

```
while ( date_to_increment.is_earlier_than( this ) )
{
   ...
```

In class **Date**, the use of the **this** keyword is not absolutely necessary. The above beginning of a **while** loop could be written alternatively as

```
while ( this.is_later_than( date_to_increment ) )
{
   ...
```

or simply in the following way

```
while ( is_later_than( date_to_increment ) )
{
   ...
```

The **this** keyword may be used to highlight that a method of "this" class, i.e., the class where the caller is located, is being called, but it is not mandatory to use the keyword in such situations because a method can refer to another member of its class simply with the name of the member.

Another use for the **this** keyword is to have it as a "name" of a constructor of "this" class. When a class has several constructors, and the constructors are not much different from each other, the **this** keyword can be used to make one constructor call another constructor. For example, in the following case

```
class SomeClass
{
   ...

   public SomeClass( int some_initial_value )
   {
      ...
   }
   public SomeClass()
   {
      this( 82 ) ;
      ...
   }
   ...
```

the second constructor, which is a default constructor, is such that the first constructor is called with the parameter 82 at the beginning of the second constructor. By using the **this** keyword, a constructor of a class can be called from another constructor. The call to another constructor must be the first statement in the calling constructor.

## More exercises with class Date

Exercise 11-3. Write a program that prints 5 such future dates that are New Year's Days (January 1) and also Sundays. This program can be made by slightly modifying program **Friday13.java**, but such a program executes rather slowly. To make a faster version of this program, you can create a `Date` object inside a `while` loop in the same way as is done in program **Birthdays.java**.

Exercise 11-4. Write a program that prints 5 future birthdays of yours that occur on Saturday.

Exercise 11-5. Write a program that asks for a month number and a year from the user, and prints the calendar of the given month.

## Exercises to improve class Date

Exercise 11-6. The fourth constructor of class `Date` accepts initialization dates either in format DD.MM.YYYY or in format MM/DD/YYYY. Improve the constructor so that it accepts initialization dates in format YYYY-MM-DD where the year is given first with four digits and the month and day are then given with two digits. All numerical fields of the date are separated by minus signs - (hyphens). This date format, where the year comes first, is recommended by the standard ISO 8601 of the International Organization for Standardization. The constructor can assume the ISO date format if it finds the character '-' in the input string. After this modification program **Columbus.java** should work with the declaration

```
Date  date_of_first_moon_landing  =  new  Date( "1969-07-20" ) ;
```

Exercise 11-7. The fourth constructor of class `Date` in **Date.java** works correctly only if the year is given with four digits, and the month and the day are given with two digits. It is possible to write the constructor so that `date_as_string` could reference dates such as "18.5.2002" or "5/18/2002" but that is not necessarily easy to do. Consider improving the constructor so that it accepts days and months given only with one digit. If that turns out to be too difficult, make the constructor such that it checks the length of `date_as_string`, and it gives an error message when the date is less than 10 characters long. This way it is possible to avoid some problems.

Exercise 11-8. Improve the constructors of class `Date` so that it is not possible to initialize `Date` objects with strange dates like 33.33.2003. The constructors must check that the day value is in the range from 1 to 31, and the month is something from 1 to 12.

Exercise 11-9. The date print format of a `Date` object cannot be changed after the `Date` object has been created. To alleviate this problem, add the method

```
public void set_date_print_format( char new_date_print_format )
{
   ...
```

to class `Date`.

Exercise 11-10. Improve class `Date` by adding the methods

```
public boolean is_in_year_of( Date another_date )
{
   ...

public boolean is_in_month_of( Date another_date )
{
   ...
```

Method `is_in_year_of()` should return true if "this" date and (the `Date` object referenced by) `another_date` belong to the same year. Method `is_in_month_of()` should return true if "this" date and `another_date` belong to the same month in the same year.

## 11.3 Graphical UML class diagrams

Various kinds of drawings are often useful when we are designing things. This is true also in the case of computer programs. When a computer program contains large classes, or if there are many classes in use, it helps in designing and understanding the program if the classes are described with some kind of graphical-textual notation.

In the world of object-oriented programming, a graphical-textual "drawing language" called UML, Unified Modeling Language, is a standard way to describe classes and relationships between classes. UML is a modeling language because it is often used to build graphical models of applications. The word "Unified" in the name of UML indicates that the language was originally created by unifying several separate modeling languages.

UML is an extensive language that provides rules for drawing many kinds of graphical diagrams. In this book, we will not attempt to achieve a thorough understanding of UML. You will merely see some of the classes described with UML graphical notations. Nevertheless, UML is quite widely used among software developers. Therefore, it is likely that you will have to study it more thoroughly in the future.

Figure 11-1 shows how the class **Date** can be described with the graphical UML notation. A class is described with a rectangle that is divided into three sections. Each section describes one aspect of the class. A graphical description of a class gives just a concise overview of the class. For this reason, only the most important methods are listed. Graphical class descriptions like the one in Figure 11-1 will be used throughout the rest of this book. These descriptions are drawn by respecting the principles of UML, but there may be slight deviations from the official UML notations.

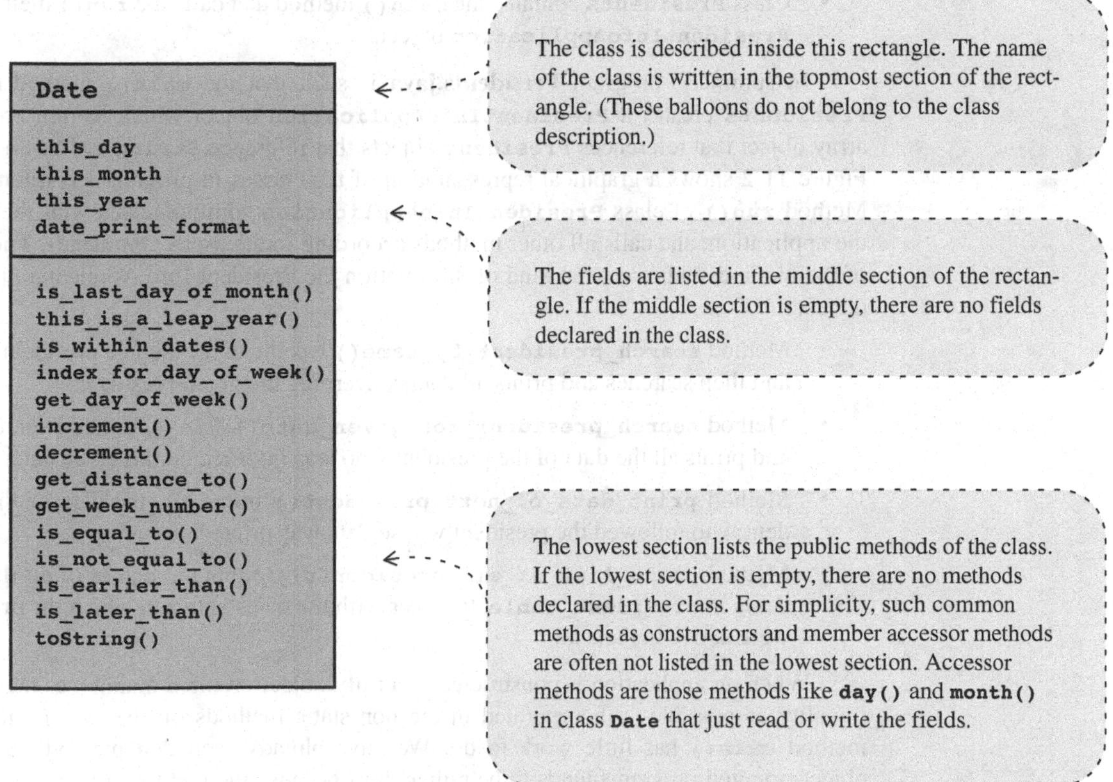


*Figure 11-1. Graphical class description for class Date.*

## 11.4 "Objects inside objects"

When a field of an object references another object, we can think that there is an "object inside object" in such a program. In reality, though, objects are quite independent creatures in the heap memory. When an object reference that belongs to some object points to some other object, there is a connection from one object to another object, and we can have the illusion of objects inside objects.

Because textual information is stored in **String** objects in Java programs, and textual information is needed in almost every program, it is very common to have Java programs that operate with objects inside objects. For example, the second example of an object-oriented program in this book, **BankSimple.java**, is a program in which **String** objects are inside (i.e., referenced by) a **BankAccount** object. Now we are going to study a somewhat larger program that has objects inside objects.

Program **Presidents.java** is an example where many classes are in use, and objects of one class are referenced in another class. Program **Presidents.java** is a "President Info Application" that can be used to ask various things about all the presidents of the United States. The following classes are used in program **Presidents.java**:

- The standard Java class **String** is used to store textual information.
- Class **Date**, which is already familiar to us, is used to store date information inside **President** objects. The **Date** class needs the short class named **DateDistance**.
- Class **President** has 7 fields to contain information about a president. The fields are references either to **String** or **Date** objects.
- Class **PresidentInfoApplication** is the heart of the entire application. The most important field of this class is **president_table**, an array of type **President[]** which references a **President** object for every American president.
- Class **Presidents** contains the **main()** method that calls the **run()** method for a **PresidentInfoApplication** object.

In summary, program **Presidents.java** is such that the **main()** method of class **Presidents** creates a **PresidentInfoApplication** object which in turn creates an array object that references **President** objects that reference **String** and **Date** objects. Figure 11-2 shows a graphical representation of the classes in program **Presidents.java**. Method **run()** of class **PresidentInfoApplication** communicates with the user of the application, and calls all other methods according to the user's commands. The names of the methods indicate what kind of information the President Info Application provides the user:

- Method **search_president_by_name()** lets the user type in a president's name, and then searches and prints all data concerning the given president.
- Method **search_president_for_given_date()** asks for a date from the user, and prints all the data of the president who was in office on the given date.
- Method **print_data_of_next_president()** prints all the data of the president who followed the president whose data was printed before.
- Method **print_list_of_all_presidents()** prints the names of all the presidents in **president_table**, together with the dates between which the presidents were active in their job.

When an application is constructed in a truly object-oriented manner, as much functionality as possible is incorporated in the non-static methods of classes, and the static method **main()** has little work to do. We have already seen that method **main()** in object-oriented programs tends to be rather short because the methods of classes do most of the work. In program **Presidents.java**, method **main()** is extremely short, consisting only of a few lines where an object of type **PresidentInfoApplication** is created, and method **run()** is called for that object. You will see these kinds of short **main()** methods in many object-oriented applications.

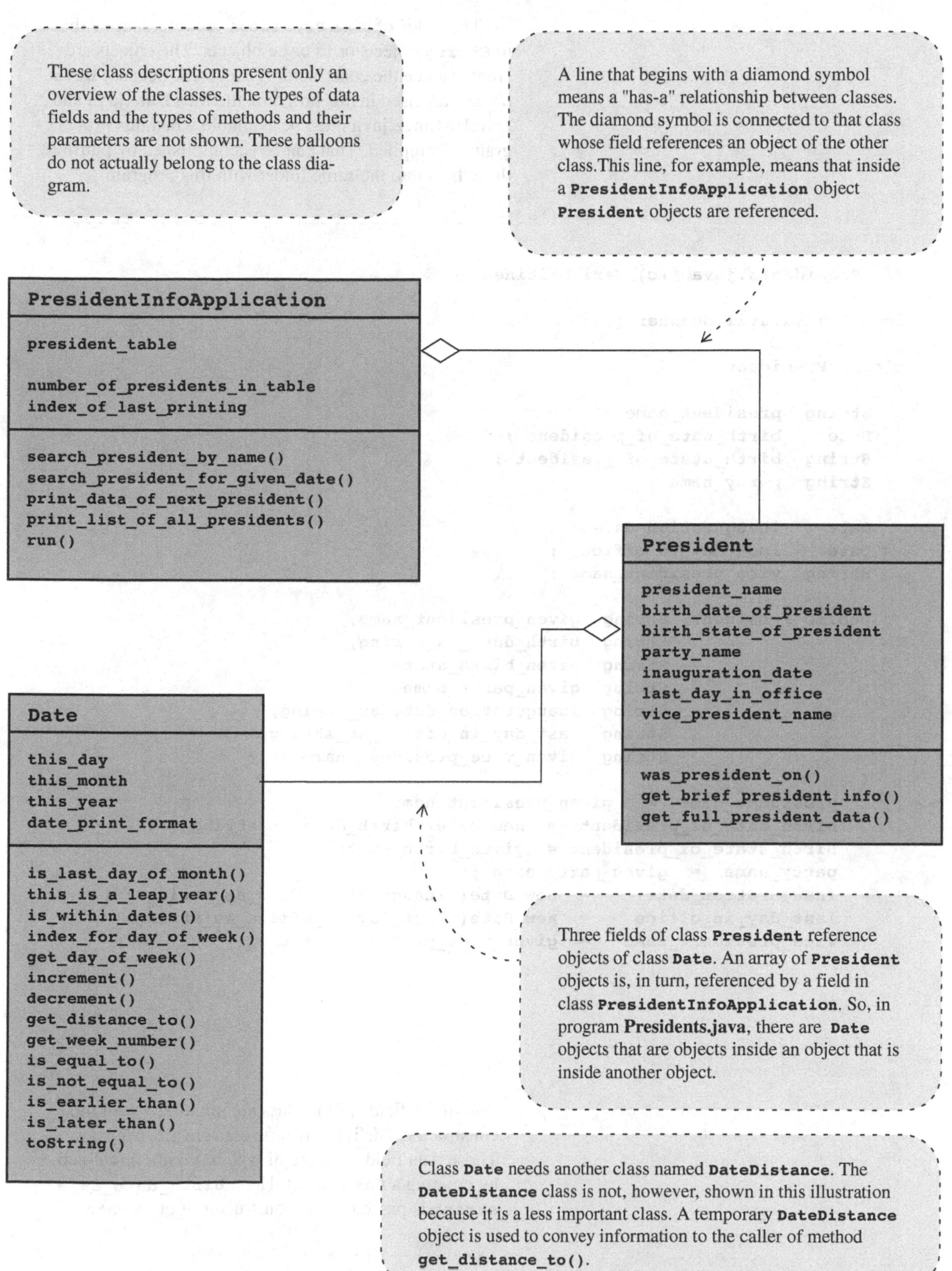
These class descriptions present only an overview of the classes. The types of data fields and the types of methods and their parameters are not shown. These balloons do not actually belong to the class diagram.
A line that begins with a diamond symbol means a "has-a" relationship between classes. The diamond symbol is connected to that class whose field references an object of the other class. This line, for example, means that inside a PresidentInfoApplication object President objects are referenced.
PresidentInfoApplication
president_table
number_of_presidents_in_table
index_of_last_printing
search_president_by_name()
search_president_for_given_date()
print_data_of_next_president()
print_list_of_all_presidents()
run()
President
president_name
birth_date_of_president
birth_state_of_president
party_name
inauguration_date
last_day_in_office
vice_president_name
was_president_on()
get_brief_president_info()
get_full_president_data()
Date
this_day
this_month
this_year
date_print_format
is_last_day_of_month()
this_is_a_leap_year()
is_within_dates()
index_for_day_of_week()
get_day_of_week()
increment()
decrement()
get_distance_to()
get_week_number()
is_equal_to()
is_not_equal_to()
is_earlier_than()
is_later_than()
toString()
Three fields of class President reference objects of class Date. An array of President objects is, in turn, referenced by a field in class PresidentInfoApplication. So, in program Presidents.java, there are Date objects that are objects inside an object that is inside another object.
Class Date needs another class named DateDistance. The DateDistance class is not, however, shown in this illustration because it is a less important class. A temporary DateDistance object is used to convey information to the caller of method get_distance_to().

***Figure 11-2. The relationships between three classes of program Presidents.java.***

The fields of class **President** are references either to **String** objects or to **Date** objects. The objects are created when the constructor is executed. Because **Date** objects are used in this program, the files **Date.java** and **DateDistance.java** must be available when this program is compiled. That can be accomplished by putting these files into the same folder with this program.

```
//  Presidents.java  (c) Kari Laitinen

import java.util.Scanner ;

class  President
{
   String  president_name ;
   Date    birth_date_of_president ;
   String  birth_state_of_president ;
   String  party_name ;

   Date    inauguration_date ;
   Date    last_day_in_office  ;
   String  vice_president_name ;

   public President( String  given_president_name,
                     String  birth_date_as_string,
                     String  given_birth_state,
                     String  given_party_name,
                     String  inauguration_date_as_string,
                     String  last_day_in_office_as_string,
                     String  given_vice_president_name )
   {
      president_name  =  given_president_name  ;
      birth_date_of_president  =  new Date( birth_date_as_string ) ;
      birth_state_of_president =  given_birth_state ;
      party_name  =  given_party_name ;
      inauguration_date      =  new Date( inauguration_date_as_string ) ;
      last_day_in_office     =  new Date( last_day_in_office_as_string ) ;
      vice_president_name    =  given_vice_president_name ;
   }
```

All the fields of the class are initialized with this constructor. The initialization data are all strings. Those data fields that are of type **Date** are initialized by creating a **Date** object. Here, **birth_date_as_-string** is passed to the constructor of class **Date**.

**Presidents.java - 1: A program that provides information about U.S. presidents.**

**is_within_dates()** is a method of class **Date**. Here it is called inside a **return** statement, and it returns **true** if **given_date** comes chronologically between **inauguration_date** and **last_day_in_office**.

This method returns a string that contains just one line of presidential information: the president's name is followed by the dates between which the president was in office. The returned string is created with method **String.format()** so that when the string is printed, the president's name is shown on the left side of a printing field that is 25 character positions wide.

```
   public String get_president_name()
   {
      return  president_name ;
   }

   public boolean was_president_on( Date given_date )
   {
      return ( given_date.is_within_dates( inauguration_date,
                                          last_day_in_office ) ) ;
   }

   public String get_brief_president_info()
   {
      return ( String.format( "\n  %-25s", president_name )
            + " president from  "  +  inauguration_date
            +  " to " +  last_day_in_office   ) ;
   }

   public String get_full_president_data()
   {
      DateDistance  time_in_office  =
            inauguration_date.get_distance_to( last_day_in_office ) ;

      return (   "\n  "
           +  president_name   +  "  born   "
           +  birth_date_of_president   +   ", "
           +  birth_state_of_president
           +  "\n    Inauguration date   :  " +  inauguration_date
           +  "\n    Last day in office  : " +  last_day_in_office
           +  "\n    Total time in office: " +  time_in_office.years
           +  " years, "   +  time_in_office.months   +  " months, and "
           +  time_in_office.days   +   " days."
           +  "\n    Party: "   +   party_name
           +  "\n    Vice president(s): "   +   vice_president_name ) ;
   }
}
```

**get_distance_to()** is a method of class **Date**. It calculates the chronological distance between two **Date** objects, and returns the distance as a **DateDistance** object.

**Presidents.java - 2: The other part of class President.**

This is the main class of the application. By creating a single object of this class, it is possible to set up the President Info Application.

**president_table** references an array of objects (i.e. an array of references to objects) of class **President**. The array can reference 80 **President** objects. It can be indexed in the same way as any other type of array. The array is created here, and the actual **President** objects are created in the constructor.

These constants (i.e., "variables" whose values cannot be changed) will be used as status values when data from **president_table** is searched.

```
class  PresidentInfoApplication
{
   President[]  president_table  =  new  President[ 80 ] ;

   int  number_of_presidents_in_table ;
   int  index_of_last_printing  =  0 ;

   static final int SEARCH_NOT_READY        =  1 ;
   static final int SEARCH_IS_READY         =  2 ;
   static final int SEARCH_IS_SUCCESSFUL    =  3 ;
   static final int SEARCH_NOT_SUCCESSFUL   =  4 ;

   Scanner  keyboard  =  new  Scanner( System.in ) ;

   public PresidentInfoApplication()
   {
      president_table[ 0 ]  =  new
       President( "George Washington",   "02/22/1732",  "Virginia",
       "Federalist", "04/30/1789", "03/03/1797", "John Adams");
      president_table[ 1 ]  =  new
       President("John Adams",  "10/30/1735",  "Massachusetts",
       "Federalist", "03/04/1797", "03/03/1801", "Thomas Jefferson");
      president_table[ 2 ]  =  new
       President("Thomas Jefferson", "04/13/1743",  "Virginia", "Dem.-Rep.",
       "03/04/1801", "03/03/1809", "Aaron Burr + George Clinton");
      president_table[ 3 ]  =  new
       President("James Madison",  "03/16/1751",  "Virginia", "Dem.-Rep.",
       "03/04/1809", "03/03/1817", "George Clinton + Elbridge Gerry" );
      president_table[ 4 ]  =  new
       President( "James Monroe", "04/28/1758", "Virginia", "Dem.-Rep.",
       "03/04/1817", "03/03/1825", "Daniel D. Tompkins" );
      president_table[ 5 ]  =  new
       President( "John Quincy Adams", "07/11/1767", "Massachusetts",
       "Dem.-Rep.", "03/04/1825", "03/03/1829", "John C. Calhoun" );
      president_table[ 6 ]  =  new
       President( "Andrew Jackson", "03/15/1767", "South Carolina","Democrat",
       "03/04/1829", "03/03/1837", "John C. Calhoun + Martin Van Buren" );
      president_table[ 7 ]  =  new
       President( "Martin Van Buren", "12/05/1782", "New York",
       "Democrat", "03/04/1837", "03/03/1841", "Richard M. Johnson" );
      president_table[ 8 ]  =  new
       President( "William Henry Harrison", "02/09/1773", "Virginia",
       "Whig", "03/04/1841", "04/04/1841", "John Tyler" );
```

**Presidents.java - 3: The fields of class PresidentInfoApplication and part of its constructor.**

```
president_table[ 9 ]  =  new
 President( "John Tyler", "03/29/1790", "Virginia",
 "Whig", "04/06/1841", "03/03/1845", "" );
president_table[ 10 ]  =  new
 President( "James Knox Polk", "11/02/1795", "North Carolina",
 "Democrat","03/04/1845","03/03/1849","George M. Dallas" );
president_table[ 11 ]  =  new
 President( "Zachary Taylor", "11/24/1784", "Virginia",
 "Whig", "03/05/1849", "07/09/1850", "Millard Fillmore" );
president_table[ 12 ]  =  new
 President( "Millard Fillmore", "01/07/1800", "New York",
 "Whig", "07/10/1850", "03/03/1853", "" );
president_table[ 13 ]  =  new
 President( "Franklin Pierce", "11/23/1804", "New Hampshire",
 "Democrat","03/04/1853","03/03/1857","William R. King" );
president_table[ 14 ]  =  new
 President( "James Buchanan", "04/23/1791", "Pennsylvania",
 "Democrat", "03/04/1857", "03/03/1861","John C. Breckinridge");
president_table[ 15 ]  =  new
 President( "Abraham Lincoln", "02/12/1809", "Kentucky","Republican",
 "03/04/1861", "04/15/1865", "Hannibal Hamlin + Andrew Johnson" );
president_table[ 16 ]  =  new
 President( "Andrew Johnson", "12/29/1808", "North Carolina",
 "Democrat","04/15/1865","03/03/1869","" );
president_table[ 17 ]  =  new
 President( "Ulysses Simpson Grant","04/27/1822","Ohio","Republican",
 "03/04/1869", "03/03/1877", "Schuyler Colfax + Henry Wilson" );
president_table[ 18 ]  =  new
 President( "Rutherford Birchard Hayes", "10/04/1822", "Ohio",
 "Republican", "03/04/1877", "03/03/1881", "William A. Wheeler");
president_table[ 19 ]  = new
 President( "James Abram Garfield", "11/19/1831","Ohio",
 "Republican", "03/04/1881", "09/19/1881", "Chester Alan Arthur");
president_table[ 20 ]=  new
 President( "Chester Alan Arthur","10/05/1829", "Vermont",
 "Republican", "09/20/1881", "03/03/1885", "" );
president_table[ 21 ] = new
 President("Grover Cleveland","03/18/1837","New Jersey",
 "Democrat", "03/04/1885", "03/03/1889", "Thomas A. Hendrics" );
president_table[ 22 ]  =  new
 President( "Benjamin Harrison","08/20/1933", "Ohio",
 "Republican", "03/04/1889", "03/03/1893", "Levi P. Morton" );
president_table[ 23 ]  =  new
 President( "Grover Cleveland", "03/18/1837","New Jersey",
 "Democrat", "03/04/1893", "03/03/1897", "Adlai E. Stevenson" );
president_table[ 24 ]  =  new
 President( "William McKinley", "01/29/1843", "Ohio","Republican",
 "03/04/1897", "09/14/1901", "Garret A. Hobart + Theodore Roosevelt" );
president_table[ 25 ]  =  new
 President( "Theodore Roosevelt","10/27/1858", "New York",
 "Republican", "09/14/1901","03/03/1909","Charles W. Fairbanks");
president_table[ 26 ]  =  new
 President( "William Howard Taft", "09/15/1857", "Ohio",
 "Republican", "03/04/1909", "03/03/1913", "James S. Sherman");
president_table[ 27 ]  =  new
 President( "Woodrow Wilson", "12/28/1856", "Virginia",
 "Democrat", "03/04/1913", "03/03/1921", "Thomas R. Marshall" );
```

**Presidents.java - 4: More initialization data for president_table.**

```
   president_table[ 28 ]  =  new
    President( "Warren Gamaliel Harding", "11/02/1865", "Ohio",
    "Republican", "03/04/1921", "08/02/1923", "Calvin Coolidge" );
   president_table[ 29 ]  =  new
    President( "Calvin Coolidge", "07/04/1872", "Vermont",
    "Republican", "08/03/1923", "03/03/1929", "Charles G. Dawes" );
   president_table[ 30 ]  =  new
    President( "Herbert Clark Hoover", "08/10/1874", "Iowa",
    "Republican", "03/04/1929", "03/03/1933", "Charles Curtis" );
   president_table[ 31 ]  =  new
    President( "Franklin Delano Roosevelt","01/30/1882","New York",
    "Democrat", "03/04/1933", "04/12/1945",
    "John N. Garner + Henry A. Wallace + Harry S. Truman" );
   president_table[ 32 ]  =  new
    President( "Harry S. Truman", "05/08/1884", "Missouri",
    "Democrat", "04/12/1945", "01/20/1953", "Alben W. Barkley" );
   president_table[ 33 ]  =  new
    President( "Dwight David Eisenhover", "10/14/1890", "Texas",
    "Republican","01/20/1953","01/20/1961","Richard Milhous Nixon");
   president_table[ 34 ]  =  new
    President( "John Fitzgerald Kennedy", "05/29/1917", "Massachusetts",
    "Democrat", "01/20/1961", "11/22/1963", "Lyndon Baines Johnson" );
   president_table[ 35 ]  =  new
    President( "Lyndon Baines Johnson", "08/27/1908", "Texas",
    "Democrat", "11/22/1963", "01/20/1969", "Hubert H. Humphrey");
   president_table[ 36 ]  =  new
    President( "Richard Milhous Nixon", "01/09/1913", "California",
    "Republican", "01/20/1969", "08/09/1974",
    "Spiro T. Agnew + Gerald Rudolph Ford");
   president_table[ 37 ]  =  new
    President( "Gerald Rudolph Ford", "07/14/1913", "Nebraska",
    "Republican","08/09/1974","01/20/1977","Nelson A. Rockefeller");
   president_table[ 38 ]  =  new
    President( "Jimmy (James Earl) Carter", "10/01/1924", "Georgia",
    "Democrat", "01/20/1977","01/20/1981", "Walter F. Mondale" );
   president_table[ 39 ]  =  new
    President( "Ronald Wilson Reagan", "02/06/1911", "Illinois",
    "Republican", "01/20/1981", "01/20/1989", "George Bush" ) ;
   president_table[ 40 ]  =  new
    President( "George Bush", "06/12/1924", "Massachusetts",
    "Republican", "01/20/1989", "01/20/1993", "Dan Quayle" ) ;
   president_table[ 41 ]  =  new
    President( "Bill Clinton", "08/19/1946", "Arkansas",
    "Democrat", "01/20/1993", "01/20/2001", "Albert Gore" ) ;
   president_table[ 42 ]  =  new
    President( "George W. Bush", "07/06/1946", "Connecticut",
    "Republican", "01/20/2001", "01/20/2009", "Richard Cheney" ) ;

   //  The value of the following variable must be updated
   //  when new presidents are added to president_table.

   number_of_presidents_in_table  =  43 ;
}
```

**Presidents.java - 5: The last part of the constructor of class PresidentInfoApplication.**

The constants written with uppercase letters are data members of this class. The constants are used as status values for the variable **array_search_status**. For more information about constants, see the information box on page 498.

Method **get_president_name()**, declared in class **President**, returns here a reference to a president's name inside a **President** object referenced in **president_table**. The string method **contains()** returns **true** when the given president name is included in the president's name inside a **President** object.

```
public void search_president_by_name()
{
  System.out.print( "\n  Enter first, last, or full name of president: ") ;

   String  given_president_name   =  keyboard.nextLine() ;

   int   president_index        =  0 ;
   int   array_search_status  =  SEARCH_NOT_READY ;

   while ( array_search_status == SEARCH_NOT_READY )
   {
      if ( president_table[ president_index ].get_president_name()
                                 .contains( given_president_name ) )
      {
         array_search_status   =  SEARCH_IS_SUCCESSFUL ;
      }
      else if ( president_index  >=  number_of_presidents_in_table - 1 )
      {
         array_search_status=  SEARCH_NOT_SUCCESSFUL ;
      }
      else
      {
         president_index  ++  ;
      }
   }

   if ( array_search_status   ==  SEARCH_IS_SUCCESSFUL )
   {
      System.out.print( "\n\n  THE #"   +   ( president_index + 1 )
           +  "  PRESIDENT OF THE UNITED STATES: \n"

           +  president_table[ president_index ].
                                get_full_president_data() ) ;

      index_of_last_printing   =  president_index ;
   }
   else
   {
      System.out.print( "\n\n  Sorry, could not find \""
           +  given_president_name  +  "\" in table.\n" ) ;
   }
}
```

**get_full_president_data()** is a method of class **President**. It returns a string containing all data that is available in a **President** object.

**Presidents.java - 6: A method that asks a president name to search for data.**

The date given by the user is converted to a **Date** object.

**was_president_on()** is a method of class **President**. It returns **true** if the president represented by a **President** object was in office on the given date.

```
   public void search_president_for_given_date()
   {
      System.out.print( "\n Please, type in a date in form MM/DD/YYYY "
                      + "\n Use two digits for days and months, and "
                      + "\n four digits for year:  " ) ;

      String  date_as_string  =  keyboard.nextLine() ;

      Date  date_of_interest  =  new  Date( date_as_string ) ;

      int  president_index      =  0 ;
      int  array_search_status  =  SEARCH_NOT_READY ;

      while ( array_search_status == SEARCH_NOT_READY )
      {
         if ( president_table[ president_index ].
                        was_president_on( date_of_interest ) )
         {
            array_search_status  =  SEARCH_IS_SUCCESSFUL ;
         }
         else if ( president_index  >=  number_of_presidents_in_table - 1)
         {
            array_search_status  =  SEARCH_NOT_SUCCESSFUL ;
         }
         else
         {
            president_index  ++  ;
         }
      }

      if ( array_search_status  ==  SEARCH_IS_SUCCESSFUL )
      {
         System.out.print( "\n\n  ON "   +  date_of_interest
               + ", THE PRESIDENT OF THE UNITED STATES WAS: \n"

               + president_table[ president_index ].
                           get_full_president_data() ) ;

         index_of_last_printing  =  president_index ;
      }
      else
      {
         System.out.print( "\n\n  Sorry, no president was on duty on "
                         + date_of_interest + ".\n" ) ;
      }
   }
```

The value of field **index_of_last_printing** will be checked by method **print_data_of_next_president()**.

**Presidents.java - 7: A method that asks a date for a search operation.**

This method allows the user to move through the entire **president_table**. When data of some president has been printed, this method lets the user read the data of the next president.

**index_of_last_printing** is a field of this class. It is set by the methods that search data in **president_table**. Here it is incremented so that it points to the next president in the table.

```
public void print_data_of_next_president()
{
   if ( index_of_last_printing  <  number_of_presidents_in_table - 1 )
   {
      index_of_last_printing   ++  ;

      System.out.print( "\n\n  THE #"  +  ( index_of_last_printing + 1 )
           + " PRESIDENT OF THE UNITED STATES:  \n"

           + president_table[ index_of_last_printing ].
                                get_full_president_data() ) ;
   }
   else
   {
      System.out.print( "\n Sorry, no more presidents in table." ) ;
   }
}

public void print_list_of_all_presidents()
{
   int  president_index  =  0 ;

   while ( president_index  <  number_of_presidents_in_table )
   {
      System.out.print( president_table[ president_index ].
                                 get_brief_president_info() ) ;
      president_index  ++ ;

      if ( ( president_index  %  15 ) ==  0 )
      {
         System.out.print( "\nPress <Enter> to continue ....." ) ;
         String  any_string_from_keyboard  =  keyboard.nextLine() ;
      }
   }
}
```

The user is asked to press the Enter key after every 15 lines of printing. This way, the user has time to read the information on the screen.

Method **get_brief_president_info()** of class **President** is called for each object referenced in **president_table**. The method returns a string that contains the president's name and the dates served.

**Presidents.java - 8: Two shorter methods of PresidentInfoApplication.**

The user selects an activity by typing in a single letter. The letter is supposed to be the first letter of the **String** object referenced by **user_selection**. If the user hits the Enter key without typing in any characters, the input string is a string of zero length, and this program terminates so that **StringIndexOutOfBoundsException** is thrown. All indexes are invalid for a string that has no characters.

```
   public void run()
   {
      String  user_selection  =  "????"  ;

      System.out.print("\n This program provides information about all"
                    +  "\n presidents of the U.S.A. Please, select from"
                    +  "\n the following menu by typing in a letter. ") ;

      while ( user_selection.charAt( 0 )  !=  'e' )
      {
         System.out.print("\n\n   p   Search president by name."
                       +  "\n   d   Search president for a given date."
                       +  "\n   n   Print data of next president."
                       +  "\n   a   Print list of all presidents."
                       +  "\n   e   Exit the program.\n\n   " ) ;

         user_selection  =  keyboard.nextLine() ;

         if ( user_selection.charAt( 0 )  ==  'p' )
         {
            search_president_by_name() ;
         }
         else if ( user_selection.charAt( 0 )  ==  'd' )
         {
            search_president_for_given_date() ;
         }
         else if ( user_selection.charAt( 0 )  ==  'n' )
         {
            print_data_of_next_president() ;
         }
         else if ( user_selection.charAt( 0 )  ==  'a' )
         {
            print_list_of_all_presidents() ;
         }
      }
   }
}

class  Presidents
{
   public static void main( String[] not_in_use )
   {
      PresidentInfoApplication  this_president_info_application
                                   = new PresidentInfoApplication() ;

      this_president_info_application.run() ;
   }
}
```

Method **run()** is called here for an object of type **PresidentInfoApplication**. When method **run()** terminates, the entire application terminates and the application object becomes garbage.

**Presidents.java - 9. Methods that run the president info application.**

```
  e   Exit the program.

  p

 Enter first, last, or full name of president: Kennedy

 THE #35 PRESIDENT OF THE UNITED STATES:
 John Fitzgerald Kennedy  born  05/29/1917, Massachusetts
   Inauguration date   : 01/20/1961
   Last day in office : 11/22/1963
   Total time in office: 2 years, 10 months, and 2 days.
   Party: Democrat
   Vice president(s): Lyndon Baines Johnson

  p   Search president by name.
  d   Search president for a given date.
  n   Print data of next president.
  a   Print list of all presidents.
  e   Exit the program.

  e

D:\javafiles3>
```

Because method **`contains()`** is used in the search operation, it is not necessary to give the full name of a president. The program can find the data of president Kennedy also with inputs like "John F" or "Kenn" because these substrings are contained in the string "John Fitzgerald Kennedy".

**Presidents.java - X. Data has been searched for with the input name "Kennedy".**

## Exercises with program Presidents.java

Exercise 11-11. Modify the boolean expression of the `while` loop in method `run()` in program **Presidents.java** so that it is possible to quit the program with both letters e and q.

Exercise 11-12. Improve class `PresidentInfoApplication` in program **Presidents.java** by adding a new method `print_data_of_previous_president()`. You should make this new method selectable from method `run()`. This new method should function in a similar manner to method `print_data_of_next_president()` but it should print the data of an earlier president.

Exercise 11-13. Improve class `PresidentInfoApplication` in program **Presidents.java** with a new method `print_presidents_born_in_certain_state()`. This method should ask for a state name (Ohio, Virginia, etc.) from the user, and go through the entire `president_table` searching for presidents born in the given state. Method `get_brief_president_info()` should be called to print `President` objects in `president_table`. You need also to modify class `President` so that you can compare the state names. One possibility is to add a method that begins

```
public String get_president_birth_state()
{
   ...
```

to class `President` and compare the birth states outside the class. Another possibility is to add a method like

```
public boolean was_born_in_state( String given_state )
{
   ...
```

to class `President` and let this method compare the state names. And of course, you need to modify method `run()` so that it uses the new feature in the program.

Exercise 11-14. The `while` loop in method `run()` in program **Presidents.java** has the problem that the program terminates if the user hits the Enter key without typing in a letter. Modify the `run()` method so that this problem is eliminated.

Exercise 11-15. If you live in a country other than the United States, you may find the rulers (presidents, chancellors, prime ministers, kings and queens, etc.) of your own country more interesting than the American presidents. So if you want information also for rulers other than the American presidents, you should modify program **Presidents.java** in suitable ways. The program can be written so that it is possible to select whether you want information about American presidents or other rulers. You must find the information about other rulers from relevant sources. You might implement the new program so that the information in `president_table` can be changed with a special method of class `PresidentInfoApplication`. If you want to use kings and queens in your improved program, you should also change the terminology used in the entire program. `president_table` might become `ruler_table`, `ruler_name` should be used instead of `president_name`, etc. The entire program might be called **Rulers.java**.

Exercise 11-16. By using program **Presidents.java** as a model, try to invent and implement your own programs that provide information from some special area.

## 11.5 Using object references as method parameters

When a method that takes parameters is called in a Java program, the parameters can convey information only from the caller to the called method, not vice versa. In some other programming languages (e.g. C++ and C#), method parameters can be declared as output parameters, which means that the parameters convey information from the called method to the caller. The absence of output parameters in the Java language can be considered problematic (a shortcoming). However, on the other hand, since Java does not provide too many features, it is a relatively easy and simple programming language. Like other programming languages, Java provides the **return** statement to transfer information from a called method to the caller.

When a reference to an object is passed as a parameter in a method call, the memory address of an object is copied from the caller to the called method. Thus, when an object reference is passed as a parameter, both the called method and the caller are able to reference and modify the same object, and such an object can be used to transfer data from the called method to the caller. Such an object can actually be used like an output parameter.

Program **LargestWithIntParameter.java** is an example in which an object reference of type **IntParameter** is used as a method parameter. The program works in the same way as program **LargestWithReturn.java** which we studied in Chapter 9. Program **LargestWithIntParameter.java** does not use a **return** statement. Instead, an **int** value is transferred from the called method inside an **IntParameter** object. The program has the lines

```
IntParameter  found_largest_integer  =  new  IntParameter();

search_largest_integer( first_array, 5,
                        found_largest_integer ) ;
```

and after the call to method **search_largest_integer()** has been executed, the largest integer found is inside the object which is referenced by **found_largest_integer**.

It is important that the object which is used to transfer the **int** value from the called method is created by the caller. If, for instance, the last statement of method **search_-largest_integer()** were replaced with the statement

```
largest_integer_to_caller  =
              new  IntParameter( largest_integer ) ;
```

the program would not work. Although this statement creates an **IntParameter** object which contains the largest integer, the caller of the method could not get hold of the object because it is referenced only by **largest_integer_to_caller** which is a local variable. Thus it is important that method **search_largest_integer()** receives a reference to an existing **IntParameter** object that is created before the method is called.

Classes like **IntParameter** in program **LargestWithIntParameter.java** may sometimes be needed, but usually the **return** statement is sufficient for transferring information from a called method. Sometimes, when a method has to transfer several pieces of information to its caller, it may be necessary to introduce special classes that can contain the pieces of information. **DateDistance** is such kind of class, and it is used by method **get_distance_to()** in **Date.java** to transfer three numerical values to its caller.

An object of type **`IntParameter`** can store only a single value of type **`int`**. This is thus not a very clever class. Class **`IntParameter`** is used in this program to demonstrate how an object reference works as a method parameter.

```
//  LargestWithIntParameter.java

class IntParameter
{
   protected int int_value  =  0 ;

   public IntParameter()  {}

   public IntParameter( int  given_initial_value )
   {
      int_value  =  given_initial_value ;
   }

   public int get_value()
   {
      return  int_value ;
   }

   public void set_value( int given_new_value )
   {
      int_value  =  given_new_value ;
   }
}

class LargestWithIntParameter
{
   static void search_largest_integer( int[] array_of_integers,
                                       int   number_of_integers_in_array,

                                       IntParameter largest_integer_to_caller )
   {
      int  largest_integer     =  array_of_integers[ 0 ] ;
      int  integer_index  =  1 ;

      while (  integer_index  <  number_of_integers_in_array  )
      {
         if ( array_of_integers[ integer_index ] > largest_integer )
         {
            largest_integer  =  array_of_integers[ integer_index ] ;
         }

         integer_index   ++  ;
      }

      largest_integer_to_caller.set_value( largest_integer ) ;
   }
```

With the **`set_value()`** method a value of type **`int`** is stored inside an **`IntParameter`** object. Because the object reference **`found_largest_integer`** in the **`main()`** method is pointing to the same object as the reference **`largest_integer_to_caller`**, it is possible to read the stored **`int`** value in the **`main()`** method.

**LargestWithIntParameter.java - 1: A rewritten version of LargestWithReturn.java.**

This statement creates an **IntParameter** object by invoking the default constructor. The value inside the object is initially 0. When a reference to this object is passed to the **search_largest_integer()** method, it will return an **int** value inside the object.

```
   public static void main( String[] not_in_use )
   {
      int[]  first_array    =  { 44, 2, 66, 33, 9 } ;
      int[]  second_array   =  { 888, 777, 66, 999, 998, 997 } ;

      IntParameter  found_largest_integer  =  new  IntParameter() ;

      search_largest_integer( first_array, 5,
                              found_largest_integer ) ;

      System.out.print( "\n The largest integer in first_array is "
                      +  found_largest_integer.get_value()  +  ".\n" ) ;

      search_largest_integer( second_array, 6,
                              found_largest_integer ) ;

      System.out.print( "\n The largest integer in second_array is "
                      +  found_largest_integer.get_value()  +  ".\n" ) ;
   }
}
```

Method **get_value()** returns the **int** value that is currently stored inside the **IntParameter** object. The returned **int** value is converted to a string when the + operator concatenates it to the other strings.

The same **IntParameter** object is used twice to get an **int** value from the **search_largest_integer()** method.

**LargestWithIntParameter.java - 2. The other part of the program.**

```
D:\javafiles3>java LargestWithIntParameter

 The largest integer in first_array is 66.

 The largest integer in second_array is 999.
```

**LargestWithIntParameter.java - X. The program works like LargestWithReturn.java.**

## 11.6 Chapter summary

- An important class in this chapter is the general-purpose class **`Date`** that is used in several example programs. Such classes are usually placed in separate source program files.
- **`this`**, a reserved keyword in Java, can be used as a special object reference. Inside a method, the **`this`** keyword references the object for which the method was called. With the **`this`** keyword it is possible to make a constructor call another constructor of a class.
- When several classes are in use in a program, the relationships between the classes can be described with UML (Unified Modeling Language) class diagrams.

# CHAPTER 12

## INHERITANCE AND CLASS HIERARCHIES

The concept of inheritance is at the heart of object-oriented programming and object-oriented thinking. Just as a person in real life can inherit the features of his or her mother's face, a Java class can inherit the features of another class. In the computer world, the inheritance mechanism is more accurate and predictable than in real life. Inheritance makes it easier to declare new classes. That's why it is so important in object-oriented programming.

In this chapter, we shall first study some simple cases of inheritance. Later, we shall study some more complex cases and a special kind of methods called polymorphic methods. We shall see that polymorphic methods are a kind of exception to the general inheritance mechanism.

## 12.1 Base classes and derived classes

In the previous chapter, we studied a class named **Date**. Objects of the class **Date** contain the necessary data fields to store information about dates, and the class provides many useful methods to do various things with the information inside **Date** objects. With those methods we can compare **Date** objects, print **Date** objects, increment **Date** objects, etc.

One might think that class **Date** is so complete that we do not need other classes to be concerned with date information. Unfortunately things are not usually so simple. In different applications, slightly different date classes might be the most suitable classes to handle date information. In a large software project, for example, some people would like to modify class **Date** by adding new methods to it, while others would like to make it behave so that it automatically copies the computer system's date into the **Date** object being created. If different groups of people tried to modify class **Date** for their own purposes, there would most likely be different versions of the class. That might be dangerous in a software project because people might end up using the wrong class versions.

Inheritance is a mechanism that helps to manage classes which produce closely related objects. By using inheritance, it is easy to make slightly different versions of an existing class without having to modify the existing class. Inheritance is one of the key concepts in object-oriented programming. With inheritance it is possible to derive a new class from an existing class. Inheritance extends an existing class and produces a new class.

If a source program contains a class declaration that begins

```
class  UpperClass
{
      ...
```

it is possible to write later in the same program or in some other program file

```
class  LowerClass  extends  UpperClass
{
      ...
```

The latter declaration specifies that class **LowerClass** inherits class **UpperClass**. The keyword **extends** tells the compiler that the members (fields and methods) of class **UpperClass** must be inherited to **LowerClass**. Those members that are declared with access modifiers (keywords) **public** or **protected** in **UpperClass** become similar members in **LowerClass**. Those members that are declared without access modifiers in **UpperClass** become similar members in **LowerClass** provided that the classes belong to the same package of classes.

In the discussion above, the classes are named **UpperClass** and **LowerClass**. These names are chosen to indicate the fact that a class that inherits another class is on a lower level. It can exist only after the upper-level class has been declared. In the terminology of object-oriented programming, we say that **UpperClass** is a superclass or base class of **LowerClass**, **LowerClass** is a subclass of **UpperClass**, and **LowerClass** is derived from **UpperClass**. When a class inherits another class, the classes form a class hierarchy. The class that inherits is in a lower position in the hierarchy. Later on, we shall see that there can be more than just two classes in a class hierarchy.

Program **BetterDate.java** is an example where inheritance is used to derive a new class from class **Date**. The name of the derived class is **BetterDate**. Although the declaration of class **BetterDate** fits on a single page, **BetterDate** contains practically everything that is in class **Date** that needs ten pages to be described. The derived class **BetterDate** contains all fields of class **Date**, all methods excluding the constructors of class **Date**, its own constructor, and its own two methods **to_string_with_month_name()** and **to_american_format_string()**. It must be noted that a derived class needs, in most cases, a constructor of its own. Constructors are not inherited from the upper class.

Class **BetterDate** is better than class **Date** because it has two new methods. The first method allows a date to be shown so that the month is expressed with letters instead of numbers. The second method prints the date in the American format, also in the case when the object is created with the European format specifier. In addition to these new methods, it is possible to call the old class **Date** methods for **BetterDate** objects.

In one respect class **BetterDate** is worse than class **Date**. Because there is only one constructor method in class **BetterDate**, there remains only the following way to create **BetterDate** objects:

```
BetterDate  date_of_reunification_of_germany
                    =  new  BetterDate( "03.10.1990");
```

The constructor of **BetterDate** only accepts strings as its parameter. **Date** objects can also be constructed by supplying the initialization date as values of type **int**:

```
Date  date_of_independence_of_finland
                    =  new  Date( 6, 12, 1917 ) ;
```

The sole constructor of class **BetterDate** passes the string that it receives as a parameter to the constructor of class **Date**. The constructor consists of the lines

```
public BetterDate( String date_as_string )
{
   super( date_as_string ) ;
}
```

This constructor calls the constructor of class **Date** with the help of the **super** keyword. The keyword **super** refers to the constructor of the superclass. It is thus the constructor of class **Date** that actually processes the string and extracts the date information from it. Only the constructor of the immediate superclass can be called by using the **super** keyword. If there are higher classes above the immediate superclass, their constructors cannot be accessed in this way.

In general, it is possible to declare the constructor of a derived class in two ways. The first way is to call the constructor of the immediate superclass before the other statements of the constructor:

```
public DerivedClass( declarations of formal parameters )
{
   super( actual parameters to the constructor of superclass ) ;
   zero or more other statements
}
```

The second possibility is to write the constructor without an explicit call to the constructor of the superclass:

```
public DerivedClass( declarations of formal parameters )
{
   zero or more statements
}
```

In the first case above, the constructor of the superclass is executed before the constructor of **DerivedClass**. In the second case, where the explicit call is missing, the compiler generates an implicit call to the default constructor of the superclass before executing the body of the constructor of **DerivedClass**. Implicit calling means that the call is not visible in the source program text, and the compiler generates it automatically. Because the compiler generates these automatic calls to the constructors of upper classes, there usually has to be a default constructor (i.e. a constructor that can be called without supplying parameters) in every class that is to be inherited.

Class **BetterDate** is better than class **Date** because it has two additional methods. We can say that class **BetterDate** is the same as class **Date** plus the two methods. **BetterDate** is thus an extended version of class **Date**.

By writing **extends Date** after the name of the new class, we can inherit the fields and methods from class **Date**.

Constructors are not inherited when a class inherits the members of another class. Constructors need to be written in most cases when new classes are derived from existing classes. Here the constructor of **BetterDate** is written so that it calls the constructor of class **Date**. The keyword **super** refers here to a constructor in the superclass.

```
//  BetterDate.java

class BetterDate  extends  Date
{
   public BetterDate( String date_as_string )
   {
      super( date_as_string ) ;
   }

   public String to_string_with_month_name()
   {
      String[]  names_of_months  =

         { "January", "February", "March", "April",
           "May", "June", "July", "August",
           "September", "October", "November", "December" } ;

      return (  names_of_months[ this_month - 1 ]  + " "
                + this_day  +  ", "  +  this_year ) ;
   }

   public String to_american_format_string()
   {
      char  saved_date_print_format  =  date_print_format ;

      date_print_format  =  'A' ;

      String  string_to_return  =  this.toString() ;

      date_print_format  =  saved_date_print_format ;

      return  string_to_return ;
   }
}
```

**date_print_format** is a field in class **Date**. Because **BetterDate** inherits class **Date**, this field can be used in a method of **BetterDate** as if it was declared in class **BetterDate**.

Method **toString()** is inherited from class **Date**, and here it is called for "this" **BetterDate** object. **toString()** returns a string representation of "this" date in its current printing format. The method could also be called without the **this** keyword and the dot operator.

**BetterDate.java - 1: Deriving a new class from an existing class.**

The **toString()** method is called automatically for a **BetterDate** object when operator + is used as the string concatenation operator.

Objects of derived classes are created in the normal way. We cannot see anything here indicating that **BetterDate** is derived from class **Date**.

```
class  BetterDateTester
{
   public static void main( String[] not_in_use )
   {
      BetterDate  birthday_of_einstein  =  new  BetterDate("14.03.1879");

      System.out.print( "\n Albert Einstein was born on "
                         +  birthday_of_einstein   ) ;

      birthday_of_einstein.increment() ;

      System.out.print( "\n Albert was one day old on "
                         + birthday_of_einstein.to_string_with_month_name() ) ;

      birthday_of_einstein.increment() ;

      System.out.print( "\n Albert was two days old on "
                         + birthday_of_einstein.to_american_format_string() ) ;
   }
}
```

This statement is, for example, "hard evidence" confirming the fact that inheritance has indeed taken place. The object reference **birthday_of_einstein** is pointing to a **BetterDate** object, and method **increment()** is invoked for the object. Because the **BetterDate** class does not contain a method named **increment()**, the method must have been inherited from class **Date**.

**BetterDate.java - 2. Using a BetterDate object.**

```
D:\javafiles3>java BetterDateTester

 Albert Einstein was born on 14.03.1879
 Albert was one day old on March 15, 1879
 Albert was two days old on 03/16/1879
```

**BetterDate.java - X. Dates printed with different methods.**

Program **CurrentDate.java** is another example where a new class is derived from class **`Date`**. The name of the class is **`CurrentDate`**. Classes **`Date`** and **`CurrentDate`** only differ from each other in that they have different kinds of constructors. The constructor of class **`CurrentDate`** reads the date information that is maintained by the operating system of the computer. The constructor gets this information by using the standard Java classes **`Calendar`** and **`GregorianCalendar`**. The used standard method gets the computer's date by interacting with the operating system of the computer which, in turn, interacts with the clock electronics of the computer.

Programs **Titanic.java** and **Weddingdates.java** are examples in which objects of class **`CurrentDate`** are created and used. When a **`CurrentDate`** object is created, its date is the current computer's date. It is, nonetheless, possible to change the initial date with the methods that class **`CurrentDate`** has inherited from class **`Date`**. For example, methods **`increment()`** and **`decrement()`** modify a **`CurrentDate`** object just as they modify a **`Date`** object.

**`CurrentDate`** objects are, by default, American style dates, which means that they are shown in format MM/DD/YYYY. The default print format in class **`CurrentDate`** is 'A'. If you want a **`CurrentDate`** object to be shown in the European format DD.MM.YYYY, you must create the object in the following way

```
CurrentDate  date_of_today  =  new  CurrentDate( 'E' ) ;
```

The above object creation statement invokes the second constructor of class **`CurrentDate`**. There is no technical reason why **`CurrentDate`** objects are by default American dates. This book just tries to achieve some kind of "international balance". As the objects of class **`Date`** are by default shown in the European date format, objects of class **`CurrentDate`** are by default American dates. You may, of course, modify these classes to make their default settings to fit your own preferences.

Two new classes are derived from class **`Date`** in programs **BetterDate.java** and **CurrentDate.java**. Figure 12-1 shows how these class derivations can be described graphically as a UML class diagram. While studying Figure 12-1, you should note that also the empty spaces in the graphical class descriptions have a meaning.

A new class can be derived from an existing base class in the following basic ways

- The new class has the same members as its base class, but it has one or more new kinds of constructors. (Class **`CurrentDate`** is like this.)
- The new class has the same fields and methods as its base class, and it has some additional methods. (Class **`BetterDate`** is like this.)
- The new class has some new fields in addition to the inherited fields and methods. (We shall study these kinds of classes later in this book, and we shall also learn that it is not always necessary to inherit all the methods of a base class.)

In practice, new classes are usually formed by mixing all the above basic ways to derive new classes. Especially when new fields are added to a new class, it is usually necessary to add new methods as well. In most cases derived classes need their own kinds of constructors. When new fields are added to a derived class, the objects of the derived class consume more memory space from the heap memory than the objects of the base class.

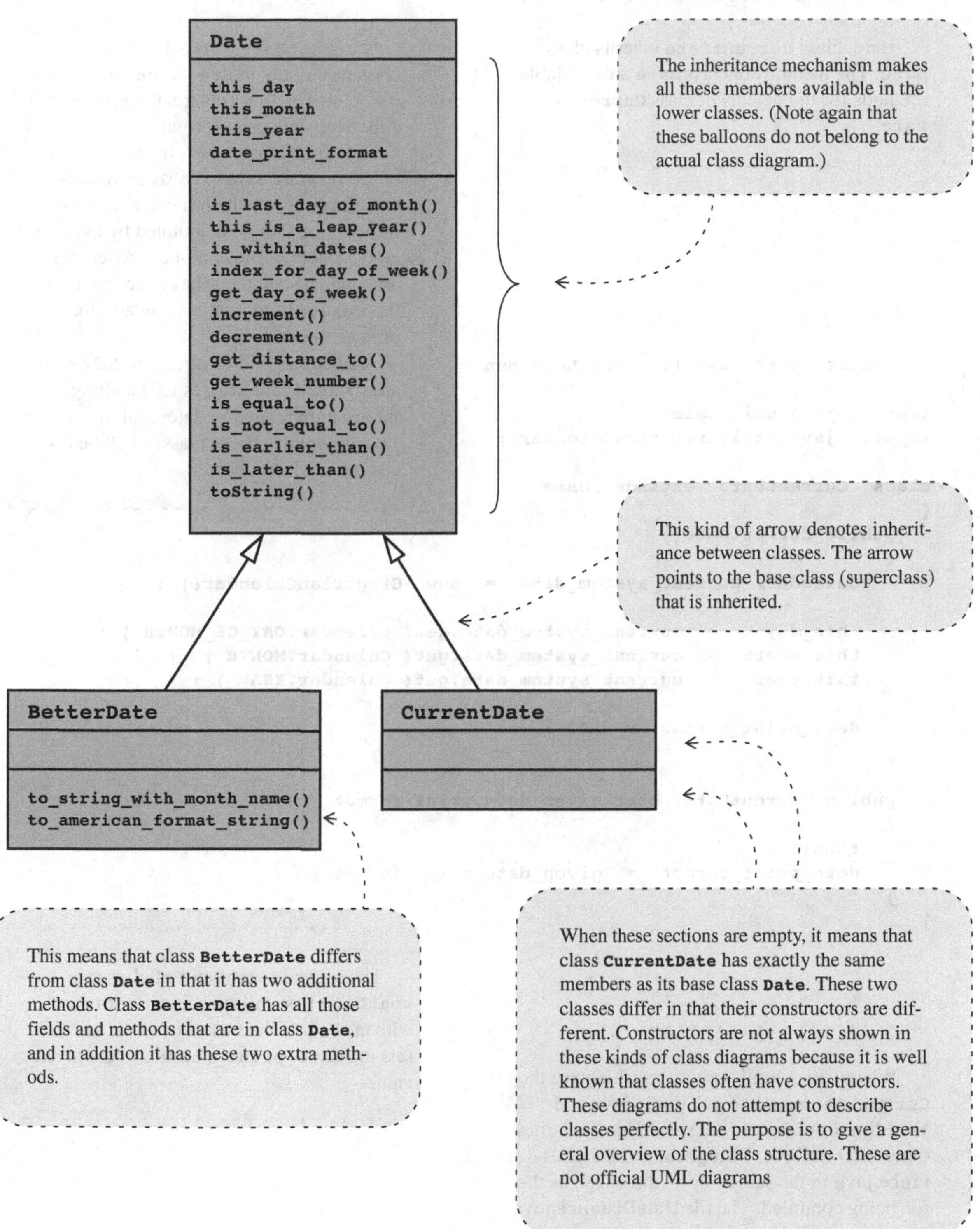


***Figure 12-1. Class diagram that describes relationships between three classes.***

Here, class **CurrentDate** inherits class **Date**. The methods of class **Date** are available methods for the objects of class **CurrentDate**.

**CurrentDate** differs from its superclass **Date** only in that its constructors are different. The first constructor assumes the American date print format.

The first constructor creates an object of the standard Java class **GregorianCalendar** from which it can read the date information that is maintained by the operating system of the computer. After these assignment statements have been executed, this **CurrentDate** object contains the date of the computer.

**Calendar** and **GregorianCalendar** are standard Java classes for handling information related to dates and time in Java programs. These classes will be discussed in a later chapter.

```
//  CurrentDate.java (c) Kari Laitinen

import  java.util.Calendar ;
import  java.util.GregorianCalendar ;

class  CurrentDate  extends  Date
{
   public CurrentDate()
   {
      Calendar  current_system_date  =  new  GregorianCalendar() ;

      this_day    =  current_system_date.get( Calendar.DAY_OF_MONTH ) ;
      this_month  =  current_system_date.get( Calendar.MONTH )  +  1 ;
      this_year   =  current_system_date.get( Calendar.YEAR ) ;

      date_print_format  =  'A' ;
   }

   public CurrentDate( char given_date_print_format )
   {
      this() ;
      date_print_format  =  given_date_print_format ;
   }
}
```

The second constructor of class **CurrentDate** first calls the first constructor with the help of the **this** keyword, and then sets the **date_print_format** to the given value.

When you compile programs which use the **CurrentDate** class (e.g. **Titanic.java** and **Weddingdates.java**), you should have the files **CurrentDate.java**, **Date.java**, and **DateDistance.java** in the same folder (directory) as the file being compiled. The file **DateDistance.java** is always needed because **Date.java** cannot be compiled without it.

**CurrentDate.java - 1. The declaration of class CurrentDate.**

Objects of class **CurrentDate** are usually created without supplying any parameters to the constructor of the class. This declaration results in that the object referenced by **date_of_today** contains the date information that is maintained by the operating system of the computer where this program is being executed.

```
//  Titanic.java  (c) Kari Laitinen

class Titanic
{
   public static void main( String[] not_in_use )
   {
      Date  date_when_titanic_sank  =  new  Date( "04/15/1912" ) ;

      CurrentDate date_of_today  =  new  CurrentDate() ;

      DateDistance time_from_sinking =

              date_of_today.get_distance_to( date_when_titanic_sank ) ;

      System.out.print( "\n Today it is " + date_of_today
                      + ".\n On " + date_when_titanic_sank
                      + ", the famous ship \"Titanic\" went to"
                      +  "\n the bottom of Atlantic Ocean."
                      + "\n That happened "
                      + time_from_sinking.years    +  " years, "
                      + time_from_sinking.months  +  " months, and "
                      + time_from_sinking.days     +  " days ago. \n\n" ) ;
   }
}
```

Because of inheritance, the methods of class **Date** can be called for **CurrentDate** objects. Here, for example, methods **get_distance_to()** and **toString()** are invoked for the **CurrentDate** object pointed by **date_of_today**.

**Titanic.java - 1. A program that uses both a Date object and a CurrentDate object.**

```
D:\javafiles3>java Titanic

 Today it is 03/01/2005.
 On 04/15/1912, the famous ship "Titanic" went to
 the bottom of Atlantic Ocean.
 That happened 92 years, 10 months, and 16 days ago.
```

**Titanic.java - X. Here the program is executed on March 1, 2005.**

Right after its creation, the object referenced by **date_to_increment** contains the current date of the computer. The object can be used like a **Date** object.

```
//  Weddingdates.java (c) Kari Laitinen

class Weddingdates
{
   public static void main( String[] not_in_use )
   {
      CurrentDate  date_to_increment  =  new  CurrentDate() ;

      int   number_of_dates_printed  =  0 ;

      System.out.print( "\n These are easy-to-remember dates for weddings and"
                     +  "\n other important events because the days and months"
                     +  "\n consist of the digits used in the year: \n" ) ;

      while ( number_of_dates_printed  <  60 )
      {
         String day_as_string    =
                 String.format( "%02d", date_to_increment.day() ) ;
         String month_as_string =
                 String.format( "%02d", date_to_increment.month() ) ;
         String year_as_string   =  ""  +  date_to_increment.year() ;

         if ( year_as_string.indexOf( day_as_string.charAt( 0 ) )  != -1  &&
              year_as_string.indexOf( day_as_string.charAt( 1 ) )  != -1  &&
              year_as_string.indexOf( month_as_string.charAt( 0 ) )  != -1  &&
              year_as_string.indexOf( month_as_string.charAt( 1 ) )  != -1  )
         {
            // Now we have found a date that meets our requirements.

            if ( number_of_dates_printed %  5  ==  0 )
            {
               System.out.print( "\n" ) ;
            }

            System.out.print( "   "  +  date_to_increment ) ;

            number_of_dates_printed  ++  ;
         }

         date_to_increment.increment() ;
      }
   }
}
```

The object referenced by **date_to_increment** is incremented to the next date. This program simply checks hundreds of dates to see which dates fulfil the criteria for a nice wedding date.

A valid wedding date has been found here. A newline is printed after every 5th date. The string concatenation operator + converts the **CurrentDate** object to a string. The method **toString()** that is provided in class **Date**, and inherited to class **CurrentDate**, is invoked automatically in the conversion operation.

**Weddingdates.java - 1.+ Using a CurrentDate object to find the next best wedding dates.**

This boolean expression tests whether the object referenced by **date_to_incrememt** contains a nice wedding date. The beginning of the **if** construct could be put into words like: "If the day of the date and the month of the date contain only such digits that can be found in the year of the date, ...". Method **indexOf()** returns the value -1 only when it cannot find the given character in the string for which it was called.

For example, date 02/06/2006 would be found to be an acceptable wedding date because all digits in strings "02" and "06" can be found in string "2006".

The three "components" of the date are converted to **String** objects here. The format specifier **%02d** ensures that single digit days and months are converted to strings that have a leading zero digit. The **format()** method of class **String** uses the same format specifiers as the method **System.out.printf()**.

```
while ( number_of_dates_printed  <  60 )
{
   String day_as_string    =
            String.format( "%02d", date_to_increment.day() ) ;
   String month_as_string =
            String.format( "%02d", date_to_increment.month() ) ;
   String year_as_string   =  ""  +  date_to_increment.year() ;

   if ( year_as_string.indexOf( day_as_string.charAt( 0 ) )  != -1  &&
        year_as_string.indexOf( day_as_string.charAt( 1 ) )  != -1  &&
        year_as_string.indexOf( month_as_string.charAt( 0 ) )  != -1  &&
        year_as_string.indexOf( month_as_string.charAt( 1 ) )  != -1  )
   {
      // Now we have found a date that meets our requirements.
```

**Weddingdates.java - 1 -1. The mechanism to find a nice wedding date.**

```
D:\javafiles3>java Weddingdates

 These are easy-to-remember dates for weddings and
 other important events because the days and months
 consist of the digits used in the year:

  02/02/2006  02/06/2006  02/20/2006  02/22/2006  02/26/2006
  06/02/2006  06/06/2006  06/20/2006  06/22/2006  06/26/2006
  02/02/2007  02/07/2007  02/20/2007  02/22/2007  02/27/2007
  07/02/2007  07/07/2007  07/20/2007  07/22/2007  07/27/2007
  02/02/2008  02/08/2008  02/20/2008  02/22/2008  02/28/2008
  08/02/2008  08/08/2008  08/20/2008  08/22/2008  08/28/2008
  02/02/2009  02/09/2009  02/20/2009  02/22/2009  09/02/2009
  09/09/2009  09/20/2009  09/22/2009  09/29/2009  01/01/2010
  01/02/2010  01/10/2010  01/11/2010  01/12/2010  01/20/2010
  01/21/2010  01/22/2010  02/01/2010  02/02/2010  02/10/2010
  02/11/2010  02/12/2010  02/20/2010  02/21/2010  02/22/2010
  10/01/2010  10/02/2010  10/10/2010  10/11/2010  10/12/2010
```

**Weddingdates.java - X. The program prints 60 dates in the MM/DD/YYYY format.**

This class must have a default constructor because it has a subclass. The default constructor is executed before the constructor of the derived class.

This program is another example in which a derived class differs from the base class so that it has a special constructor. This program is also an example of designing a base class so that it is easy to derive new classes from it. Class **EnglishCalendar** can be used to print month calendars with English texts. Texts that are printed are accessed by using these object references. When new classes are derived from this class, these references are made to point to new texts.

```
//  Calendars.java  (c) Kari Laitinen

class  EnglishCalendar
{
   protected  int  this_month ;
   protected  int  this_year ;

   protected  String[]  names_of_months ;
   protected  String    week_description ;

   public EnglishCalendar() {}

   public EnglishCalendar( int given_month, int given_year )
   {
      String[]  english_names_of_months  =

         { "January", "February", "March", "April",
           "May", "June", "July", "August",
           "September", "October", "November", "December" } ;

      String  english_week_description  =

         " Week   Mon  Tue  Wed  Thu  Fri  Sat  Sun" ;

      names_of_months   =  english_names_of_months ;

      week_description  =  english_week_description ;

      this_month  =  given_month ;
      this_year   =  given_year  ;
   }
```

An array whose type is **String[]** can be created by giving a list of string literals inside braces.

**names_of_months** is a reference to an array of type **String[]**. This statement makes **names_of_months** point to the array referenced by **english_names_of_months**. Although the array reference **english_names_of_months** ceases to exist after this constructor terminates, the actual array in the heap memory is saved from the destruction as it is referenced by **names_of_months**.

**Calendars.java - 1: A program with which calendars can be printed.**

An object of class **Date** is exploited to generate the calendar. Because our calendar is "built" into the methods of the **Date** class, it is possible to print calendars by calling the **Date** methods.

Because indexes start counting from zero, **names_of_months** needs to be indexed with a value one less than the actual month.

```
   public void print()
   {
      Date a_day_in_this_month  =  new  Date( 1, this_month, this_year ) ;

      int day_of_week_index    =  0 ;

      int day_of_week_of_first_day  =
                          a_day_in_this_month.index_for_day_of_week() ;

      System.out.print(
            "\n\n   "  +  names_of_months[ this_month - 1 ]
         +  "  "  +  this_year  +  "\n\n"+  week_description   +  "\n\n" );

      System.out.printf( "%4d  ",  a_day_in_this_month.get_week_number() ) ;

      // The first week of a month is often an incomplete week,
      // i.e., the first part of week belongs to the previous
      // month. In place of the days that belong to the previous
      // month we print just spaces.

      while ( day_of_week_index != day_of_week_of_first_day )
      {
         System.out.print( "     " ) ;
         day_of_week_index   ++ ;
      }

      while ( this_month   ==  a_day_in_this_month.month() )
      {
         if ( day_of_week_index   >=  7 )
         {
            System.out.printf( "\n%4d  ",
                               a_day_in_this_month.get_week_number() ) ;

            day_of_week_index   =  0 ;
         }

         System.out.printf( "%5d", a_day_in_this_month.day() ) ;

         a_day_in_this_month.increment() ;

         day_of_week_index   ++  ;
      }

      System.out.print( "\n" ) ;
   }
}
```

**Calendars.java - 2: Method print() of class EnglishCalendar.**

Class **SpanishCalendar** differs from its superclass **EnglishCalendar** only so that its constructor is different. The constructor makes the references **names_of_months** and **week_description** point to objects that contain Spanish texts. When the inherited method **print()** uses these references, it automatically prints those texts contained in the referenced objects.

This string literal contains the Spanish names for the days of a week in abbreviated form. The full names for Spanish days of week are: lunes, martes, miércoles, jueves, viernes, sábado, and domingo, lunes meaning Monday and domingo meaning Sunday.

```
class  SpanishCalendar  extends  EnglishCalendar
{
   public SpanishCalendar( int given_month, int given_year )
   {
      String[]  spanish_names_of_months  =

         { "Enero", "Febrero", "Marzo", "Abril",
           "Mayo", "Junio", "Julio", "Agosto",
           "Septiembre", "Octubre", "Noviembre", "Deciembre" } ;

      String   spanish_week_description  =

           "Semana  Lun  Mar  Mie  Jue  Vie  Sab  Dom" ;

      names_of_months    =  spanish_names_of_months ;
      week_description   =  spanish_week_description ;

      this_month  =  given_month ;
      this_year   =  given_year  ;
   }
}


class  Calendars
{
   public static void main( String[] not_in_use )
   {
      EnglishCalendar  an_english_calendar  =
                           new  EnglishCalendar( 2, 2008 ) ;

      an_english_calendar.print() ;

      SpanishCalendar  a_spanish_calendar  =
                           new  SpanishCalendar( 5, 2011 ) ;

      a_spanish_calendar.print() ;
   }
}
```

**Calendars.java - 3. Class SpanishCalendar the class with method main().**

```
   February  2008

 Week    Mon  Tue  Wed  Thu  Fri  Sat  Sun

   5                             1    2    3
   6      4    5    6    7    8    9   10
   7     11   12   13   14   15   16   17
   8     18   19   20   21   22   23   24
   9     25   26   27   28   29


   Mayo  2011

 Semana  Lun  Mar  Mie  Jue  Vie  Sab  Dom

  17                                       1
  18      2    3    4    5    6    7    8
  19      9   10   11   12   13   14   15
  20     16   17   18   19   20   21   22
  21     23   24   25   26   27   28   29
  22     30   31

D:\javafiles3>
```

In both of these months, the first week belongs partially to the previous month. The printing method thus prints only spaces in those day positions that belong to the previous month. The weeks begin here with a Monday, because class **Date** follows the ISO 8601 standard that specifies such weeks.

**Calendars.java - X. Objects of different calendar classes printed with the same method.**

### Reserved keyword static

The Java keyword **static** can be used in the following ways:

- A method of a class can be made static by writing a method declarator (method header) like

  ```
  public static SomeType some_method( ... )
  ```

  As we have already learned, a static method can be called without creating an object of the class:

  ```
  ClassName.some_method( ... ) ;
  ```

- A field of a class can be made static by declaring it in the following way

  ```
  static SomeType some_member ;
  ```

  A static field is a common data item for all objects of the class. The methods of the class can read and write a static field but it is the same field for all objects. A static field may be useful in some special situations, but those fields should not be favored too much in programming. One possible usage for a class-wide static variable is to use it to count how many objects of a class have been created. Among the extra programs of this book, in the **javafilesextra** folder, you can find a file named **StaticFieldTested.java**, and in that program a static variable is used to count the number of objects created. Static variables are sometimes called class variables, whereas the non-static variables are instance variables.

## Access modifiers

Members of classes include data fields, constants, constructors, and methods. Members are often marked with keywords like **public**, **protected**, and **private**. These keywords are access modifiers that specify how methods of other classes can access the members. Access modifiers are also called visibility modifiers because they specify how visible members of a class are. In addition to access modifiers, the visibility of class members depends on the package into which a class belongs. In Java, all classes belong to some package. As explained in Section 10.8, a class belongs to the default package if no **package** statement is present in its source program file. A package is usually a collection that contains many classes. In general, classes that belong to the same package may quite freely access each other's members.

Access modifiers determine the visibility of class members in the following way:

- When a member of a class is declared without an access modifier, its visibility is within the package into which the class belongs, i.e., the member is visible to all methods in all classes in the same package.
- Members declared with keyword **public** are visible to methods of all classes in "this" package and other packages. With the "this" package I mean the package of the class whose member is in question.
- Members declared with the keyword **protected** are like members declared without an access modifier except that the **protected** members are visible in derived classes that belong to other packages.
- Keyword **private** specifies that a member is visible only to the methods inside "this" class. A **private** member is not visible even to the methods of derived classes or methods of the classes in the same package.

Making data fields **protected** or **private**, and methods **public**, is the general principle of encapsulation. Data is encapsulated in **protected** and **private** data fields of a class, and the data is accessed by calling the **public** methods.

In the example programs of this book there are no **package** statements, and therefore the programs belong to the default package. This means that a class in a **.java** file is visible to other **.java** files which are placed in the same folder (directory). Because the use of packages can make small programs somewhat complicated, I have not used them in this book. However, it is a good practice to group classes into packages when large Java applications are developed.

When classes belong to the same package, the **protected** keyword has no effect within these classes. The classes in the example programs of this book are mostly these kinds of classes. I have, however, used the **protected** keyword in some classes, and those classes are the ones that act as base classes for other classes. When you see that a member of a class in this book is declared with the **protected** keyword, you know that some other classes will be derived from that particular class.

If a class belongs to a named package of classes, and the intention is that the class will be used by classes in other packages, the class should be declared with the keyword **public** in the following way

```
public class  SomeClass
{
   ...
```

The **public** keyword at the beginning of a class declaration specifies that the class is fully accessible, i.e., objects of the class can be created inside all classes regardless of which package the classes belong to. If the keyword **public** is omitted from a class declaration, the class is an internal class that can be accessed only by classes that belong to the same package as the class itself. For simplicity, the classes in this book are not declared **public**, but that does not cause any problems because the classes that need each other belong to the same, default, package.

## Exercises related to inheritance

Exercise 12-1. Add a new constructor to class **BetterDate** in program **BetterDate.java** so that **BetterDate** objects can be created in the following way

```
BetterDate  day_of_french_revolution  =
                         new  BetterDate( 14, 7, 1789 ) ;

BetterDate  end_date_of_first_world_war  =
                         new  BetterDate( 11, 11, 1918 ) ;
```

Exercise 12-2. Write a program that prints

- your current age in years, months, and days;
- your current age in just days; and
- the number of days until your next birthday.

You should use a **CurrentDate** object to obtain the current date for this program, and **Date** objects for any other purposes. You might call this program **Now.java**.

Exercise 12-3. By using Figure 12-1 as an example, draw a class diagram that describes the classes **EnglishCalendar** and **SpanishCalendar**.

Exercise 12-4. Modify program **Calendars.java** so that you derive a new class like **GermanCalendar** or **FrenchCalendar** from class **EnglishCalendar**, and use the new class to print a calendar in method **main()**. It is also possible to derive the new calendar from class **SpanishCalendar**.

Exercise 12-5. Write a program that you can command from the command line in the following ways

```
java  Yearcalendar  spanish  1984
java  Yearcalendar  english  2009
```

The idea here is that you can supply information to the program from the command line, and the program prints either an English or Spanish calendar of the given year. You can take program **Calendars.java** as a basis for this program, and declare parameters for method **main()**. With method **contains()** or **indexOf()** it is possible to compare a command line parameter to strings "spanish" and "english". When you create a calendar object inside a loop in the following way

```
for ( ...
{
   SpanishCalendar spanish_month_calendar  =  new  ...

   spanish_month_calendar.print() ;
}
```

a new object is always created when the loop is executed. When your program is ready, you can execute it in a command prompt window also in the following way

```
java  Yearcalendar  english  2009 >calendar2009.txt
```

The above command directs the output of the program into a text file named **calendar2009.txt**, and no output is generated to the screen. After you have executed the program, you can view the text file with a normal text editor. The symbol > is interpreted on the command line as an order to send the output of the program to a text file. That symbol and the file name that follows it are not counted as command line parameters. It is possible to direct the output of any program to a text file, but usually this works well only when the program in question does not input anything from the keyboard. In place of the symbol > it is possible to use the symbol >>. The command

```
java  Yearcalendar  spanish 2010 >>calendar2009.txt
```

does not delete the previously existing file **calendar2009.txt** but it appends the output of the program to the end of that file.

## 12.2 Larger class hierarchies

In this section, we shall study programs in which there are more than just two classes in inheritance chains. In the first example program, **Highmiddlelow.java**, you can examine theoretical classes that demonstrate how constructors are called automatically when inheritance takes place. You should remember that constructors are methods that are not inherited by lower classes. Constructors are, however, very important for the functionality of classes.

The hierarchy of classes in **Highmiddlelow.java** is described as a graphical class diagram in Figure 12-2. Class named **`HighClass`** is the topmost class in the hierarchy. Class **`MiddleClass`** is derived from **`HighClass`**, and class **`LowClass`** is derived from **`MiddleClass`**. To speak more accurately about class hierarchies, we can use the classes of **Highmiddlelow.java** to clarify our terminology:

- Class **`HighClass`** has two subclasses, **`MiddleClass`** and **`LowClass`**. **`MiddleClass`** is an immediate subclass to **`HighClass`** because there are no intermediate classes between them.
- Class **`MiddleClass`** has one immediate superclass (**`HighClass`**) and one immediate subclass (**`LowClass`**).
- Base class is an alternative term to refer to a superclass. Class **`HighClass`** is the base class for **`MiddleClass`** and **`LowClass`**.
- Derived class means a subclass.

Program **Highmiddlelow.java** was written primarily to demonstrate how the constructors of superclasses are called when an object of a low class is created. By studying the output of the program, you can see what happens in a practical example. The rule according to which the Java compiler generates automatic calls to the constructors of superclasses is such that before the statements of the body of a constructor are executed, the default constructor of the immediate superclass is called. If the immediate superclass has an immediate superclass, this rule is applied again. This results in that the constructor that is executed first is the constructor of the class that is on the top of the class hierarchy.

Constructors usually initialize the fields of a class. The automatic calls to superclass constructors are generated because superclass fields need to be initialized before the fields of a derived class. The initialization mechanism becomes, however, somewhat more complicated when classes have fields (data members) that are initialized with an initializer. An initializer can be an object-creation expression as in the statement

```
MemberClass another_data_member  =
                  new  MemberClass( "another_data_member" ) ;
```

In the above statement, field **`another_data_member`** is initialized by creating an object of class **`MemberClass`**. When a class contains these kinds of field declaration and initialization statements, these initializations are carried out before constructors are executed. By studying the output of program **Highmiddlelow.java**, you will find that the field initializations of "this" class are executed before the statements of the constructor of "this" class are executed. Field initializations are executed as if they were written at the beginning of a constructor.

Because the Java compiler generates the automatic calls to constructors when objects are created, there usually has to be default constructors in the upper classes in a class hierarchy. A default constructor is such that it can be called without supplying any parameters. If there are no constructors written in a class declaration, the Java compiler generates a default constructor of the form

```
public ClassName() {}
```

This is just a dummy constructor that does nothing, but it is needed in the inheritance mechanism. It is important to note that the compiler does not automatically write this constructor if there are some other constructors declared in the class.

The Java compiler implicitly calls the default constructor of the immediate superclass before it executes the constructor of the current class. This implicit calling does not happen when there is an explicit call to some constructor of the immediate superclass. If the constructor that is being executed is of the form

```
public ClassName( ... )
{
   super( ... ) ;
   ...
}
```

the compiler does not call the superclass constructor, because the writer of the program has already done it. This kind of constructor can be found in program **BetterDate.java**.

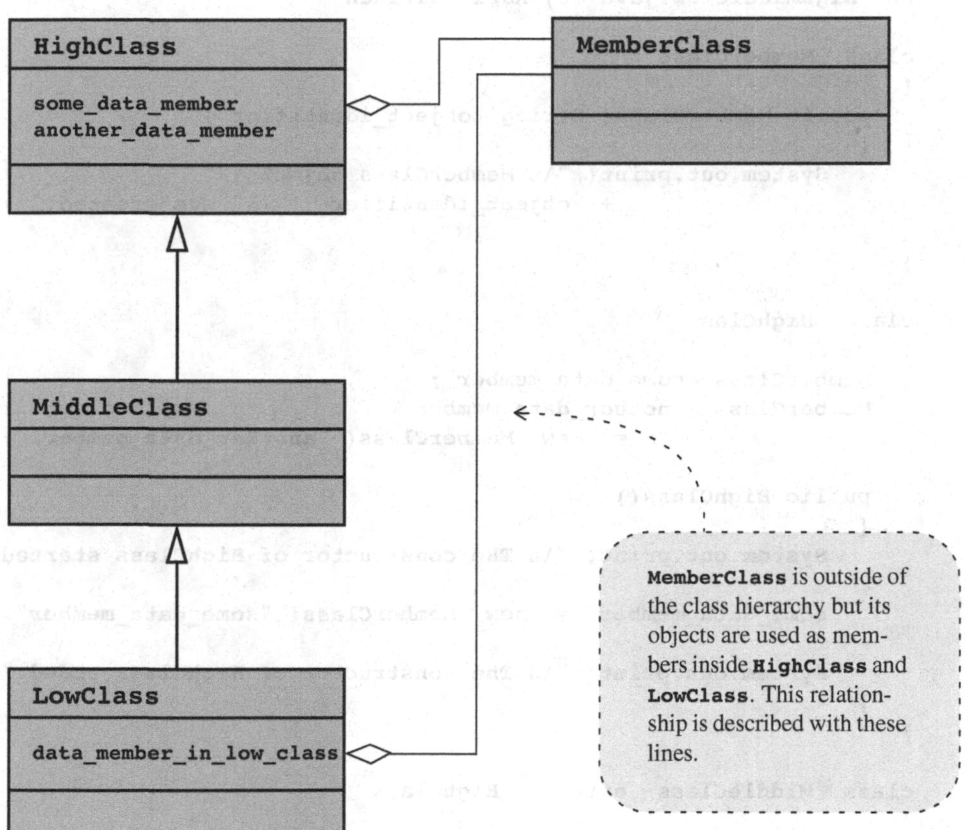


***Figure 12-2. The class hierarchy in Highmiddlelow.java.***

All classes in this program are merely theoretical. The purpose here is to demonstrate the order in which constructors are called in a class hierarchy. Objects of this **MemberClass** are used as fields inside **HighClass** and **LowClass**. The class between these two classes, **MiddleClass**, does not have any fields.

```
//  Highmiddlelow.java (c) Kari Laitinen

class  MemberClass
{
   public MemberClass( String  object_identifier )
   {
      System.out.print( "\n MemberClass object \""
                     +  object_identifier  + "\" was created." ) ;
   }
}

class  HighClass
{
   MemberClass  some_data_member ;
   MemberClass  another_data_member
                    =  new  MemberClass( "another_data_member" ) ;

   public HighClass()
   {
      System.out.print( "\n The constructor of HighClass started.") ;

      some_data_member   =  new  MemberClass( "some_data_member" ) ;

      System.out.print( "\n The constructor of HighClass ended.") ;
   }
}

class  MiddleClass  extends  HighClass
{
   public MiddleClass()
   {
      System.out.print( "\n The constructor of MiddleClass started.");
      System.out.print( "\n The constructor of MiddleClass ended.");
   }

}
```

The constructors of all these classes are such that they just print text lines indicating which constructor was called.

**Highmiddlelow.java - 1: Declarations of classes MemberClass, HighClass, and MiddleClass.**

This initialization statement is executed after the constructors of the upper classes and before constructor of this class.

```
class  LowClass  extends  MiddleClass
{
   MemberClass data_member_in_low_class  =
                     new MemberClass( "data_member_in_low_class" ) ;

   public LowClass()
   {
      System.out.print( "\n The constructor of LowClass started." ) ;
      System.out.print( "\n The constructor of LowClass ended." ) ;
   }
}

class Highmiddlelow
{
   public static void main( String[] not_in_use )
   {
      LowClass  low_class_object  =  new  LowClass() ;
   }
}
```

This program is a test program that studies the construction mechanisms of objects. You should modify this program to further examine these mechanisms. It is usual that, in order to find out the features of a programming language, it is necessary to write and modify test programs.

This object becomes garbage to be collected (i.e. a non-referenced object) immediately after its creation because there are no other statements in the `main()` method. The call to the `LowClass` constructor causes many other calls to the constructors of the upper classes.

**Highmiddlelow.java - 2. Class LowClass and method main().**

```
D:\javafiles3>java Highmiddlelow

 MemberClass object "another_data_member" was created.
 The constructor of HighClass started.
 MemberClass object "some_data_member" was created.
 The constructor of HighClass ended.
 The constructor of MiddleClass started.
 The constructor of MiddleClass ended.
 MemberClass object "data_member_in_low_class" was created.
 The constructor of LowClass started.
 The constructor of LowClass ended.
```

Although a `LowClass` object is being created in the program, the statements in the body of the `LowClass` constructor are the last ones executed.

**Highmiddlelow.java - X. All output is generated by constructors.**

Program **Windows.java** is another example where we have a longer class hierarchy. As shown in Figure 12-3, the class hierarchy consists of four classes. Despite its name, **Windows.java** is a conventional Java program that runs in a command prompt window. The program does, however, give us a glimpse of what Windows programming is about. In Windows programming it is common to use special class libraries that contain windowing classes. The classes in **Windows.java** resemble the windowing classes a little bit.

The windows that we see on the screens of our computers are usually graphical windows that contain pictures and text in various sizes and fonts. A graphical window consists of points. A graphical window can be, for example, 300 points wide and 200 points high, and a program can adjust the colors of all of those 60,000 (300 times 200) points. The console windows or command prompt windows where we run our programs are not graphical but character-based windows. In a character-based window, there is a certain number of places for characters. A typical console window can contain 25 lines of text, and each line can have 80 characters. Such a window can show 80 x 25 characters. There are thus 2000 character positions where a program can write a different character.

The window classes that are declared in **Windows.java** are character-based classes. With those classes it is possible to create window objects that are a certain number of character positions wide and a certain number of character rows high. These character-based windows can then be printed in the console window of a computer.

Different character positions in the windows of program **Windows.java** have numerical x and y coordinates. The upper left corner of a window is the zero position where both x and y coordinates are zero. The x coordinate increases when we move horizontally to the right from the zero position. The y coordinate increases when we go vertically downwards from the zero position. The character positions of a window can be described with a pair of coordinates (x, y). The upper left corner of a window is thus (0, 0). In the window

the letter e is in the position (6, 3), letter o in the position (9, 3), and the lower left corner in the position (0, 6). The above window could be of type **`DecoratedTextWindow`** of program **Windows.java**.

Objects of classes that belong to the same class hierarchy are relatives to each other. It is possible to write methods so that they accept objects of a certain class hierarchy as their parameters. In **Windows.java**, class **`Window`** has the method

```
public void move( int     destination_x_index,
                  int     destination_y_index,
                  Window  another_window )
{ ...
```

that takes a reference to an object of type **`Window`** as its third parameter. Although the parameter is clearly specified as of type **`Window`**, it means, in practice, types **`Window`**, **`FrameWindow`**, **`TextWindow`**, or **`DecoratedTextWindow`**. The third parameter of method **`move()`** can reference an object of any class in the windows class hierarchy. When a parameter is an object reference, only the address of an object is passed in the method call. Therefore, **`another_window`** can also contain the addresses of objects of the lower classes in the class hierarchy. Generally, a statement like

```
SomeClass  some_object ;
```

specifies an object reference that can point to an object of class **`SomeClass`** or to an object of some subclass of **`SomeClass`**.

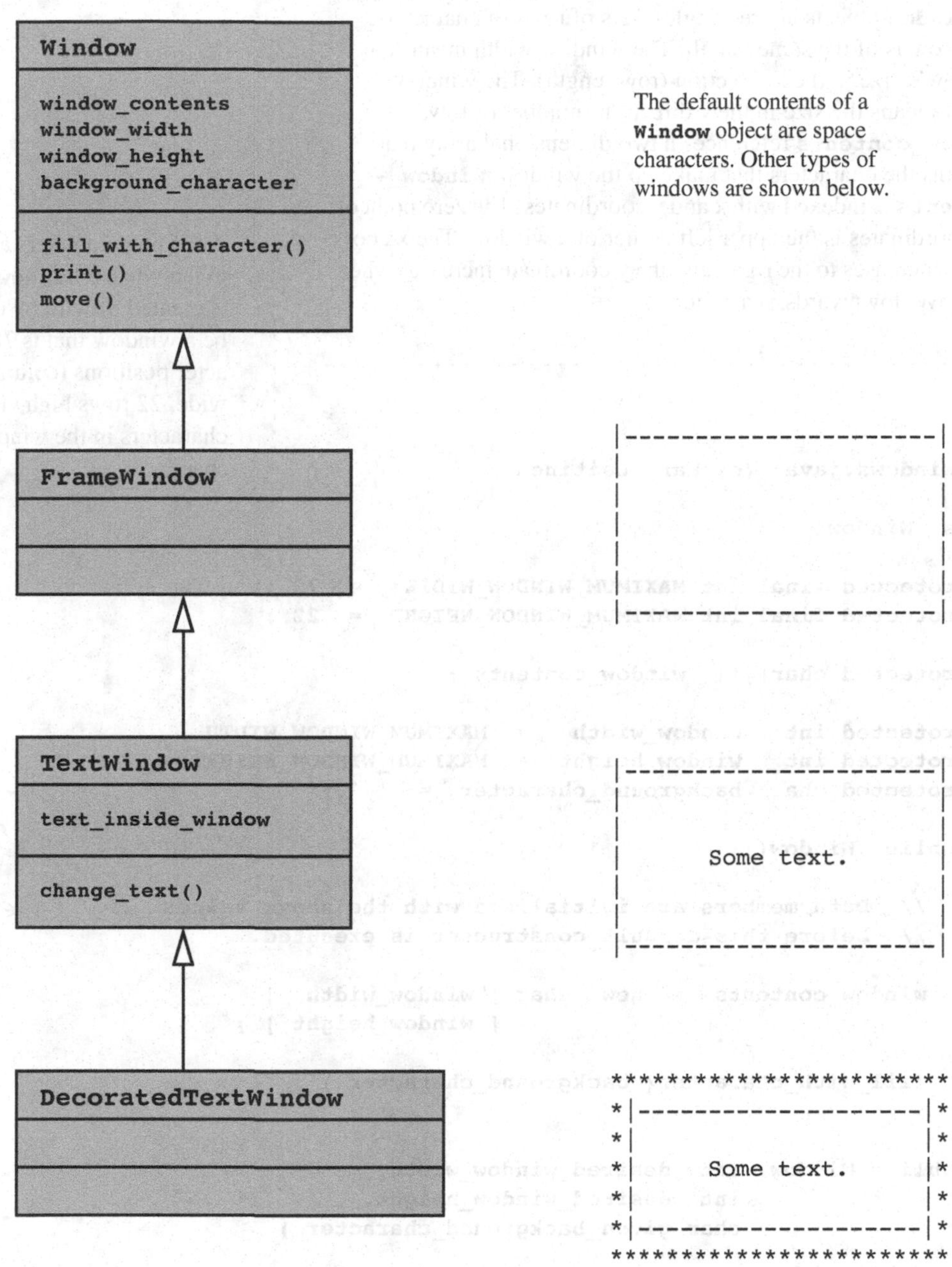


*Figure 12-3. Windows class hierarchy (left) and example windows (right).*

**Window** objects are rectangles, sets of rows of characters. Each row is of the same length. The window width means the window's size in the x direction (row length). The window height means the size in the y direction (number of rows). **window_contents** references a two dimensional array that contains the characters that make up the window. **window_-contents** is indexed with x and y coordinates. The zero point of the coordinates is the upper left corner of a window. The x coordinate increases to the right, and the y coordinate increases when we move downwards in a window.

If no parameters are given when a **Window** object is created, it will, by default, be a window that is 78 character positions (columns) wide, 22 rows high, and all characters in the window are spaces.

```
//  Windows.java  (c) Kari Laitinen

class  Window
{
   protected final int MAXIMUM_WINDOW_WIDTH   =  78 ;
   protected final int MAXIMUM_WINDOW_HEIGHT  =  22 ;

   protected char[][]  window_contents ;

   protected int   window_width    =  MAXIMUM_WINDOW_WIDTH ;
   protected int   window_height   =  MAXIMUM_WINDOW_HEIGHT ;
   protected char  background_character  =  ' ' ;

   public  Window()
   {
      //  Data members are initialized with the above values
      //  before this default constructor is executed.

      window_contents  =  new  char [ window_width  ]
                                    [ window_height ] ;

      fill_with_character( background_character ) ;
   }

   public  Window( int  desired_window_width,
                   int  desired_window_height,
                   char given_background_character )
   {
      window_width          =  desired_window_width ;
      window_height         =  desired_window_height ;
      background_character  =  given_background_character ;

      window_contents  =  new  char [ window_width  ]
                                    [ window_height ] ;

      fill_with_character( background_character ) ;
   }
```

The second constructor copies all of its parameters to the fields of the class. The window is also filled with the background character.

**Windows.java - 1: A program with a long class hierarchy.**

An index variable that is declared inside the parentheses of a **for** loop is visible only inside the loop.

When we use a two-dimensional array, we must index it with two indexes

```
   public void fill_with_character( char filling_character )
   {
      for ( int row_index  =  0  ;
                row_index  <  window_height ;
                row_index  ++  )
      {
         for ( int column_index  =  0 ;
                   column_index  <  window_width ;
                   column_index  ++ )
         {
            window_contents[ column_index ] [ row_index ]  =
                                              filling_character ;
         }
      }
   }

   public void print()
   {
      System.out.print( "\n" ) ;

      for ( int row_index  =  0  ;
                row_index  <  window_height ;
                row_index  ++  )
      {
         for ( int column_index  =  0 ;
                   column_index  <  window_width ;
                   column_index  ++ )
         {
            System.out.print(
                    window_contents[ column_index ] [ row_index ] ) ;
         }

         System.out.print( "\n" ) ;
      }
   }
```

This method actually makes a **Window** object visible on the screen. **Window** objects are sets of characters that are stored in the array (referenced by) **window_contents**. This method places the characters in the right positions on the screen.

**Window** object is printed by outputting single characters from the two-dimensional array. Method **print()** can be used to print all the window objects that can be created with classes derived from class **Window**.

Note that, because of overloading, there exist many versions of the **print()** method. The version that is used here takes a **char** value as a parameter.

**Windows.java - 2: Class Window methods fill_with_character() and print().**

This method moves another window over "this" window. The first two parameters specify the coordinates where the upper left corner of the other window should be. Part of "this" window is overwritten in the moving operation.

The third parameter specifies the window that is moved. **another_window** can reference an object of class **Window** or an object of any subclass of **Window**. In the **main()** method, this method is called to move objects of the subclasses of the **Window** class.

```
public void move( int     destination_x_index,
                  int     destination_y_index,
                  Window  another_window )
{
   int  source_y_index  =  0 ;

   while ( source_y_index  <  another_window.window_height )
   {
      if ( destination_y_index  >=  0   &&
           destination_y_index  <   window_height )
      {
         int  source_x_index  =  0 ;
         int  saved_destination_x_index  =  destination_x_index ;

         while ( source_x_index < another_window.window_width )
         {
            if ( destination_x_index  >=  0  &&
                 destination_x_index  <   window_width )
            {
               window_contents [ destination_x_index ]
                               [ destination_y_index ]  =

                  another_window.window_contents[ source_x_index ]
                                                [ source_y_index ] ;
            }
            source_x_index       ++ ;
            destination_x_index   ++ ;
         }
         destination_x_index  =  saved_destination_x_index ;
      }
      source_y_index         ++ ;
      destination_y_index    ++ ;
   }
  }
}
```

The moving operation may look somewhat complicated. The **if** statements of this method ensure that if the window object referenced by **another_window** is so large that it does not fit entirely inside "this" window, the excess parts of the other window are not copied. This **if** statement ensures that the moving operation goes well in the x direction.

**Windows.java - 3: Method named move() of class Window.**

Class **FrameWindow** differs from its base class because it has rudimentary frames. The frames are formed in a somewhat subtle manner by using the constructor of the superclass, and by creating windows that are moved over this window. The frames are made of characters | and -. The vertical frames are made with the | character. Here the constructor of class **Window**, the superclass, is called so that "this" window is filled with the | character and looks like the drawing on the right.

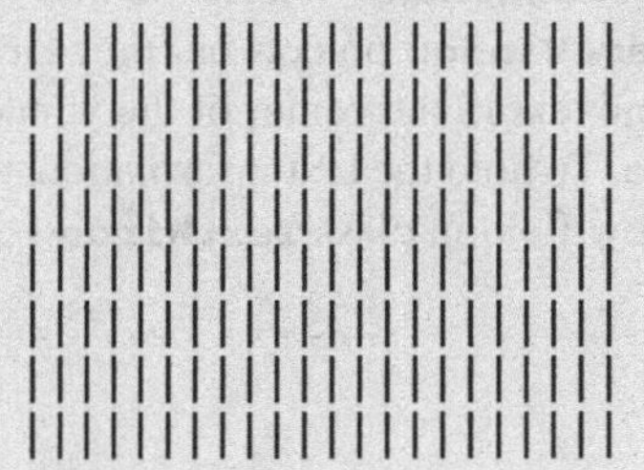

```
class  FrameWindow  extends  Window
{
   public FrameWindow()
   {
      this( 40, 10 ) ;  // Calling the other constructor below.
   }

   public FrameWindow( int  desired_window_width,
                       int  desired_window_height )
   {
      super( desired_window_width, desired_window_height, '|' ) ;

      Window horizontal_frames  =  new Window( window_width - 2,
                                               window_height, '-' ) ;

      Window spaces_inside_window  =  new Window( window_width - 2,
                                                  window_height - 2, ' ');

      move( 1, 0, horizontal_frames ) ;
      move( 1, 1, spaces_inside_window ) ;
   }
}
```

Window **horizontal_frames** is slightly narrower than "this" window, and is filled with characters -. When **horizontal_frames** is moved into the middle of "this" window, we get a window that looks like

```
|--------------------|
|--------------------|
|--------------------|
|--------------------|
|--------------------|
|--------------------|
|--------------------|
|--------------------|
```

In the last phase of the construction of a **FrameWindow** object, the constructor moves spaces into the middle of "this" window, causing the "this" window to look like

```
|--------------------|
|                    |
|                    |
|                    |
|                    |
|                    |
|                    |
|--------------------|
```

**Windows.java - 4: The declaration of class FrameWindow.**

**TextWindow** objects are like **FrameWindow** objects but they have some text in the center of the window area. To hold the text information, there is a new field in class **TextWindow**.

**embed_text_in_window()** is marked as **protected**, which means that it is supposed to be called only by methods in this class hierarchy. The method is used to copy the text stored as **text_inside_window** to the center of the window.

```
class  TextWindow  extends  FrameWindow
{
   protected String text_inside_window ;

   protected void embed_text_in_window()
   {
      int  text_length  =  text_inside_window.length() ;
      int  text_row     =  window_height / 2 ;

      int  text_start_column = (window_width - text_length) / 2 ;

      for ( int character_index  =  0 ;
                character_index  <  text_length ;
                character_index  ++ )
      {
         window_contents [ text_start_column + character_index ]
                         [ text_row ]  =

                 text_inside_window.charAt( character_index ) ;
      }
   }

   public TextWindow( int     desired_window_width,
                      int     desired_window_height,
                      String  given_line_of_text )
   {
      super( desired_window_width, desired_window_height ) ;

      text_inside_window  =  given_line_of_text ;
      embed_text_in_window() ;
   }

   public void change_text( String  new_line_of_text )
   {
      text_inside_window  =  new_line_of_text ;
      embed_text_in_window() ;
   }
}
```

**Windows.java - 5: The declaration of class TextWindow.**

Window of type **DecoratedTextWindow** is a **TextWindow** that has a decoration around the normal frame. The extra decoration frame consists of asterisks *. The decoration frame is made by first creating a window that is full of asterisk characters.

**given_line_of_text** is passed as a parameter to the constructor of class **TextWindow**. That text is, however, overwritten later when windows are moved.

```
class DecoratedTextWindow  extends  TextWindow
{
   public DecoratedTextWindow( int    desired_window_width,
                               int    desired_window_height,
                               String given_line_of_text )
   {
      super( desired_window_width,
             desired_window_height,
             given_line_of_text ) ;

      Window decoration_frame  =  new  Window( desired_window_width,
                                               desired_window_height,
                                               '*' ) ;
      TextWindow  window_inside_window  =
                  new  TextWindow( desired_window_width - 2,
                                   desired_window_height - 2,
                                   given_line_of_text ) ;

      decoration_frame.move( 1, 1, window_inside_window ) ;

      move( 0, 0, decoration_frame ) ;
   }
}
```

**window_inside_window** references a **TextWindow** object that is slightly smaller than the object referenced by **decoration_frame**. When **window_inside_window** is moved inside the **decoration_frame**, we get a window that looks like

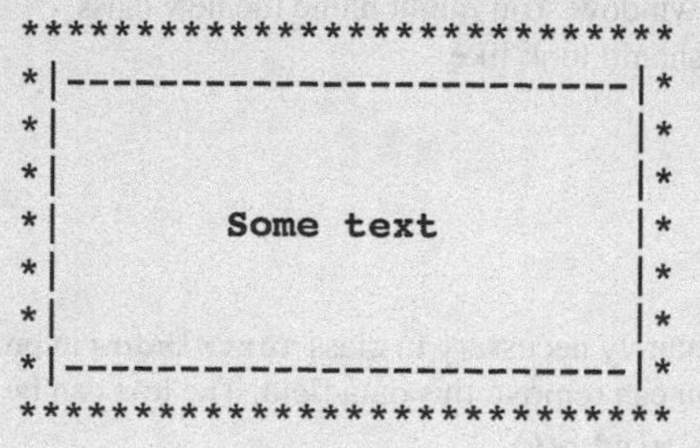

```
****************************
*|------------------------|*
*|                        |*
*|                        |*
*|       Some text        |*
*|                        |*
*|                        |*
*|------------------------|*
****************************
```

At the end, **decoration_frame** references a window that has the features that were specified when this constructor was called. Therefore, the window referenced by **decoration_frame** is moved over "this" window.

**Windows.java - 6: The declaration of class DecoratedTextWindow.**

The **FrameWindow** object referenced by **empty_window** is 24 character positions wide and 7 rows high.

The **TextWindow** object referenced by **greeting_window** is 30 character positions wide and 8 rows high, and the text "Hello, world." is put as the text inside the window.

```
class Windows
{
   public static void main( String[] not_in_use )
   {
      Window  background_window  =  new  Window( 76, 22, '/' ) ;

      FrameWindow  empty_window     =  new  FrameWindow( 24, 7 ) ;
      TextWindow   greeting_window  =
                       new  TextWindow( 30, 8, "Hello, world." ) ;
      DecoratedTextWindow  smiling_window  =
                       new  DecoratedTextWindow( 28, 11, "Smile!" ) ;

      background_window.move(  6,  2, empty_window ) ;
      background_window.move(  4, 12, greeting_window ) ;

      greeting_window.change_text( "HELLO, UNIVERSE!" ) ;
      background_window.move( 43, 11, greeting_window ) ;

      background_window.move( 40,  3, smiling_window ) ;

      background_window.print() ;
   }
}
```

Here, the object (referenced by) **empty_window** is moved over the background window so that the upper left corner of **empty_window** is in position (6, 2) inside **background_window**. Position (6, 2) means the 7th character position to the right and the 3rd row downwards from the upper left corner of the window.

When the background window is printed, all the smaller windows that were moved over it are printed as well.

**Windows.java - 7. Method main() that experiments with window objects.**

## Exercises with program Windows.java

Exercise 12-6. Derive a new class from **DecoratedTextWindow**, and make the new class such that the window objects have two asterisk frames around the window. You might name the new class **ExtraDecoratedTextWindow**. The new frame should look like

```
***************************
***************************
**|--------------------|**
**|                    |**
```

Exercise 12-7. The data field **text_inside_window** is not absolutely necessary in class **TextWindow** in program **Windows.java**. Modify the class so that you can remove this data field. The text can be given as a parameter to method **embed_text_in_window()**.

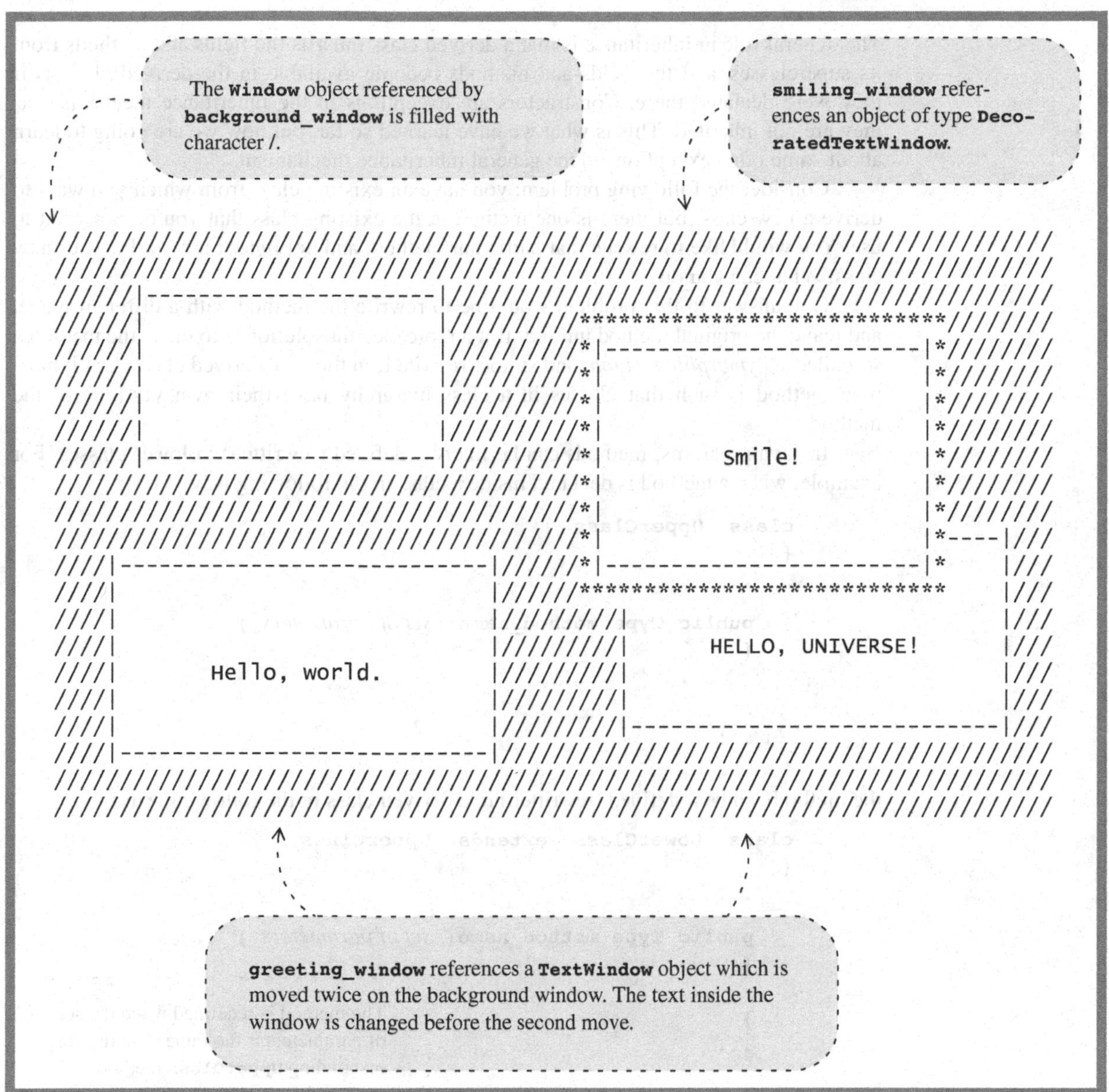


**Windows.java - X. The object referenced by background_window is the printed window here.**

## 12.3 Polymorphism – redefining methods in derived classes

The general rule in inheritance is that a derived class inherits the fields and methods from its superclasses, and the fields and methods become available in the derived class as if they were declared there. Constructors are exceptions in the inheritance mechanism as they are not inherited. This is what we have learned so far, but now we are going to learn about some other exceptions to the general inheritance mechanism.

Consider the following problem: you have an existing class from which you want to derive a new class, but there is one method in the existing class that you do not want to use. You would like to rewrite that particular method, and not inherit it at all for your new class. What can you do?

One answer to this problem would be to rewrite the method with a different name, and leave the original method unused. But a more elegant solution is to make the method a so-called *polymorphic method*, and simply rewrite it in the new derived class. A polymorphic method is such that classes in a class hierarchy have their own versions of the method.

In Java programs, methods can be freely redefined (rewritten) in lower classes. For example, when a method is declared inside a class in the following way

```
class  UpperClass
{
   ...
   public Type method_name( set of parameters )
   {
      ...
   }
   ...
}
```

the method can be redefined (rewritten) in a derived class in the following way:

```
class  LowerClass  extends  UpperClass
{
   ...
   public Type method_name( set of parameters )
   {
      ...
   }
   ...
}
```

The method is redefined when the set of parameters is the same as in the corresponding **UpperClass** method.

When a method is redefined in a derived class, the method declaration looks just like any other method declaration. Nothing in the new class indicates that there is a method with the same name and the same set of parameters in an upper class. You just have to know that the method is a redefined method.

In programming terminology, the verb *override* is also used to describe the redefinition of methods in lower classes. When a method replaces a corresponding method in an upper class, we can say that the upperclass method is overridden by the new method. When no method overrides a method that is inherited from an upper class, the method is inherited in the normal way, as we have learned earlier.

A method can be redefined in every class in a long class hierarchy. When a method is redefined in a class hierarchy, there exist several forms (versions) of the same method in the class hierarchy. Therefore, such a method can be called a polymorphic method. (The word polymorphic is of Greek origin. *Poly* means many and *morph* means form.) A class that contains one or more polymorphic methods is a *polymorphic class*. The term *polymorphism* means the use of polymorphic methods and classes.

Program **BankPolymorphic.java** is an example in which a method of our familiar banking application is replaced with rewritten methods in derived classes. The class hierarchy of **BankPolymorphic.java** is described in Figure 12-4. The two new classes that are derived from class **`BankAccount`** in **BankPolymorphic.java** can be described in the following way

- Class **`AccountWithCredit`** allows the balance of an account object to be negative. The user of the account can thus loan money from the bank by letting the account balance become negative. When objects of class **`AccountWithCredit`** are created, a credit limit must be specified. Method **`withdraw_money()`** is rewritten for class **`AccountWithCredit`** so that it allows the account balance to be negative up to the specified credit limit.
- Objects of class **`RestrictedAccount`** do not allow excessive withdrawals from bank accounts. A withdrawal limit is specified when a **`RestrictedAccount`** object is created, and the rewritten method **`withdraw_money()`** of class **`RestrictedAccount`** guards that the withdrawal limit is not exceeded.

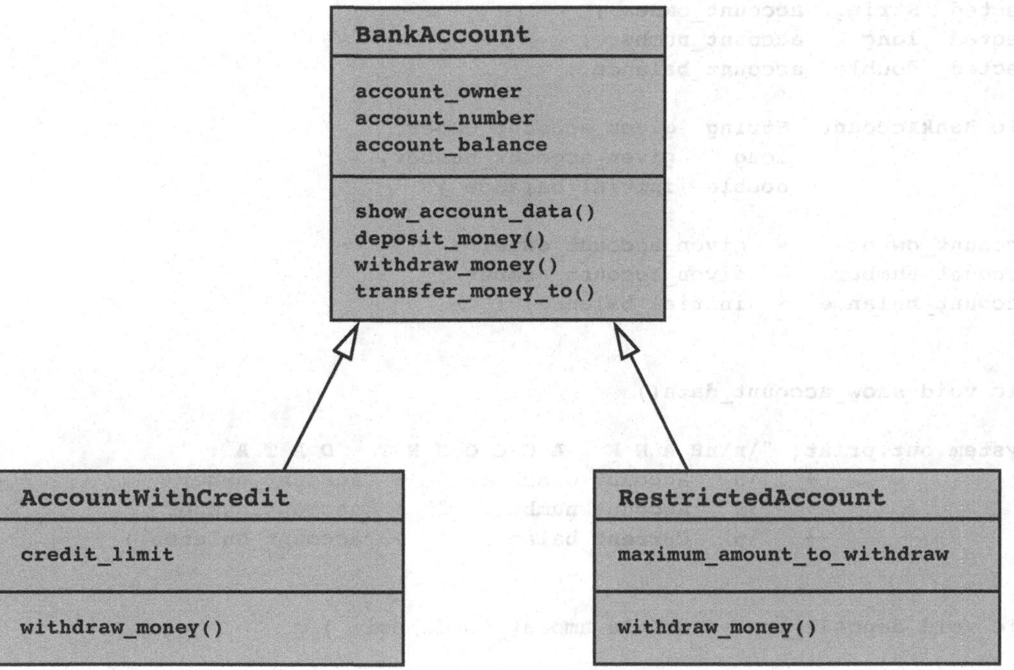


***Figure 12-4. The class hierarchy in BankPolymorphic.java.***

## Polymorphic methods vs. method overloading

Method overloading means that the same method name can mean different methods. Basically, this is true also in the case of polymorphic methods. A different version of a polymorphic method must, however, have exactly the same kinds of parameters. In the case of overloaded methods, the different methods that bear the same name must differ to the extent that either they have different number of parameters or different types of parameters. The compiler can distinguish overloaded methods with the same name because the methods have different kinds of parameters. A single class can contain several versions of an overloaded method, whereas different versions of a polymorphic method must exist in different classes in a class hierarchy.

The class **BankAccount** declared in this program is almost the same as the **BankAccount** class declared in program **BankBetter.java**. The only difference between these classes is that the fields of this class are declared with the keyword **protected**. The use of this access modifier does not actually affect the operation of this program. In this book, the fields of those classes which act as base classes for other classes are marked as **protected**.

```
//  BankPolymorphic.java  (c) Kari Laitinen

class  BankAccount
{
   protected  String   account_owner ;
   protected  long     account_number ;
   protected  double   account_balance ;

   public BankAccount( String  given_account_owner,
                       long    given_account_number,
                       double  initial_balance )
   {
      account_owner    =  given_account_owner ;
      account_number   =  given_account_number ;
      account_balance  =  initial_balance   ;
   }

   public void show_account_data()
   {
      System.out.print( "\n\nB A N K   A C C O U N T   D A T A : "
                     + "\n   Account owner :   "  +  account_owner
                     + "\n   Account number:   "  +  account_number
                     + "\n   Current balance:  "  +  account_balance ) ;
   }

   public void deposit_money( double amount_to_deposit )
   {
      System.out.print( "\n\nTRANSACTION FOR ACCOUNT OF " +  account_owner
                     +  " (Account number " +  account_number  + ")" ) ;
      System.out.print( "\n   Amount deposited: "  +  amount_to_deposit
                     +  "\n   Old account balance: "  +  account_balance ) ;
      account_balance  =  account_balance  +  amount_to_deposit ;
      System.out.print( "   New balance: "  +  account_balance  ) ;
   }
```

**BankPolymorphic.java - 1: A program with several bank account classes.**

In Java, almost all instance methods can be redefined (overridden) in derived classes. Only those methods that are declared with the **final** keyword cannot be overridden. Nothing in this method declaration indicates that this particular method is redefined in the other classes of this program. When the compiler finds a method with the same name and the same parameter declaration in a derived class, it knows that this method is overridden in the derived class.

```
   public void withdraw_money( double amount_to_withdraw )
   {
      System.out.print( "\n\nTRANSACTION FOR ACCOUNT OF " +  account_owner
                      + " (Account number " +  account_number  + ")" ) ;

      if ( account_balance  <  amount_to_withdraw )
      {
         System.out.print("\n   -- Transaction not completed: "
                + "Not enough money to withdraw " + amount_to_withdraw ) ;
      }
      else
      {
         System.out.print("\n   Amount withdrawn:      "  +  amount_to_withdraw
                        + "\n   Old account balance: "  +  account_balance ) ;
         account_balance  =  account_balance  -  amount_to_withdraw ;
         System.out.print("   New balance: "  +  account_balance ) ;
      }
   }

   public void transfer_money_to( BankAccount  receiving_account,
                                  double        amount_to_transfer )
   {
      System.out.print( "\n\nTRANSACTION FOR ACCOUNT OF " +  account_owner
                      + " (Account number " +  account_number  + ")" ) ;

      if ( account_balance  >=  amount_to_transfer )
      {
         receiving_account.account_balance  =
            receiving_account.account_balance  +  amount_to_transfer ;

         System.out.print("\n    " + amount_to_transfer + " was transferred to "
              + receiving_account.account_owner  +  " (Account no. "
              + receiving_account.account_number +  ")."
              + "\n   Balance before transfer: " +  account_balance ) ;
         account_balance  =  account_balance  -  amount_to_transfer ;
         System.out.print("   New balance:  " +  account_balance ) ;
      }
      else
      {
         System.out.print( "\n   -- Not enough money for transfer." ) ;
      }
   }
}
```

**BankPolymorphic.java - 2: The other part of class BankAccount.**

The constructor of superclass **BankAccount** is called here in order to handle the first three constructor parameters. The fourth parameter is copied to the new field of this class.

```
class  AccountWithCredit  extends  BankAccount
{
   protected  double  credit_limit ;

   public  AccountWithCredit( String  given_account_owner,
                              long    given_account_number,
                              double  initial_balance,
                              double  given_credit_limit  )
   {
      super( given_account_owner,
             given_account_number,
             initial_balance ) ;

      credit_limit  =  given_credit_limit ;
   }

   public void withdraw_money( double amount_to_withdraw )
   {
      System.out.print( "\n\nTRANSACTION FOR ACCOUNT OF " +  account_owner
                 + " (Account number " + account_number  + ")" ) ;

      if ( account_balance  +  credit_limit  <  amount_to_withdraw )
      {
         System.out.print(
               "\n   --  Transaction not completed: "
             + "Not enough credit to withdraw "+ amount_to_withdraw ) ;
      }
      else
      {
         System.out.print(
                "\n   Amount withdrawn:      "  +  amount_to_withdraw
              + "\n   Old account balance: "  +  account_balance ) ;
         account_balance  =  account_balance  -  amount_to_withdraw ;
         System.out.print( "   New balance: "  +  account_balance ) ;
      }
   }
}
```

This method overrides the **withdraw_money()** method of the superclass **BankAccount**. All other methods, excluding the constructor method, are inherited from the **BankAccount** class in the usual way.

**BankPolymorphic.java - 3: Class AccountWithCredit and its redefined withdraw_money().**

This is another class that has been derived from class **BankAccount** so that method **withdraw_money()** is redefined. The bank account objects of class **RestrictedAccount** do not allow withdrawals that exceed the value of this field. This restriction ensures that the money that is in the account is not spent too quickly.

```
class  RestrictedAccount  extends  BankAccount
{
   protected double  maximum_amount_to_withdraw ;

   public RestrictedAccount( String  given_account_owner,
                             long    given_account_number,
                             double  initial_balance,
                             double  given_withdrawal_limit  )
   {
      super( given_account_owner,
             given_account_number,
             initial_balance ) ;

      maximum_amount_to_withdraw  =  given_withdrawal_limit ;
   }

   public void withdraw_money( double amount_to_withdraw )
   {
      if ( amount_to_withdraw  >  maximum_amount_to_withdraw )
      {
         System.out.print(
               "\n\nTRANSACTION FOR ACCOUNT OF " +  account_owner
            +  "  (Account number " +  account_number  + ")" ) ;

         System.out.print(
              "\n  -- Transaction not completed: Cannot withdraw "
            +  amount_to_withdraw   + "\n   -- Withdrawal limit is "
            +  maximum_amount_to_withdraw + "." ) ;
      }
      else
      {
         super.withdraw_money( amount_to_withdraw ) ;
      }
   }
}
```

In the case that the withdrawal is acceptable, when the amount to be withdrawn is not too large, the **withdraw_money()** method of superclass **BankAccount** is called to perform the actual withdrawal. With the help of the reserved keyword **super** it is possible to call the same method in the superclass.

**BankPolymorphic.java - 4: Class RestrictedAccount and its version of withdraw_money().**

stones_account references an object of type AccountWithCredit. It is possible to withdraw 2500.00 from this account because the credit limit allows the account balance to go negative.

```
class BankPolymorphic
{
   public static void main( String[] not_in_use )
   {
      BankAccount  beatles_account  =
                   new  BankAccount( "John Lennon", 222222, 2000.00 ) ;

      AccountWithCredit  stones_account  =
                   new  AccountWithCredit( "Brian Jones", 333333,
                                           2000.00,  1000.00 ) ;

      RestrictedAccount   doors_account  =
                   new  RestrictedAccount( "Jim Morrison", 444444,
                                           4000.00,  1000.00 ) ;

      beatles_account.withdraw_money( 2500.00 ) ;
      stones_account.withdraw_money( 2500.00 ) ;
      doors_account.withdraw_money( 2500.00 ) ;
   }
}
```

Here method withdraw_money() is called for each created bank account object. Because withdraw_money() is a polymorphic method that has several versions of itself, a different method is executed in each case.

There is a withdrawal limit of 1000.00 in the object referenced by doors_account. Although the account's initial balance is 4000.00, it is not possible to withdraw 2500.00 because that exceeds the withdrawal limit.

**BankPolymorphic.java - 5. Withdrawing money from different bank accounts.**

```
D:\javafiles3>java BankPolymorphic


TRANSACTION FOR ACCOUNT OF John Lennon (Account number 222222)
   -- Transaction not completed: Not enough money to withdraw 2500.0

TRANSACTION FOR ACCOUNT OF Brian Jones (Account number 333333)
   Amount withdrawn:     2500.0
   Old account balance: 2000.0   New balance: -500.0

TRANSACTION FOR ACCOUNT OF Jim Morrison (Account number 444444)
   -- Transaction not completed: Cannot withdraw 2500.0
   -- Withdrawal limit is 1000.0.
```

**BankPolymorphic.java - X. The withdrawal succeeds only for stones_account.**

### Exercise with program BankPolymorphic.java

Exercise 12-8. Modify program **BankPolymorphic.java** by deriving a new class named **RichPersonAccount** from class **BankAccount** and redefining (overriding) the method **deposit_money()** in the new class. The new version of **deposit_money()** should be such that small deposits in the account are not allowed. The idea here is that a rich person deposits only large sums of money. A minimum deposit limit must be given when a **RichPersonAccount** object is created. For example, the following program lines

```
RichPersonAccount  rockefeller_account  =  new
     RichPersonAccount( "John D.", 55555, 900000.00, 9000.00 ) ;

rockefeller_account.deposit_money( 8000.00 ) ;
```

should result in some kind of error message from method **deposit_money()** because the sum 8000.00 is below the minimum deposit limit 9000.00.

If some method is a polymorphic method of which there are several versions in a class hierarchy, the Java interpreter (the Java virtual machine) is able to find the right version of the polymorphic method. When a program is executed, and a method is called for an object, a suitable method is selected according to the type of the object. If it is necessary in some method of a class to use a non-standard version of a polymorphic method, that is possible too. Let's consider a hypothetical class hierarchy:

```
class  HigherClass
{
   ...
   public void some_method()
   {
      ...
   }
   ...
}

class  LowerClass  extends  HigherClass
{
   ...
   public void some_method()
   {
      ...
   }

   public void another_method()
   {
      ...
      some_method() ;
      ...
   }
}
```

In this example, there is a separate version of **some_method()** in both classes, but method **another_method()** is declared only in **LowerClass**. If the source code of **another_method()** is written as above, the version of **some_method()** that is declared in **LowerClass** is called. This is the most typical situation. But if, for some more or less peculiar reason, it was necessary to call the version of **some_method()** that is declared in **HigherClass**, **another_method()** would have to be written

```
public void another_method()
{
   ...
   super.some_method() ;
   ...
}
```

By using the reserved keyword **super**, it is possible to specify a call to the method that is declared in the superclass. These kinds of method calls are sometimes useful when methods are rewritten in derived classes. It may make things easier to call the superclass' version of a method inside a new version of the same method. In program **BankPolymorphic.java** this arrangement is used in class **RestrictedAccount**. Method **withdraw_money()** is rewritten there in the following way

```
public void withdraw_money( double amount_to_withdraw )
{
   ...

      super.withdraw_money( amount_to_withdraw ) ;
   }
}
```

where an existing version of method **withdraw_money()** is called inside a new version of the same method. This makes things easier because it is not necessary to repeat the source code of the existing method inside a new method. If a modification is made to the existing method, the same modification is automatically brought inside the new method.

In **BankPolymorphic.java**, method **withdraw_money()** is declared in class **BankAccount**, and new versions of this method are introduced in lower classes. The original **withdraw_money()** in class **BankAccount** is a perfectly working method, and class **BankAccount** could be used even without deriving any lower classes from it. It is not, however, always necessary that a class where a method is declared is a useful class for creating objects.

Sometimes, it is a nice solution in an object-oriented application to use classes that are designed just to act as superclasses for other classes, and not as classes for object creation. Such classes are said to be abstract classes. These classes are abstract because they contain methods that are not real methods, but merely declarators of methods. These unreal methods are called abstract methods. An abstract class with an abstract method is declared by using the keyword **abstract** in the following way

```
abstract class ClassName
{
   ...
   abstract public Type method_name( ... ) ;
   ...
}
```

The method **method_name()** in the above hypothetical class is an abstract method that does not have a method body. Instead, there is a semicolon in place of the method body. The method cannot do anything. An abstract method declaration specifies the name, type, and parameters of the method, but the actual implementation of the method must be specified in lower classes. An abstract method is like other methods of a class with the exception that an abstract method <u>must</u> be rewritten in a lower class whereas other methods <u>can</u> be rewritten in a lower class.

The purpose of an abstract class is that it specifies the general structure of the classes that are below it in a class hierarchy. An abstract class specifies the methods that are to be found in lower classes, but it does not specify how all the methods are implemented. Each subclass of an abstract class must provide suitable implementations for the abstract methods.

Program **Times.java** is an example that demonstrates how a class is made an abstract class by declaring an abstract method inside it, and how usable classes are derived from the abstract superclass. The class hierarchy of **Times.java** is described in Figure 12-5. In the two derived classes in **Times.java** the abstract method **print()** is declared in different ways:

- Method **print()** in class **AmericanTime** prints the time in 12-hour format so that a.m. or p.m. is written after the numbers depending on whether the time is before or after midday.
- The printing method in class **EuropeanTime** prints the time in 24-hour format that goes from 00:00:00 to 23:59:59, midday being 12:00:00.

It is probably not entirely true that the 12-hour a.m./p.m. time format is used everywhere in America, and the 24-hour format is used everywhere in Europe, but the class names **AmericanTime** and **EuropeanTime** just happen to be convenient names to distinguish these two time formats. To clarify the differences between these two time formats, the following pairs are equivalent time expressions in different formats.

```
12:30:15 a.m.             0:30:15
11:59:59 a.m.            11:59:59
12:30:15 p.m.            12:30:15
 1:40:19 p.m.            13:40:19
11:35:05 p.m.            23:35:05
```

Method **main()** in **Times.java** prints the current time either in American or European format. The time is printed by the method call

```
time_to_show.print() ;
```

The interesting thing here, is that when the above statement is executed, it is not always the same version of method **print()** that is called; the version of **print()** is decided at the time when the program is executed. The object reference **time_to_show** points either to an **AmericanTime** object or to a **EuropeanTime** object, depending on what the user of the program selected. Therefore, the above statement executes that version of method **print()** that is associated with the object that is referenced by **time_to_show**.

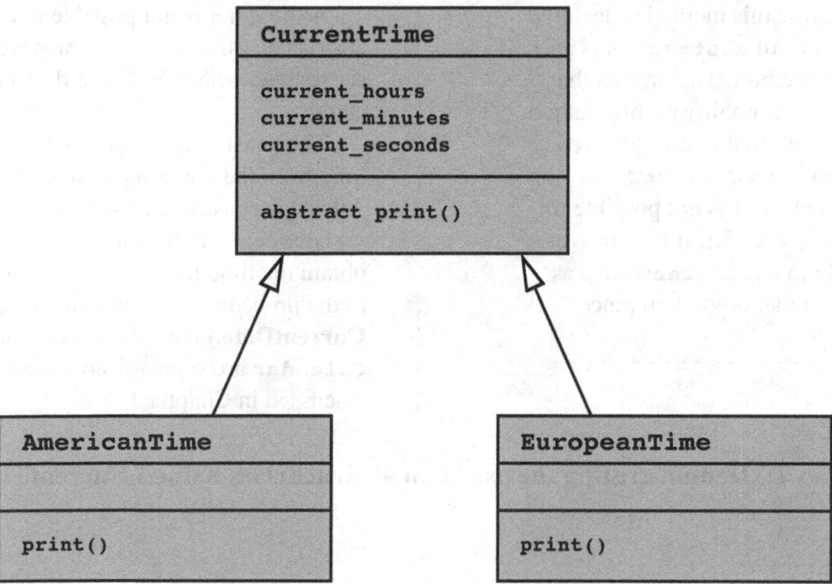


*Figure 12-5. The time-related classes of Times.java*

The reserved keyword **abstract** declares that this class is an abstract class. An abstract class contains at least one abstract method. The declaration of such a class must begin with the **abstract** keyword.

```
//  Times.java  (c) Kari Laitinen

import java.util.* ;

abstract class CurrentTime
{
   protected int current_hours ;
   protected int current_minutes ;
   protected int current_seconds ;

   public CurrentTime()
   {
      Calendar  current_system_time  =  new GregorianCalendar() ;

      current_hours    =  current_system_time.get( Calendar.HOUR_OF_DAY ) ;
      current_minutes  =  current_system_time.get( Calendar.MINUTE ) ;
      current_seconds  =  current_system_time.get( Calendar.SECOND ) ;
   }

   abstract public void print() ;
}
```

Because this method is declared with keyword **abstract**, it is an abstract method. That means that the real functionality of this method will be specified in each derived class. As class **CurrentTime** is an abstract class, it is not possible to create objects of it. It is, however, possible to use **CurrentTime** as the type of an object reference.

Although it is not possible to create objects of an abstract class, such a class can have a constructor that is executed when objects of derived classes are created.

The constructor of class **CurrentTime** gets the time from the operating system of the computer. After this constructor has been executed, the member variables contain the current time. The procedure to obtain the time from the operating system is similar to the procedure for obtaining the current date (see **CurrentDate.java**). **Calendar** and **GregorianCalendar** are standard Java classes which will be discussed in Chapter 15.

**Times.java - 1: Demonstrating the use of an abstract class named CurrentTime.**

An abstract method declared in an upper class is overridden in a derived class in the same way as other methods are overridden in derived classes. This method looks like any other normal method. Nothing indicates here that an implementation is being provided for an abstract method.

**current_hours** holds an hour value in the range from 0 to 23. By using this value as an index, it is easy to convert this hour value to an American hour.

```
class  AmericanTime  extends  CurrentTime
{
   public void print()
   {
      int[]  american_hours  =

        { 12, 1, 2, 3, 4, 5, 6, 7, 8, 9, 10, 11,
          12, 1, 2, 3, 4, 5, 6, 7, 8, 9, 10, 11  } ;

      System.out.printf( "%d:%02d:%02d", american_hours[ current_hours ],
                         current_minutes, current_seconds ) ;

      if ( current_hours  <  12 )
      {
         System.out.print( " a.m." ) ;
      }
      else
      {
         System.out.print( " p.m." ) ;
      }
   }
}

class  EuropeanTime  extends  CurrentTime
{
   public void print()
   {
      System.out.printf( "%d:%02d:%02d", current_hours,
                         current_minutes, current_seconds ) ;
   }
}
```

This **if** construct specifies that hours from 12:00:00 to 23:59:59 are considered the p.m. hours.

The format specifier **%02d** is used to stipulate that the value stored in **current_minutes** is printed so that the number is expressed in the decimal base-10 numbering system, the number is printed with two digits, and a leading zero is added if necessary.

**Times.java - 2: The classes that are derived from class CurrentTime.**

This object reference can point to an object of any subclass of **CurrentTime**. Therefore, this reference can reference both **AmericanTime** and **EuropeanTime** objects. When this program is started, it is not known which kind of object will be referenced. That depends on the user response.

```
class Times
{
   public static void main( String[] not_in_use )
   {
      Scanner keyboard = new Scanner( System.in ) ;

      CurrentTime  time_to_show ;

      System.out.print( "\n Type 12 to see the time in 12-hour a.m./p.m format."
                      +  "\n Any other number gives the 24-hour format. " ) ;

      int  user_response  =  keyboard.nextInt() ;

      if ( user_response  ==  12 )
      {
         time_to_show  =  new  AmericanTime() ;
      }
      else
      {
         time_to_show  =  new  EuropeanTime() ;
      }

      System.out.print( "\n  The time is now " ) ;

      time_to_show.print() ;

      System.out.print( "\n" ) ;
   }
}
```

Method **print()** is invoked here for the object that was created earlier. Here, it is not known which version of method **print()** is called. The special calling mechanism of polymorphic methods takes care that the right version of **print()** is executed.

**Times.java - 3. Current time is printed here either in American or European format.**

```
D:\javafiles3>java Times

 Type 12 to see the time in 12-hour a.m./p.m format.
 Any other number gives the 24-hour format. 12

  The time is now 7:50:04 p.m.

D:\javafiles3>java Times

 Type 12 to see the time in 12-hour a.m./p.m format.
 Any other number gives the 24-hour format. 24

  The time is now 19:50:13
```

Measuring time is always somewhat complicated. Although the mathematical difference between these two time values is 9 seconds, the time difference between these two program executions can be close to 10 seconds if the first execution took place at the beginning of second 04 and the second execution took place at the end of second 13.

**Times.java - X. The program is executed here twice within 10 seconds.**

We started studying method calls in Chapter 9 by exploring static methods, the methods that can be called without first creating any objects. In the case of the static methods, it is the compiler that decides which method is called in a certain situation. Now we have ended up studying instance methods with programs like **Times.java** in which the version of a method is selected at runtime. Although instance methods receive parameters in the same way as static methods, the execution of instance methods differs from the execution of static methods. The Java runtime environment (the Java virtual machine) selects a suitable instance method when a program like **Times.java** is executing. The term *late binding* (or *dynamic binding*) is used to describe the situation where the version of a method is selected during the time when a program is running. Correspondingly, the term *early binding* (or *static binding*) means that the method is selected at compilation time.

In Java programs, methods are polymorphic methods if they are not declared with keywords **`static`**, **`final`**, or **`private`**. Generally, if we have a class hierarchy where **`HighestClass`** is the topmost class from which all other classes are derived, and a method named **`polymorphic_method()`** is declared in **`HighestClass`** and redefined in every derived class, an object reference like

```
HighestClass  some_object ;
```

can refer to any type of object from the class hierarchy. **`some_object`** can store an address of a **`HighestClass`** object or any object that is created by using a subclass of **`HighestClass`**. When we write

```
some_object.polymorphic_method() ;
```

the calling mechanism of instance methods ensures that the correct version of **`polymorphic_method()`** is called. The calling mechanism selects that version of **`polymorphic_method()`** which is declared in that class whose object is pointed by **`some_object`**.

In program **BankPolymorphic.java** different kinds of bank account objects are created with the statements

```
BankAccount  beatles_account  =
                         new  BankAccount( ... ) ;
AccountWithCredit  stones_account  =
                         new  AccountWithCredit( ... ) ;
RestrictedAccount  doors_account   =
                         new  RestrictedAccount( ... ) ;
```

In each of these statements, the type of the object reference is the same as the type of the created object. This is not, however, the only possibility to write these statements. It would be possible to write the above statements in the following way

```
BankAccount  beatles_account  =
                         new  BankAccount( ... ) ;
BankAccount  stones_account  =
                         new  AccountWithCredit( ... ) ;
BankAccount  doors_account =
                         new  RestrictedAccount( ... ) ;
```

and the behavior of the program would not be altered. In these statements all object references are of type **`BankAccount`**, and the references are set to point to different types of objects. Because the calling mechanism of instance methods is somewhat "intelligent", the mechanism would be able to select the correct version of the **`withdraw_money()`** method if the above statements were put to program **BankPolymorphic.java**.

## 12.4 Chapter summary

- When a class inherits another class, members of the class being inherited become visible members in the inheriting class. Members declared with keyword **private** are not visible in derived classes. Constructors are not inherited.
- In a class hierarchy, the inheriting class is said to be the derived class, while the class that is inherited is the superclass or the base class. The term subclass is also used to describe lower classes in a class hierarchy. A superclass is sometimes called the parent class.
- Before the constructor of a class is executed, the default constructor of the immediate superclass is called automatically (implicitly). This rule is applied to every constructor call in a hierarchy of classes. The automatic calling of the superclass default constructor does not take place if a superclass constructor is called explicitly with the help of the **super** keyword.
- When a method, that already exists in the superclass, is rewritten to a derived class with the same name and the same set of parameters, the method in the derived class overrides the method of the superclass. This kind of a method is a polymorphic method.
- An object reference like

  ```
  SomeClass  some_object ;
  ```

  can reference objects of **SomeClass** and objects of classes that are derived from **SomeClass**. If a polymorphic method named **some_polymorphic_method()** is declared in **SomeClass** and redefined in its subclasses, the statement

  ```
  some_object.some_polymorphic_method() ;
  ```

  automatically selects the correct version of the polymorphic method.
- A method that is specified with the keyword **abstract** is an abstract method of which implementation must be provided in lower classes. A class that contains an abstract method is an abstract class that must be declared with the keyword **abstract**. Although it is not possible to create objects of an abstract class, an abstract class can be the type of an object reference.

### Exercise with program Times.java

Exercise 12-9. Modify program **Times.java** by deriving a third class named **TextualTime** from class **CurrentTime**. Rewrite the **print()** method for class **TextualTime** so that it prints, for example,

```
22 minutes and 25 seconds past nine in the evening
```

when the time is 21:22:25 (9:22:25 p.m.). You should test the new class by modifying method **main()** so that the object reference **time_to_show** points to a **TextualTime** object if a certain code number is given from the keyboard. Again it is important that the type of the created object is decided at the time when the program is executed.

The **print()** method of the **TextualTime** class could use the following kind of array of strings to print the textual hours

```
String[]  textual_hours  =
   { "midnight", "one", "two", "three", "four", "five",
     "six",  "seven",    "eight", "nine", "ten", "eleven",
     "noon", "one", "two", "three", "four", "five",
     "six",  "seven",    "eight", "nine", "ten", "eleven" } ;
```

## Final classes and methods

With the keyword **final** it is possible to specify that it is forbidden to derive new classes from an existing class. When the declaration of a class begins

```
final class ClassName
{
   ...
```

new classes cannot be derived from the class. The **final** class modifier is a kind of opposite to the **abstract** modifier. When you declare a class with the keyword **abstract**, it means that new classes must be derived from it, i.e., an **abstract** class is useful only as a base class for other classes. The **final** keyword says that new classes may not be derived. Many of the standard Java classes are **final** classes. For example, you cannot derive your own class from the standard class **String**. The compiler will issue an error message if you write the following lines into your program

```
class SpecialString extends String
{
   ...
```

The **final** keyword can also be used in the declaration of methods. When a method declarator (method header) contains the word **final**, it means that the method may not be overridden in derived classes. For example, if a method is declared inside a class in the following way

```
class UpperClass
{
   ...
   public final void some_method()
   {
      ...
```

it is not possible to write a derived class in the following way

```
class DerivedClass extends UpperClass
{
   ...
   public void some_method()
   {
      ....
```

**final** methods are needed in some special cases. When a method of a class is a **final** method, the class does not need to be a **final** class. On the other hand, if a class is a **final** class, there is no need to declare any method of the class as **final** because none of the methods can be inherited or overridden.

In some other programming languages (e.g. C++ and C#) all methods are supposed to be final methods unless they are declared with a special keyword (e.g. **virtual**) as methods that can be overridden in derived classes. In Java classes, instance methods are generally such that they can be overridden in derived classes, but with the **final** keyword overriding of a method can be prevented.

# CHAPTER 13

## SOME STANDARD JAVA CLASSES

A standard class is a class that belongs to a programming language, so that when you buy or otherwise acquire a compiler for the language, the standard class comes with the compiler. Some standard Java classes (e.g. **String** and **StringBuilder**) have already been discussed in the previous chapters. In this chapter we shall study some fundamentally important standard classes, which can now be explained as you are familiar with inheritance.

All the standard Java classes form a class library. This library is a huge collection of classes, and it is simply not possible to explain all the library classes in a single book. Fortunately, the library classes are explained in the electronic Java documentation. More standard classes will be studied in the following chapters, and, through these studies, I hope that you'll become competent enough to read and understand the electronic documentation and other sources.

The library of standard classes is organized so that certain kinds of classes are put to certain packages of classes. The standard packages of classes form an API (Application Programming Interface). The classes in the standard packages provide an interface through which application programs can access the resources of the computer. The classes which we will explore in this chapter belong to the **java.lang** package, which contains the most important standard classes. The **java.lang** package is automatically available for every Java program.

I must warn you that this chapter 13 is somewhat theoretical, and it does not contain many exercises. You'll need, however, to read this chapter in order to understand the Java language well. A nice feature of this chapter is that it is short!

## 13.1 Wrapper classes Byte, Short, Integer, Long, Float, Double, etc.

The most important standard Java classes are placed in a package named **java.lang**. This package of classes is automatically available to every Java program. Other, less fundamental, class packages can be brought into use with **import** statements.

One category of classes that can be found in the **java.lang** package is the so-called wrapper classes **Byte**, **Integer**, **Long**, **Short**, **Double**, etc. These classes are needed in some special situations to store inside objects the values of the basic variable types **byte**, **int**, **long**, **short**, **double**, etc. Here it is important to remember that the basic variable types are value types which store values in memory locations reserved from the stack memory, whereas classes are reference types which need memory locations from the stack memory to refer to objects that are created to the heap memory.

The wrapper classes and corresponding variable types are listed in Table 13-1. For example, the standard class **Integer** can store a value of type **int**. You can store the value of an **int** variable to an object of type **Integer**, for example, in the following way

```
int       some_int_variable  =  77 ;
Integer   some_integer_object  =
                    new Integer( some_int_variable ) ;
```

Actually it is not necessary to always use the **new** operator to create **Integer** objects. For example, the last two of the following statements

```
int       another_int_variable  =  88 ;
Integer   another_integer_object  =  another_int_variable ;
Integer   third_integer_object  =  99 ;
```

would automatically create **Integer** objects of the expressions that are written to the right side of the assignment operator =. When the last statement above is compiled, the compiler would recognize 99 to be a literal of type **int**, but as this literal is assigned as a value to an **Integer** object, the **int** value would automatically be stored inside a new **Integer** object, and **third_integer_object** would be made to reference the new object. This kind of automatic object creation is called autoboxing or simply boxing.

It is even possible to write arithmetic expressions by using objects of the wrapper classes. For example, if the above-mentioned **Integer** objects were available in a program, it would be possible to write

```
some_integer_object  =  another_integer_object  +
                        third_integer_object ;

System.out.print( some_integer_object ) ;
```

and the number 187 would be printed to the screen. What actually happens when **Integer** objects are used in an arithmetic statement like the one above, is that the values stored inside the **Integer** objects are automatically converted to **int** values, and the arithmetic operation is carried out with the **int** values. This automatic transformation from an **Integer** object to an **int** value is called unboxing. In the above arithmetic statement, automatic unboxing operations produce **int** values before the addition operation, and, after the result of the addition is available as an **int** value, it is boxed inside a new **Integer** object and **some_integer_object** is made to reference the created object.

Although it is possible to perform arithmetic operations with **Integer** objects and with objects of the other wrapper classes, it is better and computationally more efficient to calculate with traditional variables. It is, however, important to understand that there exist the wrapper classes and sometimes values stored in variables are "wrapped" inside objects of the wrapper classes.

The electronic Java documentation provides accurate information about the standard wrapper classes that correspond with the basic variable types. The following are a few examples of the public constants and methods of the **Integer** class:

- The static constant fields **MAX_VALUE** and **MIN_VALUE** contain the maximum and minimum values that can be stored in a variable of type **int**. For example, the statement

```
System.out.print( Integer.MAX_VALUE ) ;
```

would print the number 2147483647. (Table 5-1 also shows the storage capacities of different variable types.)

- **compareTo()** is a method that can be used to compare "this" **Integer** object to another **Integer** object. The method returns an **int** value that is less than zero when "this" object is less than the other object, a zero when the objects are equal, and a greater than zero value when "this" object is greater than the other object.
- The **equals()** method tests whether two objects contain the same value. The method returns **true** if the object given as a parameter is also an object of type **Integer** and it contains the same value as "this" object.
- The static method **parseInt()** can be used to extract a value of type **int** from a string. The string being parsed can be treated as a decimal string, hexadecimal string, or a binary string. In general, the term "parsing" means identifying certain kinds of numerical values or certain textual patterns in textual information.
- The **toString()** method converts an **int** value to a string. There are also several static methods to convert **int** values to strings. The static methods **toHexString()** and **toBinaryString()** convert **int** values to hexadecimal and binary strings, respectively.

Some of the methods of class **Integer** are demonstrated in program **IntegerClassTests.java** which you can find in the **javafilesextra** folder.

Some of the above-mentioned methods are overridden version of methods inherited from class **Object**, the topic of the next section. Other standard wrapper classes that represent other basic variable types provide similar methods as class **Integer**. For example, the standard class **Double** has a method named **parseDouble()** that can parse a value of type **double** from a string, and it has a **toString()** method that can convert a **double** value to a string. On the other hand, the other wrapper classes contain members that are specific to the numerical type in question. For example, the **Double** class has a public constant field named **NaN**, "not a number", that represents an undefined numerical value, such as the result of dividing zero by zero.

**Table 13-1. Java variable types and corresponding wrapper classes.**

| Variable type | Wrapper class in the java.lang package | Comments |
|---|---|---|
| **int** | **Integer** | 32-bit integer variable. |
| **short** | **Short** | 16-bit integer variable. |
| **long** | **Long** | 64-bit integer variable. |
| **byte** | **Byte** | 8-bit integer variable. |
| **boolean** | **Boolean** | Boolean variable that can have values **true** and **false**. |
| **char** | **Character** | 16-bit integer variable to store a Unicode character code. |
| **float** | **Float** | Single-precision floating-point variable. |
| **double** | **Double** | Double-precision floating-point variable. |

## 13.2 Object: the class above all classes

The standard class named **Object** is a very special class in the Java library of standard classes. The **Object** class serves as a universal superclass for all classes, and all classes implicitly inherit the **Object** class. Thus, when you declare a class by writing something like

```
class  SomeClass
{
   ...
```

the compiler interprets it as if you wrote

```
class  SomeClass  extends  Object
{
   ...
```

The compiler always automatically inherits the **Object** class irrespective of whether or not you, the programmer, would like that inheritance to happen. When you write

```
class  SomeDerivedClass  extends  SomeUpperClass
{
   ...
```

the **Object** class is inherited because **SomeUpperClass** or some of its superclasses has already inherited it.

All the standard Java classes as well as the user-declared classes have **Object** as their superclass. What every class inherits from class **Object** is a set of methods. Many of these methods are intended to be overridden in derived classes. The **Object** methods include the following:

- Method **clone()** looks like

  ```
  protected Object clone()
                    throws CloneNotSupportedException
  {
     ...
  ```

  The **clone()** method that is provided by class **Object** is a **protected** method, and can thus be called only by instance methods of derived classes. It makes a shallow copy of an object. A shallow copy is such that fields are copied, but other objects possibly referenced by the fields are not copied. If a deep copy were made, the objects referenced by the fields would also be copied.

- The **equals()** method, which compares two objects, begins with the following kinds of lines inside the **Object** class

  ```
  public boolean equals( Object another_object )
  {
     ...
  ```

  The implementation of this method in class **Object** tests whether two object references point to the same object, but it is recommended that classes override this method and implement it so that it tests whether two objects are of the same type and have the same internal content.

- Method **finalize()** looks like

  ```
  protected void finalize() throws Throwable
  {
     ...
  ```

  This is a **protected** method but it can be overridden in derived classes. Those activities that need to be done before an object is deleted should be programmed inside this method when it is overridden in derived classes. The garbage collector calls this method before it deallocates an object's memory area from the heap memory.

- A method named **getClass()** can reveal the runtime type of an object, and it begins with the somewhat strange declaration

```
public final Class<? extends Object> getClass()
{
   ...
```

  This method, which is a **final** method and thus cannot be overridden in derived classes, returns a reference to an object of type **Class**. The **Class** object then contains the type information. You can print type information to the screen with a statement like

```
System.out.print( "Class is: "  +  some_object.getClass()) ;
```

- The **hashCode()** is a method that might be needed when objects are stored in a so-called hashtable. The method begins with the following lines

```
public int hashCode()
{
   ...
```

  A hash code is a numerical value that can be used to identify an object in a collection of objects. By overriding this method, a class can generate its own kinds of hash codes for its objects. (We will not study hash codes further in this book.)

- Perhaps the most widely used method that has its origins in the **Object** class is the **toString()** method. It begins with the lines

```
public String toString()
{
   ...
```

  This method produces a string representation of an object, and it is generally overridden in classes. The class **Object** version of this method returns a string that contains the name of the class followed by hexadecimal hash code of the object. An overridden version of the **toString()** method should return a string that describes the object in textual form.

  As every object has some kind of **toString()** method available, every object can be converted to a string. The **toString()** method is invoked automatically when an object is joined to a string with the string concatenation operator (+). When a statement like

```
System.out.print( "\n The object is: "  +  some_object ) ;
```

  is executed, a version of the **toString()** method is called for the object referenced by **some_object**. If **some_object** points to a **String** object, the **toString()** of class **String** is called. If **some_object** points to an object of class **Date**, the **toString()** method of class **Date** is invoked. If **some_object** points to an object of a class that does not have its own **toString()** method, the **toString()** of class **Object** is called.

- Methods **notify()**, **notifyAll()**, and **wait()** can be used when objects are created by so-called threads that execute in parallel. Threads will be discussed in Chapter 16.

Some of the methods of the **Object** class are demonstrated in a program named **ObjectClassTests.java** which you can find in the **javafilesextra** folder.

One benefit of having such a class as **Object** is that it makes it possible to write methods that can take all kinds of objects as parameters. Such a method looks like

```
public void some_method( Object given_object )
{
   ...
```

The parameter of this method is a reference to type **Object**. In general, an object reference of certain type can reference objects of its own type as well as objects of classes that are derived from its own type. Because type **Object** is the superclass of all classes, a reference of type **Object** can reference all types of objects. For this reason, a method like the one above can be called, for example, in the following ways:

```
some_method( some_string_object ) ;
some_method( some_date_object ) ;
some_method( some_bank_account_object ) ;
...
```

A different problem is then how this kind of method processes the various kinds of objects, but, nevertheless, sometimes it is useful to have a method that takes a parameter of type **Object**.

An interesting situation is when a method that accepts a parameter of type **Object** is called by supplying a value type as a parameter. This kind of situation happens when the above **some_method()** is called with the statement

```
some_method( 123 ) ;
```

where 123 is a literal constant that is of the value type **int**. How a method that accepts all kinds of objects as parameters should behave when it is given a parameter that is not an object but a value? In Java, this problem is solved with a boxing (autoboxing) operation. In a boxing operation an object is created and a value is stored inside the object. Values of type **int** are stored inside **Integer** objects, values of type **long** are stored in **Long** objects, values of type **double** are stored in **Double** objects, etc. Boxing operations are automatic (implicit). Program **Boxings.java** is an example in which both boxing and unboxing operations take place.

```
D:\javafiles3>java Boxings

  Incremented value :  223
  Decremented value :  332
```

This program is not very practical. At this phase of your studies you probably know that there are better ways to increment or decrement the value of a variable.

**Boxings.java - X. 222 is incremented to 223 and 333 is decremented to 332.**

**increment_integer()** is a method whose parameter is an object reference of type **Object**. An object reference can reference an object of its own type or any type that is a subclass of its own type. As all classes are subclasses of class **Object**, an object reference of type **Object** can reference any object.

Because of the boxing operation that takes place when this method is called in method **main()**, the **int** value is received boxed inside an **Integer** object in the heap memory. This statement first converts the object reference to type **Integer**. Then an automatic unboxing operation takes place and an **int** value is extracted from the **Integer** object.

```
//  Boxings.java

class Boxings
{
   static int increment_integer( Object integer_as_object )
   {
      int integer_to_increment  =  (Integer) integer_as_object ;

      integer_to_increment  ++ ;

      return  integer_to_increment ;
   }

   static Integer decrement_integer( int integer_to_decrement )
   {
      integer_to_decrement  -- ;

      return  integer_to_decrement ;
   }

   public static void main( String[] not_in_use )
   {
      int  some_integer  =  222 ;

      int  incremented_integer  =  increment_integer( some_integer ) ;

      System.out.print("\n  Incremented value :  "  +  incremented_integer ) ;

      Integer  some_integer_object  =  333 ;

      int  decremented_integer  =  decrement_integer( some_integer_object ) ;

      System.out.print("\n  Decremented value :  "  +  decremented_integer ) ;
   }
}
```

Because the return type of this method is **Integer**, the returned **int** value is automatically boxed inside an **Integer** object.

Two unboxing operations take place when this statement is executed. The parameter for **decrement_integer()** is unboxed in the method call, and an **int** value is unboxed from an **Integer** object before the assignment operation.

A boxing operation takes place when method **increment_integer()** is called. It is found out that a value type is being supplied to a method that is expecting an object. In this situation an **Integer** object is created to the heap memory, and the value of variable **some_integer** is stored inside the created object. The created object is a kind of box that transfers the value of the variable, and, hence, I believe, the operation is called boxing.

**Boxings.java - 1: Boxing and unboxing activities demonstrated.**

## 13.3 Exception classes

Exception objects are used to handle exceptional situations in programs. Often the exceptional situations are some kind of errors. We have already found out that the execution of the statement

```
int  integer_from_keyboard  =  keyboard.nextInt() ;
```

is terminated so that a method called by the **nextInt()** method throws an **InputMismatchException** if the user of the program types in something that cannot be interpreted as a value of type **int**. The **InputMismatchException** that may be thrown when the above statement is executed is an object of the standard class **InputMismatchException**, one of the many exception classes in the Java class library.

Exceptions can be thrown by some methods and caught by some other methods. Many of the methods of the standard Java classes throw exceptions. When methods are explained in the electronic Java documentation, a list of exceptions that may be thrown is given for each method.

A method can throw an exception object by using the **throw** keyword in the following kind of statement

```
throw  new  ExceptionClassName() ;
```

This statement is called a **throw** statement. A **throw** statement throws a reference to a created exception object, and stops the execution of the method where the statement is located. What happens after the execution of a **throw** statement is a search for a suitable **try-catch** construct where the exception can be processed. For example, let's suppose that an exception is thrown in the following kind of program structure

```
void  throwing_method() throws SomeException
{
   ...
   if ( ... )
   {
      throw  new  SomeException() ;
   }
   ...
}

void  immediate_caller()
{
   ...
   throwing_method() ;
   ...
}

void  less_immediate_caller()
{
   ...
   immediate_caller() ;
   ...
}

void  least_immediate_caller()
{
   ...
   less_immediate_caller() ;
   ...
}
```

In this theoretical example, it is not shown which of these methods contain suitable **try-catch** constructs to handle exceptions of type **SomeException**. As I'll explain later in this section, it is usual that those of these methods which do not catch **SomeExceptions** must have the text **throws SomeException** in their method headers.

In this theoretical example, a method named **throwing_method()** is called by method **immediate_caller()** which is called by method **less_immediate_caller()** which is called by method **least_immediate_caller()**. When the **throwing_method()** throws the exception, the program execution continues in the nearest caller that has a **try-catch** construct like

```
try
{
   //  The call to an "upper" method
   //  must be inside the try block.
   ...
}
catch ( SomeException  caught_exception )
{
   //  Handling the exception of type SomeException.
   ...
}
```

This type can alternatively be some superclass of **SomeException**.

which is able to catch an exception of type **SomeException**. If a suitable **try-catch** construct is found inside the method **immediate_caller()**, the program execution continues there. If **immediate_caller()** does not have a suitable **try-catch** construct, the execution of the program continues in a less immediate caller if that method has a suitable **try-catch** construct. If no suitable **try-catch** construct is found, the execution of the program is terminated.

Program **ExceptionalNumbers.java** is an example about throwing and catching exceptions. Two custom exception classes have been derived from the standard class **Exception**, and these exceptions are caught inside different methods. In addition, program **ExceptionalNumbers.java** catches exceptions of type **Exception**.

The standard class **Exception** is one possible base class for user-defined exception classes in Java. As shown in Figure 13-1, class **Exception** is a subclass of a standard class named **Throwable** which is the superclass for all exceptions and errors in Java. The **Throwable** class provides methods with which it is possible to get information related to the caught exception. In program **ExceptionalNumbers.java**, method **printStackTrace()** is called for the caught exception in order to print some information.

It is possible to catch many kinds of exceptions with a single **try-catch** construct. For example, the construct

```
try
{

   ...
}
catch ( Exception  caught_exception )
{
   ...
}
```

catches exceptions of type **Exception** and exceptions that are objects of some subclass of class **Exception**.

Two exception classes are derived from the standard exception class **Exception**. These classes differ from their base class **Exception** only in that they have different names.

This method throws exceptions if the value of variable **number_from_keyboard** is not within the range from 100 to 998. After an exception is thrown, the execution of the program continues in a calling method that has a suitable **catch** block to handle the exception.

This method returns the value 1234 in the case it catches a **NumberTooSmallException**.

```
//  ExceptionalNumbers.java

import java.util.* ;

class  NumberTooSmallException  extends  Exception
{
}

class  NumberTooLargeException  extends  Exception
{
}

class ExceptionalNumbers
{
   static int get_number_from_keyboard()  throws  NumberTooSmallException,
                                                  NumberTooLargeException
   {
      Scanner keyboard = new Scanner( System.in ) ;

      int number_from_keyboard   =   keyboard.nextInt() ;

      if ( number_from_keyboard   <=  99 )
      {
         throw new NumberTooSmallException() ;
      }
      else if ( number_from_keyboard   >=   999 )
      {
         throw new NumberTooLargeException() ;
      }

      return number_from_keyboard ;
   }

   static int get_number()  throws  NumberTooLargeException
   {
      int number_from_above_method   =   1234 ;

      try
      {
         number_from_above_method   =   get_number_from_keyboard() ;
      }
      catch  ( NumberTooSmallException   number_too_small_exception )
      {
         System.out.print( "\n NumberTooSmallException caught. " ) ;
      }

      return   number_from_above_method ;
   }
```

**ExceptionalNumbers.java - 1: Throwing and catching some exceptions.**

If method **get_number_from_keyboard()** throws the **NumberTooLargeException**, the execution of the program jumps to this statement, passing the method **get_number()**.

```
public static void main( String[] not_in_use )
{
   System.out.print( " Please, type in a number: " ) ;

   try
   {
      int  number_read_via_several_methods   =   get_number() ;

      System.out.print( "\n The number from keyboard is : "
                        +  number_read_via_several_methods   ) ;
   }
   catch ( NumberTooLargeException number_too_large_exception )
   {
      System.out.print( "\n NumberTooLargeException caught. " ) ;
   }
   catch ( Exception caught_exception )
   {
      System.out.print( "\n Some Exception was caught. Some info:   " ) ;
      caught_exception.printStackTrace() ;
   }
}
```

The second **catch** block works only if the first **catch** block could not catch the exception.

The **printStackTrace()** method is called for the exception object to produce information about the caught exception.

**ExceptionalNumbers.java - 2. Method main() with two catch blocks.**

```
D:\javafiles3>java ExceptionalNumbers
 Please, type in a number: 555

 The number from keyboard is : 555
D:\javafiles3>java ExceptionalNumbers
 Please, type in a number: 66

 NumberTooSmallException caught.
 The number from keyboard is : 1234
D:\javafiles3>java ExceptionalNumbers
 Please, type in a number: 7777

 NumberTooLargeException caught.
D:\javafiles3>java ExceptionalNumbers
 Please, type in a number: 88.88

 Some Exception was caught. Some info:  java.util.InputMismatchException
     at java.util.Scanner.throwFor(Unknown Source)
     at java.util.Scanner.next(Unknown Source)
     at java.util.Scanner.nextInt(Unknown Source)
     at java.util.Scanner.nextInt(Unknown Source)
     at ExceptionalNumbers.get_number_from_keyboard(ExceptionalNumbers.java:26)
     at ExceptionalNumbers.get_number(ExceptionalNumbers.java:46)
     at ExceptionalNumbers.main(ExceptionalNumbers.java:62)
```

This information is printed by the **printStackTrace()** method. An **InputMismatchException** was thrown after the call to the **nextInt()** method because string 88.88 contains a decimal point and, therefore, cannot represent an **int** value.

**ExceptionalNumbers.java - X. The program is executed here four times.**

Method declarators (method headers) in program **ExceptionalNumbers.java** contain *exception specifications* which are written with the `throws` keyword. For example, the declarator of method `get_number()` looks like

```
static int get_number() throws NumberTooLargeException
```

where `throws NumberTooLargeException` is the exception specification. When this specification is written in a method declarator, it means that the method may throw an exception of type `NumberTooLargeException`, and the method does not have a suitable `try-catch` construct to catch this type of an exception. The `get_number()` method may throw a `NumberTooLargeException` because it calls the method `get_number_-from_keyboard()` which actually can throw the exception with a `throw` statement. Because `get_number()` catches exceptions of type `NumberTooSmallException`, it does not have the specification `throws NumberTooSmallException` in its declarator.

The exception specifications that are written with the `throws` keyword do not actually affect the behavior of a program. By requiring exception specifications in certain situations, the Java compiler forces a programmer to write programs according to certain rules. When you see a method declarator (method header) written with the words `throws SomeException`, you know the following things:

- The method in question either throws an exception of type `SomeException` with a `throw` statement, or the method calls another method which can throw a `SomeException` object.
- The method in question does not have a suitable `try-catch` construct to catch an exception of type `SomeException`, and if you decide to call the method from another method, you must either catch an exception of type `SomeException` in the calling method, or have the exception specification `throws SomeException` in the declarator of the calling method.

Not all methods that throw exceptions need to be called from a `try-catch` construct or the thrown exceptions be specified with the `throws` keyword. As illustrated in Figure 13-1, there exist two kinds of exceptions in Java:

- *Checked exceptions*, which are objects of a class derived from the standard class `Exception` (but not objects of a subclass of `RuntimeException`), need to be handled as shown in program **ExceptionalNumbers.java**.
- *Unchecked exceptions*, which are objects of a class that is derived either from the `Error` class or from the `RuntimeException` class, do not necessarily need to be taken care of with `try-catch` constructs or the `throws` keyword. On the other hand, it is possible to catch unchecked exceptions. We have already done that, for example, in program **MeanvalueException.java**.

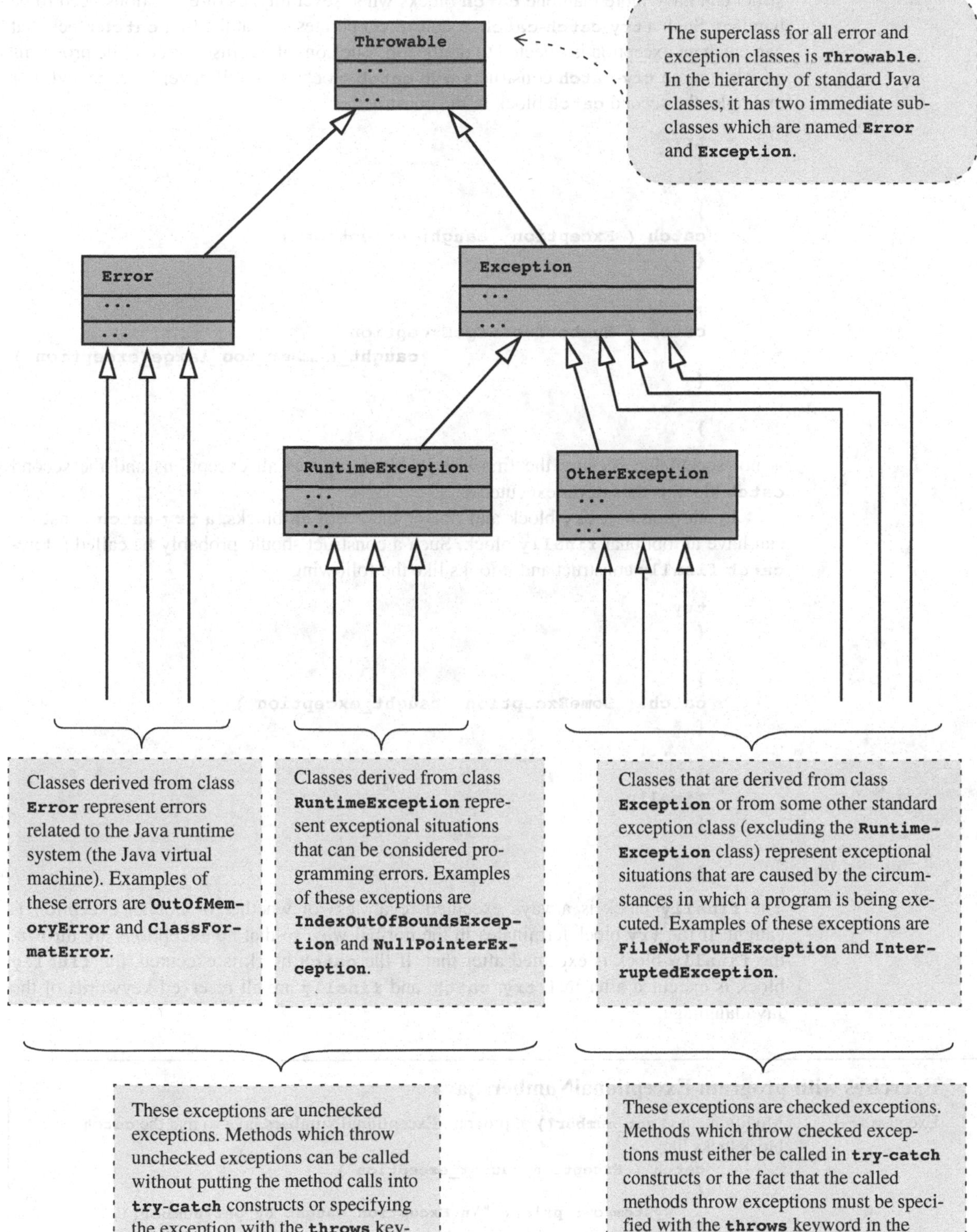


***Figure 13-1. Relationships between exception classes.***

As you can see by studying program **ExceptionalNumbers.java**, a **try-catch** construct can have more than one **catch** blocks when several types of exceptions need to be handled. Such a **try-catch-catch-**... construct operates so that the first **catch** block that can catch an exception is selected to do the job. The compiler refuses to compile programs which contain **try-catch** constructs with **catch** blocks that will never be executed. For example, the second **catch** block in the construct

```
try
{
   ...
}
catch ( Exception  caught_exception )
{
   ...
}
catch ( NumberTooLargeException
                              caught_number_too_large_exception )
{
   ...
}
```

is not acceptable because the first **catch** block catches all exceptions and the second **catch** block is thus never executed.

In addition to a **try** block and one or more **catch** blocks, a **try-catch** construct can have an optional **finally** block. Such a construct should probably be called a **try-catch-finally** construct and it looks like the following

```
try
{
   ...
}
catch ( SomeException  caught_exception )
{
   ...
}
finally
{
   ...
}
```

The **finally** block is always executed regardless of whether or not an exception is caught. If the **try** block terminates in the normal way, so that no exceptions are thrown, the **finally** block is executed after that. If the **catch** block is executed, the **finally** block is executed after that. **try**, **catch**, and **finally** are all reserved keywords of the Java language.

## Exercises with program ExceptionalNumbers.java

Exercise 13-1. Modify method **get_number()** of program **ExceptionalNumbers.java** so that the **catch** block looks like

```
catch ( Exception caught_exception )
{
   System.out.print( "\n Exception caught by get_number(). " ) ;
}
```

and study how the behavior of the program changes.

Exercise 13-2. Test what happens when you add **finally** blocks to the **try-catch** constructs of program **ExceptionalNumbers.java**.

### Operator `instanceof` and the implementation of an equals() method

The **`equals()`** method that is inherited from class **`Object`** to every Java class tests if two object references point to the same object. It is usual, and even recommended, that classes implement the **`equals()`** method so that it tests whether two objects contain the same data. When an **`equals()`** method is implemented this way, it should first test whether the two objects are of compatible type, i.e., whether it is possible to compare them, and then it should compare the actual data inside the two objects. For example, if an **`equals()`** method were written for class **`Date`** in program **Date.java**, the method should look like

```
public boolean equals( Object another_object )
{
   boolean  objects_are_equal  =  false ;

   if ( another_object  !=  null  &&
        another_object  instanceof  Date )
   {
      Date  another_date  =  (Date) another_object ;

      if ( this_day    ==  another_date.day()    &&
           this_month  ==  another_date.month()  &&
           this_year   ==  another_date.year() )
      {
         objects_are_equal  =  true ;
      }
   }

   return  objects_are_equal ;
}
```

In the above method, the first **`if`** construct ensures that **`another_object`** is indeed referencing an object (i.e., the object reference is not **`null`**), and it is referencing an object that can be compared to "this" **`Date`** object. An operator named **`instanceof`** is used to find out if the object referenced by **`another_date`** is a **`Date`** object. **`instanceof`** is a reserved keyword in Java, and it is useful when we need to ensure that the given object is of a certain type. Operator **`instanceof`** works so that it returns **`true`** if the left operand is of the same type as the right operand, if the left operand is of type that is derived from the type of the right operand, or if the left operand implements an interface specified by the right operand. (Interfaces will be discussed in Chapter 15.)

The current version of class **`Date`** has a method named **`is_equal_to()`** to test the equality of **`Date`** objects. The "official" comparison method **`equals()`** is not implemented in class **`Date`** because it was necessary to keep the class simple.

Methods like **`equals()`** need to be implemented in a class when we want to design classes that work well with other Java classes. When there exists an **`equals()`** method in a class, it is recommended that there should also be an implementation for the method **`hashCode()`**. When two objects are equal, they should have equal hash codes.

## 13.4 Class Math provides static mathematical methods

The first computers that were invented soon after World War II were used mostly to perform mathematical calculations. Although purely mathematical calculations are nowadays less typical computing tasks, computers are still being made to do calculations, and programming languages provide classes and methods which help in mathematical computing tasks. So, to end this chapter, let's take a look at what Java provides for mathematicians. (The mathematical methods that are going to be explored on these pages, are not needed in the subsequent chapters. If you are in a hurry, you can skip this section. On the other hand, studying some mathematical methods after the difficult concepts of inheritance and exceptions may be something to make you relax.)

A class named **`Math`** in the **`java.lang`** package provides static methods for making mathematical calculations. As the methods are static, you do not need to create any objects for calculations. The **`Math`** class contains, for example, the following categories of methods and constants:

- two important mathematical constants **`Math.PI`** and **`Math.E`**
- methods that carry out the traditional trigonometric functions **`Math.sin()`**, **`Math.cos()`**, **`Math.tan()`**, etc.
- methods **`Math.toRadians()`** and **`Math.toDegrees()`** to convert angles measured in degrees to angles measured in radians and vice versa
- exponential and logarithmic methods like **`Math.pow()`**, **`Math.exp()`**, and **`Math.log()`**
- methods to find absolute, maximum, and minimum values: **`Math.abs()`**, **`Math.max()`**, and **`Math.min()`**
- methods to round floating-point values in mathematically correct way: **`Math.rint()`** and **`Math.round()`**

Some of the above and other **`Math`** methods are demonstrated in program **MathDemo.java**.

As mathematical calculations usually result in numbers that are not whole numbers but numbers with a decimal point, the parameters and return types of the **`Math`** methods are frequently of type **`double`**, the double-precision floating-point type.

```
D:\javafiles3>java MathDemo

 The sine of an angle of 45 degrees is 0.7071067811865475

 Earth diameter in kilometers:              40080
 Earth diameter in miles:                   24906
 Earth area in square kilometers:       511346242
 Earth area in square miles:            197442684

 And here is a random integer in the range from 0 to 49:  15
```

Because the form of our planet Earth is not exactly a ball, the diameter and surface area that are calculated here are not exactly correct.

**MathDemo.java - X. The program produces some numerical values.**

An angle of 45 degrees is drawn on the right. The sine of the angle is calculated after the 45 degrees are converted to radians.

45 degrees

```
//  MathDemo.java

class MathDemo
{
   static final double  EARTH_RADIUS_IN_KILOMETERS  =  6379  ;

   public static void main( String[] not_in_use )
   {
      double  an_angle_in_radians  =  Math.toRadians( 45 ) ;

      double  sine_of_an_angle  =  Math.sin( an_angle_in_radians ) ;

      System.out.print( "\n The sine of an angle of 45 degrees is "
                      + sine_of_an_angle + "\n" ) ;

      double  diameter_of_the_earth =
                  2  *  Math.PI  *  EARTH_RADIUS_IN_KILOMETERS ;

      System.out.printf( "\n Earth diameter in kilometers:   %15.0f",
                         diameter_of_the_earth ) ;

      System.out.printf( "\n Earth diameter in miles:        %15.0f",
                         diameter_of_the_earth / 1.6093 ) ;

      double  surface_area_of_the_earth  =
                4  *  Math.PI  *  Math.pow( EARTH_RADIUS_IN_KILOMETERS, 2 );

      System.out.printf( "\n Earth area in square kilometers:%15.0f",
                         surface_area_of_the_earth ) ;
      System.out.printf( "\n Earth area in square miles:     %15.0f\n",
                        surface_area_of_the_earth / Math.pow( 1.6093, 2 ) );

      int  a_random_integer  =  (int) ( Math.random() * 50 ) ;

      System.out.printf( "\n And here is a random integer in the range "
                      +  "from 0 to 49:  "  +  a_random_integer  +  "\n\n" ) ;
   }
}
```

Method **Math.random()** can be used to generate random numbers. The method returns a random **double** value so that the value is greater than or equal to zero and less than 1. When some larger number is multiplied by the value that is generated by the **Math.random()** method, it is possible to get random numbers that are distributed over a longer range. The random **double** value is here converted to an **int** value. As computers always round integers downwards, the resulting **int** value is always less than 50.

With the **Math.pow()** method it is possible to raise the first parameter to the power of the second parameter.

**MathDemo.java - 1. Using some mathematical methods of the standard class Math.**

## 13.5 Chapter summary

- Standard classes **Byte**, **Short**, **Integer**, **Long**, **Float**, **Double**, **Character**, and **Boolean**, declared in the **java.lang** package, are so-called wrapper classes for the basic Java variable types **byte**, **short**, **int**, **long**, **float**, **double**, **char**, and **boolean**.
- In certain situations, values of variables are automatically put inside created wrapper objects (e.g. an **int** value is put inside a created **Integer** object). This is called boxing or autoboxing. When numerical values are automatically extracted from wrapper objects, such an action is called unboxing.
- A class named **Object** is the superclass of all Java classes. This class is inherited automatically by all classes.
- Exception classes are needed to handle problematic situations in programs. Exception objects are thrown by **throw** statements, and caught with **try-catch**(**-finally**) constructs.
- Checked exceptions need to be handled "more carefully" than unchecked exceptions. If a method does not catch a checked exception, the method header (declarator) must specify with the **throws** keyword that the exception in question is not caught by the method.

# CHAPTER 14

## STORING INFORMATION IN FILES

The hard disk memory of a computer is a place for storing files. Computers also allow files to be stored on other memory devices such as CDs, floppy disks, and flash memory devices. The memory devices which store files are different from the main memory in that they keep their memory contents even when the electricity is switched off from the computer. A computer program may create files to the hard disk when it wants to store information that must be preserved after the program terminates.

In this chapter we shall study how Java programs can handle files, i.e., how programs can read information stored in files and write information to files. The file handling mechanisms of Java are based on standard Java classes whose objects can represent files on a computer's disk memory. By calling the methods of the standard classes, it is possible to read data from files and write data to files. You will learn that files can be treated either as text files or as binary files. There exist different standard classes for these two file types.

The classes for file operations are declared in the **`java.io`** package. By using the electronic Java documentation you can find additional information about these classes. There exist many Java classes to do file operations, and objects of these classes can be made to co-operate in various ways. Don't panic if the **`java.io`** package seems somewhat confusing. In this chapter I will introduce only a few of those classes, but with the chosen classes it is possible to learn the basics of file handling.

## 14.1 Classes to read and write files

The operating system of a computer takes care, among other things, of the files in the computer's hard disk memory. Rotating hard disks are the most common memory devices to which information is moved from the main memory for permanent storage. On a hard disk bits are stored magnetically on the surface of a special disk. A hard disk can be called an auxiliary memory device because it cannot be accessed as easily as the main memory that can be addressed by the processor. A hard disk can also be called a mass memory device because its storage capacity is usually larger than that of the main memory. Other auxiliary memory devices used in computers include floppy disks, optical disks, and flash memory devices. From a programmer's point of view, all the memory devices outside the main memory are basically the same. They contain just files. Therefore, when you have learned to use the hard disk files of a computer, you will probably be able to use files stored on other memory devices as well.

For every file on a hard disk, the operating system always contains at least the following information:

- the name of the file,
- the size of the file in bytes,
- date and time information related to the file,
- the status of the file (open or closed), and
- the location of the file on the hard disk.

An application program that uses the files on the hard disk does not need to know as much about files as the operating system does. In Java, files are accessed by using standard Java classes for the basic file processing activities. The methods of the file accessing classes communicate with the operating system of the computer, and the operating system, in turn, communicates with the hardware and electronics of the computer in order to access information stored on the hard disk. Figure 14-1 clarifies the file accessing mechanism.

In order to use files in a Java program, you do not need to know the details about how the operating system accesses the files. You just need to learn to use the standard Java classes. The classes that we are going to study in this chapter include the following:

- **`FileReader`**: a class to read files as text files
- **`FileWriter`**: a class to write files as text files
- **`BufferedReader`**: a class that helps reading files as text files
- **`PrintWriter`**: a class that helps writing files as text files
- **`FileInputStream`**: a class with which a file can be opened as a binary file for reading operations
- **`FileOutputStream`**: a class with which a file can be written as a binary file
- **`DataOutputStream`**: a class that helps to write binary data to a file
- **`DataInputStream`**: a class with which it is easy to read data that has been written with the help of the **`DataOutputStream`** class

These are not all the standard classes that Java provides for file handling, but with these classes we can perform some traditional file handling operations. The electronic Java documentation provides information about all classes related to file handling.

The word "stream" is frequently used when file operations are discussed. It is used in some standard class names. A file can be regarded as a stream of information, a stream of bytes or a stream of characters. When a computer program, for example, reads a file, the data that is coming from the file can be thought of as a stream of bytes. Although in this chapter we'll concentrate on information streams related to files, the word stream can have even a wider meaning. For example, information retrieved from a network can be considered a stream of information. When an e-mail message is sent to you over the Internet, the characters of the message make a stream of information.

When a file is processed by a program, the program usually performs a certain set of activities. The general procedure of file usage in a program is the following

- Before a file can be used, it must be opened. Usually the constructor or a special method of a standard class opens a file. The file name (and possibly the entire path that describes the directory hierarchy) must be specified in the opening operation. Usually files are opened either for reading or writing operations.
- After a file is successfully opened, it usually is either read or written. We shall see later that there are several possibilities to read and write files.
- When file reading and writing operations are finished, the program must close the file(s) it has opened earlier. Closing a file means that it can no longer be used in the program. If a program does not close a file it has used, it is possible that the file is not properly written to the hard disk.

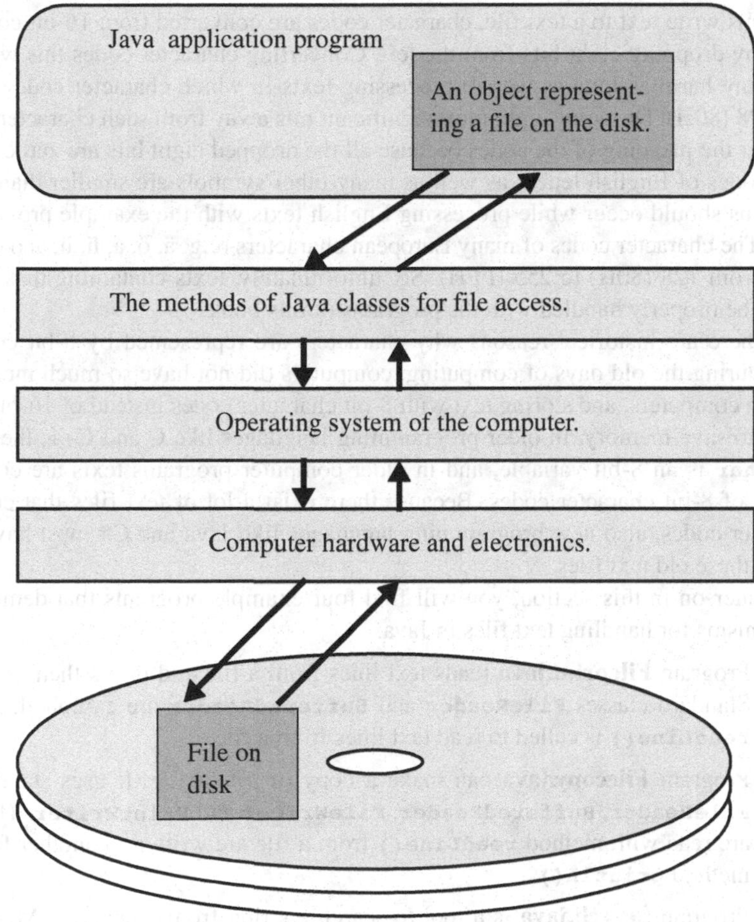


The hard disk is usually a pack of magnetic disks inside the computer. Files can also be stored on optical disks (CDs) and on other storage media.

*Figure 14-1. Accessing files in Java.*

## 14.2 Reading and writing text files

A text file is usually a list of character codes of visible characters and line termination characters. In addition to the line termination characters, text files may contain special codes such as the codes of tabulation characters. Examples of text files are source program files (e.g. **.java** files) and all other files that can be written with program editors such as EditPad and Notepad. **.txt** is a common file name extension for text files. Not all files containing text are text files. For example, files created with word processing tools (e.g. Microsoft Word) are not text files because they contain special codings that only the word processing tools can understand. Figure 14-2 shows what a small text file looks like in a file on a computer's hard disk.

Inside Java programs texts are handled so that each character of text is represented by a 16-bit character code. A variable of type **`char`** is a 16-bit (2-byte) variable, and a **`String`** object can store a sequence of 16-bit **`char`** values. In traditional text files, however, each character is stored as an 8-bit (1-byte) value, and this is the format in which the example programs of this section assume text files to be. The file handling classes of Java can handle text files in which characters are stored as 8-bit bytes. When we read text files with a Java program, the 8-bit character codes are automatically converted to 16-bit character codes by adding eight zero bits to the left of the 8-bit code. Similarly, when our Java programs write text to a text file, character codes are converted from 16-bit codes to 8-bit codes by dropping eight bits from the left. Converting character codes this way does not cause any harm as long as we are processing texts in which character codes are smaller than 128 (80H). Dropping eight most significant bits away from such character codes does not alter the meaning of the codes because all the dropped eight bits are zeroes. The character codes of English letters as well as many other symbols are smaller than 128, so no problems should occur while processing English texts with the example programs of this book. The character codes of many European characters (e.g. ä, ö, å, ñ, ü, and é) are in the range from 128 (80H) to 255 (FFH). So, unfortunately, texts containing these characters cannot be properly handled with the programs of this book.

There are historical reasons why characters are represented by 8-bit codes in text files. During the old days of computing, computers did not have so much memory as the modern computers, and storing text with 8-bit character codes instead of 16-bit codes was a way to save memory. In older programming languages like C and C++, the variable of type **`char`** is an 8-bit variable, and in older computer programs texts are considered to consist of 8-bit character codes. Because there exist a lot of text files that contain 8-bit character codes, also new programming languages like Java and C# must have means to handle these old text files.

Later on in this section, you will find four example programs that demonstrate the mechanisms for handling text files in Java:

- Program **Fileprint.java** reads text lines from a file and prints them to the screen. Standard classes **`FileReader`** and **`BufferedReader`** are exploited, and method **`readLine()`** is called to read text lines from a file.
- Program **Filecopy.java** can make a copy of a text file. It uses standard classes **`FileReader`**, **`BufferedReader`**, **`FileWriter`** and **`PrintWriter`**. The lines that are read with method **`readLine()`** from a file are written to another file by using method **`println()`**.
- Program **Search.java** is a tool to search a string from a text file. Method **`readLine()`** is used to read the file line by line, and string method **`contains()`** is used to search for the given string on each line.
- Program **Findreplace.java** replaces all occurrences of a string with another string in a text file. This program uses the same classes and methods for file handling as the other programs. In addition, this program uses objects of class **`ArrayList`** to store text lines temporarily.

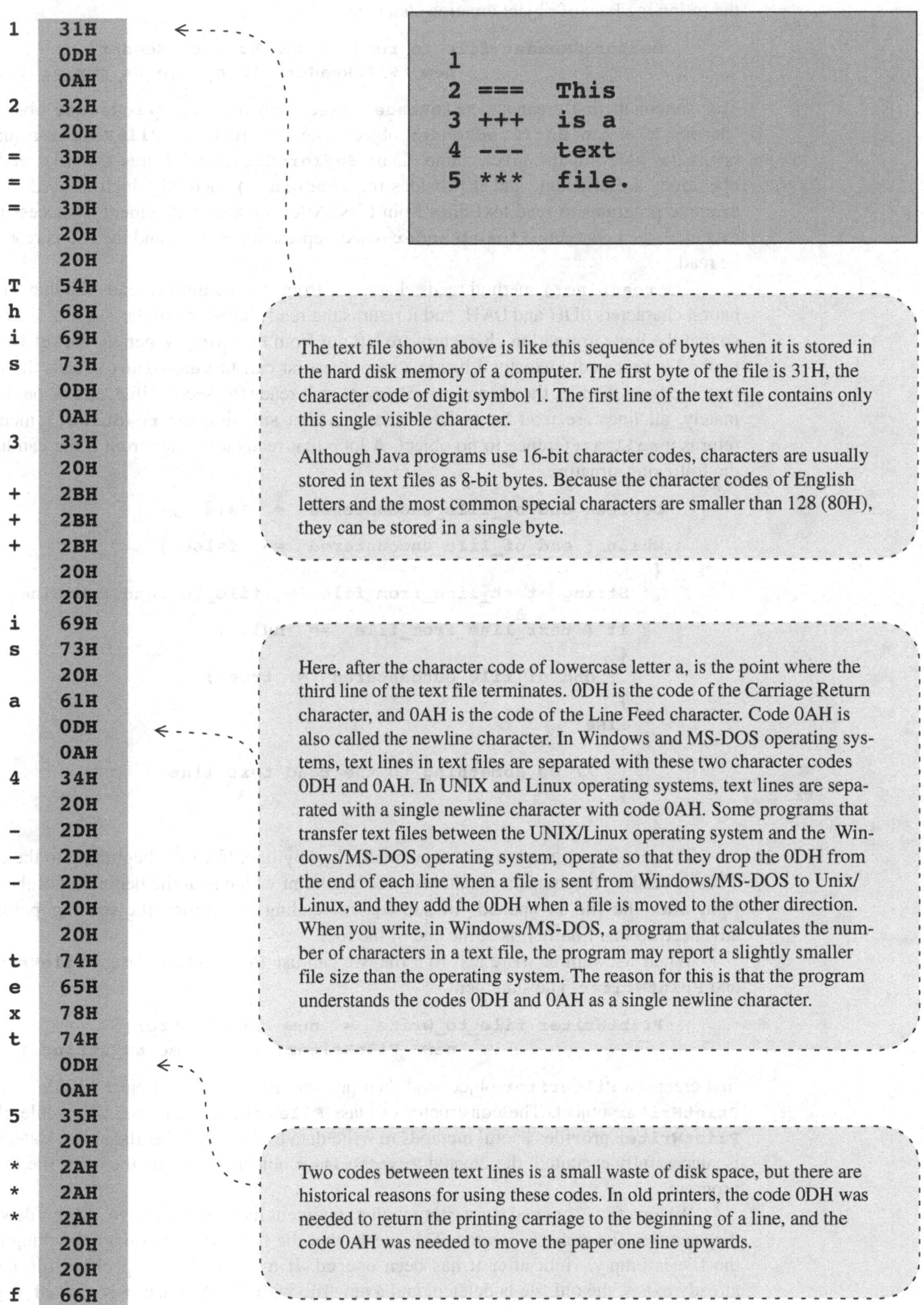

1 31H
0DH
0AH
2 32H
20H
= 3DH
= 3DH
= 3DH
20H
20H
T 54H
h 68H
i 69H
s 73H
0DH
0AH
3 33H
20H
+ 2BH
+ 2BH
+ 2BH
20H
20H
i 69H
s 73H
20H
a 61H
0DH
0AH
4 34H
20H
- 2DH
- 2DH
- 2DH
20H
20H
t 74H
e 65H
x 78H
t 74H
0DH
0AH
5 35H
20H
* 2AH
* 2AH
* 2AH
20H
20H
f 66H
1
2 === This
3 +++ is a
4 --- text
5 *** file.
The text file shown above is like this sequence of bytes when it is stored in the hard disk memory of a computer. The first byte of the file is 31H, the character code of digit symbol 1. The first line of the text file contains only this single visible character.
Although Java programs use 16-bit character codes, characters are usually stored in text files as 8-bit bytes. Because the character codes of English letters and the most common special characters are smaller than 128 (80H), they can be stored in a single byte.
Here, after the character code of lowercase letter a, is the point where the third line of the text file terminates. 0DH is the code of the Carriage Return character, and 0AH is the code of the Line Feed character. Code 0AH is also called the newline character. In Windows and MS-DOS operating systems, text lines in text files are separated with these two character codes 0DH and 0AH. In UNIX and Linux operating systems, text lines are separated with a single newline character with code 0AH. Some programs that transfer text files between the UNIX/Linux operating system and the Windows/MS-DOS operating system, operate so that they drop the 0DH from the end of each line when a file is sent from Windows/MS-DOS to Unix/Linux, and they add the 0DH when a file is moved to the other direction. When you write, in Windows/MS-DOS, a program that calculates the number of characters in a text file, the program may report a slightly smaller file size than the operating system. The reason for this is that the program understands the codes 0DH and 0AH as a single newline character.
Two codes between text lines is a small waste of disk space, but there are historical reasons for using these codes. In old printers, the code 0DH was needed to return the printing carriage to the beginning of a line, and the code 0AH was needed to move the paper one line upwards.

***Figure 14-2. A text file on a computer's hard disk.***

In the example programs on the following pages, files are opened for reading with the following kind of object creation statement

```
BufferedReader file_to_read  = new BufferedReader(
                         new  FileReader( file_name_as_string ) ) ;
```

This statement first creates a **FileReader** object, and then the **FileReader** object is "put inside" a new **BufferedReader** object. The constructor of **FileReader** actually opens the file with the given name. Class **BufferedReader** ensures that file reading operations are efficient, and it provides the **readLine()** method which is used in the example programs to read text lines from files. After the above statement is successfully executed, the created **BufferedReader** object represents the file, and the file is ready to be read.

The **readLine()** method reads characters from the file until it reads the line termination characters 0DH and 0AH, and it returns the read characters to the caller as a string, so that the line termination characters are left out from the string. When the **readLine()** method is repeatedly executed inside a loop, the first call to **readLine()** reads the first text line from the file, the second **readLine()** call reads the second line, and so on. Ultimately, all lines are read from the file, and in that situation the **readLine()** method returns a **null**, a reference to no object. A loop that reads text lines from a file can have the following structure

```
boolean end_of_file_encountered  =  false ;

while ( end_of_file_encountered  ==  false )
{
   String  text_line_from_file  =  file_to_read.readLine() ;

   if ( text_line_from_file  ==  null )
   {
      end_of_file_encountered  =  true ;
   }
   else
   {
      // Do something to the read text line.
   }
}
```

The above loop reads a file sequentially, line by line, from the beginning to the end. The file reading mechanism maintains a reading point which is at the beginning of the file right after the file is opened. In subsequent reading operations the reading point is advanced so that finally it is at the end of the file.

When we want to write text to a file, we can use the standard classes **FileWriter** and **PrintWriter**. The statement

```
PrintWriter file_to_write  =  new  PrintWriter(
                         new  FileWriter( file_name_as_string ) ) ;
```

first creates a **FileWriter** object and then puts the **FileWriter** object "inside" a new **PrintWriter** object. The constructor of class **FileWriter** opens the file, while class **PrintWriter** provides useful methods to write data to the file. After the above statement is successfully executed, the created **PrintWriter** object represents the open file in the program.

When a file is opened for writing with a statement like the one above, a new file with the specified file name is created. This means that the file does not contain anything (i.e. the file is empty) right after it has been opened. If a file with the specified file name already exists, the old file is deleted, and a new file with the same name is created. If you do not want to delete an existing file in a file writing operation, you have the following possibilities to construct your program:

- You can open a file so that the program appends text to the end of the file in the case that the file already exists. A text file can be opened in appending mode when a **PrintWriter** object is created with a statement like

```
PrintWriter file_to_write  =  new  PrintWriter(
                      new  FileWriter( file_name_as_string, true ) ;
```

where the constructor of the **FileWriter** class is given a second parameter. The second parameter must be a boolean value. **true** means that text must be appended to the end of the file if the file already exists. **false** would mean that an existing file should be overwritten.

- Before you actually open a file, you can find out if the file already exists. In the standard class **File** there is a method named **exists()** which returns **true** or **false** depending on whether or not a file with a certain name exists. You can have in your program a test like

```
File  file_to_use  =  new  File( name_of_file_as_string ) ;

if ( file_to_use.exists() )
{
   //  The file already exists.
   ...
```

and then you can ask the user of the program to decide if he or she wants an existing file to be overwritten.

Once a **PrintWriter** object is created, writing data to the opened file is rather easy. The **PrintWriter** class provides a method named **println()** to write a line of text to a file. This method automatically adds line termination characters to the end of each line. When the **println()** method is called repeatedly inside a loop, the lines go to the file so that each **println()** call places a line after the text line that was written by the previous **println()** call. For example, the loop

```
for ( int line_number  =  1 ;
          line_number  <  4 ;
          line_number  ++ )
{
   file_to_write.println( "This is line " + line_number ) ;
}
```

would put the following lines to a text file:

```
This is line 1
This is line 2
This is line 3
```

In Java programs, it is necessary to close files when they are not needed any more, and especially before the termination of a program that has been using the files. The standard Java classes that can be used in file handling provide a method named **close()** that closes a file. The **close()** method can be called in the following way

```
file_object.close() ;
```

When a program closes a file, it informs the operating system that it does not need the file any more. After a file has been closed, it can be reopened for other activities, even by other programs. A call to the **close()** method ensures that all data that is supposed to be in a file is really written to the hard disk. In file writing operations, data does not always go immediately to the disk. Data that is supposed to go to a file may be kept in an intermediate buffer which is written to the hard disk only when considered necessary. In a file closing operation all data that is possibly kept in an intermediate buffer is moved to the hard disk. (The file handling classes provide also a method named **flush()** that can be called to flush intermediate buffers.)

When you write programs which handle files, your programs must ensure that the files are opened correctly. File opening can be unsuccessful for various reasons:

- A program may try to open a non-existent file for reading.
- Although modern computers are quite reliable, a hardware problem can occur with the hard disk of the computer.
- A disk or other memory device can be full of data which prevents the writing of new files.
- Some files cannot be written when they are set as read-only files with special operating system commands. Some memory devices can be made write-protected which prevents writing files on them.
- A program may fail to open a file if the file in question has already been opened by some other program.

Although it can be a very rare situation that a file cannot be opened properly, it is important that your program is able to handle such a situation. The methods and constructors of the file handling classes throw exceptions if the file opening operations are not successful. One such exception is **`FileNotFoundException`** which is caught by those example programs that read files.

File opening problems are not the only troubles that may face a program that is reading or writing a file. File writing operations can be especially problematic from a security point of view. If a file-related problem occurs while a program is performing file writing activities, data may be lost. Possible file problems include hardware failures and disk capacity problems. The methods that write data to a file throw exceptions in such problem situations, and the application program is responsible for ensuring that no data is lost.

The example programs of this book that write files (e.g. **Filecopy.java** and **Findreplace.java**) do catch all the exceptions, but they do not take any particular actions to deal with the file writing problems. One possibility to increase the reliability of file writing operations is to use **`try-catch-finally`** constructs in programs that write files. Another possibility is to design programs so that, from time to time, backup copies can be taken from files that contain important data.

## UTF-8 Encoding

In the example programs of this book, text lines are written to a file so that each 16-bit character code of the text is stored as a single 8-bit byte. The storing of text works this way provided that the text consists of characters whose character codes are in the range from 0 to 127 (7FH). When our Java programs convert a string that consists of 16-bit character codes to a sequence of 8-bit bytes, they use a so-called UTF-8 encoding. UTF is an abbreviation of Unicode Transformation Format. UTF-8 is one format for converting 16-bit Unicode character codes to 8-bit bytes. The UTF-8 conversion works as follows:

- Character codes within the range from 0 to 127 (i.e. character codes whose 9 most significant bits are zeroes) are converted to a single byte, and the byte contains the character code. In practice, this conversion means that the 8 most significant bits of the character code are left out. This conversion does not alter the value of the character code because the 8 left-out bits are zeroes. The English letters and symbols belong to this category of characters.
- Character codes within the range from 128 to 2047 (i.e. character codes whose 5 most significant bits are zeroes) are converted to a two-byte sequence 110?????B 10??????B, in which the ????? of the first byte contains the 5 most significant bits that are left when the top 5 zero bits are left out from the original code, and ?????? of the latter byte contains the 6 least significant bits of the original code.
- Character codes that are greater than 2047 are converted to a three-byte sequence according to certain conversion rules. (For more information, please visit *http://www.unicode.org*)

## Writing data to a file with try-catch-finally constructs

I have wanted to make the example programs of this book short and as easy to read as possible. For this reason, I have not used **try-catch-finally** constructs in the example program that read or write files. Although the programs work well, they might be more secure if at least file writing operations were carried out in **try-catch-finally** constructs. The **finally** block, which is executed regardless of whether or not an exception is caught, can be used to close a file. If a file is closed in a **finally** block, the closing operation is performed also when an exception is caught. The following is an example in which text lines are written to a file in a **try-catch-finally** construct

```
public static void main( String[] not_in_use )
{

   PrintWriter  file_to_write  =  null ;

   try
   {
      file_to_write  =  new  PrintWriter(
                            new  FileWriter( "some_text_file.txt" ) ) ;

      for ( int line_number  =  1 ;
                line_number  <  4 ;
                line_number  ++ )
      {
         file_to_write.println( "This is line " + line_number ) ;
      }
   }
   catch ( IOException  caught_io_exception )
   {
      System.out.print( "\n File error. Cannot write to file. " ) ;
   }
   finally
   {
      if ( file_to_write  !=  null )
      {
         file_to_write.close() ;
      }
   }
}
```

In the above program the call to the **close()** method is inside the **finally** block. This program structure is more secure than the program structure of the other example programs because, if a file problem occurs and an exception is thrown during the execution of the **for** loop, the **finally** block closes the file before the program terminates, and those text lines that were written before the file problem occurred are saved. It is a rare situation that such a problem occurred in the middle of the execution of a loop, but if you some day write programs that handle important data, it may be a good idea to use **try-catch-finally** constructs in file writing operations. The above program structure can also be used when files are treated as binary files.

```
//  Fileprint.java

import java.io.* ;
import java.util.* ;
class Fileprint
{
   public static void main( String[] not_in_use )
   {
      Scanner keyboard = new Scanner( System.in ) ;
      System.out.print( "\n This program prints the contents of a text"
                      + "\n file to the screen. Give a file name: " ) ;

      String  file_name_from_user  =  keyboard.nextLine() ;

      try
      {
         BufferedReader file_to_print =
             new BufferedReader( new FileReader( file_name_from_user ) ) ;

         int line_counter  =  0 ;
         boolean  end_of_file_encountered  =  false ;

         while ( end_of_file_encountered  ==  false )
         {
            String text_line_from_file  =  file_to_print.readLine() ;

            if ( text_line_from_file  ==  null )
            {
               end_of_file_encountered  =  true ;
            }
            else
            {
               System.out.print( text_line_from_file  +  "\n" ) ;
               line_counter  ++  ;
            }
         }

         file_to_print.close() ;
         System.out.print( "\n  " + line_counter + " lines printed." ) ;
      }
      catch ( FileNotFoundException  caught_file_not_found_exception )
      {
         System.out.print( "\n \"" + file_name_from_user + "\" not found.\n" ) ;
      }
      catch ( IOException  caught_io_exception )
      {
         System.out.print( "\n\n  File reading error.  \n" ) ;
      }
   }
}
```

**`file_to_print`** references a **`BufferedReader`** object. That object represents a file that can be read. The file is opened by the constructor of class **`FileReader`**.

An exception of type **`FileNotFoundException`** is thrown by the constructor of class **`FileReader`** if it cannot find a file with the name that the user specified. If the exception is thrown, the execution of the program continues so that only this statement is executed, and no file reading activities are carried out.

The text file is read line-by-line in this program. Therefore, it is possible to count how many lines the input file contains.

**Fileprint.java - 1.+ A program that reads a text file and prints the text lines to the screen.**

The file input mechanism works so that in the beginning, when a file has just been opened, the "reading point" of the file is at the beginning of the file. But when pieces of data are read from the file, the "reading point" is advanced towards the end of the file. At the end, all data has been read from the file, and the file end has been reached.

When we read text lines with the **readLine()** method, the first **readLine()** call after file opening reads the first text line, the second call reads the second line, and so on. Finally, when all lines of the file have been read, the **readLine()** method returns a **null**, indicating that it could not create a **String** object because no more text is available in the file.

```
while ( end_of_file_encountered  ==  false )
{
   String text_line_from_file  =  file_to_print.readLine() ;

   if ( text_line_from_file  ==  null )
   {
      end_of_file_encountered  =  true ;
   }
   else
   {
      System.out.print( text_line_from_file  +  "\n" ) ;
      line_counter  ++  ;
   }
}
```

A method named **readLine()** is used to read a line of text from a file that is represented by the object referenced by **file_to_print**. This **readLine()** method is provided by class **BufferedReader**, and it resembles the **nextLine()** of class **Scanner** which we use to read a line of text from the keyboard. Here method **readLine()** reads a text line from the file, converts the read text to a **String** object, and **text_line_from_file** is made to reference the created object.

Method **readLine()** reads the input file until it encounters the line termination characters. **readLine()** does not, however, include the line termination characters in the string that it returns to its caller. Therefore, a newline character (\n) must be written after the text line that is output to the screen.

**Fileprint.java - 1 - 1. The loop that reads the file line-by-line.**

```
D:\javafiles3>java Fileprint

 This program prints the contents of a text
 file to the screen. Give a file name: story.txt
----- This is a very simple story. ----------
----- This text is in file "story.txt". -----
----- This is now the end of the story. -----

  3 lines printed.
```

**Fileprint.java - X. Printing a test file named story.txt.**

This statement specifies that this program uses a package named **java.io**. The classes for file handling exist in that package. This statement must thus be written at the beginning of programs that read or write files.

```
//  Filecopy.java  (c) Kari Laitinen

import java.util.* ;
import java.io.* ;     //  Classes for file handling.

class Filecopy
{
   public static void main( String[] not_in_use )
   {
      Scanner keyboard = new Scanner( System.in ) ;

      System.out.print( "\n This program copies text from one file"
                      + "\n to another file. Please, give the name of"
                      + "\n the file to be copied: " ) ;

      String name_of_file_to_be_copied  =  keyboard.nextLine() ;

      System.out.print( "\n Give the name of the duplicate file: " ) ;

      String name_of_new_duplicate_file  =  keyboard.nextLine() ;

      try
      {
         BufferedReader file_to_be_copied  = new BufferedReader(
                     new FileReader( name_of_file_to_be_copied ) ) ;

         PrintWriter new_duplicate_file  =  new PrintWriter(
                     new FileWriter( name_of_new_duplicate_file ) ) ;

         System.out.print( "\n Copying in progress ... \n" ) ;

         int  text_line_counter  =  0 ;
         boolean  end_of_input_file_encountered  =  false ;
```

Two objects of standard file handling classes are created in this program because the program opens two files. The file that is going to be read is represented by a **BufferedReader** object. The file that is going to be written is represented by a **PrintWriter** object. Both of these object-creation statements use other classes to actually open a file. The constructor of class **FileReader** opens a file for reading. The **FileWriter** constructor opens a file for writing. Both statements are able to throw exceptions that will be caught by the **catch** blocks at the end of the program.

**Filecopy.java - 1: A program that makes a copy of a text file.**

Method **println()** of class **PrintWriter** is used to write the text line that was previously read by method **readLine()** from the other file. The **println()** method automatically adds correct line termination characters to the end of the text line.

```
         while ( end_of_input_file_encountered  ==  false )
         {
            String text_line_from_file  =  file_to_be_copied.readLine() ;

            if ( text_line_from_file  ==  null )
            {
               end_of_input_file_encountered  =  true ;
            }
            else
            {
               new_duplicate_file.println( text_line_from_file ) ;

               text_line_counter  ++  ;
            }
         }

         System.out.print( "\n Copying ready.  " + text_line_counter
                         +  " lines were copied. \n" ) ;
         file_to_be_copied.close() ;
         new_duplicate_file.close() ;
      }
      catch ( FileNotFoundException  caught_file_not_found_exception )
      {
         System.out.print( "\n\n  File \"" + name_of_file_to_be_copied
                              + "\" not found.\n" ) ;
      }
      catch ( IOException  caught_io_exception )
      {
         System.out.print( "\n\n  File error. Probably cannot write to \""
                              +  name_of_file_to_be_copied + "\".\n" ) ;
      }
   }
}
```

**Filecopy.java - 2. The second part of the program which copies the text lines.**

```
D:\javafiles3>java Filecopy

 This program copies text from one file
 to another file. Please, give the name of
 the file to be copied: story.txt

 Give the name of the duplicate file: story_copied.txt

 Copying in progress ...

 Copying ready. 3 lines were copied.
```

**Filecopy.java - X. Making a copy of text file story.txt.**

```
//  Search.java

import java.io.* ;
import java.util.* ;

class Search
{
   static void search_string_in_file( String  file_name_from_caller,
                                      String  string_to_be_searched )
   {
      try
      {
         BufferedReader file_to_read  =
             new BufferedReader( new FileReader( file_name_from_caller ) ) ;

         System.out.print( "\n Searching ... \""
                     +  string_to_be_searched  + "\"\n" ) ;

         int  line_counter  =  0 ;
         boolean  end_of_file_encountered  =  false ;

         while ( end_of_file_encountered  ==  false )
         {
            String  text_line_from_file   =  file_to_read.readLine() ;

            if ( text_line_from_file  ==  null )
            {
               end_of_file_encountered  =  true ;
            }
            else
            {
               line_counter  ++ ;

               if ( text_line_from_file.contains( string_to_be_searched ) )
               {
                  System.out.print( "\n String \"" +  string_to_be_searched
                              + "\" was found on line "  +  line_counter ) ;
               }
            }
         }

         file_to_read.close() ;
      }
      catch ( FileNotFoundException caught_file_not_found_exception )
      {
        System.out.print( "\n Cannot open \"" + file_name_from_caller + "\"");
      }
      catch ( IOException caught_io_exception )
      {
         System.out.print( "\n\n  File processing error.  \n" ) ;
      }
   }
```

This method takes a file name and a string to be searched for from its caller. The method does not know whether these were initially given via the command line or whether method **main()** asked for the information from the user.

Method **readLine()** is used to read the file line by line in the same way as in program **Fileprint.java**.

Method **contains()** returns the value **true** when the string that is given as a parameter is included in the string for which the method was called. For example, string "bbc" is included in "aabbccdd", but string "bbbc" is not included in it. We can say also that "bbc" is a substring of "aabbccdd". Method **contains()** thus checks whether a string has a certain substring.

**Search.java - 1: A method that searches for a string in a text file.**

If the number of command line parameters equals 2, the program supposes that the user of the program gave the file name and the string to be searched for from the command line.

```
public static void main( String[] command_line_parameters )
{
   Scanner keyboard = new Scanner( System.in ) ;

   if ( command_line_parameters.length  ==  2 )
   {
      search_string_in_file ( command_line_parameters[ 0 ],
                              command_line_parameters[ 1 ] ) ;
   }
   else
   {
      System.out.print( "\n This program can search a string in a "
                      + "\n text file. Give first the file name :  " ) ;

      String  file_name_given_by_user  =  keyboard.nextLine() ;

      System.out.print( "\n Type in the string to be searched: " ) ;

      String  string_to_be_searched    =  keyboard.nextLine() ;

      search_string_in_file( file_name_given_by_user,
                             string_to_be_searched ) ;
   }
}
```

Here, **search_string_in_file()** is called with the data that was asked from the user.

**Search.java - 2. Method main() that calls method search_string_in_file().**

```
D:\javafiles3>type testlines.txt
----------- This is first line --------------------
XXXXXXXXXX  THIS IS SECOND LINE XXXXXXXXXXXXXXXXXXX
==========  THIS IS THIRD LINE  ===================
----------- This is last line of testlines.txt ----

D:\javafiles3>java Search testlines.txt This

 Searching ... "This"

 String "This" was found on line 1
 String "This" was found on line 4
```

"This" is not found on the second and third line because on those lines it is written with uppercase letters.

**Search.java - X. Searching for the word "This" in text file testlines.txt.**

This program can replace all occurrences of a string with another string in a text file. This method will be called twice at the end, when strings have been replaced on the text lines, and when both the original text lines and the modified text lines need to be stored back to files in the disk memory.

An **ArrayList** object containing text lines is given as a parameter to this method. An **ArrayList** object is a dynamic array. **ArrayList** arrays will be studied more thoroughly in the following chapter.

```
//  Findreplace.java  (c) Kari Laitinen

import java.util.* ;  // ArrayList, Scanner, etc.
import java.io.* ;    // Classes for file handling.

class Findreplace
{
   static void
   store_text_lines_to_file( ArrayList<String> given_array_of_text_lines,
                             String            given_file_name )
   {
      try
      {
         PrintWriter output_file  =
                new PrintWriter( new FileWriter( given_file_name ) ) ;

         for ( int line_index  =  0 ;
                   line_index  <  given_array_of_text_lines.size() ;
                   line_index  ++ )
         {
            output_file.println(
                      given_array_of_text_lines.get( line_index ) ) ;
         }

         output_file.close() ;
      }
      catch ( IOException caught_io_exception )
      {
         System.out.print( "\n\n Cannot write to file \""
                        +  given_file_name  +  "\"\n" ) ;
      }
   }
```

The exceptions that may be thrown by the methods that perform file operations are so-called checked exceptions which must be caught. Writing to a file may be unsuccessful, for example, when the file is a read-only file.

An element of an **ArrayList**-based array can be read by supplying an index value to a method named **get()**. The index values start counting from zero, in the same way as in the case of conventional Java arrays. This statement reads a text line from the **ArrayList** object referenced by **given_array_of_text_lines**, and stores the line to a file by using the **println()** method. A newline character is automatically added to the end of each text line.

**Findreplace.java - 1: A program to replace a string with another string in a text file.**

Two **ArrayList**-based arrays are created here to store the original text lines and the modified text lines. The array for the modified text lines will contain lines on which the given replacement string has been put in place of the string being replaced. By writing **<String>** after the class name **ArrayList**, we specify that we will store **String** objects to the array. These arrays are used for intermediate storage. At the end of this method, the data in the arrays will be written to files.

```
static void replace_string_in_file( String  original_file_name,
                                    String  string_to_replace,
                                    String  replacement_string )
{
   try
   {
      BufferedReader original_file =
          new BufferedReader( new FileReader( original_file_name ) ) ;
      ArrayList<String>  original_text_lines  =  new  ArrayList<String>() ;
      ArrayList<String>  modified_text_lines  =  new  ArrayList<String>() ;

      int  line_counter  =  0 ;
      boolean end_of_file_encountered  =  false ;

      while ( end_of_file_encountered  ==  false )
      {
         String  text_line_from_file   =  original_file.readLine() ;

         if ( text_line_from_file  ==  null )
         {
            end_of_file_encountered  =  true ;
         }
         else
         {
            line_counter  ++ ;
            original_text_lines.add( text_line_from_file ) ;

            if ( text_line_from_file.contains( string_to_replace ) )
            {
               text_line_from_file  =
                     text_line_from_file.replace( string_to_replace,
                                                  replacement_string ) ;

               System.out.print( "\n \""  +  string_to_replace
                    +  "\" was replaced with \""  +  replacement_string
                    +  "\" on line "  +  line_counter   ) ;
            }

            modified_text_lines.add( text_line_from_file ) ;
         }
      }
```

String method **replace()** replaces all occurrences of the given string.

Method **add()** of class **ArrayList** is used here to insert a new **String** object to the end of the array object. An **ArrayList** array is dynamic, i.e., the array grows automatically when new objects are inserted to the array. **ArrayList** method **size()** tells how many objects are stored in an array.

**Findreplace.java - 2: A method to replace a given string in a given file.**

Here it is necessary to close the original file with a call to method **close()**. The file will be reopened for writing by the **store_text_lines_to_file()** method.

The original text lines are stored in a file with file name extension **.bak**, a backup file. The modified text lines are stored in the file with the original file name.

```
         original_file.close() ;

         String  backup_file_name  =  original_file_name  +  ".bak" ;

         store_text_lines_to_file( original_text_lines,
                                   backup_file_name     ) ;
         store_text_lines_to_file( modified_text_lines,
                                   original_file_name ) ;
      }
      catch ( FileNotFoundException caught_file_not_found_exception )
      {
         System.out.print( "\n Cannot open file " + original_file_name ) ;
      }
      catch ( IOException  caught_io_exception )
      {
         System.out.print( "\n Error in reading " + original_file_name ) ;
      }
   }
```

If the file could not be found, it is likely that the user of the program gave a wrong file name.

**Findreplace.java - 3: The other part of method replace_string_in_file().**

```
D:\javafiles3>type shortstory.txt
  This is the beginning of the story.
  This is the end.

D:\javafiles3>java Findreplace shortstory.txt the XXX

 "the" was replaced with "XXX" on line 1
 "the" was replaced with "XXX" on line 2
D:\javafiles3>
D:\javafiles3>type shortstory.txt
  This is XXX beginning of XXX story.
  This is XXX end.
```

Note that the program is able to replace multiple occurrences of a string on a single text line.

**Findreplace.java - X. Replacing "the" with "XXX" in "shortstory.txt".**

It is possible to activate the program by supplying data from the command line. The first parameter given from the command line is the name of the file to be processed.

```
public static void main( String[] command_line_parameters )
{
   Scanner keyboard = new Scanner( System.in ) ;

   String  file_name_given_by_user ;
   String  string_to_replace ;
   String  replacement_string ;

   if ( command_line_parameters.length  ==  3 )
   {
      file_name_given_by_user  =  command_line_parameters[ 0 ] ;
      string_to_replace        =  command_line_parameters[ 1 ] ;
      replacement_string       =  command_line_parameters[ 2 ] ;
   }
   else
   {
      System.out.print( "\n This program can replace a string in a "
                    +  "\n text file. Give first the file name :  " ) ;

      file_name_given_by_user  =  keyboard.nextLine() ;

      System.out.print( "\n Type in the string to be replaced: " ) ;
      string_to_replace        =  keyboard.nextLine() ;

      System.out.print( "\n Type in the replacement string:    " ) ;
      replacement_string       =  keyboard.nextLine() ;
   }

   if ( string_to_replace.equals( "" )  ||
        string_to_replace.equals( replacement_string ) )
   {
      System.out.print( "\n Cannot replace \""  +  string_to_replace
             +  "\" with \""  +  replacement_string  +  "\"\n\n" ) ;
   }
   else
   {
      replace_string_in_file( file_name_given_by_user,
                              string_to_replace,
                              replacement_string ) ;
   }
 }
}
```

The program will not try to search for an empty string. Neither does it make sense to replace a string with itself. The equality of **String** objects can be tested with the **equals()** method. Operator == cannot be used here because it can only test whether two object references point to the same object.

**Findreplace.java - 4. Method main() that calls replace_string_in_file().**

## Exercises related to text files

Exercise 14-1. Modify program **Fileprint.java** so that it informs a user how many (visible) characters are found in the file that is printed to the screen. Currently, the program counts only the number of printed lines. You can use the method `length()` of the `String` class to find out how many characters a text line contains. You should declare a variable like

```
int  character_counter  =  0 ;
```

to count the characters of the input file.

Exercise 14-2. Modify program **Filecopy.java** so that the user can invoke it from the command line in the following way

```
java  Filecopy  story.txt  story_copied.txt
```

You can write a separate method that performs the file copying and organize the program in the same way as program **Search.java** is organized.

Exercise 14-3. Write a truly useless program that prints a file to the screen so that the characters of all lines are printed in reverse order. You can use program **Fileprint.java** as a basis for this program. The program might be named **Mirror.java**. A text file that contains the lines

```
Hello.
This is simple text
in a file.
```

would be printed by **Mirror.java** in the following way

```
.olleH
txet elpmis si sihT
.elif a ni
```

Exercise 14-4. Write a program that is a simple text editor which reads text lines from the keyboard and stores the lines to a text file. The program should store the text lines temporarily to an array of strings and write the lines to a file when the user stops entering text. The user should mark the end of text by typing in a line where the first character is a dot (.). After this, the program must ask the file name if the user did not give it from the command line.

Exercise 14-5. Improve program **Search.java** so that it is possible to search for more than one word in a text file. For example, by commanding

```
java  Search  somefile.txt  xxxxx  yyyyy
```

the program should display lines where either of the words "xxxxx" and "yyyyy" can be found. To do this modification, method `search_string_in_file()` should probably be changed to

```
static void search_strings_in_file(
                                  String   file_name_from_caller,
                                  String[] strings_to_be_searched )
{
   ...
```

where the second parameter is an array of strings. (To further improve the program, there could be a possibility to give words like AND and OR on the command line. These words could dictate whether both strings or just one string should specify a match.)

## 14.3 Handling files as binary files

Although all files on a computer's hard disk contain only bits, binary digits, we say that some files are text files while others are considered binary files. Categorizing files into text files and binary files is thus somewhat arbitrary. A binary file can be considered a series of bytes, and so can a text file. It is possible to open a text file as a binary file. The essential distinction between these two file types is that a binary file can contain any bytes, but a text file contains only character codes of visible characters, line termination characters, and such text formatting characters as tabulator characters. It is possible to view a text file with an editor program (e.g. JCreator, EditPad or Notepad). Binary files, on the other hand, usually contain data that is not readable by the human eye, and may even cause strange behavior in an editor program.

When we want to process binary files in a Java program, we use different standard classes depending on whether we want to read data from a file or to write data to a file. A file can be opened for binary reading operations with a statement like

```
FileInputStream  file_to_read  =  new
                     FileInputStream( file_name_as_string ) ;
```

In this statement the constructor of class **FileInputStream** opens a file with the given file name. After the statement is successfully executed, the file is represented by the **FileInputStream** object, and it can be read by using the file reading methods of class **FileInputStream**.

The basic **FileInputStream** method for reading a file in binary form has the name **read()**. Actually, there are several versions of the **read()** method. The version of the **read()** method which we use in this book can be called to read a certain number of bytes from a file. The method puts the bytes it reads to an array of type **byte[]**, and returns a value that indicates how many bytes it was able to read. Normally, the **read()** method reads as many bytes as it was asked to read, but when the end of the file has been reached, it is possible that it may not be able to read all the bytes that were requested. One possible way to call the **read()** method is the following:

```
byte[]  bytes_from_file  =  new  byte[ 50 ] ;
int number_of_bytes_read  =
                  file_to_read.read( bytes_from_file ) ;
```

This method call could be "translated" as follows: "Here is this array of bytes. Please, read bytes from the file and put them to the array, starting from the array position that has index 0. Read 50 bytes at maximum because that is the length of the array; it cannot hold any more bytes." After receiving these orders, the **read()** method would do its job and return the number of bytes it was able to read. The **read()** method checks the length of the given array of type **byte[]**, and automatically delivers as many bytes as is the length of the array.

Files are typically read with a loop, but the loop that uses method **read()** becomes somewhat complicated as the above method call must be fitted into it. One possibility to construct a loop that calls method **read()** is the following one which calculates the size of a file by counting how many bytes the file contains:

```
byte[]  bytes_from_file  =  new  byte[ 50 ] ;

int  file_size_in_bytes  =  0 ;

int  number_of_bytes_read  =  0 ;

while (( number_of_bytes_read  =
            file_to_read.read( bytes_from_file ))  >  0 )
{
   file_size_in_bytes  =  file_size_in_bytes  +
                          number_of_bytes_read ;

   //  This loop does not do anything to the read data.
}
```

In the above case, method **read()** is called in the somewhat complicated boolean expression of the **while** loop. When the boolean expression is evaluated, the **read()** method is called, and as a result variable **number_of_bytes_read** gets a new value, and that value is then compared to zero. The boolean expression is true as long as the **read()** method is able to read bytes from the file.

Method **read()** works with binary files in the same manner as method **readLine()** works with text files. In the loop above, when method **read()** is called for the first time, it reads the first 50 bytes from the file, and subsequent calls read the file from the position where the previous reading operation stopped. The above loop reads 50-byte data blocks from the file until it has read the last block. Only the last block is likely to be less than 50 bytes in length. In file reading operations it is usually not known when the final data at the end of a file is going to be read. Therefore, a loop that reads a file must always be prepared to encounter the end of file.

The above loop can be made easier to understand if a boolean variable is used in the following way:

```
byte[]  bytes_from_file  =  new  byte[ 50 ] ;

int  file_size_in_bytes  =  0 ;

boolean  bytes_still_available_in_file  =  true ;

while ( bytes_still_available_in_file  ==  true )
{
   int  number_of_bytes_read  =
                 file_to_read.read( bytes_from_file ) ;

   if ( number_of_bytes_read  >  0 )
   {
      file_size_in_bytes  =  file_size_in_bytes  +
                             number_of_bytes_read ;

      //  This loop does not do anything to the read data.
   }
   else
   {
      bytes_still_available_in_file  =  false ;
   }
}
```

This loop is, however, somewhat longer than the first loop. For this reason I ended up using a loop like the first one in program **FileToNumbers.java**.

Program **FileToNumbers.java** demonstrates how a file is read as a binary file. It also shows that a text file can be treated as a binary file. The program reads a file in 16-byte blocks and displays the bytes as hexadecimal numbers on the screen. Those bytes that represent character codes of visible characters are also shown as characters.

When you want to write data to a binary file, you can use class **FileOutputStream** to create an object that represents a binary file for writing operations. One possible file opening statement is the following

```
FileOutputStream  binary_file_for_writing  =  new
                            FileOutputStream( file_name_as_string) ;
```

Here, the constructor of class **FileOutputStream** opens the file whose name it gets as a parameter. The file is opened so that it is created if it does not exist, and if it exists, it is overwritten with new data.

Just as class **FileInputStream** provides methods named **read()** to read bytes from binary files, the **FileOutputStream** class provides methods named **write()** for writing bytes to binary files. Supposing that a file is opened with the above statement, and that there is the array

```
byte[]  some_array_of_bytes  =  new  byte[ 300 ] ;
```

containing some data, the statement

```
binary_file_for_writing.write( some_array_of_bytes ) ;
```

would write all the 300 bytes from the array referenced by **some_array_of_bytes** to the file represented by the **FileOutputStream** object referenced by **binary_file_-for_writing**, and the statement

```
binary_file_for_writing.write( some_array_of_bytes,
                               2,
                               5 ) ;
```

would use a different version of the **write()** method, and write the five bytes starting from the third array position that has index 2. The first parameter for the **write()** method specifies the byte array from which bytes should be copied to a file, the second parameter specifies the array position from which the writing operations should begin, and the third parameter says how many bytes should be written. As there are several versions of the **write()** method, there is also a version with which it is possible to write just a single byte to a file. This **write()** method could be called with a statement like

```
binary_file_for_writing.write( 0x22 ) ;
```

which would write the hexadecimal value 0x22 to the binary file that was opened above.

**NumbersToFile.java** is a program that demonstrates how data can be written to a binary file. The program uses class **FileOutputStream** to open a file for binary writing operations. In addition, the program uses a class named **DataOutputStream** in the writing operations. In program **NumbersToFile.java**, a file named **NumbersToFile_output.data** is first opened for binary writing operations with the statement

```
FileOutputStream  file_output_stream  =
      new FileOutputStream( "NumbersToFile_output.data" ) ;
```

and then the **FileOutputStream** object is used to construct a **DataOutputStream** object with the statement

```
DataOutputStream  file_to_write  =
         new  DataOutputStream( file_output_stream ) ;
```

and it is the **DataOutputStream** object that is used later to write data to the file.

The **DataOutputStream** class provides many methods for writing operations, and it is therefore useful in a program like **NumbersToFile.java**. Figure 14-3 describes how a **DataOutputStream** object co-operates with a **FileOutputStream** object when data is written to a file. Class **DataOutputStream** has a "sister class" named **DataInput-Stream**. The methods of **DataInputStream** class are convenient when we need to read data that is written with the **DataOutputStream** methods. In the next section a program named **Collect.java** uses both **DataOutputStream** and **DataInputStream** objects in file operations.

Program **NumbersToFile.java** destroys the previous content of its output file if the file already exists. If you want to write data to a binary file without destroying the previously written data, you must open the file in appending mode. If the file opening statement of program **NumbersToFile.java** were written in the following way

```
FileOutputStream  file_output_stream  =  new
          FileOutputStream( "NumbersToFile_output.data", true ) ;
```

where the constructor of class **FileOutputStream** is given two parameters, the program would append data to the end of the **NumbersToFile_output.data** file, and the file would grow always when the program is executed. When the second constructor parameter is the literal value **true**, or a **boolean** variable whose value is **true**, the file is opened in appending mode. Also in the appending mode the file is created if it does not yet exist.

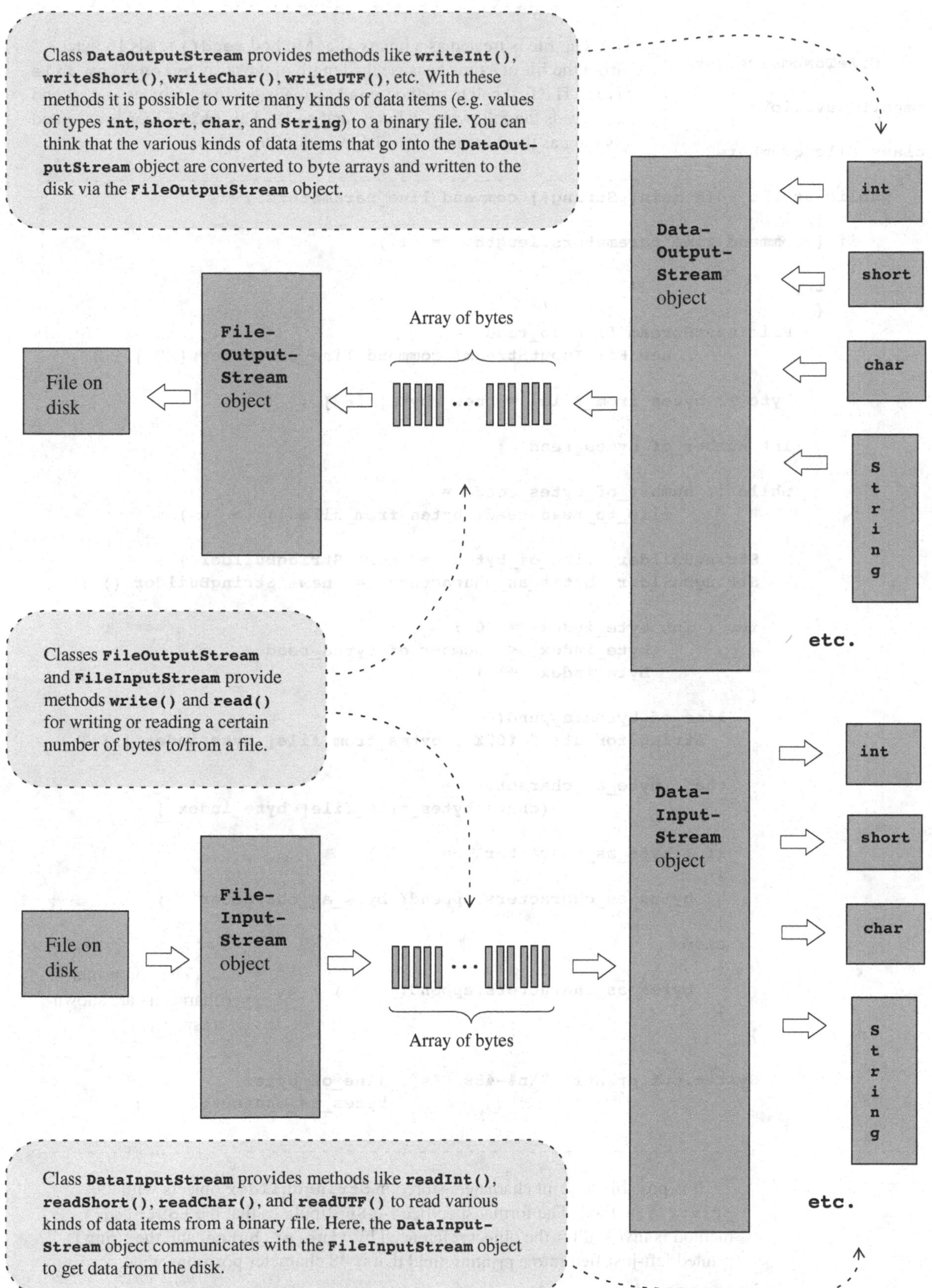


***Figure 14-3. Co-operation of classes in binary file access.***

The file is treated as a binary file. Method **read()** reads 16 bytes from the file at a time because the length of the array **bytes_from_file** is 16. The first call to method **read()** reads the first 16 bytes, the second call reads the following 16 bytes, and so on. This **while** loop is executed as long as there are bytes available in the file.

```
//  FileToNumbers.java

import java.io.* ;

class FileToNumbers
{
   public static void main( String[] command_line_parameters )
   {
      if ( command_line_parameters.length  ==  1 )
      {
         try
         {
            FileInputStream file_to_read  =
                       new FileInputStream( command_line_parameters[ 0 ] ) ;

            byte[]  bytes_from_file  =  new  byte[ 16 ] ;

            int number_of_bytes_read  ;

            while (( number_of_bytes_read  =
                       file_to_read.read( bytes_from_file ))  >  0 )
            {
               StringBuilder  line_of_bytes  =  new  StringBuilder() ;
               StringBuilder  bytes_as_characters  =  new  StringBuilder () ;

               for ( int byte_index  =  0 ;
                         byte_index  <  number_of_bytes_read ;
                         byte_index  ++ )
               {
                  line_of_bytes.append(
                    String.format( " %02X", bytes_from_file[ byte_index ] ) ) ;

                  char  byte_as_character  =
                             (char) bytes_from_file[ byte_index ] ;

                  if ( byte_as_character  >=  ' ' )
                  {
                     bytes_as_characters.append( byte_as_character ) ;
                  }
                  else
                  {
                     bytes_as_characters.append( ' ' ) ;
                  }
               }

               System.out.printf( "\n%-48s  %s", line_of_bytes,
                                                 bytes_as_characters ) ;
            }
```

The non-printable characters are shown as spaces.

It is possible to print characters stored in **StringBuilder** objects with the **printf()** method. The format specifier **%-48s** stipulates that the **toString()** method is invoked for the object referenced by **line_of_bytes**, and the string is printed left-justified into a printing field that is 48 character positions wide.

**FileToNumbers.java - 1: A program to show the contents of a file as hexadecimal bytes.**

It is important that all files, both binary and text files, are closed with a **close()** method after they are not used any more.

**FileNotFoundException** is thrown by the constructor of class **FileInputStream** if it cannot find a file with the specified file name.

```
            file_to_read.close() ;
         }
         catch ( FileNotFoundException  caught_file_not_found_exception )
         {
            System.out.print( "\n Cannot open file "
                             +  command_line_parameters[ 0 ] ) ;
         }
         catch ( IOException  caught_io_exception )
         {
            System.out.print( "\n Error while processing file "
                             +  command_line_parameters[ 0 ] ) ;
         }
      }
      else
      {
         System.out.print( "\n You have to command this program as: \n"
                         + "\n  java FileToNumbers file.ext \n") ;
      }
   }
}
```

The only way to give a file name to this program is to write it on the command line.

**FileToNumbers.java - 2. The last part of the program.**

```
D:\javafiles3>type ministory.txt
1 == ministory.txt ===
2
3 aaa AAA bbb BBB
4
5 This is the end.


D:\javafiles3>java FileToNumbers ministory.txt

 31 20 3D 3D 20 6D 69 6E 69 73 74 6F 72 79 2E 74  1 == ministory.t
 78 74 20 3D 3D 3D 0D 0A 32 0D 0A 33 20 61 61 61  xt ===  2  3 aaa
 20 41 41 41 20 62 62 62 20 42 42 42 0D 0A 34 0D   AAA bbb BBB  4
 0A 35 20 54 68 69 73 20 69 73 20 74 68 65 20 65   5 This is the e
 6E 64 2E 0D 0A 0D 0A                             nd.
```

The contents of the **StringBuilder** object referenced by **bytes_as_characters** are printed after the contents of the object referenced by **line_of_bytes**.

All bytes from the file are shown in hexadecimal form. A newline character is represented by two character codes, 0DH and 0AH, inside the file. There are two newlines at the end of the file.

**FileToNumbers.java - X. Showing the contents of file "ministory.txt".**

A **FileOutputStream** object that represents a file on the disk is created first, and then that object is used to create a **DataOutputStream** object. You can think that the **FileOutputStream** object is controlled by the **DataOutputStream** object. The standard class **DataOutputStream** provides useful methods to write binary values to a file.

If a file with the specified name already exists, it will be written over.

```
//  NumbersToFile.java

import java.io.* ;

class NumbersToFile
{
   public static void main( String[] not_in_use )
   {
      try
      {
         FileOutputStream  file_output_stream  =
                    new FileOutputStream( "NumbersToFile_output.data" ) ;

         DataOutputStream  file_to_write  =
                          new  DataOutputStream( file_output_stream ) ;

         int integer_to_file  =  0x22 ;

         while ( integer_to_file  <  0x77 )
         {
            file_to_write.writeInt( integer_to_file ) ;

            integer_to_file  =  integer_to_file  +  0x11 ;
         }

         file_to_write.writeShort( (short) 0x1234 ) ;
         file_to_write.writeDouble( 1.2345 ) ;
         file_to_write.writeBoolean( true ) ;
         file_to_write.writeBoolean( false ) ;
         file_to_write.writeUTF( "aaAAbbBB" ) ;

         byte[] bytes_to_file  =  { 0x4B, 0x61, 0x72, 0x69 } ;

         file_to_write.write( bytes_to_file, 0, 4 ) ;

         file_to_write.close() ;
      }
      catch ( Exception caught_exception )
      {
          System.out.print( "\n File error. Cannot write to file." ) ;
      }
   }
}
```

Class **DataOutputStream** provides many methods that can write data items of different types to a file. Here, a method named **write()** writes four bytes from the array (referenced by) **bytes_to_file**. The writing begins from the array position whose index is 0 (the first array position). The bytes that are put to the array 0x4B, 0x61, 0x72, and 0x69 are the character codes of letters K, a, r, and i, respectively.

**NumbersToFile.java - 1. A program that stores numerical values to a binary file.**

The execution of the program does not produce any output to the screen. All output goes to a file whose contents are shown here by using the previous example program.

The **while** loop of the program puts five values of type **int** to the file. Each **int** value occupies four bytes in the file, and the bytes are in such an order that the most significant byte is the first in the file.

```
D:\javafiles3>java NumbersToFile

D:\javafiles3>java FileToNumbers NumbersToFile_output.data

 00 00 00 22 00 00 00 33 00 00 00 44 00 00 00 55      "   3   D   U
 00 00 00 66 12 34 3F F3 C0 83 12 6E 97 8D 01 00      f 4???? n??
 00 08 61 61 41 41 62 62 42 42 4B 61 72 69            aaAAbbBBKari
```

The contents of a string are stored in UTF-8 format. Each character code occupies only a single byte. Before the character codes, there is a two-byte (16-bit) value that tells how many bytes are stored. In this case there are 8 bytes. The UTF-8 encoding is such that the characters whose codes are less than 0x80 (i.e., the normal characters and symbols in the English alphabet) are represented by a single byte. The UTF-8 encoding used by the **writeUTF()** method differs slightly from the official UTF-8 format. (See page 456 for more information about UTF-8.)

The **double** value 1.2345 is stored in eight bytes, but the number is encoded so that it is not possible to read it. The boolean values **true** and **false** are stored as bytes containing 1 and 0, respectively.

**NumbersToFile.java - X. Examining the contents of file "NumbersToFile_output.data".**

## Exercises related to binary files

Exercise 14-6. Write a program that compares two files to find out if the files have the same contents. Two files are equal if their lengths are equal, and they contain the same bytes in the same order. You can use method **read()** of class **FileInputStream** to read equal size byte blocks from two files. After each reading operation you must test if the byte blocks are the same.

Exercise 14-7. Write a program (e.g. **FilecopyBinary.java**) that makes a copy of a file by using binary file access. You can use the **read()** and **write()** methods of classes **FileInputStream** and **FileOutputStream** to move byte blocks from one file to another. You do not need to use the **DataOutputStream** class because class **FileOutputStream** has a suitable **write()** method.

Exercise 14-8. Program **FileToNumbers.java** may be a useful program when you work with files, but the program is not convenient to use when large files are examined with it. The contents of a large file do not fit to a single screen. Improve the program so that when it prints the contents of a file it asks the user of the program to press the Enter key before it shows the following 20 or so lines on the screen.

## 14.4 A larger program that uses a binary file

Program **Collect.java**, the only example program of this section, is an application that a collector could use to maintain information about his or her collected items. Many people like to collect something. Some people collect music albums or books. Others collect stamps or pictures of sports heroes. There are people who collect labels of alcohol bottles. Program **Collect.java** is a general-purpose application that could be used to handle data of various kinds of collection items. If you collect something, program **Collect.java** could be of help to you, or you can modify the program to make it suitable for your own special purposes.

When we start developing a new software system, it's imperative to consider what are the needs of the users of the system. Who will be using the system? When and how often will the system be used? What kinds of data must be maintained by the system? These kinds of questions should be answered when the software development for the system begins. From its user's point of view, program **Collect.java** fulfills the following requirements

- The program can be used by a person who is collecting something. The purpose of the program is that its user can easily view and maintain collection data with it.
- For every collection item, the user can store the following information
  -- the name of the collection item (string)
  -- the maker of the collection item (string)
  -- the type of the collection item (string)
  -- the year when the collection item was made (integer)
- The user can add and remove collection items, one item at a time.
- The user can print collection item data to the screen. It is possible to print data of all collection items, items of certain maker, or items of certain type.
- The user can store the data of all collection items in a file named **collection_-items.data**. The purpose of this feature is that the data is stored in a file when the program is not in use. When the user wants to view the data of his or her collection items, the program can load the file from the computer's hard disk memory.

The best way to learn how program **Collect.java** works is to test its features on your own computer. The program provides the possibility to load test data into the system. It is often useful, when you write a larger program, to include features that helps you test the program. The possibility to use test data in program **Collect.java** is such a feature. When you start the program, you should first load the test data, and then examine what you can do with the program.

Program **Collect.java** is a menu-based system, i.e., the user can select what to do from a menu. After the program has displayed the menu

```
Choose what to do by typing in a letter
according to the following menu:

   a   Add a new collection item.
   r   Remove a collection item.
   p   Print data of collection items.
   s   Store collection data to file.
   l   Load collection data from file.
   i   Initialize collection with test data.
   q   Quit the system.
```

the user may type in a letter, and the program will act according to the command given by the user. Figure 14-4 presents a class diagram and explains the structure of program **Collect.java**.

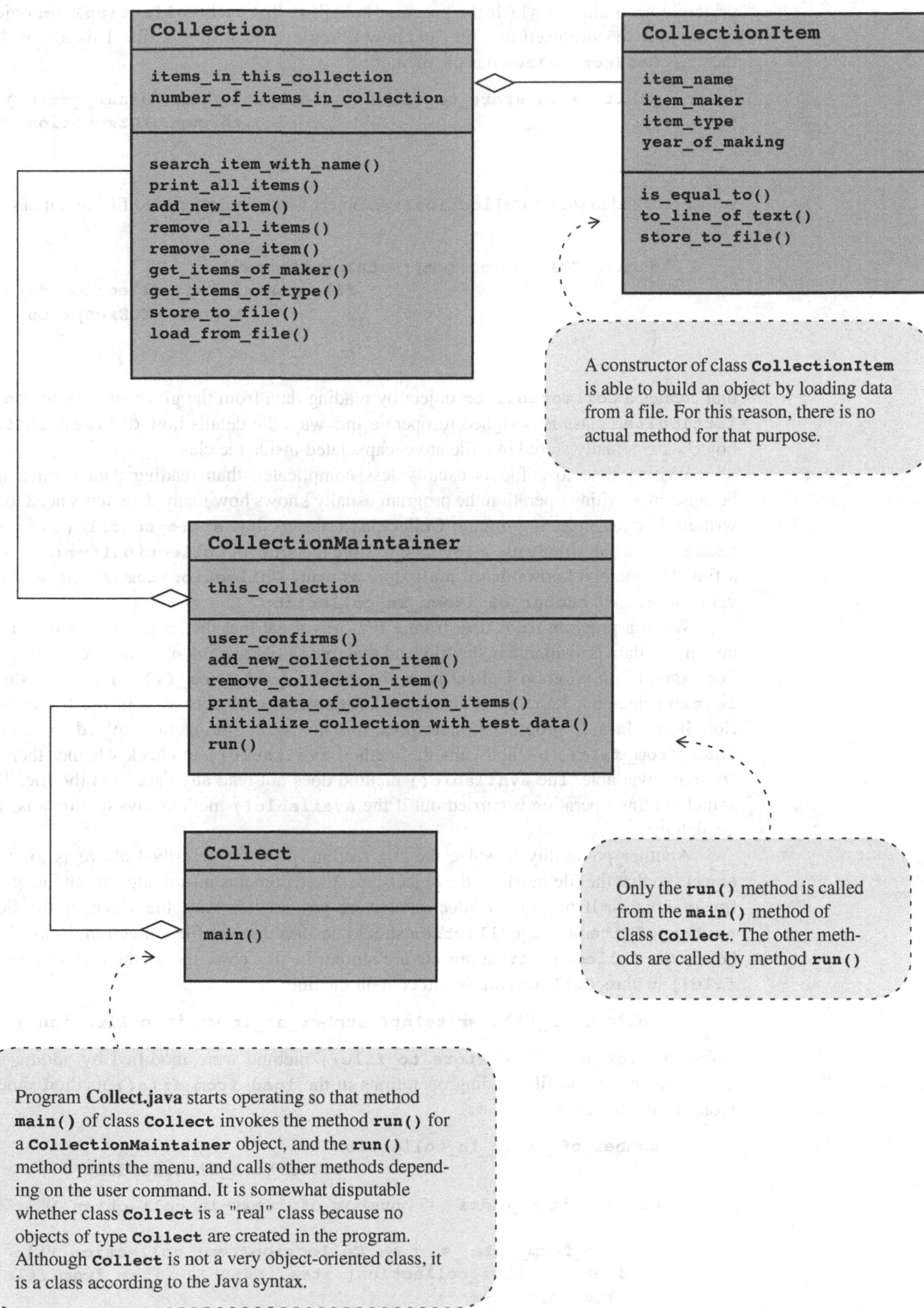


*Figure 14-4. The classes of program Collect.java.*

Program **Collect.java** uses a file to store an array of **CollectionItem** objects. The principle according to which the program is built is that each **CollectionItem** object knows how to store itself to a file, and how to retrieve itself from a file. This means that the class **CollectionItem** has the method

```
public void store_to_file( DataOutputStream  binary_file )
                                        throws  IOException
{
   ...
```

which is called to store a **CollectionItem** object to an already opened file, and it has the constructor

```
public CollectionItem( DataInputStream
                              file_containing_collection_data )
                                        throws  IOException
{
   ...
```

that creates a **CollectionItem** object by reading data from the given file. As the **CollectionItem** class is designed to operate this way, the details how **CollectionItem** objects are actually stored in a file are encapsulated inside the class.

Writing data to a file is usually less complicated than reading data from a file because in a writing operation the program usually knows how many data items need to be written. For example, in program **Collect.java**, the method **store_to_file()** of class **Collection** can simply use a **for** loop to store the array of **CollectionItem** objects to a file. The method knows that it must store as many **CollectionItem** objects as is the value of the field **number_of_items_in_collection**.

When a program reads data from a file, it is usual that the program does not know how much data is available in the file, and that makes file reading operations complicated. For example, in program **Collect.java**, the method **load_from_file()** of class **Collection** does not know how many **CollectionItem** objects exist in the file **collection_items.data**. In program **Collect.java**, this file reading problem is solved so that the **load_from_file()** method calls the method **available()** to check whether there is still data available. The **available()** method does not read any data from the file. The actual reading operation is carried out if the **available()** method says that data is still available.

Another possibility to solve the file reading problem described above is to store objects so that the file in which the objects are stored contains information about the quantity of objects. If program **Collect.java** were written this way, the value of the field **number_of_items_in_collection** should be stored in the file **collection_items.data** before the **CollectionItem** objects are stored. In this case, the method **store_to_file()** in class **Collection** should contain the line

```
collection_file.writeInt( number_of_items_in_collection ) ;
```

before the **for** loop. If the **store_to_file()** method were modified by adding the above statement, the file reading operations in the **load_from_file()** method should look like the following

```
number_of_items_in_collection  =
                              collection_file.readInt() ;

while ( item_index  <  number_of_items_in_collection )
{
   item_from_file  =  new  CollectionItem( collection_file );
   items_in_this_collection[ item_index ] = item_from_file;
   item_index  ++  ;
}

collection_file.close() ;
```

In the above case, the number of **CollectionItem** objects in the file is known before objects are actually read from the file. It is important to note that if program **Collect.java** were modified as described above, the new **collection_items.data** file would no longer be compatible with the file that is produced with the current version of **Collect.java**. This means that the **collection_items.data** file produced by the current version of **Collect.java** could not be read with the new version of the program because the data file would not contain the necessary extra data at the beginning of the file. (Among the extra programs of this book, you can find a file named **CollectAlternative.java**. In that program the modifications described above have been made.)

## Exercises with program Collect.java

Exercise 14-9 Run the program so that it generates the file **collection_items.data**. After that examine the generated file with program **FileToNumbers.java**, and clarify for yourself how data is stored in the file.

Exercise 14-10. Method **add_new_collection_item()** in program **Collect.java** can only add one item to the collection. Modify the method so that it allows the user to add several items once the method is called. You should rename the method to **add_new_collection_items()**. Inside the new method, you will need a loop that creates a new **CollectionItem** object each time the loop is executed. The loop can terminate when the user gives an empty string as the item name. The following boolean expression might be used to test if the given item name is an empty string:

```
( item_name_of_the_new_item.length()  ==  0 )
```

Exercise 14-11. Modify method **print_data_of_collection_items()** in program **Collect.java** so that the user can type in letter n to print collection items that have a certain name.

Exercise 14-12. Modify program **Collect.java** so that when the user quits the program, he or she is asked to store the collection data to a file if the collection data has been modified. One way to do this is to add the data field

```
boolean  collection_data_has_been_modified  =  false ;
```

to class **Collection** and assign the variable value **true** whenever new collection items are added, or when collection items are removed from the collection. If this variable has value **true** when the program is terminating, the program should ask the user to say whether the modified data should be saved.

Exercise 14-13. Write the **equals()** method for class **CollectionItem** in program **Collect.java**. You should override the **equals()** method inherited from class **Object**, and use the **equals()** method in place of the **is_equal_to()** method. See page 445 for advice.

Exercise 14-14. Program **Collect.java** always stores the collection data in a file named **collection_items.data**. The user of the program cannot select the file name and have several collection files. Modify the program so that the user can give the file name when the collection is either stored to a file or loaded from a file. The program could work in a flexible manner, so that if the user gives an empty string (i.e. just hits the Enter key) for a file name, the program uses the default file name **collection_items.data**. (A more advanced system would be such that the name of the collection file is stored in another file. This kind of program could have a line like "select collection file" in its main menu, and a special method that would update the file, where the name of the actual collection file is stored.)

Exercise 14-15. You can use program **Collect.java** as a basis and example when writing programs that can store data of special collections. Special collections can, for example, be collections of cooking recipes, old coins, stamps, cars, books, music CDs, etc. Select a topic for a special collection, and implement a program that can handle data related to the special collection. In your special collection program, you need a class type like **CookingRecipe**, **Coin**, **Stamp**, **Car**, **Book**, or some other type in place of the **CollectionItem** class. You might also need a class like **CookingRecipeCollection**, **CoinCollection**, or **StampCollection** to replace the **Collection** class of program **Collect.java**. Your new classes must have fields and methods that are specific to your "application domain".

The purpose of this program is to handle data related to collection items. These items can be paintings, original manuscripts, or other kinds of collectables. A **CollectionItem** object stores the data of a single item in the collection.

```
//  Collect.java  (c) Kari Laitinen

import java.util.* ;
import java.io.* ;

class CollectionItem
{
   String  item_name ;
   String  item_maker ;
   String  item_type ;
   int     year_of_making ;

   public CollectionItem( String given_item_name,
                          String given_item_maker,
                          String given_item_type,
                          int    given_year_of_making )
   {
      item_name      =  given_item_name ;
      item_maker     =  given_item_maker ;
      item_type      =  given_item_type ;
      year_of_making   =  given_year_of_making ;
   }

   public CollectionItem( DataInputStream file_containing_collection_data )
                                         throws  IOException
   {
      item_name      =  file_containing_collection_data.readUTF() ;
      item_maker     =  file_containing_collection_data.readUTF() ;
      item_type      =  file_containing_collection_data.readUTF() ;
      year_of_making   =  file_containing_collection_data.readInt() ;
   }
```

The file reading methods may throw exceptions of type **IOException**. Because the exceptions are not caught by this constructor, they must be specified with the **throws** keyword.

Class **CollectionItem** is designed so that it is easy to keep **CollectionItem** objects in a file. This constructor will be used when a **CollectionItem** object is read from a file. A **DataInputStream** object represents here a file from which data can be read in binary form. It is assumed that the caller of this constructor has already opened a suitable file by creating a **DataInputStream** object.

With methods **readUTF()** and **readInt()** of class **DataInputStream** it is possible to read data items that have been stored with methods **writeUTF()** and **writeInt()** of class **DataOutputStream**. Data is stored in pure binary form, which means, for example, that a value of type **int** is stored as four bytes in the file. This constructor reads the fields of the class in the same order as the method **store_to_file()** writes them.

**Collect.java - 1: The first part of a program to maintain data about a collection.**

Each of these four accessor methods fit on a single line.

Method **is_equal_to()** tests whether "this" **CollectionItem** object contains the same data as the other **CollectionItem** object, that is given as a parameter.

```
   public String get_item_name()  { return item_name ; }
   public String get_item_maker() { return item_maker ; }
   public String get_item_type()  { return item_type ; }
   public int    get_year_of_making() { return year_of_making ; }

   public boolean is_equal_to( CollectionItem another_collection_item )
   {
      return ( item_name.equals(  another_collection_item.item_name  ) &&
               item_maker.equals( another_collection_item.item_maker ) &&
               item_type.equals(  another_collection_item.item_type  ) &&
               year_of_making  ==  another_collection_item.year_of_making ) ;
   }

   public String to_line_of_text()
   {
      return ( String.format( "\n  %-30s%-20s%-15s%-10d",
                              item_name, item_maker, item_type,
                              year_of_making )  ) ;
   }

   public void store_to_file( DataOutputStream binary_file )
                                                throws  IOException
   {
      binary_file.writeUTF( item_name ) ;
      binary_file.writeUTF( item_maker ) ;
      binary_file.writeUTF( item_type ) ;
      binary_file.writeInt( year_of_making ) ;
   }
}
```

Method **store_to_file()** stores "this" **CollectionItem** object to a file that has already been opened by the caller of this method. The **writeUTF()** method stores a **String** object so that the 16-bit character codes of the string are stored as 8-bit bytes according to the UTF-8 transformation format. It is supposed that the object will be later read with the second constructor of this class, and that constructor reads the fields of the object in the same order as they are stored here.

Method **to_line_of_text()** converts "this" **CollectionItem** object to a **String** object that has a newline at the beginning. The text line is ready to be printed to the screen. The **String.format()** method returns a formatted string. With suitable format specifiers it is ensured that the fields (e.g. **item_name**) will be seen left-justified on the screen. For example, the format specifier **%-15s** says that the string referenced by **item_type** is shown left-justified in a printing field that is 15 character positions wide.

**Collect.java - 2: The second part of class CollectionItem.**

The purpose of an object of type **Collection** is to hold a set of **CollectionItem** objects. The length of the array that stores references to **CollectionItem** objects is specified by a constant. Initially, when a **Collection** object is created, the collection is empty, but there is space for the data of 100 collection items.

```
class  Collection
{
   static final int  MAXIMUM_NUMBER_OF_ITEMS  =  100 ;

   CollectionItem[] items_in_this_collection  =
                     new  CollectionItem[ MAXIMUM_NUMBER_OF_ITEMS ] ;

   int  number_of_items_in_collection  =  0 ;

   public int get_number_of_items()
   {
      return number_of_items_in_collection ;
   }

   public CollectionItem search_item_with_name( String given_item_name )

   {
      boolean item_has_been_found  =  false ;
      int     item_index           =  0 ;

      while ( item_has_been_found  ==  false  &&
              item_index  <  number_of_items_in_collection )
      {
         if ( items_in_this_collection[ item_index ].
                     get_item_name().contains( given_item_name ) )
         {
            item_has_been_found    =  true  ;
         }
         else
         {
            item_index  ++  ;
         }
      }

      if ( item_has_been_found  ==  true )
      {
         return  items_in_this_collection[ item_index ] ;
      }
      else
      {
         return  null  ;
      }
   }
```

Method **contains()** is used to compare the item name from the caller to an item name in the array of **CollectionItem** objects. **contains()** does not require a complete equality between the two strings. The method returns the value **true** when the given item name is included in the item name field of the **CollectionItem** object.

**Collect.java - 3: The beginning of class Collection.**

**to_line_of_text()** is a method of class **CollectionItem**. The method returns a string that is ready to be printed to the screen. Each **CollectionItem** object thus knows how it should look on the screen.

```
public void print_all_items()
{
   int  item_index  =  0 ;

   while ( item_index  <  number_of_items_in_collection )
   {
      System.out.print(
         items_in_this_collection[ item_index ].to_line_of_text() ) ;
      item_index  ++  ;
   }
}

public void add_new_item( CollectionItem new_collection_item )
{
   if ( number_of_items_in_collection  >=  MAXIMUM_NUMBER_OF_ITEMS )
   {
      System.out.print( "\n Cannot add new collection items!!!! \n" ) ;
   }
   else if ( new_collection_item.get_item_name().length()  ==  0 )
   {
      System.out.print( "\n Invalid collection item data!!!! \n" ) ;
   }
   else
   {
      items_in_this_collection[ number_of_items_in_collection ]
                                   =   new_collection_item ;
      number_of_items_in_collection  ++ ;
   }
}

public void remove_all_items()
{
   number_of_items_in_collection  =  0 ;
}
```

**new_collection_item**, that is received as a parameter to this method, is written to the first free position in the array of (references to) **CollectionItem** objects. The new collection item thus becomes the last object in the array. The field **number_of_items_in_collection** tells how many positions are used in the array of collection items. The number of free positions is **items_in_this_collection.length** minus **number_of_items_in_collection**.

**Collect.java - 4: Three methods of class Collection.**

A **CollectionItem** object is removed from the collection only if it contains exactly the same data as the object referenced by **item_to_remove**. **is_equal_to()** is a method of class **CollectionItem** that returns **true** in the case of equal object contents.

```
public void remove_one_item( CollectionItem  item_to_remove )
{
   boolean item_has_been_found  =  false ;
   int     item_index           = 0 ;

   while ( item_has_been_found  ==  false  &&
           item_index  <  number_of_items_in_collection )
   {
      if ( items_in_this_collection[ item_index ].
                         is_equal_to( item_to_remove )  )
      {
         item_has_been_found     = true   ;
      }
      else
      {
         item_index ++  ;
      }
   }

   if ( item_has_been_found  ==  true )
   {
      //  Item will be removed by moving later items one
      //  position upwards in the array of items.

      while ( item_index  <
                    ( number_of_items_in_collection - 1 ) )
      {
         items_in_this_collection[ item_index ]  =
                   items_in_this_collection[ item_index + 1 ] ;
         item_index  ++  ;
      }

      number_of_items_in_collection  --   ;
   }
}
```

Object references are moved one position towards the beginning of the array. What happens here is that the **CollectionItem** object that is being removed becomes a non-referenced object, and ultimately the garbage collection mechanism destroys the object.

**Collect.java - 5: The method to remove a single item from a Collection object.**

The methods on this page return references to **Collection** objects. A method of a class can create objects of the class itself. This method produces a **Collection** object that contains **CollectionItem** objects in which the field **item_maker** is the same.

References to those **CollectionItem** objects that are found to contain the given item maker are added to the collection referenced by **collection_to_return**. Note that no new **CollectionItem** objects are created here. The collection that is returned references the objects of "this" collection.

```
public  Collection  get_items_of_maker( String given_item_maker )
{
   Collection  collection_to_return  =  new  Collection() ;

   for ( int item_index  =  0 ;
             item_index  <  number_of_items_in_collection ;
             item_index  ++ )
   {
      if ( items_in_this_collection[ item_index ].
                          get_item_maker().contains( given_item_maker ) )
      {
         collection_to_return.add_new_item(
                            items_in_this_collection[ item_index ] ) ;
      }
   }

   return  collection_to_return ;
}

public  Collection  get_items_of_type( String given_item_type )
{
   Collection  collection_to_return  =  new  Collection() ;

   for ( int item_index  =  0 ;
             item_index  <  number_of_items_in_collection ;
             item_index  ++ )
   {
      if ( items_in_this_collection[ item_index ].
                        get_item_type().contains( given_item_type ) )
      {
         collection_to_return.add_new_item(
                            items_in_this_collection[ item_index ] ) ;
      }
   }

   return  collection_to_return ;
}
```

This method is almost identical to the other method on this page. The difference is that this method returns a collection whose items are of the desired type.

Method **contains()** is used to test if the string referenced by **given_item_type** is included as a substring in the item type string of a **CollectionItem** object. **contains()** returns the value **true** if a substring is found.

**Collect.java - 6: Methods that return subcollections from an existing collection.**

The constructor of class **`FileOutputStream`** opens the file **collection_items.data** for writing. The file is opened as a binary file. If the file already exists, it will be written over. The created **`FileOutputStream`** object is passed as a parameter to the constructor of class **`DataOutputStream`**. The **`DataOutputStream`** class provides suitable methods for writing various data items to a file.

```
public void store_to_file()
{
   try
   {
      FileOutputStream  file_output_stream  =
                 new FileOutputStream( "collection_items.data" ) ;

      DataOutputStream  collection_file  =
                 new DataOutputStream( file_output_stream ) ;

      for ( int item_index  =  0 ;
                item_index  <  number_of_items_in_collection ;
                item_index  ++  )
      {
         items_in_this_collection[ item_index ].
                        store_to_file( collection_file ) ;
      }

      collection_file.close() ;

      System.out.print( "\n Collection items have been stored.  \n\n" ) ;
   }
   catch ( Exception caught_exception )
   {
     System.out.print("\n\n Error in writing file collection_items.data. "
                 +  "\n Collection items are not stored.  \n\n" )  ;
   }
}
```

The **`try-catch`** construct catches an exception if the opening of the file is not successful, or if there occurs problems when the file is written. File opening can be unsuccessful, for example, if there is not enough disk space for a new file, or if the file being written already exists as a read-only file.

Both classes **`CollectionItem`** and **`Collection`** have a method named **`store_to_file()`**. **`CollectionItem`** objects are stored to the opened file by calling method **`store_to_file()`** for each object referenced in the array. The **`store_to_file()`** method of class **`CollectionItem`** takes care of the storing of the individual fields of the **`CollectionItem`** object.

**Collect.java - 7: The method to store the items of a collection to a file.**

An object of type **FileInputStream** is created here first. That object is passed to the constructor of class **DataInputStream**, and the **DataInputStream** object represents the file that is being read. Figure 14-3 explains how **DataInputStream/DataOutputStream** and **FileInputStream/FileOutputStream** objects co-operate.

Method **available()** is used to check whether there is more data available in the file being read. That method tells how many bytes are still available to be read.

```
   public void load_from_file()
   {
      try
      {
         FileInputStream  file_input_stream  =
                     new  FileInputStream( "collection_items.data" ) ;

         DataInputStream  collection_file  =
                     new  DataInputStream( file_input_stream ) ;

         int  item_index  =  0 ;

         CollectionItem   item_from_file    ;

         while ( collection_file.available() > 0 )
         {
            item_from_file  =  new  CollectionItem( collection_file ) ;

            items_in_this_collection[ item_index ]  =  item_from_file ;

            item_index  ++  ;
         }

         number_of_items_in_collection  =  item_index   ;

         collection_file.close() ;

         System.out.print( "\n Collection items have been loaded.  \n\n" ) ;
      }
      catch ( FileNotFoundException caught_file_not_found_exception )
      {
         System.out.print("\n File collection_items.data does not exist.\n" ) ;
      }
      catch ( Exception caught_exception )
      {
         System.out.print("\n Error in reading collection_items.data.\n" ) ;
      }
   }
}
```

The second constructor of class **CollectionItem** performs the actual file reading operations when a reference to a **DataInputStream** object is passed to it. New **CollectionItem** objects are created from the data that is obtained from the file. If the array **items_in_this_collection** already references **CollectionItem** objects before this loop is executed, the old references will be written over, and the old **CollectionItem** objects become garbage to be collected.

**Collect.java - 8: The method to load a collection from file (last method of class Collection).**

**CollectionMaintainer** is a class that interacts with the user of this program. It maintains a **Collection** object that contains the individual collection items. The **run()** method of this class is the method that actually manages the maintenance of the collection. The **run()** method decides which other methods are called.

As several methods of this class need to read data from the keyboard, it is best to create a single "keyboard" object. All keyboard input in this program is read with the **nextLine()** method, because the other **Scanner** methods do not necessarily work well with **nextLine()**.

```
class  CollectionMaintainer
{
   Scanner keyboard = new Scanner( System.in ) ;

   Collection  this_collection  =  new  Collection() ;

   boolean user_confirms( String text_to_confirm )
   {
      //  This method returns true if user types in 'Y' or 'y'.

      boolean  user_gave_positive_answer  =  false ;

      String  user_response  =   "?????" ;

      while ( user_response.charAt( 0 )  !=  'Y'  &&
              user_response.charAt( 0 )  !=  'N'  )
      {
         System.out.print( text_to_confirm ) ;
         user_response  =  keyboard.nextLine().toUpperCase() ;

         if ( user_response.length()  ==  0 )
         {
            user_response  =  "?????" ;
         }
         else if ( user_response.charAt( 0 ) == 'Y' )
         {
            user_gave_positive_answer  =  true ;
         }
      }

      return  user_gave_positive_answer ;
   }
```

This boolean method returns either **true** or **false** to the calling program. The text that the user should confirm is received as a parameter from the caller. This variable has value **true** if the user typed in 'y' or 'Y' or **false** if the user typed in 'n' or 'N'. The **while** loop is executed as long as the user types in one of these letters. With other letters it is not possible to exit from the method.

With this assignment we prevent the throwing of **StringIndexOutOfBoundsException** in case the user gives an empty string, i.e., hits only the Enter key.

**Collect.java - 9: The beginning of class CollectionMaintainer.**

```
void  add_new_collection_item()
{
   System.out.print( "\n Give new collection item name: " ) ;
   String  item_name_of_the_new_item   =  keyboard.nextLine() ;
   System.out.print( " Give the artist name: " ) ;
   String  item_maker_of_the_new_item  =  keyboard.nextLine() ;
   System.out.print( " Give collection item type: " ) ;
   String  item_type_of_the_new_item   =  keyboard.nextLine() ;
   System.out.print( " Give the year of making: "  ) ;
   int year_of_making_of_the_new_item  =
                 Integer.parseInt( keyboard.nextLine() ) ;

   CollectionItem  new_collection_item  =
         new  CollectionItem( item_name_of_the_new_item,
                              item_maker_of_the_new_item,
                              item_type_of_the_new_item,
                              year_of_making_of_the_new_item ) ;

   this_collection.add_new_item( new_collection_item ) ;
   System.out.print( "\n New item has been added to collection. " ) ;
}

void  remove_collection_item()
{
   System.out.print( "\n Give the name of the item to remove: " ) ;
   String  item_name_from_user  =  keyboard.nextLine() ;

   CollectionItem  item_to_remove  =
      this_collection.search_item_with_name( item_name_from_user ) ;

   if ( item_to_remove  !=  null )
   {
      //  An item was found in the collection.

      System.out.print( "\n This collection item was found: "
                      +  item_to_remove.to_line_of_text() ) ;

      if ( user_confirms( "\n Remove this item ( Y/N )?" ) )
      {
         this_collection.remove_one_item( item_to_remove ) ;
      }
      else
      {
         System.out.print( "\n No item was removed. " ) ;
      }
   }
   else
   {
      System.out.print( "\n The item being searched was not found!!!!" ) ;
   }
}
```

**to_line_of_text()** is a method of class **CollectionItem**. It converts all data of a **CollectionItem** object to a string. (Question: how could we simplify this statement if the method would be implemented as a **toString()** method?)

**Collect.java - 10: Methods for adding and removing single collection items.**

When the user types in letter a, it means that he or she wants data of all collection items to be printed. Therefore, **items_to_print** is set to reference the **Collection** object that contains all collection items.

The first letter in the input string specifies what the user wants this method to do.

```
void  print_data_of_collection_items()
{
   Collection  items_to_print  =  null ;

   System.out.print(  "\n Type in a letter according to menu: \n"
                   +  "\n    a    Print all collection items. "
                   +  "\n    t    Print certain types of items. "
                   +  "\n    m    Print items according to maker's name."
                   +  "\n\n    " ) ;

   String  user_selection  =  keyboard.nextLine() ;

   if ( user_selection.charAt( 0 )  ==  'a' )
   {
      items_to_print  =  this_collection ;
   }
   else if ( user_selection.charAt( 0 )  ==  't' )
   {
      System.out.print( "\n Give the type of the items to be printed: " ) ;
      String  item_type_from_user  =  keyboard.nextLine() ;

      items_to_print  =  this_collection.
                               get_items_of_type( item_type_from_user ) ;
   }
   else if ( user_selection.charAt( 0 )  ==  'm' )
   {
      System.out.print( "\n Give the name of the maker of the item: " ) ;
      String  item_maker_from_user  =  keyboard.nextLine() ;

      items_to_print  =  this_collection.
                               get_items_of_maker( item_maker_from_user ) ;
   }

   if ( items_to_print  !=  null )
   {
      items_to_print.print_all_items() ;
   }
}
```

All items are printed from the **Collection** object that is referenced by **items_to_print**.

Method **get_items_of_maker()** returns a **Collection** object that contains a subset of the **CollectionItem** objects in the collection referenced by **this_collection**.

**Collect.java - 11: A method to print collection items according to the selected criteria.**

**CollectionItem** objects are created with the **new** operator, and references to the created objects are passed as parameters to the **add_new_item()** method.

```
void  initialize_collection_with_test_data()
{
   this_collection.remove_all_items() ;

   this_collection.add_new_item(  new  CollectionItem(
     "Les Demoiselles d'Avignon","Pablo Picasso",   "painting", 1907 ) );
   this_collection.add_new_item(  new  CollectionItem(
     "The Third of May 1808", "Francisco de Goya", "painting", 1808 ) );
   this_collection.add_new_item(  new  CollectionItem(
     "Dejeuner sur l'Herbe",    "Eduard Manet",     "painting", 1863 ) );
   this_collection.add_new_item(  new  CollectionItem(
     "Mona Lisa",              "Leonardo da Vinci", "painting", 1503 ) );
   this_collection.add_new_item(  new  CollectionItem(
     "David",                  "Michelangelo",      "statue",   1501 ) );
   this_collection.add_new_item(  new  CollectionItem(
     "The Night Watch",        "Rembrandt",        "painting", 1642 ) );
   this_collection.add_new_item(  new  CollectionItem(
     "Guernica",               "Pablo Picasso",     "painting", 1937 ) );
   this_collection.add_new_item(  new  CollectionItem(
     "Ulysses",                "James Joyce",      "manuscript", 1922 ));
   this_collection.add_new_item(  new  CollectionItem(
     "The Egyptian",           "Mika Waltari",     "manuscript", 1946 ));
   this_collection.add_new_item(  new  CollectionItem(
     "For Whom the Bell Tolls", "Ernest Hemingway","manuscript", 1941 ));
}

public void run()
{
   String  user_selection   =   "???????" ;

   System.out.print( "\n This program is a system to help a collector"
                   + "\n to maintain information about his or her"
                   + "\n valuable collection items.\n" ) ;
```

**run()** is the only public method of class **CollectionMaintainer**. It calls other methods according to what the user of the program decides to do. The other methods of this class are not called by methods outside this class, though they would also be accessible for methods of classes in the same package. The "package" in this case means the same directory (folder) on the hard disk.

**Collect.java - 12: A method to initialize the collection with test data.**

Each time the user makes an acceptable selection, one method is chosen for execution by this large **if - else if - else if ...** construct. After that, the menu is displayed again.

This **while** loop is executed as long as the user does not type in the letter q.

```
      while  (  user_selection.charAt( 0 )  !=  'q' )
      {
         System.out.print( "\n\n There are currently "
            +  this_collection.get_number_of_items()
            +  " items in the collection. "
            +  "\n Choose what to do by typing in a letter "
            +  "\n according to the following menu: \n"

            +  "\n     a    Add a new collection item. "
            +  "\n     r    Remove a collection item. "
            +  "\n     p    Print data of collection items. "
            +  "\n     s    Store collection data to file. "
            +  "\n     l    Load collection data from file. "
            +  "\n     i    Initialize collection with test data. "
            +  "\n     q    Quit the system.\n\n     " ) ;

         user_selection  =  keyboard.nextLine() ;

         if ( user_selection.length()  ==  0 )
         {
            System.out.print( "\n Please type in a letter." ) ;
            user_selection  =  "?" ;
         }
         else if ( user_selection.charAt( 0 )  ==  'a' )
         {
            add_new_collection_item() ;
         }
         else if ( user_selection.charAt( 0 )  ==  'r' )
         {
            remove_collection_item() ;
         }
         else if ( user_selection.charAt( 0 )  ==  'p' )
         {
            print_data_of_collection_items() ;
         }
         else if ( user_selection.charAt( 0 )  ==  's' )
         {
            this_collection.store_to_file() ;
         }
         else if ( user_selection.charAt( 0 )  ==  'l' )
         {
            this_collection.load_from_file() ;
         }
         else if ( user_selection.charAt( 0 )  ==  'i' )
         {
            initialize_collection_with_test_data() ;
         }
      }
   }
}
```

If the user presses the Enter key without typing in anything, the input string is an empty string. In such a situation the string literal "?" is used as an "artificial" input string. Without this artificial input string, the program would terminate abruptly because it is not possible to read the first character of an empty string.

**Collect.java - 13: The last part of method run() of class CollectionMaintainer.**

It would be possible to include this **main()** method inside the class **CollectionMaintainer**, but it is my habit to put the **main()** method inside a separate class.

The whole application is activated by calling the **run()** method for a **CollectionMaintainaer** object.

```
class Collect
{
   public static void main( String[] not_in_use )
   {
      CollectionMaintainer  collection_maintainer =
                                    new  CollectionMaintainer() ;
      collection_maintainer.run() ;
   }
}
```

**Collect.java - 14. The short method main() in class Collect.**

```
     a    Print all collection items.
     t    Print certain types of items.
     m    Print items according to maker's name.

     m

   Give the name of the maker of the item: Picasso

    Les Demoiselles d'Avignon      Pablo Picasso      painting      1907
    Guernica                       Pablo Picasso      painting      1937

   There are currently 10 items in the collection.
   Choose what to do by typing in a letter
   according to the following menu:

     a   Add a new collection item.
     r   Remove a collection item.
     p   Print data of collection items.
     s   Store collection data to file.
     l   Load collection data from file.
     i   Initialize collection with test data.
     q   Quit the system.
```

These lines are part of the standard initialization data. Here, the user has commanded i (initialize) before giving the command p (print).

**Collect.java - X. The screen after the user printed collection items by maker "Picasso".**

## 14.5 Chapter summary

- Files on hard disks and other auxiliary memory devices are needed to reliably store information for longer periods of time. Traditionally files are treated in programming either as text files or binary files. Text files contain lines of text. Usually the text lines are sequences of character codes of visible characters, and each line is terminated with special line termination characters (codes 0DH and 0AH in Windows, code 0AH in UNIX/Linux, and code 0DH in Macintosh). Binary files are such that they may contain any kind of data. Text files can easily be printed on the screen or viewed with a text editor, whereas binary files can usually be handled only with a special program.
- The standard classes with which we can handle files in Java are declared in the package **java.io**. Therefore, the statement

  ```
  import  java.io.* ;
  ```

  must exist at the beginning of a program which utilizes files.
- Before a file can be read or written in a Java program, it must be opened. A file can be opened as a text file for reading with a statement like

  ```
  BufferedReader file_to_be_read  =  new  BufferedReader(
                 new  FileReader( "text_file_to_read.txt" ) ) ;
  ```

- A file can be opened as a text file for writing operations with a statement such as

  ```
  PrintWriter file_to_be_written  =  new  PrintWriter(
                new  FileWriter( "text_file_to_write.txt" ) ) ;
  ```

- A file can be opened as a binary file for reading operations with a statement like

  ```
  FileInputStream file_to_read  =
            new  FileInputStream( "file_to_read.data" ) ;
  ```

- A file can be opened as a binary file for writing operations with a statement like

  ```
  FileOutputStream file_to_write  =
            new  FileOutputStream( "file_to_write.data" ) ;
  ```

- If you want to write data to a text file so that the text is appended to the end of an existing file, you have to create the **FileWriter** object in the following way

  ```
  PrintWriter file_to_be_written  =  new  PrintWriter(
         new  FileWriter( "text_file_to_write.txt", true ) ) ;
  ```

- In order to append data to the end of a binary file, a **FileOutputStream** object must be created with a statement like

  ```
  FileOutputStream file_to_write  =
          new  FileOutputStream( "file_to_write.data", true ) ;
  ```

- A line of text can be read from a text file with the **BufferedReader** method **readLine()**. The method returns **null** if no more lines are available in the file.
- A line of text can be written to a text file with **PrintWriter** method **println()** which automatically adds the correct line termination characters to the file.
- A certain number of bytes can be read from a binary file with the **read()** method of class **FileInputStream**, for example, in the following way

  ```
  int number_of_bytes_read  =
              file_to_read.read( array_of_bytes,
                                 first_array_position_to_use,
                                 desired_number_of_bytes ) ;
  ```

  The **read()** method returns the number of bytes it was able to read. That can be less than the desired number of bytes when file end has been reached. If the **read()**

method is given only the first parameter, a different version of **read()** is selected, and the method attempts to read as many bytes as is the length of the array of bytes.

- A certain number of bytes can be written to a binary file with a statement like

```
file_to_write.write( array_of_bytes,
                     first_position_in_array_to_use,
                     number_of_bytes_to_write ) ;
```

  where **write()** is a method of class **FileOutputStream**. If the **write()** method is given only the first parameter, a different version of **write()** is selected, and all bytes from the array are written to the file.

- Classes **DataInputStream** and **DataOutputStream** provide methods for reading and writing data items of types **int**, **char**, **short**, **String**, etc. from/to a binary file. Programs **Collect.java** and **NumbersToFile.java** show how these classes can be used together with classes **FileInputStream** and **FileOutputStream**.

- It is important that files are closed after they are used. A file closing operation ensures that all data that should be on the hard disk is moved there. The file handling classes provide a method named **close()** that must be called after file reading and writing operations have been completed.

## More programs related to file handling

From the directory **javafilesextra** you can find some programs that are not shown on the pages of this chapter:

- Programs **Fileput.java** and **Showfile.java** show how a text file can be written and read in character-by-character basis.

- Programs **Encrypt.java** and **Decrypt.java** are examples of reading and writing files in binary form.

- Program **DateToJPGFileNames.java** demonstrates high-level file operations with standard class **File**. The program is able to rename the **.jpg** files of a directory (folder) so that the last write time of each file is included in the file name. When **.jpg** files are named this way, the photos are automatically listed in correct chronological order. This works provided that the camera with which the **.jpg** photos were taken was able to set the file write times correctly.

## Declaring constants with keyword final

**final** is a reserved Java keyword that has been used in some example programs of this book. When you declare a class with the **final** keyword, you stipulate that no new classes may be derived from the class. When the **final** keyword is used in the header of an instance method, it means that the method may not be overridden in derived classes. With keyword **final** it is possible to indicate that a local variable of a method or a field of a class is a constant that does not change when the program is being executed. Constants (or "constant variables") are declared with statements like:

```
final int      RADIUS_OF_SUN_IN_KILOMETERS  =  695950 ;
final double  VALUE_OF_PI    =  3.1416 ;
```

It is a tradition in programming to write the names of constants with uppercase letters.

One special use of the **final** constants is to exploit them as status values for status variables. For example, in program **Presidents.java** in Chapter 11 we use in class **PresidentInfoApplication** the following constant declarations

```
static final int SEARCH_NOT_READY          =  1 ;
static final int SEARCH_IS_READY           =  2 ;
static final int SEARCH_IS_SUCCESSFUL      =  3 ;
static final int SEARCH_NOT_SUCCESSFUL     =  4 ;
```

These are constant fields of the class, and their values cannot be changed although they are like variables. Usually the **final** fields are also declared as **static** because one such field can serve all objects of the class. The above constants serve as status values inside the methods that search for certain kinds of objects from an array of objects. In program **Presidents.java**, they are used in program constructs of the form

```
int  array_search_status   =   SEARCH_NOT_READY ;

while ( array_search_status   ==   SEARCH_NOT_READY )
{
   if ( ... )
   {
      array_search_status   =   SEARCH_IS_SUCCESSFUL ;
   }
   else if ( ... )
   {
      array_search_status   =   SEARCH_NOT_SUCCESSFUL ;
   }

   ...
}
```

**array_search_status** is a status variable (or a state variable) that is given certain status values during the execution of this loop. It is important that the constants that are used in the above loop have different numerical values. The values themselves are not important as long as they are different. The names of the constants are important because they make the above loop understandable. An equivalent version of the above loop would be

```
int  array_search_status   =   1 ;

while ( array_search_status   ==   1 )
{
   if ( ... )
   {
      array_search_status   =   3 ;
   }
   else if ( ... )
   {
      array_search_status   =   4 ;
   }

   ...
}
```

This latter version is harder to read because it contains less textual information. Constants like the ones in program **Presidents.java** thus improve the readability and understandability of programs.

## Enums specify sets of constants

As the box on the previous page explains, named constants are sometimes useful in programs. Named constants improve the readability of programs. When constants are used as status values for a status variable, the numerical values of the constants are not important as long as the numerical values differ from each other within the used set of constants. As giving numerical values to such constants is a rather mechanical activity, Java provides a mechanism to make this activity automatic. This automatic constant declaration mechanism is enums or enum types. Enum is an abbreviation of the word "enumeration", and **enum** is a Java keyword with which you can declare enums. An enum is a type as well as a set of constants that can serve as values of the enum type.

The constants that are declared in the box on the previous page could be declared as an enum in the following way

```
enum Status
{
   SEARCH_NOT_READY,
   SEARCH_IS_READY,
   SEARCH_IS_SUCCESSFUL,
   SEARCH_NOT_SUCCESSFUL
}
```

This declaration specifies an enum type named **Status**. The constants that are listed inside the braces are possible values for a variable of type **Status**. The constants inside the braces are automatically given numerical values so that the first constant is given value 0, the second constant gets value 1, the third constant is 2, and so on. The numerical values represented by the above enum are thus not exactly those used on the previous page, but that does not matter as long as the values are different.

If we wanted to use the above enum in the loop shown on the previous page, we should write the loop in the following way

```
Status  array_search_status  =  Status.SEARCH_NOT_READY ;
while ( array_search_status  ==  Status.SEARCH_NOT_READY )
{
   if ( ... )
   {
      array_search_status  =  Status.SEARCH_IS_SUCCESSFUL ;
   }
   else if ( ... )
   {
      array_search_status  =  Status.SEARCH_NOT_SUCCESSFUL ;
   }
   ...
}
```

As you can see by studying the above source program lines, an enum can be used as a type. The enum type **Status** above can be assigned only those constant values that are specified in the enum **Status**.

The enum types are actually classes, but they cannot be used in the same way as traditional Java classes. All enum types automatically inherit the standard class **Enum**, but you cannot derive new classes from enum types. Some methods are available for all enum types. For example, there is a method named **values()** which returns an array containing all enum constants of the enum type in question. A method named **ordinal()** returns the numerical value that is associated with an enum constant. With the following loop it is possible to print all the numerical values and textual values that are defined by the above enum **Status**:

```
for ( Status current_status : Status.values() )
{

   System.out.print( "\n The Status value "  +  current_status
                   +  "  has number  "  +  current_status.ordinal() ) ;
}
```

*(This box continues on the following page.)*

## Enums specify sets of constants (Continued)

As enums are classes, it is possible to write methods to enums and override methods inherited from class **`Enum`**. For example, in the following enum the **`toString()`** method has been overridden:

```
enum DayOfWeek
{
   Monday   ( "lunes" ),
   Tuesday  ( "martes" ),
   Wednesday( "miercoles" ),
   Thursday ( "jueves" ),
   Friday   ( "viernes" ),
   Saturday ( "sabado" ),
   Sunday   ( "domingo" ) ;

   String  spanish_day_of_week ;

   DayOfWeek( String given_spanish_day_of_week )
   {
      spanish_day_of_week  =  given_spanish_day_of_week ;
   }

   public String toString()
   {
      return ( name() + " (" + spanish_day_of_week + ")" ) ;
   }
}
```

In this enum there is a constructor that is automatically called for each constant that is defined at the beginning. The **`toString()`** method first prints the constant name, which is obtained by calling the **`name()`** method, and then prints the Spanish version of the day of week in parentheses. For example, the statement

```
System.out.print( " DayOfWeek.Monday as string is "
                +  DayOfWeek.Monday ) ;
```

would print

```
 DayOfWeek.Monday as string is Monday (lunes)
```

To find more information about enums, you can study the programs **EnumTests.java**, **PresidentsWith-Enum.java**, and **PlanetsWithEnum.java**, which you can find in the **javafilesextra** folder. The **PlanetsWith-Enum.java** is a rewritten version of program **Planets.java** which finds information about the planets in our Solar System.

# CHAPTER 15

## MORE STANDARD JAVA TYPES

The two preceding chapters have introduced standard Java classes. This chapter continues with the same theme. As we have now studied the basic features of Java, there are only the huge number of standard classes and other types that are left to be learned. Fortunately, you do not have know them all. You can study them gradually, as is necessary. I hope that after this book has introduced some of the standard classes, you will be able to learn the other standard classes from the electronic Java documentation and other sources.

**ArrayList** is a standard class that is useful in applications in which dynamic arrays are needed. A dynamic array is such that its length (or size) is not fixed. Instead, the array length may increase or decrease while the array is used in a program. Class **ArrayList**, the first subject of this chapter, provides methods which automatically increase or decrease the length of an array in operations that insert or remove new objects to/from an array.

Interfaces, and especially standard interfaces like **Comparable**, is the second subject of this chapter. Interfaces specify methods. A class can implement an interface, which means that the class is equipped with certain methods.

The third subject of this chapter is the standard class **GregorianCalendar**, the official Java type for handling information related to dates and time. **GregorianCalendar** is a subclass of a class named **Calendar**. You will be shown how class **GregorianCalendar** can be used instead of the **Date** class which was introduced in Chapter 11.

## 15.1 ArrayList class

We have learned a long time ago that an array of type **int[]** is a data structure that can contain a certain number of data items of type **int**. Similarly, an array whose type is, say, **President[]** is an array that can contain a certain number of references to objects of type **President**. These traditional Java arrays are created with statements like

```
int[]        array_of_integers  =  new  int[ 50 ] ;
President[]  president_table    =  new  President[ 80 ] ;
```

and individual array elements can be accessed by giving an index expression inside brackets:

```
array_of_integers[ integer_index ]  =  77 ;
president_table[ 0 ]  =  new  President( ... ) ;
```

When a traditional array is created, the length of the array is specified by the value that is given in brackets. The length of an array, which can be read from the array field **length**, is the number of array elements. For example, the above **array_of_integers** has 50 array elements to store values of type **int**, and its length is thus 50.

A shortcoming of a traditional array is that its length cannot be changed after the array has been created. A traditional array is efficient, which means that not much computing time is required to read and write the array elements, but in some programs the fixed length of an array causes problems, or at least makes programming difficult. For this reason, Java provides a standard array class named **ArrayList**. **ArrayList**-based arrays are less efficient than the traditional Java arrays, but in some programs they are very useful. The most important feature of **ArrayList**-based arrays is that they can grow dynamically, i.e., the memory space of an array is increased automatically if necessary.

**ArrayList** arrays can store only (references to) objects. When you create an **ArrayList** array, you should specify what kinds of objects you intend to store with the array. An **ArrayList**-based array can be created with a statement like

```
ArrayList<Integer>  array_of_integers  =
                            new  ArrayList<Integer>() ;
```

By writing **<Integer>** after the class name you can specify that the array will store objects of type **Integer**. There is no need to specify a length or a capacity for the array because the array can grow automatically when necessary. **ArrayList** is a so-called *generic class* whose characteristics can be fine-tuned at the moment when an object of the class is created. By writing a class name inside angle brackets, < >, after the name **ArrayList**, we can stipulate what kinds of objects the array will store. The class name inside the angle brackets is a *type parameter* for the generic class. In general, an **ArrayList** array like

```
ArrayList<SomeClass>  some_array  =
                          new  ArrayList<SomeClass>() ;
```

can store objects of **SomeClass** or objects of some subclass of **SomeClass**.

The simplest way to add elements to an **ArrayList**-based array is to use the method **add()** which can add a new element to the end of an array. For example, the statements

```
array_of_integers.add( 123 ) ;
array_of_integers.add( 456 ) ;
array_of_integers.add( 789 ) ;
```

would add three elements of type **int** to the array of type **ArrayList<Integer>** that is created above. When these statements are executed right after the creation of the array, the number of array elements becomes 3. The integer values that are added to the array by the above statements are values, not objects. Therefore, automatic boxing operations happen when the above statements are executed. In a boxing operation, a value type is automatically converted to an object. The above **int** values are converted to **Integer** objects. As a result of the execution of the above statements, the first three positions in the array reference "boxes" that contain the integer values.

An **ArrayList** array has a specific capacity in regard to the amount of elements it can hold. This capacity is consumed gradually when new array elements are added to the array. When the capacity to add new elements has been exhausted, it is enlarged automatically. The capacity of an array is enlarged so that a new and larger memory area is allocated for the array, the old array elements are copied to the new memory area, and the new memory area becomes the official internal memory area of the array.

Traditional arrays have the **length** field which can be read when we want to know how many elements the array contains. Because **ArrayList** arrays have, at least in theory, an unlimited capacity to store data, **ArrayList** arrays do not have the **length** field. Instead, the **ArrayList** class provides the **size()** method which returns a value that tells how many elements an array currently contains.

**ArrayList**-based arrays cannot be indexed with index expressions inside square brackets. To access individual array elements, the **ArrayList** class provides methods named **get()** and **set()**. With these methods an element in certain index position can be read or written.

We get a particularly interesting **ArrayList**-based array with the statement

```
ArrayList<Object>  miscellaneous_objects  =
                          new  ArrayList<Object>() ;
```

This statement creates an array that can store objects of the standard class **Object** and objects of all subclasses of the **Object** class. Because **Object** is the superclass of all Java classes, the array created by the above statement can store all kinds of objects. All the following statements would thus be acceptable:

```
miscellaneous_objects.add( 555 ) ;
miscellaneous_objects.add( 66.77 ) ;
miscellaneous_objects.add( "This is a string literal." ) ;
miscellaneous_objects.add( new  Date( "03.02.2004" ) ) ;
```

These statements add objects of types **Integer**, **Double**, **String**, and **Date** to the same array, and each element of the array points to a different type of object.

It is easy to add different kinds of objects to the above array, but when we want to do something with the objects, the situation can be somewhat more complicated. For example, if we want to take a substring that contains the first three characters of the **String** object that is the third one added to the above array, we might first write

```
miscellaneous_objects.get( 2 ).substring( 0, 3 )
```

The compiler would not, however, accept this because the method call **get( 2 )** returns a reference to type **Object**, and class **Object** does not have a method named **substring()**. In order to make the above method call acceptable to the compiler, we would have to convert the array element to type **String** in the following way

```
((String) miscellaneous_objects.get( 2 )).substring( 0, 3 )
```

Things must not, fortunately, always be this difficult. For example, all the objects that are stored by the above array could be printed with the loop

```
for ( int object_index  =  0 ;
          object_index  <  miscellaneous_objects.size() ;
          object_index  ++ )
{
   System.out.print( "\n "
            +  miscellaneous_objects.get( object_index ) ) ;
}
```

In the case of the above loop, there are no problems with compilation because for all objects there is a method named **toString()**, and that method will be called automatically when the string concatenation operator (+) is applied to an object in the array. Inside the above loop, **miscellaneous_objects.get( object_index )** returns an element of an **ArrayList**-based array, and that element is an object reference of type **Object**. When the string concatenation operator (+) is used to concatenate something to **"\n"**, the **toString()** method is invoked for the referenced object. As **toString()** is a polymorphic method that is declared in class **Object** and redefined in its subclasses, the method is executed so that first the type of the referenced object is checked, and then the **toString()** method of the class of the referenced object is invoked.

On the following pages you can find example programs **ArrayListDemo.java**, **MorseCodes.java**, and **Translate.java** that demonstrate the use of **ArrayList**-based arrays and **ArrayList** methods. Program **Findreplace.java** in the previous chapter also uses class **ArrayList**. In the following section there is a program named **Events.java**, but because that program introduces a new concept called interface, it is presented in a new section. Briefly described, the following are the most important **ArrayList** methods:

- To add elements to an **ArrayList** array you can use methods **add()** and **addAll()**. When these methods are called, the number of elements in the **ArrayList** array is increased. The more powerful of these methods is **addAll()** because with that method you can insert all the elements of another **ArrayList** array or some other collection to any position of an **ArrayList** array. The operation of method **addAll()** is described in Figure 15-1. Method **add()** can insert only a single element to a specified position of an **ArrayList** array. There are two versions of both methods. One that adds elements only to the end of an array, and one that is capable of inserting elements in the middle of an array.
- To remove or delete elements from an **ArrayList** array, you can use methods **remove()** and **clear()**. When these methods are called, the number of array elements is reduced. There are two versions of method **remove()**. One version removes the first occurrence of a certain object, while the other removes the element of a certain array position. Method **clear()** removes all elements from an **ArrayList** array.
- To make copies of an **ArrayList** array, you can use methods **clone()** and **toArray()**. Method **clone()** creates a shallow copy of an **ArrayList** array. Method **toArray()** converts the whole **ArrayList** array to a conventional array.
- To search for a certain element from an **ArrayList** array, you can use methods **indexOf()**, **lastIndexOf()**, and **contains()**. Method **indexOf()** can search for an object in an **ArrayList** array and return its index. The value -1 is returned if the object is not found. Method **lastIndexOf()** works like **indexOf()** but it starts the search from the last position of an array and proceeds towards the beginning of the array. Method **contains()** is a boolean method that can be used to check whether a certain object is in an **ArrayList** array. Method **contains()** returns **false** in the same situation when method **indexOf()** returns -1.

By using the electronic Java documentation you can find more accurate information about the methods of class **ArrayList**. It is normal that sometimes it is hard to understand how a method of a class works. In such a situation, one possibility is to write a test program in which the method is used. You could, for example, use **ArrayListDemo.java** as a test program by adding new method calls to it.

In addition to the actual **ArrayList** methods, you can use the static methods of class **Collections** when you work with **ArrayList** arrays. Some of the **Collections** methods are used in the programs of this section. In the **javafilesextra** folder, there is the program **CollectionsMethods.java** which demonstrates some of the **Collections** methods.

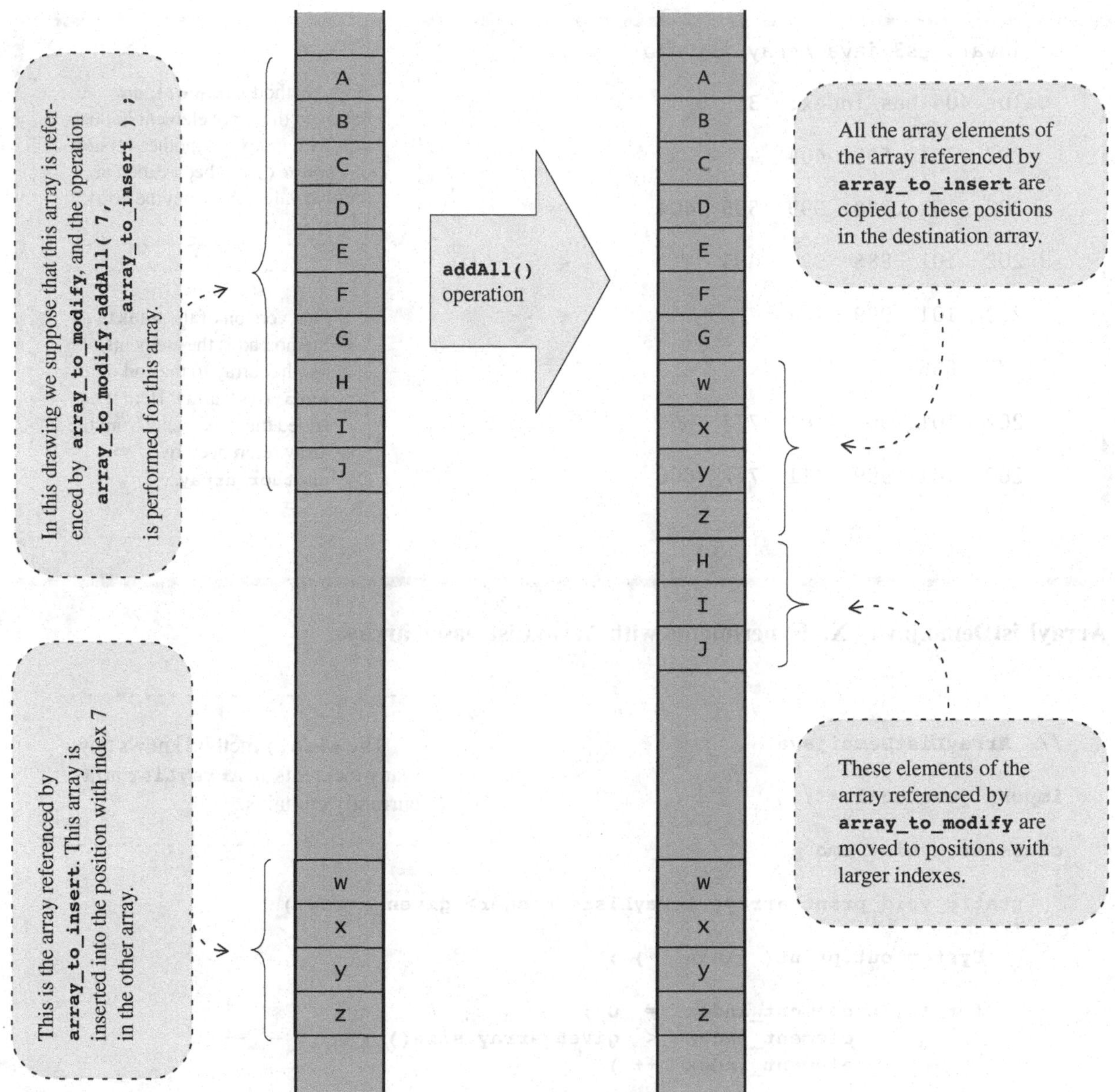


***Figure 15-1. Performing an addAll() operation with ArrayList arrays.***

## "Old-fashioned" ArrayList arrays

In older Java versions the **ArrayList** class was not a generic class. This means that **ArrayList**-based arrays were declared without specifying the type of the objects that were intended to be stored to the array. To be compatible with older Java versions, the latest Java versions still accept **ArrayList** arrays that are created without a type parameter. For example, the array referenced by **miscellaneous_objects**, that is discussed in this section, can be declared and created with the statement

```
ArrayList  miscellaneous_objects  =  new  ArrayList() ;
```

This array works in the same way as an array that is created with the statement

```
ArrayList<Object>  miscellaneous_objects  =  new  ArrayList<Object>() ;
```

but an **ArrayList** array that is declared without a type parameter is less reliable in some situations, and, therefore, such arrays should not be used. Also the compiler prints warning messages when such arrays are declared.

```
D:\javafiles3>java ArrayListDemo

 Value 404 has index:  3

   202  101  505  404

   202  101  888  999  505  404

   202  101  888  999  404

   202  101  999  404

   777  666

   202  101  999  404  777  666

   202  101  999  411  777  666
```

Here, method **remove()** has removed the array element in position with index 4. Another version of **remove()** has been called to remove value 888 from the array.

One version of the **addAll()** method adds the elements of another array to the end of an **ArrayList** array. Here it has added the 2 elements from the array referenced by **another_array**.

**ArrayListDemo.java - X. Experiments with ArrayList-based arrays.**

```
//  ArrayListDemo.java

import java.util.* ;

class ArrayListDemo
{
   static void print_array( ArrayList<Integer> given_array )
   {
      System.out.print( "\n\n " ) ;

      for ( int element_index  =  0 ;
                element_index  <  given_array.size() ;
                element_index  ++ )
      {
         System.out.printf( "%5s", given_array.get( element_index ) ) ;
      }
   }
```

The **size()** method knows how many elements an **ArrayList** array currently contains.

Method **print_array()** prints the array versions that are created in method **main()**. When the array elements are printed with the format specifier **%5s**, they appear right-justified on the screen. The **s** in the format specifier refers to the word "string". When the elements are printed as strings, the **toString()** method is automatically invoked for the objects.

An element of an **ArrayList** array can be read with the **get()** method which takes an index as a parameter.

**ArrayListDemo.java - 1: Demonstrating the standard class ArrayList.**

Here, the standard class **ArrayList** is used to create an array. As the type parameter is **<Integer>**, the array will store **Integer** objects. It is not necessary to specify any length or size for the array. Initially, this array does not contain any elements, but the array grows automatically when objects are added to it.

Method **add()** pushes an object to the end of the array. An **add()** operation increases the number of array elements by one. The **int** values that are given to the **add()** method are automatically boxed inside **Integer** objects.

```
public static void main( String[] not_in_use )
{
   ArrayList<Integer> array_of_integers  =  new  ArrayList<Integer>() ;

   array_of_integers.add( 202 ) ;
   array_of_integers.add( 101 ) ;
   array_of_integers.add( 505 ) ;
   array_of_integers.add( 404 ) ;

   System.out.print( "\n Value 404 has index:  "
                 +  array_of_integers.indexOf( 404 )  ) ;
   print_array( array_of_integers ) ;

   array_of_integers.add( 2, 999 ) ;
   array_of_integers.add( 2, 888 ) ;
   print_array( array_of_integers ) ;

   array_of_integers.remove( 4 ) ;
   print_array( array_of_integers ) ;

   array_of_integers.remove( new Integer( 888 ) ) ;
   print_array( array_of_integers ) ;

   ArrayList<Integer> another_array  =   new  ArrayList<Integer>() ;
   another_array.add( 777 ) ;
   another_array.add( 666 ) ;
   print_array( another_array ) ;

   array_of_integers.addAll( another_array ) ;
   print_array( array_of_integers ) ;

   array_of_integers.set( 3, array_of_integers.get( 3 )  +  7 ) ;
   print_array( array_of_integers ) ;
 }
}
```

With method **get()** it is possible to read an array element in certain array position, and the **set()** method writes a new value to a specified array position. As the index values start from zero, 3 refers to the fourth array element. This statement thus adds 7 to the fourth element.

Another version of the **add()** method is used to insert new array elements to the array position with index 2. As a result of the insertion operation, the elements in positions with indexes 2, 3, 4, ... are moved to positions with indexes 3, 4, 5, ..., respectively.

**ArrayListDemo.java - 2. Using the methods of class ArrayList to modify arrays.**

## Iterators

Many standard classes in the Java class library provide the possibility to use so-called iterators. For example, class **`ArrayList`** has inherited a method named **`iterator()`** that returns an iterator that can be used to read the objects that are stored by an **`ArrayList`**-based array. The returned iterator implements the standard interface **`Iterator`**. Iterators can be used instead of index variables when **`ArrayList`** objects are processed. For example, the loop inside method **`print_array()`** of program **ArrayListDemo.java** could be rewritten by using an iterator in the following way:

```
Iterator  element_to_print  =  given_array.iterator() ;

while ( element_to_print.hasNext() == true )
{
   System.out.printf( "%5s", element_to_print.next() ) ;
}
```

An iterator is a kind of pointer or a special reference to the objects of an array. In the above loop, the iterator **`element_to_print`** points to the objects of an **`ArrayList`**-based array. You can think that after the creation of the iterator, it points to a position that is one position behind the first object in the array. When the **`Iterator`** method **`next()`** is called, the iterator is advanced to the next object in the array, and a reference to the object is returned. The first call to **`next()`** makes the iterator point to the first object of the array. With the **`Iterator`** method **`hasNext()`** it is possible to check whether the array has more elements, i.e., whether a call to the **`next()`** method will be successful.

By comparing the above loop to the corresponding loop in program **ArrayListDemo.java**, you can see that using an iterator can simplify loops, or at least make a loop shorter. Instead of iterators, however, it is better to use "foreach" loops which are shorter than traditional loops. The above program lines can be replaced, for example, with the following "foreach" loop:

```
for ( Object element_in_array : given_array )
{
   System.out.printf( "%5s",  element_in_array ) ;
}
```

Invented by Samuel Morse in the U.S. in 1844, Morse codes were the first widely-used method for transmitting textual information. Each letter of the alphabet is coded with a sequence of signals. A signal can be either short or long. If two communicating parties know the Morse codes, they can communicate, for example, with a flashlight. To transmit letter L, for example, you first show the light for a short time, then once for a longer time, and finally you show it twice for a shorter time. Before telephones and computers became popular, Morse codes were widely used to send textual messages through electric lines and radio waves. Although these codes have less importance these days, they remain an important invention in the history of information processing. (The "code" for the space character is my invention in this program.)

```
D:\javafiles3>java MorseCodes

  Type in your name: Kari Laitinen

  Your name in Morse codes is:

   -.-   .-   .-.   ..         .-..  .-  ..  -   ..   -.   .   -.
```

**MorseCodes.java - X. The string "Kari Laitinen" written with Morse codes.**

With the static method **addAll()** of class **Collections**, all elements of a conventional Java array are added to the end of an empty **ArrayList** array. The array referenced by **array_of_morse_codes** is an array of strings, and, after this statement has been executed, the **ArrayList** array is an **ArrayList** version of the conventional array. Both arrays contain characters and their Morse codes as strings. The Morse code of a character is always in the following array position.

```
//  MorseCodes.java

import java.util.* ;

class MorseCodes
{
   public static void main( String[] not_in_use )
   {
      Scanner keyboard = new Scanner( System.in ) ;

      String[]  array_of_morse_codes  =

       { "A", ".-",    "B", "-...", "C", "-.-.", "D", "-..", "E", ".",
         "F", "..-.",  "G", " --.", "H", "....", "I", "..",  "J", ".---",
         "K", "-.-",   "L", ".-..", "M", "--",   "N", "-.",  "O", "---",
         "P", ".--.",  "Q", "--.-", "R", ".-.",  "S", "...", "T", "-",
         "U", "..-",   "V", "...-", "W", ".--",  "X", "-..-","Y", " -.--",
         "Z", "--..",  "1", ".----","2", "..---","3", "...--","4","....-",
         "5", ".....","6", "-....","7", "--...","8", "---..","9","----.",
         "0", "-----"," ", "       " } ;

      ArrayList<String> arraylist_of_morse_codes = new ArrayList<String>() ;

      Collections.addAll( arraylist_of_morse_codes, array_of_morse_codes ) ;

      System.out.print( "\n  Type in your name: " ) ;

      String  given_name  =  keyboard.nextLine().toUpperCase() ;

      System.out.print( "\n  Your name in Morse codes is: \n\n" ) ;

      for ( int character_index  =  0 ;
                character_index  <  given_name.length() ;
                character_index  ++ )
      {
         int index_of_character_in_arraylist  =
                arraylist_of_morse_codes.indexOf(
                ""   +  given_name.charAt( character_index ) ) ;

         if ( index_of_character_in_arraylist  !=  -1 )
         {
            System.out.print( "    "  +
                      arraylist_of_morse_codes.get(
                              index_of_character_in_arraylist + 1 ) ) ;
         }
      }
   }
}
```

Because the Morse code of a character always follows the character in the array, we add one to the index in order to get the Morse code.

**MorseCodes.java - 1. Using class ArrayList to store String objects.**

This program can make translations between words of two or three natural languages. **BilingualTranslation** is a class that is used to translate words between two natural languages like English and Spanish. Objects of class **BilingualTranslation** contain a pair of words which translate to each other.

```
//  Translate.java (c) Kari Laitinen

import java.util.ArrayList ;

class  BilingualTranslation
{
   protected String first_word ;
   protected String second_word ;

   public BilingualTranslation() {}

   public BilingualTranslation( String  given_first_word,
                                String  given_second_word )
   {
      first_word    =  given_first_word ;
      second_word   =  given_second_word ;
   }

   public boolean translate( String given_word )
   {
      boolean  translation_was_successful  =  false ;

      if ( given_word.equals( first_word ) )
      {
         System.out.print( "\n \"" + given_word + "\" translates to \""
                         + second_word  + "\"" ) ;

         translation_was_successful  =  true ;
      }

      if ( given_word.equals( second_word ) )
      {
         System.out.print( "\n \"" + given_word + "\" translates to \""
                         + first_word  +  "\"" ) ;

         translation_was_successful  =  true ;
      }

      return  translation_was_successful ;
   }
}
```

Here, there must be a default constructor (i.e. a constructor which can be called without giving any parameters) because another class is derived from this class. The default constructor of this class is executed before the constructor of the derived class.

This method returns **true** if it can translate the given word. Translation is possible if the given word is the same as some of the words inside the object itself. A line of text is printed only if translation is possible.

Method **translate()** is a polymorphic method of which there exist several versions in this class hierarchy. In the derived class **TrilingualTranslation** there is a different version of this method.

**Translate.java - 1: The declaration of class BilingualTranslation.**

Being an enhanced version of its superclass, class **TrilingualTranslation** works with three natural words. The words are supplied to the constructor when a translation object is created.

```
class  TrilingualTranslation  extends  BilingualTranslation
{
   protected String third_word ;

   public TrilingualTranslation( String given_first_word,
                                 String given_second_word,
                                 String given_third_word )
   {
      first_word    =  given_first_word ;
      second_word  =  given_second_word ;
      third_word   =  given_third_word ;
   }

   public boolean translate( String given_word )
   {
      boolean  translation_was_successful  =  false ;

      if ( given_word.equals( first_word ) )
      {
         System.out.print( "\n \"" + given_word + "\" translates to \""
                  + second_word + "\" and \"" + third_word + "\"" ) ;
         translation_was_successful  =  true ;
      }

      if ( given_word.equals( second_word ) )
      {
         System.out.print( "\n \"" + given_word + "\" translates to \""
                  + first_word  + "\" and \"" + third_word  + "\"" ) ;
         translation_was_successful  =  true ;
      }

      if ( given_word.equals( third_word ) )
      {
         System.out.print( "\n \"" + given_word + "\" translates to \""
                  + first_word  + "\" and \"" + second_word  + "\"" ) ;

         translation_was_successful  =  true ;
      }

      return  translation_was_successful ;
   }
}
```

Because this method works with three natural languages, it prints longer lines of text than the corresponding method in class **BilingualTranslation**. Note that if you want to include double quote characters inside a string literal, you must use a backslash \ before the double quote character.

**Translate.java - 2: Class TrilingualTranslation and its version of method translate().**

Here, translation objects are created to the heap memory, and references to the objects are added to the end of **array_of_translations**.

An **ArrayList**-based array is used to store references to translation objects. When an **ArrayList** array is created this way, the array can store references to objects that are either objects of class **BilingualTranslation** or objects of some subclass of **BilingualTranslation**. As **TrilingualTranslation** is a subclass of **BilingualTranslation**, **TrilingualTranslation** objects can be stored as well.

```
class Translate
{
   public static void main( String[] command_line_parameters )
   {
      ArrayList<BilingualTranslation>  array_of_translations  =
                             new  ArrayList<BilingualTranslation>() ;

      array_of_translations.add(
             new BilingualTranslation( "week", "semana" ) ) ;
      array_of_translations.add(
             new TrilingualTranslation( "street", "calle", "rue" ) ) ;
      array_of_translations.add(
             new BilingualTranslation( "eat", "comer" ) ) ;
      array_of_translations.add(
             new TrilingualTranslation( "woman", "mujer", "femme" ) ) ;
      array_of_translations.add(
             new TrilingualTranslation( "man", "hombre", "homme" ) ) ;
      array_of_translations.add(
             new BilingualTranslation( "sleep", "dormir" ) ) ;

      if ( command_line_parameters.length  ==  1 )
      {
         int  translation_index  =  0 ;

         while ( translation_index  <  array_of_translations.size() )
         {
            array_of_translations.get( translation_index ).
                              translate( command_line_parameters[ 0 ] ) ;

            translation_index  ++  ;
         }

         System.out.print( "\n" ) ;
      }
      else
      {
         System.out.print( "\n Give a word on command line.\n\n" ) ;
      }
   }
}
```

Method **translate()** is called here to possibly produce a translation. Depending on what type of object is referenced by the array element of **array_of_translations**, the appropriate version of the two versions of method **translate()** is selected automatically.

**Translate.java - 3. A simple translation application which uses the translation classes.**

```
D:\javafiles3>java Translate week

 "week" translates to "semana"

D:\javafiles3>java Translate woman

 "woman" translates to "mujer" and "femme"

D:\javafiles3>java Translate rue

 "rue" translates to "street" and "calle"
```

In this case the given word was found as the last word inside an object of type **TrilingualTranslation**.

**Translate.java - X. The program is executed three times here.**

## Exercises with program Translate.java

Exercise 15-1. Modify program **Translate.java** so that it informs the user if it is not able to translate the given word. Method **translate()** returns **true** or **false** depending on whether or not the translation was successful, but in the current version of the program that information is ignored. (It is possible to call a non-**void** method in the same way as methods of type **void** are called.) You could declare a variable like

```
boolean  word_has_been_translated  =  false ;
```

in method **main()** and set that to value **true** when a translation has been made.

Exercise 15-2. Improve program **Translate.java** so that it is capable of translating between four different languages. You can derive a class named **FourLanguageTranslation** from class **TrilingualTranslation**.

Exercise 15-3. Make program **Translate.java** to read its translation data from a file. You could convert the program to a translator application with which it would be possible to add new word combinations to the translation data. The program could be a menu-based application similar to program **Collect.java**. If you can find, for example from the Internet, an existing file which contains translations of words from one language to another, you could make a translation program which uses those existing translations. To make this task simpler, it might be best to translate only between two languages.

## Exercises related to ArrayList-based arrays

Exercise 15-4. In Chapter 7, a program named **Reverse.java** is introduced. That program uses a conventional Java array to store values of type **int**. Rewrite the program so that **int** values are stored to an **ArrayList** array instead of a conventional array.

Exercise 15-5. An **ArrayList**-based array is particularly useful in an application in which objects are dynamically inserted to an array and removed from an array. Program **Collect.java** is this kind of application. Rewrite program **Collect.java** so that you use inside class **Collection** an **ArrayList** array in place of the conventional array. This modification should simplify the methods of class **Collection**. (If you have developed some other program that is similar to **Collect.java**, it might be a useful idea to use an **ArrayList**-based array in that program.)

## 15.2 Comparable and other interfaces

A Java class can inherit the members of only one immediate superclass. A class cannot have several immediate superclasses. Sometimes, however, it is necessary that classes can be specified so that they possess certain qualities in addition to the qualities that are inherited from the immediate superclass and classes that are superclasses of the immediate superclass. The concept of *interface* has been invented to specify additional qualities of classes.

When a class is declared, it can inherit one class, and in addition it can *implement* one or more interfaces. Java has the reserved keyword **implements** which can be used in the following way

```
class SomeClass  extends  SomeSuperclass
                 implements SomeInterface, SomeOtherInterface
{
   ...
```

In this case **SomeClass** implements two named interfaces **SomeInterface** and **SomeOtherInterface**. When a class implements several interfaces, the names of the interfaces are separated by commas in the class declaration.

An interface usually specifies a set of methods. In addition an interface can specify constants. An interface contains only method declarators (method headers). It does not provide implementations (i.e. method bodies) for the specified methods. It is the responsibility of the class that implements an interface to provide implementations for the specified methods.

To explore the nature of interfaces, let's suppose that the interface **SomeInterface**, which is implemented by **SomeClass** above, is declared in the following way:

```
interface SomeInterface
{
   int calculate_something( int given_value ) ;
   void do_something() ;
}
```

When **SomeClass** implements this interface, it means that **SomeClass** must have a method named **calculate_something()** which takes an **int** value as a parameter and returns an **int** value, and it must have a method named **do_something()** that neither takes parameters nor returns anything. As the above **SomeClass** also implements the other interface **SomeOtherInterface**, it means that **SomeClass** contains also all the methods specified by that interface.

Interface declarations clearly resemble class declarations. The keyword **interface** is used in place of the **class** keyword. Like classes, interfaces are usually written to their own source program files, and the file name must correspond to the name of the interface. An interface named **SomeInterface** should be kept in a file named **SomeInterface.java**.

Java provides standard interfaces in addition to standard classes. Many of the standard interfaces are *generic interfaces*, which means that when a class implements an interface, it is necessary to specify the type of objects with which the methods of the interface will operate. The class **Event** in program **Events.java** implements the standard interface **Comparable** in the following way

```
class  Event  extends Date
              implements Comparable<Event>
{
   ...
```

This class declaration means that class **Event** has a method named **compareTo()** which can compare **Event** objects. By writing **<Event>** after the interface name we specify that the **compareTo()** method, that is the only method required by the **Comparable** interface, will take an **Event** object as a parameter. The **compareTo()** method of class **Event** thus begins in the following way

```
public int compareTo( Event event_to_compare_to )
{
   ...
```

The declaration of the **Comparable** interface can be found in file **Comparable.java** among the Java system programs, and it looks like

```
public interface Comparable<T>
{
   public int compareTo( T object_to_compare_to ) ;
}
```

where **T** marks the type that is given when the interface is used. You can find these kinds of type specifications when you study the standard classes presented in the electronic Java documentation. These type specifications may appear somewhat obscure and incomprehensible. You are not supposed to understand the generic types completely as they are not fully explained in this book.

An interface is useful because it makes it possible to say that a certain class has certain characteristics. In the case of class **Event**, which implements the **Comparable** interface, an experienced Java programmer knows by reading the first two lines of the class declaration that this class is such that its objects can be compared with the **compareTo()** method. Moreover, as there is the **compareTo()** method in class **Event**, it is possible to sort **Event** objects when they are stored in, for example, an **ArrayList**-based array. In the case of program **Events.java**, sorting means that **Event** objects are put in chronological order. The **sort()** method of class **Collections**, which is used in **Events.java** to sort **Event** objects, expects that there is a **compareTo()** method available for the objects it is supposed to sort, i.e., the **sort()** method expects that the class whose objects it sorts implements the **Comparable** interface.

The **sort()** method of class **Collections** expects that the **compareTo()** method returns

- a negative value when the object given as a parameter is larger than "this" object,
- a zero when the objects are equal, or
- a positive value when "this" object is larger than the object given as a parameter.

This behavior of the **compareTo()** method is, however, not specified by the interface **Comparable**. The interface specifies only that a **compareTo()** method must be implemented so that it returns an **int** value. When a programmer writes a **compareTo()** method, he or she must, however, know that the method must be written so that it returns values consistent with those mentioned above.

```
//  Events.java (c) Kari Laitinen

import java.util.ArrayList ;
import java.util.Collections ;

class  Event  extends Date
              implements Comparable<Event>
{
   protected String event_description ;

   public Event( int  day_of_event,
                 int  month_of_event,
                 int  year_of_event,
                 String given_event_description )
   {
      this_day   =  day_of_event ;
      this_month =  month_of_event ;
      this_year  =  year_of_event ;

      event_description  =  given_event_description ;
   }


   public String toString()
   {
      Date  date_of_event  =  new Date( this_day,
                                        this_month,
                                        this_year,
                                        date_print_format ) ;

      return ( date_of_event  +  "   "  +  event_description ) ;
   }

   public int compareTo( Event event_to_compare_to )
   {
      int  comparison_result  =  0 ;  //  Events of the same date.

      if ( this.is_earlier_than( event_to_compare_to ) )
      {
         comparison_result  =  -1 ;   //  "this" has earlier date.
      }
      else if ( this.is_later_than( event_to_compare_to ) )
      {
         comparison_result  =  1 ;    //  "this" has later date.
      }

      return  comparison_result ;
   }
}
```

**Event** is a class derived from class **Date**. **Event** objects are **Date** objects equipped with a text string which describes what happened on that particular date. Class **Event** also implements the **Comparable** interface, which means that it has a method named **compareTo()** that takes an **Event** object as a parameter.

The **toString()** method of class **Date** is used to convert the date to a string and the text that describes the event is joined to the date information. The **toString()** of class **Date** is invoked automatically when the string concatenation operator + is used with a **Date** object.

The **compareTo()** method is invoked automatically when **Event** objects are sorted with the **Collections.sort()** method.

**Events.java - 1: The declaration of class Event.**

**list_of_events** references an **ArrayList** array which is used to store objects of type **Event**. Right after the execution of this object creation statement the array is still empty, i.e., it does not contain any elements.

Here, three **Event** objects are added to the end of **list_of_events** by using method **add()**. The last **Event** object is created just before the **add()** operation.

```
class  Events
{
   public static void main( String[] not_in_use )
   {
      Event  birth_of_lennon    =  new  Event(
                 9, 10, 1940, "John Lennon was born.") ;
      Event  birth_of_einstein =  new  Event(
                14,  3, 1879, "Albert Einstein was born." ) ;

      ArrayList<Event>  list_of_events  =  new  ArrayList<Event>() ;

      list_of_events.add( birth_of_lennon ) ;
      list_of_events.add( birth_of_einstein ) ;
      list_of_events.add( new
          Event( 8, 12, 1980, "John Lennon was shot in New York." ) ) ;

      System.out.print( "\nEvents of list_of_events: \n" ) ;

      int event_index  =  0 ;

      while ( event_index  <  list_of_events.size() )
      {
         System.out.print( "\n   " +  list_of_events.get( event_index ) ) ;
         event_index  ++  ;
      }
```

This program is an example in which three different kinds of loops are used to perform the same activity, the printing of **Event** objects stored by an **ArrayList** array. Here, a **while** loop is used to do the printing. On the following page you can see how the same printing operation is done either with a traditional **for** loop or with a "foreach" loop.

**Events.java - 2: Using an ArrayList array that stores Event objects.**

These two **add()** operations insert objects to the first position of the **ArrayList** array referenced by **another_event_list**. The second inserted object takes the place of the first object so that Marilyn's birth comes after her death in the array of events.

The static method **sort()** of class **Collections** sorts an **ArrayList** array by calling method **compareTo()** for the objects stored by the array. **compareTo()** is declared in class **Event** so that it returns -1, 0, or 1 depending on how two **Event** objects relate chronologically to each other. The **sort()** method requires that the **compareTo()** method returns these kinds of values. After these **sort()** operations, both arrays are such that the oldest **Event** object is the first in the array.

```
      ArrayList<Event>  another_event_list  =  new  ArrayList<Event>() ;

      another_event_list.add( 0,
         new Event( 1, 6, 1926, "Marilyn Monroe was born." ) ) ;
      another_event_list.add( 0,
         new Event( 5, 8, 1962, "Marilyn Monroe died." ) ) ;
      another_event_list.add(
         new Event(15, 8, 1769, "Napoleon Bonaparte was born." ) ) ;
      another_event_list.add(
         new Event(25,10, 1881, "Pablo Picasso was born." ) ) ;


      System.out.print( "\n\nEvents of another_event_list: \n" ) ;

      for ( event_index  =  0 ;
            event_index  <  another_event_list.size() ;
            event_index  ++ )
      {
        System.out.print( "\n    " +  another_event_list.get( event_index ) );
      }

      Collections.sort( list_of_events ) ;
      Collections.sort( another_event_list ) ;

      list_of_events.addAll( 0, another_event_list ) ;

      System.out.print( "\n\nEvents of list_of_events: \n" ) ;

      for ( Event event_on_list : list_of_events )
      {
         System.out.print( "\n    " +  event_on_list ) ;
      }
   }
}
```

This call to **ArrayList** method **addAll()** copies all object references from the array (referenced by) **another_event_list** and inserts them into the beginning of **list_of_events**. The zero means the array position with index 0. The contents of the array (referenced by) **another_event_list** are not modified in this operation.

**Events.java - 3. Sorting and combining ArrayList arrays.**

```
D:\javafiles3>java Events

Events of list_of_events:

   09.10.1940   John Lennon was born.
   14.03.1879   Albert Einstein was born.
   08.12.1980   John Lennon was shot in New York.

Events of another_event_list:

   05.08.1962   Marilyn Monroe died.
   01.06.1926   Marilyn Monroe was born.
   15.08.1769   Napoleon Bonaparte was born.
   25.10.1881   Pablo Picasso was born.

Events of list_of_events:

   15.08.1769   Napoleon Bonaparte was born.
   25.10.1881   Pablo Picasso was born.
   01.06.1926   Marilyn Monroe was born.
   05.08.1962   Marilyn Monroe died.
   14.03.1879   Albert Einstein was born.
   09.10.1940   John Lennon was born.
   08.12.1980   John Lennon was shot in New York.
```

Two arrays are joined here. The objects of **another_event_list** are copied before the objects of **list_of_events**. Note that both arrays are sorted into a chronological order before any objects are copied.

**Events.java - X. Three lists printed with different kinds of loops.**

## Exercise related to program Events.java

Exercise 15-6. Test what happens when you add the lines

```
list_of_events.add( 1,
  new Event( 30, 7, 1947, "Arnold Schwarzenegger was born." ) ) ;
list_of_events.add( 2,
  new Event( 26, 7, 1943, "Mick Jagger was born." ) ) ;
list_of_events.add( 2,
  new Event( 16, 8, 1958, "Madonna was born.") ) ;
list_of_events.add( 2,
  new Event(  6, 2, 1945, "Bob Marley was born." ) ) ;
Collections.reverse( list_of_events ) ;
```

after the line where method **addAll()** is called in method **main()** in **Events.java**.

## Exercise related to sorting of arrays

Exercise 15-7. If you have done the earlier exercises related to program **Collect.java**, you could continue that work by adding a selectable command "Sort collection" to the main menu of the program. A collection can be sorted into an alphabetical order according to the **CollectionItem** member **item_maker**. To implement the sorting feature, you should make class **CollectionItem** implement the **Comparable** interface. The **compareTo()** method, which you have to write, should work so that a **CollectionItem** object is smaller than another **CollectionItem** object if the field **item_maker** is alphabetically smaller than the **item_maker** of the other **CollectionItem** object. The string method **compareTo()** can be used to compare strings this way. Class **Collection** should be equipped with method **sort_collection()** that can be called from the **run()** method.

## More facts related to interfaces

- An interface definition specifies a type that can be used to declare object references. For example, let's suppose that you modify program **BankPolymorphic.java** so that you first define the interface

```
interface MoneyStore
{
   void deposit_money( double amount_to_deposit ) ;
   void withdraw_money( double amount_to_withdraw ) ;
}
```

and then make class `BankAccount` implement the declared interface in the following way

```
class BankAccount implements MoneyStore
{
   ...
```

You do not have to make any other modifications to class `BankAccount` because it already has the required methods `deposit_money()` and `withdraw_money()`. After you have made the above modifications, you can use interface type `MoneyStore` to declare an object reference and create an object, for example, in the following way

```
MoneyStore  queen_account  =
                        new  RestrictedAccount( "Freddie Mercury", 99999,
                                                 7000.00,  3000.00 ) ;
```

After this declaration, you can call method `withdraw_money()` with the statement

```
queen_account.withdraw_money( 2500.00 ) ;
```

but you cannot make the method call

```
queen_account.transfer_money_to( beatles_account, 500.00 ) ;
```

because interface `MoneyStore` does not specify method `transfer_money_to()`, though the method is available for objects of type `RestrictedAccount`. When an object reference is of some interface type, the reference can be used to invoke only those methods that are specified by the interface.

- An interface can inherit or extend another interface. For example, by writing

```
interface MoneyMover extends MoneyStore
{
   void transfer_money_to( BankAccount account_to_transfer_to,
                           double      amount_to_transfer ) ;
}
```

we define a subinterface named `MoneyMover` that requires its implementors to have the specified `transfer_money_to()` method and all the methods that are defined in interface `MoneyStore`.

- An interface is similar to a pure abstract class that has nothing but abstract methods. One essential difference between interfaces and pure abstract classes is in the inheritance mechanism. A class can implement several interfaces but it can inherit only one class. Interfaces are useful because they allow a class to inherit another class and simultaneously implement one or more interfaces.

- All the methods defined by an interface are automatically considered as `public` methods. The methods do not need to be declared with the `public` keyword.

- An interface definition cannot contain any data fields, but it is possible to include constants in an interface definition. The constants are automatically considered to be `public` and `static`. For example, you could declare the constants used in program **Presidents.java** in the following way

```
interface  SearchStatusConstants
{
   int  SEARCH_NOT_READY         =  1 ;
   int  SEARCH_IS_READY          =  2 ;
   ...
```

For more information, see **PresidentsWithInterface.java** in the **javafilesextra** folder.

## *15.3 Class GregorianCalendar and its superclass Calendar*

An important example program in Chapter 11 is **Date.java**. With the **Date** class that is declared in that program we can manage information related to dates, calculate chronological distances between dates, compare dates, print calendars, etc. Although the **Date** class in **Date.java** can be useful in many programs, it is probably not good enough if you want to make serious applications with the Java language. For this reason, it is better to learn to use the **GregorianCalendar** class that is the standard Java mechanism for handling information related to dates and time. **GregorianCalendar** is a class declared in the **java.util** package. The **java.util** package also contains a standard class named **Date**, but many of the methods of that class are deprecated, which means that the class is somewhat old-fashioned.

A **GregorianCalendar** object contains the data of both date and time. A **GregorianCalendar** object encapsulates the data of a particular point in time. For example, the statement

```
Calendar  right_now  =  new GregorianCalendar() ;
```

creates a **GregorianCalendar** object that contains the current date and time of the computer. **Calendar** is the superclass of the **GregorianCalendar** class. It is normal that the type of an object reference is a superclass of the class of the referenced object. In order to get the current date and time, the constructor of **GregorianCalendar** interacts with the operating system of the computer, and the operating system in turn communicates with the electronic clock devices of the computer. The electronic clock devices inside a computer work so that they can provide the correct time once the correct date and time have been set via the operating system. The electronic clock devices contain some kind of batteries which run the clock even when the power source has been switched off from the computer.

The **GregorianCalendar** class is useful because with it we can both read the computer's time information and create objects that contain a certain date and time. A **GregorianCalendar** object can be set to contain a certain date with a statement like

```
Calendar  birth_of_winston_churchill  =
                    new GregorianCalendar( 1874, 10, 30 ) ;
```

This statement creates an object whose date is November 30, 1874. It sets, by default, the time of day of the **GregorianCalendar** object to midnight 00:00:00. If you want to create a **GregorianCalendar** object that contains an exact time of the day, you can use a statement like

```
Calendar  birth_of_charles_darwin  =
          new  GregorianCalendar( 1809, 1, 9, 14, 39, 48 ) ;
```

The object created by this statement contains the date February 9, 1809, and time 14:39:48 which means 2:39:48 p.m. (Charles Darwin was born on the mentioned date but the time is not certain.) The **GregorianCalendar** class uses the 24-hour system to measure time, but it is possible to print time in the 12-hour a.m./p.m. format. The **GregorianCalendar** constructors receive the month number as a month index (e.g. 0 means January).

Learning to use the **GregorianCalendar** class should not be a difficult task for you if you have studied the **Date** class of this book. Class **GregorianCalendar** is similar to class **Date**, and almost all programs that can be written by using class **Date** can be implemented with class **GregorianCalendar**. In order to show how the **GregorianCalendar** class works, I have rewritten a couple of **Date**-based programs by using the **GregorianCalendar** class. Program **BirthdaysGregorianCalendar.java** is a **GregorianCalendar** version of program **Birthdays.java**, and **Friday13GregorianCalendar.java** is a rewritten version of program **Friday13.java**. In addition to these rewritten versions of old programs, you can find on the following pages a program named **Showtime.java**. Program **Showtime.java** demonstrates, among other things, how the **System.out.printf()** method can be used to print time-related information.

With this statement we make the **Scanner** object referenced by **keyboard** behave so that the **nextInt()** method treats also character - as a delimiter in the input. **\\s** specifies that whitespace characters are delimiters.

```
//  BirthdaysGregorianCalendar.java

import java.util.* ;

class BirthdaysGregorianCalendar
{
   public static void main( String[] not_in_use )
   {
      Scanner keyboard = new Scanner( System.in ) ;

      System.out.print( "\n Type in your date of birth as YYYY-MM-DD"
                     +  "\n Please, use four digits for the year:  " ) ;

      keyboard.useDelimiter( "[-\\s]" ) ;

      int  year_of_birth    =  keyboard.nextInt() ;
      int  month_of_birth   =  keyboard.nextInt() ;
      int  day_of_birth     =  keyboard.nextInt() ;

      Calendar date_of_birth  =  new  GregorianCalendar(
                    year_of_birth, month_of_birth - 1, day_of_birth ) ;

      System.out.printf( "\n   You were born on a %tA",  date_of_birth ) ;
      System.out.print(  "\n   Here are your days to celebrate. You are\n" ) ;

      int  years_to_celebrate  =  10 ;

      while ( years_to_celebrate  <  80 )
      {
         Calendar  date_to_celebrate  =  new  GregorianCalendar(

                          year_of_birth  +  years_to_celebrate,
                          month_of_birth  -  1,
                          day_of_birth ) ;

         System.out.printf( "\n    %1$d years old on %2$tF (%2$tA)",
                                 years_to_celebrate,
                                 date_to_celebrate  ) ;

         years_to_celebrate  =  years_to_celebrate  +  10 ;
      }
   }
}
```

As variable **years_to_celebrate** is incremented by 10 at the end of the loop, the program prints the dates for when the person is 10 years old, 20 years old, 30 years old, etc.

A new **GregorianCalendar** object is created each time the internal statements of the loop are executed. Months are described with index values so that 0 means January, 1 means February, 2 means March, etc.

**BirthdaysGregorianCalendar.java - 1. A rewritten version of program Birthdays.java.**

This program differs from the original **Birthdays.java** in that the input date is given in a different format. This program does not work if you include a space character in the input string, but it can interpret single-digit months and days correctly.

```
D:\javafiles3>java BirthdaysGregorianCalendar

 Type in your date of birth as YYYY-MM-DD
 Please, use four digits for the year:  1977-07-14

   You were born on a Thursday
   Here are your days to celebrate. You are

   10 years old on 1987-07-14 (Tuesday)
   20 years old on 1997-07-14 (Monday)
   30 years old on 2007-07-14 (Saturday)
   40 years old on 2017-07-14 (Friday)
   50 years old on 2027-07-14 (Wednesday)
   60 years old on 2037-07-14 (Tuesday)
   70 years old on 2047-07-14 (Sunday)
```

These lines are printed with the **`System.out.printf()`** method for which a reference to a **`GregorianCalendar`** object is given as a parameter. By using suitable format specifiers, desired time information can be printed to the screen. In the format specifiers that are used to print these lines

- **`1$`** refers to the first parameter after the format string
- **`2$`** refers to the second parameter after the format string
- **`t`** marks those format specifiers which print time-related information
- **`tF`** prints the date in the so-called ISO format YYYY-MM-DD
- **`tA`** prints the day of week as a string

**BirthdaysGregorianCalendar.java - X. Here the input date is July 14, 1977.**

This program differs from the original **Friday13.java** in that the user is not asked to give a date from the keyboard. Instead, the default constructor of the **GregorianCalendar** class creates a **GregorianCalendar** object that contains the current date and time of the computer. This program thus prints ten Friday 13th dates that follow the date of the computer.

```
//  Friday13GregorianCalendar.java  (c) Kari Laitinen

import java.util.* ;

class Friday13GregorianCalendar
{
   public static void main( String[] not_in_use )
   {
      Calendar  date_to_increment  =  new GregorianCalendar() ;

      int   number_of_friday13_dates_to_print  =  10 ;

      System.out.print( "\n The following are the next such dates"
                      + "\n that are Fridays and the 13th days"
                      + "\n of a month: \n" ) ;

      while ( number_of_friday13_dates_to_print  >  0 )
      {
         while ( date_to_increment.get( Calendar.DAY_OF_WEEK )   !=
                                                   Calendar.FRIDAY  ||
                 date_to_increment.get( Calendar.DAY_OF_MONTH )  !=  13   )
         {
            date_to_increment.add( Calendar.DAY_OF_MONTH, 1 ) ;
         }

         System.out.printf( "\n   %1$tF, %1$tA", date_to_increment ) ;

         date_to_increment.add( Calendar.DAY_OF_MONTH, 27 ) ;
         number_of_friday13_dates_to_print  --  ;
      }
   }
}
```

Method **add()** is used to add 27 days to a **GregorianCalendar** object. While adding days to a date, this method conforms to the Gregorian Calendar by taking into consideration varying month lengths and leap years. After a date has been printed, 27 days can be added to the **GregorianCalendar** object because those 27 days cannot contain a day that this program is searching for.

This boolean expression specifies the following operation: "Add days to the calendar object until it contains a date that is Friday and day 13 of some month of some year." **get()** is a general-purpose method to read date information from a calendar object. The constants **DAY_OF_WEEK** and **DAY_OF_MONTH** of class **Calendar** are used to specify which date fields the **get()** method should return. The constant **Calendar.FRIDAY** refers to the numerical value that indicates Friday.

**Friday13GregorianCalendar.java - 1. A rewritten version of program Friday13.java.**

```
D:\javafiles3>java Friday13GregorianCalendar

 The following are the next such dates
 that are Fridays and the 13th days
 of a month:

   2005-05-13, Friday
   2006-01-13, Friday
   2006-10-13, Friday
   2007-04-13, Friday
   2007-07-13, Friday
   2008-06-13, Friday
   2009-02-13, Friday
   2009-03-13, Friday
   2009-11-13, Friday
   2010-08-13, Friday
```

**Friday13GregorianCalendar.java - X. Here the program is executed before May 13, 2005.**

## Getting date and time information from a GregorianCalendar object

The **Calendar** class, the superclass of class **GregorianCalendar**, provides the multi-purpose method named **get()** and a set of constants with which it is possible to make the **get()** method return the values of various calendar fields. The **get()** method is called in the following way

```
int integer_value  =  some_calendar_object.get( Calendar.SOME_CONSTANT ) ;
```

By giving a suitable constant as a parameter for the **get()** method, it is possible to make the method return the value of certain calendar field. The following are examples of possible constants:

- **Calendar.YEAR** returns an **int** value that describes a year (e.g. 2005).
- **Calendar.MONTH** returns an **int** value within the range from 0 to 11.
- **Calendar.DAY_OF_MONTH** returns an **int** value within the range from 1 to 31.
- **Calendar.HOUR_OF_DAY** returns an **int** value within the range from 0 to 23. This value represents the hour of a 24-hour clock.
- **Calendar.MINUTE** returns an **int** value within the range from 0 to 59.
- **Calendar.SECOND** returns an **int** value within the range from 0 to 59.
- **Calendar.MILLISECOND** returns an **int** value within the range from 0 to 999.
- **Calendar.DAY_OF_YEAR** returns an **int** value within the range from 1 to 366.
- **Calendar.DAY_OF_WEEK** returns an **int** value within the range from 1 to 7. The numerical value 1 means Sunday, 2 means Monday, 3 means Tuesday, etc. It is best not to use these numerical values because the **Calendar** class provides the constants **Calendar.SUNDAY**, **Calendar.MONDAY**, **Calendar.TUESDAY**, etc. which correspond with the numerical values.
- **Calendar.AM_PM** returns an **int** value that equals either to constant **Calendar.AM** or **Calendar.PM**.
- **Calendar.HOUR** returns an **int** value within the range from 0 to 11. This value represents the hour of a 12-hour clock.

To find more information about these and other constants, please consult the electronic documentation of the **Calendar** class.

```
//  Showtime.java (c) Kari Laitinen

import java.util.* ;

class Showtime
{
   public static void main( String[] not_in_use )
   {
      String[]  names_of_days_of_week  =

      { "Sunday",  "Monday", "Tuesday", "Wednesday", "Thursday",
        "Friday",  "Saturday" } ;

      String[]  names_of_months  =

      { "January", "February", "March", "April", "May", "June",
        "July", "August", "September", "October", "November",
        "December"  }  ;

      Calendar  date_and_time_now  =  new GregorianCalendar() ;

      System.out.printf( "\n Current time is:  %d:%02d:%02d.%03d \n",
          date_and_time_now.get( Calendar.HOUR_OF_DAY ),
          date_and_time_now.get( Calendar.MINUTE ),
          date_and_time_now.get( Calendar.SECOND ),
          date_and_time_now.get( Calendar.MILLISECOND ) ) ;

      System.out.print( "\n Current date is:  "
         +  names_of_days_of_week
                   [ date_and_time_now.get( Calendar.DAY_OF_WEEK ) - 1 ]
         +  ", day " + date_and_time_now.get( Calendar.DAY_OF_MONTH )
         +  " of "
         +  names_of_months[ date_and_time_now.get( Calendar.MONTH ) ]
         + " in year "  +  date_and_time_now.get( Calendar.YEAR ) + ".\n" ) ;

      System.out.print(  "\n Time zone is:     "
                     +  date_and_time_now.getTimeZone().getDisplayName() ) ;
      System.out.print(  "\n Difference from UTC/GMT in hours : "
           +  date_and_time_now.get(Calendar.ZONE_OFFSET)/(60*60*1000) ) ;

      System.out.printf(  "\n\n Short 24-h time:  %tR", date_and_time_now ) ;
      System.out.printf(  "\n Long 24-h time:   %tT", date_and_time_now ) ;
      System.out.printf(  "\n Long 12-h time:   %tr", date_and_time_now ) ;
      System.out.printf(  "\n MM/DD/YY date:    %tD", date_and_time_now ) ;
      System.out.printf(  "\n ISO date:         %tF", date_and_time_now ) ;
      System.out.printf(  "\n Date and time:    %tc", date_and_time_now ) ;

      System.out.printf(  "\n Textual date:     %1$tA, %1$tB %1$td, %1$tY \n",
                                                date_and_time_now ) ;
   }
}
```

Format specifier **%02d** ensures that minutes and seconds are printed with two decimal digits.

A reference to a **GregorianCalendar** object can be given as a parameter to the **System.out.printf()** method (or to the **String.format()** method), and by using suitable format specifiers it is possible to print date and time information in different ways.

**Showtime.java - 1. Extracting time/date information from a GregorianCalendar object.**

6:02:32.476 p.m. is expressed this way in the 24-hour time format.

This line is printed with the **System.out.print()** method. Generally, if you do not mind learning to use the format specifiers, it is easier to print time information with the **System.out.printf()** method.

```
D:\javafiles3>java Showtime

  Current time is:   18:02:32.476

  Current date is:   Wednesday, day 11 of May in year 2005.

  Time zone is:      Pacific Standard Time
  Difference from UTC/GMT in hours : -8

  Short 24-h time:   18:02
  Long 24-h time:    18:02:32
  Long 12-h time:    06:02:32 PM
  MM/DD/YY date:     05/11/05
  ISO date:          2005-05-11
  Date and time:     Wed May 11 18:02:32 PDT 2005
  Textual date:      Wednesday, May 11, 2005
```

The regional settings of the computer on which this program was executed were set to English (United States). When you run this program on your own computer, some things on the screen may look different as a result of the regional settings of your computer. For example, this day of the week (Wednesday) is printed with the format specifier **"%1$tA"**, and, as **tA** prints the locale-specific day of week, the day of week is not shown in English if you have non-English settings in your computer. The regional and cultural settings of a computer are described with so-called locales. When you create **GregorianCalendar** objects in the way they are created in this chapter, the calendars use the computer's default locale, i.e., the current regional settings.

The time zone of the computer on which this program was executed was set to Pacific Time that is used, for example, in California. Therefore, the computer's time is 8 hours behind the Universal Coordinated Time, which is the time of Greenwich, England (U.K.). Greenwich is the natural place to measure Universal time because it is located at the zero longitude. The universal time is also known as Greenwich Mean Time (GMT).

**Showtime.java - X. The program is here executed 6:02:32 p.m. on May 11, 2005.**

## 15.4 Chapter summary

- **ArrayList** is a class with which you can create dynamic arrays, arrays whose size can grow during the execution of a program. **ArrayList** methods **add()** and **addAll()** are able to increase the size of an array. The method **remove()** can delete objects from an array, and thereby reduce the array size.
- An interface usually specifies a certain set of methods. When a class implements an interface, it must provide implementations for the methods specified in the interface.
- The standard interface **Comparable** requires that a class must have a method named **compareTo()**. The **compareTo()** method is called, for example, by the **Collections.sort()** method when the objects of an **ArrayList**-based array are being sorted. The **compareTo()** method of a class decides how objects of that particular class are ordered.
- Class **GregorianCalendar** is the standard Java type for handling information related to dates and time.

### Exercises with class GregorianCalendar

Exercise 15-8. Rewrite program **Weddingdates.java** by using class **GregorianCalendar** instead of the **Date** class.

Exercise 15-9. Rewrite program **Events.java** so that you derive class **Event** from the **GregorianCalendar** class. Such an **Event** class does not need to implement the **Comparable** interface because that interface is already implemented by the **GregorianCalendar** class. Thus, your new **Event** class does not need a **comparetTo()** method since the inherited **compareTo()** works also with **Event** objects. You need to rewrite the constructor and the **toString()** method for the new **Event** class. You can use the **String.format()** method and suitable format specifiers when you rewrite the **toString()** method. The behavior of the program should not change as a result of this exercise. The **main()** method of the program does not need any changes.

# CHAPTER 16

## GOING CLOSER TO THE MACHINE

Java is a high-level programming language, which means that you can write programs with it without knowing the exact details of the processor that executes the programs. It is, however, possible to carry out some low-level operations with Java, and thereby go a little bit closer to the machine that executes the programs.

The first subject of this chapter is bit operators. With these operators we can go inside variables, and, for example, find out the value of a certain bit in an integer variable, or change the value of a certain bit.

The other subject of this chapter concerns time in programming. We already studied class **`GregorianCalendar`** in the previous chapter, but this chapter will show you how programs can measure time in milliseconds. In addition, we'll study some basic characteristics of threads, which are pieces of programs running in parallel on a computer. You'll see that it is possible to write programs in which the **`main()`** method is waiting some input from the keyboard, and, simultaneously, another method is printing characters to the screen.

## 16.1 Bit operators &, |, ^, ~. >>, and <<

Computers store information in bits. A bit can be either zero or one. When we put many single-bit storage units in parallel, we get larger storage units. Integer variables consist of many single-bit storage units put in parallel. For example, a variable of type **byte** is 8 bits in parallel, and variable of type **int** is 32 bits in parallel. (See Table 5-1 for discussion about Java variable sizes.) We have seen that it is possible to perform arithmetic operations where, for example, 8-bit or 32-bit memory units are treated as a whole entity. Individual bits do not have to be taken care of in traditional arithmetic operations. In this section, however, we shall see that if necessary it is possible to manipulate individual bits in integral variables that are 8-bit, 16-bit, 32-bit, or 64-bit memory units.

Special bit operators, or bitwise operators, provide the tools for bit manipulation. These operators can be used to inspect and change bits in variables of integral types **byte**, **char**, **short**, **int**, and **long**. The Java bit operators are listed and explained in Table 16-1. Some basic bit operations are explained in Table 16-2. You should note the following points while studying the tables:

- The bitwise-AND operator & resembles the logical-AND operator && but these operators are used in different situations. The bitwise-AND operator & only returns 1 when both its operands have value 1.
- The bitwise-OR operator | resembles the logical-OR operator ||. The bitwise-OR operator returns 0 only when both its operands have value 0.
- The exclusive-OR operator ^ is similar to the bitwise-OR operator | but the exclusive-OR operator returns 1 only when its operands have different values.
- If you compare Table 16-2 to Table 6-3, you will note that 0 (zero) corresponds to **false** and 1 (one) corresponds to **true**.

The hexadecimal numbering system is convenient for us when we are working with bits. Numbers can be expressed as hexadecimal literal constants in Java when prefix 0x, a zero and letter x, is added before the digits of the number. For example, the following Java literal constants mean the same numerically

| **HEXADECIMAL** | **DECIMAL** | **CHARACTER** |
|---|---|---|
| **0xFF** | **255** | |
| **0x20** | **32** | **' '** |
| **0x41** | **65** | **'A'** |
| **0xFFFF** | **65535** | |

In books that deal with digital electronics, it is common to write hexadecimal numbers like 41H and FFFFH, but using the letter H as a suffix does not work in Java. Hexadecimal numbers are particularly convenient in bit manipulations because one hexadecimal digit corresponds always with four bits. All 8-bit byte values can be expressed with two hexadecimal digits from 0x00 to 0xFF, and all 16-bit values with 4 hexadecimal digits from 0x0000 to 0xFFFF, and so on.

Unfortunately, neither Java nor other languages with the same visual style provide a means to express binary literals in programs. There are programming languages that can do this, and it is hard to understand why the developers of C, C++, Java, and C# programming languages have left that feature out of the languages. It would be nice if binary literals could be written with prefix 0b so that 0b01000001 would mean the same as 0x41 or 65. These kinds of literals might be useful in some special situations, but they are simply not possible. In some technical documents, however, the prefix 0b is used to write binary literals.

**Table 16-1: The bit operators of Java.**

<table>
<tr><th>Operator symbol</th><th>Operator name</th><th>Explanation</th></tr>
<tr><td>&</td><td>bitwise AND</td><td>Performs an AND operation with each pair of bits in its operands:<br>(0x61 & 0xDF) produces 0x41<br>(0xF0 & 0x0F) produces 0x00</td></tr>
<tr><td>|</td><td>bitwise OR</td><td>Performs an OR operation with each pair of bits in its operands:<br>(0x41 | 0x20) produces 0x61<br>(0xF0 | 0x0F) produces 0xFF</td></tr>
<tr><td>^</td><td>exclusive OR</td><td>Performs an exclusive-OR operation with each pair of bits in its operands:<br>(0xAF ^ 0xFF) produces 0x50<br>(0xFF ^ 0xFF) produces 0x00</td></tr>
<tr><td>~</td><td>complement</td><td>This is a unary operator that takes only one operand. It complements every bit in its operand. Complementing results in a zero becoming a one and one becoming a zero. For example,<br>~ 0xE1 produces 0xFFFFFF1E<br>~ 0xF0 produces 0xFFFFFF0F</td></tr>
<tr><td><<</td><td>left shift</td><td>Bits are shifted to the left as many bit positions as the second operand specifies. Zeroes are substituted for the disappearing bits in the right part of the original bit combination. For example,<br>(0x12 << 3) produces 0x90<br>(0x12 << 4) produces 0x120</td></tr>
<tr><td>>></td><td>right shift</td><td>This is similar to the left shift operator, but bits are moved to the right. The most significant bit determines whether zeroes or ones are added to the left part of the original bit combination. For example,<br>(0x49 >> 2) produces 0x12<br>(0x49 >> 3) produces 0x09<br>(0x80000000 >> 1) produces 0xC0000000</td></tr>
<tr><td>>>></td><td>zero fill right shift</td><td>Operator >>> functions like operator >> except that it always puts zeroes to the left part of the original bit combination. For example,<br>(0x49 >>> 2) produces 0x12<br>(0x49 >>> 3) produces 0x09<br>(0x80000000 >>> 1) produces 0x40000000</td></tr>
</table>

**Table 16-2: Some bit operations with single bits a and b.**

<table>
<tr><th>Operand<br>a</th><th>Operand<br>b</th><th>Bitwise AND<br>a & b</th><th>Bitwise OR<br>a | b</th><th>Exclusive OR<br>a ^ b</th><th>Complement<br>~ a</th><th>Complement<br>~ b</th></tr>
<tr><td>0</td><td>0</td><td>0</td><td>0</td><td>0</td><td>1</td><td>1</td></tr>
<tr><td>0</td><td>1</td><td>0</td><td>1</td><td>1</td><td>1</td><td>0</td></tr>
<tr><td>1</td><td>0</td><td>0</td><td>1</td><td>1</td><td>0</td><td>1</td></tr>
<tr><td>1</td><td>1</td><td>1</td><td>1</td><td>0</td><td>0</td><td>0</td></tr>
</table>

The bitwise-AND operator & and the bitwise-OR operator | are the most useful when we want to set some bit in some variable either to one or zero, or when we want to inspect the value of some bit. Figure 16-1 shows how operator & carries out an AND operation between values 0x61 and 0xDF. Table 16-2 explains how this operator & works with a single bit. The & operation between 0x61 and 0xDF results in value 0x41 which is the same as the first operand except that a certain bit is changed to value zero. Operator & is useful when we want to set some bits to be zero. For example, supposing that variable **some_character** is of type **char**, the statement

```
some_character  =  (char) ( some_character  &  0xDF ) ;
```

sets bit 5 to zero in variable **some_character**. As explained in Figure 16-1, bit 5 in a binary number is the bit that has exponent value 5 in a binary number. As bit 5 makes a distinction between the character codes of uppercase and lowercase letters in the English alphabet, the statement above ensures that the character code is a code of an uppercase letter. In the above statement, the bitwise-AND operator & produces and **int** value, and that value must be explicitly converted to type **char** before it can be assigned to variable **some_character**. Java requires an explicit conversion like **(char)** when there is a possibility to lose information in an assignment. When a 32-bit **int** value is stored to a 16-bit **char** variable, information can be lost if the 16 most significant bits are not zeroes in the **int** value.

With the bitwise-OR operator | we can set bits to value one in integer variables. Figure 16-2 describes the operation 0x41 | 0x20. The result of this operation is 0x61 which is the same as 0x41 but bit 5 has been set to one. By using operator | and value 0x20, we can raise bit 5 to value 1. If we want to ensure in a program that a character code is a character code of a lowercase letter, it can be done with a statement such as

```
some_character  =  (char) ( some_character  |  0x20 ) ;
```

The hexadecimal integer literals 0xDF and 0x20, used in the example statements above, are commonly called masks. Masks contain either a lot of zeroes or a lot of ones, depending on whether they are used to set bits to zero or one. When we want to set bits to zero, we use operator & and a mask that contains zeroes in those bit positions we want to make zero. If we want to set bits to one, to raise bits, we must use operator | and a mask that contains ones in those bit positions that need to become ones.

Two example programs demonstrate the use of bit operators. Program **Uplow.java** shows how the letters of a string can be converted to uppercase by using operator &. Program **Binary.java** uses all the bit operators, and shows how integers can be printed in binary form. Once you have understood how bitwise AND and OR operators work, it should be relatively easy to comprehend the exclusive OR operator ^ and the complement operator ~. The shift operators, right shift >> and left shift <<, differ from the other bit operators since they move bits from a bit position to right or left. Figure 16-3 shows how the right shift operator >> works. Left shift is similar, except that bits are moved in the opposite direction.

A special bit operator in Java is >>>, which is called the zero fill right shift operator. As explained in Table 16-1, the result produced by the >>> operator differs from the result of operator >> only in those cases when the most significant bit, the sign bit, is one. Operator >>> always adds zeroes to the left part of the binary number, while operator >> adds ones when the most significant bit of the binary number is one, i.e., when the number is negative.

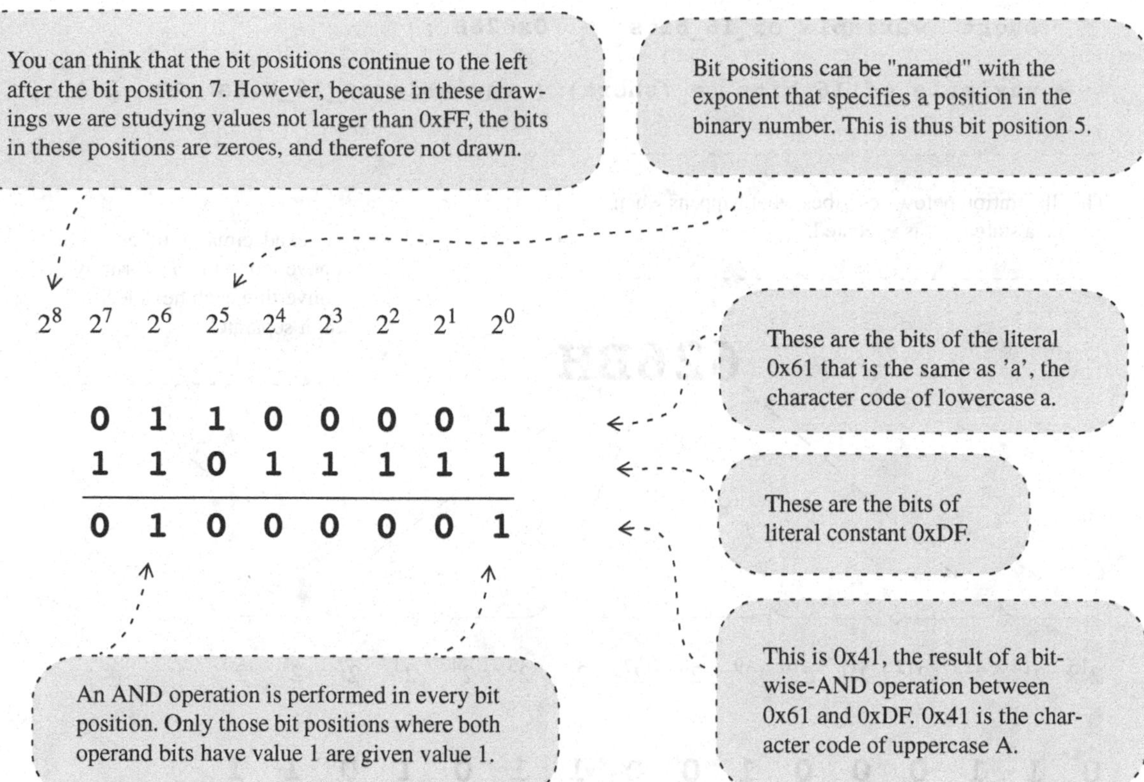


***Figure 16-1. Bitwise-AND operation between 0x61 and 0xDF.***

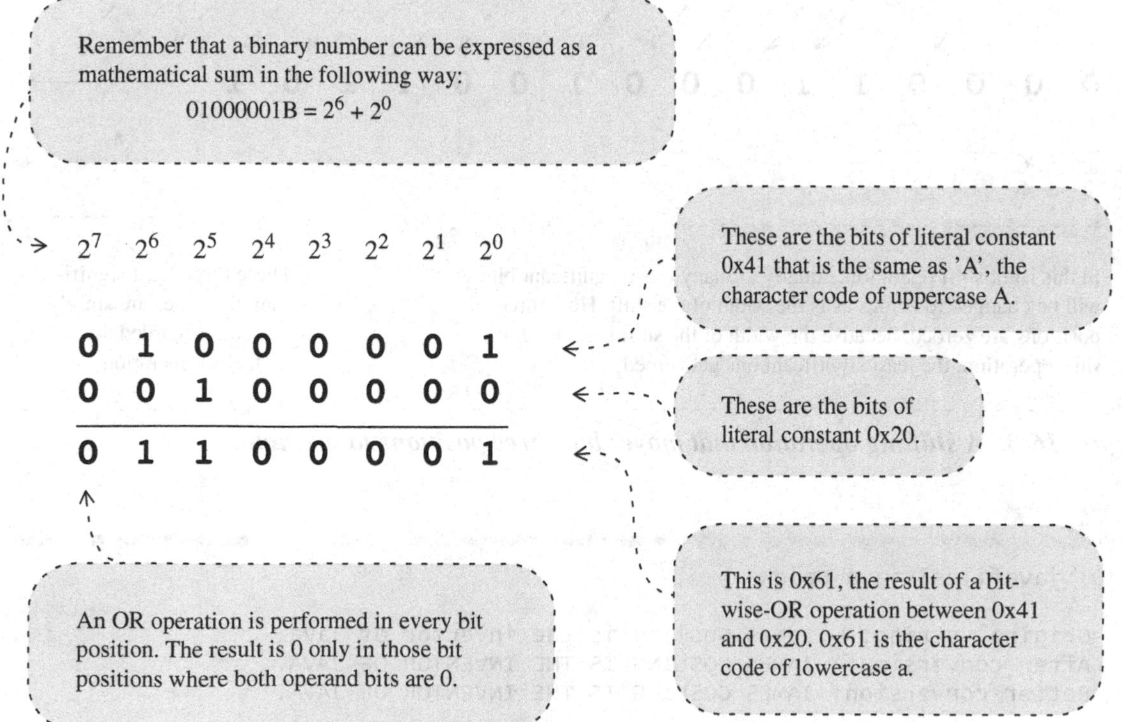


***Figure 16-2. Bitwise-OR operation between 0x41 and 0x20.***

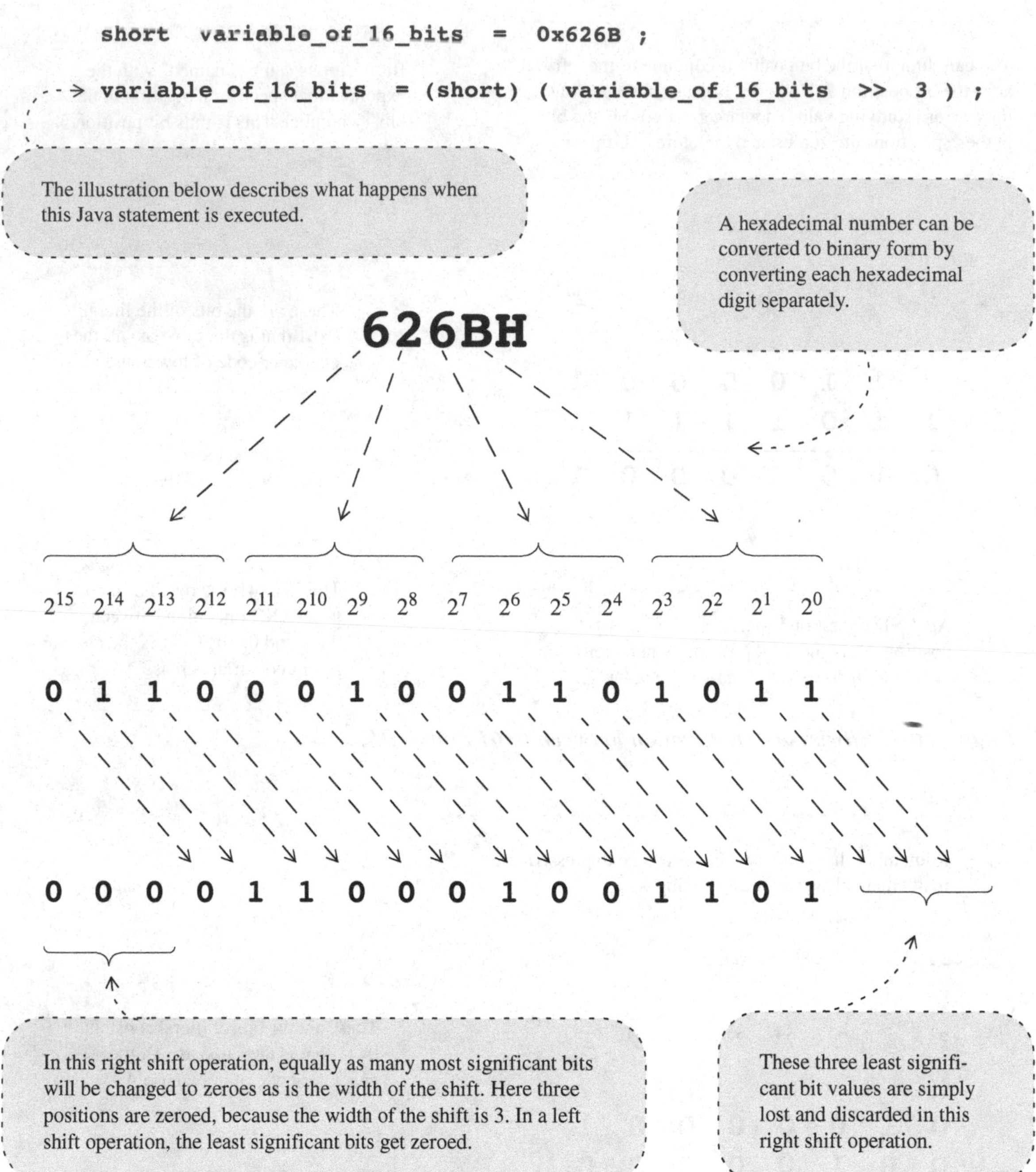

short variable_of_16_bits = 0x626B ;
variable_of_16_bits = (short) ( variable_of_16_bits >> 3 ) ;
The illustration below describes what happens when this Java statement is executed.
A hexadecimal number can be converted to binary form by converting each hexadecimal digit separately.
626BH
2^15 2^14 2^13 2^12 2^11 2^10 2^9 2^8 2^7 2^6 2^5 2^4 2^3 2^2 2^1 2^0
0 1 1 0 0 0 1 0 0 1 1 0 1 0 1 1
0 0 0 0 1 1 0 0 0 1 0 0 1 1 0 1
In this right shift operation, equally as many most significant bits will be changed to zeroes as is the width of the shift. Here three positions are zeroed, because the width of the shift is 3. In a left shift operation, the least significant bits get zeroed.
These three least significant bit values are simply lost and discarded in this right shift operation.


***Figure 16-3. A shifting operation that moves bits three positions to the right.***

```
D:\javafiles3>java Uplow

 Original string:   James Gosling is the inventor of Java.
 After conversion:  JAMES GOSLING IS THE INVENTOR OF JAVA.
 Better conversion: JAMES GOSLING IS THE INVENTOR OF JAVA.
```

**Uplow.java - X. Note that the conversion method modifies only letter characters.**

If the letter is lowercase, it is converted to uppercase with the bitwise-AND operator & and mask value 0xDF, 11011111B. This mask zeroes bit 5 which is the difference between the codes for uppercase and lowercase letters. The bitwise-AND operation returns an **int** value that is converted to a **char** value before it is written to the string.

This method modifies only the character codes of lowercase letters. Actually it would not be harmful, if the character codes of uppercase letters were processed here.

```
//  Uplow.java

class Uplow
{
   static String convert_string_uppercase( String given_string )
   {
      StringBuilder modified_string  =  new StringBuilder( given_string ) ;

      int  character_index  =  0 ;

      while ( character_index  <  modified_string.length() )
      {
         if ( modified_string.charAt( character_index )  >=  'a'  &&
              modified_string.charAt( character_index )  <=  'z'  )
         {
            modified_string.setCharAt( character_index,
             (char) ( modified_string.charAt( character_index )  &  0xDF ) );
         }

         character_index  ++  ;
      }

      return  modified_string.toString() ;
   }

   public static void main( String[] not_in_use )
   {
      String  test_string  =  "James Gosling is the inventor of Java." ;

      System.out.print( "\n Original string:   "  +  test_string ) ;

      String  uppercase_string  =  convert_string_uppercase( test_string ) ;

      System.out.print( "\n After conversion:  "  +  uppercase_string ) ;

      System.out.print( "\n Better conversion: "
                        +  test_string.toUpperCase() ) ;
   }
}
```

Method **convert_string_uppercase()** exists here to demonstrate the use of the bitwise-AND operator. It can only convert the letters of the English alphabet. If you need in your programs to convert the letters of a string to uppercase letters, you should use the standard string method **toUpperCase()**

**Uplow.java - 1. A program that demonstrates the use of the bitwise-AND operator &.**

Because the most significant binary digit, bit, needs to be printed first, the program starts with a mask value where the most significant bit has value 1. Value 0x80000000 means the binary number 1000 0000 0000 0000 0000 0000 0000 0000 B.

```
//  Binary.java  (c) Kari Laitinen

class Binary
{
   static void print_in_binary_form( int  given_integer )
   {
      int  bit_mask    =  0x80000000 ;
      int  one_bit_in_given_integer ;

      for ( int bit_counter  =  0  ;
                bit_counter  <  32 ;
                bit_counter  ++ )
      {
         one_bit_in_given_integer   = given_integer & bit_mask ;

         if ( one_bit_in_given_integer   ==   0 )
         {
            System.out.print( "0" ) ;
         }
         else
         {
            System.out.print( "1" ) ;
         }

         bit_mask   =   bit_mask   >>>   1 ;
      }
   }
```

**one_bit_in_given_integer** gets either the value zero or the same value as variable **bit_mask**.

After a bit has been printed, the bit mask is shifted one bit position to the right. This makes the mask variable suitable for finding out what is the next bit in **given_-integer**. As this loop is executed 32 times, the bit that is 1 spends some time in each bit position of the 32-bit mask variable. In the end **bit_mask** becomes zero, but that does not matter because the loop terminates. Operator >>> is used instead of operator >> because here we want zeroes to be added to the left of the binary number.

This program is quite interesting: all data in all variables and other data structures are in binary form, but it takes quite a lot of work to print the data in binary form.

**Binary.java - 1: A method that prints an integer value in binary form.**

```
public static void main( String[] not_in_use )
{
   int test_number = 0x9A9A ;

   System.out.print( "\n Original test number:           " ) ;
   print_in_binary_form( test_number ) ;

   System.out.print( "\n Twice left-shifted form:        " ) ;
   test_number  =  test_number  <<  2  ;
   print_in_binary_form( test_number ) ;

   System.out.print( "\n Back to original form:          " ) ;
   test_number  =  test_number  >>  2  ;
   print_in_binary_form( test_number ) ;

   System.out.print( "\n Last four bits zeroed:          " ) ;
   test_number  =  test_number  &  0xFFF0 ;
   print_in_binary_form( test_number ) ;

   System.out.print( "\n Last four bits to one:          " ) ;
   test_number  =  test_number  |  0x000F ;
   print_in_binary_form( test_number ) ;

   System.out.print( "\n A complemented form:            " ) ;
   test_number  =  ~test_number ;
   print_in_binary_form( test_number ) ;

   System.out.print( "\n Exclusive OR with 0xF0F0:       " ) ;
   test_number  =  test_number ^ 0xF0F0 ;
   print_in_binary_form( test_number ) ;

   System.out.print( "\n Double right shift with >>:     " ) ;
   test_number  =  test_number >> 2 ;
   print_in_binary_form( test_number ) ;

   System.out.print( "\n Double right shift with >>>: " ) ;
   test_number  =  test_number >>> 2 ;
   print_in_binary_form( test_number ) ;
}
}
```

The right shift operator >> brings **test_number** back to the original form. The number following the operator symbol specifies how many bit positions must be shifted.

Mask 0xFFF0 and operator & make the four last bits zero because those bits are zero in the mask.

The complement operator ~ is an unary operator that takes only one operand. It complements all bits in **test_number**. A bit that has value 0 becomes 1, and vice versa.

**Binary.java - 2. Method main() that calls method print_in_binary_form().**

```
D:\javafiles3>java Binary

 Original test number:        00000000000000001001101010011010
 Twice left-shifted form:     00000000000000100110101001101000
 Back to original form:       00000000000000001001101010011010
 Last four bits zeroed:       00000000000000001001101010010000
 Last four bits to one:       00000000000000001001101010011111
 A complemented form:         11111111111111110110010101100000
 Exclusive OR with 0xF0F0:    11111111111111111001010110010000
 Double right shift with >>:  11111111111111111110010101100100
 Double right shift with >>>: 00111111111111111111100101011001
```

**Binary.java - X. A 32-bit variable of type int printed many times in binary form.**

## 16.2 Playing with the time in programs – introduction to threads

Operating systems like Windows XP, UNIX, and Linux allow several programs to be executed simultaneously on a computer. These operating systems can share the processor time between several executing programs. The executing programs are represented by independent processes that are controlled by the operating system. An operating system that is able to run several processes simultaneously is called a multitasking operating system. When you work with your personal computer, you may have several windows open on the screen, and each window may belong to a different application or program that is run as an independent process by the operating system. For example, if you run a Java program in a command prompt window, that program is an independent process, and at the same time the operating system can run other independent processes like an Internet browser process or a program editor process.

A multitasking operating system that is capable of running several processes simultaneously does not really execute the processes simultaneously, but it executes a process for a while, then stops the process, and puts the next waiting process into execution. A multitasking operating system has a list of processes it has to execute, and it gives processor time for each process on the list. As each process gets frequently a small slice of processor time, it seems that all processes are executed simultaneously. As we humans are slow when compared to the processing speed of a computer, a multitasking operating system can easily give us the illusion that things are happening simultaneously.

Each running program (application) is represented by a process that is controlled by the operating system of a computer. The machine instructions of the program (application) are inside the process, and those machine instructions are executed when the operating system decides to give processor time for the process. In addition to the application processes, the operating system executes special system processes that are needed for the proper operation of the computer. In fact, the operating system itself is also a process or a set of processes that get a share of the processor time.

It is essential in the concept of a process that processes are controlled by the operating system. An application process cannot start running by itself. The operating system starts an application process after the user of the computer has commanded it to start the application. An application process, such as the Java virtual machine that executes a Java program, can, however, create subprocesses that are called threads. A thread is also an independently running piece of program but it is not so "big a player" as a process is. You can think of threads as subprocesses within a process. As we shall see very soon, it is possible that the **main()** method of a Java program creates threads that run simultaneously with the **main()** method, which is itself a thread. Such a situation is described in Figure 16-4 where a Java application program is running as a process together with other processes, and inside the Java application process there are several threads running simultaneously.

Computer programs which consist of several threads are usually such that some of the threads are inactive, i.e., they have suspended themselves. Java provides a standard mechanism for a thread to suspend itself. This mechanism is a static method named **Thread.sleep()**. On the following pages, you'll first find a program named **Sleepings.java** which demonstrates the use of the **Thread.sleep()** method in a single-threaded application. After **Sleepings.java**, you will find three other programs, **DotsAndDollars.java**, **Playtime.java**, and **Clock.java**, in which the **main()** method creates one or two threads. The method **main()** is itself a thread in the mentioned programs.

In the example programs of this section, threads are constructed by first deriving new classes from the standard class **Thread**, and then creating objects of these new classes in the **main()** method. The structure of the derived thread classes is the following:

```
class ApplicationSpecificThread extends Thread
{
   boolean  must_run_this_thread  =  true ;
   public void stop_this_thread()
   {
      must_run_this_thread  =  false ;
   }
   public void run()
   {
      while ( must_run_this_thread  ==  true )
      {
         ...
      }
   }
}
```

In the `main()` methods of the programs, thread objects are created and put in action by using the following kinds of statements

```
ApplicationSpecificThread  application_specific_thread  =
     new  ApplicationSpecificThread() ;

application_specific_thread.start() ;
```

The method `start()`, which is inherited from the `Thread` class, works so that, after it has been called, it generates a call to the `run()` method of the thread class in question. Each application-specific thread class contains an own version of the `run()` method. The execution of a thread terminates when its `run()` method terminates. In the example programs the `run()` method is made to terminate by calling the `stop_this_thread()` method which sets a `boolean` variable so that the `while` loop of the `run()` method terminates.

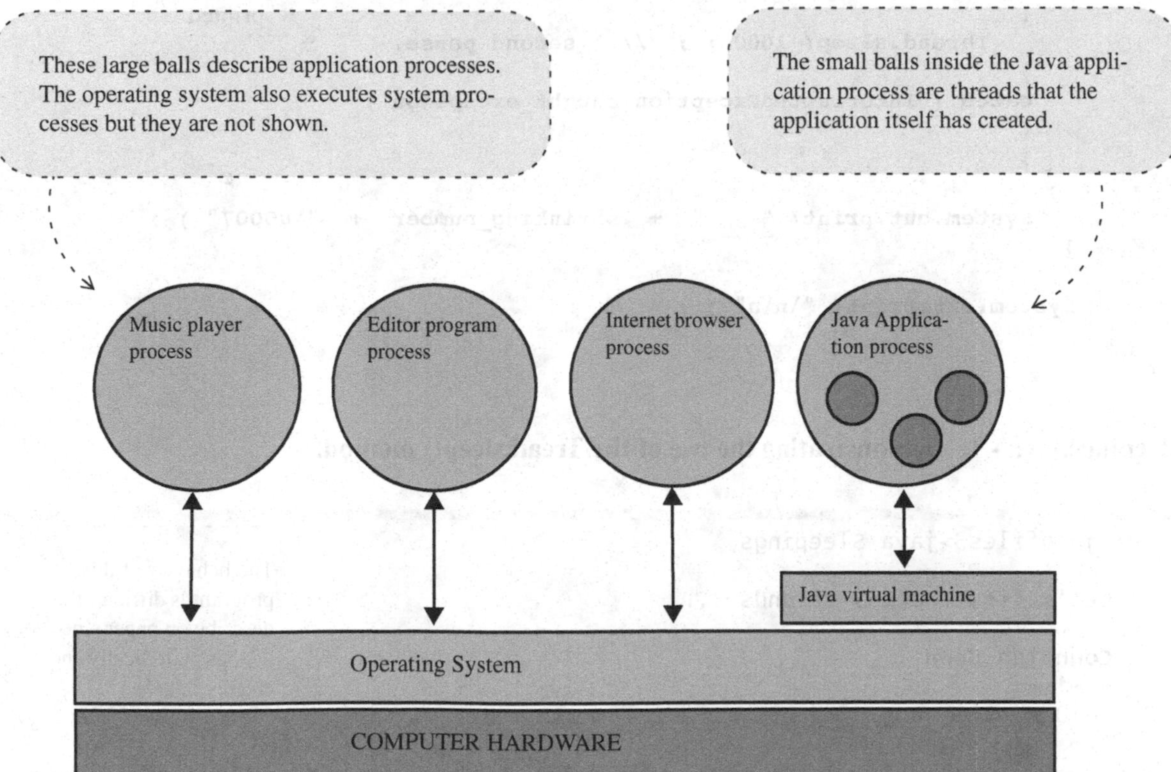


*Figure 16-4. An operating system executing application processes concurrently.*

With the method **Thread.sleep()** a thread can suspend itself for a specified number of milliseconds. As the **main()** method of a Java program is executed as an independent thread, it can stop itself if necessary. You can think that the execution of this method call takes 5 seconds, though in reality other threads may be executed when "this" thread sleeps. The **Thread.sleep()** method must be called inside a **try-catch** construct.

```
//  Sleepings.java

class Sleepings
{
   public static void main( String[] not_in_use )
   {
      System.out.print( "\n  Let's first wait 5 seconds ... \n" ) ;

      try
      {
         Thread.sleep( 5000 ) ;    //  5 s  =  5000 milliseconds
      }
      catch ( InterruptedException caught_exception )
      {
      }

      System.out.print( "\n  Counting down ... \n\n" ) ;

      for ( int shrinking_number   =  10 ;
                shrinking_number  >=  0 ;
                shrinking_number  -- )
      {
         try
         {
            Thread.sleep( 1000 ) ;  // 1 second pause.
         }
         catch ( InterruptedException caught_exception )
         {
         }

         System.out.print( "    " + shrinking_number  +  "\u0007" ) ;
      }

      System.out.print( "\n\n" ) ;
   }
}
```

This way you can express the alert or BELL character. Its Unicode value is 0007 and it produces a sound when it is "printed".

**Sleepings.java - 1. Demonstrating the use of the Tread.sleep() method.**

```
D:\javafiles3>java Sleepings

  Let's first wait 5 seconds ...

  Counting down ...

    10    9    8    7    6    5    4    3    2    1    0
```

The behavior of this program is difficult to describe on paper since it stops periodically and creates sounds.

**Sleepings.java - X. The execution of the program takes at least 16 seconds.**

In this program the **main()** method creates subprocesses that run concurrently with the **main()** method. These subprocesses are called threads. Threads can be constructed by deriving classes from the standard **Thread** class.

All the thread classes in these example programs have a **boolean** variable with which the execution of the thread is controlled. A thread starts running when the **start()** method is called for the thread object. The **start()** method is inherited from the standard **Thread** class. After **start()** is called, the **run()** method of the thread class is activated automatically, and the thread is executed as an independent subprocess as long as the **run()** method runs.

```
// DotsAndDollars.java  (c) Kari Laitinen

import  java.util.* ;

class ThreadToPrintDots extends Thread
{
   boolean  must_print_dots   =  true ;

   public void stop_this_thread()
   {
      must_print_dots   =   false ;
   }

   public void run()
   {
      while ( must_print_dots   ==   true )
      {
         try
         {
            Thread.sleep( 1000 ) ; // Wait one second.
         }
         catch ( InterruptedException caught_exception )
         {
         }

         System.out.print( " ." ) ;
      }
   }
}
```

The value of **must_print_dots** is **true** at the beginning, but the thread does not start running before the **start()** method has been called for the thread object.

The activities of a thread are programmed inside its **run()** method. This thread suspends itself with the **Thread.sleep()** method for one second, prints a dot, suspends itself again, prints a dot, suspends itself again, etc.

This thread is terminated when another thread, i.e., the **main()** method, calls the **stop_this_thread()** method. When the value of the **boolean** variable changes, this **while** loop terminates, and the entire thread terminates.

**DotsAndDollars.java - 1: A program that runs as three threads.**

```
class ThreadToPrintDollarSigns extends Thread
{
   boolean  must_print_dollar_signs  =  true ;

   public void stop_this_thread()
   {
      must_print_dollar_signs  =  false ;
   }

   public void run()
   {
      while ( must_print_dollar_signs  ==  true )
      {
         try
         {
            Thread.sleep( 4050 ) ; // Wait 4.05 seconds.
         }
         catch ( InterruptedException caught_exception )
         {
         }

         System.out.print( " $" ) ;
      }
   }
}

class DotsAndDollars
{
   public static void main( String[] not_in_use )
   {
      Scanner keyboard = new Scanner( System.in ) ;

      ThreadToPrintDots  thread_to_print_dots  =  new  ThreadToPrintDots() ;
      ThreadToPrintDollarSigns  thread_to_print_dollar_signs  =
                                         new  ThreadToPrintDollarSigns() ;
      thread_to_print_dots.start() ;
      thread_to_print_dollar_signs.start() ;

      System.out.print( "\n Press the Enter key to stop the program. \n\n" ) ;

      String  any_string_from_keyboard  =  keyboard.nextLine() ;

      thread_to_print_dots.stop_this_thread() ;
      thread_to_print_dollar_signs.stop_this_thread() ;
   }
}
```

This thread class is built like the preceding class except that the sleeping time is longer and a different character is printed.

This program starts executing like any other program, so that activities begin in the **main()** method. However, after this statement is executed, there are three threads running in parallel.

The **main()** method is also executed as an independent thread, and its main task is to wait until the user presses the Enter key. After the Enter key has been pressed, the **main()** method stops the two other threads.

**DotsAndDollars.java - 2. The main() thread creates two other threads.**

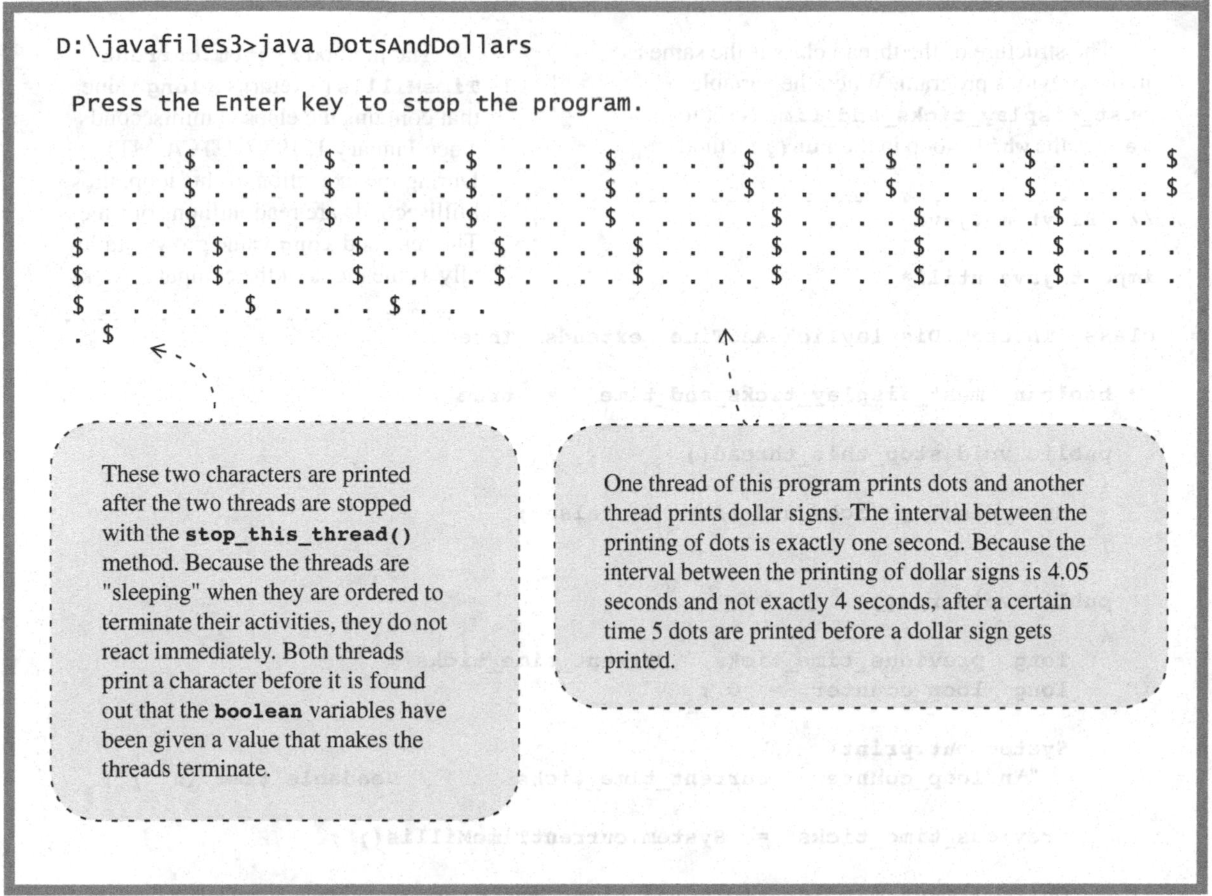


**DotsAndDollars.java - X. The program has been executing here about 173 seconds.**

The structure of the thread class is the same as in the previous program. When the variable **must_display_ticks_and_time** is set to **false**, the **while** loop in the **run()** method stops.

The method **System.currentTimeMillis()** returns a **long** value that contains the elapsed milliseconds since January 1, 1970 (UTC/GMT). During the execution of this loop, those milliseconds are read millions of times. The returned **long** value grows gradually as the clock of the computer "ticks".

```
//  Playtime.java

import java.util.* ;

class  ThreadToDisplayTicksAndTime  extends  Thread
{
   boolean  must_display_ticks_and_time   =  true ;

   public void stop_this_thread()
   {
      must_display_ticks_and_time   =  false ;
   }

   public void run()
   {
      long  previous_time_ticks,  current_time_ticks ;
      long  loop_counter   =  0 ;

      System.out.print(
        "\n loop_counter   current_time_ticks         Readable time \n" ) ;

      previous_time_ticks  =  System.currentTimeMillis() ;

      while ( must_display_ticks_and_time   ==  true )
      {
         loop_counter  ++   ;

         current_time_ticks   =  System.currentTimeMillis() ;

         if ( ( current_time_ticks  -  previous_time_ticks )  >  5000  &&
              ( ( current_time_ticks  /  1000 ) %  5 )  ==  0 )
         {
            System.out.print( "\n    "  + loop_counter
                            + "     "  + current_time_ticks  +  "       " ) ;
            System.out.printf( "%tc",  current_time_ticks  )  ;

            previous_time_ticks   =  current_time_ticks ;
            loop_counter    =  0 ;
         }
      }
   }
}
```

Variable **loop_counter** is used to count how many times the **while** loop is executed in every 5 seconds. This variable is printed and zeroed after each 5-second time period.

This **if** construct tests whether it is time to print something to the screen. Seconds must be equally divisible by 5 before anything is printed. Time is calculated here in milliseconds. 5 seconds is 5000 milliseconds.

**Playtime.java - 1: A program that displays time information after every 5 seconds.**

**WARNING!** It may be better not to run this program for a long time on your computer because the infinite loop of the other thread consumes quite a lot of processing power, and that may result in that the electronics of your computer gets too hot. In my computer the cooling fan of the processor starts operating immediately when I start executing this program.

The thread that runs in parallel with the **main()** method is created here. The **run()** method of the used thread class starts executing automatically after the **start()** method is called for the thread object.

```
class Playtime
{
   public static void main( String[] not_in_use )
   {
      Scanner keyboard = new Scanner( System.in ) ;

      ThreadToDisplayTicksAndTime thread_to_display_ticks_and_time  =
                                       new ThreadToDisplayTicksAndTime() ;

      System.out.print( "\n Press the Enter key to stop the program.\n" ) ;

      thread_to_display_ticks_and_time.start() ;

      String  any_string_from_keyboard  =  keyboard.nextLine() ;

      thread_to_display_ticks_and_time.stop_this_thread() ;
   }
}
```

**Playtime.java - 2. The main thread of the program.**

```
D:\javafiles3>java Playtime

 Press the Enter key to stop the program.

 loop_counter    current_time_ticks         Readable time

   35716704      1116197990685         Sun May 15 15:59:50 PDT 2005
   35078316      1116197995692         Sun May 15 15:59:55 PDT 2005
   35418702      1116198000699         Sun May 15 16:00:00 PDT 2005
   35643848      1116198005706         Sun May 15 16:00:05 PDT 2005
   35662022      1116198010714         Sun May 15 16:00:10 PDT 2005
   35722409      1116198015721         Sun May 15 16:00:15 PDT 2005
   35809958      1116198020728         Sun May 15 16:00:20 PDT 2005
```

The **while** loop of the program can be executed more than 35,000,000 times in 5 seconds. The number that is displayed here depends on the speed of your computer's processor. If other programs on your computer require a lot of processing power, this number is likely to be smaller.

These numbers tell how many milliseconds have elapsed since the beginning of year 1970. As you can see, 35 years, 4 months, 14 days, and 16 hours correspond to quite many milliseconds. (There are milliseconds for 7 extra hours, because the milliseconds describe GMT, while the computer's clock was set to Pacific Standard Time.)

**Playtime.java - X. Here the program is executed around 4 p.m. (16:00) on May 15, 2005.**

This statement reads the current seconds from the created **GregorianCalendar** object. The **SECOND** constant of class **Calendar** specifies that the **get()** method must return the seconds field of the current time.

```
//  Clock.java  (c) Kari Laitinen

import java.util.* ;

class  ThreadToShowSeconds  extends  Thread
{
   boolean  must_show_seconds  =  true ;

   public void stop_this_thread()
   {
      must_show_seconds  =  false ;
   }

   public void run()
   {
      while ( must_show_seconds  ==  true )
      {
         Calendar  date_and_time_now  =  new  GregorianCalendar() ;

         int seconds_of_current_time  =
                           date_and_time_now.get( Calendar.SECOND ) ;

         if ( ( seconds_of_current_time  %  20 )  ==  0 )
         {
            System.out.print( "\n" ) ;
         }

         System.out.printf( " %02d", seconds_of_current_time ) ;

         try
         {
            Thread.sleep( 1000 ) ; // Delay of one second.
         }
         catch ( InterruptedException caught_exception )
         {
            must_show_seconds  =  false ;
         }
      }
   }
}
```

This thread catches the **InterruptedException** that is thrown when the **main()** method calls the **interrupt()** method for this thread object. With the **interrupt()** method it is thus possible to awake a thread that is sleeping.

The static method **Thread.sleep()** is used to create delays inside both threads. Inside the loop of this **run()** method, the thread is stopped for one second each time after the current seconds are printed to the screen. This way the program prints something once a second, and the clock seems to be running.

**Clock.java - 1: A program which acts as a kind of clock.**

Before the **while** loop is entered, this method waits until the seconds of the current time are zero.

```
class  ThreadToShowFullTimeInfo  extends  Thread
{
   boolean  must_show_full_time_info  = true ;

   public void stop_this_thread()
   {
      must_show_full_time_info  =  false ;
   }

   public void run()
   {
      Calendar  date_and_time_now  =  new  GregorianCalendar() ;

      int  seconds_to_first_time_printing  =
                60  -  date_and_time_now.get( Calendar.SECOND ) ;

      try
      {
         Thread.sleep( seconds_to_first_time_printing * 1000 ) ;
      }
      catch ( InterruptedException caught_exception )
      {
         must_show_full_time_info  =  false ;
      }

      while ( must_show_full_time_info  ==  true )
      {
         date_and_time_now  =  new  GregorianCalendar() ;

         System.out.printf( "\n\n %tT \n\n", date_and_time_now ) ;

         try
         {
            Thread.sleep( 60000 ) ; // Delay of 60 seconds.
         }
         catch ( InterruptedException caught_exception )
         {
            must_show_full_time_info  =  false ;
         }
      }
   }
}
```

This statement is executed when the "sleep" of this thread is interrupted by calling the **interrupt()** method for this thread object. When this **boolean** variable is assigned the value **false**, the **while** loop of this **run()** method terminates. This causes the termination of the entire thread.

The format specifier **%tT** means that the printing method must output the time in 24-hour format with seconds.

**Clock.java - 2: The ThreadToShowFullTimeInfo class.**

```
class Clock
{
   public static void main( String[] not_in_use )
   {
      Scanner keyboard = new Scanner( System.in ) ;

      ThreadToShowSeconds thread_to_show_seconds =
                                    new ThreadToShowSeconds() ;

      ThreadToShowFullTimeInfo thread_to_show_full_time_info  =
                                 new ThreadToShowFullTimeInfo() ;

      System.out.print( "\n Press the Enter key to stop the clock.\n\n" ) ;

      thread_to_show_seconds.start() ;
      thread_to_show_full_time_info.start() ;

      String  any_string_from_keyboard  = keyboard.nextLine() ;

      thread_to_show_seconds.stop_this_thread() ;
      thread_to_show_full_time_info.stop_this_thread() ;
      thread_to_show_seconds.interrupt() ;
      thread_to_show_full_time_info.interrupt() ;
   }
}
```

By calling the **interrupt()** method for the thread objects, the threads are made to stop also when they are sleeping.

**Clock.java - 3. Method main() that makes the clock run.**

Two threads are printing independently time information to the screen, and the third thread is waiting for the user to press the Enter key.

```
D:\javafiles3>java Clock

 Press the Enter key to stop the clock.

 12 13 14 15 16 17 18 19
 20 21 22 23 24 25 26 27 28 29 30 31 32 33 34 35 36 37 38 39
 40 41 42 43 44 45 46 47 48 49 50 51 52 53 54 55 56 57 58 59

 11:06:00


 00 01 02 03 04 05 06 07 08 09 10 11 12 13 14 15 16 17 18 19
 20 21 22 23 24 25 26 27 28 29 30 31 32 33 34 35 36 37 38 39
 40 41 42 43 44 45 46 47 48 49 50 51 52 53 54 55 56 57 58 59

 11:07:00


 00 01 02 03 04 05 06 07 08 09 10 11 12 13 14 15 16 17 18 19
 20 21 22 23 24 25 26 27 28 29 30 31 32 33 34 35 36 37 38
```

**Clock.java - X. Here the clock was started at 11:05:12, and it was stopped at 11:07:38.**

## Exercises related to bit operators

Exercise 16-1. If the content of an integer variable is odd, bit 0, the least significant bit, is one. In Chapter 6, we studied program **Evenodd.java** that can find out if a given integer is even or odd. Modify that program so that it uses, instead of the remainder operator %, a bit operator and masking to examine the given integer.

Exercise 16-2. Modify program **Uplow.java** by writing a method there that starts

```
static String convert_string_lowercase( String given_string )
{ ...
```

Add necessary statements to method `main()` to test the new method.

Exercise 16-3. Write a program (e.g. **Showbits.java**) that can be used from the command line to check the binary value of a decimal number. The program should also show the hexadecimal value of the given decimal number. If the program is invoked from the command line in the following way

```
java  Showbits  65
```

the following should be printed to the screen

```
65  is   0100 0001 (binary)    0x41 (hexadecimal)
```

You probably need to use method `Integer.parseInt()` to convert the command line parameter to a value of type `int`. You could take method `print_in_binary_form()` from **Binary.java**, and modify it so that it prints only 8 bits if the given integer is less than 0x100, and only 16 bits if the given integer is less than 0x10000. Very many leading zeroes are not necessary in a binary number. The printing method could also output spaces so that the binary number would appear in groups of four bits.

Exercise 16-4. Improve the program that you developed in the previous exercise so that if it is invoked

```
java  Showbits  0x42
```

it prints

```
0x42 is  0100 0010 (binary)  66 (decimal)   'B' (as character)
```

The program should examine the first two characters of the command line parameter, and detect if a hexadecimal number was given. A version of method `Integer.parseInt()` can convert a string that contains a hexadecimal number. The `Integer.decode()` method might also be useful. The program should also check if the given number is a valid character code, and print the corresponding character in a positive case.

## Exercises related to timing

Exercise 16-5. Test what happens if you modify program **DotsAndDollars.java** so that the `while` loop of the `run()` method in the `ThreadToPrintDots` class is replaced with the loop

```
for ( int number_of_dots_to_print  =  0 ;
          number_of_dots_to_print  <  50 ;
          number_of_dots_to_print  ++  )
{
   //  The body of the original while loop can be used here.
}
```

Exercise 16-6. Modify program **Playtime.java** so that it prints, instead of the value of `loop_counter`, the average number of nanoseconds that is needed to execute the `while` loop once. One nanosecond is 0.000000001 seconds. If possible, you might try to run the program on different computers to see whether there are differences in execution times, or you might run the program simultaneously in two command prompt windows on a single computer. If a computer executes two programs simultaneously, that should slow down the programs because the operating system of the computer must divide processor time between several different programs.

## Exercises related to timing (continued)

Exercise 16-7. Write a program that is a simple stopwatch. You might name the program **Stopwatch.java**. The program should measure the time between two pressings of the Enter key, and print the elapsed time while awaiting the second pressing of the Enter key. You need to create a thread that prints the time to the screen while the `main()` thread is waiting input from the user. Program **Playtime.java** might be an example from which to start making this program. The loop that prints time information to the screen inside the thread that measures time could have the following form

```
while ( must_measure_time  ==  true )
{
   ...
   System.out.printf( "\r  %d:%02d:%02d",
                      elapsed_milliseconds / 60000,     //  minutes
                      (( elapsed_milliseconds % 60000 ) / 1000 ),
                      (( elapsed_milliseconds % 1000 ) / 10 ) ) ;
   try
   {
      Thread.sleep( 10 ) ;  //  Sleeping 0.01 seconds
   ...
}
```

The output statement of the above loop prints time in minutes, seconds, and hundreds of seconds. The above output statement reprints the current line because the character `\r` means a return to the beginning of a line. It is important that the loop for time measurement also contains a call to the `Thread.sleep()` method. When a thread sleeps, even for a short while, the thread consumes less computing power. If the above loop is written without the call to `Thread.sleep()`, the thread may disturb the operation of the whole computer.

Exercise 16-8. Write a program (e.g. **Alarmclock.java**) that is a simple alarm clock. The program should first ask the user to give the hour and minute when the clock should alarm, and then wait until the computer's clock shows the given hour and minute. The user should be able to stop the alarm with the Enter key. You might use the following lines in your `main()` method

```
System.out.print( "\n Give alarm hour between 0 ... 23    : " ) ;
int alarm_hour   =  Integer.parseInt( keyboard.nextLine() ) ;

System.out.print( "\n Give alarm minute between 0 ... 59 : " ) ;
int alarm_minute   =  Integer.parseInt( keyboard.nextLine() ) ;

System.out.print( "\n Press the Enter key to stop the alarm "
               +  "\n or deactivate the alarm clock.\n\n" ) ;

ThreadToMeasureTimeAndAlarm thread_to_measure_time_and_alarm  =
   new ThreadToMeasureTimeAndAlarm( alarm_hour, alarm_minute ) ;

thread_to_measure_time_and_alarm.start() ;

String  any_string_from_keyboard  =  keyboard.nextLine() ;

thread_to_measure_time_and_alarm.stop_this_thread() ;
```

Inside the `run()` method of the thread class you could have two loops, of which the first loop waits until it is time to give an alarm. The first loop could look like

```
boolean  it_is_time_to_give_alarm  =  false ;

while ( must_measure_time_and_alarm  ==  true  &&
        it_is_time_to_give_alarm     ==  false )
{
   // Check the current time and sleep if necessary.
}
```

The second loop of the `run()` method could be a loop to create the alarm sound. The loop in program **Sleepings.java** is an example of making an alarm sound.

## 16.3 Chapter summary

- The bit operators of Java are &, |, ^, ~, <<, >>, and >>>. The bitwise-AND operator & and the bitwise-OR operator | are perhaps the most commonly used bit operators. With appropriate mask values, these operators can be used to set certain bits to zero or one in an integer variable, or to find out the values of certain bits in integer variables.
- Threads are subprocesses within an application. Threads can be created in Java programs by deriving new classes from the standard **`Thread`** class.
- Method **`start()`**, which is inherited from class **`Thread`**, activates the execution of a thread. After the **`start()`** method is called, the **`run()`** method of the thread class is called automatically.
- The execution of a thread terminates when the **`run()`** method terminates. A **`boolean`** variable can be used to control the termination of a tread.
- With the static method **`Thread.sleep()`** a thread can suspend itself for a certain number of milliseconds.
- The **`System.currentTimeMillis()`** method returns a **`long`** value that tells how many milliseconds have elapsed since the beginning of January 1, 1970 (GMT) to the current time of the computer.

### Exercises related to timing (continued)

Exercise 16-9. Modify program **DotsAndDollars.java** so that the thread objects that print either dots or dollar signs are created by using a single class that looks something like

```
class  ThreadToPrintCharacters  extends  Thread
{
   boolean  thread_must_be_executed  =  true ;

   char  character_to_print ;
   long  interval_between_printings ;

   ThreadToPrintCharacters( char given_character_to_print,
                            int  given_interval_between_printings )
   {
      character_to_print  =  given_character_to_print ;
      interval_between_printings  =
                           given_interval_between_printings ;
   }

   public void stop_this_thread()
   {
      thread_must_be_executed  =  false ;
   }

   public void run()
   {
      while  ( thread_must_be_executed  ==  true )
      {
         ...
```

## Operators & and | vs. operators && and ||

The bitwise-AND operator (&) and the bitwise-OR operator (|) are used in this chapter to manipulate bits of integer variables. These operators can, though, be used with variables of type **boolean** as well. The boolean expressions which we use in **if** constructs and loops are of type **boolean**, i.e., they are either **true** or **false**. When operators & and | are used in boolean expressions, they work practically in the same way as the logical operators && and ||. For example, the boolean expression

```
( character_from_keyboard  ==  'Y'  |
  character_from_keyboard  ==  'y'  )
```

and the boolean expression

```
( character_from_keyboard  ==  'Y'  ||
  character_from_keyboard  ==  'y'  )
```

mean the same in logical sense. Similarly, the expression

```
( given_character  >=  'A'  &  given_character  <=  'Z' )
```

and the expression

```
( given_character  >=  'A'  &&  given_character  <=  'Z' )
```

are logically equal.

There is, however, a slight difference between operators & and && as well as between operators | and ||. The operators && and || work in such a way that if the first subexpression in a complex boolean expression is found to determine the truth value of the entire boolean expression, the second subexpression is not evaluated. This makes operators && and || computationally more effective than the operators & and |. For example, when the expression

```
( character_from_keyboard  ==  'Y'  ||
  character_from_keyboard  ==  'y'  )
```

is evaluated in the situation when the variable **character_from_keyboard** contains the character code of upper-case Y, it is found out that the first subexpression is true, and that makes the entire expression true regardless of the truth value of the second subexpression. In such a situation the second subexpression is not evaluated when operator || is between the two subexpressions. If operator | were used in place of operator || in the above boolean expression, both subexpressions would always be evaluated, and the boolean expression would thus be computationally less efficient. The && operator is such that if the subexpression on its left side is found to be false, the subexpression on the right side of the operator is not evaluated. For example, when the expression

```
( given_character  >=  'A'  &&  given_character  <=  'Z' )
```

is evaluated given the situation where **given_character** contains the character code of the space character, the subexpression on the left side of && is false making the entire expression false. In such a situation the right side of && is not evaluated. Because operators && and || are left-to-right associative, the left side of the operators is checked before the right side.

When operators && and || are used in boolean expressions, the evaluation of some subexpressions is conditional, i.e., they are evaluated only when necessary. For this reason, operators && and || are also called *conditional logical operators*. In this book, && and || are said to be *logical operators* and & and | belong to the *bit operators*. However, because operators & and | can be used instead of the logical operators && and ||, & and | are also called *bitwise logical operators*, and in some contexts they are called just *logical operators*, which may be confusing because && and || are the traditional logical operators.

Because operators && and || are the traditional logical operators, it is better to use them instead of & and | to form longer boolean expressions of several subexpressions.

Use empty pages for your own notes.

# APPENDIX A: SUMMARY OF IMPORTANT JAVA FEATURES

## *A - 1: Literals*

| Literals | Explanation |
|---|---|
| `'A'` (means 65 or 0x41)<br>`'0'` (means 48 or 0x30)<br>`'1'` (means 49 or 0x31)<br>`'a'` (means 97 or 0x61) | Character literals (i.e., literals of type **`char`**) are written within single quotation marks. A character literal like 'A' means the numerical value 65. |
| `'\n'` (newline, 0x0A)<br>`'\b'` (backspace, 0x08)<br>`'\r'` (carriage return, 0x0D)<br>`'\\'` (backslash, 0x5C)<br>`'\"'` (double quote, 0x22)<br>`'\''` (single quote, 0x27)<br>`'\t'` (tab, 0x09)<br>`'\0'` (NULL, 0x00)<br>`'\u0041'`(means 'A') | Special character literals are written by utilizing a so-called escape character, the backslash \. When a backslash precedes a symbol, the compiler realizes that the symbol denotes something other than the usual meaning of the symbol. With the prefix \u it is possible to give the hexadecimal Unicode character code of a character. |
| **`123`** (means 0x7B)<br>**`257`** (means 0x101)<br>**`0x31`** (means 49 or '1')<br>**`0x41`** (means 65)<br>**`0xFFFF`** (means 65535)<br>**`123L`** (a **`long`** literal) | Integer literals can be written in different numbering systems. Prefix 0x (or alternatively 0X) identifies hexadecimal literals. The compiler recognizes numerical literals on the basis that they always begin with a numerical symbol. An integer literal like 123 can be assigned to all types of integral variables. The compiler issues an error message if a literal is too large to fit into a variable. The letter L at the end of an integer literal makes it a literal of type **`long`**. Java does not have binary literals. |
| **`23.45`** (means 2345e-2)<br>**`2.345`** (means 2345e-3)<br>**`2.998e8`** (means 299800000)<br>**`3.445e-2`** (means 0.03445)<br>**`34.45e-3`** (means 0.03445)<br>**`34.45e-3F`** (**`float`** literal)<br>**`2.998e8F`** (**`float`** literal) | Floating-point literals that can be stored in variables of type **`float`** and **`double`** can be expressed either in decimal or exponential (scientific) notation. The decimal point is symbolized by . (the full stop). The comma (,) is not used in floating-point literals. Floating-point literals of type **`float`** must have an F (or alternatively an f) at the end. |
| **`"ABCDE"`** (Length is 5)<br>**`"\nABCDE"`** (Length is 6)<br>**`"\nABCDE."`** (Length is 7)<br>**`"\n\"ABCDE.\""`** (Length is 9)<br>**`"\n\n\n\n"`** (Length is 4)<br>**`"\\ABCDE\\"`** (Length is 7) | String literals are written with double quote characters. A string literal can be used to create an object of type **`String`**. Special characters can be included in string literals by using the same escape mechanism as is used in the case of character literals. |
| **`false`**<br>**`true`** | Literals of type **`boolean`** are the two words **`true`** and **`false`**. |
| **`null`** | The keyword **`null`** means that no object is being referenced. This word can be assigned as a value to object references. **`null`** is the default value when object references are fields of a class or array elements. |

## A - 2: Variables, constants, and arrays of basic types

| Declarations | Examples |
|---|---|
| Variable declarations<br><br>The built-in variable types of Java are **byte**, **char**, **short**, **int**, **long**, **float**, **double**, and **boolean**. The storage capacities of different built-in variable types are shown in Table 5-1. | `char   character_from_keyboard ;`<br>`short   given_small_integer ;`<br>`int     integer_from_keyboard ;`<br>`long    multiplication_result ;`<br><br>When variables are used as local variables inside methods, they must be assigned values before they can be used. When variables are used as fields of classes, they are automatically assigned zero values. (**boolean** fields and fields that are object references are automatically assigned values **false** and **null**, respectively.) |
| Initialized variables | `char   user_selection  =  '?' ;`<br>`byte   mask_for_most_significant_bit  =  (byte) 0x80 ;`<br>`int   character_index  =  0 ;`<br>`int   bit_mask   =  0x80000000 ;`<br>`long   speed_of_light   =  299793000L ;`<br>`float   kilometers_to_miles  = 1.6093F ;`<br>`double  value_of_pi  =  3.14159 ;`<br>`boolean  text_has_been_modified  =  false ;` |
| Constant declarations<br><br>Constants are "variables" whose values cannot be changed. | `final int  LENGTH_OF_NORMAL_YEAR  =  365 ;`<br>`final int  LENGTH_OF_LEAP_YEAR    =  366 ;`<br><br>`final double LENGTH_OF_YEAR_IN_SECONDS  =  31558149.5 ;`<br>`final float EXACT_LENGTH_OF_YEAR_IN_DAYS  =  365.256F ;` |
| Array declarations and creations | `char[] array_of_characters ;`<br>`array_of_characters  =  new  char[ 50 ] ;`<br>`int[]  array_of_integers  =  new  int[ 60 ] ;`<br>`int[]  integers_to_power_of_two =`<br>`        { 0, 1, 4, 9, 16, 25, 36, 49, 64, 81, 100, 121 } ;`<br>`int[]  two_to_power_of_integer =`<br>`        { 1, 2, 4, 8, 16, 0x20, 0x40, 0x80, 0x100 } ;`<br>`char[]  hexadecimal_digits  =`<br>`        { '0', '1', '2', '3', '4', '5', '6', '7',`<br>`          '8', '9', 'A', 'B', 'C', 'D', 'E', 'F' } ;`<br>`double[] pi_times_integer  =`<br>`          { 0, 3.1416, 6.2832, 9.4248, 12.5664 } ;`<br>`float[] centimeters_to_inches  =`<br>`        { 0, 0.3937F, 0.7874F, 1.1811F, 1.5748F, 1.9685F};`<br><br>`int[][]  some_two_dimensional_array  =  new int[ 5 ][ 9 ] ;`<br><br>If an array is created so that it is not initialized with values listed inside braces, array elements are automatically initialized with zeroes. The elements of an array of type **boolean[]** are automatically initialized with **false**. Arrays containing object references are initialized with **null**. |

## A - 3: String objects, other objects, and arrays of objects

<table>
<tr><th>Declaration</th><th>Examples</th></tr>
<tr><td>String declarations and creations</td><td><pre>
String  some_string  ;  // declares a string reference
String  another_string  =  ""  ;  // an empty string
String  third_string    =  "text inside string object" ;

char[]  some_letters    =  { 'K', 'a', 'r', 'i' } ;
String  some_name       =  new  String( some_letters ) ;
String  some_copied_string  =  new String( some_name ) ;
</pre></td></tr>
<tr><td>Object references and creations</td><td><pre>
ClassName  object_name ;  // declares an object reference
object_name  =  new  ClassName( ... ) ; // object creation

Date first_day_of_this_millennium = new Date( 1, 1, 2000 ) ;
Date last_day_of_this_millennium = new Date("12/31/2999") ;

Object  anything ;  // This can reference any object
</pre></td></tr>
<tr><td>Arrays of objects</td><td>An array of objects is actually an array of object references. Right after its creation, the elements of an array of objects contain null references.<pre>
String[]  any_array_of_strings ;

String[]  array_of_strings   =  new  String[ 9 ] ;
array_of_strings[ 0 ]  =  "some text line" ;
array_of_strings[ 1 ]  =  "another text line" ;
...

// The following is an initialized array of strings
String[]  largest_moons_of_jupiter  =
          { "Io", "Ganymede", "Europa", "Callisto" } ;

Date[]  days_of_this_millennium   =  new   Date[ 365243 ] ;
days_of_this_millennium[ 0 ]  =  new Date( 1, 1, 2000 ) ;
days_of_this_millennium[ 1 ]  =  new Date( 2, 1, 2000 ) ;
days_of_this_millennium[ 2 ]  =  new Date( 3, 1, 2000 ) ;
...

SomeClass[]  array_of_objects  =  new   SomeClass[ 10 ] ;
array_of_objects[ 0 ]  =  new  SomeClass( ... ) ;
array_of_objects[ 1 ]  =  new  SomeClass( ... ) ;
...
</pre></td></tr>
</table>

## A - 4: Expressions

The word "expression" is an important term when speaking about the grammars of programming languages. The following are examples of valid Java expressions:

```
1
254
true
some_variable
some_variable + 3
( some_variable * another_variable )
( first_variable + second_variable ) / third_variable
some_array[ 3 ]
array_of_objects[ object_index ]
some_string.length()
some_object.some_method()
some_object.SOME_STATIC_CONSTANT
```

You can see that literals, references to variables, mathematical calculations, references to objects in arrays, method calls, etc. are all expressions in Java. Expressions are parts of larger program constructs such as assignment statements, **if** constructs and loops. Expressions obtain some values when a program is being executed. When an expression represents a mathematical operation, we can say that it is a mathematical or arithmetic expression. Expressions that get the values **true** or **false** are boolean expressions.

By using the term expression it is easy to speak, for example, about the operators of a programming language. The use of the addition operator (+) can be specified

*expression* + *expression*

which can mean, for example, all the following expressions

```
some_variable + 254
some_variable + another_variable
some_variable + some_string.length()
33 + array_of_integers[ integer_index ]
```

## A - 5: Assignments and left-side expressions

When you put the assignment statement

```
1 = 1 ;
```

in a program, the compiler considers it as an error and says something like "unexpected type; required: variable; found: value" The above statement tries to assign a value to a literal, and that is not possible. I use the term "left-side expressions" to refer to expressions that are allowed on the left side of an assignment operation. A literal or a method call are not left-side expressions. Typical left-side expressions are variables, object references, references to public fields of objects, and indexed positions of arrays. The following kinds of assignment statements are thus possible

```
some_variable  =  ...
some_object  =  ...
some_object.some_public_field  =  ...
array_of_integers  =  ...
array_of_integers[ integer_index ]  =  ...
array_of_integers[ integer_index + 1 ]  =  ...
array_of_objects[ object_index ]  =  ...
```

## A - 6: The most important Java operators in order of precedence

<table>
<tr><th>Symbol</th><th>Operator name</th><th>Notation</th><th>Comments</th></tr>
<tr><td>.<br>[]<br>()</td><td>member selection<br>array indexing<br>method call</td><td>object_name.member_name<br>array_name[ expression ]<br>method_name( list of expressions )</td><td>All three operators mentioned here have the same, the highest, precedence.</td></tr>
<tr><td>++<br>--<br>~<br>!<br>-<br>+<br>( Type )<br>new</td><td>increment<br>decrement<br>complement<br>not<br>unary minus<br>unary plus<br>type cast<br>object creation</td><td>left-side-expression ++<br>left-side-expression --<br>~ expression<br>! expression<br>- expression<br>+ expression<br>( Type ) expression<br>new Type( list of expressions )</td><td>These unary operators are right-to-left asscociative. All other operators, excluding the assignment operators, are left-to-right associative.</td></tr>
<tr><td>*<br>/<br>%</td><td>multiplication<br>division<br>remainder</td><td>expression * expression<br>expression / expression<br>expression % expression</td><td>Arithmetic operators (multiplicative).</td></tr>
<tr><td>+<br>-</td><td>addition<br>subtraction</td><td>expression + expression<br>expression - expression</td><td>Arithmetic operators (additive).</td></tr>
<tr><td><<<br>>><br>>>></td><td>shift left<br>shift right<br>shift right (zero fill)</td><td>expression << expression<br>expression >> expression<br>expression >>> expression</td><td>Bitwise shift operators.</td></tr>
<tr><td><<br><=<br>><br>>=<br>instanceof</td><td>less than<br>less than or equal<br>greater than<br>greater than or equal<br>type compatibility</td><td>expression < expression<br>expression <= expression<br>expression > expression<br>expression >= expression<br>expression instanceof Type</td><td>Relational operators.</td></tr>
<tr><td>==<br>!=</td><td>equal<br>not equal</td><td>expression == expression<br>expression != expression</td><td>Relational operators or equality operators.</td></tr>
<tr><td>&</td><td>bitwise AND</td><td>expression & expression</td><td></td></tr>
<tr><td>^</td><td>bitwise exclusive OR</td><td>expression ^ expression</td><td></td></tr>
<tr><td>|</td><td>bitwise OR</td><td>expression | expression</td><td></td></tr>
<tr><td>&&</td><td>(conditional) logical AND</td><td>expression && expression</td><td></td></tr>
<tr><td>||</td><td>(conditional) logical OR</td><td>expression || expression</td><td></td></tr>
<tr><td>=<br>+=<br>-=<br>*=<br>etc.</td><td>basic assignment<br>add and assign[a]<br>subtract and assign<br>multiply and assign<br>etc.</td><td>left-side-expression = expression<br>left-side-expression += expression<br>left-side-expression -= expression<br>left-side-expression *= expression<br>etc.</td><td>Assignment operators are right-to-left associative. All arithmetic operators and most bit operators can be combined with the assignment operator =.</td></tr>
</table>

a. Operators +=, -=, *=, etc. work so that
**some_variable += 3 ;** means the same as
**some_variable = some_variable + 3 ;** and
**some_variable *= another variable ;** means the same as
**some_variable = some_variable * another_variable ;**

## A - 7: Control structures to make decisions (selections)

| Control structure | Description |
|---|---|
| Simple `if` construct | `if (` *boolean expression* `)`<br>`{`<br>One or more statements that will be executed if the boolean expression, given in parentheses above, is true. These statements will not be executed at all if the boolean expression is false (i.e. not true).<br>`}` |
| `if-else` construct | `if (` *boolean expression* `)`<br>`{`<br>One or more statements that will be executed if the boolean expression, given in parentheses above, is true.<br>`}`<br>`else`<br>`{`<br>One or more statements that will be executed if the boolean expression, given in parentheses above, is false (i.e. not true).<br>`}` |
| `if-else if` ... construct | `if (` *boolean expression 1* `)`<br>`{`<br>One or more statements that will be executed if and only if boolean expression 1 is true.<br>`}`<br>`else if (` *boolean expression 2* `)`<br>`{`<br>One or more statements that will be executed if and only if boolean expression 2 is true and boolean expression 1 is false.<br>`}`<br>`else`<br>`{`<br>One or more statements that will be executed if and only if neither boolean expression 1 nor boolean expression 2 is true.<br>`}` |
| `switch-case` construct | `switch (` *arithmetic expression* `)`<br>`{`<br>**case** $v_1$**:**<br>Statements which will be executed if the arithmetic expression has value $v_1$<br>`break ;`<br>**case** $v_2$**:**<br>Statements which will be executed if the arithmetic expression has value $v_2$<br>`break ;`<br>**case** $v_n$**:**<br>Statements to be executed when the arithmetic expression has value $v_n$<br>`break ;`<br>`default:`<br>Statements which will be executed if none of the cases matched the value of the arithmetic expression<br>`break ;`<br>`}` |

## A - 8: Control structures to perform repetitions (iterations)

<table>
<tr><th>Control structure</th><th>Description</th></tr>
<tr><td><code>while</code> loop</td><td><pre>while ( boolean expression )
{
    One or more internal statements that will be repeatedly executed as long as
    the boolean expression, given in parentheses above, is true.
}</pre></td></tr>
<tr><td><code>do-while</code> loop</td><td><pre>do
{
    One or more statements that will be first executed once, and then
    repeatedly executed as long as the boolean expression, given below in
    parentheses, is true.
}
 while ( boolean expression ) ;</pre></td></tr>
<tr><td><code>for</code> loop</td><td><pre>for ( assignment statement ;
      boolean expression ;
      increment or decrement statement )
{
    One or more internal statements that will be repeatedly executed as long as
    the boolean expression given above is true. When the boolean expression
    becomes false, the statements that follow this for loop will be executed.
}</pre>An index variable may be declared in a <code>for</code> loop in the following way<pre>for ( int some_index  = 0 ;
      ...</pre>The scope of this kind of variable is within the internal statements of the loop.</td></tr>
<tr><td>"foreach" loop</td><td><pre>for ( Type object_name : collection_name )
{
    One or more statements that will be executed for each object in the
    collection. object_name refers to the object currently being processed,
    and the loop automatically processes all objects of the collection. The
    collection being processed can be a conventional array, an ArrayList
    array, or some other kind of collection that implements the Iterable
    interface.
}</pre></td></tr>
</table>

## A - 9: Some basic Java method structures

<table>
<tr><th>Method type</th><th>Example</th></tr>
<tr><td>A static method named main() is the method that is invoked by the Java virtual machine when an executable program is run on a computer. It is mandatory to declare a formal parameter for the main() method. In this book, the name of the parameter is not_in_use when it is not used.</td><td><pre>public static void main( String[] not_in_use )
{
   ...
}</pre></td></tr>
<tr><td>The parameter that is supplied by the operating system and the virtual machine to method main() is an array of strings that contains the data that is supplied from the command line. In this book, the parameter is named command_line_parameters when it is used by the main() method.</td><td><pre>public static void main(
                 String[] command_line_parameters )
{
   ...
}</pre></td></tr>
<tr><td>A method that neither takes parameters nor outputs a return value.</td><td><pre>void method_name()
{
   ...
}</pre></td></tr>
<tr><td>A method to which two parameters of type int can be passed by value.</td><td><pre>void method_name( int first_parameter,
                  int second_parameter )
{
   ...
}</pre></td></tr>
<tr><td>A method that takes two int values as input parameters and returns an int value with a return statement.</td><td><pre>int method_name( int first_parameter,
                 int second_parameter )
{
   int value_to_caller ;
   ...
   return value_to_caller ;
}</pre></td></tr>
<tr><td>A method that takes an array of type int[] as a parameter. When arrays and other objects are passed as parameters, an array reference or an object reference is passed as a value to the called method. Thus the called method and the caller can access the same array or the same object.</td><td><pre>void method_name( int[] array_of_integers )
{
   ...
}</pre></td></tr>
</table>

## A - 10: String methods

The drawing on this page explains briefly many of the string methods. To find a more accurate description of the methods, please go to page 220.

Method **length()** returns the number of characters in a string.

Method **replace()** replaces all occurrences of a substring with a specified replacement string, or all occurrences of a character with a specified replacement character.

**indexOf()** returns the index of a substring or the index of a character in a string. If you want to know whether a string contains a certain substring, you can use the **contains()** method.

**lastIndexOf()** works like **indexOf()** but it starts the search from the last character of the string.

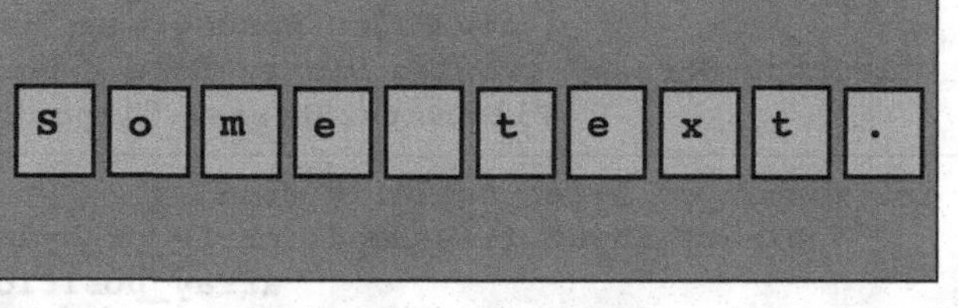


Method **startsWith()** checks whether a string begins with a certain other string. With method **regionMatches()** it is possible to check if specified regions in two strings are identical.

Method **endsWith()** checks whether the end of a string is a certain other string.

**String.format()** is a very powerful method for creating new strings.

Methods **compareTo()**, **compareToIgnoreCase()**, **equals()**, and **contentEquals()** compare strings.

**substring()** returns a string that consists of the characters in specified adjacent character positions. Method **charAt()** returns the character in a specified index position.

**toLowerCase()** and **toUpperCase()** are methods to convert the letters of a string either to lowercase or uppercase letters.

## A - 11: Mechanisms for keyboard input and screen output

The mechanisms to output data to the screen and read data from the keyboard are explained at the end of Chapter 5.

## A - 12: Input/output from/to files

| Activity | How to make it happen? |
|---|---|
| | To perform file operations in Java, the package **java.io** must be imported. |
| Open a text file for input | `BufferedReader input_file = new BufferedReader( new FileReader( "filename.txt" ) ) ;` |
| Open a text file for output | `PrintWriter output_file = new PrintWriter( new FileWriter( "filename.txt" ) ) ;`<br>`PrintWriter growing_text_file = new PrintWriter( new FileWriter( "append_here.txt", true ) ) ;` |
| Check if file opened successfully | An exception is thrown if file opening does not succeed. File operations must be carried out by using a `try-catch`(`-finally`) construct. |
| Output text to text file | `output_file.println( "This line goes to file" ) ;` |
| Input text from text file | `String text_line_from_file = input_file.readLine() ;`<br>`readLine()` returns a `null` when the end of file has been encountered. |
| Open a file in binary form for reading | `FileInputStream binary_input_file = new FileInputStream( "important.data" );` |
| Open a file in binary form for writing | `FileOutputStream binary_output_file = new FileOutputStream("important.data" ) ;`<br>`FileOutputStream growing_binary_file = new FileOutputStream( "important.data", true ) ;` |
| Read bytes from a binary file | `int number_of_bytes_actually_read = binary_input_file.read( array_of_bytes, array_position, // 0, 1, 2, ... desired_number_of_bytes ) ;`<br>`int number_of_bytes_actually_read = binary_input_file.read( array_of_bytes ) ;` |
| Write bytes to a binary file | `binary_output_file.write( array_of_bytes, array_position, // 0, 1, 2, 3, ... number_of_bytes_to_write ) ;`<br>`binary_output_file.write( array_of_bytes ) ;` |
| Close an open file | `input_file.close() ;`<br>`output_file.close() ;`<br>`binary_input_file.close() ;`<br>`binary_output_file.close() ;` |

## A - 13: Data conversions

| Conversion mechanism | How to use it? |
|---|---|
| Parsing methods | Standard Java wrapper classes (e.g. **`Short`**, **`Integer`**, **`Long`**, **`Byte`**, **`Float`**, and **`Double`**) provide static methods like **`parseShort()`**, **`parseInt()`**, **`parseLong()`**, etc., which can be used to parse a character string so that the string is converted to a numerical type. A string can be converted to a **`double`** value in the following way<br>`String value_of_pi_as_string = "3.14159" ;`<br>`double value_of_pi =`<br>`            Double.parseDouble( value_of_pi_as_string ) ;`<br>The parsing methods are useful, for example, when we want to convert a string that contains a binary or a hexadecimal value. The statement<br>`System.out.print( "\n " + Integer.parseInt( "123" )`<br>`                 + "  " + Integer.parseInt( "1111011", 2 )`<br>`                 + "  " + Integer.parseInt( "7B", 16 ) ) ;`<br>would print<br>`123   123   123` |
| **`toString()`** methods | All Java classes have a method named **`toString()`** that can convert an object to a string. A **`toString()`** method can be invoked for an object by calling it explicitly or by using the string concatenation operator (+). The statement<br>`System.out.print( "" + some_object ) ;`<br>would invoke a **`toString()`** method for the object referenced by **`some_object`**, and print the string to the screen. Some of the above-mentioned standard wrapper classes provide static methods like **`toBinaryString()`** and **`toHexString()`** with which it is possible to convert numerical values to strings in which the numbering system is not the decimal system. For example, the statements<br>`String hexadecimal_string = Integer.toHexString( 33 );`<br>`System.out.print( hexadecimal_string ) ;`<br>would print 21 to the screen. |
| **`String.format()`** method | The static **`String.format()`** method is a very powerful tool to convert numerical values to strings. You have to use format specifiers like **`%d`**, **`%X`**, **`%f`**, etc., to make the method perform the desired conversions. The conversion shown above can alternatively be carried out with the statement<br>`String hexadecimal_string = String.format( "%X", 33 );` |
| **`valueOf()`** methods | The standard class **`String`** and the above-mentioned wrapper classes provide many static **`valueOf()`** methods. For example, in the statement<br>`double value_of_pi =`<br>`            Double.valueOf( value_of_pi_as_string ) ;`<br>a string is first converted to a **`Double`** object and then unboxing takes place. |
| Casting operations | Casting is a mechanism to temporarily convert a data item to another type. Casting is usually used inside a larger statement. For example, the following statement converts a value of type **`char`** to an **`int`** value before printing:<br>`System.out.print( (int) some_character ) ;`<br>The above statement prints the character code of a character, not the character. Casting is required, for example, in assignment statements in which the value of a large variable is stored in a small variable, e.g., when the value of a **`long`** variable is copied to a variable of type **`int`**. |

## A - 14: Java class declaration

There are many different possibilities to declare classes in Java. Actually, all of Part III of this book is a long discussion of the nature of Java classes. A class declaration is identified with the reserved keyword **class**. If keyword **public** precedes the **class** keyword, the class is visible outside its package. A package is a collection that can contain many classes. Keyword **abstract** must be written before the **class** keyword if the class contains one or more abstract methods. If the **final** keyword precedes the **class** keyword, it is not possible to derive new classes from the class.

Keyword **extends** specifies that another class is inherited. Keyword **implements** specifies that one or more interfaces are implemented. A class can inherit from one superclass. It can implement one or more interfaces.

```
class ClassName  extends  SuperclassName
                 implements  SomeInterfaceName, SomeOtherInterfaceName
{
   protected int some_field ;
   ...

   public ClassName()
   {
      ...
   }

   public int get_some_field()
   {
      return  some_field ;
   }

   public void some_method( int some_parameter )
   {
      ...
   }

   public void some_other_method( ... )
   {
      ...
   }

   public String toString()
   {
      ...
      return object_as_string ;
   }
}
```

Usually classes have several constructors. A constructor has the same name as the class. A constructor is called automatically when an object (instance) of a class is created. A default constructor is one that can be called without giving any parameters.

An accessor method is one that is used to either read or write a field of a class.

All classes have a method named **toString()** because such a method is declared in class **Object** that is the superclass of all Java classes. If a class declaration does not contain a **toString()** method, it is inherited from class **Object** or from some other class in a class hierarchy.

All non-**static** and non-**private** methods of Java classes can be polymorphic methods that are overridden in lower classes. When a polymorphic method is called for an object, the correct version of the method that corresponds with the object's type is automatically selected. If you want to prevent the overriding of a method, you can declare it with the **final** keyword.

# APPENDIX B: JAVA KEYWORDS (RESERVED WORDS)

Keywords of a programming language are words that have a special meaning for the compiler of the language. Keywords may not be used as names in a program. They are thus "reserved words". All the Java keywords are listed and briefly explained below. We have not studied all the Java keywords in this book because some of them are needed only in very rare situations. The list below explains something about the keywords that we did not study.

| | |
|---|---|
| **abstract** | The **abstract** keyword is a modifier that is used when abstract methods and abstract classes are declared. A class that contains an abstract method is an abstract class that serves as a base class for other classes. An abstract class cannot be instantiated. |
| **boolean** | This keyword identifies the boolean type that can get values **true** and **false**. |
| **break** | With a **break** statement it is possible to break out from a loop or a **switch-case** construct. I recommend that **break** statements should be used only in **switch-case** constructs. Using a **break** statement inside a loop is not logical. By using state variables it is possible to avoid **break** statements inside loops. |
| **byte** | 8-bit integral type to store values in the range -128 ... 127. |
| **case** | This keyword is used in **switch-case** constructs. |
| **catch** | Keywords **catch**, **finally**, **throw**, **throws**, and **try** are needed when exceptions are handled in Java programs. Exceptions are "error objects" which Java programs can throw and catch in problem situations. **catch** begins the **catch** block of a **try-catch**(-**finally**) construct. |
| **char** | This keyword specifies the built-in (variable) type that has 16 bits, and can store the Unicode character code of a character. |
| **class** | This keyword begins class declarations. |
| **const** | **const** is a Java keyword that is not yet in use. The developers of Java have wanted to reserve this word for future use. |
| **continue** | A **continue** statement inside a loop causes a jump to the end of the internal statements of the loop. **continue** statements have not been studied in this book, and I recommend that they should not be used in programs because they are similar to **goto** statements. Instead of **continue** statements, more logical program constructs like **if** constructs should be favored. |
| **default** | This keyword is used inside **switch-case** constructs to identify the default case. |
| **do** | This keyword is used to build **do-while** loops that execute at least once. |
| **double** | The keyword that identifies the 8-byte double-precision floating-point type. |
| **else** | The keyword that is used in **if-else** constructs. |
| **enum** | This keyword can be used to specify enum types. An enum declaration specifies both an enum type and the constants that can be assigned as values to the type. |
| **extends** | With the **extends** keyword a class can be made to inherit another class. |
| **false** | A possible value for a variable of type **boolean**. The other possible **boolean** value is **true**.Officially, **false** and **true** are not keywords in Java, but they are **boolean** literals. |
| **final** | This keyword specifies that a local variable or a field is a constant whose value may not change. In addition, the **final** keyword can specify that a class is a "sealed" class from which it is not possible to derive new classes, or it can specify that a method may not be overridden in derived classes. |

| | |
|---|---|
| **finally** | Keyword **finally** begins the optional **finally** block of a **try-catch**(-**finally**) construct. The statements of a **finally** block are always executed regardless of whether or not an exception is caught. |
| **float** | The keyword used to identify the 4-byte single-precision floating-point type. |
| **for** | When the compiler sees this keyword, it knows that a **for** loop begins. In Java, the **for** keyword identifies both the traditional **for** loops and the "foreach" loops. |
| **goto** | This keyword has a bad reputation. By using this keyword it has traditionally been possible to write so-called **goto** statements with which it is possible to jump to a certain location in the program. It is one of the earliest findings in research related to computer programming that **goto** statements make programs illogical and difficult to understand. Therefore, **goto** statements should not be used in computer programs. **goto** statements can be avoided when state variables are used. Although **goto** is a keyword in Java, it does not work, i.e., it is not possible to write **goto** statements in Java. |
| **if** | This keyword begins an **if** construct. |
| **implements** | The **implements** keyword is used when a class implements one or more interfaces. |
| **import** | With this keyword a certain package can be imported to a program. Classes and other types in the package that is taken to use with an **import** statement can be referred to without mentioning the name of the package. An **import** statement can alternatively be written so that it imports only a single class of a package. |
| **instanceof** | A relational operator with which it is possible to check if something is of certain type. The **instanceof** operator returns **true** when the type of its left operand is the type specified by the right operand, or when the type of the left operand is derived from or implements the type specified by the right operand. |
| **int** | This keyword specifies that a variable, a field, a method, etc. is of the basic integer type. **int** is a 32-bit (4-byte) type. |
| **interface** | A keyword that begins an interface declaration. When a class implements an interface, it provides implementations for the methods that are specified in the declaration of the interface. |
| **long** | Type **long** is an integral type that uses 8 bytes (64 bits) to store integer values. |
| **native** | The **native** keyword specifies that a method is a native method, which is implemented so that it is compiled to native machine instructions of the computer. Usually native methods are written with a programming language other than Java, and compiled with the compiler of the used language. Native methods can be called from a Java program when method declarators are introduced with the **native** keyword. |
| **new** | An operator that is used to create objects. The **new** operator allocates memory space from the heap memory and invokes a constructor. |
| **null** | **null** means that no object is being referenced. This literal can be assigned to object references. **null** is the default value when object references are fields of a class or array elements. |
| **package** | A keyword that can be used to specify that certain classes, enums, and interfaces belong to a certain named package. |
| **private** | This keyword is an access modifier which specifies that a class member is accessible only in the class in which it is declared. |
| **protected** | This access modifier specifies that a class member is accessible for methods in classes that belong to the same package as well as for methods in derived classes in other packages. |

| | |
|---|---|
| `public` | The keyword to specify public members in a class declaration. Public members can be accessed by methods of all classes in all packages. If a type (e.g. class, enum, or interface) is marked with the **public** keyword, the type is accessible to all types outside the package of the type. A package can contain a set of types, and those types that are not marked as **public** are accessible only within the package. |
| `return` | A statement that causes a return to the calling method. Usually **return** statements supply a value to the calling method. Because a **return** statement is a kind of **goto** statement that causes a jump to the end of a method, **return** statements should be used sparingly and only at the end of methods. |
| `short` | An integral type that uses 2 bytes (16 bits) to store values in the range -32,768 ... 32,767. |
| `static` | A keyword to specify that a method or a field is static. A static method can be called without creating an object of a class. A static field is shared by all objects of a class. |
| `super` | With the **super** keyword it is possible to call the constructors and polymorphic methods of the superclass. |
| `switch` | **switch-case** program constructs begin with the **switch** keyword. |
| `synchronized` | The **synchronized** keyword can be used in programs which run several threads simultaneously, and in which a method is called from several threads. When a method is declared with the **synchronized** keyword, only one thread at a time can use it. Other threads automatically wait until a thread has executed the code of a **synchronized** method. If it is not possible to make an entire method a **synchronized** method, a set of statements of a method can be put inside a **synchronized** block of statements. |
| `this` | When the **this** keyword is used inside a method, it references the object for which the method was called. With the **this** keyword, a constructor can call another constructor of the same class. |
| `throw` | A **throw** statement throws an exception object in an error situation. A **throw** statement results in a jump to the nearest **catch** block where the exception can be handled. |
| `throws` | With the **throws** keyword it is possible to write a so-called exception specification, which specifies exceptions that may be thrown by a method. |
| `transient` | A field of a class can be marked with the **transient** keyword to indicate that its value does not need to be stored when an object of the class is serialized. Serialization of objects means that the data stored in an object is converted to such a form that it is easy to store it, for example, to a file. Object serialization is not covered by this book. |
| `true` | A value that can be given for a variable of type **boolean**. Officially, **true** is not a keyword in Java, but it is a **boolean** literal. |
| `try` | Keyword **try** begins a **try-catch**(-**finally**) construct. |
| `void` | When written in a method declaration, this keyword says that the method does not return a value with a **return** statement. |
| `volatile` | A field of a class can be declared **volatile** in order to increase reliability of applications that consist of several threads. |
| `while` | This keyword is needed when **while** loops and **do-while** loops are written. |

# APPENDIX C: PRACTICAL ADVICE FOR PROGRAMMING EXERCISES

You should attempt programming exercises with a computer in order to learn programming. In this book, there are special exercise boxes that give you smaller and larger programming tasks to do. The purpose of this appendix is to act as a guide for doing those exercises.

## C - 1: Starting an exercise

In many cases, an exercise is to modify a program that is presented in this book. In these cases, it is important that you invent your own file name for the program that you modify. For example, if your task is to make a modification to program **Game.java**, you should make a copy of **Game.java** with a different file name, and modify the program that has the new file name. In the case of **Game.java**, the new file might have a name like **GameNew.java**, **GameMy.java**, or **MyGame.java**. You should develop your own file naming policy for those situations when you make copies of the book programs. Adding the word **My** to the original file name may be one such policy. Remember also that the class name inside a **.java** file must correspond with the file name.

By using a new file name for your own version of a program, you ensure that you can find your program later, and you still have the original program stored in the original file. It may also be a good idea to have a separate directory (folder) in which you keep those programs that you have made by modifying the book programs. A directory with the name **myjava** might be one possible place for your own **.java** files.

Also in those cases when you have been asked to write a completely new program, it is often useful to start the programming task by making a copy of some existing **.java** file. In my computer I have a file named **Empty.java** of which I can make a copy when I start writing a new Java program. My **Empty.java** file looks like

```
//  .java  (c) 2005 Kari Laitinen

import java.util.* ;

class
{
   public static void main( String[] not_in_use )
   {
      Scanner keyboard = new Scanner( System.in ) ;

   }
}
```

## C - 2: Writing your program

In the beginning, when you are writing your first computer programs, there are many things that may confuse you. It may be difficult to follow any programming guidelines because you are still learning the basic concepts of programming. It is important, however, that as soon as you learn the basics of program writing, you develop for yourself a standard way to write programs. I recommend that you write your programs in the same way as the programs of this book are written.

The first programming techniques you should take into use are indentation and proper placement of braces. This means that you indent the internal statements of such program constructs as `if` statements and loops, and use braces around the indented statements in a uniform manner. According to the programming style that is used in this book, a `while` loop, for example, may not look like

```
while ( character_index  <  given_string.length() )
{
System.out.print( "  "
           +  given_string.charAt( character_index ) ) ;
character_index  ++ ;
}
```

In the above loop the internal statements of the loop are not indented. Neither may a **while** loop look like

```
while ( character_index  <  given_string.length() )
   {
   System.out.print( "  "
              +  given_string.charAt( character_index ) );
   character_index  ++  ;
   }
```

In the latter version above, the braces are indented to the same character column as the internal statements of the loop. The correct way, according to this book, is to write the **while** loop in the following way

```
while ( character_index  <  given_string.length() )
{
   System.out.print( "  "
              +  given_string.charAt( character_index ) );
   character_index  ++  ;
}
```

where the internal statements of the loop are indented but the braces are left in the same column as the keyword **while**.

Another important programming style factor is the naming of variables, arrays, constants, methods, classes, objects, etc. Throughout this book, a naming approach called natural naming is used, and I recommend that you also start writing your programs with natural names. Natural naming means that variable names and other names are constructed by using preferably several natural words. Abbreviations are not allowed in natural names. Compilers accept variables like

```
char c ;
int  linecnt ;
```

but it is better to name variables with natural names like

```
char character_from_keyboard ;
int  number_of_lines_printed ;
```

Using a uniform programming style in your programs is important, not because compilers require it, but because it helps you in your programming work. When you write a new program, it is best to write it at once so that the programming style rules like indentation and natural naming are followed. This way the program gets a logical structure, and it is likely to contain less errors. Some people try to write their programs quickly, saying that they will correct the programming style later, but that does not produce high-quality programs. Programs that are written quickly without a proper programming style usually contain many errors, and it takes a lot of time to find and correct those errors.

## C - 3: Compiling and executing your program

Before you compile a program, you should consider the following:

- Try to ensure just by using your eyes and brains that the program is consistent with your programming style rules and it is syntactically correct, i.e., written according to the rules of the Java programming language. It is always an advantage, if you learn to detect errors just by reading the program code.

- Remember to save your program with the editor before you start compiling it.
- If you compile and execute your programs in a command prompt window, don't forget that by using the Arrow Up and Arrow Down keys on the keyboard, you can find the previously typed commands, and that enables you to compile and execute the programs faster without retyping the commands.

## C - 4: Correcting compilation errors

When you try to compile your program and the Java compiler detects that the program is not written according to the rules of Java, it will display one or more error messages on the screen. The following points may help you to correct your program after unsuccessful compilation:

- Java compilers generate both error messages and warnings. Warnings are the text lines which begin "Note: ..." When even a single error message appears, it means that the program could not be compiled, and no executable file was generated. A warning is a less serious problem. An executable file is produced also when warnings are given.
- When the compiler issues an error message and gives a line number where the error was detected, the error is not necessarily on the line given by the compiler. In many cases when the compiler claims that on a certain line there is an error, the error is actually on the previous line or on the following line. Sometimes the error may be in a totally different place in the program.
- Always when you find and correct an error in a program, recompile the program. It is possible that several error messages are caused by a single error.
- Many errors that the compiler detects are writing errors. The compiler does not, unfortunately, say that "now you have most likely made a writing error" but it claims something else in such a situation. For example, if you wrote

```
int charactr_index    =  0 ;

while ( character_index   <  given_string.length() )
{ ...
```

  the compiler would say something like "Cannot find symbol character_index" although the real problem in the above case is that the name of the index variable was not written correctly when the variable was declared. You have to get used to the fact that the error messages that the compiler displays are rather mechanical, and you need to learn to interpret them.

Sometimes it is hard to find an error in a program. If you have a compilation error in a program and you cannot find its reason, you can try to locate the error by systematically doing the following checks:

- Check that all lines that need a semicolon at the end do actually have the semicolon.
- Check that there are equally many opening parentheses ( and closing parentheses ) in the boolean expressions of your **`if`** constructs and loops.
- Ensure that each opening brace { has its counterpart, a closing brace }.
- Check that you have not accidentally used an opening parenthesis ( in a place where you should have written an opening brace { or an opening bracket [. You can do these same checkings for closing parentheses ), closing braces }, and closing brackets ].

## C - 5: Searching for errors that compilers do not detect

You should remember that compilers are rather mechanical tools that can detect only some rudimentary errors in a program. Therefore, it is very important that you always attempt to write your programs so that you try not to make any errors. Never trust that the compiler will detect your programming errors.

It is a very usual moment in the development of a computer program that the program can be compiled without errors, but for some strange reason it does not work as it should. In such a situation there is a logical error in the program. The following are some typical logical errors that people, including you and me, may make

- An extra semicolon is accidentally written after the boolean expression of a loop or after the boolean expression of an **if** construct. The following examples clarify this problem

```
while ( ... ) ;
{
   ...
}


if ( ... ) ;
{
   ...
}
```

A semicolon may not usually follow the boolean expression of a loop or an **if** construct. If a semicolon is written here, the compiler interprets it as the statement that is executed when the boolean expression is **true**.

- Operator >, "greater than", is used where operator <, "less than", should be in use. These kinds of mistakes can easily be made also with operators >= and <=. These kinds of logical errors can cause many kinds of problems. One typical problem is that the internal statements of a loop are never executed because the boolean expression is **false** at the beginning. The following is an example of this

```
int integer_index  =  0 ;

while ( integer_index  >  number_of_integers_in_array )
{
   ...
```

- Because of the use of a wrong logical operator, a boolean expression can be such that it is always **true** or always **false**. For example, the boolean expression of the **if** construct

```
if ( character_from_keyboard  >=  'A'   ||
     character_from_keyboard  <=  'Z'   )
{
   ...
```

  is always **true** because the logical OR operator || is used instead of the logical AND operator &&.

So, if your program compiles but it does not work, you can make the following checks:

- Check for semicolons that may be accidentally written after boolean expressions.
- Ensure that all loops are entered and exited.
- Search for boolean expressions that may be always **false** or always **true**.

Logical errors in programs are sometimes hard to detect. When you are in a situation that your program does not work properly, and you do not know why it does not work as it should, you have, at least, the following possibilities to try:

- Print the program on paper and read it through, trying to find possible places that could cause problems. When your program is on paper, you can even test the program manually using a pencil. This means, for example, that you give values to some variables by writing them down on paper, and then you "execute" the program on paper by writing down the changing values of other variables.
- Stop thinking about the problem for a while. Let your subconscious work with the problem, and return to it the next day.
- Use some kind of debugging aid. Either insert extra statements to your program, or use a debugging tool.

The word "bug" means an error in a program, and debugging tools are computer tools with which it is possible to try to locate the error. Commercial program development environments have debugging tools which allow you to execute your program step by step, and inspect the contents of variables and other data items. These tools are certainly useful in some situations. You just need to learn to use them.

If you do not have debugging tools available, or you do not want to learn to use them, you can modify your program temporarily to see how far it executes without problems. You have, at least, the following possibilities to make temporary modifications to your program:

- By inserting extra output statements that print the values of essential variables, you can examine how the values change while your program is being executed. Even temporary output statements that just print something can be useful. For example, if you add the statement

  ```
  System.out.print( "\n This is inside a loop." ) ;
  ```

  inside a loop, and the text never appears on the screen when the program is being executed, you can deduce that the internal statements of the loop are never entered. Similar statements can be added inside **if** blocks and **else** blocks in **if** constructs.
- You can temporarily make some statements as comments by writing the double slash // at the beginning of the program lines. This way you can make your program simpler, and perhaps find the mistake more easily.
- If you suspect that some particular method in your program is causing trouble, you can take that method out from the program, and test it in a separate test program. The test program should call the method by using some test data as parameters. Actually, all general-purpose methods should be tested this way.

## C - 6: Programs that do not terminate

Especially when you begin working with loops, you are likely to write a program that never terminates. Such a program may keep displaying something forever, or it just waits for something forever. The reason for this kind of program behavior is most likely a loop that never terminates. The first thing you have to do when your program does not terminate is to make it stop somehow. Here are the things you can do, and please apply these tricks in the given order:

- First try typing Control-C. This means that you keep the Ctrl key of the keyboard down and press the C key simultaneously. Control-C character is a classic way to terminate programs that run in a command prompt window.

- In the operating systems Windows XP, Windows 2000, and Windows NT, there is a tool called Task Manager. To make your program stop, you can try to use the Task Manager to end the command prompt window task (process) where your program is running.
- You can try to shut down the operating system of your computer and restart the computer.
- The modern operating systems of personal computers are quite reliable, and they should recover from problems that are caused by small programs, but it may still be possible that your computer gets so jammed that it does not react to the mouse or the keyboard even after you have waited for its recovery for some time. In such a situation there is no other way than to switch off the electricity of the computer and restart it after that.

As it is possible that you can accidentally produce a program that can disturb the entire computer, or even require a restart of the computer, it is important, that when you test your programs, you do not have any other activities going on in your computer. So it is a good idea to close all documents and other important files when you start programming and testing.

## C - 7: Incremental program development

Especially if your programming task is to write a somewhat larger program, it is always an advantage if you can develop the program so that you start first with a smaller program and then add new features to the program. When you work this way, you should always ensure that the existing smaller program compiles and works before you start adding new features to it. This kind of programming approach can be called incremental program development, or even incremental software development. For example, let's suppose that your programming task is to write a program that reads integers from the keyboard, stores them into an array, and when the user types in number zero, the program displays the integers in reverse order. You could develop this program incrementally in the following way:

- First you might just write a program with a **`while`** loop where integers are read from the keyboard until the user types in a zero. You could test that the loop indeed terminates when the zero is entered from the keyboard.
- Then you could improve the program so that the integers that are read from the keyboard are stored in an array. Again you should compile the program and ensure that it still stops when a zero is entered.
- Before making the final version of the program, you could add two temporary output statements at the end of your program so that the first and the last integer in the array are displayed by the temporary output statements. This way you can be quite sure that the integers indeed are stored correctly in the array.
- In the final stage of the program development you could remove the temporary output statements and add the loop that prints the integers in reverse order.

## C - 8: Printing your program on paper

Paper copies of programs are important because it is often easier to study a program, and search for errors from a program, when it is on sheets of paper. For historical reasons, paper copies of programs are often called program listings. To ensure that your programs look good on paper, you should consider the following points:

- When you print a program on paper, use a font like **`courier`** in which all characters have the same width. It is also important that you use a sufficiently small font so that the lines that you see on the screen fit also on paper.
- To ensure that programs print correctly, it is better not to use tabulator characters in program texts. Most modern program editors can be configured so that they insert a certain number spaces into the program text when the tabulator key is pressed.

## C - 9: Program versions and backups

When you have to do a lot of experimentation to make a program work, you will most certainly be tempted to produce different versions of your **.java** file. You might produce program files like **MyGame.java**, **MyGame2.java**, **MyGame3.java**, etc. My advice is to avoid this. You just get confused with many similar program files. It is better to fully concentrate on a single file and try to make that working.

Remember that your **.java** files are valuable pieces of information. It is very important that you learn to make backup copies of your source program files. Hard disks of computers are quite reliable these days, but it is possible that they may break and important information can be lost. So, even if making copies of your **.java** files and other important files is sometimes frustrating and seems to be unnecessary because no problems seem forthcoming, it is important to have copies.

### Tabulator characters can be harmful in source programs

The tabulator character, or "tab", which has the character code 09H, may seem to be useful when you write a computer program with a program editor. You can put a tabulator in all those places where a space is allowed. A tabulator character corresponds to, for example, 4 spaces in the program editor. But the use of tabulator characters causes problems in the long run. If your program editor treats tabulators equal to 4 spaces, your printer may think that they are 8 spaces, and you end up having different kinds of programs on the screen and on paper. Similar problems may occur if you start editing a program with a new program editor. To avoid these kinds of problems, it is better not to use the tabulator character in source programs. It is always possible to use several spaces instead of a tabulator, and most program editors can be configured so that they insert 3 or 4 spaces into the program when the tabulator key is pressed.

# INDEX

The purpose of this index is to help you to search for information in this book. After each term mentioned in the index, there are page numbers that help you to locate the pages where the term is discussed. Each page number indicates a page on which the discussion of a term begins. In some cases, the discussion continues on the following pages.

The file names of the example programs (e.g. **First.java**, **Sum.java**, **Game.java**, etc.) are not mentioned in this index. To locate the example programs in this book, please use the alphabetical list on the introductory pages of this book.

Terms related to the imaginary computer (Chapter 4) are not widely listed in this index. Because the imaginary computer is a special subject that is discussed only in a single chapter, it should be possible to manage that information by using the table of contents.

## Symbols


! NOT operator 146
!= not equal operator 135
" double quote character 102, 121, 203, 555
$ in format specifiers 125
% in format specifiers 125
% remainder operator 138, 265, 280
%s format specifier for strings 506
& bitwise AND operator 531
&& logical AND operator 146
&& operator vs. & operator 552
( opening parenthesis 134
() empty parentheses 108, 244, 252
) closing parenthesis 134
* multiplication operator 113
*/ terminates a comment 313
*= multiply and assign operator 559
+ addition operator 113, 121
+ concatenation operator 121
++ increment operator 155, 157
+= add and assign operator 559
- subtraction operator 113
-- decrement operator 157
-= subtract and assign operator 559
... means "some program lines" 12, 274
... specifies zero or more parameters 274
.bak, name extension for backup files 466
.class, name extension for executable Java files 10
.exe files vs. .class files 28
.java, name extension for Java source files 10
.jpg files 497
.txt, name extension for text files 452
/ division operator 113
/* begins a comment 313
// double slash, begins a comment line 17, 18, 73, 313
; semicolon 14, 18
< less than operator 135
<< left shift operator 531
<= less than or equal operator 135
= basic assignment operator 113
== equal operator 135
> greater than operator 135
>= greater than or equal operator 135
>> right shift operator 531
>>> zero fill right shift operator 531
[] empty (square) brackets 178, 188
\ backslash character 203, 555
\0 NULL character 555
\b backspace character 203, 555
\n newline character 102, 203, 225, 555
\r carriage return character 203, 225, 453, 550, 555
\t tabulator character 203, 225, 555
^ exclusive OR operator 531
_ underscore character 108
| bitwise OR operator 531
|| logical OR operator 146
|| operator vs. | operator 552
~ complement operator 531
' single quote character 141, 203, 555


## Numerics


0x, prefix to form hexadecimal literals 117
1$, 2$, etc. in format specifiers 125
10-finger typing system vi
24-hour time format 423


## A


a.m./p.m. time format 423
abbreviated names 17
abstract classes 422, 424, 520
abstract classes vs. final classes 429
abstract keyword 424, 567
abstract methods 422
access modifiers 298, 398
    protected keyword 416
accessing files in Java programs 451
accessor methods 313, 339, 343, 351, 365
AccountWithCredit, an example class 418
acres, unit of area 319
action statements 99, 100
action statements vs. declaration statements 14
actual parameters 250, 268
add and assign operator += 559
add(), ArrayList method 465, 502, 507, 517, 518
add(), Calendar method 524
add_new_collection_item() method 491
add_new_item(), Collection method 485
addAll() method of class Collections 509
addAll(), ArrayList method 505, 518
addition operator + 113, 121

additive arithmetic operators 559
addresses, numerical 51
advice for studying v
age, calculation of 347, 523
algorithms, sorting 262
allocation of memory 188, 190, 272
alphabetical comparison of strings 220
American date format MM/DD/YYYY 342, 388
AmericanTime, an example class 425
Animal, an example class 308, 362
API (Application Programming Interface) 431
Apollo 11 landing 344
append(), StringBuilder method 229
appending data to the end of a file 472
appending text to the end of a file 455
applications 9
Arabic numbers 32, 33
argument lists of variable length 274
arguments vs. parameters 250
arguments, see "parameters" 244
arithmetic expressions 138, 558
    in array references 179
arithmetic operators 113, 138, 280
ArrayList class 502–512, 518
    add() method 465, 502, 507, 517, 518
    addAll() method 505, 518
    get() method 507
    set() method 507
    size() method 503
    type parameters 505
arrays
    array creation statement 189
    array declaration statement 189
    arrays of integers 178–185
    arrays of objects 557
    arrays of strings 231, 234
    as method parameters 257
    declaring arrays 178, 556
    default values 192
    "foreach" loops process arrays 176
    initialized array of strings 231
    initialized arrays 191
    jagged arrays 196
    length of an array 183
    multidimensional arrays 196, 406
    ragged arrays 196
    rectangular arrays 196
    referring to array elements 179
Arrow Down key 26, 573
Arrow Up key 26, 573
ASCII coding system 45, 105
ask_numbers_to_array() method 260, 265
assembly languages are difficult 94
assignment operator = 113, 115
assignment statements 113, 115, 558
    left-side expressions 558
associativity of operators 112, 121
associativity of the dot operator . 323
astronomical facts 342
autoboxing 432, 502
automatic calls 385, 400
automatic memory management 301, 325
automatically generated constructors 400
auxiliary memory devices 5, 50
available() method 489

## B

Babbage, Charles 205
backslash character \ 203, 555
backspace character \b 203, 555
backup (.bak) files 466
backup copies of programs 577
balloons of text viii
BankAccount, an example class 296
BankAccount, another version of the class 302
BankAccount, third version of the class 416
base class 384
base-10 system, base-16 system, etc.
    see "numbering systems"
BetterDate, an example class 386
big-endian order of bytes 106
BilingualTranslation, an example class 510
binary files vs. text files 469
binary literals do not exist 530
binary numbering system 33
binary numbers 42
    printing integers in binary form 536
binary-to-decimal conversion 36
binding, dynamic (late) vs. static (early) 427
birthdays, day of week 347, 523
birthdays, planning celebrations 347, 523
bit operators 530–537
bit, binary digit 40
bitwise AND operator & 531
bitwise logical operators 552
bitwise OR operator | 531
blocks of statements 167, 171, 276
blocks, nested program blocks 276
body of a loop 159
body of method 259
Boole, George 134
boolean expressions 134, 140, 470, 558
boolean keyword 567
boolean literals (true, false) 174
boolean methods 490
boolean type 105, 175
Boolean, standard wrapper class 433
boxing 432, 502
boxing vs. unboxing 436, 437
braces { }, rules for using 167, 571
brackets [] 188
break keyword 567
break statements 147, 150
BufferedReader class 454, 458
    readLine() method 459
bug can mean any small insect 96
byte keyword 567

byte type 105
Byte, standard wrapper class 433
bytecode instructions 268, 270

*C*

C programming language 272, 452
C# programming language 112, 452
C++ programming language 112, 305, 452
Caesar, Julius 237, 347
calculate_mean_value() method 261
Calendar class 390, 521
Calendar constants 524, 525
calendar reform 347
callee, a method that is called 242
caller, a method that calls 242
calling methods 240, 513
    stack usage 268–273
calling superclass version of a method 419
calories, unit of energy 319
capacity(), StringBuilder method 226
capitalization of names iv, 252
carriage return character \r 203, 225, 453, 555
case keyword 147, 567
case sensitivity 22
casting 565
catch keyword 171, 567
celebrations, planning 347, 523
centimeters, unit of length 319
change_text(), TextWindow method 410
char keyword 567
char type 105
character codes 141, 160, 200, 452, 453, 532
    whitespace characters 225
character codes, hexadecimal output 206
character coding 45, 46
character literals 141, 555
Character, standard wrapper class 433
charAt() String method 204, 205, 220
checked exceptions 442, 443
chronological distance between dates 345, 357
Churchill, Winston 521
.class file, executable Java file 10
.class files vs. .exe files 28
class keyword 567
class methods vs. instance methods 208
class variables 397
classes
    abstract classes 422, 424
    access modifiers 398
    accessor methods 339, 343, 351, 365
    base class 384
    calling another instance method 352
    class declarations 566
    class hierarchy 404
    class scope 277
    constructor methods 300
    copy constructors 306
    default constructors 307
    fields of classes 290
    final classes 429
    graphical class descriptions 365
    hierarchies of classes 401, 405, 415
    inheritance between classes 384
    initialization of data fields 316
    polymorphic methods 414, 510
    several constructors in a class 306
    subclasses and immediate subclasses 400
    superclass 384
    superclasses and immediate superclasses 400
classwide data 277
classwide variables 275
clock signal 54
clone() method of class Object 434
close(), method to close files 455, 457, 466
coding of textual information 45, 46, 452
Collection, an example class 484
CollectionItem, an example class 482
CollectionMaintainer, an example class 490
Collections.addAll() method 509
Collections.sort() method 518
Columbus, Christopher 344, 347
command line
    command line parameters 467
    directing screen output to file 399
command prompt window, opening and adjusting 19
command prompt window, working with 26
command_line_parameters, parameter of main() 278
commands, MS-DOS operating system 19
comments
    comments inside /* and */ 313
    double slash // comments 17, 73, 313
    text ignored by the compiler 17
    using comments in program testing 575
Comparable interface 514, 515, 516
compareTo() method of class Event 516
compareTo() method of Comparable 515
compareTo() String method 212, 220
compareToIgnoreCase() String method 220
comparison operators 135
compilation 8, 350
    compiling Java programs 25, 26
    compiling with JCreator 29
    process of compilation studied 130
    recompiling programs 26
    several .java files in compilation 344
compilation errors, correcting 573
compiler generated calls 385
compiler, installation of 20
complement operator ~ 531
complementing truth values 145
compound interest 194
computer system 9
concat() String method 221
concatenating String objects 214
concatenation operator + 121
conditional logical operators 552
console window 19
const keyword 567

constants 370
constants, literal constants 113
constructors 300, 306
automatic calling of superclass constructor 400
constructor calling another constructor 363
constructors and inheritance 385, 386
copy constructors 306
default constructors 307, 385, 400
implicit calling of constructors 385
initialization of data fields of a class 316
constructors of class String 221
contains() String method 213, 221, 320, 377, 462
contentEquals() String method 221
contents of this book x
continue keyword 567
continuing a statement on following line 109
control structures 560, 561
Control-C character 575
conventions for writing hexadecimal numbers 39
conventions for writing method names 252
Conversion, an example class 318
conversions
explicit type conversions 161, 164, 267
summary of some mechanisms 565
conversions, explicit 532
convert(), Conversion method 318, 320
convert_string_uppercase() method 535
copy constructors 306
copying objects 434
copyValueOf() String method 221
CR, carriage return character 453
creating arrays 189
creation of objects 300
CurrentDate, an example class 390
CurrentTime, an example class 424
currentTimeMillis(), method of class System 544

## D

Darwin, Charles 521
data encapsulation 339
DataInputStream class 472, 473, 482, 489
DataOutputStream class 471, 472, 473, 476, 488
date formats 342, 388
Date, an example class 350–360, 384
DateDistance, an example class 361
day(), Date method 351
deallocation of memory 272
decimal numbering system 101
decimal numbers 101
decimal-to-binary conversion 37
decisions, see "if constructs", "switch-case constructs"
declaration statements vs. action statements 14
declarations
array declarations 178, 189, 556
class declarations 566
String declarations 200
variable declarations 100, 556
vs. executable statements 100
declarators of methods 244, 259
DecoratedTextWindow, an example class 411
decrement operator -- 157
decrement(), Date method 356
default constructors 307, 385
automatically generated 400
default keyword 567
default package 336
default values 192
definitions of variables 100
delete(), StringBuilder method 229
deposit_money(), BankAccount method 296, 302, 416
designing programs 332
destruction of objects in heap memory 301
destructors do not exist in Java 305
digits 32
dimensions of arrays 196
directing screen output to file 399
dividing by zero 280
division operator / 113, 280
do keyword 567
do-while loops 164–165, 561
documentation, Java API 22
dollar sign $ in format specifiers 125
dot operator .
associativity of 323
double keyword 567
double quote character " 121, 203, 555
double slash // begins a comment line 313
double type 110
Double, standard wrapper class 433
Double.parseDouble() method 565
downloading
Java compiler 20
programs presented in this book 23
dynamic binding 427
dynamic memory allocation 326
dynamic strings 226

## E

e-mail 46
e.g. means "for example"
early binding 427
Earth, equatorial radius 110
Earth, length of equator 115
echoing 88
Einstein, Albert 387
electronic Java documentation 22
elements
referring to array elements 178
else keyword 567
embed_text_in_window(), TextWindow method 410
empty (square) brackets [] 188
empty parentheses () 108, 244, 252
empty string 204, 467
Empty.java 571
encapsulation of data 294, 339, 398
endian, little-endian vs. big-endian 106

endless loop 154
endsWith() String method 221
EnglishCalendar, an example class 394
enum keyword 567
enums 499, 500
equal operator == 135
equality of String objects 210, 467
equals() method of class Object 434
equals() method, how to write it 445
equals() String method 210, 212, 222
equalsIgnoreCase() String method 222
Error class 443
errors in programs
  correcting compilation errors 573
  typical logical errors 574
errors made by users 171
escape character, backslash \ 203, 555
escape sequence characters 203
etc. means "et cetera", "and so on"
European date format DD.MM.YYYY 342, 388
EuropeanTime, an example class 425
evaluation of expressions 112, 113, 179
even numbers vs. odd numbers 197
Event, an example class 516
example programs, downloading 23
example programs, list of xiv
Exception class 443
exceptions 171, 438–444
  checked exceptions 442
  exception specifications 442
  unchecked exceptions 442
  unhandled exceptions 120
exclusive OR operator ^ 531
.exe files vs. .class files 28
executable programs 8
execution of Java programs 25, 28
exercises in this book, list of xvii
exercises, practical advice for 571
exists(), method of class File 455
explicit type conversions 161, 164, 267
exponential notation 110
expressions 558
  arithmetic expressions 138, 558
  boolean expressions 140, 558
  parentheses, meaning in expressions 123
  relational expressions 141
extending an interface 520
extends keyword 567

## F

F, suffix for float literals 117
factorial, mathematical term 252
false, boolean literal 174, 567
feed(), Animal method 308
feet, unit of length 319
fields of classes 290
File class
  exists() method 455
file name extension 5
FileInputStream class 473, 489
FileNotFoundException 458, 475
FileOutputStream class 473, 488
  write() method 471
FileReader class 454, 458, 460
files
  accessing files in Java programs 451
  close() method 466
  opening files 451, 456, 472
  storing objects in file 480
  storing screen output to file 399
  summary of file handling 564
  text files 452
FileWriter class 454, 455, 460
fill_with_character(), Window method 407
final classes and methods 429
final keyword 370, 429, 498, 567
finalize() method 305
finalize() method of class Object 434
finally blocks 457
finally keyword 444, 568
finding errors in programs 573
findInLine(), Scanner method 169
Finland, date of independence 385
flip-flops 42
float keyword 568
float type 110
Float, standard wrapper class 433
floating-point literals 117, 192, 555
floating-point variables 110
floppy disk drive 5
flowcharts 153
flush() method 455
for keyword 568
for loops 158–163, 276, 561
"foreach" loops 176, 217, 508, 517
formal parameters 250, 268
format specifiers 116, 128, 523, 526
  %s format specifier for strings 506
format() String method 126, 222, 274, 360, 369
Formatter class 128
formatting screen output 125–128
FrameWindow, an example class 409

## G

gallons, unit of volume 319
garbage collection 209, 435
garbage collector 301, 325
generic classes and types 502
generic interfaces 514
Germany, date of reunification 385
get(), ArrayList method 507
get(), Calendar method 524
get_brief_president_info(), President method 369
get_date_print_format(), Date method 351
get_day_of_week(), Date method 355
get_distance_to(), Date method 357

get_full_president_data(), President method 369
get_index_of_smallest_number_in_array() method 267
get_items_of_maker(), Collection method 487
get_items_of_type(), Collection method 487
get_planet_name(), Planet method 321
get_president_name(), President method 369
get_value(), IntParameter method 380
get_week_number(), Date method 358, 362
get_year(), Olympics method 313
getBytes() String method 222
getChars() String method 222
getClass() method of class Object 435
getter methods 339
GIF, Graphics Interchange Format 48
golf, the game of 3
goto keyword 568
grams, unit of weight 319
graphical descriptions
    flowcharts 153
    graphical class descriptions 365
greater than operator > 135
greater than or equal operator >= 135
Greenwich Mean Time (GMT) 527
Gregorian Calendar 347, 353
GregorianCalendar class 390, 521, 525, 526
GUI, graphical user interface 169

## H

hard disk 5
hardware 4
hashCode() method of class Object 435
header of a method 259
heap memory 326
    automatic management of 325
heap memory vs. stack memory 189, 324
hectares, unit of area 319
hexadecimal input from the keyboard 120
hexadecimal literals 117, 163, 555
hexadecimal numbering system 33, 101
hexadecimal numbers, conventions for writing 39
hexadecimal output 206
hexadecimal-to-binary conversion 38, 534
hexadecimal-to-decimal conversion 36
hierarchies of classes 401, 404, 405, 415
high-level programming languages 94
HighClass, an example class 402
hyphenation 109

## I

i.e. means "in other words"
IBM Personal Computer 65
IC8 simulator 80
ICOM simulator 80
identifiers, see also "names" 108
if constructs (statements) 134–143, 560
if keyword 568
if-else if-else constructs 140
imaginary computer 54
    imaginary processor 56
    instruction decoding table 60
    internal registers 56
    machine instructions 59
    state diagram of operation 67
    vs. real computers 79
IML language 73
IML programming
    address names 76
    keywords STRING, DATA, CONSTANT 78
    loop in a program 82
    loop inside another loop 88
    program that never terminates 96
    reserving memory locations 78
    stack and subroutine calls 86
    subroutine is called 84
    subroutine to read the keyboard 89
immediate access memory 5
immediate subclass 400
immediate superclass 400
immutability of strings 204
implements keyword 514, 568
implicit calling of constructors 385
import keyword 568
import statements 334
in, static field of class System 333
inches, unit of length 319
increment operator ++ 155, 157
increment(), Date method 355
incremental program development 576
incremental software development 576
indentation of statements 167, 571
index variables 179, 407
index variables, naming of 188
index_for_day_of_week(), Date method 354
indexing 179
indexing, of strings 207
indexOf() String method 213, 223, 320
inheritance 384
    abstract classes and methods 424
    access modifiers 398
    automatic calling of superclass constructor 400
    constructors and inheritance 385, 386
    final classes 429
    interfaces inherited (extended) 520
    overriding methods 414
    polymorphic methods 414, 510
    subclasses and immediate subclasses 400
    superclasses and immediate superclasses 400
initialization
    default values 192
    initialization of arrays 191
    initialization of data fields of a class 316
    initialization of multidimensional arrays 195
    initialization of variables 155
    initialized array of strings 231
initialize_account(), BankAccount method 296
initialize_collection_with_test_data() method 493

initialize_rectangle(), Rectangle method 292
input parameters 261
InputMismatchException type 438
InputStream class 333
insert(), StringBuilder method 228
instance methods 291, 352
instance methods vs. class methods 208
instance variables 397
instanceof keyword (operator) 445, 568
instances (objects) of classes 291
int keyword 568
int type 14, 15, 100
integer (integral) variables 100, 105
integer literals 113
Integer, standard wrapper class 432, 433, 437
Integer.parseInt() method 351, 565
Integer.toHexString() method 565
integrated circuits 40
interface keyword 568
interfaces 514, 520
internal statements 152, 157, 259
international standard ISO 8601 354, 358
Internet Explorer browser 24
interpreter 28, 268
interrupt(), method of class Thread 546, 548
IntParameter class 380
IOException 482
is_earlier_than(), Date method 359
is_equal_to(), CollectionItem method 483
is_equal_to(), Date method 359
is_last_day_of_month(), Date method 352
is_later_than(), Date method 359
is_not_equal_to(), Date method 359
is_within_dates(), Date method 353
iterations, see "loops"
iterators 508

## J

jagged arrays 196
Jagger, Mick 519
jar tool 24
.java files, Java source program files 10
.java files, naming of 571
Java compiler
    downloading from Internet 20
Java Development Kit (JDK) 20
Java documentation, electronic 22
Java interpreter 21, 28, 268
Java programs vs. traditional programs 10
Java runtime environment (JRE) 21, 28, 427
Java virtual machine 9, 21, 28, 268–272, 427
java.io package 460, 564
java.lang package 335
java.util package 335
javac, command to invoke Java compiler 25
JCreator 27–30
joules, unit of energy 319
JPEG, the format of Joint Photographic Experts Group 48
Julian Calendar 347

## K

keywords 108
keywords (reserved words), summary of 567
kilobits 39
kilograms, unit of weight 319
kilometers, unit of distance 111, 319

## L

L, suffix for long literals 117
laptop computers 65
lastIndexOf() String method 215, 223
leap years 342, 353
learning, discussion of v, 3
least significant bit 38, 549
least significant byte 104
least significant digit 32
left shift operator << 531
left-side expressions 558
left-to-right associativity 121
length of a string 204
length of an array 183
length() String method 204, 207, 223
length, data field 183
less than operator < 135
less than or equal operator <= 135
lexical analysis 131
lexical comparison of strings 220
light, speed of 115
lightyears, unit of distance 115, 319
Line Feed (LF) character 453
Linux computers and Java v
Linux operating system 4, 453, 538
literals
    binary literals do not exist 530
    boolean literals (true, false) 174
    character literals 141, 555
    floating-point literals 117, 555
    hexadecimal literals 117, 163, 555
    integer literals 113
    literals of type float 192
    literals of type long 117, 555
    string literals 121, 203, 555
liters, unit of volume 319
little-endian order of bytes 106
load_from_file(), Collection method 489
local variables 275
locales 527
locating errors in programs 573
logical AND operator && 146
logical errors in programs 574
logical operators 145, 552
logical OR operator || 146
long keyword 568
long type 105
long type, literals 117, 555

Long, standard wrapper class 433
loops
    body of a loop 159
    do-while loops 164–165, 561
    endless loop 154
    for loops 158–163, 276, 561
    "foreach" loops 176, 508
    loops that are never entered 154, 574
    programming style 571
    while loops 152–157, 561
LowClass, an example class 403
lowercase letters 22, 45, 532

## M

machine code 9
machine instructions 59, 268
Macintosh computers 4
Macintosh computers and Java v
Madonna 519
main memory 5, 44, 50, 54
main storage 5
main() method 14, 495
    invocation of method main() 272
    parameters for method main() 278
    placing of the main() method 293
mainframe computers 65
make_speak(), Animal method 308
mantissa 110
Marley, Bob 519
masks and bit operators 532
matches() String method 223
Math class provides mathematical methods 446
mean value, calculation of 164
megabits 39
megabytes 39, 44
member selection operator, the dot operator . 559
MemberClass, an example class 402
members of classes
    (data) fields 290
    access modifiers 298, 398
    accessor methods 313
    constants 370
    constructors 300
    instance methods 291
    order of members 316
memory
    allocation of memory 188, 190, 272
    array of integers in memory 182
    deallocation of memory 272
    heap memory 189
    int variable in memory 104
    objects in memory 295, 299
    stack memory 189
    String object in memory 202, 209
memory addresses, numerical 51
memory areas in main memory 189
memory cell 40, 44
memory locations 51, 52
memory management 301
memory management, automatic 325
menu-based program 494
meters, unit of distance 115, 319
methods
    abstract methods 422
    accessor methods 313, 339, 343, 351, 365
    actual parameters 250, 268
    arrays as method parameters 257
    body of method 259
    boolean methods 490
    calling a method 240, 513
    calling another instance method 352
    class methods vs. instance methods 208
    conventions for writing method names 252
    final methods 429
    formal parameters 250, 268
    general structure of Java methods 259
    getter methods 339
    input parameters 261
    instance methods 291
    method declarators 244, 259
    method header 259
    methods taking parameters 244
    mutator methods 339
    native methods 272
    object references as parameters 379
    output parameters 260
    outputting data to caller 254
    overloaded method names 282
    parameters passed by reference 245
    parameters passed by value 245
    polymorphic methods 414
    public methods 262
    setter methods 339
    signature of a method 259
    some basic method structures 562
    stack usage in method calls 268–273
    static methods 208, 397
    typed methods 254, 255
    typeless void methods 254, 255
Microsoft Windows 4
Microsoft Word 4
MiddleClass, an example class 402
miles, unit of distance 111, 319
minicomputers 65
modulus operator %, see "remainder operator" 138
month(), Date method 351
months, history of 237
moon, distance from Earth 117
moon, first moon landing 344
Morse codes 508
most significant bit 536
most significant digit 32
mouse, an input device 14
move(), Window method 408
MPEG, Moving Pictures Experts Group 48
MS-DOS operating system 4, 19, 65
MS-DOS window 19

multi-line statements 109
multidimensional arrays 196, 406
multidimensional arrays, initialization of 195
multiplication operator * 113
multiplicative arithmetic operators 559
multiply and assign operator *= 559
multiprint_character() method 248
multitasking operating systems 538
mutable strings 226
mutator methods 339

## N

names, rules for writing a name 109
naming
  .java files 571
  constants 498
  index variables 188
  method names 252
  names of methods that are of type bool 352
  references to objects 238
native keyword 568
native methods 272
natural names 108, 109
natural naming 572
nested program blocks 276
new operator (keyword) 188, 291, 568
newline character \n 102, 203, 225, 555
nextByte(), Scanner method 118
nextDouble(), Scanner method 118
nextFloat(), Scanner method 118
nextInt(), Scanner method 102, 120
nextLine(), Scanner method 120, 205, 490
nextLong(), Scanner method 118
nextShort(), Scanner method 118
non-negative variables 105
not equal operator != 135
NOT operator ! 146
not_in_use, parameter for method main() 12, 278
Notepad editor 27
notes displayed by compiler 573
NULL character \0 555
null keyword 231, 568
null references 231, 323
numbering systems 32, 101
  binary numbers 33
  binary-to-decimal conversion 36
  comparison 34
  decimal-to-binary conversion 37
  hexadecimal numbers 33, 101
  hexadecimal-to-binary conversion 38
  hexadecimal-to-decimal conversion 36
  octal numbers 33
numbers, important in computing 35
numerical memory addresses 51

## O

Object class 434, 436, 503
object-oriented design
  data encapsulation 339
objects
  creation of objects 300
  destruction of objects in heap memory 301
  initialization of objects 300
  object creations 557
  object references 291
  objects of type String 200
  referencing objects 295, 300, 404, 427
  vs. object references 238
octal numbering system 33
odd numbers vs. even numbers 197
Olympics, an example class 313
opening files 451, 456, 472
operands 117
operating system, calling method Main() 272
operating system, the role of 6
operating systems 4, 538
operators
  addition operator + 113, 121
  all used operators summarized 559
  arithmetic operators 113, 138, 280
  assignment operator = 113, 115
  associativity of operators 121
  bit operators 530–537
  bitwise AND operator & 531
  bitwise logical operators 552
  bitwise OR operator | 531
  comparison operators 135
  complement operator ~ 531
  concatenation operator + 121
  conditional logical operators 552
  decrement operator -- 157
  division operator / 113
  equal operator == 135
  exclusive OR operator ^ 531
  greater than operator > 135
  greater than or equal operator >= 135
  increment operator ++ 155, 157
  instanceof operator 445
  left shift operator << 531
  less than operator < 135
  less than or equal operator <= 135
  logical AND operator && 146
  logical operators 145, 552
  logical OR operator || 146
  modulus operator %, see "remainder operator" 138
  multiplication operator * 113
  not equal operator != 135
  NOT operator ! 146
  operator && vs. operator & 552
  operator || vs. operator | 552
  precedence and associativity of operators 112
  precedence of operators 145, 559
  relational operators 135
  remainder operator % 138, 280
  right shift operator >> 531
  subtraction operator - 113
  unary operators 145

zero fill right shift operator >>> 531
ounces, unit of weight 319
out, static field of class System 333
output parameters 260
output statements 12
output, formatting 116
outputting data to caller 254
overloading
    method overloading vs. polymorphic methods 415
    overloading constructors 306
    overloading method names 282
overriding methods 414


## P


package keyword 568
packages 334, 398
    default package 336
    java.io package 460
    java.lang package 335
    java.util package 335
palindromes 206
palmtop computer 65
paper copies of programs 577
parameters 244–261
    actual parameters 250, 268
    arrays as method parameters 257
    formal parameters 250, 268
    input parameters 261
    object references as parameters 379
    output parameters 260
    parameters for method main() 278
    passing by reference 245
    passing by value 245
    to instance methods 296
    varying in number 274
parameters vs. arguments 250
parentheses, meaning in expressions 113, 123
parseDouble(), method of class Double 433, 565
parseInt(), method of class Integer 351, 433, 565
parsing 433
percent sign % in format specifiers 125
Person, an example class 298
personal computers 65
pints, unit of volume 319
Planet, an example class 321
polymorphic methods 414, 504, 510
    calling superclass version of a method 419
    polymorphic methods vs. method overloading 415
pop(), Stack method 330
Pope Gregory XIII 347
pounds, unit of weight 319
precedence of operators 112, 145, 559
precision, of floating-point variables 107
prefix 0x in hexadecimal literals 117
President, an example class 368
PresidentInfoApplication, an example class 370
print() method 103
print(), abstract CurrentTime method 424
print(), AmericanTime method 425
print(), EnglishCalendar method 395
print(), European time method 425
print(), PrintStream method 333
print(), Window method 407
print_all_items(), Collection method 485
print_array() method 506
print_array(), overloaded method 284
print_array_of_numbers() method 265
print_calculations() method 280
print_data_of_collection_items() method 492
print_data_of_next_president() method 375
print_in_binary_form() method 536
print_lowercase_letters() method 243
print_message() method 241
print_olympics_data(), Olympics method 313
print_person_data(), Person method 298
print_planet_data(), Planet method 321
print_rectangle(), Rectangle method 292
print_sum() method 246
print_text_in_decorated_box() method 248
print_uppercase_letters() method 243
printf() method 116, 523
printf(), PrintStream method 333
printing date and time information 526
printing programs on paper 577
println(), PrintStream method 333
println(), PrintWriter method 455, 461
printStackTrace(), method of class Throwable 441
PrintStream class 333
PrintWriter class 454, 460
    println() method 455, 461
private keyword 298, 398, 568
processes 538
processors 56
program blocks, nesting 276
program control 242
program counter 268, 269
program descriptions, structure of viii
program development, incremental 576
program editors 9, 27
program listings 577
program not working, what to do 574, 575
program pointer register 268, 269
program versions 577
programmers 9
programming exercises, list of xvii
programming exercises, practical advice for 29, 571
programming languages 8
    assembly languages 94
    high-level languages 94
programming style
    see also "natural naming"
    indentation of statements 167
    loops and if constructs 571
    order of class members 316
    rules for using braces { } 167
programs
    executable programs 8

list of programs in this book xiv
making backup copies 577
printing on paper 577
source code 9
source programs 8
protected keyword 298, 398, 416, 568
pseudo-code 332
public keyword 262, 298, 398, 569
pure abstract classes 520
push(), Stack method 329

## Q

quotes, see "double quotes" or "single quotes"

## R

ragged arrays 196
RAM, random access memory 5, 50
random numbers, generation of 447
read(), FileInputStream method 469, 470
readability of programs 109
readInt(), DataInputStream method 482
readLine(), BufferedReader method 454, 459
readUTF(), DataInputStream method 482
recompiling programs 26
Rectangle, an example class 292
rectangular arrays 196
redefined (rewritten) methods 414
reference types 324
reference types vs. value types 200
references
object references 291
passing parameters by reference 245
string references 200
used as method parameters 379
vs. objects 238
referencing objects 295, 300, 404, 427
this keyword 362
referring to array elements 178
regionMatches() String method 213, 224
registers, in imaginary processor 56
registers, in typical processor 269
regular expressions 223, 234, 235
relational expressions 141
relational operators 135
remainder operator % 138, 265, 280
remove_all_items(), Collection method 485
remove_collection_item() method 491
remove_one_item(), Collection method 486
repetitions, see "loops"
replace() String method 215, 224, 465
replace(), StringBuilder method 229
replace_string_in_file() method 465
reserved words 108
reserved words (keywords), summary of 567
RestrictedAccount, an example class 419
return keyword 569
return statements 255
reuse of methods 258
right shift operator >> 531
Roman numbers 33
root directory 5
run() method in a thread class 539, 541, 542, 544
run(), CollectionMaintainer method 493
run(), PresidentInfoApplication method 376
running (executing) programs 4
runtime environment 9, 21, 28, 427
RuntimeException class 443

## S

Scanner class 118, 120, 333, 522
findInLine() method 169
nextByte() method 118
nextDouble() method 118
nextFloat() method 118
nextInt() method 120
nextLine() method 120, 490
nextLong() method 118
nextShort() method 118
Schwarzenegger, Arnold 519
scope of variables 276, 561
scope, class scope 277
screen output, directing to file 399
screen output, formatting 116
search_item_with_name(), Collection method 484
search_largest_integer() method 256, 380
search_president_by_name() method 373
search_president_for_given_date() method 374
search_string_in_file() method 462
searching for errors in programs 574, 575
selections, see "if constructs", "switch-case constructs"
semicolon ; 14, 18
serialization of objects 569
server computer 65
set(), ArrayList method 507
set_value(), IntParameter method 380
setCharAt(), StringBuilder method 227
setOut(), PrintStream method 333
setter methods 339
shallow copy of an object 434
shift operations, shifting bits 534
short keyword 569
short type 105
Short, standard wrapper class 433
show_account_data(), BankAccount method 296, 302, 416
signature of a method 259
simulation 80
simultaneous execution of programs 538
sine of an angle 447
single quote character ' 141, 203, 555
size() method of ArrayList 503
sleep(), method of class Thread 540, 546
software 4
software development, incremental 576
sort(), Collections method 518
sort_to_ascending_order() method 266

sorting algorithms 262
source code 9
source programs 8
source programs, downloading 23
SpanishCalendar, an example class 396
specifications of exceptions 442
speed of light 115
split() String method 224, 234, 235
stack
  role of stack in method calls 268–273
  stack implemented with software 326
  stack pointer register 268
stack frame 270
stack memory vs. heap memory 189, 324
Stack, an example class 328
stack_is_not_empty(), Stack method 330
standard input device 118
standard Java classes 434
start(), method of class Thread 539, 541
startsWith() String method 224
statements
  assignment statements 113, 115, 558
  break statements 147, 150
  do-while loops 164–165, 561
  for loops 158–163, 561
  if constructs 134, 560
  import statements 334
  internal statements 152, 157, 259
  method calls 242
  output statements 12
  return statements 255
  switch-case constructs 147–150, 560
  the role of semicolon ; 100
  throw statements 438
  try-catch constructs 171, 173, 438
  while loops 152–157, 561
static binding 427
static keyword 397, 569
static methods 208, 397
status variables (state variables) 498
stop_this_thread() method 541, 542
store_text_lines_to_file() method 464
store_to_file(), Collection method 488
store_to_file(), CollectionItem method 483
string arrays 234
String class 200
  constructors 221
string constants, see "string literals"
string literals 121, 203, 555
String methods 208, 220
  charAt() method 204, 205, 220
  compareTo() method 212, 220
  compareToIgnoreCase() method 220
  concat() method 221
  contains() method 213, 221, 320
  contentEquals() method 221
  copyValueOf() method 221
  endsWith() method 221
  equals() method 210, 212, 222
  equalsIgnoreCase() method 222
  format() method 126, 222, 274, 360, 369
  getBytes() method 222
  getChars() method 222
  indexOf() method 213, 223, 320
  lastIndexOf() method 215, 223
  length() method 204, 207, 223
  matches() method 223
  regionMatches() method 213, 224
  replace() method 215, 224, 465
  split() method 224, 234, 235
  startsWith() method 224
  substring() method 213, 216, 224
  toCharArray() method 225
  toLowerCase() method 218, 225, 323
  toString() method 225
  toUpperCase() method 225
  trim() method 219, 225
  valueOf() method 225
StringBuffer class 230
StringBuilder class 226, 474
  append() method 229
  delete() method 229
  insert() method 228
  replace() method 229
  setCharAt() method 227
StringIndexOutOfBoundsException 490
strings
  arrays of strings 231
  concatenating String objects 214
  creating String objects 216
  dynamic (mutable) strings 226
  empty string 204, 467
  equality of String objects 210, 467
  finding substrings in String objects 223
  immutability of strings 204
  length of a string 204
  searching for substrings inside strings 213
  String object in memory 202, 209
  taking substrings from String objects 224
strong typing 267
subclasses 400
subinterfaces 520
subroutines 240
subscripting, see "indexing"
substring() String method 213, 216, 224
substrings in String objects 223
subtract and assign operator -= 559
subtraction operator - 113
suffix F identifies float literals 117
suffix L identifies long literals 117
Sun Microsystems 20
Sun, radius of 498
super keyword 385, 386, 419, 569
superclass 384, 396
supercomputers 65
superstitious friends, how to help them 342
switch keyword 569
switch-case constructs 147, 150, 560

symbols, see also "names" 108
synchronized keyword 569
syntax of a programming language 12
System class 333
System.currentTimeMillis() method 544
System.in 333
System.out.print() method 103
System.out.printf() method 116, 125, 128, 523
systems 9

## T

tab, see "tabulator character"
table of contents x
tabulator character \t 203, 225, 555
tabulator character, avoiding 577
Task Manager in Windows 576
text balloons viii
text files 452
text files vs. binary files 469
TextWindow, an example class 410
this keyword 362, 363, 569
this_is_a_leap_year(), Date method 353
Thread class 541
Thread.sleep() method 540, 546
threads 538–548
ThreadToDisplayTicksAndTime, an example class 544
ThreadToPrintDollarSigns, an example class 542
ThreadToPrintDots, an example class 541
ThreadToShowFullTimeInfo, an example class 547
ThreadToShowSeconds, an example class 546
throw keyword 438, 569
throw statements 438
Throwable class 443
throwing exceptions 438
throws keyword 442, 482, 569
TIFF, Tagged Image File Format 48
time measurement 426
time printing formats 423
to_american_format_string() method 386
to_line_of_text(), CollectionItem method 483
to_string_with_month_name() method 386
toCharArray() String method 225
toHexString(), method of class Integer 565
toLowerCase() String method 218, 225, 323
toString() method in class Event 516
toString() method of class Object 435, 504
toString() String method 225
toString(), Date method 360
toUpperCase() String method 225
traditional programs vs. Java programs 10
transfer_money_to(), BankAccount method 303, 417
transient keyword 569
transistors 40
translate(), a polymorphic method 510, 511, 512
TrilingualTranslation, an example class 511
trim() String method 219, 225
true, boolean literal 174, 569
truth values 134, 174
try keyword 171, 569
try-catch constructs 171, 173, 438
try-catch-finally constructs 444, 457
Turing machine 65
Turing, Alan 207
.txt, name extension for text files 452
type parameter of generic type 502
type parameters of ArrayList arrays 505
typed methods 254, 255
typeless void methods 254, 255
types
    explicit type conversions 161, 164, 267
    reference types vs. value types 200, 324
typing with 10 fingers vi

## U

UML, Unified Modeling Language 365
    describing inheritance between classes 389
    examples of class diagrams 389, 401, 405, 415
    has-a relationship between classes 367
unary operators 145
unboxing 432
unchecked exceptions 442, 443
underscore character _ 108
unhandled exceptions 120
Unicode character coding 46, 47, 105
Unicode Transformation Format 456
Universal Time 527
UNIX computers and Java v
UNIX operating system 4, 453, 538
unsigned variables 105
uppercase letters 22, 45, 532
UTF-8 456, 477

## V

value types 324
value types vs. reference types 200
valueOf() methods 565
valueOf() String method 225
varargs 274
variables
    boolean type 105
    byte type 105
    char type 105
    classwide variables 275
    double type 110
    float type 110
    floating-point variables 110
    initialization of variables 155
    instance variables vs. class variables 397
    int type 100
    local variables 275
    long type 105
    non-negative variables 105
    parameter variables 247
    short type 105
    table of all types 107, 433

variable declarations 100, 556
varying number of parameters 274
versions of programs 577
virtual keyword (C++ and C#) 429
virtual machine 9, 28, 268–272, 427
visibility modifiers 398
visibility of class members 298
void keyword 254, 569
volatile keyword 569
vs. means "versus" or "against"

## W

warnings given by compiler 573
was_president_on(), President method 369
weak typing 267
week numbers 358
while keyword 569
while loops 152–157, 561
whitespace characters 225
whole numbers (integers) 14
Window, an example class 406
Windows operating system 4
Windows XP operating system 538
windows, character-based 404
Windows/MS-DOS operating system 453
withdraw_money(), BankAccount method 303, 417
withdraw_money(), redefined method 418, 419
workstation 65
World Calendar 347
write(), FileOutputStream method 471
writeInt() and other DataOutputStream methods 476
writeInt(), DataOutputStream method 482
writeUTF(), DataOutputStream method 477, 483
writing about objects and their references 238

## Y

yards, unit of distance 115, 319
year(), Date method 351
year, definition of 342

## Z

zero fill right shift operator >>> 531
.zip files, unzipping (extracting files) 23

# USEFUL TABLES

On the following pages, you will find tables that are useful when you work with computer programs. Don't hesitate to use this page to write down important information that you need to remember in your programming work.

## Character codes from 0 to 127.

| DEC | HEX | CHARACTER | DEC | HEX | CHAR | DEC | HEX | CHAR |
|---|---|---|---|---|---|---|---|---|
| 0 | 00 | NULL | 48 | 30 | 0 | 96 | 60 | ` |
| 1 | 01 | | 49 | 31 | 1 | 97 | 61 | a |
| 2 | 02 | | 50 | 32 | 2 | 98 | 62 | b |
| 3 | 03 | | 51 | 33 | 3 | 99 | 63 | c |
| 4 | 04 | | 52 | 34 | 4 | 100 | 64 | d |
| 5 | 05 | | 53 | 35 | 5 | 101 | 65 | e |
| 6 | 06 | | 54 | 36 | 6 | 102 | 66 | f |
| 7 | 07 | BELL | 55 | 37 | 7 | 103 | 67 | g |
| 8 | 08 | BACKSPACE | 56 | 38 | 8 | 104 | 68 | h |
| 9 | 09 | TABULATOR | 57 | 39 | 9 | 105 | 69 | i |
| 10 | 0A | NEWLINE,LF | 58 | 3A | : | 106 | 6A | j |
| 11 | 0B | | 59 | 3B | ; | 107 | 6B | k |
| 12 | 0C | | 60 | 3C | < | 108 | 6C | l |
| 13 | 0D | CR | 61 | 3D | = | 109 | 6D | m |
| 14 | 0E | | 62 | 3E | > | 110 | 6E | n |
| 15 | 0F | | 63 | 3F | ? | 111 | 6F | o |
| 16 | 10 | | 64 | 40 | @ | 112 | 70 | p |
| 17 | 11 | | 65 | 41 | A | 113 | 71 | q |
| 18 | 12 | | 66 | 42 | B | 114 | 72 | r |
| 19 | 13 | | 67 | 43 | C | 115 | 73 | s |
| 20 | 14 | | 68 | 44 | D | 116 | 74 | t |
| 21 | 15 | | 69 | 45 | E | 117 | 75 | u |
| 22 | 16 | | 70 | 46 | F | 118 | 76 | v |
| 23 | 17 | | 71 | 47 | G | 119 | 77 | w |
| 24 | 18 | | 72 | 48 | H | 120 | 78 | x |
| 25 | 19 | | 73 | 49 | I | 121 | 79 | y |
| 26 | 1A | | 74 | 4A | J | 122 | 7A | z |
| 27 | 1B | ESCAPE | 75 | 4B | K | 123 | 7B | { |
| 28 | 1C | | 76 | 4C | L | 124 | 7C | \| |
| 29 | 1D | | 77 | 4D | M | 125 | 7D | } |
| 30 | 1E | | 78 | 4E | N | 126 | 7E | ~ |
| 31 | 1F | | 79 | 4F | O | 127 | 7F | DELETE |
| 32 | 20 | SPACE | 80 | 50 | P | | | |
| 33 | 21 | ! | 81 | 51 | Q | | | |
| 34 | 22 | " | 82 | 52 | R | | | |
| 35 | 23 | # | 83 | 53 | S | | | |
| 36 | 24 | $ | 84 | 54 | T | | | |
| 37 | 25 | % | 85 | 55 | U | | | |
| 38 | 26 | & | 86 | 56 | V | | | |
| 39 | 27 | ' | 87 | 57 | W | | | |
| 40 | 28 | ( | 88 | 58 | X | | | |
| 41 | 29 | ) | 89 | 59 | Y | | | |
| 42 | 2A | * | 90 | 5A | Z | | | |
| 43 | 2B | + | 91 | 5B | [ | | | |
| 44 | 2C | , | 92 | 5C | \ | | | |
| 45 | 2D | - | 93 | 5D | ] | | | |
| 46 | 2E | . | 94 | 5E | ^ | | | |
| 47 | 2F | / | 95 | 5F | _ | | | |

In the first column:
LF = Line Feed
CR = Carriage Return

You get the 2-byte (16-bit) Unicode character codes of these 1-byte codes if you add 8 zero bits before each code.

**Numbers expressed in different numbering systems.**

| DEC | HEX | BINARY | DEC | HEX | BINARY |
|---|---|---|---|---|---|
| 0 | 00 | 0000 0000 | 48 | 30 | 0011 0000 |
| 1 | 01 | 0000 0001 | 49 | 31 | 0011 0001 |
| 2 | 02 | 0000 0010 | 50 | 32 | 0011 0010 |
| 3 | 03 | 0000 0011 | 51 | 33 | 0011 0011 |
| 4 | 04 | 0000 0100 | | | |
| 5 | 05 | 0000 0101 | ... | | |
| 6 | 06 | 0000 0110 | | | |
| 7 | 07 | 0000 0111 | 61 | 3D | 0011 1101 |
| 8 | 08 | 0000 1000 | 62 | 3E | 0011 1110 |
| 9 | 09 | 0000 1001 | 63 | 3F | 0011 1111 |
| 10 | 0A | 0000 1010 | 64 | 40 | 0100 0000 |
| 11 | 0B | 0000 1011 | 65 | 41 | 0100 0001 |
| 12 | 0C | 0000 1100 | 66 | 42 | 0100 0010 |
| 13 | 0D | 0000 1101 | 67 | 43 | 0100 0011 |
| 14 | 0E | 0000 1110 | | | |
| 15 | 0F | 0000 1111 | ... | | |
| 16 | 10 | 0001 0000 | | | |
| 17 | 11 | 0001 0001 | 126 | 7E | 0111 1110 |
| 18 | 12 | 0001 0010 | 127 | 7F | 0111 1111 |
| 19 | 13 | 0001 0011 | 128 | 80 | 1000 0000 |
| 20 | 14 | 0001 0100 | 129 | 81 | 1000 0001 |
| 21 | 15 | 0001 0101 | 130 | 82 | 1000 0010 |
| 22 | 16 | 0001 0110 | | | |
| 23 | 17 | 0001 0111 | ... | | |
| 24 | 18 | 0001 1000 | | | |
| 25 | 19 | 0001 1001 | 254 | FE | 1111 1110 |
| 26 | 1A | 0001 1010 | 255 | FF | 1111 1111 |
| 27 | 1B | 0001 1011 | 256 | 100 | 0001 0000 0000 |
| 28 | 1C | 0001 1100 | 257 | 101 | 0001 0000 0001 |
| 29 | 1D | 0001 1101 | 258 | 102 | 0001 0000 0010 |
| 30 | 1E | 0001 1110 | | | |
| 31 | 1F | 0001 1111 | ... | | |
| 32 | 20 | 0010 0000 | | | |
| 33 | 21 | 0010 0001 | 510 | 1FE | 0001 1111 1110 |
| 34 | 22 | 0010 0010 | 511 | 1FF | 0001 1111 1111 |
| 35 | 23 | 0010 0011 | 512 | 200 | 0010 0000 0000 |
| 36 | 24 | 0010 0100 | 513 | 201 | 0010 0000 0001 |
| 37 | 25 | 0010 0101 | | | |
| 38 | 26 | 0010 0110 | ... | | |
| 39 | 27 | 0010 0111 | | | |
| 40 | 28 | 0010 1000 | 1022 | 3FE | 0011 1111 1110 |
| 41 | 29 | 0010 1001 | 1023 | 3FF | 0011 1111 1111 |
| 42 | 2A | 0010 1010 | 1024 | 400 | 0100 0000 0000 |
| 43 | 2B | 0010 1011 | 1025 | 401 | 0100 0000 0001 |
| 44 | 2C | 0010 1100 | 1026 | 402 | 0100 0000 0010 |
| 45 | 2D | 0010 1101 | | | |
| 46 | 2E | 0010 1110 | ... | | |
| 47 | 2F | 0010 1111 | | | |

## Important numbers in computing.

| $2^n$ | DECIMAL | HEX | "slang" |
|---|---|---|---|
| $2^0$ | 1 | 1H | |
| $2^1$ | 2 | 2H | |
| $2^2$ | 4 | 4H | |
| $2^3$ | 8 | 8H | |
| $2^4$ | 16 | 10H | |
| $2^5$ | 32 | 20H | |
| $2^6$ | 64 | 40H | |
| $2^7$ | 128 | 80H | |
| $2^8$ | 256 | 100H | |
| $2^9$ | 512 | 200H | |
| $2^{10}$ | 1024 | 400H | 1 k |
| $2^{11}$ | 2048 | 800H | 2 k |
| $2^{12}$ | 4096 | 1000H | 4 k |
| $2^{13}$ | 8192 | 2000H | 8 k |
| $2^{14}$ | 16384 | 4000H | 16 k |
| $2^{15}$ | 32768 | 8000H | 32 k |
| $2^{16}$ | 65536 | 10000H | 64 k |
| $2^{17}$ | 131072 | 20000H | 128 k |
| $2^{18}$ | 262144 | 40000H | 256 k |
| $2^{19}$ | 524288 | 80000H | 512 k |
| $2^{20}$ | 1048576 | 100000H | 1 M |
| $2^{21}$ | 2097152 | 200000H | 2 M |
| $2^{22}$ | 4194304 | 400000H | 4 M |
| $2^{23}$ | 8388608 | 800000H | 8 M |
| $2^{24}$ | 16777216 | 1000000H | 16 M |
| $2^{25}$ | 33554432 | 2000000H | 32 M |
| $2^{26}$ | 67108864 | 4000000H | 64 M |
| $2^{27}$ | 134217728 | 8000000H | 128 M |
| $2^{28}$ | 268435456 | 10000000H | 256 M |
| $2^{29}$ | 536870912 | 20000000H | 512 M |
| $2^{30}$ | 1073741824 | 40000000H | 1 G |

ISBN 141208152-1

9 781412 081528

Printed in the United States
By Bookmasters